ZEMLINSKY

Antony Beaumont

ZEMLINSKY

Antony Beaumont

CORNELL UNIVERSITY PRESS
ITHACA, NEW YORK

First published in the USA in 2000
by Cornell University Press
512 East State Street, Ithaca, NY 14850

Photoset by Agnesi Text Hadleigh
Printed in England by Clays Ltd, St Ives plc

Musical examples prepared by the author

A CIP record for this book
is available from the Library of Congress

ISBN 0–8014–3803–9

This book was researched, written and published with the generous support of
the Alexander Zemlinsky Fonds bei der Gesellschaft der Musikfreunde in Wien.

Acknowledgement is made to the following publishers and copyright holders
for permission to reproduce music examples from the works listed below:

Boosey & Hawkes, London: Richard Strauss, *Elektra*; Bosworth's, Munich: Richard
Heuberger, *Der Opernball*; Breitkopf und Härtel, Wiesbaden: Zemlinsky, Ländliche Tänze
op. 1; Edition Wilhelm Hansen, Copenhagen: Zemlinsky, Lieder op. 2, *Irmelin Rose und
andere Gesänge* op. 7, *Turmwächterlied und andere Gesänge* op. 8; Mobart Music
Publications: Zemlinsky, Songs op. 22, *Das bucklichte Männlein*, Songs op. 27; G. Ricordi
& Co., Munich: Zemlinsky, Posthumous Songs, *Frühlingsbegräbnis*, *Es war einmal . . .*,
Ein Tanzpoem, *Der Traumgörge*, Hochzeitsgesang, *Der König Kandaules*, Two movements
for string quartet; Schott's Söhne, Mainz: Erich Wolfgang Korngold, Sinfonietta op. 5,
Viktor Ullmann: Three Sonnets from the Portuguese op. 29; N. Simrock, London–Hamburg:
Zemlinsky, Clarinet Trio op. 3, String Quartet no. 1; Universal Edition, Vienna: Zemlinsky,
Symphony in B♭ major, *Die Seejungfrau*, *Kleider machen Leute*, Six Maeterlinck Songs,
Psalm 13, Psalm 23, String Quartet no. 2, *Eine florentinische Tragödie*, *Der Zwerg*, Lyric
Symphony, String Quartet no. 3, Symphonische Gesänge, *Der Kreidekreis*, Sinfonietta, String
Quartet no. 4; Alban Berg, Piano Sonata op. 1, String Quartet op. 3, *Wozzeck*; Alma Maria
Schindler-Mahler, Vier Lieder; Arnold Schoenberg, Gesänge op. 2, *Pelleas und Melisande* op. 5,
String Quartet no. 2 op. 10, Three Piano Pieces op. 11, Five Orchestral Pieces op. 16

2 4 6 8 10 9 7 5 3 1

Victoria Beaumont
née Fischmann

*Salonika 1921
†Oxford 1995

IN MEMORIAM

Ja, renn nur nach dem Glück
Doch renn nur nicht zu sehr!
Denn alle rennen nach dem Glück
Das Glück rennt hinterher.

Brecht, *Die Dreigroschenoper*

On ne t'a point promis le bonheur.
Travaille, c'est tout ce qu'on te demande.

Claudel, *L'Annonce faite à Marie*

Contents

IX Berlin 1927–1933

X The Humpbacked Mannikin 383

XI Vienna 1933–1938

XII Lieder (III) 439

XIII The Exile

XIV EPILOGUE 'Zemlinsky can wait' 467

List of Plates

Acknowledgements

1 Historisches Museum der Stadt Wien; 2 (photograph by Franz Köhler, Vienna), 3 (photo-graph by Georg Wassmuth, Vienna), 4 (photograph by L. Bachrich, Vienna), 7, 9, 16 by per-mission of The Houghton Library, Harvard University; 5, 6, 18 from Otto Biba, *Bin ich kein Wiener?* (Vienna, 1992); 8 Arnold Schönberg Center, Vienna; 10 unidentified press photo, by kind permission of Dr Jürgen Schebera; 11 from Walter Firner, *Wir von der Oper* (Vienna, 1932); 12 Nachlass Louise Zemlinsky, Gesellschaft der Musikfreunde in Wien; 13 by kind per-mission of Arnold Greissle-Schoenberg and Nancy Bogen; 15 Bayerische Staatsbibliothek, Munich; 19, 20 Österreichisches Theatermuseum, Vienna, by kind permission of Dr Dietrich Roller; 18, 19 Theatermusuem Cologne; 21 by courtesy of the Vienna Volksoper; 22, 23, 24, 25 Österreichische Galerie, Vienna, private collection, and Collection Leopold, Vienna (from K. A. Schröder, *Richard Gerstl 1883–1908* (Vienna–Zurich, 1993); 26 photograph by the author; 27 photograph by Silvia Kargl; 28 photograph by Peter Schramek, Musikverein Wien

Abbreviations

ACl	Alfred Clayton, *The Operas of Alexander Zemlinsky*, dissertation (Cambridge, 1982)
AeSU	Hartmut Krones (ed.), *Alexander Zemlinsky. Ästhetik, Stil und Umfeld*, (Wiener Schriften zur Stilkunde und Aufführungspraxis, Sonderband 1, Vienna–Cologne–Weimar, 1995)
ASD	Antony Beaumont and Susanne Rode-Breymann (eds.), *Alma Mahler-Werfel: Diaries 1898–1902* (London, 1998)
AT	*Der Auftakt* (Prague), October 1921, special Zemlinsky number
AZ–AMW	Zemlinsky's unpublished letters to Alma Schindler, Alma Mahler and Alma Mahler-Werfel, van Pelt–Dietrich Library Center, University of Pennsylvania
BikW	Otto Biba, *Alexander Zemlinsky. Bin ich kein Wiener?*, exhibition catalogue (Vienna, 1992)
B–SC	J. Brand, C. Hailey, D. Harris (eds.), *The Berg–Schoenberg Correspondence* (Basingstoke, 1987)
Hil-Kat	Ernst Hilmar (ed.), *Arnold Schönberg Gedenkausstellung 1974* (Vienna, 1974)
LoC	Alexander Zemlinsky Collection, The Library of Congress
MolA	Moldenhauer Archive, The Houghton Library, Harvard University
NLZ	Nachlass Louise Zemlinsky, Gesellschaft der Musikfreunde in Wien
SPH	Felicitas Heimann-Jelinek and Kurt Schubert (eds.), *Spharadim – Spaniolen – Die Juden in Spanien – Die sephardische Diaspora*, (Studia Judaica Austriaca XIII, Eisenstadt, 1992)
St-Id	Arnold Schoenberg, *Style and Idea*, (London, 1972)
St-Sch	H. H. Stuckenschmidt, *Schönberg. Leben, Umwelt, Werk* (Zurich, 1974); English version, translated by Humphrey Searle (London, 1977)
Tan	Pamela Tancsik, 'Die Prager Oper heisst Zemlinsky', *Theatergeschichte des Neuen Deutschen Theaters Prag in der Ära Zemlinsky von 1911 bis 1927* (Vienna, 2000)
TiU	Otto Kolleritsch (ed.), *Alexander Zemlinsky. Tradition im Umkreis der Wiener Schule*, (Studien zur Wertungsforschung VII, Graz, 1976)

vP/D   van Pelt–Dietrich Library Center, University of Pennsylvania
Web-Br   Horst Weber (ed.), *Briefwechsel Zemlinsky mit Schoenberg, Berg, Webern und Schreker* (Berlin, 1995)
Web-ZW   Horst Weber, 'Zemlinsky in Wien 1871–1911', in *Archiv für Musikwissenschaft* XXVIII/2, 1971, 77–93
ZTuA   Werner Loll, *Zwischen Tradition und Avantgarde. Die Kammermusik Alexander Zemlinskys*, (Kieler Schriften zur Musikwissenschaft XXXIV, Kassel, 1990)

Introduction

Travelling around Vienna by tram, as the story goes, Zemlinsky would sometimes break into song, or rather a wordless caterwaul of moans and groans.
One day a fellow traveller asked him what he was singing. 'My own music,' he
replied. And with a wry smile he added, 'Like this, with a bit of luck, somebody
might take an interest in it.'[1] *Se non è vero è ben trovato.* Zemlinsky's life story
is that of a man running after luck, only to discover that luck was running
behind him – far behind him. 'My time will come after my death,' he would say.
Success crowned his earliest endeavours with golden laurels, then abandoned
him; life became a struggle for recognition.

When this book was first conceived, in the spring of 1990, there seemed little
chance of filling the extensive gaps in Zemlinsky's biography. Few people
remembered him, and at the age of ninety even his widow was finding her
memory had grown confused and uncertain. He himself kept no diary and he
collected press cuttings only sporadically. He was a man of deeds not words.
Newspaper interviews were few and far between; his surviving correspondence,
though copious, offers surprisingly little biographical information or clear
insight into his artistic personality, and before emigrating to America in 1938,
rather than allowing his personal papers to fall into the hands of the Gestapo,
he destroyed them.

Under the circumstances, it seemed only logical to summarize the available
information in two or three introductory chapters, before moving on to a discussion of Zemlinsky's music, which itself can often be read as pages of a secret
diary. Soon it became clear, however, that such an intuitive–emotional approach
to his art would be fraught with technical and ethical problems, and that there
could be no substitute for a hard backbone of verifiable information.

I therefore set out on a fact-finding mission, which soon grew into something
of an industry. Inspection of manuscript material in the Zemlinsky Collection
at the Library of Congress revealed that several works of substance were still
unpublished and unperformed; a cursory glance at Alma Mahler-Werfel's
almost illegible early diaries indicated that, once deciphered, they would probably reveal the truth about her complex relationship with Zemlinsky; contrary
to rumour, the short score of *Der König Kandaules*, his last opera, proved to be
complete. The project and its by-projects became interactive and mutually inter-
dependent. Some twenty works from the Zemlinsky Collection were edited and
prepared for publication,[2] Alma Mahler-Werfel's diaries took wing as a book

project of its own,[3] and the process of discovery concluded (symbolically at least) on 6 October 1996, with the world première at the Hamburg Staatsoper of the re-constructed *Kandaules*.[4]

Certain areas of Zemlinsky's life are still only partly charted. Little is known of his childhood, and mystery surrounds his activities as a Freemason. Information on his later years, when he no longer corresponded with Schoenberg or Alma Mahler, is scant. Beyond Vienna and Prague there is little information on his conducting engagements, and an important collection of letters to Heinrich Jalowetz is inaccessible to research, pending publication.[5] The most fully documented of his compositions, ironically, is the three-act ballet *Der Triumph der Zeit*, which he never completed.[6]

In discussing an artist as complex as Zemlinsky, analysis is indispensable, if only to draw attention to the discipline and precision with which he deploys his seemingly unbridled reserves of nervous energy. Rather than trying to offer comprehensive analyses of every major work, however, and well aware that it would be perfectly possible to write an extensive monograph on each one in turn, I have instead devoted an entire chapter to the detailed investigation of a single shorter piece, *Das bucklichte Männlein* (part x), including the complete score as a point of reference. Even here, however, my approach is essentially that of a performing artist in search of interpretative insights, rather than that of an academic, who may consider analysis to be an end in itself. Analysis, as Schoenberg often stressed, can demonstrate how a piece is 'made', but scarcely explain 'what it is'. In this spirit, I have often supplemented or even supplanted technical discussion with considerations of a more speculative or esoteric nature: the symbolism of number, theories of colour and of key, the use of musical ciphers and talismans, the influence of cabbala.

In a book of evident cyclopaedic ambition, the lack of a dedicated section of bibliography may appear surprising. The explanation is simple but also chastening: apart from a handful of essays in musicological periodicals or composite publications, and a few excellent dissertations (such as those of Clayton, Oncley and Rooke), readers in search of further English-language reading material on Zemlinsky will draw a complete blank. Those conversant with German will discover a wide range of analytical and biographical material, however, much of which is listed on pp. xiii–xiv; a brief foray through the Notes (pp. 487–515) will bring to light further, often more specific titles and references.

A fair portion of my text makes use of German-language source material quoted verbatim. For the sake of stylistic consistency, I have translated most of these quotations myself, even where other translations already existed. Exceptions to this rule are identified in the corresponding bibliographical reference by the inclusion of the translator's name.

Individually to list the names of those who contributed to the researching and writing of this book would fill several pages. I would therefore like to express my thanks in more concise but no less heartfelt form to all the archivists, librarians and scholars who have given of their time and professional assistance in Barcelona, Basle, Berlin, Bremen, Cincinatti, Cologne, Copenhagen, Frankfurt, Hamburg, Harvard, London, Los Angeles, Madrid, Munich, New Haven, New York, Oxford, Philadelphia, Prague, San Diego, St Petersburg, Sydney, Turin, Vienna, Washington DC and Zurich. Of the many private individuals who contributed information and advice, practical help and constructive criticism, I would like to thank Max Nyffeler, Irmtraud Jo and Georg Himmelheber in Munich, the late David Tristram in New York, the Česky Hudební Fond in Prague, Cathy Steven, Silvia and Edmund Morris in Washington DC, Susanne and Stefan Harpner in Vienna, and Nelly and Jacques Lasserre in Zurich for their generous hospitality. Alessandra Seledec and Silvia Kargl at the Musikverein helped to open doors in Vienna that would otherwise have remained closed. Lotte Klemperer sent copies of rare and valuable items from her 'Archiv OK'. Horst Weber kindly allowed access to his edition of the Zemlinsky–Schoenberg correspondence long before it was published, and Pamela Tancsik likewise made available a pre-proof version of her invaluable thesis on Zemlinsky in Prague. Long discussions with the Viktor Ullmann specialist Ingo Schultz have done much to support my theories of number symbolism. With a perfect balance of encouragement and admonishment Belinda Matthews at Faber and Faber managed to hold me to my deadline. Jill Burrows edited and typeset the book with effortless expertise and awesome rapidity. Finally my thanks go to Peter Dannenberg and his colleagues on the Board of the Alexander Zemlinsky Fonds in Vienna. Without their generous and unbureaucratic support, this book could never have been written.

ANTONY BEAUMONT
October 1999

I PROLOGUE

The Sephardic Diaspora

Zemlinsky was one-quarter Jewish. Yet he grew up in an entirely Jewish milieu, attended a Jewish primary school and played the organ in the synagogue. Ida, his first wife, and Louise, whom he married in 1930, were both of Jewish parentage; the majority of his colleagues and closer friends were Jews. His father, who was of pure Catholic descent, converted to Judaism out of conviction. He himself later converted to Protestantism, but conviction scarcely played a part in it: to be a Christian was simply more convenient.

Though he turned away from the faith of his forefathers, their mentality was deeply instilled in him, their pride and humility, their humour, their willingness to accept whatever destiny had in store for them. An understanding of his Semitic roots is essential to an understanding of his art.

His background was untypical. The majority of Viennese Jews were of Central European (Ashkenazic) origin, but he was of Sephardic stock, descended from those tribes of Israel that had settled in Spain.

The Spharadim

According to legend, the first Jews came to Spain during the reign of King Solomon. A thousand years later, after the destruction of the Second Temple (AD 70), many fugitives made their way to the Iberian peninsula. Around 586 BC, Obadiah had prophesied a triumphant homecoming for these exiled tribes: 'The captivity of Jerusalem, *which is in Sepharad*, shall possess the cities of the south.'[1] The Jews of Spain mistakenly interpreted his words as pertaining to themselves, chose Sepharad as the name for their new home,* and called themselves *Spharadim* or Sephardis. At first they concentrated in the southern coastal areas, subsisting chiefly from agriculture; later they also established colonies inland. During the Roman Occupation, these pioneers were no better or worse treated than Jews in other regions of Europe or the Middle East.

The fall of Rome led in Spain to the rise of the Visigoths. The first rulers of this heathen dynasty recognized the Jews' right of citizenship and treated them with respect and tolerance. But their King, Reccared, eventually decided to embrace the Christian faith. Supported by the new, clerical power of Rome,

---

* Biblical research has since established that Sepharad was the name given to the area surrounding Sardis, capital city of Lydia.

the Visigoths created an atmosphere of harassment, coercing the Jews into serfdom and depriving them of their rights.

In 711 Cordoba, Toledo and other strategic cities fell to invading forces from North Africa. The Jews welcomed the Moorish invaders as liberators, while the Arabs and Berbers – minorities in need of indigenous support – soon came to appreciate the organizational ability and commercial skill of their Sephardic allies. With the founding of the Omayyad Dynasty in 755 dawned an era of unprecedented racial tolerance, economic and social growth, cultural and spiritual advance. The rule of the Caliphate, from the ascent of 'Abd-ar-Rahman III (912–961) to the overthrow of the last of the Omayyad princes in 1031, brought prosperity and social acceptance in equal measure. No Jewish community in exile was ever to experience comparable or better living conditions until the later eighteenth century.

Upon the collapse of the caliphate followed the rule of the Almoravidas and Almohadas, religious fanatics, who tolerated neither Christian nor Jew in their midst. Disillusioned and embittered by the atmosphere of discrimination and mistrust, many Jews, including the celebrated philosopher Maimonides of Cordoba, emigrated to North Africa; others settled in the Catholic kingdoms of Castille, Aragon and Navarre. Here they were received with open arms and, under Alfonso X and Jaime I, they prospered once again, holding important ministerial posts, playing leading roles in public life and contributing substantially to the arts and crafts of the region.

Irrespective of higher politics, and prompted less by wise ideals of tolerance and brotherly love – as then advocated by the Norman kings of Sicily – than by an inborn Hispanic nonchalance, a mentality of 'live and let live', Christians, Muslims, Jews and conversos* coexisted peacefully for centuries. The latter often lived in the juderia (Jewish quarter), even if this was no longer required of them, and many whose reasons for embracing Catholicism were material rather than religious (the so-called marranos) continued secretly to observe Jewish rites.

With the reconquista, the struggle of Spanish Catholics to oust their Moorish invaders, began a reign of bigotry and terror. By the mid-fourteenth century over half of Spain was again under Christian rule. Now there was talk of a 'Spain for the Spaniards', of Catholicism as the sole and universal faith, of limpieza de sangre (racial purity); those in public office or positions of authority were required to submit proof of their Christian ancestry. One of the bitterest opponents of Judaism, Archdeacon Ferran Martinez of Seville, repeatedly preached anti-Semitic propaganda from the pulpit. In 1391 he provoked an attack on the juderia, triggering off a full-scale pogrom, massacre, pillage and plunder. The example of Seville was followed in many other cities: a wave of violence swept the country.

* Converts, normally from Judaism to Christianity but also between all other faiths.

With the fall of Granada, in January 1492, the *reconquista* was complete. Having ousted the Moors, Spain was on the way to becoming a purely Catholic country. In the eyes of the authorities, the time was now ripe to purge the land of all remaining non-Christian elements. At the end of March the *reyes catolicos* consequently proclaimed an edict that required all Jews resident in the united kingdoms of Aragon and Castille either to embrace the Catholic faith or to forfeit their possessions to the state and leave the country within four months. The penalty for non-compliance was death.

Fifty thousand opted for conversion, 150,000 for exile. Many fled to the Netherlands, establishing communities in Amsterdam and the Flemish cities. Under the rule of Oliver Cromwell some were admitted to England; some followed Columbus and the *conquistadores* to the Americas. Many remained in the Mediterranean regions, settling in the ports and trading centres of France, Italy and North Africa; others found refuge in the Ottoman Empire, establishing large communities in Constantinople, Salonika and (from 1565) Sarajevo.

At first the indigenous Jews of Turkey (the so-called Romaniots) reacted to these newcomers with hostility, for the Sephardis, who prided themselves in their noble ancestry and purity of descent, were disdainful of those whom they considered of lower rank. In due course, however, the Romaniots merged and intermarried with the *Spharadim*, adopted their culture and learned their language. In Spain the Jews had customarily conversed in Arabic mixed with Hebrew, but in Turkey they cultivated a Hispano-Judaic tongue known as Ladino, based on the Castilian of Cervantes but also incorporating elements of Hebrew, Arabic and Turkish.

A major source of revenue for the *Spharadim* in Spain was the production of codices and illuminated manuscripts. In Turkey they were quick to learn the new craft of typesetting and printing. Half a century after Gutenberg and only twenty years after Caxton, a family of Sephardis in Constantinople set up the first Ottoman printing press, establishing a tradition of Sephardic publishing that was to thrive for over four centuries.

Shem Tov Semo

Several of Zemlinsky's ancestors worked in the Sephardic publishing trade. Foremost amongst them was Shem Tov[2] Semo, his maternal grandfather. Semo (c. 1810–c. 1880) was a journalist who specialized in questions of social integration, propagated the ideal of enlightenment (*Haskala*) and advocated an early form of Zionism. He is said to have been an itinerant scholar, but despite his Zionist ideals he never visited the Holy Land. In accordance with his theories of cultural assimilation, he married a Muslim bride and settled in Sarajevo, where Serbian Catholics, Bosnian Muslims and Sephardic Jews had lived in harmony for centuries. There, in 1848, his wife gave birth to a daughter, whom they named Clara. During the 1860s, probably at the behest of the Alliance Israélite Universelle,* Semo moved to Vienna. Together with his brother Alexander,† he founded a monthly journal, *El Correo de Viena*, intended primarily for the city's local Sephardic community, but also circulated in Istanbul and other Jewish enclaves in southern Europe and the Balkans. Evidently Semo saw his sojourn in Vienna as a temporary measure, for he retained his Turkish citizenship. In the early 1870s he probably returned to the Balkans.

Whether the Semo family was purely Sephardic is uncertain: isolated references in the Ottoman Empire to Semos *before* the expulsion of the Jews from Spain suggest that they may have been of Romaniot origin. David Semo, a Greek Jew, is reported to have negotiated the surrender of Corfu to Venice in 1386,[3] and during the fifteenth century a Romaniot named Abraham Semo was Chief Rabbi at Sophia.[4] Yet there can be little doubt that Shem Tov Semo was a man of typically Sephardic temperament and outlook, self-assured and quick-witted, proud yet humble.

The Spharadim in Vienna

In Vienna, Semo was reunited with several relatives who had been born there, including Moses Semo (1851–1917), a printer, who presumably worked for *El Correo*, and Markus Semo (1848–1919), a beadle at the Sephardic synagogue, who in 1887 received a silver watch from Sultan Abdul-Hamid II in recognition of his long service to the community.[5]

At the beginning of the nineteenth century Kaiser Franz II had granted a Christian publisher named Anton Schmidt a monopoly for books in Hebrew. Under his leadership, Vienna soon became the centre of a flourishing trade, despite competition from Amsterdam and Venice, and Schmidt's Ladino and Hebrew publications circulated throughout the Sephardic world.

After 1850 the Jewish population of Vienna increased rapidly. Attracted by the growing prosperity of the Habsburg Empire and the prevailing climate of tolerance, immigrants from the Bukovina, Hungary, Galicia and Russia made their

* 'An organization of emancipated Jews [founded in Paris in 1860] bridging national barriers, for the purpose of furthering the emancipation of other Jews and stimulating their mutual advancement.' (Jacob Katz, *Out of the Ghetto. The social background of Jewish emancipation, 1770–1870* (Cambridge, Mass., 1973), 216). 'The *Alliance* sent out representatives, who propagated ideology combining ideas of "progress", "civilization" and the "unity of the Jewish people" with loyalty towards the regional administration of those countries in which Jews lived.' (Edwin Seroussi, 'Die sephardische Gemeinde in Wien: Geschichte einer orientalisch-jüdischen Enklave in Mitteleuropa', *SPH*, 145–53).
† It was probably Alexander Semo to whom Alban Berg was introduced in 1918: 'In the evening at the Schoenbergs', met an old uncle of Mathilde's, a blockhead [*Sumper*]' (*Letters to his Wife*, 22 September 1918, 398). There was a further encounter in March 1923 (ibid., 31 March 1923, 498).

way in droves to the Austrian capital. There was no official ghetto, but the majority, particularly those of limited means, settled in the Leopoldstadt, known as the II. *Bezirk* (second district), an island bounded on the west by the Danube Canal and on the east by the river itself. As in other heterogeneous Jewish communities, the *Spharadim* held themselves aloof from their Ashkenazic neighbours, upheld their traditional customs and prayed in their own synagogue; they even spoke a Hebrew that differed in pronunciation from that of their eastern European kinsmen.

Little had changed in the Sephardic way of life since the middle of the sixteenth century. When Semo arrived in Vienna, he joined forces with a group of seriously minded young men who were determined to introduce social and religious reforms. The most influential member of this lobby was Marcus Russo, of whom Semo wrote approvingly in *El Correo* as 'a young man who is a little better educated than most'.

'Education is the mother of enlightenment and civilization,' he added; 'civilization is the mother of the human race.'[6]

In 1881 Russo was elected president of the community. During his quarter-century of leadership, the 'Turkish-Israelites' of Vienna, as they were known, experienced halcyon days. Private donations enabled the community to found a society for the distribution of clothing to children of the needy and an institution offering accommodation to poorer itinerant Jews, to provide welfare for the aged and care for the sick. A particularly munificent benefactor, Abraham Elias, put a spacious apartment building in the Novaragasse, which housed a day school, a library and living quarters for community officials, at the community's disposal.

Throughout their long history, the *Spharadim* had been content to leave the intoning of the service to the *chasan* (officiating priest, cantor). Now it was decided to beautify the liturgy with choral music, presented in a style designed to appeal to the younger generation. There being no tradition of such music, an Ashkenazic cantor from Graz, Jacob Bauer, was engaged as musical director and commissioned to compose sacred music based on traditional Sephardic folksong. Bauer in turn appointed Isidor Loewit, a fine tenor and an experienced composer of temple music, as his assistant. Michael Papo, son of the community's then acting Chief Rabbi, recalls:

My father held session after session with the cantor and the musician, at which he sang all the melodies, while Loewit, with his admirable knowledge of music, transposed the old Oriental melodies into modern music [. . .]. The choir, consisting of ten to fifteen boy sopranos and contraltos, one tenor, two baritones and one bass, was taught the modern Sephardi tunes. The adult members of the choir were excellent singers, since most of them were members of the choir of the Imperial Royal Court Opera.[7]

'The congregation accepted the innovation with great enthusiasm,' wrote Bauer.

'When the old, well-loved tunes rang out in the house of worship [. . .], even the most conservative faction gradually came to accept them.'[8]

In 1885 Russo laid the foundation stone for a new synagogue in the Zirkusgasse, financed by a few wealthy sponsors and built to lavish designs by the architect Hugo von Wiedenfeld. The building, designed in Moorish style and quoting motifs from the Alhambra,[9] was completed within two years and inaugurated on 17 September 1887. Space was provided for a sizeable choir, and a large organ was installed, but only on condition that it 'would never in any circumstances be played on any day on which the playing of a musical instrument was forbidden by Orthodox Jewish Law'.[10]

Over the years, Bauer and Loewit expanded their repertoire of sacred music and published much of it in an anthology entitled *Shir ha-kavod* ('Songs of Praise', 1889). Bauer also founded a weekly journal, the *Oesterreichisch-ungarische Cantoren-Zeitung*,[11] which included an editorial column on matters of non-musical concern, commentaries on affairs in world Jewry (pogroms in Russia, massacres in Basra, the murder of a Jewish girl at Constantinople), news of cantors from other German-speaking cities, articles on the history of synagogal chant, and occasional musical supplements. In an early issue,[12] Bauer recorded that the doyen of Austrian cantors, Solomon Sulzer, had attended a service at the Sephardic synagogue and was well pleased with the 'exact' performance of his music. Guest of honour at a wedding ceremony in December 1888 was the (Catholic) composer Franz von Suppé.[13]

These years of Sephardic prosperity were short-lived. In 1890 the Austrian government moved to incorporate the community into the Ashkenazi-dominated central organization of Viennese Jews, the Israelitische Kultusgemeinde. In 1908 Marcus Russo lost his fortune and resigned the presidency. During the First World War the flags of both Turkey and Austria were flown in the Zirkusgasse, but living conditions in post-war Vienna proved unfavourable, and in 1929 the Sephardic Chief Rabbi emigrated to Paris, followed by many of his flock. In the later 1920s the Viennese community experienced a resurgence of vitality; but in the night of 9–10 November 1938 (the so-called *Reichskristallnacht*) the synagogue was looted, desecrated and set ablaze by Nazi thugs. So sturdy was the substance of the building that explosives subsequently had to be used to destroy it. A cupboard in the vestry, which housed irreplaceable manuscript copies of Loewit's music, went up in flames.

Adolf von Zemlinszky

By no means all the Jews of Vienna dwelt in the Leopoldstadt – there was no legal obligation to reside there, nor was it ever considered a particularly salubrious neighbourhood – and those who were better off settled in higher-class urban areas and suburbs. The *II. Bezirk* was conveniently close to the city centre, however, and rents were affordable. Hence it was a natural gathering point for all those who came to Vienna from the further reaches of the Austrian Empire, whatever their religious or cultural background.

One of the many Catholic settlers in the II. *Bezirk* was Anton Semlinsky,* who had come to Vienna from the small Hungarian town of Zsolna (Sillein in der Zips, today the Slovakian Žilina),† where his father Josef was the postmaster. In 1832, aged thirty-four, Anton Semlinsky married Cäcilie, daughter of a musician named Wenzel Pulletz, who was probably employed at the Theater an der Wien. Upon arriving in Vienna, he found work as an official on the recently opened Schönbrunn railway; in 1845 he was appointed clerk to the Imperial waterworks. Three years later he retired from the Civil Service and opened a tobacco shop in the Leopoldstadt.

His son Adolf was born on 23 April 1845[14] and baptized at the Catholic parish church of St Josef on the Taborstrasse. Of Adolf Semlinsky's youth and early adulthood nothing is known. His education was evidently thorough, and military service will have been unavoidable. According to some reports, he followed in his father's footsteps and became a railway official. But he had also inherited something of grandfather Wenzel's artistic flair, and fostered ambitions as a writer. Evidently considering his name detrimental to a literary career (the Viennese have always tended to look on their Slav neighbours as country bumpkins), he adopted a more ambiguous orthography (Zemlinszky),[15] added a spurious 'von' for good measure, and set out, as Adolf von Zemlinszky, to make his mark in the world of letters.

Like many a struggling writer, he had to pay his way with a clerical job. Around 1870, perhaps through his involvement in the publishing trade, perhaps merely because he was a close neighbour, Adolf von Zemlinszky met and fell in love with Clara Semo. On 8 July 1870 he formally renounced his membership of the Catholic Church, and on 20 November, having partaken of the obligatory religious instruction and undergone the ritual of circumcision (performed by Rabbi S. W. Freud), he was admitted into the Turkish-Israelite community and adopted the sacred name of Aharon ben Avraham (which he never used). The marriage was celebrated at the Sephardic synagogue on 8 January 1871; ministrants were Moses Haim and Gabriele Papo, the witnesses were Alexander Semo[16] and a horse-dealer named Samuel Koritschoner. At that time Semlinsky

---

* Details of the Zemlinsky family tree are taken from Heinz Schöny's article on the composer, 'Musikgeschichte und Genealogie' no. 56, *Genealogie*, April 1978, vol. 14, 97–101. Schöny traces the ancestry of the Pulletz family as far back as 1616, and of the Semlinskys to the beginning of the nineteenth century, but makes no reference to the Viennese scions of the Semo family, whose records are preserved at the Zentralfriedhof and in the registry of the Israelitische Kultusgemeinde.

† Žilina lies at the foot of the Carpathians in Northern Slovakia, 96 miles due east of Brno. According to Zemlinsky's own childhood recollections, his paternal grandfather came from Neustadt (Nove Město), 6 miles further north.

(*sic*) was living at Taborstrasse 59 and employed as *Privatbeamter* (private official) by the insurance company 'Donau'; in the registry, the bride's father is
described as editor of the newspaper *Correo di Vienna* (*sic*).

Shem Tov Semo left Vienna soon afterwards to continue his life of travel,
leaving his brother in charge of the *Correo* and the chief editorship in the hands
of his Austrian son-in-law,[17] who by this time had presumably acquired a working knowledge of Ladino. In 1872 Zemlinszky was also appointed Secretary to
the Turkish-Israelite community. Without doubt this was a great honour and a
token of acceptance but also, as the Secretary was accountable for the community's entire administrative and legal affairs, a heavy responsibility. The salary
was negligible.[18] In recompense, a small apartment was placed at his disposal
on the second floor of the new synagogue. The Zemlinszkys never lived there,
however, and later it was reassigned to the janitor.

On his marriage certificate, on the birth certificate of his third child,
Mathilde, (1878) and on his death certificate (1900), Adolf von Zemlinszky's profession is declared as *Beamter* (civil servant).[19] Yet there is no evidence that he
worked for an insurance company or any other state-run body or institution
after 1871, nor do his son's recollections of poverty and hunger indicate that the
family benefited from the privileges accorded to government officials. While
retaining his status as civil servant, in 1882 Zemlinszky changed his registered
profession to *Schriftsteller* (writer)[20] and found employment as chief editor of
the fortnightly journal *Wiener Punsch* (modelled on the English *Punch*, but
written for and circulated almost exclusively among Jewish readers). The occupation must have been time-consuming, for he contributed several regular
columns: 'Vermischte Nachrichten des Dr. Confusius' (general news and gossip),[21] 'Professor Dideltapp' (satirical comments on art and artists), 'Simele
Krach an der Börse'[22] (news from the stock market, invariably illustrated with
an engraving of a hook-nosed confidence trickster), and 'Heulmeyer am
Clavier' (poetry in cabaret style). From the early 1890s the magazine appeared
weekly and gradually shifted its emphasis from verbal to pictorial humour,
bringing it more closely in line with its English counterpart. Literary supplements appeared every month, but to these Zemlinszky never contributed.

Most of his more serious literary work was devoted to novels and short
stories on themes from Jewish history: 'Jehuda ben Halevi', 'Der Verfluchte' and
'Die Tochter des Chasan' were serialized in Bauer's *Cantoren-Zeitung*;[23]
Salomo Molcho, *Der Graf von Montfort* and *Der Vagabund* appeared as paper-
backs.[24] His most valuable book, however, and the only one for which he is
now remembered, was a monograph on the history of the Sephardic community
in Vienna, published in 1888 in a dual-language edition with Ladino translation
by Gabriele Papo.[25] A slender volume, beautifully presented and printed, today
it counts as the only authentic and reliable history of a community – indeed of a
world – that has vanished without trace.

II

Vienna 1871–1901

I

Childhood in the Leopoldstadt

Adolf and Clara von Zemlinszky* moved into a cramped but conveniently situated apartment at Odeongasse 3, a few paces from the synagogue in the Zirkusgasse and only two blocks away from the community's administrative building in the Novaragasse. The city centre was within easy reach too, only a few minutes walk over the bridge across the Danube Canal; nearer still lay the Prater, Vienna's largest park and recreation area, with its champagne pavilions and beer halls, carousels and bowling alleys; and midway between the Odeongasse and the park, on the Praterstrasse, stood one of Vienna's most popular playhouses, the Carltheater.

On 14 October 1871, in the apartment on the Odeongasse, Clara gave birth to a son. In deference to the boy's uncle, and perhaps with the intention of helping their child on his path to fame and fortune, his parents named him Alexander.[1] Eight days after his birth he entered the Jewish Covenant.[2]

Adolf von Zemlinszky had served in the war against Prussia,[3] which culminated in 1867 with the rout of the Austrian army at Königgratz. Hostilities were ended by the *Ausgleich*, a political agreement by which Hungary acquired independent status within a newly founded state of Austro-Hungary. In Austria a severe depression ensued, causing the country, in A. J. P. Taylor's words, to become 'the second Sick Man of Europe'.[4] The following five years, however, were a time of almost miraculous abundance. Harvests were exceptional, leading to a boom in the export of agricultural products; the resultant economic growth provided funds for public development on a lavish scale; this in turn caused an upsurge of private investment. The network of railways doubled, demand for consumer goods trebled, and public money was made available for a monumental scheme of urban expansion (conceived twenty years before), conversion of the moat surrounding the old city of Vienna into the Ringstrasse. Along its spacious, tree-lined boulevards the Kaiser laid foundation stones for the new Town Hall, the Burgtheater, the University, the Museums of Ethnology and Art History and the Stock Exchange; in 1869 the new Hofoper was inaugurated with a performance of *Die Meistersinger*, and on 1 May 1873, proudly demonstrating that his Empire had again reached its zenith, Franz-Josef opened the World Exhibition.

---

* The composer's name will henceforth be cited as 'Zemlinsky', that of his parents as 'von Zemlinszky'.

Yet the explosive pace of economic growth also gave rise to a wave of uncontrolled financial speculation. Only a week after the opening of the Exhibition, on Austria's Black Friday, the bubble burst: 330 firms, including forty banks, six insurance companies, a railway line and fifty-two major private companies, became insolvent overnight. The Exhibition itself proved cripplingly expensive and failed to draw the expected crowds; the harvest was calamitous; a severe cholera epidemic broke out in the capital and spread rapidly throughout the country.[5] Unemployment rose steeply; prices soared and incomes fell in inverse proportion; dubious dealings on the money markets caused countless smallholders and investors to forfeit their savings or to be bankrupted outright. In 1874 a Viennese newspaper reported, 'The cost of living is just as high as it was last year, while – surprisingly – rent, even for the poorest of living quarters, garrets, cellars and lodging-houses (*Bettmiete*), is not even marginally cheaper.'[6]

Notwithstanding the difficult economic situation, the Zemlinszkys were obliged to move into a more spacious apartment, at Springergasse 6, for Clara was expecting a second child. On 26 March 1874 she gave birth to a girl, Bianca (named, presumably, after Clara's aunt), but the child was afflicted with severe gastro-enteritis and lived only five weeks.[7] Later that year Adolf von Zemlinszky took in a lodger, a friend of the family and a keen amateur pianist, who had come to Vienna to study. He brought his piano with him: to the four-year-old Alexander that instrument came as a revelation. Years later he recounted his childhood recollections to Alma Schindler, who recorded them in her diary:

He learned the piano by chance. The son of one of his father's friends was allowed to take piano lessons. And this friend let little Alex learn along with him. – Naturally he soon surpassed the other fellow. He was given a teacher of his own, whose fee was 3 fl. per month and high tea [*Jause*].[8]

Alexander made rapid progress. His talents were encouraged but also exploited:

Wherever he was invited, he had to play 'The Monastery Bells', 'The Maiden's Prayer', etc. Mozart sonatas, which he knew by heart, were forbidden. Once the whole family was in a restaurant in the Prater, and the proprietor's daughter played a piece, 'Maria', which moved all the guests to tears. His mother promptly borrowed the music and he had to learn it.[9]

When the temple choir was founded in 1881, Alexander was just ten years old. As a budding musician and son of the community secretary, he could scarcely have avoided being enrolled; perhaps he also numbered amongst those children of the underprivileged who at the annual Hanukkah festival received gifts of warm clothing. Three years later, when his voice broke, accompanying choir practice and playing the synagogue organ on high days and holidays evidently furnished him with a source of pocket money.

Apart from a brief motet, composed in 1896 for the wedding of Jacob

Bauer's daughter (see p. 47–8), Zemlinsky's early involvement in the musical life of the Sephardic synagogue is documented just once, in a report on the service to celebrate Abdul-Hamid II's fiftieth birthday in 1892, published in *Wiener Punsch*:

Specially for the occasion Herr Heinrich Elias composed a spirited festive hymn, which met with such success that at the end of the service the well-deserving composer was requested to be presented to his Excellency the ambassador. It should also be mentioned that the distinguished organ playing of Herr Alex. Zemlinszky and of the harp virtuosi Herr and Frau Professor Moser made a notable contribution to the complete success of the occasion.[10]

The Sephardic sacred music of Bauer and Loewit, which Zemlinsky heard regularly during his childhood, exerted no discernible influence on his own musical development. For a child already steeped in Mozart and rapidly discovering Brahms and Wagner, the traditional melodies, decorously harmonized by the Cantor and his *chasan*, can have held little appeal. But, judging by the anthems and motets published in *Shir ha-kavod*, the quality of singing must have been uncommonly high. The solo passages for *chasan* confirm Michael Papo's assertion that Loewit possessed a voice of considerable range and agility, and the demands placed upon the choir far exceed those of other synagogal anthologies of the period, such as those of Solomon Sulzer or Louis Lewandowsky. Thus Zemlinsky grew up in an atmosphere of discerning musical professionalism, and acquired already during his childhood an intrinsic knowledge of the human voice and its expressive powers.

On 7 September 1877 Clara von Zemlinszky gave birth to a third child, Mathilde,[11] and in 1882 the family moved house once again, to Pillersdorfgasse 3,[12] where they remained for ten years.

Clara seems to have brought her children up with clear-cut ideals, a well-defined code of moral and social behaviour, and a characteristically Sephardic pride, bordering on arrogance. In his letters to Schoenberg, Zemlinsky never omitted to send (or later, request) news of his mother.[13] Yet his comments are confined to her often delicate state of health, or to card parties, railway timetables and other such trivia. Never do his letters betray any feelings towards her, whether positive or negative, nor do they disclose much about her as a person.[14] Only once, writing to Alma Schindler, did he allow an outsider a glimpse of the family circle:

It was always a rather curious [life] which, at face value, lacked warmth. – But in fact each family member made sacrifices for the sake of the others. For the others there was nothing but anxiety and suffering. My father lived for nothing but his family. [. . .] My mother [is] a very retiring, withdrawn woman, who has more deep-seated qualities [*Innenleben*]. I have inherited much from her – her sharp tongue, her recklessness – but I also have good qualities from my father.[15]

Clara Semo's *Innenleben* must have included many aspects of Zemlinsky's own, self-contradictory personality: impetuousness and composure, conviviality and reserve, boundless self-esteem and profound humility, exquisite courtesy and sharp-tongued sarcasm. And where his father was the artist of the family, whose dreams of fame and fortune remained largely unfulfilled, his mother was more the pragmatist. Evidently it was she who shouldered much of the responsibility for bringing up her children as respectable citizens, and for fulfilling her father's precept, 'Civilization is the mother of the human race.'

Shem Tov Semo's golden word, 'Education is the mother of enlightenment and civilization', must also have been graven on her heart. Whatever hardships and deprivations Zemlinsky experienced during his childhood – and he later recalled that he and his family were well acquainted with hunger – few composers of comparable background enjoyed an education more thorough than his, a regular schooling of seven years and a further eight years of study at the Vienna Conservatoire. When he was six, his parents sent him to the Sephardic school *Midrash Eliahu* in the Novaragasse.[16] There he learnt the 'three Rs', but also '*Torah* and *Tefillot* (Bible reading and prayer), also in translation, as well as the Sephardic *Minhag* (ritual)'.[17] Two years later he was transferred to a state-run *Volksschule* (primary or grade school), which offered higher academic standards. He did well and was often top of the class.[18] In due course his musicality also came to notice:

Later, at high-school (*Gymnasium*[!]), the teachers took note of him and advised his parents to send the boy to the Conservatoire. – They were persuaded that they would save themselves the tuition fees. That helped – but they were mistaken. They had to go on paying for a further two years, for nothing.[19]

Little else is known of the composer's childhood except that he was once taken to see *Lohengrin* at the Hofoper. For days after the performance he remained, as he liked to recount, 'in a fever of excitement'.[20]

On 6 September 1884, as Alexander was approaching his thirteenth birthday, his father sent a letter of application on his behalf to the Conservatoire of the Gesellschaft der Musikfreunde.[21] An audition was arranged, the application accepted, and that same autumn Zemlinsky was able to begin his studies at the preparatory school (*Vorbildungsschule*) of the Conservatoire, in the piano class of Wilhelm Rauch.

2

The Vienna Conservatoire

Zemlinsky's curriculum at the *Vorbildungsschule* included piano and theory; he should also have attended choral class, but since his voice was breaking,* he was exempted. At first he relied entirely on family support, but after three years his progress was reviewed, his teachers declared themselves well satisfied, and he was awarded a Rubinstein scholarship to the value of 1000 fl. per annum. With this income, supplemented by money won in Conservatoire competitions or earned from private tuition, he was just able to provide for himself.

In 1887 he graduated to the senior school (*Ausbildungsschule*) and enrolled in the piano class of Anton Door.[1] A pupil of Czerny and one of Brahms's closer friends, Door had in his youth enjoyed some success as a soloist. Since 1869, however, when he was appointed professor at the Conservatoire, he had all but abandoned his solo career and established a niche in Viennese musical life as a solid but inspiring teacher, noted more for technical than interpretative insight. For two years Zemlinsky also attended the theory classes of Robert Fuchs and Franz Krenn. Fuchs's course, though nominally restricted to harmony and counterpoint, in fact amounted to a comprehensive course in composition.[2]

As his piano studies drew to a close, Zemlinsky made a few notable solo appearances. At a Conservatoire concert on 1 September 1889 he played the solo part in Robert Fuchs's Piano Concerto in B♭ minor op. 27, and in the final round of the annual Conservatoire piano competition, on 26 June 1890, he gave a much admired performance of Brahms's Handel Variations, which won him a gold medal and a Bösendorfer grand piano.† His diploma concert,[3] which followed on 12 July, included the Scherzo in canonic form for two pianos by Josef Labor[4] and the first movement of the Schumann Concerto. Despite these early successes, showmanship and delight in virtuosity were aspects of music-making towards which he felt an instinctive antipathy. His sensitive nature, combined with his knowledge and understanding of the human voice, made him an ideal lieder accompanist. But he made no attempt to follow a soloist's career, nor did the virtuosity of any fellow musician ever inspire him to compose a concerto or any other *morceau de bravoure*.

* According to the records, Zemlinsky's voice continued to break for over four years(!), from 1885 to 1889 (cf. Otto Biba, 'Alexander Zemlinsky und die Gesellschaft der Musikfreunde in Wien', *AeSU*, 210).
† In later years, Zemlinsky lent and finally – under aggravating circumstances – gave the piano to the critic Julius Korngold (see p. 286n).

Brahms, who took a genuine and lively interest in young talent, frequently attended Conservatoire concerts. From time to time there was even talk of offering him a professorship, but he knew that he was temperamentally unsuited to teaching. His presence was intimidating, his sarcasm biting, and from anyone who came to him for advice he expected deference and unconditional compliance. Robert Fuchs stood ideologically and personally close to him, but possessed a less forbidding exterior. Brahms himself spoke well of him – 'an excellent musician, everything so fine, so able, so delightfully thought out'[5] – but off the record he also observed, 'Fuchs is never profound; only in his symphonies does one occasionally gets a glimpse of something deeper.'[6]

Judging by the few of his works that have stood the test of time, Fuchs was a competent orchestrator and capable of imaginative, even popular melodic invention. His lighter pieces, particularly the five serenades for strings, brought him international acclaim. But in his more ambitious compositions the grace and lyricism of the serenades is filtered away, leaving a sediment of unmemorable themes, dry textures, restless modulations and unmotivated dramatic outbursts. After 1885 his musical style stagnated. Already in 1901 the ever outspoken Alma Schindler remarked, 'With every word he apologizes, so to speak, for being alive. His voice is soft and insignificant, he doesn't move with the times, and he lacks self-confidence.'[7] And Wilhelm Bopp, who was appointed Director of the Conservatoire in 1907, complained in a report to his superiors that 'the man is rooted in an idyllic past, has not been to concerts or the opera in years, he lives as a stranger among strangers, a loner who has remained untouched by the waves of a new age'.[8] Yet many composers of distinction and of widely differing temperament attended his class, including George Enescu, Leo Fall, Richard Heuberger, Gustav Mahler, Joseph Marx, Robert Stolz, Franz Schmidt, Franz Schreker and Hugo Wolf.

Little has been written of Fuchs as a teacher, and no common denominator in the music of his pupils can directly be attributed to his influence. Most of his students found him helpful and kind-hearted, but in later life they spoke disparagingly of him, and he was prepared only grudgingly to acknowledge their success. Sibelius, who studied privately with him for a few months in 1890, wrote that he was 'a highly skilled orchestrator, a professional to his fingertips',[9] but later asserted that he had learned little from him.[10] Hugo Wolf, who was in his early teens when he enrolled in the Conservatoire, found his teacher sympathetic and was anxious to please him. 'My G major Sonata met with Prof. Fuchs's warmest approval, because it shows better command of sonata form,' wrote the sixteen-year-old to his parents.[11] But as a music critic he later poured scorn on his ex-teacher's 'boring' serenades, and composed his own brilliant Italian Serenade perhaps to show how he felt the form should be handled.[12] The case of Mahler was particularly acute: Henry-Louis de La Grange claims that Fuchs can be 'considered responsible for making Mahler conscious of the essential problems of musical form';[13] yet there was little love lost between them. Remembering the fifteen-year-old Mahler as 'already then [. . .] so horrendously impertinent', and protesting against his re-orchestrations of Beethoven,[14] Fuchs was evidently unwilling to take any credit for helping to launch his career. As a student, Franz Schreker received his teacher's enthusiastic support; but when, in 1905, he asked Fuchs for a considered opinion of his opera *Der ferne Klang*, he was told that it was 'mad rubbish' (*verrücktes Zeug*).[15] Zemlinsky retained more affection for his teacher than most of his classmates, and included the E minor Serenade op. 21 no. 3 in at least one of his concert programmes. But when asked to mark Fuchs's sixtieth birthday (in 1907) with a production of the opera *Die Königsbraut* at the Volksoper, he sent a polite note of refusal.[16]

Study in the class of Robert Fuchs was dedicated primarily to formal analysis of the classics, with courses of strict counterpoint based on the *Gradus ad Parnassum* of Johann Joseph Fux, and of harmony based on the figured-bass method of Simon Sechter, published in 1835. The entire 'new German' school, from Liszt onward, was disallowed; Wagner, of course, was taboo. In lieu of study and analysis of contemporary music, Fuchs seems to have set great store by pastiche technique, giving students the opening bars of a Haydn quartet, a Beethoven sonata or a Schubert song, and requiring them to write an exposition, a development section or indeed a whole movement in the style of the original.[17] In one area of his teaching, motivic economy, Fuchs was ahead of his time. One small motivic cell, or even a single interval, he taught, could suffice to generate the thematic material for a whole movement or even a whole work. The cell can be subjected to a multitude of variative processes: augmentation and diminution, inversion, retrograde, addition or subtraction of notes, selective octave displacement of individual pitches. By stressing that this technique was rooted in the past rather than prophesying its potential for the future, Fuchs never followed his own ideas through to their logical conclusion. Indeed, he seems to have been quite unaware that this hermetic system of motivic interrelationships – later propagated by Schoenberg as the technique of 'developing variation' – contained the seed of a revolution.

Musical life in Vienna was so multifarious that Conservatoire restrictions could easily be ignored. During his years of study, Zemlinsky is scarcely likely to have missed such important events as the Viennese premières of Verdi's *Otello* (1888) and *Falstaff* (1893), the world première of Massenet's *Werther* (16 February 1892), the complete Wagner cycle from *Rienzi* to *Götterdämmerung* (1–20 December 1888) or Hans Richter's celebrated interpretation of *Tristan*. In the Musikverein there were historic performances of Bruckner (the world première of the Third Symphony, in its final revised version, on 21 December 1890, and of the Eighth on 1 December 1892), Viennese premières of Richard Strauss

(*Don Juan* on 10 January 1892, *Tod und Verklärung* almost exactly a year later) and important concerts of Brahms. Zemlinsky himself was evidently much in demand as pianist and accompanist, often in the salons of the well-to-do. Much of his income was spent on books. He took a particular interest in modern literature from France and Scandinavia, kept himself abreast of contemporary German trends and experienced at first hand the emergence of Richard Dehmel, Detlev von Liliencron, Hugo von Hofmannsthal, Arthur Schnitzler and the group of writers formed by Hermann Bahr, known as 'Jung-Wien'.

Having completed his diploma course as a pianist in 1890, Zemlinsky remained at the Conservatoire for a further two-year course of composition study. His new teacher was Johann Nepomuk Fuchs, who had joined the staff of the Conservatoire only shortly before, in 1888. While his brother Robert was probably the finer craftsman and the more discerning theoretician, J. N. (or Hans) Fuchs was the more experienced practitioner and, by all accounts, the more agreeable personality. He had held conducting positions at the opera houses in Bratislava, Brno, Cologne, Hamburg and Leipzig, was an accomplished composer of operas and incidental music, had prepared performing editions of operas by Handel, Gluck and Schubert and served as adviser to Breitkopf und Härtel's complete Schubert Edition. Since 1880 he had been a *Kapellmeister* at the Hofoper, a post he retained, despite altercations with Mahler, until his death in 1899.[18] J. N. Fuchs instructed Zemlinsky in formal analysis and practical composition, later also in orchestration, vocal writing and score-reading.[19] He appears to have taken an instant liking to his pupil, and when, in 1891, Zemlinsky's father submitted his annual application for fee exemption, J. N. Fuchs endorsed it with the words: 'In consideration of the applicant's talent, as well as his enthusiasm and diligence, he can be warmly recommended.'[20]

Early Works

Zemlinsky's earliest known manuscripts are preserved[21] in an album of miscellanea, written between 1887 and 1890, that includes short pieces, sketches and fragments of piano music, lieder, and chamber music, unfinished cadenzas for Beethoven's G major Piano Concerto (which he was presumably learning at the time) and even a brief sketch for a piano concerto of his own. All in all, the collection reveals that he was no infant prodigy, and that his path to mastery, though relatively swift, was no easy one. The choice of key for the piano concerto, B♭ minor, could be interpreted as a homage to Tchaikovsky, whose music, scorned as it was by Hanslick and his circle, exerted a considerable influence on the young composer.

There is little evidence of Tchaikovsky, however, in the Ländliche Tänze (Rustic Dances) op. 1 (1891), which follow the tradition of the German Dances

of Schubert, Schumann's *Papillons* (of which Zemlinsky quotes the opening
bars) and Brahms's *Liebeslieder* waltzes. There are twelve dances in all, of
which nos. 1–10 comprise a series of waltzes and *Ländler* in ternary form, contrasting tempi and a wide range of keys, while the two closing numbers, which
run without a break, amount to a pot-pourri in the manner of the waltz codas
of Johann Strauss. Here the tonal stability of the foregoing pieces gives way to
transitional modulation, and the scale figure of *Papillons* climbs vertiginously
from D through E♭ to F major[22] before a theatrical return to A major ushers in
a closing page of pyrotechnics.

Everything emanates directly or indirectly from a simple cell of two notes,
the falling major 2nd A–G, introduced in the opening bar of the work.
Expanded from crotchet to dotted minim units, the cell outlines in nos. 2, 3, 8
and 10 the harmonic structure; in no. 4 it is contracted and inverted to generate
a distinctive left-hand figure; in no. 7 it reappears in its original guise, but
expanded from two notes to three; the finale reinstates the two-note form,
rhythmically augmented into a hemiola:

EX. I

Zemlinsky's partiality for modulation into distant keys, as demonstrated
here and in most of his early compositions, can be ascribed primarily to the
influence of Robert Fuchs, but may also be symptomatic of J. N. Fuch's

enthusiasm for the music of Schubert. In the opening dance, for instance, the relative minor is established within three bars, and later the tonal centre moves in quick succession through e, g, E♭ and c before returning to the tonic, C. There is also some early evidence of Zemlinsky's unending search for novel chords and startling harmonic progressions. The coda of no. 7, for instance, surprises with a 4ths chord, resolved in a manner strangely prophetic of Schoenberg's First Chamber Symphony;[23] no. 10 introduces the 'Fate' chord, a D minor triad with added G♯, later to become Zemlinsky's identifying harmonic fingerprint; and in the finale a rising sequence of 9th chords over a dominant pedal[24] generates a passage of Bizet-inspired dissonance that must have caused raised eyebrows at the Conservatoire.

Zemlinsky rarely confided his innermost thoughts and feelings to the piano. While his lieder abound in refined colours and textures, his handling of the solo instrument is surprisingly lacklustre. There is little in op. 1 to match the intricate sonorities of his orchestral music or the tense, often exploratory sound-world of the quartets. The ideas often lie awkwardly under the fingers, moreover, as if they had been transcribed from an imaginary orchestral score.

While Zemlinsky would expend meticulous care on structural and motivic coherence, the notation of his manuscripts and printed editions, particularly that of his earlier works, is plagued by inaccuracies, ambiguities and inconsistencies.* Schoenberg once wrote of Zemlinsky, that when he first met him he was a *Schnellschreiber* (speed-writer), and recalled that while waiting for the ink to dry on a page of manuscript he would practise for his next concert.[25] Evidently he found even less time for the delicate business of correcting his fair copies and checking printers' proofs. While demonstrating an endearingly casual disregard for posterity, the texts of his early works present even the most diligent interpreter with intractable problems.

In the first April 1892 number of *Wiener Punsch* Adolf von Zemlinszky included a paragraph of unabashed propaganda for his son's *opus primum*:

Breitkopf & Härtel in Leipzig have just published a work entitled *Ländliche Tänze* for piano by the brilliant young composer Alexander Zemlinszky, and its appearance has been greeted from all sides with great enthusiasm. The work [. . .] can warmly be recommended to anyone interested in good music.[26]

To the twenty-one-year-old composer this kind of publicity was distasteful. 'Let me give you this advice,' he told his wife Louise many years later. 'Never run after anything in life. Everything to which you are destined will come to you. I never lifted a finger for myself – everything came to me. If you want to force something to happen, it can only lead to difficulties, because it is not in your

---

* The published edition of op. 1 no. 8, for example, includes at least four misprints and one inconsistency within the space of a few bars.

destiny.'[27] He must have said as much to his father too, for never again did his name appear in the columns of *Wiener Punsch*.

In retrospect Zemlinsky must have felt that the impetuous decision to 'publish and be damned' was misguided:* he had presented himself to the world with a visiting card as composer of light music. But by no means did this represent his ambition or adequately reflect his ability. And when he agreed to teach Alma Schindler, one of his conditions – possibly a rueful reflection on the Ländliche Tänze – was that she was to publish nothing without his prior approval.[28] He himself waited five years before again venturing into print.

With the Symphony in D minor Zemlinsky completed his course of study with J. N. Fuchs. The first three movements were probably composed during the spring semester of 1892, and the finale added later the same year.[29] At an end-of-term concert at the Conservatoire on 11 July, attended by Brahms,[†] Zemlinsky conducted the first movement on its own. The complete work was performed on 10 February 1893, again with the orchestra of the Conservatoire, this time conducted by J. N. Fuchs. Seated amongst the rank-and-file of the violin section, presumably on both occasions, was the twelve-year-old George Enescu. Sixty years later, in a series of conversations with Bernard Gavoty (broadcast by Radio France under the title *Entretiens*), he recalled his years of study in Vienna, spoke in glowing terms of Zemlinsky, then seated himself at the piano and played a substantial extract from the D minor Symphony – by heart.[30]

In a large-scale symphonic work, classical sonata form and developing variation, as Zemlinsky soon discovered, are uneasy bed-fellows. And when a first-movement exposition is itself rich in motivic variation, the scope for further elaboration of the same material in the development section itself is limited. Having exhausted most of the variative possibilities in his exposition, Zemlinsky sustains the momentum of his development section chiefly with histrionic gestures and sequential build-ups. The first-subject reprise is compressed to a mere fifteen bars, underpinned (in the manner of the 'Choral' Symphony) by a *forte* roll on the timpani, while the second subject returns, in the manner of Schubert, as a literal, undeveloped repetition in the tonic major. After a contracted reprise, the thirty-six-bar coda appears disproportionately long. The Scherzo poses no such structural problems: here Zemlinsky is in his element, relishing abrupt changes of register and dynamic, long crescendos and short, breathless silences.

The Trio, a relaxed ländler with a stately, Schubertian climax, furnishes an ideal contrast. Would that the ensuing slow movement, *Sehr innig und breit*, fulfilled the promise of its opening theme, a fervent adagio worthy of Bruckner,

* Zemlinsky's work was presumably recommended to Breitkopf und Härtel by J. N. Fuchs.
† Evidently this was the occasion on which Zemlinsky and Brahms first met.

a seamless arch of melody, exquisitely orchestrated and eloquently harmonized. But the second subject is introduced as a stormy *tempo doppio*, from which the movement never regains equilibrium. Instead of expanding and intensifying the opening theme, Zemlinsky contents himself with a literal reprise decorated by a descant of semiquavers in the violins, a slow-tempo repeat of the second subject and, again, a protracted coda. The fourth movement, too, is notable more for avoiding formal problems than for grappling with them. This is essentially a serenade finale, relaxed, rambling, good-natured and, in its closing pages, unpretentiously bombastic.

Within the limits of classical orchestral style, Zemlinsky demonstrates an innate sense of clarity, colour and blend. Conservatoire students doubtless received dire warnings against imitating Wagner's handling of the brass, and in the first three movements the participation of trumpets, trombones and timpani is minimal. Observing Viennese tradition, Zemlinsky also writes for natural horns and trumpets, but in the finale he abandons this stricture, finds more meaningful contributions for the brass and allows himself the luxury of three timpani.

The *Wiener Tageblatt* reviewed the work sympathetically:

The D minor Symphony of Zemlinsky, a composer who is still very young, reveals a decided melodic flair, fairly mature technique and a good ear for sound. We were particularly struck by his striving to express himself aptly and concisely. Most of the themes have a clearly defined outline and make a natural, unforced, level-headed and clear effect. The principal ideas of the first movement imprint themselves clearly on the listener's memory, and one can follow their subsequent progress without difficulty. The development section seems to be not quite on the same level of invention [. . .] but is nevertheless a solid achievement. There follow a dashing Scherzo (in F major) and a somewhat world-weary (*weltschmerzelnd*) Andante [*sic*]; the Finale is brisk, but its serious theme loses its contours too rapidly. It opens with great promise but soon loses itself in effusiveness. The composer's desire to make an impact through harmonic audacity is clearly noticeable in every movement.[31]

The critic of the *Deutsche Kunst- und Musik-Zeitung* commented – with some disdain – on Zemlinsky's latent talent as an opera composer:

The entire accoutrement indicates that an old hand, Mr Hans Fuchs, stood by the young composer with unsparing advice, the result being that traces of the most modern operatic technique, which seeks to make effect through stupefaction, have crept into Zemlinsky's symphony. Certain passages – for a beginner – are simply too showy, too forcible, too rustically chivalrous (*cavalleristisch rustikanisch*).[32]

In Vienna, every new work stood or fell with its reception in the *Neue Freie Presse*. These anonymous words of laconic praise, penned perhaps by Eduard Hanslick in person, acknowledged that Zemlinsky was considered a talent to be reckoned with:

EX. 2   Symphony in D minor – motivic relationships

Abbreviations   a = intervals augmented; c = condensed (one or more notes omitted); d = intervals diminished; e = extended (one or more notes added); i = inverted; r = retrograde.

Commentary   The principal motif is built from two separate cells, *x* and *y* (*y*ⁱ is in this case identical to *y*ʳ); *x* and *y* combine to form the opening theme; further motifs included in the first and second subject groups of the first movement are built principally from variants of *y*. The Scherzo begins with *x* in the timpani, answered by *y*ⁱ in the strings; the main theme of the Trio is an ornamented inversion of *x*+*y*. In the slow movement, *y* is reduced to its outline, a falling 3rd. Similar procedures are applied to the three principal themes of the finale.

[He] is a pupil of *Hofopernkapellmeister* J. N. Fuchs and has already learned a thing or two. Nowadays, sadly, this counts as praise; once upon a time it was a matter of course. [. . .] The work is well scored, logically constructed, and reveals talent and temperament. Although this or that betrays the hand of a novice, on the strength of this trial a propitious future can be prophesied for Mr Zemlinski [*sic*].[33]

3

The Polyhymnia

Early in 1892, conscript no. 1723 ('Surname: Zemlinszky; Religion: Mosaic') received the call to arms. His medical report, dated 11 March, was unpromising: 'Height: 158 cm. [5 ft 2 in.], currently unsuitable, temporarily deferred.' An identical report was filed on 7 April 1893, and a third examination, on 23 April 1894, set the seal on his military career: 'Height: 159 cm., unsuitable for armed service, constitution weak; rejected.'[1] Until September 1914 the military authorities troubled him no further.

But his parents had not named him Alexander for nothing, and it was his ambition to conquer the world. He may have been slight of stature, but his pride and self-assurance were boundless. Nor did he feel in any way handicapped by an appearance that, at first glance, was anything but attractive (caricaturists later revelled in it). 'Believe me, he really *was* ugly,' recalls his great-nephew, Arnold Greissle-Schönberg.[2] Hans Heinsheimer recalled a 'sharp [. . .] owl-like' face,[3] and Elias Canetti observed, 'I could never look at him without searching for his chin.'[4] Beneath bulging, oval eyes – only a sympathetic observer could perceive their soft, dreamy expression – protruded a long, triangular nose. A cigar often drooped sensuously from his lower lip. Within the limits of his budget, Zemlinsky dressed elegantly. In the winter he would swathe himself in dark suits and ankle-length overcoats; during the summer months he sported a white three-piece suit and a straw boater,* a soft collar being his only concession to the torrid Viennese heat.[5] Despite the devastating verdict of the military commission, he enjoyed physical exercise. Vacations were customarily spent at lakeside resorts, where it was his delight to swim, row and wander in the mountains. In 1901 he penned this candidly venal self-portrait:

Short and skinny (low marks: unsatisfactory, ß-). Face and nose: impossible; every facial feature: ditto. Hair too long, but that can be dealt with. I took an even closer look at myself in the bath (by your leave!!): no protuberances or deformities, muscles none too feeble, potency potential (*Kraft-Fähigkeiten*) astonishingly well developed! Everything else as outlined above. Hence summa summarum: hideous!![6]

From an early age Zemlinsky possessed a voracious appetite for the opposite sex. In many senses an ascetic, he was in erotic matters an epicure, who rode the wave of his sexual energy with abandon, wherever it might lead him.

---

* See the portrait by Richard Gerstl (plate 17).

Looking back on his youthful period of *Sturm und Drang*, he wrote to Alma Schindler:

If ever you believed me to be a 'well brought up', 'chaste' young man, then I must disillusion you. On the contrary, my last years have been wild, to say the least; I have also had disgustingly good 'luck' in this respect! I really can't understand why![7]

And in 1912 Schoenberg chronicled the following scene in a Prague restaurant:

Curious: at table nobody bothered to talk to me for fifteen minutes at a time. Alex, naturally, was involved with a young lady: Horwitz's sister-in-law, an insignificant but very lively girl, who draws attention to herself with her good looks. [. . .] Alex had promised that I could be home by 11 o'clock, but I had to accompany them to the coffee-house. Home at two in the morning.[8]

Nowhere does Zemlinsky's carnally passionate nature manifest itself more explicitly or with greater *élan* than in his music. A lengthy tribute in verse, written by a female admirer upon his departure from Prague in 1927, makes the point with doggerel exactitude:

Du hast, ich weiss es, seit früher Zeit / für Frauen besonderes Faible. / Sie waren für Dich – in Leben und Kunst – / für all Dein Schaffen der Hebel.

Since early days, I know, your heart / the fairer sex desired. / For you they have – in life and art – / your greatest works inspired.[9]

Almost to his last breath he exuded erotic charisma. Louise Zemlinsky recalled with an enigmatic smile that even the young American nurse, hired to care for the semi-paralysed seventy-year-old, succumbed to his charm.[10]

Dramatis personae

During his student years, apart from dallying with the opposite sex, Zemlinsky laid the foundations for many enduring friendships.

Arthur Bodanzky (1877–1939) studied the violin at the Conservatoire and composition, privately, with Zemlinsky. In 1895 he joined the orchestra of the Vienna Hofoper; five years later he was appointed conductor at Budweis (České Budějovice). During the 1901–2 season he worked with Zemlinsky at the Carltheater, subsequently becoming an assistant to Mahler at the Hofoper. In 1904 he succeeded Zemlinsky at the Theater an der Wien. Further stages in his conducting career were Prague (at the Neues Deutsches Theater as a colleague of Otto Klemperer) and Mannheim (Musical Director). In the autumn of 1914 he was appointed Chief Conductor for German repertoire at the Metropolitan Opera, a post he held, in tandem with Toscanini, until his death. In 1938 he played a key role in bringing Zemlinsky and his family to America.[11] His brother

Robert Bodanzky (1879–1923), for a brief period an actor at the Theater an der Wien and later librettist for Lehár, Kálmán and Oscar Straus, married Schoenberg's cousin and early flame, Malvina Goldschmied.

Hugo Botstiber (1875–1942) studied law before joining the class of Robert Fuchs at the Conservatoire. He enrolled in Guido Adler's musicology course at Vienna University, simultaneously studying composition with Zemlinsky. After a period as assistant to Eusebius Mandyczewsky he was appointed Secretary to the Gesellschaft der Musikfreunde and, in 1913, Director of the newly founded Wiener Konzertverein. Schoenberg painted his portrait. During the 1930s he was a neighbour of the Zemlinskys at the Kaasgrabengasse in Grinzing. After the Anschluss he found refuge in London.

Friedrich Buxbaum (1869–1948) studied at the Conservatoire until 1889. In 1895 he joined the Fitzner Quartet, playing in the first performance of Zemlinsky's Quartet op. 4. In 1898 he joined the Rosé Quartet and subsequently, at the request of Mahler and Arnold Rosé, also became principal cellist at the Hofoper, an appointment that caused considerable friction with the composer Franz Schmidt, at that time co-principal of the cello section.[12] In 1921 Buxbaum left the Rosé Quartet and founded his own ensemble, the Wiener Streichquartett. After the Anschluss he fled to London, joining Rosé and other Viennese colleagues in concerts of chamber music.

A senior member of the Brahms circle was Hugo Conrat (d. *c.* 1910), a businessman of Hungarian-Jewish origin, who for many years served as Treasurer to the Tonkünstlerverein. In artistic circles he played an unassuming but vital role: in their spacious apartment on the Wallfischgasse he and his wife Ida opened their salon to composers, painters, singers and writers. Chez Conrat, Zemlinsky came into contact with Karl Kraus, Fernand Khnopff, the Secessionists and other famous artists; here he also first met Alma Schindler. Ilse Conrat, the youngest of three daughters, created the monument for Brahms's grave in the Zentralfriedhof.

Richard Heuberger (1850–1914) qualified as a construction engineer before studying composition with W. A. Rémy in Graz. He became influential in Vienna as Director of the Singakademie and music critic for the *Wiener Tageblatt*, later also assisting Hanslick on the staff of the *Neue Freie Presse*. In 1894 he is reported to have encouraged Schoenberg to a career in music.[13] In his *Erinnerungen*, Heuberger describes an informal composition lesson with Brahms, a two-hour ordeal that followed much the same pattern of *sparagmos* and *catharsis* that Zemlinsky was later to experience:

By the time he had finished pulling my poor songs to pieces, I was in a state of complete dejection (*Deliquentenstimmung*). [. . .] Those mangled lieder never did get published.[14]

Posterity remembers Heuberger for his operetta *Der Opernball*. Unable to

complete the score in time for the first performance, at the Theater an der Wien
on 5 January 1898, he enlisted the help of Zemlinsky, who orchestrated most
of the first act for him and, it would appear, composed the scintillating overture.[15] In lieu of a fee, Heuberger is said to have presented his colleague with a
box of cigars. The *Opernball* overture is a pot-pourri of the most memorable
tunes, but the thematic material with which it opens is Zemlinsky's own,
impregnated with his musical monogram, D–E–G, repeated over and over:

EX. 3   Heuberger: *Der Opernball* overture

Zemlinsky's contribution to the success of *Der Opernball* remained officially
unacknowledged, but in Viennese musical circles it was an open secret. When
Josef Hellmesberger conducted Heuberger's Schubert Variations, at a concert of
the Vienna Philharmonic on 15 December 1901, Karl Kraus made it public:

One could scarcely imagine a harsher verdict on Heuberger's competence than that
pronounced by Mr Max Kalbeck: 'Today, Heuberger would probably have clad his
music in more brilliant colours. [. . .] The Variations do not approach the beguiling
orchestral colours of his *Opernball*, for example.' But who, other than Mr Kalbeck
and a few others, is aware that the beguiling orchestral colours of *Der Opernball*
were provided not by the composer but by Alexander von Zemlinsky, who orchestrated the greater part of the operetta?[16]

Zemlinsky also provided an overture and 'beguiling' orchestration for Eduard
Gärtner's operetta *Die verwunschene Prinzessin*.[17] But Gärtner (1862–1918),
who not only composed and painted but also possessed a fine baritone voice,
reciprocated in full measure, regularly including Zemlinsky's lieder in his
concert programmes. On several occasions he and Zemlinsky also performed
Schoenberg songs,[18] including the world premières of the lieder op. 1 and 2.[19]
After the first public performance of the latter, on 1 December 1901, there were
protests from the audience. 'From then on the scandal never ceased,' was
Schoenberg's rueful comment to Egon Wellesz.[20] Later contact between Gärtner

and Zemlinsky is not documented, but Schoenberg is known to have cultivated his friendship at least until 1912.[21]

Rudolf Stephan Hoffmann (1878–1938) graduated in medicine, and studied piano and music theory privately with Zemlinsky.[22] Finding himself unable to make his way as a creative artist, he embarked on a career as critic and writer, publishing important monographs on Schreker (1921) and Korngold (1922). Since he maintained close contact with Zemlinsky, his biographical and critical essays offer valuable insights. In 1938 he emigrated to Palestine.

Alexander, Arnold and Eduard Rosé (originally Rosenblum) came from Iaşy in Romania. Alexander, the eldest (1858–1904), was a viola-player; in Vienna he was active as impresario and music dealer. Eduard (1859–1943), a cellist, joined with his brother Arnold in 1882 to form the celebrated Rosé Quartet. In 1898 he married Mahler's sister Emma and moved to Weimar, his place in the quartet being taken by Buxbaum. He perished in the Terezín ghetto. Arnold (1863–1946), the violinist of the family, was appointed *Konzertmeister* of the Hofoper Orchestra at the age of eighteen. He became a close ally of Mahler, who was known to consult his opinion even over the quality of his singers.[23] He studied composition with Robert Fuchs at the same time as Zemlinsky, and in 1902 he married Mahler's sister Justine. Despite the fracas that led to Mahler's withdrawal from the Hofoper in 1907, Rosé retained his post until 1938, when he was obliged to resign. After one of the longest careers in the history of violin-playing, he died in London, a fugitive from the Nazis.

While still in his teens, Franz Schreker (1878–1934) conducted and composed for the Döbling Männergesangsverein. At the Conservatoire he studied the violin with Ernst Bachrich and Arnold Rosé, later joining the composition class of Robert Fuchs. In 1895 he founded his own musical society, the Verein der Musikfreunde Döbling, which comprised a choir and a small instrumental ensemble. His biographer Christopher Hailey recounts:

This very nearly led to Schreker's expulsion from the institution [i.e. the Conservatoire], for such extra-curricular, semi-professional activity by students was strictly prohibited. Only a deputation headed by the Mayor of Döbling (and in which Zemlinsky is said to have participated) was able to convince the Conservatoire administration to allow Schreker to continue both his studies and his concert activities. [. . .] It is quite likely that Schreker knew Zemlinsky from the Conservatoire, [. . .] though there is no evidence that either was in any way associated with the other's group.[24]

Hailey also mentions the 'somewhat fantastic combination' of instrumentalists Schreker had at his disposal at Döbling: 'according to [Paul] Stefan [. . .] four violins, flügelhorn, harp, piano and harmonium.'[25] Assuming that memories might have dimmed by the time Paul Stefan published his biographical essay on Schreker in 1920,[26] it seems not inconceivable that Zemlinsky's *Minnelied*, a light-hearted Heine setting for male-voice choir accompanied by two flutes, two horns and harp, which dates from c. 1895, was composed for Schreker's odd assortment of Döbling musicians. Zemlinsky was never particularly close to Schreker, but for many years they remained loyal colleagues. In 1908 Schreker worked briefly under Zemlinsky's direction as Assistant Chorusmaster at the Volksoper. Later Zemlinsky was to call on his expertise both as conductor of the Philharmonic Chorus and as librettist, and in Prague he ensured that *Der ferne Klang* and *Der Schatzgräber* were added to the repertoire. Ultimately the friendship cooled. Schreker, whose popularity had far exceeded Zemlinsky's, began to lose favour and in consequence grew hostile towards those younger composers whom he considered to be usurping his position. Zemlinsky, in contrast, retained an objective outlook and acknowledged Hindemith, Krenek and Weill as new leaders of the German avant-garde.

Richard Specht (1870–1932) studied architecture before taking piano lessons with Ignaz Brüll and theory with Zemlinsky and Schreker. Embarking on a career as a writer and music critic, he founded *Der Merker*, one of the few periodicals in Vienna that remained loyal to Zemlinsky even during the difficult years preceding his move to Prague.

Karl Weigl (1881–1949) studied the piano, harmony and counterpoint with Zemlinsky from 1896 to 1899 before taking classes with Anton Door and Robert Fuchs at the Conservatoire and enrolling in Guido Adler's musicology course at the University. After a brief period as repetiteur at the Hofoper, he led a composition class at the Conservatoire. In 1938 he emigrated to the US. Whether he resumed contact with Zemlinsky in New York is uncertain. His substantial *œuvre* includes six symphonies and eight string quartets.

Lacking the means to study at the Conservatoire, the composer–pianist Erich J. Wolff (1874–1913) was mostly self-taught. In the later 1890s he was the inseparable companion of Schoenberg and Zemlinsky. During a season as assistant to Zemlinsky on the music staff of the Carltheater (1901–2), he composed music for Hofmannsthal's mime drama *Der Schüler*. In 1908 he moved to Berlin, where he was active as an accompanist. He died in New York during a concert tour, aged thirty-eight. A volume of sixty lieder, published posthumously, was highly acclaimed; he also composed a violin concerto and a string quartet.

For shelter from the storms of his self-avowedly 'wild' life-style Zemlinsky looked primarily to Melanie Guttmann (1872–1961), daughter of a transport agent from Brno. A talented soprano, in 1890 she enrolled in the class of Joseph Gänsbacher at the Conservatoire. At the end of her preliminary year she won a Hofoper scholarship and joined the class of Johann Ress, whose roster of pupils also included Mahler's future prima donna, Selma Kurz. Her schooling, apart from voice lessons, included harmony and counterpoint, piano, mime, fencing, Italian language, German literature and classical mythology. In 1895 she graduated with a first-class diploma and a modest Conservatoire prize. Melanie

Guttmann's friendship with Zemlinsky is sparsely documented. By all accounts she was no beauty, and he looked to her for sympathy rather than sensual pleasure. Presumably they met at the Conservatoire; later they were affianced, but the relationship cooled, partly as a result of Zemlinsky's affair with Alma Schindler, and in August 1901 she emigrated to the US. In 1905 she married the painter William Clarke Rice; during a belated honeymoon at the Traunsee in the summer of 1907 she introduced him to Schoenberg and his circle.

The Tonkünstlerverein (1)

The Wiener Tonkünstlerverein was founded by Anton Door and his colleague Julius Epstein in 1884; Brahms was Honorary President and, as far as his schedule permitted, never missed a concert. Under his aegis the *Verein* became renowned for first-rate performances of lieder and chamber music, and with his encouragement and sponsorship the society regularly held competitions for new music. Placing one's name on the list of active *Verein* members soon became the most effective entrée into the higher echelons of Viennese musical society.

Zemlinsky enrolled at the beginning of the 1893–4 season, together with Alexander Rosé, Friedrich Buxbaum and Erich J. Wolff,[27] making his début, both as composer and performer, on 20 November 1893 with a Piano Quartet in D major. The following 23 April Buxbaum premièred his Cello Sonata,* and in December 1895 he accompanied the violinist Carl Flesch, who had recently completed his studies at the Paris Conservatoire, in a concert that included the César Franck Sonata, Paganini's D major Violin Concerto and miscellaneous virtuoso show-pieces.[28]

In 1896 a competition was held for chamber works including at least one wind instrument. On 11 December, under the *nom de plume* of 'Beethoven', Zemlinsky submitted his Clarinet Trio op. 3, which won third prize.† At a concert on 16 January 1897, he made a rare solo appearance, joining Moritz Violin in a performance of Julius Röntgen's Ballade for two pianos on a Norwegian Folk Song.

At the beginning of the 1897–8 season Schoenberg enrolled in the *Verein*, making his bow on 17 March 1898 with the D major Quartet in a concert that also included three items with Zemlinsky at the piano: four songs from his own op. 2, Robert Fuchs's Fantasiestücke for violin, viola and piano op. 57 and an aria from Hermann Goetz's *The Taming of the Shrew*.

After Brahms's death in April 1897, Eusebius Mandyczewsky was elected President. Many members had grown dissatisfied with the predominantly conservative programmes, but just as many others supported the *Verein* for that

* Neither of these works has survived.
† The first and second prizes were awarded to Walter Rabl and Miroslav Weber.

very reason. It was found mandatory to form a subcommittee, which included
Zemlinsky and Heuberger, to revise the statutes. As a result of their delibera-
tions the 'monthly lamentations at Brahms's graveside' ceased,[29] but they succeeded in reaching only a nominal consensus between the opposing factions.

As a performer, Zemlinsky was particularly active in the 1898–9 season. On
13 January 1899 he accompanied Josef Lewinsky, the great Burgtheater actor,
in a performance of the melodrama *Enoch Arden* by Richard Strauss, and on
7 April he joined Karl Prohaska in a performance of Brahms's F minor Sonata
for two pianos. On 24 November the avant-garde was represented by
Pfitzner's Piano Trio, while on 15 December, for the benefit of the reactionaries,
Zemlinsky played the harmonium in Dvořák's Bagatelles op. 47. On 28 December
he accompanied Melanie Guttmann in a performance of his own Walzer-
Gesänge op. 6.

The *Verein*'s polarization was further reflected in the elections for the
1899–1900 season: Heuberger, as liberal conservative candidate, succeeded
Mandyczewsky; Zemlinsky, as moderate progressive, was elected Vice-President,
and Schoenberg, the revolutionary *in petto*, was voted on to the committee.

Brahms

Since joining the Tonkünstlerverein, Zemlinsky had enjoyed sporadic contact
with Brahms, and at a concert with the orchestra of the Conservatoire on 18
March 1895 he was even accorded the honour of sharing the rostrum with
him.* Later that year, hard at work on the score of *Sarema*, he applied to the
Minister of Culture and Education for a grant. The Ministry committee,
whose members included Brahms and Hanslick, unanimously endorsed the
application and, in a report dated 10 October 1895, stressed 'the young man's
fine talent, serious leanings and creditable artistic achievements in the mastery
of form'.[30]

On 5 March 1896 the Hellmesberger Quartet gave the first performance of
Zemlinsky's D minor String Quintet.† 'It's bursting with talent,' was Brahms's
verdict,[31] but he was also critical of its progressive tendency. As Zemlinsky
recalled:

He asked for the score and, with a brief and somewhat ironic interjection – 'Of
course, only if you are interested in discussing it' – invited me to call on him. It was a

* A Conservatoire concert to celebrate the twenty-fifth anniversary of the opening of the
Musikverein, at which Zemlinsky conducted his Suite for orchestra. Brahms, who finished the
programme with his *Academic Festival* Overture, had a contretemps with a clarinettist during
rehearsal. After the concert he left the hall in a rage (cf. Richard Heuberger, *Erinnerungen an
Johannes Brahms. Tagebuchaufzeichnungen aus den Jahren 1875 bis 1897* (Tutzing, 1976), 78).
† The world première of Brahms's Four Serious Songs was given at a concert of the
Tonkünstlerverein on 30 October 1896; after the interval the Hellmesberger Quartet repeated
the Zemlinsky Quintet. Due to failing health, Brahms did not attend.

decision not to be taken lightly: [. . .] a conversation with Brahms was no easy matter. Question and answer were curt, gruff, seemingly cold and often highly sarcastic.

Arriving at the master's apartment on the Karlsplatz, he hesitated long before ringing the doorbell.[32]

He read my quintet through at the piano, at first making light corrections, examining one passage or the other in greater detail, but with no actual word of praise or encouragement, eventually growing more vehement [. . .] Having reduced me to a state of utter despair, he soon restored my good humour, asked about my material needs and offered me a monthly grant, which would enable me to reduce my teaching schedule and spend more time composing.[33]

For some years, Zemlinsky wrote, he had been an ardent 'Brahmin' with a thorough knowledge of the master's works: 'At that time it was my aim to possess and command his singular, marvellous technique.'[34] Yet it was no easy matter to hold a steady course between the Scylla and Charybdis of Brahms and Wagner, the opposing forces of classicism and modernism prevalent in musical Vienna. The D minor Symphony and E minor String Quartet reflect divided loyalties; *Archibald Douglas*, the first of the Ballades for piano (1893–4), is closely modelled on Brahms's *Edward* op. 4 no. 3, but in the other three pieces of the published set, despite allusions to Gounod, Tchaikovsky, Schumann and Hugo Wolf, Zemlinsky found a more personal voice. Those works which Brahms recommended to Simrock (opp. 3, 4 and 6) are, understandably, the most Brahmsian, while the Wagnerian echoes of *Sarema* and *Es war einmal . . .* approach the opposite extreme. Not until the turn of the century, encouraged by the rising influence of Jung-Wien and the Secessionists, did Zemlinsky entirely liberate himself from classicist influence.

When, in 1915, Zemlinsky decided to include Brahms's First Symphony in a concert programme, he commented on his choice in a letter to Schoenberg with two exclamation marks.[35] But by 1922 Brahms had for him acquired the patina of a historical figure: 'Today, when I conduct a symphony or play one of his wonderful chamber works,' he wrote, 'I fall once again under the spell of my early memories.'[36]

The Brahmsian technique of developing variation provided the basis for all of Zemlinsky's music. A less axiomatic but no less consistent influence of Brahms can also be detected in his use of musical ciphers and symbols. During the later 1890s he adopted personalized equivalents to the dual mottoes of Brahms and Joachim, 'F–A–E' (*frei aber einsam* – 'free but lonely') and 'F–A–F' (*frei aber froh* – 'free but happy').* Where Brahms had followed Schumann in transliterating names and initials, Zemlinsky's chosen mottoes were numerical, hence freely transposable.† His cipher 2–3–5 (in its basic form: D–E–G), represents the

---

* The German word 'frei' in this context signifies 'unattached, unmarried'.
† The choice may have been prompted by the paucity of usable letters in his name.

inner self; its inversion, 4–3–1, symbolizes the world.* These dual images enter his music in 1896: *Waldgespräch*, completed in the first week of that year, opens with two emphatic statements of the 'World' motif; its counterpart (for want of an authenticated name, let it be known as the 'Self' motif) was undemonstratively introduced in the revised finale of the D minor String Quintet, completed just eight days later.[37]

The Polyhymnia

The Musikalische Verein Polyhymnia was inaugurated by Zemlinsky in order to co-ordinate the activities of several interrelated amateur groups within the II. *Bezirk*. Meetings were held at Hotel Rabl on the Fleischmarkt, and a first public concert, featuring music for strings by Volkmann and Grieg, was given on 30 November 1895 at the Hotel Zur goldenen Ente.[38] In 1896 Hugo Botstiber's father Alois, a dentist by profession, was elected President.† Weekly orchestral rehearsals were now held at Hotel National on the Taborstrasse (II. *Bezirk*); later the group moved to a central and presumably more capacious venue in the beercellar of a restaurant on the Graben, Zur grossen Tabakspfeife. On 2 March 1896, with an orchestra of some thirty string-players, the Polyhymnia presented a programme of Bach (D minor Piano Concerto), Boccherini and Grieg (Elegiac Melodies) at the Kaufmännische Vereinshaus in the Johannesgasse. Zemlinsky also introduced two novelties, his own *Waldgespräch* for soprano and small orchestra and Schoenberg's 'very atmospheric'[39] Notturno in A♭ major for solo violin, harp and strings.‡ Melanie Guttmann sang the solo part in *Waldgespräch* and performed a group of lieder by Eduard Schütt, Heinrich Hofmann and Lucien Lambert; Beatrix Goldhaar, the pianist in the Bach concerto, contributed solo items by Rubinstein and Schumann.

Despite enthusiastic notices, the concert appears to have broken the bank. *Frühlingsglaube* and *Geheimnis*, two brief poems for chorus and string orchestra, which Zemlinsky composed in October 1896, may have been intended for a collaboration between the Polyhymnia and Schoenberg's workers' choir in Mödling,[40] but the March concert was destined to be the group's last public appearance.

---

* The connotation 'motif of the "World"' was Zemlinsky's own (cf. Rudolf Stephan Hoffmann, 'Zemlinskys Opern', *AT*, 213). For a detailed discussion of the origin, application and possible significance of these motifs, the reader is referred to Part v.
† As the group's most prominent benefactor, it was probably Alois Botstiber who sponsored a competition for original compositions, which Schoenberg won with his *Schilflied*, composed in 1893 (cf. Willi Reich, *Arnold Schönberg, oder der konservative Revolutionär* (Vienna–Frankfurt–Zurich, 1968), 15–16).
‡ The manuscript of Schoenberg's Notturno in A♭ major was long believed lost, but in 1995 the autograph of an untitled Andante for strings and harp, in the Moldenhauer Archive at the Library of Congress, was identified beyond any reasonable doubt as the missing work.

Schoenberg

Accounts of Zemlinsky's first meeting with Schoenberg differ widely. According to Schoenberg's sister Ottilie:

My brother [. . .] was engaged as conductor of several workers' choral societies. At that time he made the acquaintance of Zemlinsky and a little while later, together with him and other young musicians, he founded the Polyhymnia, where they performed their compositions.[41]

In his Schoenberg biography of 1925 Egon Wellesz writes:

A musician [David Joseph Bach] to whom he submitted his compositions for an opinion, advised him to show them to Alexander von Zemlinsky, who was held in high regard by the young musicians. [. . .] Zemlinsky recognized the talent in the works submitted and undertook to give Schoenberg lessons in counterpoint. For several months, whenever he could find the time, he gave him formal tuition, the only such which Schoenberg ever had.[42]

Stuckenschmidt dates the first meeting to 1893, but Wellesz's assertion that they first met at rehearsals of the Polyhymnia orchestra, i.e. in 1895,* is confirmed by Zemlinsky's own account, written in 1934:

The orchestra was not large: a few violins, one viola, one cello and one double-bass. We were young and thirsting for music, and we met once a week to play, no matter what or how. [. . .] At the one desk of cellos sat a young man who maltreated his instrument with more fire than accuracy. [. . .] This cellist was none other than Arnold Schoenberg. At the time he was junior clerk at a bank, but he cared little for his job, preferring sharps and flats to stocks and shares. In this manner I made Schoenberg's acquaintance, which soon grew into an intimate friendship.[43]

Any Viennese artist worth the name would frequent at least one of the coffee-houses, making his choice according to the clique to which he belonged. Zemlinsky was a regular of Café Landtmann, close to the Burgtheater, and Café Griensteidl, situated between the Hofburg and the Volksgarten.† At the latter he introduced Schoenberg to his circle. The music critic Max Graf recalls:

---

* Recalling their early friendship in his essay 'Heart and Brain in Music' (*St-Id*, 55), Schoenberg wrote, 'While studying at the Vienna Conservatoire, [Zemlinsky] prepared at the same time for a competition in piano which he later won', seeming to imply that they had known each other even longer (the only piano competition Zemlinsky is known to have won was the Bösendorfer Prize in the spring of 1890). Schoenberg's remark may however refer to the autumn of 1895, when Zemlinsky was putting the finishing touches to the score of *Sarema* and simultaneously practising César Franck's Violin Sonata for a forthcoming performance with Carl Flesch.

† Griensteidl, popularly known as 'Café Megalomania', was the favoured meeting place for the Jung-Wien writers.

One day Zemlinsky came along with a young man whom he introduced as his pupil, and of whose compositions, as he told us, we would one day hear much more. The new arrival was indeed quite remarkable. His Pierrot-like face bubbled over with energy and defiance, he had the strangest ideas. [. . .] It was Arnold Schoenberg.[44]

Schoenberg's cousin Hans Nachod adds:

They were rebels, attractive rebels, especially attractive for the younger generation [. . .] because they were unconventional in the conventional surroundings of old traditional Vienna. They used to meet in the old café Griensteidl or in the Winterbierhaus [in the Stadtgarten]. Every night they discussed their problems until dawn and then went home drunk.[45]

Graf also recalls Sunday morning chamber-music sessions at the Zirkusgasse apartment of Alexander Rosenzweig, a violinist in the orchestra of the Burgtheater, at which the two friends joined with the operetta composer Edmund Eysler in heated debates on the music of the masters:

Schoenberg's thirst for knowledge was not easy to quench, he always argued his theoretical case in depth and with the energy of conviction.[46]

In a tribute to Zemlinsky on his fiftieth birthday, Schoenberg declared, 'He has remained the man whose attitude I try to imagine when I need advice.'[47] An informal teacher–pupil relationship began soon after their first meeting (Wellesz writes of a period of 'several months' devoted to the study of counterpoint). Yet neither Schoenberg nor Zemlinsky ever described in any detail how or when they worked together, nor is much evidence of a correcting hand to be found in Schoenberg's early manuscripts.[48] Discussion must have centred on style and aesthetics, analysis of the classics, harmony and orchestration, comparative studies of Wagnerian leitmotiv technique and Brahmsian developing variation – 'I had been a "Brahmsian" when I met Zemlinsky,' wrote Schoenberg, 'his love embraced both Brahms and Wagner and soon thereafter I became an equally confirmed addict.'[49] Modern trends in literature must also have been a favourite topic, and it was almost certainly Zemlinsky who introduced Schoenberg to the poetry of Dehmel and Hofmannsthal, Jacobsen and Maeterlinck.

There is no evidence of any subsequent period of formal tuition. Louise Zemlinsky recalled that, 'in conversation, Schoenberg and Zemlinsky restricted themselves to essentials',[50] and Schoenberg's laconic comment, 'the rest I had to find out for myself',[51] while referring primarily to his cello-playing, dispels any notion of regular musical schooling. In an essay written in 1912, Webern observed, with characteristic concision, 'Arnold Schoenberg is self-taught. For a short period he received advice on composing from Alexander von Zemlinsky, not so much in the form of tuition as of congenial conversation.'[52] For six years, until his move to Berlin in December 1901, Schoenberg was Zemlinsky's inseparable companion; that in itself was a complete musical education.

In an interview given in 1913, Zemlinsky outlined his ideas on teaching, with a characteristically elliptical allusion to his former pupil:

My 'method' is based on the principle that my pupils must learn everything that has hitherto been accepted as good and necessary, and only then can they learn – or, if need be, relearn – what their talent requires for free development. Only those who have acquired a thorough knowledge and command of traditional and outmoded ideas can entirely be liberated from them. In the case of a genius, matters are perhaps different. But geniuses have no need of tuition.[53]

In October 1896 came news that Zemlinsky's opera *Sarema* had been awarded the Luitpold Prize. A production was scheduled in Munich for the following autumn, and it became a matter of urgency to prepare the performing materials. Wellesz recounts that Zemlinsky and Schoenberg spent the summer of 1897 in the mountain resort of Payerbach, working on the vocal score. The task afforded Schoenberg invaluable practical experience as well as an opportunity to study Zemlinsky's orchestration at first hand.* As the summer drew to a close, Zemlinsky returned to Vienna, while Schoenberg stayed on to finish his String Quartet in D major. Influences of Brahms and Dvořák abounded, as he was the first to admit, and later, at Zemlinsky's behest, he made numerous alterations to the first movement and entirely rewrote the second and third.

During 1898–9 Schoenberg composed two poems to songs by Karl von Levetzow, *Dank* and *Abschied*.[54] These too were revised under Zemlinsky's critical eye, but now he limited his advice to practical considerations, such as piano texture and vocal tessitura.[55] The summer of 1899 was again spent at Payerbach, where Schoenberg composed several settings of poems by Dehmel, including *Erwartung* op. 2 no. 1 and *Warnung* op. 3 no. 4. The climax of his Dehmel period, however, was the string sextet *Verklärte Nacht*, completed in just three weeks, a musical declaration of love for Mathilde Zemlinsky. 'There's still much *Tristan* to be heard in it,' grumbled her brother, even after the score had been revised,[56] but he was aware that his friend's musical education was now complete. 'After having acquired a certain ability himself,' wrote Schoenberg many years later, 'everybody must start producing something that has not been said before.'[57]

---

* The title page of the autograph vocal score (preserved at the Bavarian State Library in Munich) credits Schoenberg with the piano arrangement ('Clavierauszug mit Text /: von Arnold Schönberg :/'), but the manuscript reveals that Zemlinsky himself prepared the first four scenes (pp. 1–45 of the printed edition), several passages of the following scene and the last 29 bars of act 1. The remainder, by Schoenberg, includes numerous corrections and erasures in Zemlinsky's hand. Neither of them appears to have expended much energy on proofreading the printed edition (Berté, Leipzig, 1899).

Sarema

Luitpold, who was instated as Prince Regent of Bavaria in 1886, could look back on a long and distinguished military career. But he was also passionately interested in the arts, and almost as lavish a patron as the hapless Ludwig II. On 1 November 1893 it was announced that he was sponsoring an opera competition, open to German and Austrian composers and endowed with a munificent prize of 6000 Marks. The response was overwhelming: 103 entries were submitted, and the adjudicators were occupied with the scores for the best part of a year. When they convened, being unable to decide on an outright winner, they agreed to award three prizes of equal value. At the first ballot, *Theuerdank* by Ludwig Thuille and *Der tolle Eberstein* by Arthur Könnemann received the required number of votes, while *Sarema* and Richard Lederer's *Hiob* tied for third place; in a second ballot the vote went to Zemlinsky.[58] During the 1897–8 season, all three scores were performed at the Munich Hofoper. *Theuerdank*, despite the persuasive conducting of Thuille's friend Richard Strauss, was a flop; Könnemann's score fared little better, and his name has since vanished from the annals of music history.* *Sarema*, on the other hand, was greeted with an ovation and well received by the press. Nevertheless the work was revived only once, at Leipzig in 1899, and slumbered for nearly a century in the archives of the Bavarian State Library before being heard again.[59]

As source material Zemlinsky chose *Die Rose vom Kaukasus*, a verse drama by Rudolf von Gottschall.[†] When it was published in 1852, the play's theme was topical. Under Ottoman rule the indigenous peoples of the Caucasus had always enjoyed cultural, religious and administrative freedom. But by the Treaty of Adrianople of 1829 Turkey was obliged to cede extensive territories in the region to Russia. Unwilling to accept Russian colonization, the Abkhasians and Circassians, led by Shamyl (*c.* 1797–1871), Imam of Daghestan, waged an embittered and protracted war of resistance. After the fall of Sevastopol in 1856

---

* Arthur Könnemann (1861–?), active as *Kapellmeister* at Brandenburg, Paderborn and Münster, later Musical Director at Ostrava. He composed several operas to his own librettos, including *Die versunkene Stadt*, performed at Leipzig in 1895. Ludwig Thuille (1861–1907) withdrew the score of *Theuerdank* (with the exception of the overture) after the Munich production. His second opera, *Lobetanz*, to a libretto by Otto Julius Bierbaum, premièred at Karlsruhe in 1897, enjoyed considerable popularity. It was subsequently produced at the Vienna Hofoper under Mahler (1901) and the Metropolitan Opera, New York, under Hertz (1911). Today Thuille is principally remembered for his chamber music.
† At first Zemlinsky considered using a libretto by Salomon Mosenthal, *Die Folkunger*, based on the medieval saga of Magnus Ericsson, King of Norway and Sweden (its theme of conflict between Christian and heathen cultures inspired Strindberg in 1899 to his historical drama *Folkungasagan*). Mosenthal's libretto was set to music in 1875 by Edmund Kretschmer. Of Zemlinsky's projected opera only a few sketches have survived.

the Russians increased their concentration of troops in the Caucasus; the Circassian stronghold was stormed, and Shamyl taken captive.

In the original, one-act version of the play, the leader of the Circassian partisan army bore Shamyl's name. But when in 1862, three years after the ill-fated mullah's seizure by the Russians, Gottschall published a revised, two-act version, he changed the name to 'The Prophet' and introduced a new character, Amul Beg, Sarema's father. It was from this version, republished in 1874 as a low-price paperback, that Zemlinsky drew his libretto. The tragedy of *Sarema* may well have appealed to him for its relevance to his own family background, and it is not insignificant that he dedicated the score to his parents.

Gottschall was a prolific writer,* active not only in theatre but also as novelist, journalist and editor. Though a declared follower of the philosopher Ludwig Feuerbach and his concept of religion as man's 'consciousness of the infinity of his own nature', no such atheist principle applies to *Die Rose vom Kaukasus*. A more palpable influence on the play was Pushkin's epic poem on the antithesis of nature and civilization, *The Captive in the Caucasus*, of which the German edition was published in 1840. Like Sarema, Pushkin's unnamed Caucasian heroine falls in love with a captive Russian soldier and frees him from his chains; aware that she has betrayed the cause of her own people, she commits suicide.†

Cast

Count Tcherikov,‡ Russian colonel (bar); Godunov, captain (bass); Sarema (sop); Amul Beg, her father (bar); Asslan [Circassian prince] (ten); the Prophet (bass). Women, Russian soldiers, Circassians. Time: 1841§

Synopsis

1 *The Russian camp*   Over a game of dice, Tcherikov recounts to Godunov how he rescued Sarema from a band of marauding Cossacks. Though betrothed to Asslan, she returned his love and took refuge with him. Sarema is torn between duty to her home country and love for Tcherikov. Asslan appears, disguised, to lead her to safety from an impending Circassian assault. She begs him to spare Tcherikov.

---

* His list of works includes some twenty-five dramas, a dozen large-scale novels, verse anthologies, translations from the French, literary criticism, a critical edition of the works of Hermann Grabbe and much else.
† Pushkin's poem was set to music by César Cui, using a libretto by Victor Krilov (composed 1857–8; revised 1881–2). It seems unlikely that Zemlinsky was familiar with the work.
‡ In the vocal score, the orthography varies (title page: 'Tscherikoff', musical text: 'Dscherikoff'). Spelling of Russian names is here anglicized.
§ The year is specified by Gottschall, but not in the libretto. In 1841 dissension arose between Russia and the European powers over the free passage of naval vessels through the Dardanelles, and war was only narrowly avoided.

Asslan is discovered and taken captive. Sarema intercedes, but Tcherikov brusquely rejects her. She prays for justice and guidance.

II *The Circassian stronghold*   The Prophet leads his people in a prayer for victory. Sarema breaks the news of Asslan's capture, but Amul Beg, blinded by a stray Russian bullet, exhorts his people to disregard his traitorous daughter. She urges that only an immediate attack can save Asslan's life. The Prophet places his trust in her and, with her father's blessing, she leads the Circassians into combat.

III *The Russian camp*   Asslan, sentenced to death, pours scorn on Tcherikov and declares that he alone loves Sarema. Sounds of a distant skirmish delay his execution. The Circassians, victorious, hasten to his rescue; Tcherikov is captured. Sarema, tormented by guilt, refuses Asslan's offer of reconciliation. Though aware that Tcherikov's love is insincere, she frees him from his chains. Drawing a dagger, she stabs herself. The camp is plundered and razed to the ground.

Zemlinsky worked at *Sarema* with impressive rapidity, composing acts I and II between February and April 1894 and completing act III on 22 June. The orchestration, which he interrupted to compose the Suite for orchestra and the Lustspielouvertüre (Comedy Overture), was completed on 28 August 1895, just three days before the closing date of the competition.[60]

The authorship of the libretto is uncertain, for neither autograph full score nor printed vocal score mentions any name other than Gottschall's. The critic of the *Allgemeine Musik-Zeitung* dwelt at some length on textual cuts and alterations ('the latter, unfortunately, do not always equal the impetus and noble sentiment of Gottschall's muse, and frequently recall the phraseology of an outmoded operatic style') and stated explicitly that 'the composer, still young of years, wrote the libretto [. . .] himself';[61] the *Neue Musikalische Presse*, a periodical published in Vienna and with whose editors Zemlinsky was in close contact, asserted that the composer had 'adapted Gottschall's dramatic poem with the help of his friend Arnold Schoenberg';[62] Louise Zemlinsky maintained that the libretto was written by the composer's father.[63] Since the cost of a professionally written libretto was almost certainly beyond Zemlinsky's means, there seems little reason to doubt any of these three claims.* Presumably he himself adapted the play to his musical requirements, abbreviating the action, smoothing out verse rhythms and apportioning the text into ensembles and choruses. The play is written in blank verse, but in the opera several sections – notably Sarema's act I arias – are recast in rhyming couplets. It seems not improbable that Adolf von Zemlinszky, an adept versifier (if only in the satirical columns of

* The manuscript vocal score includes textual alterations in a hand that is neither Schoenberg's nor Zemlinsky's. These could be Adolf von Zemlinszky's, but it is not inconceivable that they were implemented by the stage director at the Munich Hofoper, Robert Müller, or some other person involved in the first production.

Wiener Punsch) was responsible for these. He probably also contributed the Hymn to Allah, absent in the play, which opens act II. By the time Zemlinsky made Schoenberg's acquaintance, in the autumn of 1895, the orchestration was all but complete. Schoenberg's contribution to the libretto can therefore have consisted only of modifications that occurred to him while working on the vocal score. Considering that none of the librettists had any practical experience of the theatre, the result is surprisingly workmanlike and well paced. Extended monologues are rigorously shortened, and the role of Godunov, depicted by Gottschall as an unscrupulous, drunken desperado, is reduced to a few words. Although the libretto follows the formal outline of the play, scarcely a line remains unaltered.

From the outset Sarema is ensnared by her passion for a stranger. By the time she comprehends the consequences of her reckless erotic drive and the true character of the man whom she adores, her involvement is irreversible. Not only is Tcherikov guilty of genocide, but his actions, even towards those whom he purports to love, are ruthless, and treacherous.* In following her sensual instinct, Sarema betrays her own blood. Lust triumphs over loyalty, a transgression that can be expiated only by self-destruction. The situation, in itself powerful, calls for skilful dramatic architecture and a climactic denouement. But instead of pulling the threads of his drama together in the coda, as it were, of a gripping symphonic finale, Gottschall expounds his heroine's dilemma in the first-movement exposition. Sarema lives on to see Asslan rescued and Amul Beg avenged, to be forgiven by her kith and kin, admired for her courage and determination, and triumphant over the dastardly Tcherikov: her sins are expiated. At this stage in the drama her suicide appears gratuitous, melodramatic and ultimately unmotivated.

Gottschall's play depicts the violation of a Caucasian idyll by a horde of brutal, dull-witted and drunken invaders. But by depicting the Circassians as noble savages, he patronizes them; and by dwelling recurrently on the scenic beauties, quaint costumes and picturesque rituals of the region, he trivializes his message. When *Die Rose vom Kaukasus* was published, relations between Russia and the European states were at their lowest ebb; but by the 1890s Tsar Alexander III had long since established peaceful relations with Germany, and memories of the internecine struggle had faded. Zemlinsky accordingly toned down the aspect of political agitation and expunged Gottschall's purple passages – silver-clad warriors etched against golden Caspian sunsets – concentrating the action on the timeless themes of *eros* and *agape*, national identity

---

* Gottschall introduces a reference to Tcherikov's mistress in St Petersburg, a Countess Shumla. Contemplating his promotion to a high-ranking position at court, for which she has intrigued on his behalf, he muses: 'And Sarema? [. . .] She shall accompany me – I shall find a way of concealing the affair from the Countess.'

and religious belief. For his purpose a precise geographical or racial background was unimportant, and his score, apart from a few mild orientalisms in the Hymn to Allah, avoids *couleur locale*.

His music is often Wagnerian, with recitatives punctuated by *Lohengrin*-inspired orchestral interjections, *gruppetto* figures similar to those which adorn the melodic lines of *Der fliegende Holländer* and *Tannhäuser*, softly pulsating figures for solo timpani introduced, as in the *Ring*, at moments of quiet suspense. In some instances Zemlinsky is drawn further – dangerously far – into Wagner's gravitational field: the harmonization of Asslan's arioso (pp. 39–41) pays undisguised homage to *Tristan*; animated syncopations combined with a running melody in the bass (pp. 109–11) paraphrase the opening of *Siegfried* act III. Several contemporary commentators complained of a lack of individuality in the melodic invention of *Sarema*, but none expressed surprise or even annoyance at the Wagnerisms; indeed Zemlinsky was praised for them. 'We were regaled with *Tristan*s, *Ring*s and *Meistersinger*s, and it was done with absorbing deftness', wrote one critic.[64]

Yet *Sarema* cannot be dismissed as mere Wagnerian pastiche. Neither the swift pace of the action nor the luminous scoring in any way reflects the tradition of Bayreuth; the solo vocal and choral writing, remarkably assured for a composer with no previous operatic experience, owes less to Germanic declamation than to Slavic cantilena, and many an elegiac turn of phrase reflects Zemlinsky's youthful enthusiasm for Tchaikovsky. In lieu of object-orientated leitmotiv technique, a small repertory of motifs and melodic figures is used to symbolize affect and atmosphere.* In the D minor Symphony and the E minor Quartet Zemlinsky had demonstrated his technical skill in the manipulation of small motivic cells. Now he was confronted for the first time with the problem of integrating these techniques into a larger structure. In later operas he sought the 'brief, forceful motif, whose meaning is unambiguously established within two or four bars'.[65] Where in *Sarema* he lacked experience in moulding drama to musical infrastructure, he resorted, like most of his contemporaries, to the operatic lingua franca of his time: the language of Bayreuth.

At the première, the title role was sung by the legendary Milka Ternina.[†] Much of the success of *Sarema*, according to critical opinion, was hers. Yet Zemlinsky, too, was greeted by the public – already after act II – with spontaneous and heartfelt enthusiasm. The critic of the *Münchener Neueste Nachrichten* described the occasion in graphic detail:

* The most prominent motif, a 'Circassian' rhythm representing energy and defiance –

♩♩ ♪ ♩ ♩ – sounds in the opening bar of the orchestral Prelude. It reappears frequently in Zemlinsky's later works.
† Famed for her Kundry at Bayreuth, Ternina was one of the finest Wagner singers of her generation. She appeared regularly at Covent Garden and the Met.

The public was utterly amazed by the uncommonly youthful appearance of the fragile, cleanshaven little man, who repeatedly came onstage and gratefully kissed the hand of his leading lady. An evident wave of surprise went through the house, and the applause swelled appreciably – a scene that was repeated after act III, when the singers, joined by the conductor and producer, took countless curtain-calls.[66]

Piano Music

Zemlinsky never entered any of his piano pieces for competitions, and few after the Ländliche Tänze were even intended for public consumption. They are private utterances and, in the best sense, salon music: intimate thoughts, clandestine greetings, messages of love and desire.

The Four Ballades, composed c. 1893–4, shortly after the D minor Symphony, constitute a four-movement sonata. A discarded title page, with a dedication to J. N. Fuchs, reveals that the work was originally intended to be published as op. 2. In the event, it remained unpublished until 1996.

Archibald Douglas, based on a poem by Theodor Fontane, is a brooding, D minor triptych in the romantic 'Scots' tradition of Bruch and Mendelssohn. In *Der König von Thule*, based on Gretchen's song in Goethe's *Faust I*, Zemlinsky submits the motivic particles of the D minor Symphony to new, preponderantly chromatic scrutiny. *Der Wassermann* (Justinus Kerner), a lilting, A♭ major ländler with an eruptive, tonally unstable trio, recalls the more picaresque aspect of Hugo Wolf. The A minor *Intermezzo* finale is based on a secret programme. After a 'passionately animated' opening section, the music dissolves into a chromatic two-part canon, in which the pianist's hands meet and entwine: a music-room seduction, an unchronicled teacher–pupil romance? In the coda Zemlinsky quotes a famous line of Goethe, 'Nur wer die Sehnsucht kennt, weiss was ich leide.'* His manuscript offers no clue as to its relevance.

Perhaps the *Albumblatt*, composed in May 1895 and subtitled 'Erinnerung aus Wien' ('Souvenir from Vienna'), can be read as a page from the same secret diary. Composed in Zemlinsky's key of despair, E♭ minor, the piece is 'dedicated in friendship to my dear pupil Catharina Maleschewski'. An impetuous middle section dies away with an allusion to the *Tristan* Prelude,[67] and the reprise is abandoned after five bars to make way for an identified quotation from Tchaikovsky's setting of *Nur wer die Sehnsucht kennt* (op. 6 no. 6, composed in 1869). Nothing in Zemlinsky's early music matches the despondency of the closing bars.

The Skizze in C minor, a *danza grotesca* published in 1896, is the revised version of a miniature for piano, composed c. 1891. In a languorous trio section,

---

* Mignon's song from *Wilhelm Meister*, popularly known in English as 'None but the lonely heart'. In this context a more exact translation would be: 'Only he who knows desire can understand my anguish.'

absent from the earlier version, Zemlinsky once again introduces the characteristic falling minor 7th of the Tchaikovsky song. The predominantly whimsical
atmosphere of the piece suggests, however, that the 'anguish' of the Mignon
episode had by now faded.

In the autumn of 1898 Zemlinsky composed a suite of four brief tone-poems
in ternary form, entitled Fantasien über Gedichte von Richard Dehmel
(Fantasies on Poems by Richard Dehmel). *Stimme des Abends* is based on one
of Dehmel's most elliptical texts, a filigree study of silence and near-silence,
with an undertone of *Angst*. At a technical level, the poem is remarkable for its
asymmetrical metre and irregular rhyme scheme. Zemlinsky responds more
eagerly to these than to the fragile mood of suspense (EX. 4A). In his setting of
Dehmel's *Erwartung*, composed the following year, Schoenberg paid homage to
the fluttering piano figures of *Stimme des Abends* (EX. 4B)[68]

The third Dehmel Fantasy was originally headed by the poem *Ideale Landschaft*:

EX. 4A   Zemlinsky, *Stimme des Abends*, op. 9 no. 1

EX. 4B   Schoenberg, *Erwartung*, op. 2 no. 1

Du hattest einen Glanz auf deiner Stirn, / und eine hohe Abendklarheit war, / und sahst nur immer weg von mir, / ins Licht, ins Licht – / und fern verscholl das Echo meines Aufschreis.

Your forehead was aglow with light, / the evening sky was clear and tall, / you turned your gaze away from me / towards the light – / my cry of pain re-echoed in the distance.

The choice of text may have reflected a crisis in Zemlinsky's relationship with Melanie Guttmann, whose gaze at that time was evidently already turned 'towards the light' of a new life in America.* Yet the warm, glowing colours and lyric melodic lines of the piece scarcely echo Dehmel's 'cry of pain'. On 11 May 1901 Zemlinsky signed a contract to publish the Dehmel Fantasies. The following day he wrote to Alma Schindler:

I'd like to dedicate the volume to you, I must do so. But your name should not appear, that would be compromising. What should I do? Think it over![69]

For this delicate problem he himself found the characteristically secretive solution. Instead of 'Ideale Landschaft' he headed the piece with another poem, 'Liebe', Dehmel's quintessential vision of spiritual union:

Du sahst durch meine Seele in die Welt, / es war auch Deine Seele: still versanken / im Strom des Schauens zwischen uns die Schranken – / Es ruhten Welt und Du in mir gesellt.

You looked straight through my soul into the world, / it was your soul as well: softly in the stream of / our gaze the barriers between us fell – / You and the world, at one, reposed in me.

A first proof copy of the Dehmel Fantasies was ready by the end of September. Zemlinsky dispatched it to Alma at once. In his accompanying letter, while revealing nothing of the music's past history, he hinted darkly at the change of dedication:[†]

You should play through the opening bars of the piece entitled *Liebe* from time to time. They were conceived in an atmosphere of warmth and greater contentment, also of greater calm. At that time, three years ago, I didn't know you. Today a piece of the same sort would probably be more yearning, more turbulent, more pessimistic.[70]

A Jewish Wedding

On 25 May 1896, Dr Isidor Kahan, Rabbi from Novogrudok, age thirty-six, married Helene Bauer, age twenty, daughter of Cantor Jacob Bauer, at the

---

* The song *Der Tag wird kühl*, with a dedication 'to my Mela as farewell greeting', was composed in June 1897.
† The opening bars of *Liebe* are reproduced in EX. 63 (p. 305).

Sephardic synagogue in the Zirkusgasse. As Michael Papo recalls, these wedding ceremonies were graded by tariff:

There was an enlarged choir for a first-class wedding, and two harps reinforced the organ music. [. . .] Special liturgical music had been composed. [. . .] Second-class weddings were simpler. The canopy was still very beautiful, but not to be compared with the first-class canopy, and it could be put up by the caretaker. There were no harps, only the organ and the normal choir, using different music.[71]

Evidently the Kahan–Bauer wedding was a second-class affair, for no harps were played. As the bridegroom stepped under the canopy, the ministrant greeted him with the traditional words from Psalm 118:26, 'Baruch aba' ('Blessed be he [that cometh in the name of the Lord]'). Normally the congregation would have responded with a prayer of benediction, 'Mi adir'. Artistically speaking, however, this was a more than a first-class wedding, for the prayer had been set to music specially for the occasion by Zemlinsky. 'Baruch aba; Mi adir' for cantor, mixed chorus and organ, published in 1995 as *Hochzeitsgesang*, is his only surviving setting of a Jewish liturgical text. His Hebrew was rusty,[72] and a few turns of phrase from *Waldgespräch*, composed a few weeks earlier, crept into the opening tenor solo. Nevertheless, euphonious vocal writing and effortless technical command raise the *Hochzeitsgesang* above the level of a mere occasional piece. Zemlinsky was later to recall it, if only subconsciously, in his settings of Psalms 23 and 13.

Rabbi Kahan and his wife later settled in Brno. On 31 March 1942 they were arrested by the Gestapo and transported to the ghetto of Terezín; Helene perished there on 1 October 1942, her husband on 30 November.

Chamber Music

At the Tonkünstlerverein it was standard practice to submit new scores for trial performance before including them in public concerts. If the verdict was negative, the committee could effectively hinder a work's further dissemination. As long as Brahms was alive, this system functioned satisfactorily, indeed he took genuine pleasure in guiding young composers along what he considered the path of righteousness. His positive attitude was also reflected in the annual *Verein* competitions, which had the practical effect of promoting and simultaneously subsidizing the prize-winners. After his death the system became subject to abuse.

An interesting case of a work that evidently failed to pass its trial was Zemlinsky's String Quartet in E minor, composed c. 1893 and first published in 1997. As Werner Loll has shown in his perceptive analysis,[73] the first movement, despite a dense network of motivic relationships, harmonic ambiguities and metrical irregularities, is a model of logic and clarity. For a beginner in the

art of quartet composition, Zemlinsky's command of string texture is also outstanding. Neither the scherzo nor the ensuing andante attain the same level of
proficiency or artistry, however, while the finale is notable for harmonic piquancy
rather than for melodic or structural originality. The opening bar combines an
accented passing-note in the violin with a chromatic descent in the viola, jolt-
ing the listener momentarily into D♯ major before the basic key, E minor, has
even established itself. Legitimate though the voice-leading may be, the aural
effect is startling, Zemlinsky stands before his judges, as it were, with the self-
assurance of a truculent schoolboy.

EX. 5

From a set of parts among the composer's posthumous papers it transpires
that the E minor Quartet was played through at least once, and that modifications and corrections were implemented by the players during rehearsal. More
far-reaching alterations are pencilled into the autograph score, but only as far as
the exposition repeat in the first movement. *Toujours en avant*: since it was not
in Zemlinsky's nature to brood over setbacks, the score and parts were stowed
away in his music cupboard, and remained in oblivion for over a century.

The String Quintet in D minor, composed in 1894–5, must also have been
subjected to private screening, probably in the autumn of 1895. Presumably at
this juncture – rather than after the first public performance, as Zemlinsky
implies in his 'Recollections' – he was summoned to his historic audience with
Brahms:

As I shyly attempted to defend a passage in the development section which seemed
to me, in the Brahmsian sense, quite successful, he opened the score of a Mozart
string quintet and demonstrated the perfection of its 'still unsurpassed formal
design'. And his concluding remark sounded perfectly objective and matter-of-
course: 'That's the method handed down from Bach to myself!'[74]

Persuaded of the need for thorough revision, Zemlinsky discarded the finale, an
Allegro molto in D minor, and substituted a delightful major-key *Prestissimo*
which, as the critic of the *Wiener Tageblatt* reported, was 'dashed off in just
a couple of days'.[75] A virtuoso caprice of epic proportions (336 bars), the

movement is motivically related to its predecessor, but with an added dash of Hungarian temperament. Contrast is provided by a yearning second subject in F major, whose syncopated sigh later establishes rhythmic independence and is ultimately transformed into the 'Circassian' rhythm of *Sarema*. In the transition from first to second subject Zemlinsky surreptitiously hints at the leitmotiv of the 'Guileless Fool' from *Parsifal*. A recitative-like passage inserted before the reprise correspondingly introduces the 'Self' motif.*

It was generally agreed that the D minor Quintet was the finest of Zemlinsky's earlier chamber works. He nevertheless appears either to have mislaid or destroyed the manuscript fair copy, retaining only the original, unrevised version of the first movement and a separate score of the new finale.† Some impression of the lost scherzo and adagio can at least be gleaned from press reports of the first public performance, given by the Hellmesberger Quartet on 5 March 1896. Hanslick, who would have preferred the 'witty' scherzo to have a 'more keenly pointed conclusion', described the slow movement as 'somewhat aphoristic, with a deeply soulful note';[76] Krtsmary from the *Neue Musikalische Presse* added, 'The adagio (in Ab major), in a key slightly too far removed from the preceding scherzo (A major) and, in particular, from the ensuing finale (D major), is a movement bathed in euphony and imbued with a warm, profound sensibility';[77] the *Neues Wiener Tageblatt* mentioned 'the delicate, hopping waltz rhythm of the scherzo theme and the ardently persuasive melody of the adagio',[78] and the critic of the *Sonn- und Montagszeitung* concluded, 'In all four movements, particularly the middle ones, the Quintet contains moments of striking beauty; but its roses are embedded in wreaths of thorns which, for all the skill with which they are woven, prick no less keenly.'[79]

Zemlinsky's vocabulary of melodies and rhythms reveals the devout 'Brahmin' at every turn. But where the E minor Quartet respects the classical concept of chamber music as civilized discourse between like-minded individuals, the Quintet places its protagonists on a stage, with five actors declaiming epic texts in tones of feverish exaltation. By and large the first-movement exposition respects musical convention, but the development section, an uncompromisingly polyphonic case history of hysterical outbursts and nervous relapses, grinding dissonances and jagged cross-accents, repeatedly violates classical syntax. Composure is momentarily restored in the recapitulation, but the coda again plumbs Cimmerian depths.

Had Zemlinsky continued in this boldly theatrical vein, his position *vis-à-vis* the conservative élite of the Tonkünstlerverein would soon have become

---

* The reference to *Parsifal* is at bars 77–81, the 'Self' motif at bars 146–50. The Skizze for piano, written a few months later, encompasses a comparably whimsical quotation from the 'Good Friday Spell' (bars 14–15).
† These two movements were published in 1994. The surviving autograph also includes fragmentary sketches for the three remaining movements.

untenable. Brahms must have indicated to him, in plain language, where and how he had overstepped the mark. In a situation where Schoenberg would have scowled defiance, he humbly followed the call to order.

The Serenade (or Suite) in A major for violin and piano, composed in the aftermath of this traumatic experience, was first performed by Rudolf Fitzner, with the composer at the piano, on 24 January 1896. The opening intrada begs the vexed question of a development section by avoiding sonata form altogether. In the ensuing movements (adagio, scherzo, waltz and finale) a self-conscious air of rustic nonchalance prevails but, apart from some surface appeal, the work has little to offer. The melodic invention is arid and short-breathed; a handful of piquant textures scarcely conceal the lack of inner compulsion.

In the light of the circumstances under which it was composed, the Clarinet Trio in D minor op. 3, following only a few months after the String Quintet and in the same key, can be understood as Zemlinsky's considered reaction to what he clearly felt was justified criticism. The effusiveness and elation of the earlier work are now tempered by discipline and circumspection; on every page the music reflects a spiritual and stylistic debt to Brahms. Yet this is no declaration of bankruptcy: the beauty and expressive power of the music speak for themselves. Technically speaking, the work is a miracle, a feeding of the five thousand. Every melodic idea originates in the three-note ur-motif D–E–F with which the work begins:

EX. 6

Commentary In bar 2, using a rhythmic formula frequently found in the chamber music of Robert Fuchs, the ur-motif is interverted to generate a *Drehfigur* (pivotal figure). Bar 3 expands the idea to D–E–G, Zemlinsky's 'Self' motif, rhythmically iterated as an augmentation of the dotted figure in bar 2. Bar 4 is at once the retrograde of bar 1 and an interversion of the *Drehfigur*. In the piano, bars 1–2,

Zemlinsky inverts and augments the ur-motif, thereby evolving an asymmetrical rhythmic figure of 2(5+3) quavers – a trump card which he holds in reserve for the climax of the development section.[80] In bars 2–3 the inverted ur-motif overlaps with its diminished interversion B♭–G♯–A. The minor 3rd, D–F, introduced as an oscillating accompaniment in the piano l.h., delineates the outer boundaries of the ur-motif while also serving as a flashback to the D minor String Quintet, in which the same figure plays a prominent role. (The *Poco mosso con fantasia* section of the andante uses the same oscillating minor 3rd to set the scene for a dramatic, quasi-improvised 'Zigeuner' music, reminiscent of the *minore* section in the adagio of Brahms's Clarinet Quintet.) The motivic cell D–E–G♯ in the second half of bar 2 anticipates the 'Self' motif of the following bar. From bars 1–4 the piano r.h. traces the contour of a subsidiary figure in 4ths, D–A–D, repeated and inverted in the bass line of bars 4–5. The motivic significance of this seemingly nondescript thematic particle is revealed only in the andante; later it dominates the entire third movement.* Similarly, in bars 3–4, the piano r.h. outlines the 'Self' motif (A–B♭–D). In these opening four bars, only the E♭ major arpeggiated figure in the piano l.h. originates neither directly nor indirectly from the ur-motif. But here too, economy is of the essence: arpeggio is the only ornament used in the entire composition. At the summary restatement of the first subject in bar 16, moreover, the figure acquires a structural function. Combined with the 4ths motif, the arpeggio also furnishes a fanfare-like main theme for the middle section of the andante; transformed into a *ppp* wash of D major, it becomes the *envoi* of the finale.

This rigorous concentration of motivic relationships is sustained throughout, indeed to a degree far in excess of anything in the music of Brahms himself. Some commentators have interpreted Zemlinsky's choice of clarinet,[†] cello and piano as a gesture of homage. If that was his intention, then he limited his gesture to the choice of instruments. The writing itself is far removed from the spare textures and autumnal colouring of Brahms's op. 114 Trio, composed five years earlier; and where Brahms is amiably conversational, Zemlinsky is passionately rhetorical. Behind the mask of conformity, his op. 3, like the String Quintet, is essentially a wordless psychodrama.

The String Quartet in A major op. 4, composed in the summer of 1896, is less economical and less earnest a work than op. 3. A major was Zemlinsky's key of joy, a quality reflected in every bar. Each movement explores the key from a different aspect: the opening *Allegro con fuoco* modulates widely; the scherzo juxtaposes Lydian major with subdominant minor; the slow movement opens in the tonic minor but soon moves into the major key, in which it also

---

* In the finale, V–I progressions generally supplant the mediant relationships of the previous movements. D–A–D takes its final bow as bass line of the closing bar, as a simple cadential formula.
† The Trio was composed at a time when capable clarinettists were rare but talented amateur string-players abundant. Accordingly it was published with a substitute part for violin. Whether Zemlinsky adapted the score himself is uncertain, but the imagination with which it is done – with liberal use of octave displacements, double-stops and pizzicati – implies authenticity.

closes; in the closing *Vivace e con fuoco* Zemlinsky combines the tonal gregar-
iousness of the opening movement with the Lydian inflexion of the scherzo and
the plagal connection of the trio.

The opening movement teases the ear with constantly varying asymmetries
of rhythm and metre. Structurally speaking, its first subject group is assembled
from three contrasted subsections. These can be further subdivided into nine
distinct rhythmic figures, which are varied, contracted, expanded and reversed,
much in same way as the pitch material. Loll remarks on the resultant 'disjunctive' quality of the exposition, and adds, 'Even in the works of Brahms,
such systematic use of rhythmical complexity is nowhere to be found.'[81] To
offset these irregularities, the movement luxuriates in the expansiveness of an
unabridged recapitulation.

The formal outline of the scherzo corresponds to that of Brahms's Second
Symphony: a *Prestissimo* middle section flanked by *Allegretto* outer sections. In
a question-and-answer scheme of major 2nds (<u>C♯–D♯–</u> F♯–E), the opening bars
cite the 'Self' motif; in bars 5–6 the motif is diminished and interverted
(<u>C♯–E–B♯</u>), in bars 8–11 a three-part contrapuntal array combines two further
variants (<u>B–C♯–[E]</u>–D and [E]–<u>D–C♯–F♯</u>). The motif is also a constitutive
element of the *Prestissimo*, where it is, however, ultimately swept aside by the
vigorous rhythm of a *furiant*.

In the slow movement, marked *Breit und kräftig*, the 'World' motif (A–G–E)
is combined with its transposed retrograde in the bass (A–C–D), and answered
by an interversion of the 'Self' motif (B–D–A). The melodic line of bars 3–4
repeats this procedure in varied form, while the inner voices and bass-line move
sequentially (EX. 7).

The first performance of op. 4, given only a few days before that of the
Clarinet Trio, was an unqualified success. '[The work] is more clearly articulated
and less encumbered by juvenile utterances than the String Quintet introduced
last year,' enthused one of the critics, while also encouraging the composer to
still greater independence: 'Brahms is just as dangerous a model as Wagner. He
who considers himself a follower promptly becomes a duplicator. Zemlinsky
has too many original ideas to betray himself entirely.'[82] W. W. Cobbett, the
great connoisseur, considered the A major Quartet 'an enjoyable experience for
both players and audience',[83] and Rudolf Stephan Hoffmann wrote in 1912 of
a 'classical purity and richness, which some may today find outmoded, but
offers every one of us joyous relaxation and gathering of strength'.[84]

Orchestral Music

At the jubilee concert on 18 March 1895* honours were shared between Zem-

* See p. 34.

EX. 7*

linsky and his near-contemporary Robert Gound,† the former conducting his new Suite for Orchestra, the latter a melodrama entitled *Der Ilsenstein*. More than two years had passed since the performance of the D minor Symphony, and this concert afforded Zemlinsky an ideal opportunity to test his progress in the field of orchestration before proceeding with the scoring of

* At the reprise (bars 86–7), the boldness of the harmony is heightened by homophony:

† Robert Gound (1865–1927) was born near Heidelberg and studied in Leipzig and Vienna. He was active primarily as accompanist and voice teacher. In 1923, returning to Vienna after nearly a decade spent in Switzerland, he changed the spelling of his name to Gund.

Sarema. The unfortunate Gound received a roasting in the press. 'This kind of melodrama is an aesthetic absurdity, and we are astounded that the Conservatoire encourages its production. [. . .] The work affords neither a negative nor a positive opinion about its composer', wrote Gustav Schoenaich.[85] For the 'warm-hearted poetry, [. . .] imagination and passion' of Zemlinsky's score, on the other hand, he found nothing but praise. The *Oesterreichische Rundschau* was equally enthusiastic: 'The three pieces [. . .] offer a rich diversity of melody and rhythm, and enthral the listener with youthful freshness and fire.'[86]

In the eyes of the Viennese critics the young Zemlinsky could do no wrong. But he himself must have been aware that these early triumphs were short-lived. Proudly he collected and displayed his trophies, but honest self-appraisal left him in little doubt of the actual worth of these works, none of which he ever troubled to publish or even revive. Despite the unison chorus of praise, the melodic invention of his Suite was insipid, its 'rhythmic diversity' meagre. The opening movement, *Legende*, emulates the style and architecture of *Archibald Douglas* (no. 1 of the Ballades for piano), with minor-key outer sections flanking an animated, major-key hunting scene. In the ensuing *Reigen* (round-dance) and scherzo-finale (*Humoreske*), clear textures, clean lines and precisely spaced chording indicate that Zemlinsky had shaken off the outmoded house style of the Conservatoire and begun to assimilate the more sophisticated orchestral techniques of Tchaikovsky and Bizet, Johann Strauss and Suppé.

Sterling craftsmanship coupled with unsophisticated charm and unexceptional melodic invention is also found in the Lustspielouvertüre to Wartenegg's *Der Ring des Ofterdingen*. Wilhelm Wartenegg, Edler von Wertheimstein, was Custodian of the Imperial Art Gallery. His award-winning four-act comedy was published by Reclam, Leipzig, and first performed at the Deutsches Volkstheater in February 1891. Presumably Zemlinsky composed his overture for a stage production of the play, but there is no documentary evidence of a commission or other theatrical connection. Begun in the autumn of 1894, the score was completed in March of the following year, three days before the jubilee concert. The main theme was later salvaged for the mime drama *Ein Lichtstrahl*.

Waldgespräch, a ballad for soprano, strings, two horns and harp, was composed in 1895–6 for the Polyhymnia. Zemlinsky evidently considered that the jaunty ländler rhythm of Schumann's *Liederkreis* setting (op. 39 no. 3) failed to reflect the eerie atmosphere of Eichendorff's poem. Already in 1890 he had composed a setting of the text in E♭ minor as a dramatic *scena* for voice and piano. The more expansive instrumental setting, in G minor, accentuates the poem's theatrical potential, ingeniously exploits the colouristic possibilities offered by the small ensemble and opens up reserves of dramatic intensity which the music of the previous months had left untapped. Once again the critics were on Zemlinsky's side:

The work's fresh, original ideas and genuinely exalted, youthful fire made a great impression on the audience and unleashed an intense salvo of applause, which was directed as much towards the talented young composer as at Miss Gutmann [*sic*], who helped him to his triumph with a beautiful, well-schooled voice and sensitive interpretation.[87]

With the Symphony in B♭ major, composed in 1897, Zemlinsky won the Beethoven Prize, an award sponsored by the Tonkünstlerverein and partly financed by Brahms. Of all the Viennese musical prizes this was the most prestigious. However, as with the Luitpold Prize, the honours had to be shared, this time with Robert Gound and his Symphony in G major. Gound and Zemlinsky presented their prize-winning works to the public at a Vienna Philharmonic concert on 5 March 1899. Zemlinsky had handed in his manuscript with a *nom de plume* taken from *Die Meistersinger* (act III, scene II):*

Wer Preise erkennt und Preise stellt, / der will am End auch, dass man ihm gefällt.

The prizes are granted, the prizes supplied, / and he who presents them will be satisfied.

If these words imply a self-assurance bordering on arrogance, they are amply confirmed by the music, indeed to such an extent that one critic wrote that 'Zemlinsky sometimes bites off more than he can chew, as if to say: look what I can do!'[88]

The work is cyclic in form. A motto theme (itself prefaced by a fanfare of falling 5ths) encircles the first movement, appears as a distant reminiscence in the coda of the scherzo and provides much of the motivic substance for the adagio. Epithets of potency accompany the *Allegro* marking of the first movement: *mit Feuer und Kraft* (with fire and strength), and after a *Don Juan*-esque upward rush of semiquavers the first subject, *fortissimo* on horns and cellos, is marked *mit Schwung* (with energy). For all his individual vitality and orchestral brilliance, Zemlinsky does little to suppress stylistic allegiances. The third subject emulates Dvořák's habit of adorning a lyric theme with a rhythmically animated counter-subject, and a Slavonic spirit also imbues much of the scherzo. Wagner's *Meistersinger* apprentices rush on to the stage for the *breiter* section of the second-subject group in the first movement; young Siegfried forces the transition from development to recapitulation, and in the slow movement the 'Self' motif, disguised as a soft A♭ major brass chorale, points unambiguously in the direction of *Parsifal*. Shadows of Schubert and Bruckner pass across the scherzo, but the finale, a set of twenty-six variations with interpolated fugato on an eight-bar *cantus firmus*, bears the unmistakable stamp of a devoted

---

* Though intended merely as an identification tag for administrative purposes, the motto is included in the Universal Edition full score, published in 1977.

'Brahmin'. Even if the movement lacks the power and purposefulness of its model – the passacaglia finale of Brahms's Fourth Symphony – the layout is innovative, the plan ambitious, its execution imaginative. Webern's Passacaglia op. 1 and Schoenberg's Variations for Orchestra op. 31 can both be traced to these roots. The weakness of passacaglia form, however, particularly in a symphonic context, is the lack of larger paragraphs and clearly defined points of culmination. Brahms solves this problem with mastery; Zemlinsky tries too hard ('bites off more than he can chew') and fails. Though he does much to hold his structure together, it dissolves all too readily into its component parts, separated as they are by tempo changes, *ritardandi* and silences. He does keep a startling *coup de théâtre* in reserve for the coda, however, in the shape of the motto theme, to which the *cantus firmus* now proves itself to be a perfectly tailored countersubject. Yet even this moment of panache cannot impose cohesion on an inherently discontinuous form. Zemlinsky appears to have been more intent on long-term cohesion, however, for when in the final bars his trumpets blaze out the salient falling 5th with which the Symphony opens, they echo the jubilant *envoi* of the D minor Symphony. The message is loud and clear: this score marks the end of an apprenticeship. The years of study are over; mastery has been attained.

A Brahms Memorial

In April 1896 Zemlinsky composed *Frühlingsbegräbnis* for soprano and baritone soli, chorus and orchestra, to a poem by Paul Heyse. Judging by the textures of the first manuscript sketch, he conceived the work for small forces and with piano accompaniment, perhaps for performance at the Polyhymnia. But by the time he had penned the exultant closing bars of the coda, it must have become clear to him that larger forces would be required. The first version, composed between April and July 1896, orchestrated the following year and dedicated to the memory of Brahms, was scored for a classical orchestra with double woodwind; later (*c.* 1902–3), at the behest of the Süddeutsche Musikverlag* in Strasbourg, Zemlinsky revised the work and enlarged the orchestra to include triple woodwind and two harps.

Heyse is best remembered for translations and paraphrases, such as those immortalized by Hugo Wolf in the *Italienisches Liederbuch*. But *Frühlingsbegräbnis*, an original work, is no comparable masterpiece (the poet omitted it from the collected edition of his works). The story is allegorical: a funeral cortège of animals and fairies bears Spring, a comely youth transfixed by the first rays of Summer's sun, to his last resting place; a woodpecker preaches a

---

* The Süddeutsche Musikverlag, founded in 1899 by Fritz Müller, went into liquidation in 1992 and was taken over by Bosworth & Co.

sermon on eternity and rebirth; as the funeral draws to a close, the elfin mourners are blasted away by a violent thunderstorm. Zemlinsky did what he could for the text, with expressive melodic lines and sumptuous colours, and by moulding it into a through-composed symphonic form (dead march, scherzo-waltz, andante, allegro-finale, coda), he imposed a semblance of order upon its unbalanced structure. The principal theme, a double-motif of falling triads and a rising 4th, owes allegiance to the second movement of the *Deutsches Requiem*,* but otherwise there is less influence of Brahms than of Wagner. By introducing a brief fugato in the storm scene, lip service is also paid to the conventions of nineteenth-century choral-society tradition.

Frühlingsbegräbnis, which may have been considered unsuitable for the official Brahms memorial concerts, remained unperformed until February 1900. But then, at a concert of the Gesellschaft der Musikfreunde in the famous 'Golden Hall' of the Musikverein, it was given in style. Zemlinsky himself presided over the Vienna Philharmonic Orchestra and the three hundred voices of the Singverein. The critic of the *Neues Wiener Journal* complained of 'a lack both of melody and overall unity' but granted, if grudgingly, that 'the handling of the chorus and orchestra is ingenious and sometimes truly astounding.'[89] The public and most of the press were firmly on Zemlinsky's side. Following only three weeks after the triumphant première of *Es war einmal . . .* at the Hofoper, this performance marked the zenith – alas, too soon – of his Viennese career.

---

* As the idea is metrically altered, this affinity is more apparent to the eye than to the ear. Zemlinsky's tempo marking, *marschmässig* (in the style of a march), could be interpreted as an intentional clue to the origin of his idea for it is identical to that of Brahms, but it is equally possible that both the double-motif and its accompanying tempo marking were subconscious borrowings.

4

Fin de siècle

By the turn of the century Zemlinsky's musical style had acquired a physiognomy which, in four further decades of creative activity, was to remain fundamentally unchanged. His artistic credo could be condensed into one sentence,
which he formulated in 1902: 'A great artist, who possesses everything needed
to express the essentials, must respect the boundaries of beauty, even if he
extends them far further than ever before.'[1] In this spirit, he strove to push his
music to the furthest extremes of tonal harmony. Key, no longer an absolute
value, gradually merges into timbre; formal cohesion, emancipated from any
traditional system of tonal relationships, relies increasingly on the brief motivic
cell. But Zemlinsky also upheld the principles of functional harmony and
respected the traditions of key symbolism – attributes of tonal harmony that he
found essential to his art. And because for him tonality provided all the raw
material he ever needed for articulating his individual world of expression, he
never felt the need to move entirely beyond its domain.

Where a painter may work more productively with blues than with reds, a
sculptor in wood rather than stone, several twentieth-century tonal composers
have preferred, or perhaps were involuntarily drawn towards, one particular
key: Janáček, for instance, to Ab minor, Busoni to C major, Korngold to F#
major – and Zemlinsky to D minor. His early compositions in that key include
the Symphony of 1892–3, the String Quintet and Clarinet Trio; shorter essays
include the first Ballade, the Prelude to *Sarema* and several lieder. After the turn
of the century, as key began for him to lose structural relevance, D minor
became an area towards which all paths tended to lead. Rudolf Stephan
Hoffmann found that 'D minor characterizes in Zemlinsky specific moments of
tragic despair.'[2] But despair is only one of many affects that Zemlinsky articulates in that key. The pensive humour of the 'Schneiderlein Song' in *Kleider
machen Leute*, the emotional volatility of the Second Quartet, the grim energy
of the Sinfonietta, the finely drawn melancholy of such late songs as *Und einmal gehst du* (1933) and *Ahnung Beatricens* (1935) – all these find their expressive qualities in the colouristic potential of D minor.

In 1935, Schoenberg's pupil Viktor Ullmann published a brief systematic
study of all the major and minor keys, based on the colour theories of Rudolf
Steiner.* D minor, he wrote –

---

* Ullmann's theories of the relationship between sound and colour coincide largely with those

is always quite clearly the key of the homeless wanderer: the Flying Dutchman, Siegmund, Wozzeck, the restless, the pursued, those *compulsively* on the move. This interpretation also throws significant light on the great Ninth Symphonies of Beethoven and Bruckner. Schoenberg's First Quartet similarly displays the inner attributes of the restless wanderer.[3]

His theory does not account for the mystic solemnity of D minor in Mozart (*Don Giovanni*, Requiem), the agony of Amfortas (*Parsifal*), the nature mysticism of Mahler (Third Symphony) or the warm-blooded sensuality of Berg, who once wrote of his fiancée, Helen Nahowski, as 'my most glorious Symphony in D minor'.[4] But considering the growing restlessness and nervous energy of Zemlinsky's music, the concept of a 'wanderer' key does seem appropriate, if only in the sense that D minor was a tonal resting place from which he set out on ever more convoluted journeys through his dark forest of post-*Tristan* chromaticism.

Zemlinsky always preferred the sharpened to the diatonic subdominant. In a lifetime of composing, his major-scale patterns tended consistently towards the Lydian mode, his minor scales, conversely, to the 'Zigeuner' configuration propagated by Liszt, with its symmetrical pairs of augmented 2nds. As a logical consequence of this configuration emerges the 'Fate' chord; in due course the G♯ suffix becomes an almost integral part of the D minor triad.

A singular aspect of Zemlinsky's art is his exploitation of the *glissando* – not to be confused with the string portamento customary in the era and systematized by Mahler* – as an expressive device in its own right. He first calls for a true *glissando* – for four trombones in unison *ff* – in the second movement of *Die Seejungfrau*, composed in 1902–3. Whether this made him the first composer to incorporate what was generally considered circus music into a serious work of art is debatable: Schoenberg's use of *ppp glissandos* for muted trombones in *Pelleas und Melisande* was exactly contemporary, a fact that seems to indicate collusion. At the close of act I of *Der Traumgörge*, a *ff* passage for four trombones in unison proclaims the emancipation of the *glissando* as a dramatic effect in its own right. In the Second Quartet (1914–15) Zemlinsky discovers the 'vulgar, trivial' possibilities of string *glissando*[†] (cf. EX. 48G); in *A Florentine Tragedy* he accompanies Guido Bardi's last strangulated gasp with an obscene gesture for solo violin, sliding down the 'Fate' chord from high G♯ to low D,

---

of Messiaen. This can be explained by the fact that both based their conclusions on Goethe's *Farbenlehre* (*Theory of Colour*), 1810.

* String-players of taste were just as sparing in their use of portamento as of vibrato, as witnessed by the surviving recordings of Arnold Rosé, not to mention the draconian economy of Carl Flesch.

† Cf. EX. 48H. Of the Second Quartet, Walter William Cobbett wrote: 'There are indications for gliding the fingers which are unlikely to prove to the taste of the average chamber music player' (*Cobbett's Cyclopedic Survey of Chamber Music*, 2nd edn (London, 1963), 596).

and in *Der Zwerg* his disfigured hero is accompanied by an arsenal of *glissando* capers (e.g. EX. 65A). In the Third Quartet op. 19 he extends his repertoire of grotesque effects to a chordal *glissando pizzicato* (cf. ex. 69), and with the profound orchestral sigh which closes the Lyric Symphony (1922), he discovers the poetic potential of a soft trombone *glissando*.

Steeped in the traditions of his native city, Zemlinsky was a leading exponent, both as composer and interpreter, of the so-called 'Viennese *espressivo*'. The marking *espr.* proliferates in scores of every period, with gradations ranging from *ohne espr.* through *poco espr.* to *molto espr.* and, at points of maximum intensity, its German equivalent, *mit grossem Ausdruck*. This *espressivo* is no vague invitation to languish or swoon, but precisely defines several musical parameters. At the simplest level, it serves as a supplementary dynamic marking which, in a polyphonic context, identifies and highlights the principal voice.* The difference between a normal *piano* and a *piano espressivo* is principally one of tone quality, but the marking *espressivo* also determines many other aspects of interpretation: articulation, vibrato on a stringed instrument or pedalling on the piano, portamento and, above all, rhythmic flexibility. With a subtle *tempo rubato*, an *espressivo* line is etched against a *tempo giusto* background.†

Viennese *espressivo* was always an elusive quantity. Applied indiscriminately, it led to vulgarity; applied mindlessly, it led to that interpretative *Schlamperei* against which Mahler and Toscanini fought incessant battles. The advent of disc recording heralded its demise; today the art is all but lost.

In contrast to the seamless *legato* of Italian musical line, the Germanic ideal of melodic articulation, at least in the Romantic era, was of a *quasi legato* or *portato*.‡ Zemlinsky makes considerable use of *portato*, notated as a combination of *staccato* dot and *tenuto* line, but as a rule his phrasing is *legato* in character. Long phrases are rarely bounded by a single slur, but usually grouped into smaller units, linked by a sub-system of shorter slurs. Each individual slur demarcates a wave of intensity; a sequence of slurs thus charts larger-scale

---

* The analogous marking *poco espressivo* signifies 'subsidiary voice'. Both were later systematized by Schoenberg, who devised the signs **H⌐** and **N⌐** to identify them. The advantage of Schoenberg's system is that the performer can also see where an *espressivo* passage ends. In Zemlinsky's music this is, as a rule, self-evident.

† The theory and practice of 'Viennese *espressivo*' are exhaustively discussed in the writings of Rudolf Kolisch. One of the finest documents of this largely forgotten art is Schoenberg's 1942 recording of *Pierrot lunaire*, in which Kolisch played the violin. Discussing Zemlinsky's orchestral recordings in a sleeve-note which accompanied their LP re-issue in 1986, Helmut Haack remarks on the use of what he terms *gebundene Rubato* (tied rubato), the aim of which was 'to shape the principal voice according to its inherent expression, whereby the technique of minimal delay places greater stress on the opening and closing portions than on the main body of a thematic unit, which is taken more lightly and flowingly'.

‡ The opening of Wagner's *Tannhäuser* overture is a classic instance of Germanic *portato* culture.

patterns of harmonic flow and melodic tension. Where the ideal of Italian *legato* is a seamless, smoothly regulated stream of sound, Zemlinsky's *sostenuto* is thus discontinuous and spasmodic.

A related notational subtlety, often dismissed by performers as an eccentricity, is the *crescendo* over a rest. Here too, Zemlinsky uses traditional notation to untraditional ends. His agogical crescendo marks the transition between two neighbouring fields of tension. After a rhetorical pause, the voice resumes as if on a rising wave:

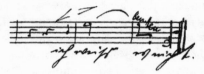

EX. 8A   Last four bars of *Auf die Nacht* (1892), autograph facsimile[5]

Ich weiss es nicht.

I know it not.

EX. 8B   *Ahnung Beatricens* (1935), bars 10–11, autograph facsimile*

Bist du mir vorbestimmt, bist du ein Wahn, und

Are you my destiny, are you unreal, and

Tempo, for Zemlinsky a further parameter of intensity, is intimately related to *legato* and *crescendo*. Though his tempo markings are strongly differentiated, the actual pulse of his music eschews extremes. As if to repress the irrepressible restlessness of his temperament, the markings most frequently used are *ruhig* (calm) and *mässig* (moderate). To prevent disintegration of the melodic line, slower tempi are often qualified by the Mahlerian admonition *nicht schleppen*; the maximum pulse of rapid tempi is determined by the demands of playability and clarity, usually leading to greater moderation than the marking itself might

* The almost illegible hieroglyphic over the first bar reads: 'mit grossem Ausdruck'.

imply. Gradations of tempo, mapped out verbosely and in minute detail, define character and affect rather than speed. As the pulse of Zemlinsky's music remains in a state of permanent flux, metronome markings are superfluous.* Modifications of tempo are usually minimal; when coupled with a change of metre, adjacent note values are, as a rule, mathematically related. Abrupt alterations of pulse are rare; *accelerandos* and *ritardandos* are exponential rather than linear.

For a meaningful analysis of Zemlinsky's larger scores, particularly the operas, it would be necessary to chart every interrelationship of pitch and rhythm, and also compare the intensity curves of register, pulse, dynamic, timbre and texture. His works offer a rich field for harmonic, motivic and formal analysis, but for most of these other parameters musicology possesses no units of measurement, and in pre-serial music they are commonly disregarded. Yet even if the processes of organic growth in Zemlinsky's large-scale works cannot precisely be measured, to the ear the intensity curves are immediately apparent. Intuitively the listener can sense that 'seismographic reactivity to the many stimuli with which he permeated himself', which Adorno[6] considered one of the most distinctive characteristics of his music.

Zemlinsky could easily have found fame and fortune as a composer of operetta and lighter music. But, while some of his colleagues sought material success in the world of show business, his Sephardic pride rebelled against the idea of bearing his goods to market, and he never seriously contemplated writing music for profit. With the gradual collapse of monarchical structures during the course of the nineteenth century, patronage of the arts in Germany and Austria waned, and often enough the legend of the starving artist became grim reality. When Richard Strauss founded the Anstalt für musikalische Aufführungsrechte, the German equivalent of the Performing Right Society, in 1903, he effectively succeeded in enforcing the Berne Copyright Convention of 1886 and in safeguarding himself and his colleagues against the crassest forms of exploitation and plagiarism. With luck on one's side, it was now theoretically possible to achieve financial success without sacrificing art to Mammon. Zemlinsky always dreamed of scoring a major box-office success – such as those he was later to witness with Korngold's *Die tote Stadt* (1920), Krenek's *Jonny spielt auf* (1927) and Weill's *Dreigroschenoper* (1928) – without compromising his artistic integrity. Yet his concept of music-theatre proved too personal, too introspective to appeal to a wider public. By the time he succeeded in composing an opera better attuned to public taste, *Der Kreidekreis* (1933), circumstances were no longer favourable.

* There are exceptions, notably in *Eine florentinische Tragödie* and *Der Zwerg*. Zemlinsky once wrote that he had not included metronome marks in the score of the Lyrische Symphonie, 'because only recently, in the performances of two operas of mine, I came to realize that they are of scarcely any use' (Zemlinsky, 'Lyrische Symphonie', *Pult und Taktstock*, I/1, 1924, 10–11).

Conversion to Protestantism

Austria's economy recovered only falteringly from the effects of the stock-market crash of 1873. Poverty remained widespread, the cost of living pro-hibitive, accommodation scarce. Nevertheless Vienna remained a Mecca for immigrants, particularly from Eastern Europe and the Balkans. Between 1848 and 1880 the city's population doubled, and by 1895 it had reached 1.5 mil-lion. Only 10 per cent was of Jewish origin, but by the turn of the century the intake of Jewish students at the *Gymnasien* (high schools) and the University was approaching 60 per cent; in banking and insurance, industry and com-merce, law, medicine, journalism, music and literature, Jews were taking an increasing part.

In 1885, Karl Lueger, a lawyer of working-class provenance, was elected into the Austrian parliament as a deputy of the Liberal Democratic party. Shortly afterwards he gave his support to legislation intended to restrict the influx of Jewish immigrants, breaking with his mainstream colleagues, and founded a new party, the Christian Socialists. With a programme of anti-Semitic reform he won votes among the under-privileged and, in due course, the Catholic middle classes, allowing him to win a landslide victory in the municipal elections of 1895. Initially the Kaiser refused to confirm him in office, and appointed a city council of his own choosing. But after two years of ineffective government by this conservative–liberal coalition, Lueger was re-elected with an even more substantial majority. Franz-Josef bowed to public opinion. The blond-bearded Lueger, popularly known as 'der schöne Karl', a fiery public speaker, was noted in his private sphere for charm and civility, even towards his Jewish friends. He implemented reforms in public transport, health and education, and began to transform suburban areas into garden cities. Despite the undeniable benefits of his ten years in office, the new strain of anti-Semitism that he and his followers implanted in the minds of the electorate proved uncommonly virulent. One of his most attentive followers was a penniless art student named Schicklgruber, later to become known to the world as Adolf Hitler.

In 1894 world Jewry was shaken by the court-martial of Alfred Dreyfus, which in France unleashed a shock-wave of anti-Semitism. An eye-witness of the trial was the Paris correspondent of the *Neue Freie Presse*, Theodor Herzl. Hitherto, in accordance with the proposals of Shem Tov Semo and other ideol-ogists associated with the Alliance, he had believed that a gradual assimilation of Jews into European society would in time eliminate problems of discrimina-tion. The violent repercussions of the Dreyfus affair convinced him that the only realistic solution could be the founding of an independent Jewish state on its own, sovereign territory. In his monograph *Der Judenstaat*, published in 1896, he proposed the establishment of Eretz-Israel; the following year, at a congress in Basle, he led two hundred delegates in founding the World Zionist Organization.

To most liberal-minded Jews, Herzl's radicality was just as unacceptable as the agitation of the Christian Socialists. Finding themselves caught between the hammer of anti-Semitism and the anvil of Zionism, many chose at this time to abandon the faith of their fathers. Within his circle, it was Schoenberg who took the initiative, embracing the Protestant faith in March 1898. The Israelitische Kultusgemeinde registered Zemlinsky's withdrawal on 30 March 1899, and his sister Mathilde followed suit on 11 October 1901, a week before her marriage to Schoenberg. No record of Zemlinsky's baptism has so far come to light, nor has it been possible to elucidate the exact circumstances that prompted it.* Judging by his comments in a letter to Alma Schindler, the decision seems to have been partly motivated by family differences:

We have virtually no contact with relatives on either side of the family. I loathe relatives anyway, and thanks to me they were all 'insulted'. Amongst them I couldn't find the understanding and warmth that I need in order to exist. Moreover I need an environment of enthusiasm – not for myself, but for everything that interests me.[7]

Adolf von Zemlinszky, who had embraced Judaism for purely idealistic reasons, may have registered surprise or disappointment, but both parents appear to have accepted their son's decision without demur. Born into a minority within a minority, Zemlinsky's fondest wish – in all matters unrelated to his art – was to vanish into the crowd, untouched by prejudice and immune to discrimination. He took little interest in world affairs, and religion played a role neither in his private nor his artistic life. Party politics were of relevance to him only in their effect on his career, and his preferred place of worship was at the altar of Venus.

It was probably at this time, shortly before the turn of the century, that he became a Freemason. Of a whole package of measures intended to speed his progress towards fame and fortune, Baptism and Masonic initiation were perhaps the most drastic. But there were other, subtler ones: he changed his official date of birth from 14 October 1871 to 4 October 1872, and modified the orthography of his name by eliminating the pseudo-Hungarian 'z' and suppressing the spurious 'von', which he retained only for conducting appearances. He would gladly have changed his name altogether. 'I envy you one thing,' he once remarked to Alma Schindler, 'your German name. Zemlinsky is in itself unobjectionable, but a musician must have a German name.'[8]

In 1899 the Zemlinskys and their dog Bogimann moved from the Pazmanitengasse, where they had been living since 1896, into an apartment at Obere Weissgerberstrasse 12 in the III. *Bezirk*. The house was a mere stone's throw from the Leopoldstadt; indeed from the window they could look across the Danube Canal to the Carltheater. But for Zemlinsky one principal objective had been achieved: he had at last moved away from the ghetto.

* Schöny dates Zemlinsky's baptism to 'approximately 1906', but gives no source.

Es war einmal . . .

In the spring and summer of 1896 Zemlinsky sketched out a few scenes for an opera about Desiderius, last king of the Lombards; shortly after winning the Luitpold Prize, he informed the press that he was working on a subject taken from a novella by Conrad Ferdinand Meyer.[9] Neither of these projects came to fruition.

In the autumn of 1897, Mahler, who had recently been appointed Musical Director of the Vienna Hofoper, wrote to Zemlinsky's publisher, expressing his interest in *Sarema*.[10] Zemlinsky instead proposed a new opera, of which he had already sketched out the opening scenes, based on Holger Drachmann's folk-tale comedy with music, *Der var engang* ('Once upon a time, or The Prince of Nordland'),[11] which he may have seen at the Raimund Theater in 1894. As librettist he secured the services of Maximilian Singer,* who worked from a German translation by Marie von Borch,[12] published in 1897. Whether Mahler commissioned the opera or merely proffered an undertaking to perform it is unclear.

Work on the short score began in August 1897 and progressed with customary rapidity. The prologue and first act[13] were ready by the end of November, the complete short score on 10 June of the following year. According to Natalie Bauer-Lechner, Mahler was immediately struck by Zemlinsky's 'incredible technique' but found his music 'full of resemblances and plagiarisms'.[14] He waited six weeks before inviting the composer to play the score through to him, but then accepted it for performance without further ado.[15]

While studying art in Copenhagen, Holger Drachmann (1846–1908) came under the influence of the celebrated literary critic and political radical Georg Brandes.[16] His career began in 1869 with an exhibition of seascapes, but in 1871 he travelled to England, where he came into contact with workers in London's East End. The experience inspired him to write poetry expressing sympathy with the Socialists, but his enthusiasm for their cause was short-lived. Passionate, volatile and self-possessed, Drachmann was a Peer Gynt-like figure whose first reaction to any personal crisis was to travel – and he spent much of his life on the road. He was contemptuous of *petit-bourgeois* Danish society, and his kinsmen found him outspoken and immoral. In London he fell in love with a sixteen-year-old Danish girl, whom he married shortly afterwards and divorced in 1875. He remarried in 1879, divorcing again ten years later due to an affair with a cabaret singer.

---

* Singer (1857–1928) wrote librettos for *Esther* (1886) and *Don Juan de Galeano* (music by Julius Stern), as well as several operettas, including *Der Weise von Cordova* (music by Oscar Straus), *Der Schwur* and *Das Jägerhaus* (music by Wilhelm Reich). His spoken dramas included *Junius Brutus* (Vienna, 1881) and *Der Wunderstein* (Prague, 1912).

Der var engang was written in the summer of 1884 at Tarvisio in the Italian Alps. At its première in 1887 the play was an instant success – thanks primarily to the incidental music and songs by the Danish composer Peter Lange-Müller – and it remained in the repertoire of the Royal Theatre, Copenhagen, for several decades. Lange-Müller's setting of the 'Hymn to the Summer Solstice', with which the play ends,[17] became in Denmark a popular national song. Performances were also frequent in Germany, and Drachmann followed the progress of *Es war einmal*, which he himself rated 'a classic in our literature',[18] with undiminished interest. He appears not to have been informed of Zemlinsky's operatic version, however, which was premièred while he was on a visit to New York. Zemlinsky took little heed of red tape – the co-librettist of *Circe*, Walter Firner, once described his attitude to international copyright law as *weltfremd* (naïve)[19] – and it is not inconceivable that he overlooked the question of obtaining the rights from Drachmann's German publisher. However, Maximilian Singer's operatic adaptation was published in Vienna shortly before the première, and it would appear that some form of copyright licence was eventually obtained.

The German *Märchen* (or Danish *Eventyr*), with its enchanted castles, doughty heroes, sleeping princesses and wicked ogres, is concerned primarily with transforming the real world into unreality, the natural into the super-natural, the familiar into the unfamiliar. Like *Wunderhorn* poetry, the *Märchen* is rooted in a centuries-old, unwritten tradition of folk culture. Since Zemlinsky's stage works, with the possible exception of *Sarema* and *A Florentine Tragedy*, are all founded on legend and myth, they are all in a sense folk-tale operas. Their subjects are approached from a psychoanalytical angle, their dramaturgy is ultra-modern,* but their thematic material is as ageless as Zemlinsky's archetypal *alter ego*, the Dwarf:

Vielleicht kaum über zwanzig alt, vielleicht alt wie die Sonne.

Perhaps scarcely more than twenty years old, perhaps as old as the sun.[20]

Singer prefaces his libretto with a thumbnail psychological sketch of the heroine:†

Once upon a time there lived a Princess who was so beautiful that she enchanted everyone who saw her. Kings' sons and commoners came from far and wide to win her hand, but all had to withdraw under a torrent of abuse and derision. Therefore

---

* 'Ultra-modern', a cult word of *fin-de-siècle* Vienna, was approximately equivalent in usage to 'avant-garde' in the 1950s and 1960s and 'post-modern' in the 1980s and 1990s.
† The title of the opera, *Es war einmal . . .*, as printed in the first libretto and on the playbills at the Hofoper, included Singer's ellipsis, which is here retained. Although of considerable significance to the drama, the preface is not included in the current edition of the vocal score, nor is any comparable apologia included in Drachmann's play.

she was considered vain and arrogant, the whole country feared her sharp repartee and trembled at her fury. But in the depths of her heart she was different. She suffered that no suitor had ever won her love and secretly she wept at her loneliness. And then, once upon a time . . .

Cast

Prince of Nordland (ten); Princess of Ilyria (sop); King of Ilyria (bass); suitor (ten); Kaspar, the Prince's aide (bar); Swiss guard (bar); gamekeeper (bass); herald (bass); three ladies-in-waiting; Christine, Johanna and Gertrude (three village girls); three students. Courtiers, ladies-in-waiting, vendors, townsfolk, soldiers; acrobats, musicians.

Synopsis

Prologue *Hall of the royal palace*   In the presence of the King and his courtiers, a luckless gallant sings the praises of the haughty Princess. Two new suitors, the Prince and Kaspar, are shown in. Unimpressed by the Prince's ardour, the Princess attempts to humiliate him. When he refuses to kneel, she storms out in a rage. Since a direct approach has failed, the prince determines to win her by guile.

I *Gate of the palace garden*   Disguised as gypsies, the Prince and Kaspar attract the Princess's attention with a melancholy ballad. For the price of a rose from her hair, they sell her a golden ball and a magic goblet. Tossing the ball from hand to hand, she and her attendants join in a carefree round-dance. The oracular powers of a magic kettle arouse her further curiosity. The Prince offers to give it to her in exchange for a kiss. Hesitantly she pays the price; but the King, alerted by Kaspar, apprehends his daughter *in flagrante*. Her punishment is banishment and degradation; no longer a Princess, she is the gypsy's bride.

II *Woodland hut by a fiord*   The Prince, still in disguise, leads his unwilling wife to a humble dwelling place. He meets her derision with forbearance, urging her to accept her new role as spouse and helpmate. Having comforted her with a tender folk song, he leaves to hunt in the royal forest. She is lonely and desolate, and her fear gradually turns to affection. When the gypsy returns, pursued by the gamekeeper and his men, she shields him; Kaspar, disguised as an innkeeper, sends them off on a false trail. As the gypsy rises to resume the hunt, she falls into his arms: 'I am yours for all eternity.'

III *Market-town in Nordland*   Amidst the hurly-burly of the annual fair, acrobats and musicians divert the crowd. The Princess, now a vendor of household utensils, tells the innkeeper (Kaspar) of her continued devotion to the gypsy. A group of students amuse themselves at her stall. Disguised as a soldier, the Prince makes uncouth advances. A brawl ensues, and her wares are smashed. Kaspar, in court attire, brings on a herald, who proclaims that the Prince of Nordland intends to marry; the bridal gown is ready, only the bride has still to be chosen. The wedding dress goes the rounds: it fits the Princess perfectly, but she refuses to abandon the gypsy. Only when the Prince reveals his true identity does she accept the crown. The curtain falls to a brief chorus of jubilation.

The *hubris* and *nemesis* of a disdainful belle is an ageless theme of world literature. It has taken the stage in various guises, notably in Shakespeare's *The Taming of the Shrew* (1594), Moreto's *El desdén con el desdén* (1654) and Nezami's mystic version of the Turandot legend (*Haft Peiker*, 1198), imported to Europe by Pétis de la Croix and dramatized by Gozzi (1762); in the realm of folk tale there are fine examples in the collections of the brothers Grimm (*King Drosselbart*) and Hans Christian Andersen (*The Swineherd* and *The Travelling Companion*); near contemporaries of *Es war einmal* . . . in the operatic repertoire on similar themes included Hermann Goetz's *Der Widerspenstigen Zähmung* (1874), Delius's *Irmelin* (1892, first performed 1953) and Reznicek's *Donna Diana* (1894).

Drachmann's comedy astutely mixes elements of several folk tales into the basic story-line of *King Drosselbart*. Andersen's *Swineherd* provides the episode of the golden goblet and the magic kettle, *Cinderella* the scene of the wedding dress. While the Turandot-inspired princess of Andersen's *Travelling Companion* is a literally man-eating *femme fatale*, Drachmann's haughty heroine is content to humiliate her suitors; but where Moreto's hero meets disdain with disdain, Drachmann's prince follows the Grimms' bearded king in destroying his heroine's pride, breaking her in like a young filly.

In a society that accepted male supremacy as a forgone conclusion, even a folk-tale princess could expect of marriage neither love nor happiness, but merely the sacrifice of her identity.[21] Drachmann accordingly depicts his heroine as a trophy, and all means, however devious, apparently justify the suitors' ends in attempting to win her. His comedy reflects the sadistically misogynous attitude of Nietzsche, the profound suspicion of Strindberg, the fear of inadequacy that motivated much of the *machismo* of nineteenth-century society. Under such circumstances, a happy ending seems plausible only in the unreal world of *Eventyr*.

These cracks in the surface of Drachmann's drama are partly closed by his concluding hymn, which serves, as in the choral finales of Russian opera, to stress the pagan, ritualistic aspect of the plot: in a folk tale, the well-being of the monarch signifies abundance and fertility for the entire populace. But by precluding popular or nationalist interest and concentrating on the drama's purely personal aspect, Singer's libretto becomes a study in mental cruelty. His heroine may at the outset sincerely 'weep at her loneliness' but, despite the happy ending, she is exploited and humiliated, and there seems little reason to presume that her situation will much improve. Love, the tale implies, is a man's prerogative; a woman's is merely obedience.

To the inherent sexist tension of the drama Zemlinsky responded with sensitivity. Much of his music is diatonic, euphonious and delicately scored. But the torments of his heroine are depicted with grating chromaticisms and dark orchestral timbres: two sound-worlds which he often juxtaposes but never

entirely resolves. There are however significant moments of symbiosis, notably
the orchestral prelude to act I and the Nordic folk song of act II.

Although the material introduced in the prelude recurs during the course of
later scenes, this is no overture in the traditional sense. As if reflecting Singer's
prefatory note, Zemlinsky presents a dream-like survey of the opera's principal
motifs, couched in the form of a brief tone-poem. The unaccompanied opening
theme –

EX. 9

– presents a subtle interweaving of the 'Self' and 'World' motifs.* Chromatic
disturbances ruffle its pentatonic calm already in the fifth bar; at bar 15 the
harmonic rhythm doubles, and from bar 22, with the introduction of a steadily
rising chromatic bass line, the clouds darken. A 'seismic' eruption of languor
and passion (the emotive words are included in the tempo markings) rises over
33 bars to a powerful climax, then rapidly dissolves, making way for a new
theme in E major. Viktor Ullmann saw in this key, as exemplified in
Schoenberg's Chamber Symphony op. 9, a mixture of yellow and red, with a
potential for 'tender warmth or blazing fire'.[22] Zemlinsky's E major theme, a
variant of the *Drehfigur* which dominated the previous section, indeed exudes
a 'tender warmth', redolent of the post-*Meistersinger* harmony that colours
much of his score. From here it is also but a small step to the opening F major:
the principal theme returns *a cappella* on the cor anglais, hanging in the air
like an unanswered question. If any resolution of the conflict is offered here,
then it is one that anticipates the later Zemlinsky: withdrawal, solitude,
resignation.

As nerve centre of the entire opera, the prelude is not advantageously placed,
and Mahler, with his sure sense of theatrical effect, decided to omit the 'seismic'
middle section altogether. Even if his cut destroyed the formal balance and lowered the dramatic temperature, it was a shrewd modification, which served to
balance the piece against the whimsical humour that pervades the following

---

* Zemlinsky's C–D–F–A motif also occurs in the slow movement of Mahler's Fourth
Symphony, composed shortly before or even during the rehearsal period for *Es war einmal
. . .*, in the autumn of 1899. Mahler introduces the motif in C major (at 15[8] in the
Philharmonia study score (i.e. the eighth bar after fig. 15; all passages in published scores without bar numbers are referred to in this way; 15⁻⁴ correspondingly signifies the fourth bar before
fig. 15) but then moves into F. A fragmented version of the motif, in E♭, also opens the Rückert
song *Ich bin der Welt abhanden gekommen*.

scenes. Zemlinsky's sense of theatre demanded *catharsis*. Later he was to find better solutions: in *Der Traumgörge* and *Der König Kandaules* a comprehensive orchestral psychogram prefaces not the first but the third act; in *A Florentine Tragedy* and *Der Zwerg* the *catharsis* is integrated into the substance of the drama.

A turning-point of a different nature is marked by the Prince's Nordic folk song. Zemlinsky invariably interpolated song into his music-dramas. While Sarema's 'Rose of Shiraz', repeated as a swan-song, can be construed as a lingering remnant of Romanticism, here the singer, in direct anticipation of Brechtian epic theatre, steps out of character. The folk melody (Hanslick was adamant that it was of Norwegian origin), supported by a harmonization that recalls the 7th-chord harmonies of the A major Quartet, is of a heart-rending simplicity, popular yet in essence 'ultra-modern'.

In 1900, with the publication of a volume of *Deutsche Chansons*, Otto Julius Bierbaum declared his resolve to establish a new, popular style of German literature. His anthology, which remained a bestseller for over twenty years, presented humorous and light-hearted lyrics by the leading German poets of the age and was intended 'to exert an improving influence upon the taste of the masses'.[23] The new century, as he envisaged it, should seek to bring to the common man the sublimity of great art; all those 'merely in search of a little entertainment will here find what they are lacking: that serenity of spirit which transfigures life, the art of the dance transformed into words and music, colours, lines and movement'.[24] Much of the score of *Es war einmal* . . . reflects this trend towards mass appeal, short-lived as it was.

Some commentators have detected in Zemlinsky's post-Brahmsian works a counterpart to the formal criteria of art nouveau. The Princess's round-dance in act I of *Es war einmal* . . . is a case in point. The scene is set in an idyllic park landscape, the air aswarm with butterflies. Lithe young maidens with blond, flowing tresses playfully toss a golden hoop from hand to hand: a typical *Jugendstil* picture. But such comparisons are entirely visual. The epithet is no more appropriate to this music than it would be to Wagner's flower-maidens in *Parsifal* or to Ravel's waltzing insects in *L'enfant et les sortilèges* – the two operatic set-pieces that roughly define the stylistic boundaries of Zemlinsky's round-dance. Certainly, the principal characteristics of *Jugendstil* – stylized imitation of nature, avoidance of straight lines, concentration on arabesque and ornament, particularly the repetition and variation of smaller ornamental units – apply to this music. But they apply just as well to the nature imitations of Jannequin and Vivaldi, Messiaen and Tippett. The rediscovery of Zemlinsky, Schreker and Korngold, which followed in the wake of the Mahler renaissance, went hand in hand with the rehabilitation of *Jugendstil* art. In our multimedia-orientated age, the separate stimuli of sight and sound have begun to coalesce. Audiences hear with their eyes, seeking the interaction of extraneous ideas instead of accepting the non-interactive disciplines of individual art forms.* A musical *Jugendstil* never existed, only a music inspired, like any other, by the visual arts of its time.

Mahler threw himself with energy and enthusiasm into preparing the new opera. The sets and costumes were lavish, his best singers were entrusted with the principal roles: Selma Kurz as the Princess and Eric Schmedes as the Prince. During rehearsal, numerous changes were made. According to Natalie Bauer-Lechner, Mahler's friend Siegfried Lipiner advised him on textual alterations,[25] and Zemlinsky was asked to recompose several passages. Some of these were needed to facilitate Mahler's cuts, others – including a new transition from the prologue to act I – smoothed the dramatic flow. The most far-reaching alterations were made to the closing pages of act I, which underwent two stages of transformation before meeting with Mahler's approval. The bold harmonies of the definitive version, which draws upon the song *Klopfet, so wird euch aufgetan*,† demonstrate Zemlinsky's continuing stylistic development. A reminiscence of the Prince's Nordic folk song, sung offstage, was interpolated in act II; extensive cuts were made in act III (a total of 177 bars), including a strophic song for the Prince in his soldier disguise, accompanied by a stage band.

The world première, on 22 January 1900, was an unqualified success, and the piece remained in the repertoire of the Hofoper for twelve performances – a rare distinction for an operatic novelty, then as now. The critics – other than those from the anti-Semitic press, who missed no opportunity to denigrate Mahler – were enthusiastic. Many commented on the echoes of Wagner and Goldmark, but as with *Sarema*, these were not necessarily considered a deficiency. Heuberger, revealing a feuilletonist's talent for purple prose, recognized Zemlinsky's innate talent for music-theatre and (perhaps as a belated gesture of personal gratitude) singled out the orchestration for lavish praise:

At present there are few composers whose sense of theatre is as acute as Zemlinsky's, few so familiar as he with every greater and lesser trade secret of dramatic effect – in the positive sense of the word. By determining in the score the exact pace of dialogue (*Rede und Gegenrede*), an opera composer commands a superb mechanism with which he can unambiguously specify his principal characters' states of mind, their moods and changes of mood. [. . .] Nevertheless, everything that happens on stage is symbolic. Only when the orchestra lends its unfathomable voice

* Cf. Hans Hollander, *Musik und Jugendstil* (Zurich, 1975) and Jürg Stenzel (ed.), *Art nouveau, Jugendstil und Musik* (Zurich–Freiburg, 1980). The latter includes contributions in English by Gerald Abraham and Derick Puffett and in French by Jean-Michel Nectoux and François Lesure. Carl Dahlhaus, in his authoritative essay 'Musik und *Jugendstil*', ultimately dismisses the question as a *Scheinproblem* (bogus problem, red herring).
† Later published as op. 10 no. 5. The insert of 47 bars was presumably composed in November or December 1899. It begins four bars before the Princess's words 'Aus Freude und Glück'.

from the depths of some mysterious crypt are these mysteries unveiled, commented, consummated, motivated.[26]

The seventy-five-year-old Hanslick attended a later performance. His lengthy review was divided into strophes, each concluding with the pugnacious refrain: 'Must they always Wagnerize?'* A devout 'Brahmin' to the last, he exhorted Zemlinsky to liberate himself from all remaining influence of Bayreuth:

Twelve years before Zemlinsky composed his opera, [. . .] I saw the folk play at the Royal Theatre in Copenhagen. [. . .] Zemlinsky's music strikes me as too artful, if not too artificial for such a comedy; the declamation too often stilted, the vocal line lacking in melody, the orchestration over-saturated and restless. [. . .] These observations, written long after the first performance of Zemlinsky's successful work, are by no means intended as censure. As such they would be unjustified, for they intentionally accentuate the negative aspects – actually just one negative aspect – of the score, prompted by a sincere interest in the future of this talented young composer.[27]

Despite the acclaim to which the opera was launched, *Es war einmal . . .* remained on the shelf of the Hofoper library for ten years. In May 1912 a new production was staged at Mannheim and in October of the same year, Zemlinsky himself conducted the work in Prague.[28] Then silence – over half a century of oblivion.

In 1987 the Danish Radio recorded the work in a new edition by Jan Maegaard (published in 1990), a reconstruction of the version performed in Mannheim and Prague, including all the cuts, alterations and retouchings implemented by Mahler.[†] Using the same edition, the opera was staged with considerable success at Kiel in 1991. Even in a theatre of relatively modest means, it became clear that Zemlinsky's sense of drama, his mastery of orchestral colour and wide expressive range had remained undimmed by the passing of time.

---

* 'Muss denn immer gewagnert sein?'

† Maegaard does not seem to have realized that the Hofoper score (in the Österreichische Nationalbibliothek) is a copy, and that there also exists an original manuscript (at the Library of Congress). This confusion about manuscript sources led him also to assume that the revised ending of act 1 was composed by Mahler himself, an assumption that in turn led him to presume that Mahler had also lent Zemlinsky a 'helping hand' in other passages. Mahler's contributions, apart from occasionally adapting vocal lines to fit his textual alterations, were in fact limited to cuts, retouchings and changes of dynamic. Despite the undisputed effectiveness of his changes, Zemlinsky did not unequivocally approve of them. When Alma Schindler asked to borrow the score, he was unwilling to part with it, explaining, 'It's the only complete copy in existence, since the one at the Opera is already an adaptation [*Umarbeitung*]' (*AZ–AMW*, 19 July 1901).

5

Alma gentil

Among those present at the world première of *Frühlingsbegräbnis* was the twenty-one-year-old Alma Schindler. Her first impression of Zemlinsky was anything but flattering:

The man [. . .] cuts the most comical figure imaginable. A caricature – chinless, small, with bulging eyes and a downright crazy conducting style. It always makes a comical effect when composers conduct their own music, because they always want to draw *too* much out of the orchestra, more than necessary.[1]

Two weeks later, at a dinner party, they met for the first time:

An evening at Spitzer's.* I went with the greatest disinclination and had a wonderful time, spoke almost all evening with Alexander von Zemlinsky, the twenty-eight-year-old composer of *Es war einmal* . . . He's dreadfully ugly [. . .] and yet I found him quite enthralling. [. . .] At table [he] asked me softly, 'And what do you think of Wagner?' 'The greatest genius who ever lived,' I answered calmly. 'And which work of Wagner's is your favourite?' '*Tristan*' – my reply, which so delighted him that he was quite transformed. He became truly handsome. Now we understood each other. I find him quite wonderful – shall ask him round.[2]

She sent him a copy of her latest song, *Stumme Liebe*, to a poem by Lenau, and on 10 March they met again, at a party thrown by Hugo and Ida Conrat in honour of the Belgian painter Fernand Khnopff.

Zemlinsky told me that he was extremely impressed by my song, that I have real talent – and other things too. I told him that he and Khnopff were the two major attractions for me. He didn't believe me. 'Fräulein, if I weren't so sensible – you could easily turn one's head.' Suddenly he grew serious. 'Fräulein [. . .] I would like to dedicate a song to you – no, more than that – a whole volume of lieder that's soon to be published' [*Irmelin Rose und andere Gesänge* op. 7]. [. . .] I was overwhelmed with joy.[3]

On 28 March Alma attended the tenth performance of *Es war einmal* . . ., accompanied by Khnopff and Ida Conrat. 'On the whole I liked the opera,' she wrote, '[but] in the first act there are too many scenic and linguistic fireworks.

* Friedrich V. Spitzer (1854–1922) was heir to a sugar factory in Moravia. A keen amateur musician, he studied chemistry and later took to photography, exhibiting his work at the Secession. The interior décor of his villa on the Hohe Warte was executed by the celebrated *Jugendstil* craftsman Josef Hoffmann.

That leaves me cold.'⁴ Later she invited Zemlinsky to call, with the intent of showing him more of her songs. But their next encounter, at a Tonkünstler-verein concert, was less cordial, for Alma became aware of the woman in Zemlinsky's life, Melanie Guttmann. After the concert she made a scene, and Zemlinsky left in a rage. Nevertheless he promised to call the following Monday, as agreed.

I played him a few of my more recent songs, and he found them very talented but poorly crafted. [. . .] At one turn of phrase he said, 'That's so good, I could almost have written it myself.' He drew my attention to a few minor errors, was kind and jovial. [. . .] He asked to take three of the songs with him. I shall copy them out and send them.⁵

Alma was at that time a pupil of Josef Labor. She revered the blind organist, but had in six years made little headway. Her knowledge of musical theory was tenuous, her output limited to piano music and songs. After Zemlinsky's cursory examination of her manuscripts, she determined to win his services as a teacher – 'if only Mama will let me', as she wrote.⁶ Her father, the painter Emil Jacob Schindler, had died intestate, and subsequently her mother had married Schindler's assistant, Carl Moll. Since then, Anna Moll had taken the purse strings firmly in hand. But she dominated not only the financial affairs of the family. They had spent the spring of 1899 with a group of Secessionist painters on an Italian 'grand tour', during the course of which Alma became passionately involved with Gustav Klimt. When the affair came to light, there was an éclat: all further contact was forbidden, and Klimt was sent packing with accusations of immoral behaviour ringing in his ears. Alma brooded for months over the forced separation. Desperate for affection, she turned to the architect Josef Olbrich, but he disregarded her; she flirted gauchely with Erik Schmedes, the heldentenor, but he was married, albeit unhappily; in the playwright and lawyer Max Burckhard she found an avuncular admirer, but Alma – even Alma – was shocked by his wantonness and hedonistic excess.

Even if he took care not to betray the fact, Zemlinsky was spellbound by her. A fortnight after the first official consultation, they met again at Spitzer's; he took the opportunity to ask for her photograph. Four days later, after carefully considering the consequences, she obliged.

Meanwhile Carl Moll was planning a special birthday surprise for his step-daughter: a printed edition of three of her songs, with an ornamental title page designed by Koloman Moser.*

---

* The songs were *Stumme Liebe* (Lenau), and two songs to texts by Dehmel and Rilke. The former, *Lobgesang*, was published in 1924, presumably with some revisions, as no. 4 of the Fünf Gesänge.

Adolf von Zemlinszky †

On 19 June Alma noted with regret that Zemlinsky had been unable to come to dinner: 'His father is sick.'[7] Ten days later, she called on him with the proofs of her projected op. 1 fresh from the engravers:

Since we had the carriage, we drove to the Prater and from there to the Weissgerberstrasse, to leave Zemlinsky my songs. I rang – and Frl. Guttmann opened the door. I asked after his father; she led me to the music room and told me that he had passed away – early that morning. I was ashamed to leave my light-hearted note and the music, but she put them on the desk and said she would not give them to him until he was calmer. 'And there you are too' – she pointed to my photo, standing at the centre of the desk. [. . .] I have a tremendous respect for Frl. Guttmann, her eyes were full of tears and her lips were quivering. She told me he had fought all night, and she had kept vigil at his bedside. [. . .] She was wearing a big apron, appears to be running the household.[8]

Adolf von Zemlinszky was only fifty-five years old when he died. The death certificate records the cause of death as 'kidney stones': his last days must have been sheer agony.

The Turkish-Israelite community appears not to have been unduly saddened by the loss of their Secretary. Michael Papo refers only obliquely to the event – 'at that time a fully qualified lawyer [. . .] took over the secretaryship and reorganized the communal administration, bringing it up to the most modern standards'[9] – implying that Zemlinszky's services had been little appreciated. Nor did the Managing Director of *Wiener Punsch* honour his Chief Editor with any public demonstration of sorrow or grief. Readers might have noticed a thin strip of paper pasted over Zemlinszky's name on the back page of the first July edition, bearing the name of his successor. That was all.

Early in July Zemlinsky began work on a memorial to his father, a setting of lines from Psalm 83 for four soli, chorus and large orchestra. He chose words not of sorrow but of anger, vengeance and, ultimately, the justice of *Elohim*:

Keep not thou silence, O God: hold not thy peace, and be not still, O God. For, lo, thine enemies make a tumult, and they that hate thee have lifted up the head. They have taken crafty counsel against thy people.

O my God, make them like a wheel, as the stubble before the wind, as the flame setteth the mountains on fire, and as the fire burneth a wood.

That men may know that thou, whose name alone is Jehovah, art the most high over all the earth.[10]

The text is divided into three sections: *Langsam* (D minor, 6/4), *Allegro molto, schnell und stürmisch im Ausdruck* (F minor, 3/4) and *Mässig bewegt* (D major, 4/4). Three ideas of contrasting affect, colour and tessitura are juxtaposed in the opening bars: (i) a brooding D minor fugato for strings, (ii) a soft, high-pitched D major chorale-like signal for wind and brass and (iii) an enigmatic major–minor figure for strings and timpani. A seismic development of (i) rises over five bars to a massively scored tutti. E♭ minor, the key of despair, is twice answered by F♯ minor, the key of anguish. The chorus enters *ff* in the principal key, D minor; F♯ minor is now answered by A minor, the key of death. A solo soprano repeats the opening words, *innig flehend* (tenderly imploring), to a simple motif in F major. 'They that hate thee have lifted up the head': the tonal centre shifts momentarily to C minor. Whirling figures in the strings illustrate the 'crafty counsel' of the enemies; with mounting tension the figures rise inexorably from D minor through E♭ minor to F minor. A reprise of (iii) followed by (i) provides a hesitant transition.

The middle section, modelled on the central *Allegro* section of Brahms's *Song of Destiny*, is cast in the form of a monolithic *perpetuum mobile*. The 'wheel' with which the psalmodist would smite his enemies prompts Zemlinsky to an omnipresent *Drehfigur*, the 'fire' to flickering mordants in wind and strings.

With an imperious gesture minor changes to major, clearing the air for the closing paean. Where in *Frühlingsbegräbnis* a few bars of fugato were included as if for propriety's sake, here Zemlinsky embarks on a full-scale choral fugue, vigorous and forthright, crowned with a triumphant, Handelian tutti. The orchestra breaks the spirit of apotheosis in the final bars with a grim and tumultuous reminder of the opening: 'Keep not thou silence.'

In 1902 Schoenberg attempted to persuade a Berlin choral society to perform the score,[11] but Psalm 83 received no hearing until 1987. Even then it failed to establish itself in the repertoire, and the first commercial recording was issued only twelve years later. Rudolf Stephan, in his essay on the psalms,[12] omits even to mention Psalm 83. Yet the three psalms, like the four quartets, constitute a coherent autobiographical entity: together they constitute a cornerstone of Zemlinsky's *œuvre*.

During the autumn and winter of 1900–1901, Zemlinsky worked on a group of songs for baritone and orchestra, probably intended for his friend Eduard Gärtner. First published in 1999 as Two Songs for voice and orchestra (*Der alte Garten*, to a text by Eichendorff, and an anonymous poem entitled *Erdeinsamkeit*), they were completed in short score but never orchestrated. A further Eichendorff setting, *Die Riesen*, survives only as a fragment. The fact that both complete autographs are signed and dated indicates that Zemlinsky considered them substantially complete. The text of *Erdeinsamkeit* could possibly have been written by his father, indeed the work may have been intended as a further memorial to him. It could however also have been written in conjunction with Zemlinsky's activities as a Freemason. Research has so far established that he was a member of the German lodge 'Freilicht zur Eintracht' in Prague,* but no

* Information kindly provided by Ingo Schultz.

information about his Masonic activities in Vienna has so far come to light. The
hypothesis of a Masonic origin is supported by certain aspects of the poem: the
secrecy surrounding its authorship, the employment of a vocabulary far
removed from the literary lingua franca of the time, the obscurantist cosmolo-
gy and unorthodox theological message, with its constantly recurring address
to 'My brothers'. Zemlinsky's use of the Masonic key, E♭ major, offers further
evidence to support the idea. Written at a time when he was largely involved
with the entertainment industry, these two songs catch him in a fine-nerved
and serious mood. *Der alte Garten*, with its lush E major harmony and
subtle enharmonic shifts, recalls Debussy's *Prélude à l'après-midi d'un
faune*; *Erdeinsamkeit*, 255 bars long, with sweeping melodic lines and dramatic
orchestral interludes, relishes the manifold possibilities of post-Wagnerian
chromaticism.

The Carltheater

Franz Ritter von Jauner was director of the Hofoper from 1875 to 1880; the
following year he took over management of the Komische Oper on the Ringstrasse. Only a few weeks after taking office, on 8 December, the theatre caught
fire during a performance, with considerable material damage and the loss of
thirty lives. Accused of negligence, he was sentenced to three months' imprison-
ment. In 1895 he returned to grace and was entrusted with the directorship of
the Carltheater. His first novelty, Suppé's *Das Modell*, was a failure, but Sidney
Jones's *The Geisha* and the Johann Strauss pasticcio *Wiener Blut* proved major
box-office attractions. Unfortunately Jauner failed to balance his books. On 23
February 1900 he opened the theatre safe and found it bare; he took a pistol
from his desk and shot himself in the head.[13] The theatre was placed in the
hands of a consortium, and the company disbanded. In the summer of 1900
Leopold Müller was entrusted with the theatre's administration and hastily
assembled a new ensemble. Under his directorship the Carltheater became host
to a new generation of composers, ushering in the celebrated 'silver era' of
Viennese operetta.

  Adolf von Zemlinszky, despite his experience in the insurance business, had
evidently made little or no provision for his family. With his unexpected death,
it now fell to his son to become the breadwinner. So far Zemlinsky had managed to scrape together an income from teaching, accompanying and arranging,
but with this revenue alone he was unable to support the rest of the family.
Notwithstanding Alma Schindler's remarks about his effusive behaviour on the
rostrum, critical opinion of his conducting was highly favourable. Indeed his
conducting of the Vienna Philharmonic in the B♭ major Symphony had won him
warmer praise than the score itself: 'As a conductor he showed remarkable
ability. He has learned much about leading (not about interpretation) from

G. Mahler,'[14] wrote one of the critics. And his performance of *Frühlings-begräbnis* had prompted appraisal as 'a genuine musician [. . .] with a good ear and a keen sense of rhythm, a true interpreter who knows how to communicate his vision, a real leader.'[15] Although Zemlinsky had no operatic experience whatsoever, Müller offered him the post of Chief Conductor at the Carltheater. Under the circumstances, it was an offer he could not refuse. For Müller, Zemlinsky was a star attraction, and, flouting Viennese tradition, he featured the young conductor's name in bold type on every playbill and newspaper advertisement.* For Zemlinsky the engagement was an irksome chore that robbed him of time for creative work and forced him into contact with music which, as often as not, he deplored. But at least he could rely on a regular income.

Of the twenty-one soloists in Müller's new ensemble, the most renowned was the tenor Louis Treumann, who later created the role of Danilo in Lehár's *Die lustige Witwe*. There was an orchestra of forty-two and a chorus of thirty-six, many of whom also took smaller solo parts (with at least two ladies of the chorus, Mitzi Dotzauer and Sofie Rakanow, Zemlinsky became amorously entangled).

Early in September, rehearsals began for Edmond Audran's *Le grand Mogol*. After nine performances, the work was taken out of the repertoire to make way for Carl Weinberger's *Die Diva*. In contrast to the elegance and esprit of Audran, this music – cheap, plagiarized but undeniably popular – turned Zemlinsky's stomach. From a cryptic comment in *Die Fackel*[16] it transpires that he had insisted on a clause in his contract exempting him from performing any work of which he did not approve. *Die Diva* was therefore entrusted to his second in command, Victor Schwarz, while Zemlinsky, with a little time on his hands, was at last able to fulfil his obligations to Alma.

Alma Again

The Zemlinskys had found solace in their bereavement by taking a few weeks' holiday in Rodaun, just outside Vienna, and later at Seeboden on the Mill-städtersee in Carinthia. From there, Zemlinsky wrote to Alma:

When I received your songs, I was, as you will appreciate, in the depths of misery. I couldn't concentrate on anything for even five minutes. And so it went on for several days. Then I took a look at the so-called brush proofs. Now please listen and don't get me wrong: the three songs contain such an incredible number of mistakes, some originating in the manuscript, others in the engraving, impossible errors of vertical alignment and non-existent musical symbols – that it made my head spin.[17]

---

* On announcements and programmes at the Hofoper, even Mahler's name never appeared in print.

There seemed little choice but to consign Alma's op. 1 to limbo. Zemlinsky was invited over for consultation. His commitments at the Carltheater occupied him throughout September, but after the première of *Die Diva* he found time for a visit. On Thursday 18 October Alma noted:

Zemlinsky is due today . . .

And he *came*. Half an hour late, admittedly, but he came. [. . .] His appearance at our house provoked a chorus of dismay. I find him neither hideous nor grotesque, for his eyes sparkle with intelligence – and such a person is never ugly.

He left with a promise to return the following Monday, but instead sent a witty, pseudo-biblical letter of apology. Delay followed delay, and on more than one occasion Alma took up her pen 'to say farewell for once and for all'.[18] Finally, on Tuesday 13 November, he arrived for her first lesson:

'Well then, what shall I teach you?' 'Form.' 'All right, show me what you've got.' I played him my latest piano piece. 'It has good moments, shows talent, but it lacks technique and aptitude.' Then he tested my knowledge of harmony, looked at my latest counterpoint exercises, and we *both* agreed that my capabilites are meagre – almost *non-existent*. [. . .] Afterwards we chatted about everything under the sun, and he stayed on for two full hours. My spirits are soaring.[19]

They began to go out together. On 1 December Alma was Zemlinsky's guest at Eduard Gärtner's song recital;* on 7 December she returned the compliment, inviting him and Koloman Moser to *Meistersinger* at the Hofoper. The following evening they dined at the Conrats', where Alma had a long conversation with Erich J. Wolff.

These fellows are so free with their opinions. They compared my face with that of a well-known actress, and Zemlinsky said, 'I would be happy if I could express in music that nuance which makes Fräulein Alma the more beautiful of the two.'[20]

On his next visit Zemlinsky started playing from a vocal score of *Tristan* lying open on the piano. According to Alma's memoirs, written thirty years later, 'I leaned on the piano, my knees trembled [. . .] we sank into each other's arms.'[21] But this was untrue. The diary records Alma's trembling knees – but when he had finished, Zemlinsky simply stood up and took his leave.

Lessons continued. On 7 January 1901 matters became more earnest:

I asked him to play the prelude to *Es war einmal* . . ., but he wouldn't. – I made so bold as to tell him that I hadn't gone to *Tristan* because he wasn't there. He said, 'You know, Fräulein, you are becoming tiresome. You may be able to keep all your other young men under your thumb, but with me – that won't work.' And he's right. *What* do I want of him? Yes, I like him – beyond words. But when he arrived – his incredible ugliness, his smell. And yet – when he's there, I grow strangely excited.[22]

* See p. 30.

At the end of the month she took a lesson at his apartment:

The room radiates unbelievable poetry. Schoenberg opened the door with his gob full – I believe poor Zem. is besieged by spongers. One wall is full of laurel wreaths etc., including a bust and a picture of Brahms. The photogravure of Wagner that I sent him for Christmas hangs over the desk, above it the sprig of mistletoe that I fixed to the wrapper. *My* photo is still standing on the desk. Even if I mean nothing to him – personally – at least he can take pleasure in looking at my picture.[23]

He also showed me the score of *Es war einmal . . .* How I envy him. 'This is *my* work, *my* talent, my heart and my love' [. . .].[24]

On 24 February they attended a concert of Weber, Dvořak and Bruckner (the Fifth Symphony) conducted by Mahler.

Today – we were sitting close together – when he turned to me, it caused me physical pain – sheer sensual over-anxiety. My greatest wish, that he should really take fire for me, will remain unfulfilled, because he knows me too well – my faults, my limitations, my stupidity. What he thinks of me, I can read in his eyes. [. . .] How I envy him! He is everything I should like to be![25]

The round of concerts, lessons and dinner parties continued. On 8 March Alma turned up unexpectedly at a Tonkünstlerverein concert in which Zemlinsky was accompanying his *Irmelin Rose* songs. At the sight of her rival, Melanie Guttmann, her hackles rose once again:

Fräulein Guttmann was there with the whole family. I don't know them, but they stared at me continually through their opera-glasses – what a cheek. Zemlinsky remained in the green room and didn't greet me. Spitzer said, 'Zem. was here, saw you and went away.' That hurt! But now, as I write this down, I couldn't care less. You Jewish sneak, keep your hooked-nosed Jew-girl. She's just right for you.[26]

The season was already drawing to a close. Since the previous September Zemlinsky had conducted ninety-nine performances at the Carltheater. Having given ample proof of his expertise on the rostrum, he was anxious to find a position with greater artistic scope. There was an opening in Breslau, which would have been ideal, had it not signified taking leave of his beloved Vienna – and of Alma. A further argument in favour of remaining in Vienna was an offer from Hugo von Hofmannsthal to compose music for his ballet *Der Triumph der Zeit* (*The Triumph of Time*). The young poet was influential and well connected, the chances of securing a première at the Hofoper seemed favourable . . .

Alma asked Zemlinsky whether he had reached an agreement with Hofmannsthal. His answer was curt and scornful: 'He told me it was none of my business, that I should disregard his artistic affairs (*Künstlerschaft*) altogether.'[27] Her gate-crashing the Tonkünstlerverein was a further bone of contention. Matters came to a head at a performance of *Tristan* on 12 March.

I told him I felt like a fallen angel. [. . .] 'I want to open your eyes above all to the minimal interest you have taken in my art,' [he said]. [. . .] 'I've been asking myself all along how it is that you are so moved by *Tristan*. There must be some very special affinity [. . .] because nothing else interests you in the least.'[28]

Realization dawned on her the following morning.

He is beautiful and so immeasurably great that my eyes cannot apprehend his full stature. I am at my wits' end. I can't compose, my eyes are full of tears. God, God, what have I lost? [. . .] I can't live without him any longer. [. . .] Not a word did I find for his wonderful songs – not a word.[29]

And Zemlinsky avenged himself by making biting comments about her compositions:

Your manner, you know, is just as transparent to the interested observer as your music – a warm, feminine, sensitive opening, but then doodles, flourishes, unstylish passage-work. Olbrich should have your songs performed by an artiste from the Barnum [& Bailey] company, wearing the customary black tails, on his head a dunce's cap.[30]

Nevertheless the lessons continued, and occasionally they still visited operas and concerts together. Above all, they began to correspond in earnest. As a rule, Zemlinsky's letters were terse and distant; to Alma, however, he was able to open his heart. Soon he had apologized for his hard words:

It was foolish of me to imagine that *you* should take a greater interest than others in my puny talent – foolish, because I never stopped to question why. But – no malice aforethought – I never make the same silly mistake *twice*![31]

Finally, at his next visit, on Wednesday 10 April, destiny took its course:

We had our regular lesson. Afterwards we sat down together. [. . .] He told me that I was playing with him, that he thanked God for his common sense. Suddenly our gaze met and didn't waver. I asked him to come on Saturday. He asked if that was important to me. I said yes. He kissed my hands, bent his head over them. I laid my head on his. We kissed each other on the cheek, held each other for an eternity. I took his head in my hands, and we kissed each other on the mouth, so hard that our teeth ached. [. . .]
He told me he had struggled all winter against his love for me.[32]

A Picaresque Interlude: The Ueberbrettl

With the founding of the 'Buntes Theater (Ueberbrettl)' in Berlin, Ernst von Wolzogen was the first to put Otto Julius Bierbaum's theory of art for the common man into practice.[33] A gregarious theatrical entrepreneur, editor of the *Bayreuther Blätter*, playwright and novelist, Wolzogen's chief claim to posterity lies today in his libretto for Richard Strauss's opera *Feuersnot* (1900). Before opening his 'literary *variété*', he had chosen Bierbaum's chanson *Der lustige*

Ehemann as a test piece, and commissioned several composers, including Zemlinsky, to set it to music. To his mind, 'Oscar Straus's version [. . .] was so far superior to those of his competitors that the question of a musical director for my Ueberbrettl was immediately decided.'[34]

In May 1901 the 'Buntes Theater' made its Viennese début at the Carltheater with chansons, recitations and sketches, to texts by Bierbaum, Dehmel, Liliencron, Morgenstern, Max Reinhardt and Wolzogen himself. The programme, which ran to packed houses for two weeks, also included a pantomime, *Pierrots Fastnacht*, to a scenario by Leo Feld.

At this time Zemlinsky composed the music for a mime drama with piano accompaniment, entitled *Ein Lichtstrahl (A Ray of Light)*, to a commission by Wolzogen. Evidently he had made only fleeting acquaintance with his librettist, for in the autograph the text is ascribed merely to 'Gellert'. There can be little doubt, however, that the credit goes to Oskar Geller, critic, playwright and actor, 'a mercurial little Jew' as Wolzogen remembered him[35] and evidently of some influence in the intrigue-ridden atmosphere of Viennese theatre. It was on his recommendation that Wolzogen became acquainted with the music of Oscar Straus, and Geller later also claimed to have played an important role behind the scenes in the appointment of Mahler at the Hofoper.[36] Applauding Wolzogen's ambition to evolve a 'refined form of *variété*', Geller was himself active for a time in the Ueberbrettl troupe, appearing under the pseudonym of Luigi Spontelli.

Cast

He, She, The Other; a simply furnished room, with a large wardrobe; early evening.

Synopsis

She is reading the paper. The door opens and *He* bursts in, accuses her of infidelity and threatens revenge. *She* appeases him, and *He* goes off to play cards. At the door *He* bumps into *The Other*. 'It's only the tailor,' *She* explains, and lewdly he takes her measurements to prove the point. Finally *He* leaves; they drink and grow amorous. A knock at the door: *The Other* clambers into the wardrobe, lights a candle and begins to read the paper. *He* rushes into the room. 'Why didn't you open at once?' – 'I fell asleep.' *He* becomes affectionate, *She* rebuffs him. *He* lights a cigar, thereby inadvertently blowing out the lamp. Darkness. A ray of light seeps through the wardrobe door. *He* rushes over and opens it. 'We shall fight, one of us shall die,' says *The Other*. *He* begs forgiveness. Kisses and embraces all round.

The scenario and music of *Ein Lichtstrahl* anticipate the silent-movie style of a slightly later era; in certain respects the drama can also be read as a prophetic parody of *A Florentine Tragedy*. Yet despite a veiled reference to the B♭ major Symphony[37] and extensive use of the principal theme of the Comedy

Overture,[38] the work stands quite alone in Zemlinsky's *œuvre*. Casting aside his technical polish, he revelled in unrefined piano textures, abrupt transitions and Klezmer-like syncopations. In contrast to Oscar Straus, however, he also went some way towards fulfilling the high-flown artistic ambitions of the Ueberbrettl idea: within a sophisticated formal structure there are passages of 'ultra-modern' harmony, and the thematic material is organized, as ever, according to the principles of developing variation.

Ein Lichtstrahl was never performed at the Ueberbrettl, perhaps because the *Decameron*-inspired bisexual implications of the *lieto fine* were considered off-colour. Probably in May–June 1902, during a guest appearance with the Carl-theater in Dresden, Zemlinsky made the acquaintance of Franz Artzt, a drama-turg associated with a *variété* theatre known as the 'Cabaret du Quartier Latin'. Carefully obliterating the original dedication, he prepared an abbreviated ver-sion of the score for him, with a more conventional ending.[39] Even then, the work remained unperformed.

The autograph of *Ein Lichtstrahl* is dated 8–17 May 1901. For this very period Alma later removed the pages from her diary,* but vague allusions in Zemlinsky's letters indicate that this was the time when matters between them finally came to a head. There is mention of a performance of *Tristan*,† during the course of which he and Alma came physically very close, and an evening *chez* Henneberg‡ at which they exchanged further intimacies. Neither at this time nor later, however, was the relationship consummated. When Alma met Mahler in November 1901 she was, despite the gossip, *virgo intacta*.

It should be added that in executing Wolzogen's commission Zemlinsky demonstrated impeccable professionalism: of the dizzy erotic heights he was scaling, his music betrays nothing.

---

* The pages were presumably removed in 1962–3, when she checked through the entire manuscript, added marginalia and struck passages out.
† During the unchronicled fortnight there was only one performance of *Tristan* at the Hofoper, on 15 May.
‡ The graphic artist and photographer Hugo Henneberg (1863–1918) and his wife Marie, customarily referred to by Alma as 'Auntie Mie'. In the summer of 1901 Klimt painted a *Portrait of Marie Henneberg*, which now hangs in the Moritzburg Gallery, Halle.

6

Alma crudel

They made an incongruous couple. Time and again Zemlinsky would stress that he was not her plaything,[1] but to Alma he was often just that. 'He's so small [. . .] that when we walk together, he reaches no higher than my shoulder.'[2] Sometimes her feelings would run away with her. 'Surely he must feel, must imagine how I love him, how the whole world dissolves when I look into his eyes. [. . .] I thirst for him, thirst for his life-fluid.'[3] At other times it was the folk tale of *Es war einmal* . . . translated back into reality: she, a trophy, only to be won by the most valiant of suitors. Already in the first weeks of their romance she grew critical of Zemlinsky's deference and formality:

A woman should be the taker, [. . .] has no right always to be the giver. I long for him to hug me tightly and *shout* 'Alma, my Alma', as Klimt once did. But he addresses me as *verehrtes Fräulein* [esteemed young lady] and is noticeably offended if I forget to call him by his first name.[4]

Carl Moll was a rabid anti-Semite,* his wife a social climber. These family traits had to a certain extent rubbed off on Alma. When Zemlinsky and Erich J. Wolff sent her a jovial postcard from a coffee-house in the Leopoldstadt, she was incensed:

Is he one of those half-Jews who never succeed in ridding themselves of their Semitism? And to think that he should sit down with a fellow like Wolff – an unwashed Jew – to drink the night away.[5]

Her dream of marital bliss with Zemlinsky was soon disrupted by the prejudices of her parents and friends. Max Burckhard was the first to dissuade her: 'For heaven's sake *don't marry* Z. Don't corrupt *good* race.'[6] Zemlinsky's hopes were centred less on marriage as an institution than on a fruitful artistic partnership. Apart from Alma's good looks, he valued her as a potential helpmate, as his muse. Soon after they had sealed their bond with a first, searing kiss, he expressed his feelings with clarity and candour:

I have gone through days of fearful expectation; unceasing hope and anxiety in the face of reality. Please understand, dear, dear Fräulein Alma! Reality has brought me nothing but disappointment. In my thoughts, my feelings, I was happy, perfectly happy. I am in the throes of a great, hopeless passion, my adoration has with time become so strong but also so firm and categorical that I can say: it can never end!![7]

* Shortly before Vienna fell to Russian troops in 1945, he committed suicide.

On 18 May the Molls left Vienna for St Gilgen, where they had rented a water-front villa on the Wolfgangsee. As soon as they arrived, Alma went to the post office and applied for a *poste restante* address. In deference to Mozart and da Ponte, she chose the number 1003.* Between then and mid-September, when the family returned to Vienna and moved into their new villa on the Hohe Warte, Zemlinsky sent a stream of letters to PO Box 1003; only official communications on musical matters were addressed directly to the house.

Already on the journey, while changing trains at Bad Ischl, Anna Moll took her daughter aside and gave her a piece of her mind:

It has come to my notice that Zemlinsky is in love with you. [. . .] That will lead to nothing. You are not the person to make sacrifices. On a diet of bread and water even the strongest love perishes. I have nothing against him – but he should at least have a few groats to his name.[8]

Two weeks later, Alma took Marie Henneberg into her confidence. But she, too, was aghast:

'Oh dear, you can't marry *him*. He's a Bohemian, you wouldn't feel the rift until you were married. He's still a nobody, and that won't change for some time yet, because he's so stubborn. As his wife, you would constantly have to put up with that.' 'You're wrong,' I said, 'nobody is easier to manage than he.' 'No, no, Alma. He's not for you.'[9]

In December 1900, a prosperous young architect named Felix Muhr had befriended the Molls; the following 23 March he proposed marriage. Alma was not attracted to Muhr in the least, but on his account her parents subjected her to massive pressure. Her letters reflected stormy discussions around the dinner table. Two powerful arguments against Zemlinsky were voiced over and over again: his poverty and his ugliness. He answered them as best he could:

Your Mama, for whom I otherwise have the greatest respect, does not ask: does he love you, but: has he got money. [. . .] Love in exchange for love, that is all I know. I can and will not be denigrated. My whole pride rises in rebellion. After all, I do have some standing – perhaps just as much as that entire band of artists, those poseurs and prigs, whose company you respectfully cultivate. [. . .] With a cruelty quite your own, you omit not even the most trivial arguments. Dr Muhr with his money bags! I retort: Mr Zemlinsky with his talent! There.[10]

I love you much more passionately than I can ever show – but as master, not as slave!! I can only be the master! [. . .] You say I am frightfully ugly? Very well! I thank God for it. And I thank God that so many young ladies have ignored that ugliness and found the path to my soul, have never so much as mentioned it; I know I need not be ashamed on that account, that I am still a person of some value.[11]

At the end of May Zemlinsky received a cancellation from Breslau. Hastily

* 'Ma in Ispania son già mille e tre' (*Don Giovanni*, act 1, no. 4).

he renewed his contract at the Carltheater for a further season, with improved working conditions and a higher salary.[12] In June he announced – almost casually – that Melanie Guttmann was leaving for America, never to return.[13] Hard at work on his Hofmannsthal ballet, he sent Alma regular progress reports. She in turn set a scene from a play by Hofmannsthal* and sent it to Zemlinsky for evaluation. As usual, his technical insight was invaluable, his criticism scathing:

Just as I often advised you with regard to poetry: in the first place you should formulate a clear plan, i.e. divide the scene up – how far will the first motif take you, how far the second, etc. Then: isolate the main idea! Even if each individual line is sharply characterized, that will be of little use. Where will that take you in an opera? Once a scene has been planned out, you must decide which motifs dominate – these you first have to invent. Then ascertain where the mood – i.e. key, tempo, rhythm, melody – *really* has to change. It's easy to be led astray, i.e. the mood appears to change with every line of dialogue. But the composer's task is to penetrate to the depths and fish out the one overriding mood which the poet conceived for the whole scene and which, notwithstanding the rhythm of the dialogue, can pervade the entire passage with only minor modifications. Get it?

But first you must learn to harmonize correctly, to build good, flexible forms. [. . .] In your piece all this is missing . [. . .] It takes more than just toying with piano keys and manuscript paper! More than just dreaming of parties, ball gowns, admirers, presents, cycling tours, etc.[14]

In August Zemlinsky set forth, with Hugo Botstiber as his travelling companion, on the pilgrimage to *Parsifal* in Bayreuth. Disappointed by the mediocrity of the singing, which he found 'easy to surpass',[15] he took a brief sightseeing trip around Nuremberg and spent two days in Munich, where he whisked through museums and art galleries, saw a new play by Hermann Sudermann at the Deutsches Schauspielhaus and a superb performance of *Figaro* at the Hofoper. Then he travelled on to Bad Ischl, where he had made an assignation with Alma for 10 August. But Anna Moll resolved to visit friends in Ischl that very day, and Alma had no choice but to cancel the rendezvous. Instead of explaining her precarious situation candidly to Zemlinsky, however, she made feeble excuses. Frustrated and angered, he travelled on to Mattsee to join Schoenberg and Mathilde for the rest of his holiday.†️ Nevertheless, as token of his undiminished affection he sent her a flower plucked from Wagner's grave.

Anna Moll had caught wind of her daughter's plan for the clandestine meeting, and now insisted that Zemlinsky could no longer be tolerated, that all

---

* Judging by Zemlinsky's description – 'a long dialogue with nothing particularly dramatic and nothing particularly lyric about it' (*AZ–AMW*, *c*.8 June 1901), 'in Alexandrine pentameters [*sic*]' (ibid., *c*.19 June 1901) – this was probably the scene for Dianora and the Nurse from *Die Frau im Fenster*.

†️ Evidently there was some tension at this time, for Zemlinsky later reported to Alma (*AZ–AMW*, *c*.21 September 1901): 'I am on good terms with Schoenberg again.'

contact, including tuition, must cease.[16] Still smarting at the evident rebuff in Ischl, he responded by taunting Alma with alternatives:

Whom could you approach for compositions lessons? Gound, I fear, is now more reactionary than ever, and although his theory teaching is uncommonly rigorous, he would set you off in a direction which neither you nor I would care for. The same with Labor. How about Schoenberg: a talented fellow, a fiery spirit in every sense, a true revolutionary! Think it over. [. . .] Wolff might also be worth considering.[17]

But Alma threatened suicide, whereupon her mother had little choice but to capitulate.

Your Mama sent me a very nice letter, I was very pleased. Amongst other things, she wrote: 'If you can't find the time, Alma will come to grief.' I replied, I think as politely as possible, but also very briefly. There wasn't much to be said, however, as I didn't want to write anything that would be untrue.[18]

As the summer progressed, the situation crystallized. Zemlinsky sketched out his dream scenario down to the last detail:

We'll sit together at the piano, lovingly, earnestly, and I'll play you my latest things. Simply, naïvely you'll say: 'That I like, that I don't.' That's what I long for. Yes, that's how we'll set things up. A small, subdued living room, cosy – but beautiful, very beautiful. And when our work is done, there we shall linger. Just as before, but much better![19]

Torn between her passion for Zemlinsky, which grew wilder from day to day, and the ever sterner censure of her parents and friends, Alma took refuge on an imaginary island of mystic rapture:

I've just been watching two flies copulating. They were so still, so imperturbable. Now and then a shiver ran through their wings. I blew at them – and they flew off lethargically, the one with the other, and resumed their activity a little further away. How I envied them. The breath of the world caressed me. How could anyone find that offensive? The flow of the one into the other – I find it beautiful, *wondrously* beautiful. How I long for it. Alex, my Alex, let me be your font. Fill me with your holy water.[20]

The Triumph of Time

In 1891, with a series of poems published under the pseudonym of Loris Melikow, the seventeen-year-old Hugo von Hofmannsthal sought to articulate funda-mental human perceptions and cosmic truths, antitheses of the individual and the collective, of moment and eternity, preordination and coincidence, thought and deed.[21] With time, he grew sceptical of the power of the printed word to express his vision, and turned, in search of a more flexible medium, to the stage. Hoping to solve his dilemma by eliminating the spoken word altogether, he experimented briefly with a theatre of mime, choreography and stage design, which relied entirely on the 'imagination of the eye'.[22] In the spring of 1900, during an extended visit to Paris, he sketched out a trilogy of such dance-dramas, *Leda and the Swan*, *The Festival of Love* and *The Visit of the Goddess*, which combined elements of classical mythology with the symbolism of *fin-de-siècle* French literature. Inspired by the lavish Renaissance masques of Leonardo in Milan and Burgkmair in Augsburg,[23] and stimulated by encounters with Maeterlinck and Rodin, he subsequently wrote a more elaborate mime drama, *The Miracle of Life*. Before returning to Vienna in June 1900, he expanded the work by adding an opening section entitled *The Crystal Heart* and sketching out an epilogue, *Hour of Recollection*. *The Miracle of Life*, now renamed *The Intermezzo*, thus became the central panel of a dance-theatre triptych entitled *The Triumph of Time*.

In March 1900 Hofmannsthal had made the acquaintance of Richard Strauss.* There was talk of a possible collaboration, and in November the poet sent the composer a copy of his new work, adding that he believed 'the choice of subject or chain of serious ideas' to be 'quite felicitous'.[24] Strauss, however, was himself working with Otto Julius Bierbaum on a ballet project, *Kythera*, and felt honour bound to turn the offer down.† 'Particularly the second act is excellent, and the first also includes moments of great poetical beauty,' he wrote to Hofmannsthal. 'With some reluctance, I bid these fine things farewell.'[25]

At a lunch party on 27 February 1901 Spitzer drew Zemlinsky aside, told him of Hofmannsthal's ballet project and advised him to contact the poet without delay.‡ Zemlinsky wrote, expressing his keen interest,[26] and on the afternoon of 6 March he arrived for Alma's lesson in great excitement, clutching under his arm the typescript of *The Triumph of Time*. Together they read it through, finding the piece 'uncommonly imaginative and poetic'.[27] Two days later Zemlinsky wrote to Hofmannsthal:

Reading the work through for a second time, I felt clearly that where the drama is carried forward solely by symbols, the interest slackens, and I could scarcely find the necessary strength for the music. [. . .] If we can reach an agreement, I shall start work on the composition of your ballet right away.[28]

---

* Strauss was in Paris to conduct the French première of *Ein Heldenleben* with the Orchestre Lamoureux.
† The ballet was never completed (cf. Franz Grasberger (ed.), *Der Strom der Töne trug mich fort. Die Welt um Richard Strauss in Briefen* (Tutzing, 1967), 130). In a letter to Mahler, dated 22 April 1900, Strauss offered him a 'burlesque ballet in one or two acts: Dances of the Comets, an astral pantomime [. . .] – by Paul Scheerbart.' Mahler accepted the work without hesitation: 'I consider it a point of honour for the Hofoper to give the première', he wrote (Herta Blaukopf (ed.), *Gustav Mahler. Richard Strauss. Briefwechsel 1888–1911* (Munich, 1980), 52–5). This project, likewise, never materialized.
‡ It may be assumed that Hofmannsthal, as a regular visitor to the Hofoper, had attended a performance of *Es war einmal . . .* in January or February 1901.

Hofmannsthal was evidently able to set the composer's mind at rest, and in April work began on a short score. Zemlinsky's particular concern was that his music should be 'sufficiently "light" for a typical ballet public.'[29]

The ballet will include a good deal of musical material, much more than a real opera. [. . .] In an opera I have much more motivic, thematic work; but here I am continually obliged to devise new pieces, particularly in acts II and III.[30]

He intended, of course, to dedicate the work to Alma. 'At one point I have worked in one of your motifs, imperceptibly, just for us!' he confided.[31] During the theatre vacation, his daily schedule was relatively relaxed:

Breakfast at 8.30, after which I work and write letters until about 11.30, then follows a stroll in the Prater. Lunch at one o'clock, then rest and reading until 2.30 or three o'clock, then work again until around six o'clock. In the evenings I either go to the Deutsches [Theater], which is simply unsurpassable, or have dinner in the Prater.[32]

Hofmannsthal delivered the long-awaited libretto of act III in mid-July. He had conceived it as 'a transfigured reminiscence of the first act, but more profound and exalted, permeated and illuminated by the cosmic forces'.[33] When the final version arrived, Zemlinsky was at first overjoyed. But he soon realized that, viewed from a practical angle, the poet's extravagant cosmography far transcended the technical possibilities of stage design, that his 'imagination of the eye' had run away with him. 'For the sake of something more lively, more droll', he suggested interpolating a dance for a troupe of fauns, who in the original scenario merely rush across the stage and vanish into the bushes. He also demanded substantial cuts and, instead of a mystic apotheosis, proposed 'a so-called *ballabile*, a finale with gaily tripping girls and children'.[34]

Hour of Recollection can be read as a preliminary version of the solemn triumphal tableau that concludes *Die Frau ohne Schatten*. The symbol of the crystal heart, common to both works (in certain respects comparable to the silver rose of *Der Rosenkavalier*), was a self-devised emblem of *eros* and *thanatos*. In act I of *The Triumph of Time*, as at the climax of act III of *Die Frau ohne Schatten*,[35] it shatters into myriad fragments. *Hour of Recollection* closes with the heart's restoration and its transformation into a gigantic torch, in whose flame the spectator may perceive 'the higher forces, transfiguration, the totality of life on earth'.[36] The idea comes uncomfortably close to the line dividing the sublime from the ridiculous, and even Hofmannsthal admitted that he was 'quite unable to judge [its] merits or demerits'.[37] Zemlinsky's suggestions for amendments, which in effect amounted to playing the work to the gallery, must nevertheless have sent a shudder down his hypersensitive spine. Agreement on a definitive version of act III was never reached. Zemlinsky informed Alma on the morning of 14 October (his thirtieth birthday) that he had just finished the short score, but the closing pages are lost – perhaps never existed.

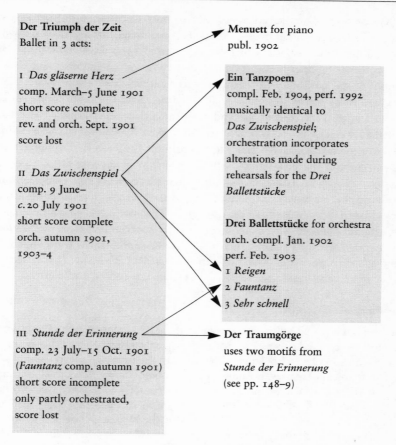

Der Triumph der Zeit
Ballet in 3 acts:

I *Das gläserne Herz*
comp. March–5 June 1901
short score complete
rev. and orch. Sept. 1901
score lost

II *Das Zwischenspiel*
comp. 9 June–
c. 20 July 1901
short score complete
orch. autumn 1901,
1903–4

III *Stunde der Erinnerung*
comp. 23 July–15 Oct. 1901
(*Fauntanz* comp. autumn 1901)
short score incomplete
only partly orchestrated,
score lost

Menuett for piano
publ. 1902

Ein Tanzpoem
compl. Feb. 1904, perf. 1992
musically identical to
Das Zwischenspiel;
orchestration incorporates
alterations made during
rehearsals for the *Drei
Ballettstücke*

Drei Ballettstücke for orchestra
orch. compl. Jan. 1902
perf. Feb. 1903
1 *Reigen*
2 *Fauntanz*
3 *Sehr schnell*

Der Traumgörge
uses two motifs from
Stunde der Erinnerung
(see pp. 148–9)

Genealogy of works related to *The Triumph of Time*

The orchestral score of act I was completed in August, and work on the short score of act III began on 15 October, parallel to the instrumentation of act II. 'I take terrific trouble; every bar has to come alive within me: only then does my highly acclaimed art of orchestration come to light,' he told Alma.[38] A copy of the text was sent to Mahler at his villa in Maiernigg on the Wörthersee, and in mid-September Hofmannsthal was summoned to the Hofoper for a brief meeting with the Director. In a distraught letter to Zemlinsky he reported, with fine understatement, that Mahler's opinion of the work was 'not very favourable' and that Heinrich Lefler, who was responsible for designing the sets, 'had not the least idea' what to make of it all. 'I should add that, as far as Mahler is concerned, everything now depends on your music.'[39] But Mahler had spoken and was not to be moved. His standpoint, as he later stressed in conversation with Alma, was that the ballet was incomprehensible.

The ambitious project collapsed like a house of cards, with poet and composer left to salvage what they could. Hofmannsthal arranged to publish his work in the September issue of *Die Insel*, and in 1902 Zemlinsky sold a piano arrangement of a brief Menuett danced in act I by an old gardener and his wife – symbol of the durability of true love – to a publisher of salon music. He also arranged three pieces from acts II and III (including the superfluous *Fauntanz* ('Faun Dance')) for concert use and performed them in February 1903 as Drei Ballettstücke. The music was well received, even by Mahler,[40] and Schoenberg tried to persuade Richard Strauss to perform the pieces in Berlin, but in vain. A plan to publish the Ballettstücke the following year likewise failed to come to fruition.[41] In 1904, realizing that the three pieces were too insubstantial for choreographic treatment, Zemlinsky revised act II of the original ballet score for performance independently of the other acts. The new score, which differed from the original version only in its more slightly more transparent orchestration, was entitled *Ein Tanzpoem*. Once again Mahler and Strauss were approached, once again to no avail. And there the case rested until the 1990s, when the work, in its final, single-act version, was staged, recorded and enjoyed.

Ein Tanzpoem: Synopsis

Daybreak, a wooded hill on Parnassus, at its peak a colossal arch. The Hours and Moments awake and dance. A horn signal rouses the Hour of Sluggishness; the Hour of Elation rushes by, in her hand a thyrsus staff. An animated general dance is interrupted by solemn fanfares, heralding a procession of Years, thirty in all, including a Bacchic youth, a wanderer, three kings in rich apparel, a barefooted fisherman and a sage led by a child. Following them in a golden carriage sits Time, the 'magna mater',[42] gently slumbering. The Hours perform the Miracle of Life: a new-born child is transformed successively into a playful boy, an ardent youth, a man in the pose of Rodin's *Thinker* and, finally, a fragile old man. Now comes the Miracle of Transfiguration: the Hour of Benediction enters, on her shoulder a white dove; the bird soars into the sky, falters, flutters to the ground and dies; the Hour of Grief leads the funeral procession; at the graveside the Hour of Sublimity steps forward to pick up the cadaver, which, in her hand, begins to glow; she flings it high into the air, and soon the dove reappears, transfigured, as a shining star. As the procession moves on, the curtain falls.

Hofmannsthal's *Intermezzo* is in effect a mystery play in three sections – dawn chorus and sunrise, Miracle of Life, Miracle of Transfiguration – which move on the discrete levels of allegorical, existential and metaphysical drama. Despite its constituent elements of dance and mime, the concept is largely static, a succession of *tableaux vivants* in the manner of the closing scene of Goethe's *Faust II*. Unity is provided, above all, by lavish recourse to ornament. In many respects a pure emanation of art nouveau, in others an orgy of classical arabesque, *Ein Tanzspiel* is a self-contradiction of styles, an ultra-modern canvas in a monstrous rococo frame.

Zemlinsky disregards the tripartite structure of the scenario, fusing the two 'miracle' sections into a single, symmetrical unit whose proportions approximately balance those of the opening 'Dance of the Hours'.* In an effort to clarify Hofmannsthal's obscure symbolism, he concentrates on the decorative outer surface of the drama, seeking with his music to beguile rather than to interpret.

On a sun-drenched Sunday morning in June, with Alma's photograph resplendent on his desk amidst a bouquet of red roses, he set to work:[43]

> The bells have been ringing for the procession since 7 o'clock this morning. [. . .] I feel young and happy, courageous and spirited. [. . .] I love you, love you unceasingly, inexpressibly. I kiss you so hard that your lip almost bleeds – can you feel it? – and go straight to work. Luck is on my side today: I am about to begin the second act of my ballet.[44]

Against a rich tapestry of rhythmic and motivic ostinati, the 'motif of the mysterious, unceasing flow of time' (Hofmannsthal's words) resounds softly in the horns –

EX. 10

– supported by symmetrical, canonic semiquaver groups in the upper strings. Offstage horns call the sleeping Hours to attention with 'the Signal', a Mahlerian *Naturlaut* in which is embedded the motif of the 'World':

EX. 11

For Zemlinsky these few scraps of melody would normally have sufficed to compose an entire score. But here, apart from a thematic lineage that often originates in a basic cell of 2nds, 4ths and 5ths,† variative technique is applied with little rigour. Long themes and regular periodic structures, lilting rhythms and

---

* Each half lasts approximately seventeen minutes.
† The bracketed notes of EX. 10 (C♯–B–F♯–C♯) can be considered as ur-motif. Identical or related shapes determine the melodic outline at 14 (D–C♯–G[–D]), the waltz theme after 32 (E–D–A–E), the general dance at 50 (A–E–F♯–C♯), the Boy's dance after 81 (F–B♭–C–B♭), etc.

translucent orchestration are the principal unifying factors; technical processes are kept discreetly out of sight.

The second section, with offstage trumpet fanfares reminiscent of Mahler's Second Symphony and a pompous E♭ major march worthy of Elgar, was begun in early July. In the music for the Blonde Hour, who leads the introductory round-dance, Zemlinsky painted a sound-picture of Alma, while the scene of the ardent youth in the 'Miracle of Life' was intended as a self-portrait:

First a stormy motif for four horns in unison against a tremolo in all the violins, then, where the first Hour dances towards him with outstretched arms, a calm, bliss-ful, powerfully amorous waltz motif.[45]

By the time the final scene was being sketched out, rehearsals had begun for the new season at the Carltheater. Time was short, and work on the closing pages of the score suffered frequent interruption. The Euphorion-inspired scene of the fluttering dove passes in the orchestra virtually without comment, the hieratic episode for the Hours of Benediction, Grief and Sublimity is absolved with almost undignified haste. The score closes as it opened, with the motif of 'Time', now ringing out imperiously in the brass.

Ein Tanzpoem is flawed by an inherent discrepancy between the idealistic proposition of the drama and the realistic disposition of the score. The poet's vivid 'imagination of the eye' nevertheless coincides with the composer's corus-cating orchestration, in joint anticipation of the Technicolor wonders that, a few decades later, were to emanate from Hollywood.

On 8 June 1901 Hofmannsthal married Gerty Schlesinger, daughter of the Director-General of the Anglo-Austrian Bank. *Hour of Recollection*, completed in the weeks immediately following the wedding, reveals itself, through a jungle of mythological and pseudo-mythological symbols, as the celebration of a fleet-ing moment of unmitigated happiness. Zemlinsky conceived the ballet in the same spirit, but for him all it could later offer were anguished memories. In his professional career, just as in his private life, the work signified a fateful turning-point. To him, the score was later little more than a token of his undying love for Alma. In 1910 he wrote to her, 'When I recall a few bars of the ballet, particularly the opening, even now I still recall their spirit, the spirit of those palmy days!'[46]

The Tonkünstlerverein (II)

During the spring of 1900, though critical of unadventurous programming, Zemlinsky continued to support the activities of the *Verein*. For a concert on 1 March he composed a brief, light-hearted singspiel entitled *Fridl*, but it was cancelled due to the indisposition of a singer (the manuscript was subsequently mislaid). In its stead he accompanied two melodramas by Max von Schillings.

A Brahms memorial concert (3 April) and an evening dedicated entirely to the chamber music and lieder of Goldmark (3 May) were programmed for the more conservative *Verein* members. On 19 April Zemlinsky led a small string orchestra in the Viennese première of a more progressive work, Josef Suk's Serenade op. 6.

Since the annual report for the 1900–1901 season has not been preserved, the sequence of events that caused Zemlinsky and Schoenberg to resign cannot reliably be reconstructed. Evidently the bone of contention was a proposal by Zemlinsky that the *Verein* should promote the first performance of *Verklärte Nacht*. A trial performance was arranged, presumably with the Rosé Quartet, who gave the work its world première in 1902. Many years later Schoenberg still smarted at Heuberger's remark, that it sounded 'as if someone had smeared over the score of *Tristan* while it was still wet'.[47] And on another occasion he recalled that the work was rejected simply because of '*one* single uncatalogued dissonance'.[48] For Schoenberg the matter was closed, and he never darkened the doors of the Tonkünstlerverein again. Zemlinsky was more conciliatory. For a while he joined Schoenberg in boycotting *Verein* concerts; and on one occasion he snidely informed Hugo Conrat: 'I've coined a new name for the *Verein*: [. . .] the Concordia Morticians' Union.' To which Conrat retorted, 'The title is not unfitting. After all, Concordia means harmony – and since you've left, that just about hits the nail on the head.'[49] But in due course he returned to the fold. Ill-health prevented him from participating in a Carnival programme on 22 February, but on 8 March 1901 he accompanied a performance of his *Irmelin Rose Gesänge* op. 7 – the songs he had dedicated to Alma.

Schoenberg and Mathilde

In May 1901 Mathilde announced that she was pregnant; on 7 October she and Schoenberg were married at a register office in Bratislava, and eleven days later they celebrated the rites of holy matrimony in Vienna at the Protestant church in the Dorotheergasse. It became imperative for Schoenberg to find regular employment. In September the Ueberbrettl had revisited the Carltheater, and Zemlinsky had taken the opportunity to introduce his future brother-in-law to Wolzogen. The vogue for literary *variété* was now sweeping across Europe, and Wolzogen, determined to maintain his leading position in the field, had built a small theatre in Berlin as permanent abode for his company. Intent on securing the services of the best talents available, he was engaging artists *en masse*, sometimes merely to prevent them from signing on elsewhere. Schoenberg, who had composed at least one song for a literary cabaret in Vienna,[50] was hired outright. In early December he and Mathilde set off for Berlin; their first child, Gertrude (Trudi) was born there on 8 January 1902.

Under Leopold Müller's direction, the Carltheater was enjoying unqualified commercial success. Zemlinsky opened the new season with Millöcker's *Der*

Damenschneider, followed in quick succession by Alfred Zamara's *Die Debütantin* and, on 25 October, Heinrich Reinhardt's *Das süsse Mädel*. The last, the forgotten masterpiece of a forgotten composer, was to run for 188 performances. Fortunately, Zemlinsky was now able to share his conducting duties with Arthur Bodanzky and could rely on the expert services of Erich J. Wolff as repetiteur, both having joined the company at the beginning of the season. Six new soloists were engaged on permanent contract, and the chorus was augmented to forty-five.

Alma Maria Mahler

Alma returned from her summer vacation on 25 September, but ten days passed before Zemlinsky found time to visit her.

I opened the gate and led him up to my room. Our kisses were less wild but more tender than in the spring. [. . .] He found me changed, but couldn't say how. He could only stay briefly, had missed the train and had a performance in the evening. He *didn't* give me a lesson.[51]

Day after day Alma confided her hopes and fears to her diary. Her ecstasy knew no bounds:

I would gladly be pregnant for him, gladly bear his children. His blood and mine, commingled: my beauty with his intellect. I would gladly serve him in his professional life, live for him and his kith and kin, breathe [for him], attend to his every happiness, serve on him with a gentle hand. God give me the strength and the willpower to do so.[52]

On 11 October he at last found time to call again. Lessons at the Moll's new villa followed a regular pattern: for an hour or so, Zemlinsky would sit at the piano and correct Alma's latest exercises, scolding and praising by turn; then they would repair to the sofa for an intensive session of extra-curricular activity. Though aware that Anna Moll could disturb them at any moment, they were in seventh heaven. The time had come, Zemlinsky felt, to consummate the union: 'I would like to possess you – possess you completely!!!' he wrote.[53] But Alma hesitated. Looking back on this turbulent period, she ascribed her diffidence to sheer cowardice:

Fool that I was, I believed in a virginal purity, which had to be upheld. Not the times were at fault, it was I who was to blame. I played hard to get. But this period was absolute music for me: perhaps the happiest and most carefree of my life.[54]

Tension mounted. In the privacy of the Moll's music room their love was undivided, but on the rare occasions when they were in company the sparks would fly. On 1 November, at dinner with Spitzer, matters came to a head. Zemlinsky fumed:

You come into the room, scarcely give me your hand, scarcely answer my questions. [. . .] The conversation revolves around trifling, childish, stupid events, with vulgar words and hysterical expletives. [. . .] And then the letter you brought with you.* Not a loving word, instead inane remarks about a yellow bed and a yellow blouse: the comforts of courtesans! [. . .] I am not complaining, not begging: that was earlier – but now no longer! [. . .] To love I cannot force you† but at least to conventional good manners.⁵⁵

His love was undiminished, but the reality of the situation began to dawn on him:

Recently, when we were alone together, your recklessly tender love-making was motivated chiefly by the desire to find out what it was like. That's my suspicion. [. . .] How tender and warm-hearted were your words: 'I want to be the mother of your children' – if only they had been sincere. But they were not! [. . .] This I know: all your views, your boundless vanity and self-indulgence, all this, for the two of us, is an obstacle to happiness! [. . .] I am constantly debating whether I should come out to visit you this week or not. Perhaps it would be better if you were not to see me for some time.⁵⁶

On 6 November Alma sent him a brief, conciliatory letter. He replied with alacrity:

You make me wild, my renewed longing for you is driving me almost mad! All my resolutions are blown to the winds!⁵⁷

On 27 October he conducted an orchestral concert in Graz, promoted by Alexander Rosé, with the violinist Jan Kubelik and the pianist Rudolf Friml as soloists. Five days later, on 7 November, the programme was repeated in Vienna. That evening, while Zemlinsky was energetically leading the orchestra of the Konzertverein through a programme of Cornelius, Spohr, Liszt, Lalo and Ernst, Alma was out visiting her friends the Zuckerkandls. The list of guests included Klimt, Burckhard, Spitzer and – Mahler. Alma's first impression of him was of sheer nervous energy, of a man 'made of nothing but oxygen'.⁵⁸ Impressed as she was, the idea of loving, let alone marrying such a man never entered her head. Two days later she sat at the piano, idly weighing up the pros and cons of consummating the bond with her 'beloved Alex':

If only I knew: 1) if he does *not* give himself entirely, whether my nerves would suffer, and 2) if he *were* to give himself entirely, whether there would be any unpleasant consequences. Both alternatives are equally dangerous, yet I madly desire his embrace. I shall never forget the touch of his hand on my most intimate parts. Such fire, such a sense of joy flowed through me.⁵⁹

Yet Mahler had not remained idle. Already at their first meeting he had invited Alma to his dress rehearsal of Offenbach's *Les contes d'Hoffmann* the following

* In order to avoid arousing Anna Moll's suspicion, most of the love letters were delivered by hand.
† 'Zur Liebe kann ich Dich nicht zwingen' (*Die Zauberflöte*, act 1).

morning; and two days later he sent her an anonymous love poem. On 18
November, after a performance of Gluck's *Orfeo ed Eurydice*, he intercepted
her and Anna Moll in the foyer and invited them into his office for a cup of tea.
From his comments it became apparent that he was the author of the poem.
Imperiously Alma asked her diary: '*Alexander v. Zemlinsky – who is he?*'[60]

Nevertheless she was torn between the two men, both as lovers and as
artists. Mahler sent her his *Wunderhorn* songs and she was aghast; she played
through act I of *The Triumph of Time* and wrote: 'It's so close to my heart'.[61]
She was also uncertain – with good reason, as was soon to transpire – whether
Mahler would respect her ambitions as a composer. For her parents, there was
no shadow of doubt: beyond the circle of his Viennese admirers, Zemlinsky
was an unknown, while Mahler was internationally accredited, occupied an
influential position, drew a good salary. He was also twenty years her senior –
and Jewish – but these objections were brushed aside. Aided by family pressure
and abetted by her persistently nagging desire for sexual fulfilment, Alma gradually succeeded in persuading herself that she loved him. On 12 December she
wrote to Zemlinsky:

You know how *very* much I loved you. You have fulfilled me *completely*. Just as
suddenly as this love arrived, it has departed – has been cast aside. Love has taken
command of me with renewed force! On my knees I beg your forgiveness for the evil
hours I have given you. Some things lie beyond our control.[62]

Four days later he came to bid her farewell:

He entered the room – paler than usual and quiet – I went to him, drew his head on
to my breast and kissed his hair. I felt so strange. Then we sat down and talked
earnestly about the whole affair – side by side – we two, whose bodies had once
coiled in love's wildest embrace. He a little sarcastic, as ever, but otherwise charming, endearingly charming. My eyes were full of tears, but my will stood firm. Today
a beautiful, beautiful love was buried. Gustav, you will have much to do to replace it.[63]

On 27 December news of Mahler's engagement was leaked to the press. The
following day Zemlinsky sent Schoenberg and Mathilde a jovial New Year's
greeting, spiked with family gossip, theatre news and flippant remarks about his
brother-in-law's Ueberbrettl début. Upon his *chagrin d'amour* he squandered all
of eight words – as if the affair had never been of any consequence: 'The latest
news: Mahler engaged to Alma Schindler.'[64] Then silence: two and a half lines
of dashes, twenty-five in all – a stifled cry of despair.

Facsimile: Zemlinsky's letter to Schoenberg (28 December 1901), second page

III

Lieder (1)

In the summer of 1901 Zemlinsky outlined the prevalent artistic situation:

Siegfrieds have become a rarity in our time, [. . .] I mean [. . .] there is a complete
lack of truly great men, heroes and spiritual leaders [*Geistestyrannen*]. The best of
our era are to be found in other walks of life. There are no geniuses; the last, in
painting, was perhaps Böcklin; in poetry – I must rack my brain – perhaps no
German since Goethe; in music, Wagner and Brahms. Today [we have] fastidious
talents but no universal capacities – experts in their field, I would say, specialists – also
in music. They exercise a virtuoso command over a specific, small area. Their nerves
are impressionable as wax; they are writing, painting and composing their own
decadence; with sickly but delicate nerves they move consciously downwards.[1]

Even if his critical view of the *status quo* was intended partly as self-reproach,
there was no question of his 'virtuoso command' being limited to a 'small area'.
And although he never composed a concerto or an oratorio, never penned an
aesthetic manifesto or a technical primer, it would be wrong to view him as a
'specialist' in any particular field. In one specific area he was nevertheless something of an expert: the lied.* The expressive, technical and intellectual possibilities of lied form opened up for him a potential of intimacy that opera, by
essence, could never attain. And in the new poetry of Austro-Germany and
Scandinavia, that admixture of symbolism, impressionism, neo-Romanticism
and aestheticism which Hofmannsthal understood as the 'anatomy of one's
own soul', he found an ideal vehicle with which to penetrate and illuminate his
personal world of feeling: his own nerves, stretched to breaking point by his
love for Alma, had become 'impressionable as wax'.

Like the Secessionist painters and the Jung-Wien poets, Zemlinsky learned to
traverse a razor's edge between emotional hypersensitivity and uninhibited
eroticism, between self-glorification and self-denigration. Even Scriabin's fanati-
cal 'I am God! I am nothing'[2] found in him a pre-echo:

I can be infinitely humble, at heart that is what I am; even more than that. But then
I can also be infinitely proud and domineering. And sometimes that quality triumphs
over everything![3]

Of the extensive repertoire of post-Wagnerian lieder, only those of Richard

---

* Zemlinsky's *œuvre* includes both *Lieder* and *Gesänge*. Some composers reserve the latter
term for larger-scale compositions (usually settings of sacred poetry or songs with orchestral
accompaniment), but his use of the nomenclature is undogmatic.

Strauss found immediate popular acceptance. Had Zemlinsky possessed any comparable talent for self-advertisement, his lieder could well have been accepted as their equals or even their superiors. Yet the best, with the exception of the Maeterlinck Songs, vanished from the public gaze within a few years of publication, and even at the time of writing four of the most important collections are still out of print.*

The lieder fall into three distinct periods: an early phase of experiment and consolidation (1889–1901), a more speculative middle period (1903–16) and, after a break of almost two decades, a late period (1933–37, anticipated in the orchestral Symphonic Songs of 1929) notable for economy and astringency. The early songs speak of the joys and torments of love, those of the middle period pose cardinal questions of mortality and human destiny, while the final period is more diversified, often masking *Weltschmerz* beneath an outer surface of dry, impish humour.

The gap of thirty years between the earlier and later periods coincides exactly with Zemlinsky's activities in the theatre. His middle-period songs (with the exception of the Two Ballads of 1907) were composed during summer vacations, to texts with which he was long familiar. In his early years he found time to scan through a wide range of classical and modern literature, and loved to enthuse about his new discoveries – Gorky, Ibsen, Mirbeau, Sudermann or Zola – in letters to his friends. But composing lieder, as he later discovered, was a pastime for a man of leisure, unencumbered by a musical director's daily of round of rehearsal, audition, crisis management and performance.

Of ninety songs written or sketched during the first period, thirty-five were published between 1898 and 1901 by Hansen, Simrock and Doblinger; a further twenty-one unpublished items, dating from 1889–97, and two chansons, composed in 1901 for the Ueberbrettl, are included in a subsidiary volume of *Posthumous Songs*, published in 1995 by Ricordi.

The earliest, which date from 1889–90, are modelled on Schumann and Mendelssohn, Tchaikovsky and Liszt. Yet few can be dismissed as mere juvenilia, and none lacks some element of individuality. Zemlinsky demonstrates an innate ability to capture the atmosphere of a poem, a keen sense of matching verse structure to musical form, a natural feeling for vocal writing and a fine ear for sonority. The piano rarely oversteps the role of accompanying instrument: preludes are brief, extended postludes rare.

Several salient musical characteristics can be traced back to these first songs. Zemlinsky's penchant for the Lydian mode is already implicit in the vocal line of *Die schlanke Wasserlilie* (1889), and the same augmented subdominant, in a minor-key context, colours the final bars of *Ich sah mein eigen Angesicht*

* Opp. 2, 5, 7 and 8, published by Hansen, Copenhagen, 1878–1901.

(1890). Here the chromatic auxiliary note (A♮ against E♭ minor) is promptly and smoothly resolved, but in the coda of *Lieben und Leben*, composed a few days later, Zemlinsky lingers pensively over a D♯ superimposed on a second-inversion A minor triad, thus arriving spontaneously at the 'Fate' chord.

Lerchengesang (October 1890) opens with an archetypal motif of 'Joy' –

EX. 13

– which later also sings out in the closing phrases of *Klagen ist der Mond gekommen* (op. 6 no. 2), in the prelude and postlude of *Blaues Sternlein* (op. 6 no. 5) and in the coda of the orchestral song *Der alte Garten*. More significant is its prominent role in *Der Traumgörge*, where the motif is complemented by a disfigured variant, the motif of 'Sorrow' (see EX. 27).

During his period of study with J. N. Fuchs, Zemlinsky's ambition to win acceptance as a Brahmsian neophyte tended to inhibit the originality he had shown in his earliest works. In answer to criticism that he modulated too frequently, he demonstrated with a setting of Heine's *Frühlingslied* (July 1892) that he was perfectly capable, given the appropriate poem, of not modulating at all. This ability to generate a seismic curve with only minimal recourse to functional harmony later stood him in good stead for more ambitious monochrome studies, such as *Geflüster der Nacht* (op. 2/1 no. 3) and *Vöglein Schwermut* (op. 10 no. 3).

Of the unpublished songs from the 1890s, the *Orientalisches Sonett* is perhaps the most striking. Painting a languid picture of harem life, the poet, Hans Grasberger, a Viennese Orientalist, poses the question of female subjugation central to *Sarema* and *Es war einmal . . .*:

Wie wird euch, schöne Frauen, zu Gemüte? / Schwand alle Sehnsucht nach der Heimat hin, / wo frei und heilig ist der Liebe Drang?

What are your feelings, lovely ladies? / Is all longing for your homeland spent, / where love's desire is free and sacred?

Zemlinsky juxtaposes a vocal line lightly spiced with augmented 2nds against a simple, unmodulating accompaniment of strummed chords in C♯ minor, shaping the song's seismic curve solely through gradations of vocal tessitura, keyboard sonority and harmonic tension. A startling turn to C major causes the curve to rise sharply, reaching its peak at the words 'tiefes Weh' ('grievous pain'). For a moment the calm of the perfumed garden is disturbed by extreme dissonance, and the song ends enigmatically with the 'Fate' chord resolving on to E major, the key of 'tender warmth'. Composed impulsively and in obvious haste, the *Orientalisches Sonett* was for Zemlinsky probably little more than a study, an experiment in 'extending the boundaries of beauty'. Two years later, for a poem of similarly exotic background, *Der Liebe Leid* (op. 2/1 no. 4), he returned to the safer ground of *Zigeuner* harmony, familiar to his public from the Hungarian Dances of Brahms and the coffee-house music of the Prater.

The texts of the Lieder op. 2 – Russian lyric poetry and Turkish folksong, Romantics (Goethe and Eichendorff), moderns (Heyse and Storm) and one ultramodern (Wertheimer)* – appear to have been selected at random. Nevertheless there is a unity. The seven poems of book I are preponderantly nocturnal, the six of book II diurnal. Read *en suite*, they describe a circle through love, despair and hope.

In *Heilige Nacht* the singer experiences love as a gift of divine grace. The eyes of his beloved shine brightly in *Der Himmel hat keine Sterne so klar*, but already in *Geflüster der Nacht* her words cast a shadow of foreboding. The dream shatters, and in *Der Liebe Leid* (based on a Turkish folk poem) the singer bewails his loss. *Mailied* skittishly depicts a lovers' game of hide-and-seek, but the game is an illusion, the beloved is gone, never to return. In Rodenberg's *Um Mitternacht* only her picture remains –

Bei Tage wird er zum Liede / und Nachts wird er zum Traum.

By day 'tis what I sing of, / by night it is my dream.

– and book I closes with a bitter-sweet humoresque, *Vor der Stadt*, a winter's tale of two strolling players in fruitless search of love and warmth.† *Frühlingstag* opens book II in a mood of tranquillity: only a few small clouds, drifting over a sunlit valley, remind the singer of his broken heart. These clouds

---

* Paul Wertheimer (1874–1937), poet and playwright, was a schoolfriend of Hofmannsthal, Schnitzler and Stefan Zweig and a member of Jung-Wien. A regular guest at Café Griensteidl, he was personally acquainted with Zemlinsky, who set five of his poems to music. Karl Kraus described him as 'a lawyer [. . .] who understands less about theatre than a cow about jurisprudence, while the latter certainly writes the better poetry' (*Die Fackel*, 622–33, mid-June 1923, 43).
† In 1893 Zemlinsky set the same poem for four-part chorus *a cappella* (only a fragment survives).

drift 'like childhood's innocent dreams', and in *Alt-deutsches Minnelied* and *Der Traum* childish fantasies are revisited. But the wounds reopen (*Im Lenz*), and the singer's agony, projected on to that of an unmarried mother, drives him almost to suicide (*Das verlassene Mädchen*). Hope ultimately triumphs over despair, and with *Empfängnis* the circle closes: the singer prostrates himself before the Saviour, his arms outspread in longing for the solace of night, for the gift of divine grace.

The experiences recorded in op. 2 may reflect a personal trauma, such as is implicit in the fourth Ballade and the *Albumblatt*, and a possible clue to the identity of the beloved may lie in the dedication of *Der Traum* (withdrawn before publication) to 'Frl. Anna M.'⁴ Yet the songs were composed out of sequence, and Zemlinsky specifically requested Hansen to publish *Der Traum* separately, sensing perhaps the imbalance caused by following it with a piece of similar character.

At a time when he was still seeking to define his personal code of values in larger-scale works, op. 2 shows him already to have attained technical and artistic mastery in smaller forms. *Heilige Nacht* and *Der Liebe Leid* betray some influence of Brahms, while the ironical joviality of *Mailied*, with its stylized cuckoo-calls, overlaps with the *Wunderhorn* style of Mahler. Yet the voice – whether beguiling or tearful, cajoling or downhearted – is consistently and unmistakably Zemlinsky's own.

Of Heyse's *Im Lenz* two settings survive. The earlier version, included in a portfolio of studies for J. N. Fuchs, is dated 1 November 1892; the op. 2 setting, which shares a sheet of manuscript paper with a sketch for the unfinished *Desiderius* project, was composed on 2 July 1896. Apart from the key of B minor common to both,* they differ radically. The first setting appears emotionally overwrought and harmonically unfocused, the second disciplined almost to the point of austerity, with finer prosody and a precisely defined tonal architecture.

The tragicomic *Vor der Stadt* evokes a wealth of musical images. Eichendorff's musicians sing and fiddle, but Zemlinsky depicts them with the roving-minstrel cliché of strummed guitar chords. They dance too, even if their repertoire is limited, and the regular quaver beat of their measure is distorted by crushed notes, Magyar snaps, fandango-like arabesques and impromptu *rubatos*. Lacking a stable centre, the tonality roves incessantly, like its protagonists. Nowhere do they show much respect for the laws of functional harmony, least of all – as they disappear over the wintry horizon – in their final, faltering cadence.

---

* Key signatures are cited from the edition for high voice, which evidently respects Zemlinsky's original tonal scheme (in the low-voice edition, key relationships are ignored). In all the early lied collections, key relationship is of structural significance. Markings in his own printed copies indicate, however, that he himself transposed individual songs, albeit within narrow limits.

EX. 14   *Empfängnis*, bars 1–4

Having so far avoided any allusion to his personal musical symbols (most of the op. 2 songs were in fact composed before he had devised them), in *Empfängnis* Zemlinsky makes use of nothing else. Pliant lines and soft-edged timbres establish a region of contemplation, in which the motifs of 'Self' and 'World' meet and entwine. These motifs were conceived as symbols of confrontation, of the individual pitted against the collective. Here that duality is momentarily resolved. The key chosen for this solemn union, Gb major,* offers an antidote to the despairing Eb minor of *Das verlassene Mädchen* while also representing the point of furthest remove from the C major of *Heilige Nacht* with which the cycle opened.

Like op. 2, the eight Gesänge op. 5 were published in two books, each unfolding a new chapter in Zemlinsky's saga of infatuation, conquest and disappointment. Book I speaks of illusions and false dreams, of the volatility of love, but book II follows the rising curve of a new passion, to culminate in a scene of turbulent summer love-making. The first three songs of book I were

---

* Ullmann, following Goethe, sees Gb major as reddish-blue, and perceives it as stimulating 'sensations of softness and longing'. With Gb major Zemlinsky also refers back to *Geflüster der Nacht* and the middle section of *Um Mitternacht*.

written in quick succession between Christmas 1896 and New Year's Day 1897, just three weeks after the first performance of the A major Quartet. *Unter blühenden Bäumen*, which opens book II, was composed at least nine months earlier and first published as a supplement to the *Neue Musikalische Presse*. The original dedication, to Melanie Guttmann, could be of biographical significance, as also for the ensuing lieder, *Tiefe Sehnsucht*, *Nach dem Gewitter* and the climactic, minor-key *Im Korn*.

No continuous story-line connects these songs, nor do they appear to have been written at the same consistently high level of inspiration as op. 2. They follow no clear scheme of tonal interrelationships, but revolve asymmetrically around an axis of D minor (*O Blätter, dürre Blätter*) and D major (*Unter blühenden Bäumen*), a duality of grief and serenity.* These two lieder, rich in 7th and 9th chords, are as fine as anything Zemlinsky ever wrote for the medium. *O Blätter* consolidates the harmonic discoveries of the A major Quartet, while *Unter blühenden Bäumen* is notable for its irregular periodic structure and a particular sensitivity in matching textual nuance to harmonic tension.

Although Zemlinsky's relationship with Melanie Guttmann is largely undocumented, it appears that *O Blätter* and the other songs in book 1 of op. 5 reflect an interim period of disaffection. In July 1897 followed a setting of Heyse's *Der Tag wird kühl* in the key of anguish, F♯ minor, and with a dedication 'to my Mela[nie] on parting'. Whether these words referred to her planned emigration to America, which she was to defer until the summer of 1901, or whether they signified a spiritual parting of the ways, the six Walzer-Gesänge op. 6 to poems by Gregorovius, composed during a break in the composition of *Es war einmal . . .* in the spring of 1898, can be interpreted as a gesture of renewed welcome.

The writer and historian Ferdinand Gregorovius (1821–1891) devoted his life's work to the culture of Italy. A pioneer in the genre of historical travelogue, he wrote absorbingly on Apulia, Capri and Corsica, Hadrian, Tiberius and Lucrezia Borgia. For sheer erudition, his eight-volume *History of the City of Rome in the Middle Ages* eclipsed all his other works, yet his collected poems, published posthumously in 1892, reached a far wider public. Stylish translations and paraphrases of Italian folk poetry, they reflect the intellectual's longing for the South and for the sunlight that inspired them.

Expressions of unclouded joy were rarely Zemlinsky's strength. The Walzer-Gesänge, written primarily to entertain, challenging but not dauntingly difficult to perform, follow in the tradition of Brahms's *Liebeslieder* waltzes. Even the

---

* In the original manuscript the two were placed back to back, with *O Blätter, dürre Blätter* as the concluding song of book 1. The same D minor/D major duality is fundamental to the tonal structure of the Second Quartet (see pp. 227–8), the Maeterlinck Songs and many other works.

ominous opening of *Klagen ist der Mond gekommen* (no. 2) soon softens into
bland euphoria. Only in *Ich geh' des Nachts*, a dialogue between Death and the
anxious bride of an abducted lover, does the mood darken. Zemlinsky is in his
element here, depicting the scene as a fleeting *Nachtstück* in Dorian-tinged
D minor, obsessively centred on the 'Fate' chord.* As Death speaks, the tonality
changes enharmonically and sinks through F minor to E♭ minor. With a simple
chromatic shift the tonic is reinstated. A sudden *forte* within the context of
piano sempre, coupled with a spasm of sextuplets in the piano, marks the
climax, which is brief and violent.

The years following Brahms's death were a period of intensive experiment, a
time for running the hands over the keyboard in search of new chords and
unorthodox harmonic progressions. The collection composed in 1898–99,
Irmelin Rose und andere Gesänge op. 7, opens with *Da waren zwei Kinder*,
which Adorno understood as

a tentative prototype for that late tonality in which the twelve semitones are virtually
emancipated, while eschewing chromatic slips from one note to the next – anticipating
that harmonic line of consciousness which led ultimately to the concept of composition with twelve tones.[5]

Writing in 1959, at a time when Zemlinsky was all but forgotten, Adorno contributed significantly to his rehabilitation. His evaluation of *Da waren zwei
Kinder* as 'a true masterpiece, looking far beyond the *Jugendstil* milieu from
which it stems'[6] was a prophet's cry in the wilderness, but his technical commentaries, evidently written without access to the printed music,† are sometimes
misleading.

   Whereas German musicians tend to scoff at all things French, the cultural
rapport between Paris and Vienna has always been free of antipathy. To
Zemlinsky and Schoenberg it was clear that since the death of Wagner the
French had taken the lead in harmonic experiment. In op. 7 Zemlinsky turned his
gaze westward and, only a few months after the Gregorovius settings and a few
weeks after the Dehmel Fantasies, began to look for new harmonic paths. In
place of integrated harmonic structure, he learned to exploit chords for their
individual properties of surface tension and colour; in place of classical modulation, he learned to shift kaleidoscopically by other means from one key centre to the next. Yet his techniques of voice-leading – *pace* Adorno – are still
largely traditional. Seemingly paradoxical chord sequences can be explained as
the logical outcome of stepwise motion –

* Zemlinsky's setting of *Nun schwillt der See so bang* (Wertheimer), composed *c.* November 1896
and published in the *Posthumous Songs*, may have served as a preliminary study for op. 6 no. 4.
† Adorno's erroneous titling of op. 7 no. 2, *Anbetung* instead of *Entbietung*, supports this sup-
position.

EX. 15A   op. 7 no. 1 (*Da waren zwei Kinder*), opening

EX. 15B   op. 7 no. 3 (*Meeraugen*), opening

or enharmonic ambiguity:

EX. 15C   op. 7 no. 2 (*Entbietung*), bars 19–23

[When your hair billows out,] the red blossoms and your blood drive it forcefully to the midnight of fulfilment.

Entbietung, chronologically the first of the series, glows with erotic tension, the anguish of F♯ minor asserting itself with magnetic force against the counter-weights of A minor, C major, A♭ minor, F minor and B♭ minor, each coloured by auxiliary notes. The vocal line, restricted in compass to little over an octave, describes triadic circles against an accompaniment obsessively pulsating in 'Circassian' rhythm. Many of the more unfamiliar harmonic effects are arrived at by a simple process of mirroring the bass line in the upper voices. Through strict technical control, Zemlinsky evokes and sustains an atmosphere of erotic frenzy.

The opening bar of *Meeraugen* (EX. 15B) combines a *Drehfigur* in minor 3rds, its mirror image and an independent four-note motif (C–E♮–F–C), fragmentarily echoed in the lower octave. Despite the contradictory notation and the pedal point on F, the ear isolates the first beat of each bar as an E major triad: the impertinent gesture of the E minor Quartet (EX. 4) is elevated to a plane of mystical ambiguity. The opening phrase also includes eleven of the twelve semitones, while the twelfth pitch (E♭), interpolated in bar 4, sets a chromaticism in motion whose potential for subversion is ingeniously exploited during the course of the song. The bass line serves as an anchor with which to stabilize the chromaticism of the upper voices, but its chain breaks three times, causing the harmony to rotate through the circle of 5ths.* In this context of tonal unrest, Adorno may even have understood the contrary chromatic motion of the closing bars as prophetic of Schoenberg's *Erwartung* monodrama, composed only ten years later:

EX. 16   *Meeraugen* (bars 39–40)

Just as the *Orientalisches Sonett* revisits the milieu of *Sarema*, *Irmelin Rose*, Jens Peter Jacobsen's ballad of a haughty princess, serves as a pendant to *Es war einmal . . .* As if to mirror the feminine caprice of his heroine, Zemlinsky plays a witty game of shifting keys. The song begins mendaciously, in A minor, with the true tonic, F major, briefly revealed in bar 7 but not properly established

---

* *Da waren zwei Kinder*, bars 6–8, progresses through a half-circle of 5ths (from D to E♭); *Meeraugen* progresses still further: in bars 5–10 nine steps (from D♭ to A♭), in bars 14–20 all eleven steps (from F to C), and in bars 32–7 ten steps (from E♭ to F).

until bar 10, and lightly veiled even then by an added 6th. Turning through the tonic minor, Irmelin moves abruptly into G♭ major, veers towards D major, then twists back to the tonic, pausing lethargically to contemplate her own beauty before setting out on a new round of playful deception. Her suitors march past in D major to the accompaniment of mock-military fanfares, but she remains non-committal, spiralling off in a chromatic ascent towards G♭ major before falling back into the false tonic of the opening. Not until she has shown the gentlemen off the premises –

Doch Prinzessin Stahlherz jagte / all die Freier schnippisch fort.

Pertly ousted all her suitors / our princess with heart of steel.

– does she allow herself the luxury of undisturbed F major, lazily sinking back on to a bed of 6th, 7th and 9th chords.

    Sonntag, to a poem by Wertheimer, returns to the contemplative atmosphere and widely arched melodic line of *Empfängnis* (op. 2/II no. 6). A simple three-note cell, D–E–F♯, furnishes the entire substance of thirteen radiant bars, with an opulent, seemingly improvised piano part, notable for its polyrhythmic irregularity. The prayer of *Empfängnis* for fulfilment is answered, if not in love, then in art. A sense of bliss – not the clear blue sky of Gregorovius, but an inner glow of pride and satisfaction – pervades the entire song.

All mein Geh'n ist heut' / ein seliges Schreiten; / kein Ton, der mich reut, / ist in meinen Saiten.

Where today I walk, / my steps are sacred; / no chord have I struck / that I regret.

With languid self-confidence the singer repeats the words 'kein Ton' to a falling 6th, a universal gesture of peace and contentment (EX. 17).*

    During the course of a social gathering, Zemlinsky spontaneously offered one of his finest works, the op. 7 songs, to Alma Schindler, a complete stranger. In her, he found the incarnation of his Princess of Ilyria, his Irmelin.† Her memories of that evening paint a vivid picture:

I said to Zemlinsky, 'Why haven't you been taking more notice of me?' 'Fräulein, you really are a mad flirt. You know just as well as I do that it's been impossible even to get near you.' And he was right – the men were hovering around me like moths around a lamp. And I felt like a queen, proud and unapproachable,

* Cf. the 6/8 section of the seduction scene in act II of *Parsifal* and the aria 'Depuis le jour' which opens act II of Gustave Charpentier's *Louise*, both of which use the falling 6th B♮–D in G major to comparable effect.
† Other dedications were less intimate: the opp. 2 and 8 collections are inscribed to distinguished lieder singers, Anton Sistermans and Johannes Messchaert, the op. 5 songs to a 'Fr. J. C.' (possibly Ida Conrat).

EX. 17   *Sonntag*, bars 12–13

exchanged three cool words with each one. [. . .] It was a veritable triumph.[7]

The songs had been composed several months before they first met, but now he found them strangely relevant:

Curious! They are all poems whose content applies to you, i.e. inspired by the way I feel about you at present. Only the first – I would wish for a happier ending! *Da waren zwei Kinder.*[8] [. . .] You, my beautiful, my most beautiful one. Your dear, deep sea-eyes [*Meeraugen*], so near, so wonderfully near. You have given wing to my Sunday [*Sonntag*] spirit.[9]

But by the time the songs appeared in print, in the autumn of 1901, the affair was reaching its end. Only a few days before her first meeting with Mahler, Zemlinsky wrote indignantly to her:

I notice that you have never again mentioned the volume of songs bearing your name, and never told me for instance what your Mama had to say. I conclude that you are carefully hiding them –! [. . .] If that's the case, then I much regret having jeopardized your position![10]

The four songs published as *Turmwächterlied und andere Gesänge* op. 8, which date from the spring of 1899, share no common theme, but are unified by an unusually narrow key range: E♭ major, A♭ major and F minor. The title song solemnly celebrates the composer's conversion to Protestantism; *Und hat der Tag all seine Qual* is an ethereal echo of *Entbietung* (op. 7 no. 2), the throbbing 'Circassian' syncopation now reduced to a rapt adagio, the harmony further refined, the textures luminous and luxuriant; *Mit Trommeln und Pfeifen* and *Tod in Ähren* are songs on the death of soldiers. The former, a saga comparable in content to Mahler's *Der Tambourg'sell*, makes extensive use of a Schubertian ostinato rhythm; the latter,* reminiscent of Duparc, contrasts

---

* Liliencron's message of pity is conveyed by the sarcastic pun of the title: 'Tod in Ehren' means 'death on the field of honour'; 'Tod in Ähren' signifies 'death in a cornfield'.

a more dramatic style with calmer interludes based on the 'World' motif.

Jens Peter Jacobsen, the world-weary poet of *Turmwächterlied* ('Song of the Watchman in the Tower'), looks down from his high vantage point to admonish his fellow men to love, hope and charity; a self-avowed agnostic, he takes it upon himself to intercede for them with the Almighty. But his words scarcely conceal his cynicism and disillusionment:

Gute und Böse, Sieche und Heile, / mit Ruf und Rede seufzend / im heiligen Zeichen des Kreuzes. / Höre sie alle in deiner Gnade, / gewähre ihnen nach deinem Willen, / lass sie christlich beten.

The good and evil, the sick and healthy, / calling and sighing pitifully / in the holy name of the Cross: / hear them all in Thy mercy, / let Thy will be done, / let them pray as Christians.

Wilfully disregarding the subversive undertone, Zemlinsky stresses the poem's rhetorical grandeur and preaches from an ecumenically unstable pulpit a musical sermon of epic proportions. At the stormy climax of *Meeraugen* (op. 7 no. 3) he had stretched the medium of voice and piano almost to its limits; here he goes still further, investing the accompaniment with orchestral sumptuousness and dynamic range. Throwing his motivic economy to the winds, he disburses a wealth of themes and motifs in an uncharacteristically loose-jointed sequence of recitative, arioso, strophe and interlude. Cyclic unity is provided by a solemn fanfare, with which the song opens:

EX. 18

While acknowledging the mystic and heroic qualities of E♭ major, here (as in the closing section of *The Triumph of Time*) it is a key of transfiguration. After a solemn 26-bar prelude, which veers towards A♭ major, the voice enters softly, steering the tonality resolutely through the subdominant and dominant into G major, and reaching its apex, E major/C♯ minor, at the words 'denn der Herr ist gut' ('for the Lord is good'). With an imperious gesture E♭ major is reinstated. Despite passing chromaticisms, the last 28 bars remain steadfastly in the tonic, an open-hearted declaration of faith.

In his printed copy of the song* Zemlinsky later replaced the word 'christ-lich' (Christian) in the last line of the poem with 'alle' (all). His Protestant zeal, though at first sincere, seems to have been short-lived.

Otto Julius Bierbaum was justifiably proud of *Der lustige Ehemann* and gave the poem pride of place in his anthology of *Deutsche Chansons*. A nonsense poem almost worthy of Lewis Carroll, it contrasts the folk-music cliché of 'Ringelringelrosenkranz' ('ring-a-ring o' roses'), with a self-devised portmanteau refrain, 'Klingklanggloribusch' (approximately: 'ding-dong-pleasure-plume'). Audiences in Berlin and Vienna smiled knowingly at the phallic implication and went home whistling the song – but in the version by Oscar Straus, which had taken the palm in Wolzogen's unofficial Ueberbrettl contest. Zemlinsky's witty setting, with its drastic chromaticisms, was evidently too sophisticated for popular taste. Had he not included it as the title song in the collection *Ehetanzlied und andere Gesänge* op. 10, it might well have fallen altogether by the wayside.[†]

The central theme of op. 10 – whether expressed in rollicking waltz rhythm (*Ehetanzlied* and *Kirchweih*), tender lyricism (*Selige Stunde*), masculine vigour (*Meine Braut führ' ich heim*) or theatrical intensity (*Klopfet, so wird euch aufgetan*) – is the joy of partnership. In many respects op. 10 thus covers the same ground as the Walzer-Gesänge op. 6. But after the stylistic breakthrough of op. 7 Zemlinsky writes with greater freedom, expressive power and stylistic variety. As in the earlier cycle, one song disrupts the general euphoria: *Vöglein Schwermut*. Morgenstern's ballad tells of a melancholy little bird that roosts upon the hand of Death:

Der streichelt's leis und spricht ihm zu: / flieg mein Vögelein! / Und wieder fliegt's flötend über die Welt.

With a sweet caress Death whispers low, / 'Fly my little bird!' / And off it flies fluting over the world.

The piano flutters nervously around the 'Fate' chord in a manner reminiscent of Schumann's *Vogel als Prophet*. But when Death speaks, the voice is lowered to a terrified whisper, the accompaniment freezes into immobility.

Only a few preliminary sketches of op. 10 survive, making it impossible to establish the exact chronology. However, since the opening phrase of *Klopfet, so wird euch aufgetan* is quoted in the revised act 1 finale of *Es war einmal . . .*, the song can be dated approximately to the autumn of 1899. And since the first

---

* Preserved in *MolA*.
[†] Of three further chansons and one duet composed for the Ueberbrettl, only the two items published in the *Posthumous Songs* have survived.

draft of *Meine Braut führ' ich heim* shares a folio with a sketch for one of Jacobsen's *Songs of Gurre* (*Mit Toves Stimme flüstert die Wald*), it can be dated to the closing months of 1899.* *Ehetanzlied*, Zemlinsky's entry for the Ueberbrettl competition, was evidently written in January or February 1900. Since the contract with Doblinger Verlag was not signed until 11 May 1901,[11] the remaining songs must have been composed during the intervening twelve months. The title of *Selige Stunde* may be an oblique reference to *The Triumph of Time*,† which would imply a composition date of March or April 1901. Wertheimer cannot approach Hofmannsthal's linguistic precision; indeed his three short verses are a jumble of mixed metaphors.‡ Yet the rapt concentration of Zemlinsky's setting, with 'Circassian' syncopation against a descending bass line, is itself a 'miracle of transfiguration'.

Discretion prevented Zemlinsky from dedicating any further pieces to Alma, but privately he considered op. 10 just as much hers as op. 7, particularly *Selige Stunde*, which she admired for its sonorous 7th chords.

The surprise for 'Dr Spitzeles'§ is complete. His name shines splendid and glorious over my song *Selige Stunde*. It's the song with your favourite chord. But then (in jest), I could always write you another piece with the same chord.[12]

The key to all the songs of op. 10 seems to lie in their dedications, all but one of which were suppressed before publication.[13] The three more extrovert numbers, *Ehetanzlied*, *Meine Braut führ' ich heim* (originally entitled *Hochzeitslied*) and *Kirchweih*, are epithalamia, dedicated respectively to Anna Norden (a family friend), Siegfried Theumann (second violinist of the Buxbaum Quartet) and Arnold Schoenberg. Rudolf Stephan Hoffmann cites *Klopfet, so wird euch aufgetan* as the *locus classicus* of the 'World' motif.[14] The song is an impassioned plea for shelter from the storms of life – and perhaps a last attempt at reconciliation. In this spirit, Zemlinsky originally intended to dedicate it to Melanie Guttmann.

And *Vöglein Schwermut*? The sad little bird, it transpires, was a prophetic self-portrait. Zemlinsky dedicated the song to the only wedding guest still without a partner: himself.

---

* The competition for which Schoenberg entered his original *Gurrelieder* song-cycle was announced on 15 January 1900, with the closing date on 15 May. Zemlinsky was invited to adjudicate (together with Heuberger, Mandyczewsky, Carl Prohaska and Anton Rückauf). It is unclear whether he abandoned the Jacobsen setting out of deference to Schoenberg, or because he had agreed to join the jury.
† In the final section of the ballet, *Miracle of Transfiguration*, it is the 'selige Stunde' ('Hour of Benediction') that leads the dance.
‡ A poem entitled *Selige Stunde* is included in Wertheimer's *Neue Gedichte* (Munich, 1904), but the text of the op. 10 song differs completely. Zemlinsky copied it down in fluent shorthand(!), presumably to the poet's personal dictation.
§ A 'Semitic' nickname. Despite his gratitude to Spitzer, Zemlinsky's opinion of him was unflattering.

IV

Vienna 1902–1911

I

Symphony of Death

Alma had long succeeded in concealing her affair with Zemlinsky from Mahler. When the truth finally emerged, he rounded on her:

Your cold-hearted attitude [. . .] is incomprehensible to me. Did you love him? Is it then fair to relegate him to the sad role of teacher? Do you consider it humane or generous that he should sit silent and courteous before you – the cause of his suffering – and simply take everything in his stride? If you really believe you loved him, could you still accept such a situation?[1]

On 12 January 1902 he presented his Fourth Symphony to an unenthusiastic Viennese public. Alma, who herself found little to admire in the work, did not even trouble to record the event in her diary. Nine weeks later, on 9 March 1902, their marriage was sanctified in the vestry of the Karlskirche, with only the Molls and the Rosés in attendance.

For Zemlinsky life went on much as before. At the Carltheater rehearsals were in progress for Carl Weinberger's *Das gewisse Etwas*, a vaudeville to a libretto by Leon Stein and Victor Léon.* *Die Fackel* observed sardonically:

An experienced conductor, noted for his ability in orchestrating operettas by others, recently confessed with a sigh, 'Were it not for amateurs, the real talents would never be able to earn a living!' Whether Mr Charles [sic] Weinberger still has his works finished by outside contractors, and who those contractors are, I cannot say.[2]

Reading between the lines, it would appear that Zemlinsky had again provided a 'beguiling' orchestration for another composer. And when the production opened, on 15 March, even Kraus granted that the piece had some merit. On 12 April followed *Der kleine Günstling* by Jenö Fejér, another 'amateur': his real name was Weiss, and he had made his fortune selling grain; the orchestration was provided by a conductor from Budapest.[3]

Day after day Zemlinsky carved his way through these flimsy pieces. It was the very treadmill depicted in the first movement of Mahler's Fourth Symphony, 'the world as eternal present-time',† fruitless, frivolous, soul-destroying. 'Everything on earth would be wonderful', he confided to his mother, 'if there were no operetta!'[4]

Beyond the confines of the Carltheater, musical life in Vienna was still rich

---

* In 1905 the same team wrote the libretto of *Die lustige Witwe*.
† Subtitle for the first movement of Mahler's Fourth Symphony, not included in the printed editions.

and stimulating. On 25 January Zemlinsky attended the world première of Franz Schmidt's First Symphony* and heard a symphonic poem, *Barbarossa*, by Siegmund von Hausegger, whom he considered 'a *highly talented fellow*'.[5] Four days later Mahler premièred *Feuersnot* at the Hofoper, and Zemlinsky wrote an appreciative letter to Strauss in Berlin. 'It will appear to him as if we were the most dedicated disciples of his muse,' he observed wryly to Schoenberg, adding that the work was 'not effective on stage'.[6] On 31 January he accompanied the fourteen-year-old prodigy Stefi Geyer in Beethoven's Violin Concerto and Jenö Hubay's *Carmen*-Fantasy. The following evening, back at the Carltheater, he conducted the 101st performance of Heinrich Reinhardt's *Das süsse Mädel*. A rare appearance at the Tonkünstlerverein followed on 21 February, when he accompanied four of his lieder opp. 7 and 8.

On 18 March the Rosé Quartet, augmented by Franz Jellinek and Franz Schmidt,[†] gave the long-awaited world première of *Verklärte Nacht*. For Schoenberg, who had been unable to attend, Zemlinsky had qualified praise:

> Apart from some moments of considerable tedium and affectedness in the middle of the work, it made a great impression on me. There are passages of true beauty and deepest feeling as well as genuinely great, uncommon artistry! You really must revise the piece, publish the score and try to disseminate it. [. . .] The success was just as you would have wished. Heartfelt, frequent recalls mixed with opposition. [. . .] Rosé had to take six bows.[7]

It was probably at this time, encouraged by the success of *Verklärte Nacht*, that Zemlinsky himself began work on two programmatic pieces for string sextet. Of the first, a slow movement in E♭ minor entitled *Ein Stück aus dem Leben eines Menschen* ('A piece of a person's life') and subtitled 'Schicksal' (fate), only fragments survive;[8] of the other, a setting of Dehmel's *Die Magd* with sextet accompaniment, a score of 210 bars has been preserved.[‡] Like *Frühlingsbegräbnis*, the opening verses of *Die Magd* tell of a young man struck down by the summer sun. But where Heyse's poem inhabits a world of playful make-believe, Dehmel presents a gruesome human tragedy. On a clear spring night a farm labourer and his lass embrace beneath the alder tree; in the heat of the summer cornfields the boy dies of exhaustion; as autumn approaches, the girl – now pregnant – is ordered to leave the farm; under Christmas lights, shining from inhospitable houses, she kills her new-born child and sinks delirious into the snow. Why Zemlinsky abandoned the project is not clear. In the surviving

---

* Schmidt's Symphony in E major was awarded the 1902 Beethoven Prize.
† Schmidt's participation in the Rosé Quartet's early performances of *Verklärte Nacht*[5] seems all the more remarkable in view of his anti-Semitic polemic against Mahler, Rosé and Buxbaum (see p. 31), included in an autobiographical sketch *c*.1914. In 1929 he dedicated his G major Quartet to Rosé.
‡ The first two sections, which constitute a thematically integrated unit, were published in 1997 as *Maiblumen blühten überall* ('Maybuds blossomed all around').

fragment of verse 3, inspiration slackens: perhaps he realized the impossibility of finding music for the suicide of the outcast mother more tragically serene than that for the death of the young man. But perhaps he instinctively sensed that the story, for him, was over. Had he himself not been struck down by Alma, his summer sun?

As soon as the Carltheater season ended, at the end of April, the ensemble set off to Dresden for a four-week guest appearance, while Clara Zemlinszky travelled to Berlin to visit the Schoenbergs. Zemlinsky had written to Strauss, asking him to recommend *Es war einmal . . .* to the Director of the Hofoper in Dresden. When Strauss finally replied, his advice was to leave the score at the stage door.[9]

In 1901 Josef Weinberger took over several smaller music-publishing businesses and amalgamated them into one large firm, Universal Edition. In urgent need of new editions of the classics for the amateur market, he commissioned a series of operatic arrangements for piano (solo or duet) from various Austrian composers. Zemlinsky was entrusted with *Fidelio*, completed in April, *Die Zauberflöte*, *Die lustigen Weiber von Windsor*, *Zar und Zimmermann* and *Der Waffenschmied*, all completed during the summer vacation. In order to meet Weinberger's deadlines, he was obliged to maintain an average output of ten pages of manuscript per day.* Assignments that he himself could not complete were passed on to Schoenberg.

The Dresden public flocked to see *Das süsse Mädel*, but towards the end of the month ticket sales dropped, and the production was replaced by Offenbach's *La princesse de Trébizonde*. Zemlinsky was only too happy to give up the rostrum to Bodanzky, and flee to the Schoenbergs in Berlin. When he returned to Vienna, later in June, prospects for the coming season seemed rosier, for he had negotiated a contract at the Theater an der Wien with better pay, more stimulating repertoire and a certain degree of artistic independence. He would have taken up his new post at once, were it not for Leopold Müller, who claimed that his contract at the Carltheater had already been renewed – verbally, if not in writing (in Austrian law, a verbal agreement can be considered legally binding). In July Müller took the matter to court and, whether by fair means or foul, won his case. Zemlinsky had no choice but to return to the Carltheater for another season of Thespian drudgery.

During the summer months, musical life in Vienna revolved largely around 'Venedig in Wien', two square miles of the Prater laid out in Venetian style, with

---

* Between 1902 and 1904 Zemlinsky prepared altogether ten arrangements for UE, delegating three further assignments (*Der Waffenschmied* for piano duet, *Rosamunde* and *Il barbiere di Siviglia*) to Schoenberg. Weinberger's policy proved unsound: between 1901 and 1907, UE published 1,500 classical titles, thereby incurring a debt of 900,000 fl. (see Norman Lebrecht, *When the Music Stops* (London, 1996), 333).

canals plied by authentically costumed gondoliers, *piazze* and connecting
wooden bridges, concert halls, theatres, restaurants and drinking places. Gabor
Steiner, the managing director, provided entertainment for every taste: popular
concerts were conducted by Karl Komzák,* Vienna's most celebrated band-
master, while more highbrow fare was offered by a *Riesenorchester* (giant
orchestra) of 150 musicians under Hermann Graedener. Steiner also commissioned operettas from popular composers, including Lehár, Zierer and Eysler,
and had them performed by the best singers he could hire. In 1898 and 1899
he also promoted concerts of Italian grand opera with a company managed
by Luigi Malipiero.† For the 1902 season 'Venedig' was transformed into a 'city
of flowers'. Oscar Nedbal and Richard Strauss gave orchestral concerts, and on
21 June no fewer than twelve conductors, including Josef Bayer, Lehár and
Zemlinsky, led the *Riesenorchester* in a 'Devil's Festival' of light music.

   After a performance of *Ein Heldenleben* with the *Riesenorchester* on 18 July,‡
Strauss joined Zemlinsky and the Rosé brothers for dinner. Ostensibly he was
willing to move heaven and earth for the young composer and his revolutionary
brother-in-law,[10] but ultimately his generosity proved little more than a gesture
of good will. Nevertheless, Zemlinsky revered Strauss his life long and saw in
him the epitome of *Glück*: a man with real talent, charisma, political acumen –
and a Christian by birth.

   August was spent at Altmünster on the Traunsee with the Schoenbergs,
Bodanzky, Weigl and other friends. A strict daily routine of composing and
transcribing was interspersed with walking tours, boating trips and outings to
nearby recreation areas. One afternoon, to his delight, Zemlinsky spotted the
veteran Carl Goldmark playing whist in a Gmunden coffee-house.

   The theatre season opened in mid-September, and on 3 October followed the
world première of Heuberger's newest *magnum opus*, *Das Baby*. Public
response was poor – after two weeks, box-office receipts were down by half –
and Heinrich Reinhardt's *Der liebe Schatz* went into rehearsal in its place.
'Horrible, hideous, hateful,' fumed Zemlinsky.[11] In December followed Lehár's
Der Rastelbinder, a Carltheater classic, which was to run for over two hundred
performances. Schoenberg had meanwhile returned to Berlin, only to find
Wolzogen's Buntes Theater on the verge of collapse. With the help of Strauss,
he succeeded in securing himself temporary employment teaching counterpoint.

   Although Mahler had insisted that Alma break off relations with Zemlinsky,
and would not tolerate him entering the house, between the two men contact

---

* In 1900 Komzák honoured Zemlinsky's success at the Hofoper by performing and publish-
ing an orchestral pot-pourri from *Es war einmal* . . .
† Father of the composer Gian Francesco Malipiero. At this time, the seventeen-year-old was
studying music theory with Eduard Stocker at the Vienna Conservatoire.
‡ The orchestra, according to Zemlinsky, was 'huge, but inadequate for the pieces' (letter to
Schoenberg, 24 June 1902, *Web-Br*, 19).

was maintained. In the spring of 1902 Zemlinsky sent Mahler the score of his Drei Ballettstücke, which was politely rejected; the following spring they discussed an idea for an opera based on *Malva*, a novella by Maxim Gorky, to a libretto by Ernst Hutschenreiter:[12] Mahler advised against it.

Neither Mahler nor Strauss professed an interest in the Drei Ballettstücke,* but finally Ferdinand Löwe agreed to include them in his regular series of Wednesday concerts. The performance, on 18 February 1903, was the first of an orchestral work by Zemlinsky in two years. He was delighted that Mahler found time to attend (with Alma at his side), grateful that Heuberger gave him a good review, and flattered by the unanimous praise of his conducting. In April he entered into negotiation with a music publisher in Strasbourg who had expressed an interest in the Ballettstücke[13] and evidently also paid him for a revised version of *Frühlingsbegräbnis*.[14] But Zemlinsky was aware that both these pieces were too insubstantial to maintain the reputation he had gained with *Es war einmal* . . . For over a year he had been working on a large orchestral score, and now it lay on his writing desk, all but complete.

The Little Mermaid

Die Seejungfrau, an orchestral fantasy on the eponymous tale by Hans Christian Andersen, was originally conceived as a through-composed symphony in two parts:

I a) on the sea-bed (entire exposition); b) the Mermaid and the mortal world, the storm, the Prince's rescue.

II a) the Mermaid's longing; in the domain of the Mer-witch; b) the Prince's wedding, the Mermaid's end.[15]

Zemlinsky appears also to have written his own programme, but apart from a few cue words scribbled into the short score, this has not survived. During the process of composition he expanded the plan to three movements, the first corresponding to the original part I, the second focusing on a subsidiary scene in Andersen's story (a ball at the Mer-king's palace), the third depicting the Mermaid's life as a mortal, her demise and reincarnation as a spirit of the air.

He began work in February 1902, a few days before the Mahler–Schindler wedding. By the end of August 1902 the first movement was finished in full score. The short score of the whole work was completed a week later, and the full score on 20 March of the following year, four weeks after the first performance of the Drei Ballettstücke. Before the world première he made substantial

---

* In a postcard to Schoenberg dated 19 January 1903, Strauss, who evidently intended to perform at least two of the three movements in concert, asked to be sent the orchestral materials. The performance never materialized (see *St-Sch*, 59).

cuts, including a sailors' bacchanal in the first movement and the entire scene of the Mermaid's ordeal with the Mer-witch, a passage of 75 bars, in the second movement.*

In a spirit of friendly rivalry, Schoenberg began work in July 1902 on a tone-poem based on Maeterlinck's *Pelléas et Mélisande* (a subject allegedly suggested to him by Strauss). The play, with its hothouse erotic atmosphere and Poe-inspired aura of decay, must have appealed to him above all on account of its affinity to *Verklärte Nacht* and the *Gurrelieder*. To the envy and admiration of his brother-in-law, he completed the short score in a matter of weeks.

The psychological process that prompted Zemlinsky to choose Andersen's tale was complex. In her little garden, under the branches of a rose-coloured weeping willow, the Mermaid kept a statue of a handsome boy, which once had fallen to the seabed from a sinking ship; surmounting a vase of red roses on his writing desk – the composer's 'little garden' – Zemlinsky cherished just such a memento: his framed photograph of Alma. In forfeiting her tongue to the knife of the Mer-witch, the Mermaid proved herself willing, for love of a mortal, to bear excruciating pain; in punishment for daring to penetrate Alma's high society Zemlinsky had suffered the pain of belittlement. 'The first morning after he marries another, your heart will break,' warns the Mer-witch, 'and you shall become foam on the crest of the wave'; now that Alma had left him, his heart was indeed broken. She was to have been his Muse, but now, instead of smiling on him like some benevolent goddess, she troubled his waking hours and tormented his dreams. To Schoenberg he confided that *Die Seejungfrau* was 'a preliminary study for my Symphony of Death';[16] and soon after completing the score he wrote, 'I feel distraught, cheerless and completely discouraged. [. . .] I lack your optimism, patience, humour and *joie de vivre*. I am *much* changed from what I was.'[17]

His resolve to compose an extended piece for large orchestra was inspired principally by *Ein Heldenleben*. Indeed, only a few days before starting work on *Die Seejungfrau* he borrowed a score of the work and studied it avidly.[18] The programme may have been egotistical and overblown,† but Strauss's bold, memorable themes and stunning orchestral effects never failed to impress. The passages of cacophony, for which it had become notorious, Zemlinsky found less convincing. He felt that they failed to satisfy the demands of motivic logic; the intricacies of the score were unfocused and disorganized, its dissonances wilful and synthetic. His own maxims, as outlined to Schoenberg, were sterner:

Where the ear [. . .] detects ugliness, where the art of tone-painting, of sharpest characterization, becomes a parody – operetta, tone-painting of the Ueberbrettl – even

---

* A brief allusion to this episode survives in the transition from the trio to the scherzo reprise (at 17⁻² in violas and cellos).
† At early performances of Strauss tone-poems, the public was invited – at extra cost – to purchase booklets containing the detailed programme.

with the greatest technique, the boundary is overstepped. The section entitled 'The Adversaries' can no longer be taken seriously! In my view it is merely motivated by the desire to pour personal venom on the critics: 'D'you hear? That's how nauseating you really are.' Only in this sense can I come to terms with such a passage. But this is not art, certainly not music. The greatest refinement dissolves into *naïveté*.[19]

He saw no reason to abandon the principles instilled in him by Fuchs and Brahms. On the contrary, even when writing for large orchestra he remained true to the ideal of total thematicism. Hence an elaborate passage of tone-painting, such as the storm scene in the first movement, was 'a hell of a job (*Sauarbeit*)', as he told Schoenberg, 'if one wishes to avoid becoming cheap and vulgar'.[20]

Work on *Die Seejungfrau* began, unusually, with a chart of motifs. The first, captioned 'Home' (*Heimat*), uses the same nuclei as those of the D minor Symphony, a 4th and a descending 3-note scale figure. But now the 4ths are presented as a mirrored pair, A–E and A–D, and the rising interval is filled in with the 'Self' motif:

EX. 19

A second motif represents the 'World of Humans' (*Menschenwelt*):

EX. 20*

Further motifs depict the seabed itself (a rising scale figure in a low register) and 'Pain, Despair' (*Schmerz, Verzweiflung*) – the falling scale of EX. 19, with its rhythmic stress transferred to the second note. A motif used frequently in the score, but not included in the chart, depicts foam flying off the crest of a wave (EX. 21).

A 'nature' figure, comparable to those filling many a page of the *Ring*, it combines the 4ths and falling scale of EX. 19 with the characteristic falling 6th of EX. 20. The significance of this 6th is explained by the Mermaid's own motif. 'The youngest of the six sisters was also the most beautiful . . .' wrote Zemlinsky in the short score at its first appearance. Her theme combines the

---

* In the score, the motif is never cited exactly in this form.

EX. 21*

rising 6th of the motif of 'Joy' (EX. 13) with the blissful falling 6th of *Sonntag* (EX. 17), transposed into A major, the key of sunlight;[21] it closes with an inter-version of the 'World' motif, identical to the *Naturlaut* of Wagner's Woodbird:

EX. 22

In the central section of the second movement, Zemlinsky introduces a new motif which, as he told Schoenberg, symbolizes 'Man's Immortal Soul':[22]

EX. 23

The idea originates in the mystical fanfare of *Turmwächterlied* (EX. 18), but the voice-leading is now refined to a scheme of 4ths and 5ths: as in EX. 18, the bass mirrors the soprano; but now there are new inner parts (Bb–F–G and G–C),[†] and the pitches of the second chord, arrayed in ascending order, climb

---

* Zemlinsky continually varies both the pitch and the rhythm of this motif. The variant quoted here, played by flute and harp in the coda of the second movement (24^{11}) probably represents the ur-form. From pitches 4 to 7 Zemlinsky extrapolates a 6/8 theme, prominent in the first movement, which is (coincidentally?) identical to the slow-movement second subject of Tchaikovsky's Fifth Symphony:

† In orchestrating this figure, Zemlinsky changes the voice-leading. The idea of combining a

the ladder of 4ths, [G]–C–F–B♭–E♭–A♭, which in Schoenberg's Chamber Symphony no.1 was soon to make musical history. 'You shall become foam on the crest of the wave,' warns the Mer-witch. But her prophecy is false: the 'Foam' motif, as quoted in EX. 21, contains the mirrored pair of 4ths of the 'Immortal Soul' motif, F–C and F–B♭.

With this carefully organized microstructure, Zemlinsky felt adequately equipped to build a cohesive work in three amply proportioned movements. During the process of composition he found the balance shifting from the programmatical to the abstract. The first movement, colourful and dramatic, follows Andersen almost literally. But in the scherzo the thematic material begins to assert its independence, and narrative flow is largely abandoned. With no recourse to fresh material whatsoever, the festivities in the palace of the Mer-king transform the sombre seascape music of the first movement into a dazzling *scène au bal** – a stunning demonstration of the possibilities of total themati-cism. The trio section presents a psychological study of the Mermaid: her love for the Prince, her vision of death and her rebirth. The third movement also provides a mere outline of the story. An ostensibly new theme for violins in 3rds (actually a varied inversion of the 'Seabed' motif) depicts the Mermaid's first, painful steps on land; with a Wagnerian downward plunge of the strings, she throws herself into the sea; with a reprise of the 'Immortal Soul' music of the second movement – reminiscent of the 'Miracle of Transfiguration' in *Ein Tanzpoem* – the work draws to a solemn conclusion.

The events of 1901 might have wounded Zemlinsky's pride and undermined his self-assurance, but from an artistic standpoint their effect was positive. His music had acquired new depth and conviction; the fine gradations of emotional intensity, which hitherto he had articulated more fully in smaller forms, notably in lieder, he now began to apply to larger-scale works. As in *The Triumph of Time*, something of his professional involvement with the entertainment indus-try still shines through, and the decorative element of *Jugendstil* still prevails. Confronted for the first time with his physical ugliness, Zemlinsky was con-cerned above all to be beautiful.

The Vereinigung

On 29 May 1903 Zemlinsky laid down his baton at the Carltheater, and in September he finally took up his promised post at the Theater an der Wien. Under the direction of Wilhelm Karczag and Karl Wallner the house had

---

motif with its mirror image in the bass dates back at least as far as the second movement of the A major Quartet (EX. 7).

* At the first climax of the festive music (2^{-1}), Zemlinsky writes a glissando for all four trom-bones *fff*, making him the first composer – or perhaps joint first with Schoenberg – to incor-porate this effect in an orchestral score.

become a shrine of classical ('golden') operetta. Yet Zemlinsky conducted not a note of Millöcker, Johann Strauss or Zeller there, and apart from Offenbach's *Contes d'Hoffmann* his repertoire was limited, as at the Carltheater, to ephemera. Neither orchestra nor chorus was appreciably better, but the ensemble was larger, and in the celebrated Alexander Girardi the theatre could boast a veritable star.

Schoenberg's contract at the Stern Conservatoire in Berlin ended in the spring of 1903. Zemlinsky advised him against returning to Vienna, warning him that musical life was in 'dire straits'.[23] While Jung-Wien had firmly established itself as leader of the literary avant-garde, and in the visual arts breakaway groups were flourishing, composers lacked any such free infrastructure and still relied on the city's established musical institutions. But Mahler had resigned his directorship of the Philharmonic, and Josef Hellmesberger, his successor, lacked flair and imagination; under Heuberger's presidency the Tonkünstlerverein remained a bastion of conservatism; the Conservatoire still viewed any form of modernism with horror; only Mahler at the Hofoper, seconded by his new stage designer, Alfred Roller, continued to blaze a trail for progress. Schoenberg's future in Berlin was less than certain, however, and in July he returned to Vienna. He and Mathilde rented an apartment in the IX. *Bezirk*, at Liechtensteinstrasse 68–70; during the summer, Zemlinsky moved out of the Obere Weissgerberstrasse and moved into an apartment on the same floor.

At the end of the 1902–3 season Zemlinsky resigned from the Tonkünstlerverein. Later that year the journalists Paul Stefan and Wilhelm von Wymetal founded a society in honour of the composer–pianist Conrad Ansorge.* With a distinguished roster of founder members, including Detlev von Liliencron, the Burgtheater actor Ferdinand Grigori, the singers Marie Gutheil-Schoder and Moriz Frauscher from the Hofoper, and the critic Franz Servaes from the *Neue Freie Presse*,[24] the *Ansorge-Verein* planned to promote concerts and poetry readings devoted to 'all great art, whether older or newer'.[25] While voicing doubts as to 'the power of Ansorge's music', on which the programmes were to concentrate, Zemlinsky accepted Stefan's invitation to become Musical Director.[26] Doubtless he hoped for opportunities similar to those offered in the past by the Tonkünstlerverein. In the event, he composed just one song for the new *Verein* (*Über eine Wiege*, in April 1904), and after appearing a few times as accompanist, his interest waned. Many of the meetings were entirely devoid

---

* Born in Silesia, Conrad Ansorge (1862–1930) studied with Liszt, toured the US and later taught in Weimar and Berlin. His compositions include orchestral and chamber music, a piano concerto and a requiem. Paul Stefan (actually Paul Grünfeldt, 1879–1943) was born in Brno but spent most of his childhood in Vienna. He published monographs on Schubert, Mahler, Schoenberg and Oskar Fried as well as several books on contemporary music; later he was editor of *Der Anbruch*. Wilhelm von Wymetal (1878–1929) was Chief Stage Director at the Hofoper under Weingartner. For many years he worked in the same capacity at the Metropolitan Opera, New York.

of music, and the aura of snobbishness surrounding the proceedings* can scarcely have been to his taste.

Since Hellmesberger and Löwe were neither capable of mastering intricate, modern scores nor particularly inclined to include them in their programmes, Zemlinsky's greatest concern was now to promote performances of *Die Seejungfrau* and *Pelleas und Melisande*, to which end he began to seek private patronage.[27] Once Schoenberg had returned to Vienna, the two co-ordinated their efforts and founded a musical society of their own, the Vereinigung schaffender Tonkünstler in Wien.† Mahler accepted the post of Honorary President, and the composer–conductor Oscar von Posa was appointed Secretary. An inaugural announcement was published on 23 April 1904, together with an appeal to composers to submit works for performance. The constitution bore Schoenberg's unmistakable stamp:

§2 The object of the society is a) the cultivation and promotion of contemporary works of musical art for the free expression of artistic individuality and b) the safeguarding of members' individual artistic standpoints and interests.

§3 [. . .] The object outlined in a) above will be achieved by the promotion of public performances of artistically significant works and of such compositions as have in Vienna not yet attained their due recognition. In this respect, the music of Austrian and German composers will be given priority.[28]

Contact with Mahler now became more frequent, and it was only a matter of time before Zemlinsky was allowed to see Alma again. Already bored with her role as 'Frau Direktor', she longed for more stimulating hours, such as those she had spent with Zemlinsky.‡ Even if she had forsworn composition, she could at least play duets with him. After their first session she sent him money; politely but firmly he returned it. But her connections with people in high places proved useful now, and she was happy to assist the Vereinigung in the search for sponsorship.[29]

At this time Schoenberg made the acquaintance of Eugenie Schwarzwald, wife of a high official and director of a girls' school in the Wallnerstrasse.[30] With characteristic generosity, she put a room at Schoenberg's disposal, free of

---

* 'The audience was required to wear evening dress, and the concerts were followed by dancing' (Paul Stefan, 'Aus Zemlinskys Wiener Zeit', *AT*, 227).
† NB the official name of the Vienna Secession was 'Vereinigung bildender Künstler Österreichs'.
‡ In *Mein Leben* (unabridged edn; Frankfurt am Main, 1963; p. 37), after mentioning the birth of her second child, Anna, on 15 June 1904, Alma bemoans her isolation: 'Mahler [. . .] will not permit anyone to visit me while he is out of the house. [. . .] If only Hans Pfitzner lived in Vienna! If only I could resume contact with Zemlinsky!' Since she actually resumed lessons with Zemlinsky some months *before* the birth of Anna, the passage can be construed as wilful distortion, perhaps intended to justify events that later occurred while Mahler was 'out of the house'.

charge, in which to hold evening classes. In the 8 October edition of the *Neue Musikalische Presse* he accordingly advertised a course, due to begin the following week, for 'professionals and serious-minded amateurs'. He himself would teach harmony and counterpoint; Zemlinsky was responsible for form and orchestration; Elsa Bienenfeld for music history. The advertisement concluded: 'The number of participants is very limited.'[31] He need not have feared. Guido Adler, lecturer in music history at Vienna University, urged his students to enrol, but only a handful of private pupils followed the call, notably Alban Berg, Karl Horwitz, Heinrich Jalowetz, Anton Webern and, a few months later, Egon Wellesz and Rudolf Weirich.

By the end of September, 127 composers had submitted a total of 885 works to the Vereinigung.[32] Ambitious plans were now forged. For the first season (1904–5) the executive committee scheduled three orchestral concerts at the Musikverein, three programmes of chamber music and lieder in the Börsendorfersaal and a supplementary concert devoted entirely to Mahler's orchestral songs.[33] On 23 November Zemlinsky conducted Hausegger's Dionysian Fantasy and three orchestral songs by Hermann Bischoff; after the interval followed the Viennese première of Richard Strauss's *Symphonia domestica*, conducted by Mahler.*

On 12 December, Schoenberg, Zemlinsky and pupils from the Schwarzwald course attended the final rehearsal of Mahler's Third Symphony at the Musikverein. Despite their sceptical attitude towards his music, they were swept aside: it was a conversion by fire. Henceforth their respect for Mahler knew no bounds. Schoenberg's letter of appreciation, written the following day, is well known:

I saw your soul naked, stripped bare. It lay before me like a wild, mysterious landscape with terrifying reefs and chasms; and at the next turning there were delightful, sunlit meadows, idyllic resting-places. [. . .] I saw the forces of good and evil locked in mortal combat, saw a man agonizedly striving for inner harmony, sensed a human being, a drama, the *truth*, the unrelenting truth.[34]

Zemlinsky, too overawed to approach Mahler directly, wrote instead to Alma. His letter, a model of urbanity and circumspection, makes a striking contrast:

From start to finish I had the impression of a music that plumbed nature's most intimate depths. I tell you frankly that only in the music of the very greatest have I heard a power and profundity comparable, for example, to the first part of the first movement or the two final movements; only in Beethoven and Brahms (disregarding the pre-Beethovenian composers) have I heard themes so precisely and expressively shaped and developed. And the second movement: the essence of charm

---

* Strauss, who was an honorary member of the Vereinigung, had originally undertaken to conduct his work himself. For these orchestral concerts, the Vereinigung hired the orchestra of the Konzertverein; for the concert of Mahler lieder they won the services of the Vienna Philharmonic.

distilled into sound, grace in final perfection. [. . .] What I long suspected is now an absolute certainty, and yesterday I told my friends: *this is one of the elect* (*Das ist Einer!*). I was so happy yesterday to have witnessed a major event in the history of music.[35]

The second orchestral concert of the Vereinigung, on 25 January 1905, featured the long-awaited premières of *Die Seejungfrau* and *Pelleas und Melisande.** Since Schoenberg's score called for a huge orchestra, and both works required copious rehearsal, the cost was exorbitant. The complexities of *Pelleas* had even Zemlinsky baffled,[†] and Schoenberg, though inexperienced, resolved to conduct the performance himself. As Egon Wellesz recalls, the decision proved ill-advised:

The rehearsal which I attended would have culminated in an ugly scene, had Mahler not been present. He was standing in the middle of the hall, still in his winter coat, a fur cap on his head, holding the score in his hand. Suddenly he called out: 'Where is the second English horn? I can't hear it.' Bemused silence, then a voice from the orchestra, 'He isn't there today.' No wonder Schoenberg hadn't noticed the player's absence: the original score, in my possession, is so complex and densely orchestrated that even in performance it was hard to distinguish the principal melodic lines; indeed even Mahler, when reading the score, had difficulty following the intricate part-writing.[36]

Experience with performances of his own symphonies had convinced Mahler of the danger of verbalization. At his insistence, both works were shorn of their programmes and presented as 'absolute music'. Max Vancsa, writing for the *Neue Musikalische Presse*, voiced his suspicion that 'scarcely fifty' members of the audience 'were really familiar with Maeterlinck's drama'.[37] And of the brutality underlying Andersen's folk tale even the critics appear to have been ignorant. Epithets such as 'charming', 'poetical', 'heart-warming' characterized their reviews – as if Zemlinsky's score were a forerunner of Edvard Erikson's winsome statue on the Copenhagen waterfront. Only Richard Specht, writing about the work five years later, perceived its latent tragedy:

One can sense that some event has occurred in the artist's life – whether positive or negative – whose consequences were disastrous.[38]

But Specht's imagination ran away with him, and he interpreted the 'disastrous' occurrence as rivalry between Zemlinsky and his brother-in-law. At the time of writing, his intuition was not far from the truth, but in 1905 the two were still staunch friends. Missing no opportunity to denigrate the man she once had

* The programme also included five orchestral songs by Oscar von Posa to texts by Liliencron.
† In a letter dated April 1903 (*Web-Br*, 40) Zemlinsky wrote, 'It is the finest work of art to have been written in our time. I believe, R. Str[auss] will not remain your friend for long!!! [. . . but] I believe that, due to the over-saturated polyphony, much, very much, cannot sound.'

worshipped, it was Alma who, during the concert in January 1905, first perceived the rift that was slowly opening:

Now I understood Zemlinsky's curious appearance: small, toothless and without the
slightest hint of a chin. [. . .] Mahler and I always used to say: 'Zemlinsky's music
has no chin!' Sequences . . . enharmonic alterations . . . mere chromaticism . . . it
makes no impression. What a shame! His talent outweighs his imagination.[39]

And later she concluded, rashly: 'At first Schoenberg's teacher, he later became
his pupil.'[40]

According to the critics, it was Zemlinsky who stole the show. His
diaphanous orchestration teased the ear; the rich harmonies and passionate
climaxes gave pleasure, and with his experience as a conductor of operetta, he
knew to articulate the finest nuance, to negotiate the subtlest of *rubatos*. During
Pelleas und Melisande, on the other hand, the audience became restless; some
left noisily, others stayed to whistle or yell their disapproval.

Despite its success, Zemlinsky took little further heed of *Die Seejungfrau*.
His promised contract with the Süddeutsche Musikverlag in Strasbourg never
materialized,* and only few further performances were given during his lifetime, notably by Walter Meyrowitz in Berlin (1907) and Bodanzky in Prague
(1908). Later he entrusted the manuscript of the first movement to his friend
Marie Pappenheim,† and today it is still treasured by her heirs. In the early
1980s, when Zemlinsky's music began to attract renewed public interest,
researchers compared this untitled fragment with a two-movement torso found
among the composer's posthumous papers, and established that the two
manuscripts together constituted a full score.‡ In 1984 Peter Gülke revived the
work at a concert with the Austrian Youth Orchestra. Since then, *Die Seejungfrau* has found its place in the concert repertoire as one of Zemlinsky's most
attractive and amenable scores.

For the Vereinigung, just as for the Polyhymnia, one ambitious project sufficed to break the bank. The third orchestral concert, scheduled for 11 March,
could not be underwritten, and a programme of lieder was presented in its place.
Since no further private sponsorship was forthcoming, the books were then closed.

* The only fruit of a planned collaboration with the Süddeutsche Musikverlag appears to have
been the publication, in 1903, of Erich J. Wolff's Sechs kleine Tänze op. 4 for piano duet.
† The dermatologist and writer Marie Pappenheim (1882–1966). She published several vol-
umes of poetry and wrote librettos for Schoenberg (*Erwartung*, 1909) and Zemlinsky (working title: *Der Graf von Gleim*, c. 1925). For many years she was a close friend of Zemlinsky
(rumours of an intimate relationship can be neither substantiated nor dismissed). Her aunt,
Bertha Pappenheim, was the 'Anna O.' whose case history was published by Freud and Breuer
in *Studies in Hysteria* (Vienna, 1895). Several other relatives and descendants were, or still are,
active in the field of psychoanalysis and psychotherapy.
‡ Credit for this discovery is divided between Peter Gülke, Ernst Hilmar and Alfred Clayton
(see Gülke, 'Zemlinskys *Seejungfrau*', *AeSU*, 57–66; Hilmar, 'Zemlinsky und Schönberg', *TiU*,
55–79 (with facsimile); *ACl*, 124–8).

2

Dreams and Delusions

The Volksoper (1)

Only a few hundred yards from Zemlinsky's apartment in the Liechtensteinstrasse stood the Kaiserjubiläums-Stadttheater, opened in December 1898 in celebration of Franz Josef's fiftieth jubilee. The house had a dry acoustic, suitable for speech but less satisfactory for music; it seated 1,400. In the statutes for the new theatre, Lueger's municipal government stipulated a repertoire of straight theatre, ranging from the German classics to modern comedy; the performance of works by Jews and the employment of Jewish artists or personnel were expressly forbidden. This policy was pursued, with steadily diminishing artistic and financial return, for four years. The company was then disbanded, and the building leased to Rainer Simons, an experienced theatre director from Cologne.* In the spirit of the Opéra-Comique in Paris and Carl Rosa's Light Opera Company in London, Simons founded a Volksopernverein (popular opera society), with which he proposed to provide high-quality, low-cost performances as an alternative to the Burgtheater and the Hofoper. The Volksoper, as a private enterprise, was immune to censorship or ministerial intervention.

Such an ambitious venture does not take wing overnight. It may be assumed that Zemlinsky entered into negotiation with Simons long before the doors of the Volksoper opened to the public; indeed he probably signed his contract even before starting work at the Theater an der Wien.† The 1903–4 season was devoted to building a repertoire of spoken drama, for which Simons engaged an ensemble of fifteen actors and twelve actresses. In September 1904 the opera ensemble moved in, with Zemlinsky as Musical Director, seconded by the conductors Josef Czerin, Ferdinand Hellmesberger and Oscar von Posa; there were

* Rainer Simons (1869–1934), was born in Cologne of Jewish parents (his father was theatre director in Düsseldorf, his mother an actress). He studied voice with Julius Stockhausen and conducting with Engelbert Humperdinck, making his début as a stage director in Düsseldorf at the age of eighteen. Later he worked in Königsberg as singer and producer, and in 1896 he was appointed Theatre Director in Mainz. After managing the Volksoper for fourteen years, he resigned in 1917 and became Professor of Stagecraft at the Vienna Musikakademie; later he was also active as Director of the Raimund Theater.
† From the Obere Weissgerberstrasse it was only a short walk to the Carltheater, only slightly further than from the Volksoper to the apartment in the Liechtensteinstrasse. From the IX. Bezirk, however, the Theater an der Wien could be reached only by cab or tram, which indicates that Zemlinsky saw his engagement there only as a stop-gap before moving to the Volksoper.

fifteen soloists on full-time contracts and a further five guests (including the soprano Emmy Destinn), four dancers, an orchestra of forty-seven and a chorus of forty-six. Within the first four months Simons presented eight operas: Weber's *Der Freischütz* (15 September), Flotow's *Martha* (30 September), Auber's *Fra Diavolo* (1 November), Lortzing's *Undine* (13 October) and *Zar und Zimmermann* (7 December), Donizetti's *La fille du régiment* (18 November), Rossini's *Il barbiere di Siviglia* (24 November) and Gounod's *Faust* (22 December). On 18 January 1905 (a week before the world première of *Die Seejungfrau*) followed the first novelty, Siegfried Wagner's *Der Kobold*; the season continued with Maillart's *Les dragons de Villars* (16 February), Bizet's *Carmen* (7 March), Auber's *La dame blanche* (23 March), Verdi's *La traviata* (10 April) and Conradin Kreutzer's *Das Nachtlager in Granada* (24 April).

As Rudolf Stefan Hoffmann recalled, the orchestra was new and inexperienced:

Der Freischütz. Zemlinsky gives the upbeat. Entry of the horns . . . they crack. A portent that becomes reality. That crack, sometimes scarcely audible, at others times embarrassingly prominent, was to remain an integral part of life at the Volksoper.[1]

In Zemlinsky's expert hands standards soon rose, and he felt confident to tackle more demanding works, such as *Figaro* (18 November 1905), *Die Zauberflöte* (3 October 1906) and *Tannhäuser* (22 November 1906). Donizetti, Rossini and Verdi were evidently not to his taste, for he delegated all the Italian repertoire to his colleagues, making an exception only for the Viennese première of *Tosca* in 1907. Operetta was also an essential part of the programme, but Zemlinsky himself conducted only *Die Fledermaus* and, on 22 December 1905, the world première of Heuberger's *Barfüssele*.

Der Traumgörge *(I)*

It was clear to Zemlinsky that his next stage work would be about Alma. Already during the summer of 1901 he had confided to her:

I'm looking for material for an opera in which you shall take the leading female role. I wouldn't include everything of you: the dazzling festivities, dinner parties, dances, admirers, etc. I have no talent for soubrette parts! But all the rest. And then myself: much of me. That could even turn out a tragedy, don't you think?[2]

Unable to share her enthusiasm for the picturesque folk-tale librettos of Bierbaum, he indicated that he was thinking along more serious lines, and that Goethe's *Werther*, Gottfried Keller's *Romeo und Julia auf dem Dorfe* ('A Village Romeo and Juliet') or Hermann Sudermann's *Der Katzensteg* would suit him better.[3]

Initially he considered none of these: during the autumn of 1902 he worked sporadically with Ernst Hutschenreiter on *Malva*, his Gorky project.* The novella tells of an ageing fisherman who leaves his wife for a younger woman; she in turn favours his twenty-two-year-old son; conflict arises, and the tale culminates in violence. Gorky's coarse-grained language, translated into opera, would have called for *verismo* treatment, much in the manner of Eugen d'Albert. How far Zemlinsky could have modified his style to meet these demands remains an unknown quantity, for neither libretto nor sketches have survived.†

Mahler had encouraged Zemlinsky to keep him informed of further operatic plans. Hence he knew at an early stage of the *Malva* project, and was presumably also acquainted with the novella. Only too conscious of the twenty years separating himself from Alma,‡ he might have sensed that the tale reflected the precariousness of his own situation, the more so since its title was all but an anagram of her name – a coincidence, but one that might well have caused irritation. Whatever the reason, he let it be known that he was 'completely opposed'[4] to the idea. Zemlinsky had little option but to notify Hutschenreiter, in April 1903, that the project had been shelved.§

A new plan soon materialized. Karczag and Wallner, the co-directors of the Theater an der Wien, ran a thriving publishing house that specialized in light music and operetta. Wallner approached Arthur Schnitzler, author of the controversial plays *Liebelei* ('Playing with Love') and *Freiwild* ('Free Game'), with a view to commissioning a triptych of one-act musical burlesques. As composers he set his sights on Heuberger, Raoul Máder¶ and Zemlinsky. On 25 June 1903 the three were summoned to Wallner's office, where Schnitzler read them several of his more recent shorter plays.[5] Zemlinsky expressed interest in a black comedy for marionettes, *Der tapfere Cassian*; Wallner held him to his word, and a contract was drawn up. But although he had ghosted several popular composers in his time, Zemlinsky was still reluctant to write anything for the entertainment industry under his own name. He remained on good terms

* From a card to Hutschenreiter, dated 23 August 1902 (*BikW*, 100), it transpires that the collaboration had already progressed as far as detailed discussion of metre and literary style.
† It was Zemlinsky's custom to sketch his first musical ideas directly into the libretto.
‡ In one of Mahler's first letters to Alma he compared their relationship to that of Eva and Hans Sachs in *Die Meistersinger* (cf. letter dated 5 December 1901 in *GoR*, 71–2).
§ On 17 March 1903 Zemlinsky wrote to Schoenberg, 'Tomorrow I shall be making a contract for a libretto, in April I want to start work' (*Web-Br*, 38), whereby it is unclear whether he was planning to finalize his agreement with Hutschenreiter or had meanwhile entered into negotiations with another librettist.
¶ Raoul Máder (1856–1940), at that time repetiteur at the Hofoper, was later active as *Kapellmeister* and *Intendant* at the Royal Opera in Budapest and, from 1921 to 1925, Director of the Volksoper. The final years of his life were spent in Budapest, where he resumed the directorship of the Opera. His one-act opera *Die Flüchtlinge* was performed at the Vienna Hofoper in 1890.

with Schnitzler for many years,[6] but of the music for *Der tapfere Cassian* he never wrote a note.*

Meanwhile the drama about Alma was taking shape in his mind, and he had found a poet, Leo Feld, in whom he felt he could place his trust. The advantage of Hutschenreiter, as Zemlinsky explained to Schoenberg, had been that he was 'no Jew, i.e. no Griensteidl type'.[7] Feld, in contrast, was a regular patron of Café Griensteidl and, from an artistic point of view, the very epitome of Jung-Wien. His first play, *Die Lumpen*, a satire on the Viennese literary scene, was staged with some success at the Carltheater in 1898, and awarded a literary prize. *Der grosse Name*, performed in 1909 with incidental music by Robert Stolz, won more widespread approval, but its success was due to the fact that Feld collaborated on it with his brother, Victor Léon. Author of such popular favourites as *Wiener Blut*, *Der Opernball* and *Die lustige Witwe* (1905, his *chef d'œuvre*), Léon possessed the surer sense of stagecraft and a keen instinct for the vagaries of public taste. Feld, as his schoolfriend Stefan Zweig recalled, was the intellectual of the family:

He possessed every quality needed for success, and only one aspect of his indefatigable energy was perhaps misplaced: the lofty idealism of his striving. He always set his literary goals too high; whatever the price, it was his ambition to cross the invisible line of the Burgtheater; an inner sense of responsibility caused him to forswear cheap effects. [. . .] A serious, self-effacing man, his attitude towards art was far purer, far nobler [. . .] than that of many a celebrated household name.[8]

Cast

Görge, a village lad (ten); Grete, his cousin (sop); the miller, her father (bass); Hans, her lover (bar); the parson (bass); the Princess (sop); Gertraud, daughter of a banished baron (sop); two dissident villagers: Züngel,† a tailor (ten) and Mathes (bar), a charcoal-burner; Kaspar, a foreman (bar); the innkeeper (ten); his wife (mezzo); Marei, a bartender (sop); a dream-voice (mezzo); a peasant (act I, bass); a peasant (act II, bar); an older peasant (act II, ten). Villagers, dream-voices, peasants, children. Time: 1820s

Synopsis

I *A village in North Germany* Görge regales Grete with a sinister tale of Black Murr, prince of cats. His imagination takes fire: 'Fairy tales must come alive,' he cries. Seeking to calm his nervous agitation, Grete reminds him that they are soon to be betrothed; he answers absently. The miller divulges to the parson that he has

---

* In 1908 Schnitzler offered the work to Max Reinhardt, suggesting that Bogumil Zepler be engaged in place of Zemlinsky (Werner Welzig (ed.), *Arthur Schnitzler: Tagebüch. 1903–1909* (Vienna, 1991), entry for 15 June 1908). In the event, the work was first performed at Leipzig the following year, in an expanded singspiel version, with music by Oscar Straus.
† In the vocal score: Züngl.

arranged the marriage in order to retain control of the mill, which is Görge's birthright. Grete, alone, reveals her vacillating sympathy for the bookish Görge. To the villagers' delight, Hans returns from military service. Disgruntled by the news of Grete's engagement, he coaxes Görge into publicly recounting his dream: the strange narrative is met with derision and disbelief. Laughing heartily, Hans takes his leave. Görge fixes his gaze on the millstream and falls into a trance: his mother appears to him and reads from a story book. 'Fairy tales must come alive,' he cries again. Suddenly the Dream-Princess stands before him, radiant in white and girdled with roses. She urges him to follow her into a miracle world of beauty and fantasy. The vision fades, the clock strikes noon and, to Görge's consternation, Grete, the parson and other guests emerge from the mill. With the Princess's words ringing in his ears, he rushes off.

II *Another village, three years later, Whitsuntide* Kaspar rails against the tyranny of the landowners. To organize a peasants' revolution, a spokesman is needed: he proposes Görge. Marei reveals her attraction to Görge, but the men warn of his liaison with Gertraud, who is suspected of arson and witchcraft. In exchange for sex, the innkeeper has offered Gertraud work in the kitchen: his wife hounds her off the premises. Görge consoles her as best he can, but is himself now a derelict. Kaspar and his henchmen invite him to canvass for their cause. In the role of popular leader he sees the possible realization of his dream. But Gertraud is shunned by the peasants, and when Görge discovers the baseness of their motives, he rejects them. Finding Gertraud on the point of suicide, he realizes that he loves her. Marei discovers them in a fond embrace and swears revenge. To the glow of Whitsun bonfires Görge pledges himself to Gertraud. Kaspar and Marei lead the villagers in a witch-hunt, and Gertraud's house is set ablaze. Görge, in sudden fury, silences the mob and leads his bride to safety.

Epilogue *Görge's village, one year later* Görge has claimed his inheritance, enlarged the mill and built a school; Gertraud has succoured the sick and needy. Hans and Grete, now also married (if less happily), lead the villagers in voicing their gratitude. Görge and Gertraud contemplate the beauty of the evening sky. In the gathering shadow, with flowers woven into her hair, Gertraud becomes almost indistinguishable from the image of the Dream-Princess.

Feld must have been aware that his libretto would need, above all, to reflect Zemlinsky's personal experiences. Life in Görge's village, as he depicts it, bears a striking resemblance to that of the Leopoldstadt, and the magic millstream seems to flow with the muddy-brown water of the Danube Canal.

He and Zemlinsky began work in the spring or early summer of 1903. Instead of concentrating on a single theme or literary source, they sought to integrate a wide range of ideas and influences. By throwing together stock characters and archetypal situations a plot would eventually emerge of its own accord. Zemlinsky's original concept, as he told Schoenberg, had been for a free adaptation of *Der arme Peter*, a cycle of three short poems by Heine:

Briefly: *der arme Peter* is the man, an idealized young visionary or dreamer (I
haven't yet decided on a milieu), full of longing for love, who lives unloved and dies
young. [. . .] Quite unlike his fellow men, misunderstood, he lives for his dreams.
[. . .] The whole thing could play in a village or small town on the Rhine. I'm not
quite sure: country-folk or petit-bourgeois? In the latter case, *der arme Peter* could
be an artist or skilled craftsman, a goldsmith or the like.[9]

Feld countered by suggesting a folk tale by Richard Volkmann, *Vom unsicht-
baren Königreiche (The Invisible Kingdom),* which tells of an orphaned boy
who finds in dreams relief from the drudgery and injustice of the real world.
Feld also presumably takes credit for introducing the subplot of the miller,
Görge's inheritance and the arranged marriage, a situation familiar from *The
Bartered Bride*. As act I evolved, the libretto became an ingenious amalgam of
these various sources, with Hans and Grete taken from Heine, the dreamer and
the Princess from Volkmann, so modified as to merge into a continuous story-
line. Where Heine depicts the relationship between Peter and Grete as a tragedy
of unrequited love, Feld underlines the couple's incompatibility; by intimating
a kinship between Peter and Vašek (Smetana's stuttering simpleton), he made
Volkmann's dreamer an object of ridicule; and in order to transform the folk
tale into an allegory of artistic striving, the title figure was upgraded from simple peasant boy to frustrated intellectual, transforming him into a tragic figure
not unlike Thomas Hardy's Jude. Feld and Zemlinsky were at first divided over
their hero's name. Following Volkmann, who called him Jörg or Traumjörg
('Jörg the dreamer'), Feld proposed 'Görge'. Zemlinsky agreed, but in his typescript copy of act I he replaced the name, wherever it occurred, with 'Peter'. In
the end, Feld won his way. Adding the definite article, the authors agreed on a
title that, flaunting theatrical superstition, consisted of thirteen letters:[†] *Der
Traumgörge*.

The libretto of act I must have been finished by the end of 1903 or soon after,
for during the spring of 1904 Zemlinsky was already able to 'croak'[10] and play
two complete scenes to Alma. By October the music of act I was finished, and
for a few days, before starting work on the orchestration, he entrusted her with

* Richard (von) Volkmann(-Leander) (1830–1889) was professor of surgery at the University
of Halle. During the Franco-Prussian War he served as consulting medical officer to the
German army in Soisy, near Paris. Here, in 1871, he wrote a collection of short stories entitled
Träumereien an französischen Kaminen ('Reveries at French Firesides'), published later the
same year in Leipzig; it includes *The Invisible Kingdom*. The book was acclaimed for its 'sub-
lime sentimentality' and its balance between irony and artistic ingenuousness.
† Schoenberg changed the orthography of 'Aaron' to avoid a thirteen-letter title (*Moses und
Aron*), and Sigmund Freud probably omitted the 'e' in his first name for the same reason. Most
early commentators on *Der Traumgörge* avoided the ominous thirteen: Wymetal wrote 'Der
Traumjörg' (*Neue Badische Landeszeitung*, 6 October 1909) and Schoenberg 'Der Traumgörg'
(*Web-Br*, 85), while Rudolf Stephan Hoffmann studiously omitted the definite article
('Zemlinskys Opern', *AT*, 211–15).

his short score.[11] The summer of 1904 was spent at Altmünster on the Traunsee, in the company of Bodanzky, Feld and his sister, Eugenie Hirschfeld.[12] Zemlinsky played them the *Gurrelieder*, and Feld, who was evidently so engrossed in his work that his every thought emerged in rhyming couplets, enthused to Schoenberg:

Die Gurrelieder waren herrlich – der Alex, der ist oft gefährlich.

The Gurrelieder were delightful – and Alex, he can be so spiteful.[13]

Due to his commitments at the Volksoper, Zemlinsky was unable to resume work until the following March. His 1905 vacation was divided between Sekirn, only a few miles from Mahler's summer house at Maiernigg, and Gmunden on the Traunsee. At Sekirn, on 6 July, he completed the first draft of act II; two days later he set to work on the epilogue (at this stage still act III). For three days he was a house guest of the Mahlers,* and in early August he joined Feld and Bodanzky in Gmunden, where they finished work on the libretto.

Once again the theatre season proved too hectic for concentrated composition. During the summer of 1906, spent at Rottach on the Tegernsee, Zemlinsky revised and orchestrated the short score of act II. Since the weather was poor and the Bavarian cuisine insipid, Zemlinsky spent whole days at his writing desk, breaking the monotony only for a brief visit to Maiernigg. In August he developed a feverish infection and had to return to Vienna, where his doctor lanced a large abscess in his throat. Convalescing, he wrote to Schoenberg, 'Gradually I am resuming work – naturally with an andante – nothing fast!'[14] And writing to Alma the same day, he added:

Before the theatre season begins in earnest, I hope to finish the opera.† It gives me pleasure – great pleasure. I still believe that it will amount to something. And as soon as I have something legible, you shall see it immediately.[15]

On 26 October he signed the final double-bar of the orchestral score.

When Görge ran off through the cornfields at the end of act I, neither Feld nor Zemlinsky had the slightest idea where he would go or what he would do next. The music of act I was composed, as Rudolf Stephan Hoffmann recalls, 'before the rest [of the text] had even been written.'[16] In the summer of 1904 a sequel had to be devised. 'Much time had elapsed,' Hoffmann continues, 'and neither poet nor musician was able to pick up the thread of his former style.'[17] In Volkmann, Jörg is reunited with his princess in the realm of dreams; her father,

---

* It was probably at this time that Mahler invited Zemlinsky to prepare the four-handed piano arrangement of his Sixth Symphony.
† In the sketchbook, the end of the epilogue is undated.

the dream-king, transforms her into a mortal; Jörg returns home, marries her, and in his humble dwelling – his 'invisible kingdom' – they live happily ever after. Feld clearly felt disinclined to follow such a predictable path, and decided instead to model much of act II, at Zemlinsky's instigation, on Sudermann's *Der Katzensteg*.

The novel, published in 1899, is set in East Prussia during the Napoleonic Wars,* with most of the action centred on the fictitious town of Schranden. Through no fault of their own, Boleslav, a young soldier of good family, and Regine, his father's former mistress, have become pariahs of the community. Living in isolation as master and servant in the burned-out ruins of Schranden castle, united only in hatred of their adversaries, a strange, animal passion kindles between them. Eventually the townspeople, intent on taking Boleslav's life, storm the castle. Regine is shot dead by her own father; Boleslav returns to active service and falls in battle.

With sharp-witted eclecticism, Feld plundered the book for everything he could use. He revelled in the rough-grained beauty of the language, in Sudermann's vivid depiction of individuals hounded by the mob, and in the unpredictable but earthy character of Regine, who provided him with an ideal contrast to the ethereal figure of the Dream-Princess.

Zemlinsky knew *Der Katzensteg* to be close to Alma's heart. She had read it in May 1899, during a period of crisis provoked by her parents, when they peremptorily terminated her clandestine affair with Gustav Klimt.

There's a strange, wild passion in it [she wrote in her diary]. I like it more than I can say. If anybody wants to know me, let them read *Der Katzensteg*. How I'd love to be as full-blooded as Regine. She's utterly and entirely human![18]

During the following weeks she read three further books by Sudermann,[19] and there can be little doubt that she later shared her enthusiasm for his work with Zemlinsky.†

In the opera Alma is hence depicted in two guises. As Dream-Princess – noble, beautiful, inspiring – she displays those attributes Zemlinsky perceived as the highest ideals of womanhood; as Gertraud she possesses those qualities – compassion, humility, sincerity – Alma herself knew she lacked.

Act II draws on numerous images and symbols. Marei, the jealous rival, and Züngel, the raucous ballad-singer, are stock figures of the Romantic stage; the political element introduced by bringing the intellectual Görge into contact with Kaspar and his band of plundering thugs can be traced back, indirectly, to Schiller's *Die Räuber*; Görge's mystic union with Gertraud – the 'Whitsun fire'

* Sudermann sets the story in 1809, shortly before Napoleon's flight from Elba; the first-edition libretto of *Der Traumgörge* cites time and place as '1815, a village in the Pfalz'.
† Zemlinsky had insisted that for a libretto based on *Der Katzensteg*, only Sudermann himself would be an adequate partner (*AZ–AMW*, 31).

episode – reflects Zemlinsky's personal memories of *Parsifal* at Bayreuth, linked as they must have been with the ensuing trauma of Bad Ischl and the cancelled rendezvous. In both acts Feld makes sporadic forays into Freudian analysis,* portraying Görge as a neurotic, his daydream a symptom of mother fixation, his literary ambition a delusion of grandeur, his love for Gertraud an Oedipal or even incestuous relationship.† There are also allusions to plant symbolism: Görge's house lies in the shade of a linden tree, symbol of endurance,‡ Grete decks the front door with pine twigs, symbol of undying love, and Gertraud's house is overgrown with vines, emblem of Bacchic carnality; roses are woven into the Princess's crown, and roses grow in Gertraud's garden, symbols of true love – and perhaps also a memory of those red roses with which Zemlinsky had adorned Alma's picture on his writing desk.

Rudolf Stephan Hoffmann, who witnessed the creative hiatus between acts I and II at first hand, expressed his concern at the resulting loss of homogeneity. Yet experience of the work in the theatre proves his fears largely unwarranted. The two acts constitute a diptych, a clearly defined duality of light and darkness. Görge's village is paved with petit-bourgeois good intentions: the corn ripens, the millwheel turns, the sun shines. The village of act II is a place of sin, its inhabitants motivated by envy, lust, hate and avarice. Feld further articulates this duality in cosmological terms: in act I the principal elements are earth (the village and its inhabitants), water (the millstream as source of Görge's vision) and air (the Princess); act II, in contrast, is permeated by fire: even the spirit of Christianity shines only as tongues of flame in distant Whitsun bonfires.

While the structure of act I is clearly defined, that of act II is nebulous. This is partly due to the haphazard revisions it underwent, with scenes rewritten, interpolated and removed, but partly also to Feld's obtuse manner of relating cause to effect. His decision to write the entire text in verse is a further source

---

* One of Freud's lectures includes a passage that amounts to a résumé of *Der Traumgörge*: 'An artist [. . .] desires to win honour, power, wealth, fame and the love of women; but he lacks the means of achieving these satisfactions. Consequently, like any other unsatisfied man, he turns away from reality and transfers all his interest, and his libido too, to the wishful constructions of his life of fantasy, whence the path might lead to neurosis' ('The Paths to the Formation of Symptoms', Lecture 23, *Introductory Lectures on Psycho-Analysis* (London, 1963)).

† Cf. Görge's declaration of love to Gertraud in act II: 'So nenn' ich dich Mutter, Schwester, Weib!' ('So I call you mother, sister, wife!'). The first to realize the theatrical potential of psychoanalysis, and convincingly to combine Freudian theory with folk-tale opera, was Franz Schreker. His first-draft libretto of *Der ferne Klang* was written at exactly the same time as Feld's act I.

For a simple but effective translation of Freudian dream interpretation into practical stagecraft, Feld might have done worse than follow the example of his brother, whose operetta *Der Herr Professor* (music by Béla von Ujj) was premièred at the Carltheater on 4 December 1903, with Zemlinsky conducting: the entire second act plays in a dream.

‡ In the spirit of *Der Winterreise*, Clayton interprets the linden tree – misleadingly – as a symbol of 'romantic longing' (*ACl*, 146).

of vexation, with linguistic clarity often sacrificed for the sake of rhyme. A note pencilled into Zemlinsky's printed copy of the vocal score[20] exposes a further weakness of the act: Kaspar is a strong-minded, persuasive and articulate fellow; why then should he need a spokesman? And if Görge is as broken as he purports to be – 'a cur, a sloth, a gut, a drunkard [. . .], a gob of saliva, just a mouth to feed'[21] – it is unclear why Kaspar should trust him to win the ear of the masses. Despite the realism implied by Feld's stage directions, the act – as it stands – can satisfactorily be interpreted only as a nightmare vision, illogical and brutish, and, as such, a negation of the miracle world represented by the Dream-Princess.

The epilogue is generally interpreted as an idyll of escapism, in which Görge finally recognizes in Gertraud his Princess and, with her at his side, finds a way of living out his dreams far from the turmoil of the outside world.* But this is oversimplification. In accepting Feld's idea of basing the action on Volkmann's *The Invisible Kingdom*, Zemlinsky agreed *de facto* that the opera would not end with the hero's death; the outcome of *Der Traumgörge* is tragic none the less. Görge's tragedy is not that he dies, but that he lives on. Meekly he capitulates to fate, well aware that the price must be eternal frustration. As much is implied, if obtusely, in a line from Goethe's *Faust II* with which Feld prefaced the printed libretto:[†]

Dem Tüchtigen ist diese Welt nicht stumm!

An able man will reap the world's acclaim!

Only a reader well acquainted with *Faust*, or one who takes the trouble to read the scene from which Feld quotes, can divine his meaning. The passage runs as follows:

An able man will reap the world's acclaim! / What need has he through Eternity to roam, / when all he apprehends, he finds at home? / So let him wander through his earthly day; / when spirits haunt him, go his quiet way; / in marching onwards, pain and fortune find, / though every moment unfulfilled in mind.

It was symptomatic of Feld's intellectualism that he chose to omit the operative word – 'unfulfilled' (*unbefriedigt*). In the final bars of the epilogue, a solo violin, accompanied only by celesta and harp, ascends to a stratospheric high A, as if Görge and his world had floated into the heavens. But as the curtain falls, a *ppppp* octave of cellos and basses seemingly echoes that terrible, unspoken word: *unfulfilled*.

* Whereas Gertraud, in the original version of the epilogue, was already the mother of Görge's child, in the final version all reference to her child was omitted. The necessary changes (on page 193 of the vocal score) were evidently made at the last minute.
† From *Faust II*, act v ('Midnight'), line 11,446. The quotation is not included in the vocal score.

EX. 24   vocal score, page 212*

The opera opens with the ur-form of this closing phrase, a solo for muted horn, which winds itself dreamily around a static column of string octaves:

EX. 25

* Page references correspond to the Ricordi vocal score, published in 1990.

These soft, high octaves open the listener's ear to far-off times and distant places. The first of countless cross-references, self-borrowings and snatches of imaginary or actual folk melody, they seem to emanate from the same world invoked by Mahler at the opening of his First Symphony, perhaps even that of Beethoven in his Fourth. Rudolf Stephan Hoffmann was critical of this eclectic element in Zemlinsky's score:

[. . .] Everything technical, particularly the richness of motivic polyphony, represents a step forward, there is a greater freedom of rhythm and harmony. Yet the very first notes of the second act reveal a distinctly different style. The long interruption, as well as fresh impressions of Strauss, Dukas, [. . .] Pfitzner, Mahler and, above all, Schoenberg, resulted in a change of style comparable to that between parts I and III of the *Gurrelieder*.[22]

His comments and criticisms invite closer examination.

Motivic polyphony. Zemlinsky's counterpoint had never been strictly linear in the sense, say, of Beethoven's later fugues. Like most nineteenth-century contrapuntists, his voice-leading follows a predetermined harmonic outline. In *Der Traumgörge*, however, the procedure is often reversed: by combining motifs and melodic lines independently or asynchronously, new chords and idiosyncratic harmonic progressions arise empirically. In act I, for example, Görge sings to a simple, homophonic accompaniment:

EX. 26A   vocal score, pages 13–14

Fairy tales must come to life

In act II the idea is expanded into a polyphonic labyrinth (EX. 26B).

Commentary Most of the argument revolves around the figure E♭–A♭–G in the bass line, one of a family of motifs related to the C–B♭–E♭ of the vocal line, itself an inversion of the principal 'Görge' motif (EX. 25). The counter-subject in cor anglais and bass clarinet (bar 8) quotes a theme from the dream vision of act I (vocal score, page 70), while the triplet figure in the last bar is derived from the 'Mill' theme (EX. 31A). For the sake of clarity, semiquaver figuration for violins and violas, adapted from the 'Millstream' music of act I, is here omitted.

EX. 26B   vocal score, page 119

Once I was kind and gentle, yearned and craved for a realm of light! Fairy-tale dreams,
bright as the sun, filled my waking hours;

This asynchronous polyphony also helps Zemlinsky to discover a new relationship between line and texture. Translated into sound, his counterpoint becomes a spirited game that follows the line of a perpetual *Klangfarbenmelodie*. Individual terraces of sound advance and recede, often with breathtaking rapidity; melodies pass deftly from one instrument to another and dissolve into ever new lines and colours. Irrespective of its dramatic affect, the score offers both performer and listener a high degree of *Spielfreude* – the sheer physical pleasure of sound.

Zemlinsky's motifs, though simple in themselves, often have a complex genealogy. One of the most striking examples is the motif of 'Joy', first heard in bars 19–22 of act I, which can be traced as far back as *Lerchengesang*, composed in 1890 (cf. EX. 13):

EX. 27A

In the interim Zemlinsky had devised a 'disfigured' variant of the motif, which played a prominent role in act III of *The Triumph of Time*:

EX. 27B

As Görge's joy turns to disillusionment, in act II of the opera, this variant is introduced and further developed (EX. 27C). In countless new variants the same motif figures prominently in *Der König Kandaules* (cf. EX. 91), composed thirty years later.

Freedom of rhythm. As in his previous works, Zemlinsky knows to avoid the tyranny of the down beat and the four-bar period, often achieving rhythmic flexibility with the aid of such well-tried Brahmsian techniques as displacement of the bar-line or asymmetrical subdivision of the bar. A further novelty of the *Traumgörge* score (which Zemlinsky was to investigate more thoroughly in the Second Quartet) is the use of polyrhythm.* Thematic ornamentation is

---

* Cf. *In blühenden Rosen*, vocal score, page 70, where Zemlinsky experiments with 5:3 and 5:6 rhythms.

Nun lie-gen wir da am Weg...... ver-fehmt,...... zer-lumpt...... und ver-lo - ren

EX. 27C   *Der Traumgörge*, vocal score, page 163

Now we lie here at the road-side, outlawed, ragged and lost.

generated, as in *Die Seejungfrau*, by rhythmic diminution, as for example in Görge's vision narrative,* where semiquaver derivates of EXX. 27 and 28A adorn the texture with flurries of arabesques. Rhythmic diminution also serves as a tool for variative development. A hemiola figure associated with the menacing figure of Black Murr (EX. 28A), for instance, later becomes a jagged rhythm associated with Gertraud's anger (EX. 28B):

EX. 28A   act I, vocal score, p. 6

EX. 28B   act II, vocal score, p. 108

Freedom of harmony. Erich W. Korngold, who studied with Zemlinsky from 1908 to 1911, recalls his teacher's 'modernist' approach to harmony:

[It was] strictly logical, while permitting freedom and audacity in the configuration of chords, in the discovery of distant pitch relationships, in his own, distinctive

* Vocal score, pages 50–51.

technique of 'delayed resolution'. One natural and rationally moulded line – this was his basic principle – suffices to allow others their freedom of movement. He was particularly strict with regard to the logical flow of the *bass line*. [. . .] A chord would 'draw' him through one pitch, as he liked to express it, to another, predetermined one.[23]

As Korngold implies, harmony and counterpoint, traditionally taught separately, were in Zemlinsky's eyes a single, all-embracing discipline. In EX. 26B asynchronous lines of polyphony, richly spiced with auxiliary and passing-notes, meet in a harmony that hovers perpetually on the fringe of unfamiliarity, and move with a harmonic rhythm so rapid that even familiar chords often pass unrecognized. Neither melody nor bass line determine the direction of the harmonic flow; no ground plan controls the tonal structure. Yet nothing is left to chance: melody, harmony, dynamic, tempo, texture, timbre and register all follow a minutely charted seismic curve, which rises or falls in unison with the drama, line for line and scene for scene. It is a highly sophisticated art.

The passage where Görge finds Gertraud on the point of committing suicide beautifully illustrates Zemlinsky's technique of 'delayed resolution' (EX. 29).

Impressions of Strauss, Dukas, Pfitzner, Mahler and Schoenberg. Writing fifteen years after the event, Hoffmann seems to have confused his chronology. If there is any influence of Strauss in Zemlinsky's score, then chiefly of *Salome*; if any of Dukas, then of *Ariane et Barbe-bleue*. But *Salome* was not performed until December 1905, by which time the short score of *Der Traumgörge* was already finished,* and Zemlinsky is unlikely to have heard or seen the score of *Ariane* – a work he profoundly admired – until after its world première in Paris on 10 May 1907. He was well acquainted with Pfitzner and his music, indeed at Alma's behest he performed the Piano Trio op. 8 at a concert of the Verein-igung in December 1904, but his music betrays no influence of that work, nor is there any evidence that *Die Rose vom Liebesgarten*, which Mahler conducted at the Hofoper in March 1905, exerted any particular influence on his act 1, as Hoffmann implies. Zemlinsky's score begins with a delicate homage to Mahler,[†] but at no other point does the influence of his music become palpable, indeed Mahler's alterations to the Vienna manuscript[‡] of *Der Traumgörge* indicate that his ideas were often diametrically opposed. The influence of Schoenberg, on the other hand, can be sensed throughout. Richly decorative polyphonic textures, such as those of the vision scenes in act 1 and the closing pages of the epilogue,

---

* Zemlinsky's triadic *crescendo–sforzato* interjections for muted trumpets (vocal score, page 141) directly anticipate a brass figure in the opening scene of *Elektra* (at 1^2 et seq.).

† Only in bar 19 of the introduction, when a high flageolet is added in violin 1, does the provenance of the string octaves become apparent; at the same time Zemlinsky obscures them behind a trill for flutes and piccolos.

‡ The manuscript score preserved at the Austrian State Library includes cuts and retouchings in Mahler's hand.

EX. 29   act II, vocal score, page 145

GÖRGE: So sweet, so still?
GERTRAUD: I'm going.
GÖRGE: You're going? (*Fiercely*) Because they. . .?
GERTRAUD: Don't I have to?
GÖRGE: Have to? Who will compel you?
GERTRAUD: (*Smiling sadly*) Compel me?

Commentary   Zemlinsky uses the technique of 'delayed resolution' primarily to establish and maintain harmonic tension between the bass line and the upper voices. The overall tonality hovers between Eb minor, C#/Db minor and D minor, but the bass line moves asynchronously, not even coinciding with the upper voices on the final shift to D minor.

draw their strength from the *Gurrelieder*; much of the new harmony in act II owes its boldness to *Pelleas und Melisande* and the Quartet op. 7, on which Schoenberg was working, parallel to Zemlinsky, between the summer of 1904 and the autumn of 1905. The whole-tone triads in contrary motion – a recurrent phenomenon of act II – seem to have been directly inspired by *Pelleas*:[24]

EX. 30A   *Schoenberg, Pelleas und Melisande, 32⁻²*

EX. 30B   *Der Traumgörge*, opening of act II

And the motif associated with Görge's village and its inhabitants –

EX. 31A–B   *Der Traumgörge*, vocal score, pages 19/30

– is distantly related to the theme of Melisande:*

EX. 31C   Schoenberg, *Pelleas und Melisande*

* The 'Melisande' motif is here reproduced in the form cited by Berg in his published analysis of *Pelleas* prepared for Universal Edition. The close relationship between the two motifs becomes clearer when Zemlinsky introduces further variants in *Der König Kandaules* (see EX. 91).

Despite these affinities, Alma Mahler's assertion that Zemlinsky had 'become Schoenberg's pupil' can be taken with a grain of salt. While Schoenberg, with his relentless forward drive, was drawing all those around him into his wake, Zemlinsky subjected his every new discovery to quizzical scrutiny – and his verdict was not always favourable. In August 1906, when Schoenberg completed his Chamber Symphony op. 9, he showed the manuscript to his pupils, who were enthralled. Webern recalls:

Already the following day, under the influence of this work, I wrote a sonata movement. [. . .] It was related to a key, but in a very strange way. Then I had to write a set of variations, but the theme which I devised was actually in no key at all. Schoenberg turned to Zemlinsky for advice, and he settled the matter – in a negative sense.[25]

Whatever their differences on musical questions, their personal bond remained firm. In no other work of Zemlinsky's can the moral and practical support of Schoenberg be more clearly felt than in *Der Traumgörge*. Schoenberg used his skill as a bookbinder to provide sketchbooks,* and of the several hands involved in copying out the conducting score, his is evident on many pages. The figure of Gertraud was probably named after Schoenberg's daughter, Gertrude; and when Mathilde gave birth to a second child, on 22 September 1906, it seemed only logical that the boy should take his name from the opera: baptized as Georg, Schoenberg's eldest son was invariably known as Görgi or Görgl.

While working on *Der Traumgörge*, Zemlinsky's own family status changed. Abandoning his role as 'little bird of melancholy', he put away his mourning clothes and, prompted by pragmatism rather than passion, got married. The first to whom he broke the news of his engagement, in the spring of 1905, was Alma:

It would make me happy to hear that you felt well disposed towards my decision – believe me, it means much to me. But I would ask you at least to remain, just as before – – – my close friend![26]

Nothing is known of the circumstances surrounding the engagement, and little is known of the bride. But the young lady with whom Zemlinsky proudly posed on the steps of the Volksoper (plate 6) can almost certainly be identified as his fiancée, Ida,† younger sister of Melanie Guttmann. And the picture itself can be dated with even greater certainty to 17 November 1905.‡ After an engagement that lasted over two years, Zemlinsky married her on 21 June 1907.

---

* Schoenberg constructed sketchbooks for act II and the epilogue, using sheets of score paper cut into oblong strips and bound in orange-red and blue covers; the sketchbook for act I has not survived.
† Ida, daughter of Jenny (*née* Fischer) and August Guttmann, was born in Brno on 26 June 1880.
‡ The playbills behind the couple's back advertise *Car[men]* (left), *Der Troubador* (*Il*

The score of *Der Traumgörge* bears no dedication, but its sobering message, that even a genius must learn to accept the shortcomings and humiliations of reality, exactly reflects this turning-point in his life.

At the Hofoper

Zemlinsky's activities at the Volksoper were largely dictated by the necessities of private enterprise. 'Here I am more slave than artist,' he complained to Alma.[27] In the spring of 1906, in search of artistic and material improvement, he entered into negotiations with the Hofoper in Dresden. But when Mahler asked him to supervise rehearsals of *Der Traumgörge* and offered him a full-time engagement at the Vienna Hofoper, he leapt at the chance. As a bonus, his new contract, originally intended to begin in August 1907, was pre-dated to 1 May. Two days later he made his début with a new production of Verdi's *Otello*. The choice was scarcely calculated to show the new *Kapellmeister* at his best, for he had never conducted a note of Verdi in his life. And with the large apparatus of the Hofoper he appears to have established no immediate rapport. A letter to Alma, written later the same month, mentions subsequent performances of *Carmen* and *Die Zauberflöte* and adds, almost apologetically, 'I'm gradually "getting to grips" with the ensemble. Given the opportunity, I hope things will soon go really well.'[28]

Long before the score of *Der Traumgörge* was even finished, Karczag and Wallner had undertaken to publish it, in conjunction with the New York branch of Breitkopf und Härtel. In September 1906 Feld's text was passed by the censor. The publishers' contract could now be ratified, and a firm order was placed for production books, chorus parts and vocal scores, the latter skilfully prepared by Bodanzky.[29] At the eleventh hour Mahler read the work through, evidently for the first time, and demanded sweeping changes; Feld and Zemlinsky had no option but to return to the drawing board. While act I was left largely unaltered, act II acquired a stronger political slant, with more attention devoted to Kaspar and less to Marei, Züngel and the villagers;* extensive cuts were

---

trovatore), Pierre Berton's *Die schöne Marseillerin* (top right) and Grillparzer's *Sappho* (bottom right). Only once were these four works performed in immediate succession at the Volksoper, namely on 16–18 November 1905.

* In the original version, Kaspar and his henchmen plot to overthrow the village prefect for levying extortionate taxes. This clarifies their motivation for choosing Görge as their spokesman, for he is the only literate person in the community. In emulation of Sudermann, Gertraud is originally shunned because her father had acted as a spy for Napoleon's troops. A complete scene ('scene 7', beginning on page 125 of the original vocal score) is devoted to Marei, who pleads with Görge to abandon Gertraud. Züngel is also presented as a more three-dimensional character. The vocal score acknowledges Johannes Wattke, a dramaturg in Chemnitz, for 'revising and editing' the text. Zemlinsky must have known Wattke from the Carltheater, for the playbills of Carl Weinberger's *Die Diva* credit him as co-author of the libretto. The nature and extent of his contribution to *Der Traumgörge* are unclear.

made to the first half of act III and its title changed to 'epilogue'. Karczag had no choice but to publish a new libretto and order the re-engraving of forty pages of vocal score. The added outlay will scarcely have passed without a grumble, but for a work confidently expected to be received by press and public as a masterpiece, no expense was spared.

With the première scheduled for 4 October, rehearsals began in early August. Zemlinsky was immersed in 'production meetings, design conferences and musical discussions', while Feld, to his annoyance, was still proposing alterations to the libretto.[30] The orchestral parts were copied, measurements taken for costumes and wigs, the sets designed and built; the singers had learned their music, and the stage manager had already taken them through blocking rehearsals.* But then, in the third week of rehearsal, disaster struck. Since the spring, rumours had been circulating that Mahler intended to leave the Hofoper, but for several months these could be neither confirmed nor denied. After the summer intermission it appeared that the differences between him and Count Montenuovo, the Kaiser's adjutant, had been settled. Behind the scenes, however, Montenuovo was frantically looking for a replacement. When news filtered through that Felix Mottl had been approached, Eduard Hanslick and other anti-Wagnerians launched a vicious campaign against him in the press. About this time, Zemlinsky wrote to Alma:

Your long-cherished wish is to be fulfilled: Director Mahler is leaving the Opera! And therewith begins *my* tale of woe. At present I simply can't imagine what's going to happen, particularly with regard to myself. As far as I am concerned, calamity is the word. I know very well that, whoever is appointed his successor, I shall inevitably be the loser. I am in a terrible state.[31]

But Mottl, as Musical Director of the Munich Hofoper, had little to gain from a move to Vienna, and withdrew his candidacy. Attention then turned to Felix Weingartner, who since 1891 had been Director of the Berlin Hofkapelle. The court of Wilhelm II was a hotbed of intrigue and artistic reactionism, and Weingartner had fallen foul of his superiors in circumstances similar to those that led to Mahler's downfall in Vienna. Only too glad for an excuse to leave Germany, he responded to Montenuovo's proposal with alacrity. Agreement was soon reached, and on 22 August he wrote to Mahler, reviving the bond of friendship that had long existed between them,[†] and gently breaking the news

---

* According to Clayton, rehearsals (i.e. coaching of the principal roles) had already begun in January (*ACl*, 143). No schedule survives, but the fact that at least one orchestral rehearsal was held is substantiated by handwritten markings by individual players in some of the parts. The surviving stage manager's score (OA 2553/3 at the Austrian National Library) includes detailed diagrams of stage movement for all three acts, as well as cuts in act I and the epilogue, which correspond to those entered in the orchestral parts.

† Weingartner prided himself on having been the first to champion Mahler's Third Symphony (he conducted the second movement in Hamburg in 1896 and a group of three movements the

of his appointment.[32] A few days later the engagement was made public, and on 2 October, only two days before the scheduled première of *Der Traumgörge*, the Kaiser signed a document officially terminating Mahler's contract.

As Weingartner saw it, the Hofoper had for some time been resting on its laurels. By contemporary standards the repertoire was limited, box-office takings were poor, most of the soloists were suffering from strain, and the ballet, which had formerly played to packed houses, was in a state of disarray. Aided and abetted by Roller, Mahler had repeatedly overrun his budget, sometimes to the extent of raiding the musicians' pension fund to cover the deficit.* Discouraged by personal attacks from court circles and the anti-Semitic press, his interest gradually shifted to a conducting career in the concert hall and abroad. He was concerned, above all, to concentrate his energy on composition, an attitude for which Weingartner expressed his deepest sympathy.

Weingartner saw himself as a Hercules summoned to clean out Augean stables. Only vaguely aware of the trouble in store for him, he took up office on 1 January 1908. A long-term project of Mahler's, the world première of Goldmark's *Ein Wintermärchen*, was realized the following day, but failed completely. Two further novelties were announced for the spring, Julius Bittner's *Die rote Gred*† and Eugen d'Albert's *Tiefland*. As a celebrated interpreter of Beethoven, Weingartner himself took the rostrum for the first time on 23 January with *Fidelio*, one of the most celebrated productions of the previous era. Deploring Mahler's practice of interpolating the third *Leonore* overture before the final scene, he ordered its omission. But since its ten-minute duration also covered the changing of Roller's monumental sets, the entire production had to be redesigned. In the eyes of his adversaries, Weingartner had besmirched the Holy of Holies.‡ A storm of protest swept through the press, and to his dismay Weingartner found himself accused of anti-Semitism.

A Catholic from Dalmatia and a newcomer to Vienna, he was totally unprepared for the extent and the vituperative articulation of the city's Semitic neurosis. In Berlin, where he had lived and worked for sixteen years, Jewish artists and musicians had for generations been accepted, applauded and honoured. He

following year in Berlin). Mahler considered these truncated performances as constituting 'a monstrous misunderstanding' of his intentions (letter to Richard Strauss, in Herta Blaukopf (ed.), *Gustav Mahler Briefe* (Vienna, 1982), 62).

* The archives of the Hofoper reveal that Roller's sets for *Der Traumgörge* were little more than an ingenious aggregation of redundant items from the scenery dock, including *Der Corregidor*, *William Tell*, *Lobetanz* and the pre-Roller production of *Siegfried* (cf. Carmen Ottner, 'Alexander Zemlinsky und die Wiener Hofoper', *AeSU*, 221).

† The Viennese composer Julius Bittner (1874–1939) was essentially self-taught. *Die rote Gred*, an opera in two acts, was first performed at Frankfurt on 26 October 1907.

‡ Bruno Walter recalls that Weingartner ruined the tense, motionless opening of the act 1 quartet in Mahler's production by introducing a meaningless piece of stage business for Jacquino (Walter, *Thema und Variationen* (Stockholm, 1947), 263).

himself had aroused the wrath of Cosima Wagner at Bayreuth by supporting Hermann Levi, prompting allegations of *pro*-Semitism, while the libretto of his opera *Genesius* (1892) had in Berlin been criticized for alleged *anti*-Semitic tendencies. After twenty years as Chief Conductor of the Vienna Philharmonic (1908–27) and four seasons as Director of the Volksoper (1919–24) he formulated a considered opinion:

It is absolutely typical [of Vienna] that the making of every new acquaintance is accompanied by inquiries concerning origin and race. [. . .] In many respects, as here, Vienna is regressive. While elsewhere in the Western world, in a process leading to kinship, certain antagonisms are slowly being levelled out, if at first only superficially, in Vienna these are strongly accentuated and still occasionally raise their ugly head.[33]

Weingartner stood aloof, a cultivated, other-worldly man, arrogant and politically naïve. In the debacle of *Der Traumgörge* he has traditionally been depicted as the villain. His actual role was more complex. Although Mahler had extracted a solemn promise that *Der Traumgörge* would be performed, and despite the Hofoper's contractual obligation to Karczag and Wallner, an instinct for self-preservation told him that the work would have to be dropped: if it succeeded, it would become a cudgel with which to administer him further beatings in the columns of the Viennese press; if it failed, all manner of reasons would be found for making him personally responsible, all the more so, since his own reputation as a composer fell far short of Zemlinsky's – and, as posterity has shown, justifiably so. While Goldmark was too old and universally respected to be drawn into racist controversy, and the music of Bittner, an Austrian Catholic, was hitherto all but unknown in Vienna, Zemlinsky, as leading survivor of the Mahler era, constituted a direct threat to his authority. Without even taking the trouble to read the score, he therefore ordered the première to be cancelled. To Karczag's enquiry, on 24 March, whether the work was to be performed, he replied that Schmedes, the leading tenor, was unavailable, as his services were required for repertoire performances. Karczag countered with news that the Neues Deutsches Theater in Prague (where Bodanzky had been engaged as First *Kapellmeister* in August 1907) was interested in performing the work. But Weingartner called his bluff (Bodanzky had little or no influence on the choice of repertoire in Prague) and pencilled on the letter: '*Traumgörge* free for Prague.'[34]

Zemlinsky's position at the Hofoper had became untenable, and as Weingartner was also unwilling to entrust him with further repertoire performances, he applied for fifteen weeks' leave of absence for guest performances at the Volksoper. On 15 February his contract at the Hofoper was officially terminated, with the proviso that he could continue to draw a salary until he found permanent employment elsewhere. Mahler, who had been kept abreast of developments, wrote somewhat absently from Philadelphia (the letter lay forgotten for several days in the pocket of his tailcoat):

Unfortunately the news of your adventures with the new regime were not altogether unexpected. Nevertheless, I would not have expected W. simply to ignore his promises, above all that he would bring out your opera. As I can imagine, for you this is truly calamitous. Altogether I feel partly to blame, even if 'blameless'. And my conscience often troubles me. But – who could have predicted all this! I would think that you must now do everything you can to get your work performed at the Volksoper.[35]

Der Traumgörge (II)

Zemlinsky returned to the Volksoper like a wounded beast to its lair. But he never made any attempt to get his new opera performed there, and when Heinrich Teweles, director of the Neues Deutsches Theater in Prague, later offered to stage the opera, Zemlinsky at first refused. Teweles recalls:

Due to his status in the theatre, he was wary of any suspicion that he might exploit his position to his own advantage, particularly as he was frequently required to pronounce verdicts upon the works of his contemporaries. So it came to pass that the still unperformed *Traumjörg* remained locked up in his closely guarded treasure-house.[36]

Shortly after signing a long-term contract with Universal Edition, in 1913, Zemlinsky did suggest to the director, Emil Hertzka, that he might acquire the rights to the work from Karczag. But he also indicated that he was dissatisfied with the libretto: 'Since the text of act II demands more urgency and conciseness, a word from you to Feld would doubtless make its effect.'[37] Hertzka's reaction was negative, and as Zemlinsky, like any true artist, was more interested in future successes than past disappointments, he put the score back into the cupboard and forgot all about it. In 1919 Webern wrote to him:

I would like to tell you: since the summer I have been avidly studying your *Traumgörge*, and it pleases me more than I can say. [. . .] The fact that this work is still unperformed demonstrates all too clearly the miserable state, the appalling iniquity of our musical establishment. [. . .] I can scarcely hear my fill of such music as on page 187 of the vocal score – epilogue: HANS: 'Du kümmere dich nur . . .' and then page 192 Allegretto – GRETE: 'Und unsere Frau, der wollen wir danken . . .' and what then follows up to that tender little entry for the chorus. The ensuing final scene counts among the most beautiful things I have ever heard.[38]

Much later – probably in the summer of 1935 – Zemlinsky did once take the vocal score from his shelf and open it out on the piano in his music room. Over three successive evenings he played it through, one act at a time. When he had finished, he turned to his wife, who had been listening, and said, 'Es ist gut.' Then he put it back where he had found it.[39]

During the 1970s the Vienna State Opera cleared out its music library. The operation was executed with great care, and items that appeared to be of value were passed on to the Austrian National Library for safekeeping. Thus, at the very time when the Zemlinsky renaissance was gathering momentum, the original performing materials of *Der Traumgörge* became accessible to music research. Thanks to the efforts of Horst Weber and Wulf Konold, the opera was exhumed, edited – and performed.

Those present at the world première in Nuremberg on 11 October 1980 were aware that they were witnessing an event of great importance. *Der Traumgörge* proved to be a score of searing beauty and, at times, overpowering intensity. The contrast between Hans, the sturdy yokel, Kaspar, the scheming villain, and Görge, the flat-footed little dreamer, were vivid and immediate; the iridescent colours and impassioned outbursts of Görge's confrontation with the Dream-Princess, the light-footed humour of the villagers' entry in the epilogue – all this and much else remains unforgettable. Only the most hardened could have been unmoved by the dream sequence of act 1 or the closing pages of the epilogue. As was now clear, fatuous political infighting had caused a terrible miscarriage of justice.

Not that everything in Nuremberg was ideal. An orchestra confronted with copies of the 1907 performing materials battled against illegible handwriting and (literally) thousands of copyists' errors. Lacking confidence to perform the work uncut – surely the only solution now acceptable, for lack of a composer and librettist to solve the dramaturgical problems – the Nuremberg production observed most of Mahler's cuts and added several more.[*] One of Mahler's omissions was particularly unkind: the extended orchestral introduction to the epilogue, in which Zemlinsky summarizes the entire inner conflict of the drama.

A sensitive area in the performing tradition of *Der Traumgörge* concerns the casting of Gertraud and the Dream-Princess. In Nuremberg the roles were doubled by one singer, implying that the two characters were in effect one and the same. Attractive as the concept may appear – opera-goers are acquainted with a similar doubling of Venus and Elisabeth in *Tannhäuser* – it serves only to obscure the message of Görge's failure, and can indeed give the impression that his dream eventually comes true. When rehearsals were abandoned in 1907, it appears that Mahler was still pondering this very question, for in the stage manager's cast list[†] the distribution of roles is noted as follows:

Prinzessin ⎫ Marie Renard
Gertraud ⎭ Fladung

Both singers learned both roles, pending a later decision.[‡]

---

[*] The first commercial recording, issued in 1985, abbreviated the work further, to the point of unintelligibility.

[†] The cast also included Erik Schmedes in the title role, Gerhard Stehmann as Kaspar, Anton Moser as Hans, Gertrud Förstel as Grete and Elisa Elizza as Marei.

[‡] For Mahler this was common practice. For instance, he cast the title role in *Salome* with no

Considerable aid to understanding and assessing the work was offered at
Nuremberg by the programme book, which included informative articles by
Konold and Weber, a finely observed musical analysis by Burckhard Rempe,
which identified many of the themes and motifs by name, but was careful to
point out that these were intended merely as identification tags, and an interesting study by Angelika Wildner-Partsch, who interpreted Görge, and with him
all Zemlinsky's operatic protagonists, as a 'passive hero'.[40] Partsch's interpretation has since found widespread acceptance and in many more recent studies
has acquired the status of a catchword. Yet the concept of passivity explains
neither Görge's restless search for fulfilment nor the Dwarf's erotic determination (in *Der Zwerg*), neither Hai-Tang's resolute struggle for justice (in *Der
Kreidekreis*) nor the *action gratuite* that causes the downfall of Kandaules. If
Zemlinsky's heros and heroines have anything in common, then it is this: they
are victims of circumstances beyond their control, prisoners in a world of
restrictions and frustrations, combatants in a futile struggle against their own
destiny.

---

fewer than three sopranos, 'so as to have a choice and, if need be, a replacement' (letter to
Richard Strauss, 19 August 1905). Some weeks later a fourth singer was added to the list: 'You
can choose the one that most nearly fulfils your expectations,' he wrote (undated letter to
Strauss, *c.*22 October 1905; both in Blaukopf, op. cit., 101–2, 108). The roles of Dream-
Princess and Gertraud were entrusted to Marie Renard and Irene von Fladung, neither of
whom were full-time members of the Hofoper ensemble (Renard left in 1900; Fladung's contract terminated in March 1907).

3

Farewell to Vienna

Dukas

Zemlinsky returned to the Volksoper in the spring of 1908, but as a guest conductor and for just one work, *Ariane et Barbe-bleue* by Paul Dukas. Since the production of Siegfried Wagner's *Der Kobold* in 1905, it was the first time that Simons had risked programming a novelty. Sandwiched between light opera and operetta, *Ariane* cut an incongruous figure on the playbill, but it was Simons's avowed intention to establish his theatre, within given financial limits, as capable of contributing to the contemporary artistic scene. His public, however, was out of its depth. *Ariane* was greeted with hisses, and the production was given only three times.*

The critics unanimously acclaimed the achievement of Zemlinsky and his orchestra, as also of the young Gusti Stagl, who coped bravely with the immense demands of the title role. Even the German nationalist press hailed the production as a 'significant artistic success' for the Volksoper, and singled out the translator, Harry la Violette, for obliquely formulated praise: 'To see the German language being treated in the France of today with such care and consideration: the German people can consider this one of their finest victories.'[1]

Elsa Bienenfeld summarized those aspects of the score which particularly recommended it to Vienna's musical avant-garde:

Dukas's harmonic style represents the consolidation of a trend towards which French music has long been striving. That apart, the work presents, at a higher level than ever before in French opera, complete motivic development of all themes, and is formally designed in a fashion foreign even to the theatre of Debussy.[2]

Debussy was undoubtedly the more popular, and his music enjoyed greater dissemination, but it was Dukas to whom Zemlinsky felt the stronger affinity. The music of *Ariane* is based, like his own, on specific relationships between key and colour; its techniques of motivic development are closely akin to those of developing variation. Like Zemlinsky, Dukas experimented with chord formations and motifs based on 4ths, delighted in a lush yet pellucid orchestral

---

* The production opened on 2 April 1908. For the New York première of *Ariane* in 1911, Gustav Kobbé added to his celebrated *Complete Opera Book* a brief résumé of the work, which concludes with the priceless remark: 'The allegory in this tale is that five out of six women prefer captivity (with a man) to freedom without him. The opera has not been popular in this country' (1919 edn, 761).

sound, and knew to fashion complex textures in such a way as to maintain clarity. Zemlinsky must also have admired the discipline and logic of his architecture, and, above all, his ability to place intellect at the service of emotion. The score achieved what Zemlinsky had attempted in *Der Traumgörge*, a theatre of contemplation rather than of action, a drama of the soul, far removed from the young Hofmannsthal's 'imagination of the eye'.

The sole evidence of personal contact between Dukas and Zemlinsky is a telegram sent to the composer in Paris on the eve of the Vienna première, countersigned by Schoenberg, Berg and Webern. It is not inconceivable that the two composers met, but probably not before August 1910, when the young Korngold was invited to play to Archduke Eugen in Munich: Dukas is known to have been present on that occasion,[3] and Zemlinsky might already have arrived to attend rehearsals for the world première of Mahler's Eighth Symphony. Yet contact was clearly tenuous, and any theories of musical cross-pollination between the two composers or of a possible influence of Dukas on the Second Viennese School inevitably remain speculative.

The Volksoper (II)

At the close of the 1906–7 season Simons disbanded his entire ensemble of actors. With 32 solo singers and 10 dancers, a chorus of 67 (supplemented when required by an extra-chorus of 46 and a children's chorus of 21) and a *corps de ballet* of 20 *élèves* and 20 children, he concentrated his activities on music-theatre and ballet. The limitations of the pit dictated the size of the orchestra, which, with a complement of 58, was small in proportion to the rest of the company. By the time Zemlinsky left for the Hofoper, however, he had succeeded in welding his players into a responsive and capable instrument. Operetta now accounted for only a small part of the repertoire, and with spectacular new productions, including *Lohengrin* and *Le prophète*, Simons largely achieved his goal of entering into competition with the Hofoper.

From mid-April to the close of the 1907–8 season Zemlinsky conducted ten productions from his former repertoire, including *Der Freischütz*, *Tannhäuser*, *Tosca*, *Die Zauberflöte* and *Don Giovanni*. Meanwhile his position at the Hofoper had been filled by Hugo Reichenberger, and Weingartner had agreed to direct the Vienna Philharmonic's series of Sunday concerts. In the winter of 1909 Zemlinsky inaugurated a rival Sunday matinée concert series. Taking note of Weingartner's preferences, he chose programmes that invited direct comparison, with an accent on Beethoven and Wagner.

From February 1907 until March 1908 (shortly after the première of *Ariane et Barbe-bleue*) Franz Schreker worked at the Volksoper as chorusmaster. He certainly profited from direct exposure to the music of Dukas, but his duties also obliged him to rehearse other works for which he often felt less sympathy.

For the 1908–9 season Simons had engaged the Czech composer–conductor Oskar Nedbal as Musical Director,* and Zemlinsky was obliged to accept a makeshift contract as First *Kapellmeister*. His only première, on 24 March 1909, was of Millöcker's *Der Bettelstudent*, an assignment far beneath his dignity, but one that he accepted presumably for the sake of re-establishing his presence within the company – and of earning a living. Once he had launched the new production, however, the repertoire performances were entrusted to his assistant, Gottfried Baldreich. A new soloist in the ensemble that season was Schoenberg's Viennese cousin, Hans Nachod. Born in 1883, he had completed his studies at the Vienna Conservatoire and was now on his way to a re-spectable career as a heldentenor.

Zemlinsky spent the rest of the spring and the summer of 1909 working on the score of *Kleider machen Leute*. No sooner had the ink dried on the last page than he swung back into action at the Volksoper, with *Fidelio* on 15 September, followed by *Lohengrin, Der Freischütz, Die Zauberflöte, Carmen, Figaro* and, on 29 October, the première of *Baron Trenck*, an operetta by the Croatian composer Srečko Albini. In the roles of Elsa, Agathe and Pamina the Volksoper presented a twenty-four-year-old newcomer from Moravia: Maria Jeritza, soon to become one of the greatest sopranos of her generation. A new addition to the music staff in the autumn of 1909 was Anton Webern. Having tasted his first theatre blood during the 1908 summer theatre season in Bad Ischl, he was determined to make his name as a conductor. But this particular path to fame, as he soon discovered, was thorny. Whether he stayed the course at the Volksoper or resigned after a few weeks, as on other occasions, is uncertain.

A Deaf Child and a Silent Woman

Five weeks after the première of *Ariane*, on 8 May 1908, Ida Zemlinsky gave birth to a daughter, Johanna Maria ('Hansi'). The baby's first weeks were over-shadowed by serious illness, and in June, once the worst was over, her anxious parents packed their bags and headed for Gmunden on the Traunsee.[4] Hansi made steady progress, and when she was nine weeks old her father composed a piece specially for her, for voice and tambourine: *Der chinesische Hund, oder der englische Apfelstrudel* ('The Chinese Dog or the English Apple Strudel'). Alas, when Papa struck his tambourine, little Hansi scarcely reacted. Whether due to a congenital defect or as after-effect of her early sickness, her hearing was impaired. Only in the final bars of the piece, when the tambourine swelled to a mighty crescendo, did she register approval in the manner intended, with a

* Having conducted four performances of *Der fliegende Holländer*, Nedbal withdrew from his contract.

vigorous burp. In later years she reacted less positively to her father's music.*

Zemlinsky's career might have been a permanent struggle for recognition, but his talents did at least guarantee him the basic potential for earning a living. Schoenberg, on the other hand, was blessed with little proficiency as a performer and found himself obliged to eke out a living from private teaching, gifts and loans. The strain of housing, feeding and clothing a family of four, coupled with the dawning realization that his genius might well remain unacknowledged until long after his death, began to cause mounting tension within the family. The outpourings of affection for Mathilde that he had expressed in *Verklärte Nacht* were forgotten, and after the birth of their first child the relationship began to cool. A secret programme for the D minor Quartet op. 7, sketched in 1904–5, reflects this growing estrangement. Beginning with 'feelings of oppression, despair; fear of being engulfed', all the motifs of the first section are involved in a 'conflict', which expresses the 'resolution to start a new life'. The third section speaks of a 'growing longing for those left at home, turning into despair at the pain caused them', and the finale dreams of 'quiet joy and the accession of peace and harmony'.[5]

In the spring of 1906, at one of Mahler's concerts, a twenty-three-year-old art student named Richard Gerstl introduced himself to Schoenberg and asked permission to paint his portrait. An avid follower of the new-music scene, he had already approached Mahler and Ansorge, but had in both cases been rebuffed. Having first made discreet enquiries as to Gerstl's artistic credentials, Schoenberg assented. Sittings were held at the apartment in the Liechtensteinstrasse, with the composer on an ottoman in a corner of the living room, his head slightly averted, his eyes raised to confront the observer with a penetrating gaze.

Gerstl soon became acquainted with Schoenberg's pupils and friends and, naturally, with Mathilde and her four-year-old daughter. A few weeks later he painted a portrait of the two, Mathilde discreetly seated at the dining table to conceal her pregnancy, and Trudi at her side. Waiving his fee for both pictures (his father, a dabbler on the stock exchange, supported him generously), he presented them to his new friends.[†] Several portraits of Schoenberg's acquaintances followed, notably of Berg's sister Smaragda, and of Webern's friend Ernst Diez.[6] A second portrait of Mathilde, this time on her own, followed in the spring of 1907. When the group repaired to the Traunsee that summer, Gerstl was invited to join them. Inspired by the vitality of his companions, his style became ever

* 'Hansi was no beauty,' recalls Arnold Greissle-Schönberg, who knew her well. 'She had her father's nose and chin and his slightly bulging eyes. Unfortunately for her she was also a rather passionate lady, not a good combination' (letter to the author, 6 August 1998).
† Schoenberg later gave both portraits to Berg, who in turn passed them on to Georg Schoenberg. Today they are preserved at the Historisches Museum der Stadt Wien (Schoenberg) and the Österreichische Galerie (Mathilde and Gertrud).

wilder and more uncompromising. Within a matter of weeks he had completed several landscape paintings, a portrait of Zemlinsky,* new studies of Mathilde, and two large family groups. Melanie Guttmann and her husband, the American painter and sculptor William Clarke Rice, joined the party on a belated honeymoon; they too, it appears, were perpetuated on his canvas.†

Gerstl, an archetypal angry young man, refused to accept the authority of his teachers‡ or to heed the advice of relatives and friends; on leaving art school, he found himself completely isolated. Schoenberg discovered in him a stimulating conversation partner, however, and a willing listener. Under Gerstl's influence, and probably with his technical advice, he himself began to paint. This new spiritual empathy strengthened Gerstl's own resolve to progress along his lonely path. Meanwhile, in his emotional solitude, he found an ally in Mathilde; their friendship soon grew into love.

A chance comment of Trudi's in the summer of 1907 revealed that the two were on intimate terms. At first Schoenberg hoped to settle the matter 'from man to man', and wrote to Gerstl to the effect that they had grown too close to allow a woman to come between them. But the relationship intensified. Gerstl rented a studio close by, at Liechtensteinstrasse 20, and although Schoenberg forbade Mathilde to go there, she took no heed. She was her lover's favourite model, but he also painted and sketched numerous self-portraits: his scowl was fearsome; more terrifying still was his laugh.

In the summer of 1908, which again was spent on the Traunsee, Mathilde and Gerstl were surprised by Schoenberg in a compromising situation. They fled to Vienna; Schoenberg reported his wife to the police as missing, then left in pursuit. With *Verklärte Nacht*, the *Gurrelieder* and *Pelleas und Melisande* he had given the world three masterpieces on the theme of marital infidelity; confronted with the situation in real life, he found himself unable to handle it.

What part Zemlinsky played in this drama is uncertain. Considering that he had once written of his sister, 'should the need arise, one of us would willingly make any sacrifice for the other',[7] and bearing his own permissive attitude in mind, it may be assumed that his sympathies were largely on her side. It was Webern who assumed the role of mediator, imploring Mathilde to return to her

---

* Gerstl's Zemlinsky portrait (plate 17), which depicts him in a white suit and straw boater, with cane in hand, was modelled on Edvard Munch's celebrated portrait of Harry Graf Kessler, painted in 1906.

† Like Gerstl, Rice had studied in Vienna. Gerstl's double portrait, sometimes known as *Couple on the Green* (Klaus Albrecht Schröder, *Richard Gerstl 1883–1908* (Vienna, 1993), 127) or *Couple Before a Meadow with Tree-stump* (Otto Breicha, *Gerstl und Schönberg. Eine Beziehung* (Salzburg, 1993), plate 16), probably depicts Melanie Guttmann-Rice and her husband.

‡ His first teacher, Christian Griepenkerl, described his work as 'shitting into snow'. Heinrich Lefler, who recommended him to Schoenberg in the spring of 1906, subsequently threw him out of his class on grounds of insubordination.

husband, if only for the sake of her children. She never forgave him for intruding into her dream of freedom,[8] but realizing the hopelessness of her situation, finally agreed to rejoin the family.

On 11 November 1907 Gerstl had been invited, as a matter of course, to a concert of chamber music and lieder by Schoenberg's pupils. For 4 October 1908 a more ambitious concert of orchestral music was scheduled at the Musikverein, which included the world première of Webern's Passacaglia op. 1. This time Gerstl waited in vain for an invitation. If he had not yet realized the consequences of his actions, he realized them now: his isolation was complete. That night he burned his personal documents and several of his pictures. He was found dead in his studio, hanging naked before the full-length mirror which he had used for his self-portraits.*

On 9 November Mathilde wrote to Gerstl's brother Alois:

Believe me, of the two of us, Richard chose the easier path. To have to go on living in such a situation is terribly hard.[9]

Schoenberg suffered no less acutely. Already in the spring of 1908 he had given musical expression to his misery in the Second Quartet and Das Buch der hängenden Gärten; now he drafted out a document that disavowed the marriage entirely:

I have wept, acted like a man in despair, [. . .] I have contemplated and been driven almost to suicide. [. . .] I am in utter despair, because I do not believe it. Cannot believe it. I do not consider it possible that I can have a wife who betrays me.[10]

Mathilde had professed her innocence, but she had lied to him. No wife worthy of his name could be anything but truthful; therefore she had never been, and no longer was, his wife. Until her death in 1923, she remained Schoenberg's loyal helpmate and Clara's caring daughter. But to outsiders she became the impersonation of unobtrusiveness, 'the silent woman'.[11]

The Mystery of Mannheim

In a curriculum vitae written for Universal Edition in February 1910, Zemlinsky wrote that from 1909 to 1910 he was engaged as First Kapellmeister at the Hofund Nationaltheater in Mannheim. He sanctioned the inclusion of this information in every biographical note printed during his lifetime, and it has been repeated in many others published long after. Likewise, an article about his arrival in New York in January 1939, based on an interview arranged for him by Bodanzky, includes the following data: 'He moved on to the [Vienna] Staatsoper [sic] in 1908, to the Mannheim Opera in 1909 and to the directorship of the

---

* Rumours that he also stabbed himself in the heart or even castrated himself are not borne out by the police report (quoted in Schröder, op. cit., 186).

Neues Deutsches Theater in Prague in 1911'.[12] Despite these authentic sources, the Mannheim phase of Zemlinsky's career remains swathed in mystery. Weber states categorically[13] that 'Zemlinsky was engaged neither in Mannheim in 1909 [. . .] nor in Weimar.'* And a careful study of playbills, newspapers and other documentation from the period confirms that he conducted at Mannheim only once: in 1912, as guest conductor in a performance of *Es war einmal . . .*

Since the archives of the Mannheim theatre were destroyed during World War II, it seems unlikely that the whole truth will ever emerge. From 1906 to 1908 the position of First *Kapellmeister* in Mannheim was occupied by Hermann Kutzschbach, who had previously been engaged at the Hofoper in Dresden. In the autumn of 1908 the First *Kapellmeister* at Chemnitz, Heinrich Grimm, fell seriously ill and was obliged to stand down. His position was hastily filled by one of Kutzschbach's former colleagues at the Dresden Hofoper, the Serbian conductor Oscar Malata. But evidently the *Intendant* in Dresden, Ernst von Schuch, was prepared to release Malata from his contract in mid-season only if a replacement could be found. An agreement was reached, whereby Kutzschbach should return to Dresden as soon as a deputy had been found for him in Mannheim. The search led to Zemlinsky, who was at that time still suspended on full pay at the Hofoper. Mannheim, a prosperous industrial centre with a large and important opera house, must have been an attractive proposition, both artistically and financially. Indeed, on 11 December 1908 the *Allgemeine Musik-Zeitung* reported: 'We hear that Alexander Zemlinsky is to leave the Vienna Hofoper for an engagement at Mannheim.' But on 25 December the Mannheim *Intendant*, Carl Hagemann, released a press announcement to the effect that 'Mr Kutzschbach is to be replaced by Artur Bodansky [*sic*] from the Deutsches Landestheater in Prague, and the position of Mr Reichwein [Kutzschbach's assistant] will be taken by Albert Coates from the Dresden Opera';[14] neither engagement was to take effect until the beginning of the following season. Six days later the *Neue Badische Landes-Zeitung* published an article by Wymetal (whom Weingartner had meanwhile appointed Chief Producer at the Vienna Hofoper), expressing qualified praise for Bodanzky, but also regret that Zemlinsky had declined the offer:

At a respectful distance behind Zemlinsky, Bodanzky rates as the most diligent and most mature conductor of his circle. He has a firm and secure command of the orchestra, knows to muster his reserves and to build. When I heard him conduct, I became aware of only one deficiency: a certain heavy-handedness, a predilection for *ritardando*.[†] If Zemlinsky was not to be won, the *Intendant* in Mannheim could have engaged no better young Viennese talent than Bodanzky.[15]

---

* The myth of Weimar is propagated in *Die Musik in Geschichte und Gegenwart*.
† If this was a consistent fault of the young Bodanzky, it was one that he soon corrected. At the Met, where he concentrated on German repertoire, he became notorious for his rapid tempi, particularly in Wagner.

There, but for an intriguing twist, the story would have ended. But the
Chemnitz *Intendant* evidently decided that he could manage for a while without a musical director. Malata therefore remained in Dresden, Kutzschbach in
Mannheim – and Zemlinsky in Vienna. Since Bodankzy was unavailable until
the autumn, Zemlinsky appears to have agreed to deputize for him at
Mannheim at least until May. But now that the *Kapellmeister* carousel had
ground to a halt, he continued to draw his salary from the Hofoper, evidently
supplemented by monthly compensation payments from Mannheim. All that
remained of the affair, as far as he was concerned, was a new entry in his curriculum vitae – and (presumably) a modest surplus at the bank.

Kleider machen Leute

The only surviving sketchbook for *Kleider machen Leute*, in blue covers
resourcefully secured with parcel string, newspaper and gum, bears a dedication
in verse from the bookbinder:

*Fehlt es an Grütze, / Vater der Mütze, / oder am Blitze / gar an der Spitze –: / Als
dann benütze / dies 'Buch der Skizze', / und schenke mir – Witze / ins
Jubiläumstheater.*

If you haven't a groat, / have sold your big coat, / if all that you wrote / with dull-
ness is smote – / this book should promote / new sketches of note, / and jokes I can
quote – / at the Volksoper.

Christmas 1905, Arnold Schoenberg*

Schoenberg's poem happens to offer the only available clue to the dating of the
libretto. Poking fun at Feld's craze for rhyming couplets, he appropriates a
rhyme verbatim from *Kleider machen Leute*:

*Was sie wert und was sie nütze,/ Sollt' ich darauf Antwort geben, / dazu reicht nicht
meine Grütze! / Doch der Mantel und die Mütze / sind mir Wert wie Luft und
Leben!*

What they're worth and how I use them? / Many reasons I could mention, / but my
brain-cells they confuse them! / My fur cap and coat, to lose them / would condemn
me to abstention.[16]

The fact that Feld's libretto was already in circulation by December 1905

---

* A literal translation is scarcely possible. 'Grütze' (groat) is here used in a slang connotation
as 'grey matter'; 'Blitz(e)' (flash) can here be read as an abbreviation of 'Genieblitz' (stroke of
genius); 'Spitze' (point) implies a pencil point. The 'Mütze' (cap) of the original has been
replaced in this translation by a 'Mantel' (coat): in the context of *Kleider machen Leute*, the
two are interchangeable.

indicates that this was no hasty sequel to *Der Traumgörge*, but a long-term project, completed at least two years before Zemlinsky began to compose the music. Feld might even have presented his work as a dowry, as it were, upon entering into partnership in 1903.

No drawing-room bookshelf in the German-speaking world used to be complete without a selection of Gottfried Keller. A leading exponent of nineteenth-century poetic realism, Keller held up a distorting mirror to middle-class society, in which his readers could see themselves reflected with sarcasm and grotesque humour. In post-Marxist society, the enlivening spark of religious scepticism* in his prose works no longer burns so brightly, and today he is more often studied at school than read at home. *Die Leute von Seldwyla*, a two-volume anthology of novellas published in 1856 and 1874, is the work for which he is best remembered. Of the five stories in volume 1, the most overtly dramatic, *Romeo und Julia auf dem Dorfe* ('A Village Romeo and Juliet'), followed the author around, as he once complained, 'like a well-trained poodle'[17] and attracted the interest of numerous composers, from Busoni (1884)[18] to Kelterborn (1991). Only one stage adaptation ever achieved any lasting success, however, namely the opera by Delius, composed to his own libretto in 1899–1906.[19]

The form of *Kleider machen Leute* ('Clothes Make the Man')[†] is episodic and open-ended, its humour dry and mordant. Keller's wit, which relies for its effect on minutely observed detail, is scarcely the stuff that opera librettos are made of. The topography is problematical too, with frequent changes of location – from dining room to drawing room, from hotel stairway to WC – that are difficult to accommodate within a theatre ground plan. In the closing paragraph, his narrative suddenly jumps ten or twelve years into the future, affording a glimpse of the hero as prosperous head of a large family. Where cinema can credibly emulate such a device, theatre cannot. These are some of the thornier problems that Feld will have encountered in adapting *Kleider machen Leute* for the operatic stage.

As most of the manuscript material is undated, the opera's genesis is vague. Zemlinsky began work in April 1907 and probably completed the short score by June 1908, for at that time he started on a new project, a string quintet in D minor.[‡]

* Like Rudolf von Gottschall, Keller was an ardent follower of Ludwig Feuerbach.
† The title is taken from a dictum of Quintilian's, 'Vestis virum reddit' (*Institutio oratoria*, 6, 1, 30). A further opera based on the same story, composed in 1934 by Joseph Suder (1892–1980) to his own libretto, was first performed in 1964. The comic situation of a commoner masquerading as a nobleman – or vice versa – is, of course, common currency in opera, whether in single scenes (e.g. *Figaro*, act IV; *Don Giovanni*, act II) or complete plots (Adam, *Si j'étais roi*; Verdi, *Un giorno di regno*, etc.).
‡ A fragment of fifty-two bars survives. The only other composition dating from this period was the cycle of Five Songs to texts by Richard Dehmel, composed in December 1907 (see pp. 268–71).

The orchestral score was finished at Steinakirchen am Forst in Upper Austria on 14 August 1909. During this entire period, Zemlinsky all but vanishes from sight.* No correspondence with Schoenberg survives for the period from September 1907 to July 1910 (such letters as may have existed were probably destroyed in the aftermath of the Gerstl crisis); and since Alma was in New York for much of the year, correspondence with her was irregular. One letter from Feld has been preserved, however, in which Zemlinsky's request for a cut in act II is met with the flattening remark: 'We are writing an opera and not a pot-pourri.'[20]

Substantial cuts were nevertheless implemented, even before the world première. The work went through several subsequent stages of modification, until in 1921, with the prospect of new productions in Munich and Prague, Zemlinsky and Feld prepared a thoroughgoing revision of the whole opera.[†] Numerous passages were rewritten, others jettisoned; two smaller roles were eliminated, and acts II and III telescoped together; more time was allowed for scene changes, with a waltz-intermezzo inserted between the prologue and act I, and an extended orchestral interlude for the new act II.[‡] The new vocal score, published in 1922, was sixty pages shorter than the original version.[§]

Cast

Wenzel Strapinski, a tailor from Seldwyla (ten); the master-tailor (bass); two tailor's apprentices (ten, bass); magistrate (bass); Nettchen, his daughter (sop); Melchior Böhni, sales representative of Quandt & Son (bar); Adam Litumlei, notary (bass); Eulalia, his wife (mezzo); [Liselein, his daughter (sop);][¶] Polykarpus Federspiel, town clerk (ten); elder son of Messrs Häberlein & Co. (ten); Mrs Häberlein (sop); younger son of Messrs Pütschli-Nievergelt (bass); coachman (bar); innkeeper of

---

* At this time he might have collaborated with Jalowetz on an analysis of Schoenberg's Second Quartet, published in *Erdgeist*, IV/February 1909, 225–34, and signed '—y' (cf. 'Arnold Schoenberg's F♯ Minor Quartet: A Technical Analysis', translated by Mark DeVoto, *Journal of the Arnold Schoenberg Institute* XVI/1 and 2, 1993, 293–322).

† Two hand-written notes (*LoC*, 15/10) furnish evidence that Feld collaborated with Zemlinsky on the 'Prague' version. The first is written on the reverse side of an undated furrier's bill made out to Magda Feld, the second on the reverse side of a calendar page for June 1921.

‡ Copies of the 1910 vocal score are rare, and the performing materials no longer exist.

§ There exist altogether three versions of the vocal score. The first, copyrighted in 1910 and published the following year by Bote und Bock (264 pp.), subtitles the work 'Komische Oper'; an abbreviated version, issued in 1913 with the same plate number as the 1910 edition, is subtitled 'Musikalische Komödie' (246 pp.). In 1918 the rights to the work were acquired by Universal Edition, who issued the 'Prague' version (196 pp.) in 1922. Credit for the authorship of the piano reduction is omitted from all three editions. As transpires from Zemlinsky's correspondence with Schoenberg, however, the 'Prague' version (i.e. the piano reduction of the modified and newly composed sections) was prepared by Schoenberg's son-in-law, Felix Greissle. For further details, including Zemlinsky's criticisms of Greissle's work, see *Web-Br*, 61, 93–4 and 229.

¶ Only in the 1910 version.

'Zur Wage' (bass); his wife (sop); [waiter (ten);]* waiter's apprentice (sop);† cook (mezzo); servant (ten); prologue (spoken). Men and women from Goldach and Seldwyla.

Synopsis

Prologue *On the road to Goldach* Business is bad in Seldwyla, and Strapinski has decided to leave. On a misty autumn morning he bids his two colleagues farewell. Clad in a silk-lined travelling coat and a high cap of sable – his journeyman's masterpieces – he sits on a milestone and stares blankly into the distance. Luck is on his side: an elegant equipage drives by, and the coachman is glad to take him as far as Goldach.

Original version (1910)	*Revised version (1922)*
I In Goldach Böhni pays court to Nettchen. She is repelled by his arrogance and contempt for small-town society, and dreams of marrying a nobleman from a distant land. Her father expresses approval of Böhni as a son-in-law.	I In Goldach Böhni pays court to Nettchen. She is repelled by his arrogance.

The carriage draws up, and the innkeeper assembles his personnel to greet it. Announcing his passenger as 'Count Strapinski from Poland', the coachman drives on. The tailor is welcomed with deference, and a table laid in his honour.

The meal is served. Strapinski refuses the soup, but hesitantly accepts a bottle of champagne; then hunger gets the better of him, and he wolfs down a large meat pie.	The meal is served. Strapinski hesitantly accepts a bottle of champagne; then hunger gets the better of him, and he wolfs down a large meat pie.

The *haute volée* of Goldach arrives for the afternoon card game. The tailor, obliged to maintain his false identity, joins the party for a cigar. When Böhni arrives with Nettchen and her father, Strapinski is captivated by the girl's charm. Böhni's suspicions are aroused, and he resolves to make enquiries about him in Seldwyla. It transpires that the coachman has driven off with his 'master's' luggage. As night falls, the townspeople therefore hasten to fetch dressing-gowns, nightcaps, etc., which they proudly present to their noble guest. Escape is out of the question; Strapinski goes pensively to his room.

II *At the magistrate's villa* While the men play *Skat*, the ladies drink coffee and exchange recipes. Böhni voices suspicions about the 'Count', but at that moment Strapinski appears, almost	II/i *At the magistrate's villa* Accompanying herself at the piano, Nettchen sings a song to a text by Heine. The guests repair to the dining room, and lunch is served.

* Only in the 1910 version.
† In the 1910 version: 'The Piccolo'.

betraying himself with critical remarks on the Goldachers' taste in clothing. Federspiel and Lieselein seek his support for their marriage, Häberlein and Pütschli ask him to sponsor them in the forthcoming municipal elections. The guests repair to the dining room, and lunch is served. Accompanying herself at the piano, Nettchen sings a song to a text by Heine.

Hoping to slip away unnoticed, Strapinski goes into the garden; but first he feels compelled to bid farewell to Nettchen. Their conversation culminates in a declaration of love. Nettchen begs her father's permission to marry the 'Count'.

Böhni, who has overheard the conversation, implies that he is aware of Strapinski's true identity. He leads the couples on to the dance floor for a rollicking waltz.	Böhni overhears the conversation. Inwardly fuming, he takes his seat at the piano and accompanies the guests in a rollicking waltz.
	Orchestral interlude: 'The deceitful Böhni'
III/i *Ballroom at the 'Waldhaus', between Goldach and Seldwyla* The master tailor and his two journeymen tell Böhni that all is ready for the forthcoming charade. Böhni explains to them that he and Strapinski are rivals in love.	II/ii *Ballroom at the 'Waldhaus', between Goldach and Seldwyla* The two journeymen tell Böhni that all is ready for the forthcoming charade.

Guests arrive from Goldach and Seldwyla, greet each other and take their places. Strapinski and Nettchen arrive in a sleigh. Böhni has invited them to a pageant, *Clothes Make the Man*, that illustrates the history of tailoring. The role of a 'wolf in sheep's clothing' is taken by the master tailor, wearing a coat and cap identical to Strapinski's. The 'Count' is exposed as a journeyman.

With the jeers of the guests ringing in his ears, Strapinski beats a hasty retreat.	Uproar; Strapinski responds furiously to the taunts of the angry guests. Only when Böhni and the magistrate have ushered them out is calm restored. Strapinski explains to Nettchen how he unwittingly acquired his false identity, then takes his leave. She stops him: he may be a tailor and no aristocrat, but he has a noble heart. To a reprise of their love music, she falls into his arms.
III/ii *On the road to Goldach* Snow is falling, and the bells of Seldwyla mingle with the sound of sleighbells. Strapinski, in despair, falls asleep in the ditch. Discovered by Nettchen, he explains how he unwittingly acquired his false identity, then takes his leave. The magistrate arrives with Böhni, who declares that he is prepared to forgive, and still wishes to marry Nettchen. But she drags Strapinski from his hiding place: he may	

be a tailor and no aristocrat, but he has
a noble heart. To a jubilant chorus of
bystanders, the curtain falls.

Reviews of the world première, on 2 December 1910 at the Volksoper, were
largely unfavourable. But since most of the critics devoted their column space
to enumerating the alleged deficiencies of the music, Feld's contribution passed
largely unremarked – an indication if not of approval then at least of forbearance. After the Prague première, at the Deutsches Landestheater on 20 April
1922, no less an authority than Max Brod wrote enthusiastically of the libretto,
'The text maintains a fine dramatic tension, its rhymes are attractively thought
out, and each scene builds effectively towards its final curtain'.[21] His only regret
was that Feld had ignored Strapinski's significance as a freedom-fighter, an aspect
of the figure for which, in Keller, the people of Goldach express their respect.

Most commentators who have since held the libretto in the balance have
found it wanting. *Kleider machen Leute* was the last work of Zemlinsky's to be
performed in pre-war Germany, in a production in Cologne that opened on 12
December 1934.* By that time, even in the liberal-minded Rhineland, the press
was firmly under Nazi control. The critic of the *Kölnische Zeitung* accordingly
belittled Feld for his implicitly Semitic 'intellectualism', quoting passages from
a lecture by Hitler's chief ideologist Alfred Rosenberg to support his argument.
Gottfried Keller, he proclaimed, was the 'most profound humorist [and]
serious-minded psychologist' of the Nordic race, hence for non-Arians a book
with seven seals.[22]

At the Swiss première, in Zurich on 21 September 1935, public response was
warm, but the critic of the *Neue Züricher Zeitung* remained unconvinced of the
viability of Keller's essentially rural art in the sophisticated, urban framework
of opera. Much of his column space was devoted to criticizing the work for its
'overpowering expressive range'. He complained, for instance, that Feld had
omitted an episode from the novella in which Strapinski, prompted to sing
something in Polish, unwittingly launches into a Silesian folk song about a pig-
farmer's daughter. Where 'Keller's idea was prompted by Homeric wit,' he concluded, 'Zemlinsky and his librettist fail to follow him.'[23]

More recently Horst Weber has expressed the very opposite opinion, namely
that Feld resorts to a 'synthetic *naïveté* which is sometimes embarrassing',
thereby 'coarsening' Keller's language. He also points out that

Keller depicts the tailor's apprentice [. . .] on the one hand as a person entirely aware

---

* *Kleider machen Leute* was substituted at short notice for *Der Kreidekreis*, which had been
banned in Germany after brown-shirt agitation at the première in Stettin (see p. 407). The production, conducted by Meinhard von Zallinger, produced by Erich Bormann and with the
twenty-six-year-old Peter Anders as Strapinski, was mounted at the instigation of Heinrich
Jalowetz, who was Musical Director at Cologne until he was obliged to resign in 1933.

of his true worth, on the other as a little scoundrel who is not averse to his involuntary role as Count, but slips into it as if into a garment. [. . .] Feld, in contrast,
eliminates Strapinski's complicity.

And he concludes:

If the work is to be revived, then it would be advisable to bring the text into line
with Keller's original.[24]

In the opera, Strapinski is introduced as a hungry wayfarer, prepared to follow wherever destiny leads him – a character closer to the roving musicians of
Eichendorff's *Vor der Stadt* (see p. 107) than to the inscrutable, 'Black Fiddler'-
inspired figure of Keller's original. If Feld had wished to depict the tailor as 'a
little scoundrel', he certainly would have done so. But his declared intention
was quite the reverse,* and his adaptation, whether by accident or design,
transforms the chief protagonist into an affectionate caricature of Zemlinsky.
The surface similarities are striking: the Polish-sounding name,[†] diminutive
stature[‡] and dapper appearance, the predilection for cigars, the inability to
resist a pretty face. But there is also a deeper affinity, implicit in the
Adelsprädikat (the fictitious 'von') of Zemlinsky's name. With no malice aforethought, Strapinski encroaches on a world into which he was not born and to
which he can never belong. But he proves himself perfectly capable of living up
to noble obligations; indeed for Nettchen's sake he wilfully prolongs the mas-
querade. Inevitably the experience ends in disaster.

Alma was painfully aware that, despite the name, no aristocratic blood
coursed in her lover's veins (*'Alexander v. Zemlinsky – who is he?'*). But when
he took final leave of her, his courtly dignity put her to shame:

I told him that I no longer loved him – and that it was actually he who should be
shamefaced – but it was *I* who felt it more deeply. He seemed so noble, so pure,
stood so *high* above me! [. . .] My poor Alex – I could see the suffering on his face.
You noble man![25]

Humble birth but noble soul – high birth but tainted character: all
Zemlinsky's stage works, with the notable exception of *Der Traumgörge*, are
founded on this antithesis. And where in his other operas heroes or heroines of
lowly origin are confronted with princes, infantas, kings or emperors, here the
antithetical elements are fused into a single character. Whatever the short-

* In his letter to Zemlinsky (quoted on p. 170), Feld argues against a suggested alteration of
the subplot in act II: 'If Strap[inski] really does something for the two [Lieselein and
Federspiel], he becomes for all intents and purposes a confidence trickster.'
† The unauthorized variant 'Zemlinski' still often occurs in dictionaries and concert programmes.
‡ Keller makes a point of introducing his hero as 'das Schneiderlein', i.e. in the diminutive
form.

comings of the work as drama, *Kleider machen Leute* presents the most rounded of all Zemlinsky's musical self-portraits.

In the scene of Strapinski's denouement, Feld and Zemlinsky bring to the surface a xenophobia and a racial intolerance that in Keller remain latent. Amid a hubbub of yells and clenched fists, the impostor is found out, the tailor humiliated. But in effect it is the people of Seldwyla and Goldach who are unmasked, revealing in their demure, well-ordered souls if only for a moment a smouldering potential for violence and racial intolerance. From here on, the work can no longer be a comedy. And when the little tailor finally embraces the bride, his triumph rings surprisingly hollow. In contrast to Keller's congenial apotheosis, the dream of *petit-bourgeois* happiness is shown, as in *Der Traumgörge*, to be a delusion.

Schoenberg had prefaced the sketchbook with a teasing salute to Zemlinsky's artistry; Zemlinsky reciprocated by beginning the opera with a subtle parody of the famous 4ths chord from the Chamber Symphony:

EX. 32*

These bars define the style and disposition of all that is to follow: motifs based largely on 4ths and 5ths, diaphanous orchestral textures and an atmosphere of

* The accidental before the piccolo E♭ in bar 6 is missing in the published vocal score; EX. 32 follows the text of the Bote und Bock copyist's score of 1910 (now in the possession of Universal Edition, Vienna). An unsigned postcard to Zemlinsky in Rottach/Tegernsee, postmarked 14 August 1906, features a further parody of the Chamber Symphony, entitled 'Motif for a symphonic poem, "The Mountaineer"', (facsimile in *Web-Br*, 347; Weber ascribes the postcard to Erwin Stein):

gentle, almost other-worldly humour. They also establish the principal key of the opera, D minor.

D minor, in a context of extreme chromaticism, is the domain of Strapinski. At the opposite end of the spectrum, a tritone apart, stands Nettchen: her Heine song in act II is radiant in the 'pure blue' (Ullmann) of A♭ major; much of the love duet is also in that key. In the dream-like atmosphere of the waltz-intermezzo, interpolated at three key moments in the drama, their two worlds meet. The dance begins in D major, softly and deliberately; as it gathers momentum, a chromatically descending bass line steers towards A♭, and the pulse increases to full waltz tempo; then, with a deft return to D, the seismic curves of tempo, dynamic and compass fall gently back to their starting-points.

Despite the lightness of touch appropriate to a musical comedy, the work opens morosely. As the curtain rises, Strapinski and his colleagues strike up a heartbroken song of farewell, with a melody built from the rising 5th of the opening bar and the motif of the 'world', harmonized as a virtuoso *trompe l'oreille* that constantly circumvents the tonic.* For the two apprentices, the border between Seldwyla and the outside world signifies the demarcation line between life and death. To stress the solemnity of this leave-taking, Strapinski thanks his colleagues for accompanying him on his 'last journey' (*letzte Geleit*). The transition accompanying their exit winds chromatically towards A minor, the key of death.

The tailor stands at the crossroads, unable to turn back, uncertain of what lies ahead. Thus his situation mirrors the composer's own. Since the autumn of 1906, when Webern had devised a theme 'in no key at all', Zemlinsky was aware that his friends were moving along a path that he, as a creative artist, could not and would not follow. In his helplessness, Strapinski breaks into a little ditty. As much an existentialist statement as a folk song, its complexity lies concealed behind *Wunderhorn*-inspired irregularities of metre and lithely skipping rhythmic figures. The 'Schneiderlein' song also voices Zemlinsky's solidarity with the underprivileged, a theme first addressed in the *Maiblumen* sextet and which, in later years, was to become obsessive. Strapinski's obsequious sales patter –

Wir brauchen Bürger und Stutzer im Frack, / Soldaten, doctores und allerlei Pack! / Und Kleider machen erst Leute!

We need honest citizens and dandies in tails, / soldiers and doctors and all that avails. / For clothes indeed make the man.

---

* After initially implying a subdominant context (bars 10–12), the key centre passes towards the relative major (23–4), the supertonic minor (28–9) and the submediant major (31–2) before returning to the tonic – only to conclude in the relative major. D minor triads sound only on the second beat of bar 18 (for the duration of a quaver) and in bar 35 (for one semiquaver).

– recalls that unidentified arranger, toiling away in obscurity to produce 'beguiling' orchestral clothing for the music of others, who once remarked to Karl Kraus, 'Were it not for amateurs, the real talents would never be able to earn a living!' Also new is the quality of self-doubt:

Was machst denn du? Wachst denn du?

What are you doing? Are you awake?

The same question, posed with greater insistence, pervades the sixth Maeterlinck song (1913) with its recurrent refrain of 'Wohin gehst du?' ('Where are you going?'), and is posed again, symbolically but no less insistently, in the Sinfonietta of 1934. Once self-doubt had entered Zemlinsky's work, it was never again entirely absent.

From a musical standpoint, the 'Schneiderlein' song (EX. 37A) is the nerve centre of the opera. Most of the melodic material evolves, directly or indirectly, from here; the harmony, which describes elliptical paths around clearly identifiable tonal centres, contains the essence of all that follows.*

With the arrival of the equipage, the comedy begins. A boisterous orchestral interlude depicting the ride to Goldach replaces the traditional overture. Contrapuntally supported by the 'Coachman' motif –

EX. 33

– the 'Schneiderlein' theme rings out confidently as first subject; two further themes of a more passionate character constitute a second-subject group. Of these, the first is kept in reserve for the end of act I, when Strapinski soliloquizes on his transformation from tailor to count. The melody climbs jaggedly and falls gently back:

---

* Like Dukas, Zemlinsky integrates two discrete elements, the 4ths chord and the augmented triad. After the musical joke of the opening bars, however, Zemlinsky confines his use of 4ths and 5ths to melodic contours. As in the op. 7 lieder, much of the harmony is based on stepwise progressions (the voice-leading of EX. 37A is a case in point). The specific harmonic style of *Kleider machen Leute* is further discussed in Horst Weber, *Alexander Zemlinsky* (Vienna, 1977), 50–51; detailed contextual, harmonic and Schenkerian analyses of the 'Schneiderlied' are included in John Williamson, 'Mahler's "Wunderhorn" style and Zemlinsky's "Schneiderlein"', in M. T. Vogt (ed.), *Bericht über den Internationalen Gustav-Mahler-Kongress* (Kassel, 1989), 293–311. Williamson's conclusions diverge substantially from Weber's.

EX. 34   vocal score, page 84*

Strange how everything has turned out – this morning I was a tailor,

In later works, the dying fall of this third bar, which encompasses the inverted 'Self' motif, acquires a specific significance, recurring at moments of rare erotic sensibility, such as in the third Maeterlinck song, to the words 'Verirrt sich die Liebe auf irdischer Flur' ('If loves goes astray in earthly realms'), and in the finale of the Lyric Symphony, as a hushed *Klangfarbenmelodie* for trumpet and violins, within the phrase 'Steh still, o wundervolles Ende für einen Augenblick' ('Stand still, o beautiful end for a moment').

The second theme, a figure of four notes, is kept in reserve for the closing scene of the opera,[†] where it serves to express Strapinski's fury and anguish. Though closely related, both harmonically and melodically, to the motif with which the Princess entices Görge into her dream-world, the idea is not left in suspense, as in *Der Traumgörge*, but makes the finite, if resigned gesture of resolving on to a flattened 7th chord:

EX. 35A   *Der Traumgörge*, vocal score, page 77

* Page numbers refer to the 1922 edition of the vocal score (UE 7106).
† In the original version, the end of act II.

Ihr___ seid, ja ihr, die Schnei - der - see - len

EX. 35B *Kleider machen Leute*, vocal score, page 183

You, yes you, are the ones with tailors' souls

Act I opens and closes in a dream, depiciting Goldach as an oasis of peace and good will. To underline the illusion, Zemlinsky lets the curtain rise and fall to a euphonious melody in D major, which incorporates a cadential figure from the 'Evening Prayer' in Humperdinck's *Hänsel und Gretel*:

EX. 36

Despite Feld's concern that the work should be 'an opera and not a pot-pourri', despite the care with which Zemlinsky organizes his thematic material into large-scale symphonic units, and conscientiously avoids the predictable or the banal, the score takes fire in its set-pieces and large-scale tableaux rather than in dialogue scenes and shorter ensembles. Admittedly the same could be said of *Der Rosenkavalier*, a direct contemporary of *Kleider machen Leute*, and a work with which it has sometimes been (unfavourably) compared. But this is arguably a problem common to all comic operas since *Figaro*. The specific dramaturgical flaw of *Kleider machen Leute* lies in its over-reliance on situation comedy and the lack of a satisfying apotheosis – but these are weaknesses inherent in the choice of subject itself.

The physiognomy of act I is determined by the 'cigar' quintet (from which

Zemlinsky later extracted the waltz-intermezzo), the impassioned monologue in which Strapinski resolves to flee, and the closing orchestral nocturne. In act II/i the beauty of Nettchen's Heine song and the vivacity of the 'engagement dance' (a brilliant reworking of *Kirchweih* from the op. 10 lieder) overshadow everything around them; in the love duet, on the other hand, both Feld and Zemlinsky only narrowly avoid lapsing into triviality. The climactic charade scene of act II/ii seeks to revive the spirit of the pageant in act III/ii of *Die Meistersinger*; despite the energetic contributions of a riotously bucolic stage band, however, the invention rarely rises above mere proficiency. The ensuing denouement scene rivals the intensity of the fire-raising act II finale of *Der Traumgörge*, but here the violence is short-lived, and the transition to the reconciliation scene awkwardly managed.

Even if Zemlinsky withdrew the original version, much can be said in its favour. Acts II and III may be over-expansive, but the music is stylistically unified, and the characters are more fully developed. Nettchen's role in the 'Prague' version is drastically curtailed; the original opening scene, in which she recounts her romantic dreams of aristocratic lovers and distant lands, serves to present her in clearer profile. Böhni's contempt for small-town mentality is also more clearly motivated in the original version, indeed he even appears a little sympathetic. But whatever musical gains it may bring, there are also losses. The advantages of the 1922 version lie primarily in its conciseness. Act II of the original version opens with an extended double quartet, which, though dramatically superfluous, is a scintillating essay in *Falstaff*-inspired contrapuntal virtuosity. The denouement of act III is followed by a haunting interlude in B♭ minor, pervaded by the sound of sleigh-bells.* Strapinski sings a poignantly beautiful monologue, and Nettchen is allowed time to confront her girlish dreams with reality before giving herself to the man she loves. Only the ending – a vigorous C major chorus based on the 'Schneiderlein' song – is disappointingly banal. But the 'Prague' version of the closing bars – a fragment of the 'Scheiderlein' theme, transformed into B♭ major fanfares – appears no less inconclusive.

Much of the revision was a skilful job of cutting and pasting. In the few instances where music had to be added, Zemlinsky proved himself no purist. This becomes most apparent in the orchestral interlude after the 'engagement dance' in act II, where the Ueberbrettl diatonicism of the op. 10 lieder is juxtaposed with music that at times abandons tonality altogether. As a drastic depiction of Böhni's spleen, the break in style is striking, particularly in the grotesque disfigurement of the 'Schneiderlein' theme:

---

* Julius Korngold criticized Feld for stipulating snow in November – a rare event even in Switzerland – but the anomaly stems from Keller himself, whose story already begins with a light snow shower (cf. J. Korngold, *Deutsches Opernschaffen der Gegenwart* (Vienna, 1922), 240–53).

EX. 37A Prologue, vocal score, page 13

Little tailor, what are you doing? Are you awake? And so busy today?

EX. 37B 'The deceitful Böhni', vocal score, page 146

Initially all augured well for *Kleider machen Leute*: the Stuttgart Hofoper, where Max von Schillings had been appointed *Generalmusikdirektor* in 1908, acquired the rights to the world première, and Rainer Simons undertook to stage the work at the Volksoper. Already in December 1909, only four months after completing the orchestral score, Zemlinsky announced to Alma:

My opera has found a publisher – Bote und Bock – and has already been engraved. It's already in rehearsal at Stuttgart, but evidently under highly adverse conditions, with opposition, etc. As soon as the performing materials are ready, I shall start rehearsing it in Vienna.[26]

In the spring of 1910 he had further news for her:

My opera is in print at last. I'm coaching it too, and want to persuade Simons to schedule it for October, as planned. Otherwise I won't get to it until next April. [. . .] Did you know, by the way, that I'm now on the programming committee of the Allgemeine D[eutsche] Musikverein? The affair has caused me a great deal of work. The quality of the pieces sent in was, again, frightful. My proposal to perform Schoenberg without him entering it was turned down. [Karl] Weigl's [First] Symphony has been accepted.[27]

The summer vacation was spent at Bad Ischl, correcting orchestral parts for
Stuttgart (as with *Der Traumgörge*, they were teeming with errors)[28] and completing the score of Psalm 23. Time also had to be found for the pilgrimage to
Munich where, on 12 September, Mahler conducted the world première of his
Eighth Symphony. In the autumn Schoenberg took up a new teaching post at
the Academy of Music, and Zemlinsky was invited to adjudicate in the
Academy's annual composition competitions – appointments made on the initiative of the new Director, Wilhelm Bopp. Vienna's most obdurately tradition-
alist musical institution was gradually moving into the twentieth century.

As far as the new opera was concerned, things began to go wrong: further
resistance to the piece by the Stuttgart ensemble made it impossible to go ahead
with the première, and even the Volksoper had to postpone its production.
Simons kept his word, however, and on 2 December the curtain rose on *Kleider
machen Leute*. Due to the débâcle of *Der Traumgörge*, it was the first time that
Vienna had heard an opera of Zemlinsky's in nine years, indeed the first time
that he had presented anything new at all since 1905. No longer the talented
newcomer, no longer Mahler's protégé, he was now too modern to be dismissed
as old-fashioned, but too conservative to become a *cause célèbre*. The critics
could find no convenient peg on which to hang him. Instead they let him fall.

This is by no means the appropriate place for music that requires analysis. And for
brevity, which as everyone knows is the soul of wit, he simply lacks the gift.[29]

Zemlinsky's music is so skilful, so richly stocked with erudite ideas, that the light,
innocuous story becomes unnaturally weighted down.[30]

This method of composition has one defect: it addresses the mind and is starved of
natural feeling [*Gemüt*]. To the devil with intellect! We want more melody![31]

One of the few still prepared to speak out in his favour was Rudolf Stephan
Hoffmann:

A highly gifted composer applies his immense talent and brilliant technique to a
story about a poor, honest, hard-working and undervalued tailor's apprentice, in
whom perhaps he has discovered something of himself. Thus the music permits rich
insights into a fascinating personality. It is wrong to confuse individuality of melodic
style with poverty of melodic invention. In truth, the opera is composed entirely of
melody [. . .]

And his review ended with harsh words to his colleagues:

Is the opera really so insignificant that it can be dismissed, as has become habitual
in certain critical quarters, with frosty obeisance or foolish jests? Do we really possess such an abundance of creative talents that we have to make life a misery for
each of them in turn?[32]

Life with the Korngolds

Another staunch supporter of *Kleider machen Leute* was Julius Korngold, who had succeeded Eduard Hanslick as chief critic of the *Neue Freie Presse* in 1903. In substance, his review differed only slightly from those of his colleagues, but where they had damned with faint praise, Korngold praised with implicit approval and respect:

All in all, *Kleider machen Leute* is the work of an artist of fine-nerved sensibility, a brilliant writer of musical prose who repeatedly rises to moments of inventive and perceptive musical poetry. As such, it stands head and shoulders above all other operatic music currently circulating in the German-speaking world.[33]

Like most critics of his generation, he readily acknowledged the mastery of Brahms and Wagner in their individual fields; in all other respects he continued in the erudite, authoritative and outspokenly conservative tradition of his predecessor. For Julius Korngold, Mahler do could no wrong, and in the summer of 1907, on the day of Mahler's resignation from the Hofoper, he was heard to exclaim, 'Whoever his successor is, we shall finish him off.'[34] It came almost as an embarrassment to discover that his own son, Erich, was a child prodigy. To make a success of the boy's career, Julius was obliged to jeopardize his supposedly unimpeachable position as a journalist; Erich, conversely, suffered frequent setbacks and embarrassments occasioned by his father's sharp pen and vitriolic tongue.

From the age of nine, the 'little' Korngold, as he became known, studied counterpoint with Robert Fuchs. The teacher–pupil relationship proved unproductive, however, and in the summer of 1907 the twelve-year-old was taken to play his compositions to Mahler. Deeply impressed, he recommended that the boy be taken to the best teacher he knew: Zemlinsky. Lessons in 'harmony, form, voice-leading and, above all, piano playing', began the following year:

My young imagination was captured by a teacher who, with his fabulous musicianship, with the originality of his opinions and convictions, with his mildly sarcastic manner of speech and behaviour, exuded an implicit authority and soon won my deepest affection.[35]

Under Zemlinsky's supervision he composed a Passacaglia in D minor on a given seven-bar theme (published, at Mahler's suggestion, as the finale of the Piano Sonata op. 1), the Second Sonata in E major, which he dedicated to his teacher, and the *Märchenbilder* op. 3, delightful miniatures on themes from children's stories, including *Wichtelmännlein* ('The Pixy'), perhaps facetiously intended as a portrait of his teacher, and *Das tapfere Schneiderlein* ('The Courageous Little Tailor'), based on the tale by Andersen.

Zemlinsky categorically refused to show the boy his own new work. '"You're a griper," he would say with a smile.'*[36] It seems more likely that he was concerned to let the boy develop a personal style, free of extraneous influence. That he nevertheless brought his influence to bear on Korngold is undeniable.

I later realized [wrote Korngold] that he was going through a sort of artistic crisis of self-assertion against the new and seductively radical theories of Arnold Schoenberg, his much-admired brother-in-law, since for him it was fundamentally impossible to suppress an instinctive feeling for tonality. [. . .] At that time, in 1910, he was composing with an enthrallingly individual style of harmony and melody, which already displayed a tendency towards modern French music and Schoenbergian 4ths.

In 1910, orchestration was added to the curriculum. Before beginning his tuition with Zemlinsky, Korngold had composed a short dance-pantomime for two pianos on a *commedia dell'arte* story entitled *Der Schneemann*. On the understanding that the work should not be performed publicly in Vienna, his father had arranged with Universal Edition to publish a two-handed version for private circulation. In April 1910, however, Erich played the piece at a charity gala hosted by Baroness Bienerth, wife of the Austrian prime minister. Count Montenuovo, who was present, was so taken with the work that he drew Weingartner's attention to it; he in turn immediately made arrangements for the ballet to be staged at the Hofoper. Though genuinely impressed by Erich's prodigious talent, Weingartner had also found a golden opportunity to embarrass Korngold's father, who was doing his best, as promised, to 'finish off' Mahler's successor in the columns of his paper. Julius Korngold took the unprecedented step of calling at the Hofoper in an attempt to have the project called off, but Weingartner also remained adamant, assuring him that father and son were for him 'two entirely distinct personalities'.[37] Since Erich was deemed too inexperienced, Zemlinsky was commissioned to orchestrate the piece, a task he accomplished with customary aplomb in a matter of days. Delightfully choreographed, and with entrancing designs by Heinrich Lefler, the première on 4 October 1910 (the Kaiser's name-day and, as it happened, Zemlinsky's 'official' thirty-ninth birthday) was an unqualified success. The ballet became a mainstay of the repertoire, with thirty-one performances between 1910 and 1919 and a revival, with new sets and costumes, in 1933. At the Hofoper (or the Staatsoper, as it was renamed after the fall of the Austrian monarchy), no original score of Zemlinsky's ever enjoyed anything approaching such success.

Those close to Korngold were astounded to observe the rapidity and ease

---

* The shrewdness of his judgement is proved by a comment made by the 'little' Korngold before a performance of *Kleider machen Leute*, reported seven years later by Alban Berg: 'If this opera doesn't come up to scratch either, I'll throw him out for good' (Berg, *Briefe an seine Frau* (Vienna, 1965), 352).

with which a boy scarcely in his teens could grasp the most complex of harmonic and contrapuntal procedures, master the art of post-Romantic orchestration and develop an individual sense of form. He was not content, however, to play at mimicking his elders. As a child, his nerves were anything but 'sickly and delicate': the overriding affect of his music was joy. Not for him the introspection and ecstasy of a Zemlinsky; to scale heights of passion or plumb depths of despair was foreign to his nature. In emulation of his teacher, he devised a musical monogram, to which he adhered throughout his career, long after the thrills of fame and early success had faded. Unlike Zemlinsky, however, who kept his small treasure of ciphers and symbols a closely guarded secret, Korngold blazoned the motto, complete with identifying tag, on the title page of his first major orchestral work, the Sinfonietta op. 5, composed in 1911–13. His 'motif of a joyous heart', an ascending flourish of 4ths –

EX. 38A

– appears to have found its inspiration in the bucolic polka of the village band in *Kleider machen Leute*:*

EX. 38B

Though temperamentally quite unlike his teacher, Korngold adhered his life long to the techniques learned during his boyhood. In the film studio, developing variation proved an invaluable aid to musical unity; in his hands the lush clarity of Zemlinsky's orchestral sound became the hallmark of Hollywood at its most glorious.

---

* Since F♯ major was as much Korngold's home key as D minor was Zemlinsky's, the 'motif of a joyous heart' often appears at the pitches of EX. 38A. In the G major third movement of the Sinfonietta, however, which shows evidence of having been influenced by Zemlinsky's Psalm 23, Korngold introduces the motif, in the bass line, to the pitches of EX. 38B, bar 2 (i.e. D–G–E–A–D).

The Volksoper (III)

For obscure contractual reasons, Simons became involved in litigation with the tenants of the Jubiläumstheater; indeed during the course of the 1910–11 season he was given summary notice to quit.[38] The dismissal was promptly revoked, and he remained in office for a further seven years, but at the time he was in no position to renew contracts or offer his artists better conditions. Zemlinsky, though musical director in all but name, had therefore to content himself with a contract that defined his position only as *Kapellmeister*. Since his first concern was financial stability for himself and his family, the uncertainty of his future at the Volksoper was just as influential on his decision to leave Vienna as the apathy towards his music shown by the press.

By now relations with Schoenberg had reached a low ebb. Their communal lifestyle in the Liechtensteinstrasse having been wrecked by the Gerstl affair, towards the end of 1908 the Schoenbergs moved to the outlying suburb of Hietzing. In the spring of 1910 the Zemlinskys also moved house, but just a few hundred yards down the road, to Fuchstallergasse 4, a few paces from the stage door of the Volksoper.

Such close proximity can only have been to Zemlinsky's advantage, for during his last season in Vienna he spent most of his waking hours in the theatre, conducting 86 performances in seven months. His repertoire consisted of *Carmen* (10 performances), *Mignon* (9), *Die lustigen Weiber von Windsor* (9), *La juive* (8) *Lohengrin* (7), *Kleider machen Leute* (6), *Die Zauberflöte* (5), *Tannhäuser* (4), *Le prophète* (3), Gounod's *Faust* (with Maria Jeritza as Marguerite; 3) *Fidelio** (2) and the most spectacular production of the season, *Salome*, which opened on 23 December and within four months was given no fewer than 21 times.[†]

For Simons this *Salome* production was a strategical triumph. Even before the world première of the opera, at Dresden on 9 December 1905, Mahler had expressed his resolve to stage the work at the Hofoper; indeed he had consulted Strauss on casting the major roles, and avidly studied the score. On 8 October Strauss was therefore surprised to receive a perfunctory note from Simons:

I have just heard that your work *Salome* will not be passed by the censor at the Hofoper. Please be so kind as to let me know whether you will now be prepared to entrust the work to me.[39]

This was the first he had heard of Mahler's battle with the censor, which had

---

* In place of the *Fidelio* overture Zemlinsky substituted the overture *Leonore* no. 3.
† The title role was sung by Clothilde Wenger, later also by Maria Jeritza; Zemlinsky conducted all but one of the performances. The most successful production of the season was not *Salome*, but *Quo Vadis?*, an opera by Jean Nouguès based on the famous novel by Heinrich Sienkiewicz. It was performed over thirty times.

actually been raging for several months. Somewhat bemused, he passed the letter on to Mahler, who greeted the Volksoper initiative with the glee of an experienced theatrical conniver. 'Dear friend!' he wrote to Strauss –

For me this letter is *most opportune*! *Salome* at the Jubiläumstheater may be *quite impossible*, but my plan now is to present the performance *as a possibility*. – If necessary, you will have to support me and even *pretend to negotiate*. – Faced with such an ultimatum, I expect that even our sagacious censor will be prepared to make concessions.[40]

But Mahler was wrong. Gradually he realized that the official line on *Salome*, though ostensibly motivated by public morality and Catholic sensibility, was actually dictated by intrigue in higher court circles. To struggle against such invisible enemies was futile; ultimately he had no choice but to admit defeat and take his bow.

As long as Mahler was in office, however, Strauss was not even prepared to countenance a production at the Volksoper. Hence the Austrian première of *Salome* was given not in Vienna but in Graz, on 16 May 1906, and the first Viennese performance, on 25 May 1907, was given neither at the Hofoper nor at the Volksoper, but at the Deutsches Volkstheater, by the theatre company from Breslau conducted by Theodor Löwe. On 24 March 1909 the Hofoper staged the Viennese première of *Elektra*, but Weingartner disliked the piece and delegated the production to Reichenberger. Simons seized his opportunity and approached Strauss once again. Strauss now agreed without further demur, setting his seal of approval on the venture by conducting the penultimate performance, on 9 April 1911, in person.*

Unobtrusively, on 29 April, with a performance of *Tannhäuser*, Zemlinsky bade the Volksoper farewell. He never conducted there again.

Mahler: The Final Years

Two weeks later, on 12 May, Mahler returned to Vienna. Six days later he was dead. Since leaving Austria, his contact with Zemlinsky had inevitably become sporadic. 'What are you and Schoenberg doing? I should be glad of some news,' he had written from New York in March 1908. 'But don't reply to this letter – I shall be arriving in Vienna at the beginning of May and will come and see you at once.'[41] That summer, Zemlinsky was again a guest at Maiernigg, where Mahler asked him to prepare the piano-duet version of the Seventh Symphony. In the event, the commission was transferred to Casella, but Zemlinsky still found time to attend the final rehearsal for the Viennese première of the work, on 3 November 1909, with the orchestra of the Konzertverein conducted by Ferdinand Löwe. In a letter to Alma in New York, he formulated with characteristic terseness his opinion of both work and performance:

* *Salome* was not staged at the Hofoper (meanwhile renamed the Staatsoper) until 1918.

Once again, strangely, it made the same impression on me as earlier in Maiernigg. The 1st, 2nd and 3rd movements went wonderfully; the finest, despite unclear interpretation, were the 1st and 3rd. – I didn't get on so well with the 4th, which I liked very well, by the way, or the finale. – This is just a fleeting, superficial judgement, but in words I can do no better.[42]

Apologizing for not writing more frequently, his letter opened with a touching declaration of friendship:

The way I treat my few friends is certainly inattentive and careless, but that doesn't mean that I'm any less fond of them than before. Perhaps during these dreadful times I have changed, grown more diffident, more suspicious and above all less communicative, hence apparently less open-hearted, but my love and reverence for these few people has not diminished on that account. You and Director Mahler can be certain for all time of my unbounded admiration and love – come what may, no matter what impression I might give you.[43]

He had read a press announcement, emanating from a news agency in Paris, that Mahler was working on an opera entitled *Theseus*.[44] 'Is it true?' he asked. 'Certainly not! But I'd still like to hear about it.'[45] A *démenti* was published three weeks later:*

Much as the idea appeals to him, [Director Mahler . . .] has at present neither time nor inclination to compose a large-scale dramatic work, and he will be quite satisfied, considering the wide range of his conducting activities, if his 'symphonic goals' can be attained in the manner he visualizes.[46]

Perhaps Alma clarified the situation in her next letter, explaining that the hero of Mahler's early libretto was not Theseus but Odysseus. At any rate, for Zemlinsky the Homeric legend became subconsciously linked to the concept of transatlantic travel. When he himself arrived in New York in 1938, a fugitive, the idea came to fruition in his last operatic project, *Circe*.

With Max Reinhardt in Munich

In the summer of 1911 Zemlinsky came into contact with an artist who, like Korngold, was later to leave an indelible impression on Hollywood: Max Reinhardt. Their collaboration centred on a festival of operetta in Munich, from June to September, at the Munich Künstlertheater (known today, in honour of Luitpold, as the Prinzregententheater). For *Orphée aux enfers*, which

---

* Mahler had asked his sister Justine to send him the manuscript of an early opera libretto, *Die Argonauten*. He received it in Hamburg, shortly before sailing for the US, on 8 November 1908. 'I read it for half an hour, as if spellbound,' he wrote to Alma (cf. Henry-Louis de La Grange and Günther Weiss (eds.) *Ein Glück uhne Ruh'. Die Briefe Gustav Mahlers an Alma* (Berlin, 1995), 371–2). During the voyage, he allegedly threw the manuscript into the sea. How the press came to hear of the story is unclear.

opened on 5 September, Reinhardt and his company, augmented by cohorts of can-can dancers, choristers and supernumeraries, and with an orchestra of 97, moved into the Musikfesthalle, where the previous year Mahler had conducted his 'Symphony of a Thousand'.

The season began on 30 June with *La belle Hélène*;* Fritzi Massary and Maria Jeritza alternated in the title role, and the production ran for 67 performances. 'What a blessing at last to hear this delightful score with a good orchestra [. . .] and a real conductor,' wrote the critic of *Die Musik*, Edgar Istel.[47] And Zemlinsky expressed his delight, in a letter to Schoenberg, at the 'estimation and respect' shown to him as 'someone who knows his job':

They want me to compose something for the coming season, which would be staged with first-class décor. They are also thinking of entrusting me with the post of Chief Artistic Director (in place of Reinhardt)![48]

Under congenial working conditions, even operetta could be palatable. On 21 July followed *Themidore*, a 'love play' in three acts to a text by F. Steffan with music by Digby La Touche.† According to press reports, Zemlinsky orchestrated the work;[49] from a letter to Schoenberg it transpires that he was also commissioned to make 'several alterations' to the score, for which he received a fee of 500 Marks.[50] Compared with Vienna, this was a princely sum; moreover the closed-pit design of the Künstlertheater, modelled on the Festspielhaus in Bayreuth, allowed him to pass the baton to his assistant whenever he felt the urge. Even so, one such piece was enough:

The next novelty, which is even more ghastly than *Themidor* [sic], I simply refused to conduct. In consequence, the directors were summoned to a committee meeting & the novelty was – cancelled. It will be replaced now, instead of in September, by *Orpheus*.[51]

Since Reinhardt was running the season on private capital, the production of *Themidore* was a financial necessity. A director of his calibre would not have squandered his time on such trifles had the production not guaranteed the support of an influential firm of theatre publishers – and doubtless their munificent sponsorship.

Together with Bodanzky and his family, who had travelled down from

---

* The revival of a production from Berlin, rehearsed by Reinhardt's assistant Berthold Held.
† The source was a celebrated erotic novel of the Napoleonic era, Claude Godard d'Aucour's *Themidore ou mon histoire et celle de ma maîtresse* (Paris, 1763); in press reports and other printed sources for the operetta, orthographical variants included *Themèdore* and *Thermidor*. F. Steffan (whose real name, it appears, was Sobotka) owned a large Berlin brewery and was co-director of a theatrical publishing house, Drei Masken Verlag. *Themidore* was written with the help of the popular Austrian humorist Roda Roda, but he withdrew from the project before it was completed. The Irish composer (Richard) Digby La Touche was descended from a family of bankers from Co. Wicklow. Fragments of a manuscript vocal score of *Themidore* act II are preserved in the Zemlinsky Collection (*LoC*, 18/8).

Mannheim, Zemlinsky had rented a small house in Berg on the Starnberger See, a few miles from the city centre.

I'm not working on anything [he wrote to Schoenberg] except the proofs of the vocal score of 'Kleid. m. Leute', which, at last, is definitely going to be published. The heat is simply too dreadful and prevents one from starting anything useful. We spend all our time bathing in the lake. Hansi too, of course, who loves every minute of it.[52]

Quite unexpectedly, on 4 August, the Schoenbergs arrived from Vienna. Trudi, who was now nine years old, had been discovered playing 'doctors and nurses' with the young son of their landlord in Hietzing. This man, Philip von Wouvermans, used the incident as an excuse for regaling his tenants with anti-Semitic abuse; Schoenberg in turn had defended his rights by threatening him with a pistol. Since mid-July the situation had become intolerable; before it escalated any further, he fled.[53] All but penniless, he and his family moved in with the Zemlinskys. Weeks of trepidation followed, while Schoenberg cast around for some new means of subsistence. Not until the end of September, when Alfred Kerr, seconded by Ferruccio Busoni, Oskar Fried, Artur Schnabel and Edward Clark, made arrangements for him and his family to settle in Berlin, was he able to venture forth from his lakeside refuge.

Another troubled soul arrived in Starnberg a few days later: Otto Klemperer. The twenty-six-year-old *Kapellmeister* was recovering from a severe depression, which had caused him to interrupt his conducting career at the Hamburg Stadttheater. After treatment at a sanatorium near Frankfurt and sojourns in Strasbourg and Lausanne, he had written to Oskar Fried in search of short-term employment. Fried, who was a close associate of Reinhardt, secured him a commission to compose incidental music for a new production of the *Oresteia* of Aeschylus, due to open in the Künstlertheater at the end of August. Klemperer set to work in early July, and when he arrived in Munich on 12 August the score was already complete. Having found lodgings at Feldafing, on the opposite side of the lake, he doubtless lost little time in calling on Zemlinsky, for it was he who was to conduct the new score.

Klemperer was well acquainted with Bodanzky, for they had worked together for two seasons in Prague; to Zemlinsky and the other members of the household, however, he was a newcomer. Due to Schoenberg's nervous condition and Klemperer's unstable temperament, the situation was tense. Klemperer found Schoenberg 'proud and distant'; Schoenberg, for his part, passed a 'distinctly unappreciative' judgement on Klemperer's music.[54] Admittedly, the *Oresteia* music had been written at lightning speed and (according to Peter Heyworth) 'in a mildly manic condition',[55] but Zemlinsky supported it to the last. Yet to no avail: it was abandoned before the opening night and never seen or heard of again. Many years later, Klemperer was still unwilling to discuss the episode.

The affair did have one positive outcome, however: the bond of friendship extended to him *in angustiis* by Zemlinsky proved durable and mutual.

Several other friends and acquaintances visited Munich that summer: Paul Stefan, who was writing a book on Mahler,[56] Richard Strauss, who was conducting a festival of Mozart opera in the Residenztheater, and Oskar Fried, who introduced himself to Zemlinsky at a banquet and talked at length about Schoenberg's *Pelleas und Melisande*, which he had conducted in Berlin the previous October.[57] As Max Reinhardt's son Gottfried recalls,

At the rehearsals of *La belle Hélène* one often saw a fourteen-year-old pupil of the conductor Alexander von Zemlinsky. The latter used to say, however, that he had nothing more to teach him, and if anyone still had anything to learn, then it was he from his pupil. His name: Erich Wolfgang Korngold. [. . .] At the time, admittedly, nobody ever imagined that Korngold would one day become Reinhardt's closest musical collaborator.[58]

As so often, Zemlinsky's jest contained a seed of bitterness. At fourteen, Korngold had already acquired the knack of being in the right place at the right time, of winning friends and influencing people, of taking his wares to market and selling them at a good price – aspects of art his teacher never succeeded in mastering.

Beside the Still Waters

On 14 October 1910 Zemlinsky entered his fortieth year. During the past decade he had lost the greatest love of his life and entered into a marital relationship that left him unfulfilled; his daughter had been born handicapped, his mother had grown old and frail, his sister was living a life of anxiety with a suspicious husband, and his friendship with Schoenberg, shaken by the Gerstl affair and complicated by growing artistic differences, had begun to cool. Since the turn of the century his path to fame and fortune had grown tortuous. He had watched men of lesser talent rising to positions of influence and prosperity, while he, both as composer and as performing artist, continued to languish in obscurity. With Dante, he might have said,

Nel mezzo del cammin di nostra vita / mi ritrovai per una selva oscura / ché la diritta via era smarrita.

Midway upon our life's journey / I found myself in a dark forest, / for the straight pathway had been lost.[59]

In 1908 the three largest Viennese choral societies amalgamated to form a new, imposing body of singers, the Philharmonic Choir. Schreker left the Volksoper in mid-season to become its musical director, and as far as possible he resolved to include at least one contemporary work in every concert.

Asked to write a short piece for the Philharmonic Choir, Zemlinsky unhesitatingly chose Psalm 23. He sketched out the short score in July 1910 and, between sessions of proof-reading *Kleider machen Leute*, completed the orchestration the following month. Thus in December he was able to present three significant new scores to the Viennese public in quick succession: *Kleider machen Leute*, given six times at the Volksoper, Psalm 23 premièred by Schreker at the Musikverein on 10 December,* and the first four Maeterlinck songs (composed immediately after the Psalm), which received their first public performance the following evening.

Just as *Der Traumgörge* offers the key to Zemlinsky's stage works, Psalm 23 stands at the focal point of his music for the concert hall, as the most complete and concise representation of his art. As such, it was only logical that he should choose verses that stand at the centre of both Jewish and Christian doctrines, a psalm that pays homage to Yahweh in all his five aspects: the good shepherd, the provider of worldly needs, the God of peace, the God of healing, the God of righteousness.

The work is a fascinating hybrid, at once sacred and secular, subjective and objective. While never entirely masking a deep-seated spirit of contemplation, the text is clad in the rich colours of an imaginary temple music. With a bright-sounding array of flutes, harps, celesta, glockenspiel, triangle and cymbals, Zemlinsky relives childhood memories of the sunlight that flooded into the synagogue through high stained-glass windows set into the dome.† The stately processional of the opening section and the coda, with its symmetrically structured walking bass (formed from the D–E–G of the 'Self' motif), opens with a pentatonic oboe solo, a sub- or semi-conscious recollection of the wedding anthem that he had once composed for the cantor's daughter (EXX. 39A and B) but which also recalls the music for the Youth in *The Triumph of Time*, that 'powerfully amorous waltz motif' with which Zemlinsky painted his idealized self-portrait (EX. 39C).

The principal key of Psalm 23 is G major, 'the key of the victor' (Ullmann) and the 'yellow' key, whose attributes, according to Goethe's *Theory of Colour*, are 'serenity, cheerfulness and gentle delight'. As in Psalm 83, the writing is largely polyphonic, but the Brahmsian manner and self-consciously learned forms of the earlier work are now supplanted by the flexible counterpoint of *Der Traumgörge*. A comparable grace and natural flow prevails in the harmony, which moves logically from pentatonicism through diatonicism to free, tonally

---

* Psalm 23, which runs for *c*.12 minutes, was dwarfed at least quantitatively by the other item on the programme, *Gloria!* by Jean Louis Nicodé, a 2½-hour symphonic ode for alto solo, men's voices, organ and orchestra.
† As daily reminder of his musical roots, Zemlinsky needed look no further than the orchestra of the Volksoper, where he could call on the services of Franz Moser, the same harpist who twenty years before, in duet with his wife, had joined him to make music at the Sephardic Synagogue. In the orchestration of Psalm 23 the two harps take pride of place.

EX. 39   (A) *Hochzeitsgesang* (1896); (B) Psalm 23, opening phrase

He who is supremely praised, He who is supremely great.

EX. 39C   *Ein Tanzpoem* (1901/1904)

unstable chromaticism, before culminating in the (Masonic) grandeur of E♭ major. The coda then returns to the serene G major of the opening.

During the course of the work it becomes apparent that the pentatonic oboe motif of EX. 39 (2–3–6) serves as a preliminary or condensed variant of the 'Görge' motif (ex. 25). The 'Görge' motif itself is introduced in the violas, two bars before the first chorus entry, but only once. In the final moments of the piece, to the words 'Goodness and mercy shall follow me all the days of my life', it reappears, talisman-like, in fivefold reiteration. Each of these five iterations is differently harmonized, and while the first four – *pp* in octaves on trumpet and horn – emerge only indistinctly through the choral sound, like a distant fanfare, the fifth stands alone, mysterious in pastel shades of flute and clarinets in their lowest register. The mystery of this fifth iteration also lies in its mathematics, a pattern of semitones arranged to form a sequence of 9th chords. While the bass line asymmetrically mirrors the motif, the inner parts open and close, fan-like, in symmetrical array:

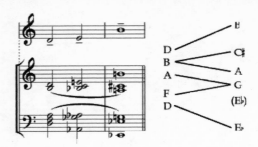

EX. 40

With these three sphinx-like chords Görge himself traverses the valley of the shadow of death. The double-bar marks the frontier: 'So far and no further.' No Dream-Princess awaits him beside the still waters of his millstream. Her miracle-world lies far ahead, at the end of life's journey.

V

Surface and Symbol

All art is at once surface and symbol. Those who go beneath the surface do so at their peril. Those who read the symbol do so at their peril.

Oscar Wilde, *The Picture of Dorian Gray*

Observe, however, that of man's terrestrial possessions and attainments, unspeakably the noblest are his Symbols, divine or divine-seeming.

Thomas Carlyle, *The French Revolution*

On 9 June 1917 Zemlinsky conducted a concert in Prague with just two works on the programme: Bach's Concerto for three pianos (BWV 1063) and Beethoven's 'Choral' Symphony – both in D minor. 'Was this a coincidence?' asked the critic of the *Prager Tagblatt*, Erich Rychnovsky. Having closely observed Zemlinsky as composer and interpreter over a period of six years, he felt qualified to answer the question himself:

The devotees of key-affect might look for some profound mystery in such programming; in search of a solution to the riddle, they might even seek out Schumann's passage on choice of key, written three generations ago. Those who know Zemlinsky's ways, and are aware that *he is an artist who does nothing that is not carefully considered*,* might be able to divine his intentions.[1]

To the musical scholar Zemlinsky's scores open up a broad field for historical, analytical and aesthetical evaluation; to the stage director his operas present a detailed psychogram of *homo austriacus* in the era of Sigmund Freud; for the interpreter and listener perhaps the most immediately striking attributes of his music are its textural richness and emotional intensity. But there is a further aspect to his art, which to him was evidently as essential as all else: the use of secret symbols. Awareness of their presence neither enhances nor detracts from appreciation of the music, and to go beneath the surface in search of them may be perilous – but to ignore them on that ground alone would be to disregard a salient aspect of the creative process and, ultimately, to misconstrue the message of the music.

Since time immemorial, numerologists have postulated that everything under the sun can be expressed as number, a notion that in the age of digitalization has been amply verified. Yet many musicologists are still unwilling to accept the study of numerical symbols as a valid tool of their trade, particularly when applied to music of the Romantic and post-Romantic eras. Hans Heinz Stuckenschmidt complained of this in 1957:

Our predominantly emotional view of nineteenth-century music has suppressed our awareness of its symbols. Whoever draws attention to the existence of such phenomena is greeted with an undertone of condescension and contempt, as if people who indulged in such superstitious practices could not be taken entirely seriously. [. . .]

* Author's italics.

Masters of such legendary repute as Pérotin, Guillaume de Machaut, Dufay and Josquin Desprez played outlandish and devout glass-bead games of notation, but our later, emotional attitudes towards music have actively hindered their acceptance.[2]

Ten years later, the discovery of a score of Berg's Lyric Suite, marked up with the composer's authentic and exhaustive exposition of the work's hidden numerical symbols,[3] offered irrefutable proof of creative processes whose very existence had in many quarters long been denied or, at best, dismissed as irrelevant. Zemlinsky, to whom the Lyric Suite was dedicated, left no comparable traveller's guide to any of his works – at least, none that has so far come to light – but he delighted in scattering hints and veiled allusions. No particular psychic ability is needed to divine the presence of his secret messages or even to intercept them; reading them is far harder. A close examination of the creative processes nevertheless reveals that this invisible area of his art testifies no less than the visible area to a musician 'who does nothing that is not carefully considered'.

The rise of the *ars nova* coincided in Spain with an upsurge of interest in cabbala, the 'secret wisdom'. Cabbala, a study of the Holy Word, seeks to explain the Creation as a process involving the ten divine numbers of God (*Sefirot*) and the twenty-two letters of the Hebrew alphabet. During the thirteenth century, under the leadership of Moses de Léon, the *Spharadim* became leaders in this field, and in exile cabbala study remained widespread within their communities.

Despite his part-Sephardic ancestry, Zemlinsky is unlikely to have possessed any detailed knowledge of cabbala;* nevertheless, his early education in *Torah* and *Tefillot* will have provided him with a basic understanding of its concepts and, perhaps, of its technical principles. Over the centuries, superstition and mystical speculation gave rise to various alternative systems of number interpretation, many of which are still in use today. Some of these are closely related to the authentic cabbala, others make use of basic cabbalistic techniques but also include elements drawn from Hinduism, Buddhism, Rosicrucianism, the Tarot and the Book of Revelation. This layman's cabbala, as practised by astrologers, soothsayers and other devotees of the esoteric, was probably the variety with which Zemlinsky was better familiar.

Of the three methods of cabbalistic textual analysis, the best-known and most universally applied is *Gematria* (substitution of numerical values for letters), a technique familiar to and frequently employed by Bach.† Schumann developed its principles to evolve his own musical alphabet, with which he incorporated a diversity of secret messages in his music,[4] and from him the

---

* According to Jewish tradition, only men over forty years of age were eligible for cabbala study.
† Only with the advent of composition with twelve semitones, as evolved by Hauer and Schoenberg, did it become possible to apply other cabbalistic techniques, *Notariqon* (acrostical permutation) and *Temura* (anagrammatical permutation), to music.

concept, if not the technique, was passed on to Brahms. Brahms appears to have made no use of *Gematria* in the stricter sense, however, and, apart from adopting Schumann's 'Clara' motif, confined his ciphers to simple letter combinations, notably 'F–A–F' and 'F–A–E'. Musical research has paid little attention to this aspect of his art,[5] yet a summary inspection of just one work, the D minor Violin Sonata, indicates that much still awaits discovery and evaluation:

EX. 41   Brahms: Violin Sonata op. 108

Where Brahms took delight in such devices, it seems plausible that Zemlinsky should have followed his example. Unlike the ciphers of Brahms, however, his 'Self' motif and its derivates do not represent specific letters of the alphabet. In many instances the motif appears as the pitch-class D–E–G, i.e. (taking C as the first step of the scale) 2–3–5; sometimes this numerical sequence is transformed into rhythm, for instance as groups of 2(5+3) quavers. Obscured by the context of triplet movement, a rhythmic symbol of this variety is first hinted at in the opening bars of the Clarinet Trio (EX. 6, piano part). It appears undisguised, towards the end of the development section, in the piano right hand, while the cello articulates groups of 2+3+3 semiquavers and the piano left hand augments the same figure to groups of [2]+3+3 quavers:

EX. 42   Clarinet Trio op. 3, bars 128–31

As principal theme of *Ein Tanzpoem* – the 'motif of the mysterious, unceasing flow of time' – the rhythmic formula 2(5+3) acquires even greater prominence (EX. 10).

Since the 2–3–5 sequence is freely transposable, it clearly can bear no alphabetical connotation. However, this does not rule out the possibility that its origin could be found in an alphabetical sequence. Bearing in mind that many composers, from the Bach family to Shostakovich, have incorporated musical transliterations of their names in their music, the first step must be to examine the names 'Zemlinsky', 'Alexander Zemlinsky', 'Z–E–M', or even 'S–E–M' (the three letters common to both 'Semo' and 'Semlinsky') for possible numerical transliterations. When applying popular *Gematria* to names, numerologists consult equivalence tables already known to the ancients, the most common of which are the Cheiro system, based on the relationship of the letters of the Hebrew alphabet to the numbers 1 to 8, and the Pythagoratic, based on the numbers 1 to 9 and the Greek alphabet. In Zemlinsky's case, neither system offers any viable solution,* nor does the simple extrapolation of usable notes of the scale, as practised by Berg in his Chamber Concerto, lead to any meaningful result.

When Zemlinsky went on stage to take his bow at the world première of *Sarema* in 1897, his youthful appearance was commented on in the Munich press with surprise and admiration.[6] Although there was clearly no necessity to make himself any younger than he already was, during the later 1890s he changed his year of birth, whenever cited in biographical notes, almanacs or musical dictionaries, from 1871 to 1872, and moved the date forward by ten days, from 14 to 4 October. Like the *Adelsprädikat* of his name, this fictitious

* The numerical values of E and M, 5 and 4, are common to both systems.

date of birth must have been inspired by a spirit of artistic licence – the numerical equivalent of a pseudonym,* a fact of which those closer to him were well aware.† The apparent error, which meanwhile had crept into numerous lexica and other works of reference, was corrected by researchers in the early 1970s.[7] However, no attempt was made to explain it.

But there is an explanation, and it proves the accuracy of Rychnowsky's remark that Zemlinsky did nothing 'that was not carefully considered'. The true date and false date are interrelated, namely, in that the sum of their integers is identical:

$$(1+4) + (1+0) + (1+8+7+1) = 4 + (1+0) + (1+8+7+2) = 23$$

Following numerological practice, this process of integer summation is repeated until only one integer remains, which is the secret or cardinal number. In this case

$$2 + 3 = 5$$

Thus the origin of the 2–3–5 sequence stands revealed. As it happens, the integer sum of 14, the day of Zemlinsky's birth, is identical:

$$1 + 4 = 5$$

According to secular cabbala, this convergence of two numbers on the secret number 5 could be interpreted as follows:

1 א *aleph* power 4 ד *daleth* imagination	5 ה *he* reason	2 ב *beth* attention 3 ג *gimel* memory

In other words, 'power of imagination', attribute of the creative artist, and 'attention' and 'memory', attributes essential to the performing artist, emanate from or together lead to 'reason' or 'logic'. Analogous to Shem Tov Semo's dictum, that 'education is the mother of enlightenment and civilization', these values could be expressed as a metaphysical equation –

Logic is the mother of imagination and awareness

– a reflection of Zemlinsky's ideal of equilibrium between expressive freedom and technical discipline.

---

* The false date appears to have first been made public in a biographical note on the composer in the programme book for the world première of *Frühlingsbegräbnis* (11 February 1900).
† E.g. the special number of *Der Auftakt*, issued to mark Zemlinsky's fiftieth birthday, which was published at the correct time, in October 1921. On official documents such as passports, visa applications and tax forms, Zemlinsky invariably used his true date of birth.

The origin of the 2–3–5 sequence is thus explained, but it is still unclear why Zemlinsky felt any necessity to change his date of birth. No better explanation can be offered than to quote the opening words of *Der König Kandaules*:

Der, der ein Glück hält, soll sich gut verstecken! Und besser noch, sein Glück vor andern.

He who possesses fortune should hide himself well! And better still, hide his fortune from others.

Kandaules is the tragedy of a man who, instead of hiding his fortune, reveals it to the world and shares it over-generously with others. His fortune is thus defiled: a sin against destiny, for which the penalty is death. For Zemlinsky, whose trust in the power of destiny served as a substitute for more orthodox forms of religious belief, the act of falsifying or concealing his date of birth was a means of safeguarding his fortune.

Our frame of observation varies according to dogma or creed. To Zemlinsky, who stood between three faiths and adhered to none, his cardinal number, 5, was open to numerous numerological interpretations. As indivisible combination of the 'masculine' 3 and the 'feminine' 2, 5 is the number of love; as sum of the 'origin', 1, and of 'material order', 4, it is the number of power. The number 5 is sacred to both Jew and Christian, the number of the pentagram and of the wounds of Christ. According to the divine laws of cabbala, the fifth *Sefiroth*, or Quinquary, represents strength or fortitude, that creative energy which sets the world in motion:[8]

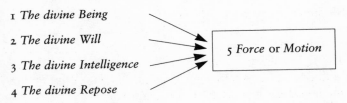

1 *The divine Being*

2 *The divine Will*

3 *The divine Intelligence*   5 *Force or Motion*

4 *The divine Repose*

Translated into musical terms, the sequence possesses a further paradoxical attribute: whether read as steps of the diatonic scale (2–3–5) or counted out in units of semitones, the pitch-class is the same:

whole-tone + minor 3rd = perfect 4th
2 semitones + 3 semitones = 5 semitones

No other three-note pitch-class possesses this particular form of ambiguity; it is a marvel of musical mathematics, unique to 2–3–5 and its permutations.

The number 5 itself, as a pitch-class, possesses comparable, magical properties. Read as an interval, it defines the perfect 5th; measured in semitones, it defines the perfect 4th: the one is the inversion of the other.

References to 14 in Zemlinsky's music assume varied forms. In some instances 14 determines the lengths of periods or phrases, in others it appears as a unit of semitones, i.e. the major 9th. On two occasions Zemlinsky quotes from or alludes to the Evening Prayer from *Hänsel und Gretel* (*Kleider machen Leute*, EX. 36, and *Das bucklichte Männlein*, EX. 78 bars 73–6). Thereby he invokes the *Vierzehnheiligen* (fourteen guardian angels) of German folk mythology:

Abends, will ich schlafen gehn, / Vierzehn Engel um mich stehn.

When at night I go to sleep / Fourteen angels watch do keep.[9]

In the Second Quartet Zemlinsky contrasts 14, as a period length, with 13, thus aligning his secret number with that of Schoenberg, to whom the work was dedicated.* This same juxtaposition, expressed intervallically, is also found in the opening bars of *Der König Kandaules*. The theme EX. 43A, which is built on a framework of 5s (perfect 4ths and 5ths), includes Zemlinsky's secret number in the rising major 9th C–D (14 semitones) and Schoenberg's in the falling phrase D–A–C♯ bounded by the minor 9th (13 semitones):

EX. 43

Zemlinsky also attached special significance to 14 in the calendar. It can scarcely have been coincidental that he completed the short score of *The Triumph of Time* on his birthday, that the orchestral score of *Kleider machen Leute* bears the date 14 October 1909, that *A Florentine Tragedy* was begun on 14 March 1915 and completed exactly twelve months later, or that the short score of *Der König Kandaules* was begun on 14 June 1935.

By nature of its cardinal significance, 5 often appears in the opening bars of Zemlinsky's compositions: the B♭ major Symphony opens with the perfect 5th F–B♭ as a fanfare, and 5, in its dual function as perfect 4th and perfect 5th, is prominent in every theme; both *Ein Tanzpoem* and *Die Seejungfrau* open with softly sustained perfect 5ths in a low register; in *Der Traumgörge* a pair of 5ths interlocks within the opening theme (EX. 25).

The Triumph of Time is permeated by 5. Both the 'Time' motif itself (EX. 10)

* E.g. the second-subject group, from 16 to the double-bar before 20, which consists of two sections of 14 bars (from 16 to 17⁻¹ and from *Tempo I* to the double-bar), framing two sections of 5 bars each. The Quartet ends with a 13-bar period, beginning at 112 (rehearsal numbers from the Philharmonia pocket score).

and the 'Signal' (EX. 11) are built from 5ths (the latter in combination with the 'World' motif), as are the musical self-portrait of the 'ardent youth' (EX. 39C) and the brass fanfare that opens the 'Dance of the Hours':

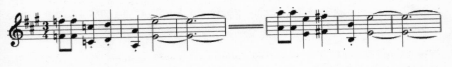

EX. 44

Of greater significance is the occurrence of five 5s, whether horizontally or vertically. The second chord of the motif of 'Man's Immortal Soul' in *Die Seejungfrau* (EX. 23), rearranged as Ab–Eb–Bb–F–C, forms such a sequence, a five-note 5ths chord. Another example is the fivefold repetition of the 'Görge' motif (see p. 193) in Psalm 23, Zemlinsky's personal prayer for 'Goodness and mercy'. And in the opening bars of *Kleider machen Leute* (EX. 32), ostensibly intended as a jovial allusion to Schoenberg's Chamber Symphony, one note of the original 4ths chord is omitted. Zemlinsky salutes his friend, but with an array of five 5ths in a row he also invokes his own lucky, five-pointed star.* It is not inconceivable that the irregular 4ths chord with which he signed his name on the manuscript of the ballad *Der verlorene Haufen* (see p. 267n) represents a 'disfigured' variant of the same idea.

In later incipits 5 remains prominent: the orchestral version of the first Maeterlinck song, written in 1913, prefaces the original piano version with a four-bar introduction of parallel 5ths; the opening trumpet fanfare of *A Florentine Tragedy* compresses a rising 5th and the 'World' motif into four notes; the opening theme of *Der Zwerg* is harmonized in parallel 5ths, the *Ballade* of the Sinfonietta is based on a motif of falling 5ths. But as Zemlinsky moves into new spheres of influence, his number symbolism grows more complex. By the early 1930s his system of relating pitch, rhythm and period to number has evolved to a secret language in its own right. Any attempt to 'read' this would indeed be perilous.

In cabbalistic systems of numerology, 23 possesses no designated attributes, which may explain why Zemlinsky consistently interpreted the number as the sum of its parts, 2 and 3. Nevertheless, he will have been aware that he shared his secret number with Berg. Nor will it have escaped Berg that Zemlinsky's date of birth stood in harmony with his own 'fateful number', indeed for him

---

* Even as careless a proof-reader as Zemlinsky must have spotted the missing accidental in bar 6 (see p. 175n). It may even have been his intention to leave the fortuitous engraver's error unaltered, as a means of 'hiding his fortune from others'.

that fact alone will have reinforced, perhaps even explained, his instinctive empathy for Zemlinsky. In June 1915 Berg enlarged on the subject in a letter to Schoenberg:

I remain unshaken in my firm belief in this fate, I could write a book on the subject; but even more interesting is the fact that it always involves a fateful number. The number 23![10]

And a few days later he revealed that discoveries associated with the number 23 by the biologist Wilhelm Fleiss confirmed his 'old belief':

For dates of birth and death, stages of life, periodicity of illness, in whole families, royal dynasties, generations, indeed nations, [. . .] the conclusion is that the woman's number is 28, that of the man 23.[11]

As amply borne out by Berg's annotated score of the Lyric Suite, such considerations played a major part in the formal structure and pitch content of his music. Yet number, in his case, was by no means the only factor that determined the nature of the symbol beneath the surface.

In 1989 the American musicologist Brenda Dalen published an essay on the secret programme of Berg's Chamber Concerto.[12] One of her most startling discoveries was that, apart from the names Arnold Schoenberg, Anton Webern and Alban Berg (A–D–S–C–H–B–E–G, A–E–B–E and A–B–A–B–E–G), which are spelled out at the beginning of the first movement, in the *Adagio* Berg undemonstratively introduces a theme derived from the name of Zemlinsky's sister Mathilde: A–H–D–E. As Dalen points out, the 'Math' theme, as Berg refers to it in his sketches, appears 47 bars before the central point of the movement and disappears 47 bars later, corresponding to Mathilde's life-span of forty-seven years (she died in 1923, while Berg was at work on the score). By introducing Schoenberg's 'Melisande' theme into the passage, Berg also alludes to the love triangle Schoenberg–Mathilde–Gerstl, and a quotation from *Wozzeck*, played by the solo violin in bars 303–5, associates the 'Math' theme, in a gesture of horrifying implication (horrifying, in that the work was written to honour Schoenberg on his fiftieth birthday), with the painter's violent death. The text to which Berg alludes is taken from the scene immediately preceding Wozzeck's suicide (act III/iv):

Aber ich muss mich waschen, ich bin blutig.

But I must wash myself, there's blood on me.

Not surprisingly, the 'Math' theme is also found in the work in which Zemlinsky documented and attempted to resolve the crisis engendered by the Gerstl affair, his Second Quartet. Unlike Berg, however, Zemlinsky introduces the theme not at original pitch but a 5th lower. A–H–D–E, modified by subtracting the secret number 5, thus becomes D–E–G–A,* the 'Self' motif extended by an additional pitch: a symbol of brotherly love and a reiteration of Zemlinsky's assertion that every member of the family was prepared to make 'sacrifices for the sake of the others'.

Schoenberg incorporates the same musical symbols into several works composed in the aftermath of the Gerstl affair. The first of his Five Orchestral Pieces op. 16, *Vorgefühle* ('Premonitions'), begins with a double iteration of Zemlinsky's 'Self' motif, combined with its inversion in parallel 5ths, reaching its apex in a variant of the 'Fate' chord:

EX. 45   Schoenberg: op. 16 no. 1

The 'Fate' chord also provides the framework of the second of the Five Orchestral Pieces, *Vergangenes*,[†] where it appears four times: in the opening and closing bars, at the end of the first section (bar 145) and at the reprise (bar 205). Here, as in the first piece, the chord is presented in a D minor context but, stripped of its mediant, as the open 5th, D–A, above it the G♯. This denuded variant of the 'Fate' chord also appears at key moments in the last movement of Schoenberg's Second Quartet, a tragic echo of the adoring words he had once addressed to Mahler: 'I saw your soul naked, stripped bare.'

In the second of the Piano Pieces op. 11, composed in the summer of 1909, the characters are assembled as if for one of Gerstl's contorted family portraits (EX. 46). Zemlinsky's 'Self' motif rises sequentially to an impassioned climax, dragging his sister's theme, as it were, in its wake. The second chord (EX. 46A) incorporates Schoenberg's initials, A–S; and the pitches with which he surrounds them, G and D, can be read as representing the names of his children, Görgi and Trudi.[‡]

---

* Cf. EX. 48D.

† *Vergangenes* is generally understood as signifying 'memories', 'past experiences'. However, the root, *Vergehen*, also signifies 'violation', indeed in present-day German the word is used as a euphemism for rape. Schoenberg's title could hence also be interpreted as signifying 'Crimes' or 'Sins'.

‡ Trudi's son, Arnold Greissle-Schönberg, recalls that superstition was an essential part of

EX. 46   Schoenberg: op. 11 no. 2 (bars 45–7)

EX. 46A

Is it legitimate to read so much into a single chord, a chord, moreover, that is by no means unique to the music of Schoenberg? His own professed attitude towards musical symbols – which differed little from that of Berg or Zemlinsky – confirms rather than denies the possibility of such an interpretation, far-fetched as it may at first appear. Requested by his publisher to devise titles for the Five Orchestral Pieces, Schoenberg debated this very question in his *Berlin Diary* and concluded:

Music is miraculous in that one can say everything in such a way that those in the know can understand it all, and yet one's own secrets, those which one will not even admit to oneself, remain undivulged.[13]

Zemlinsky's own musical symbols are in principle just as elusive. The 2–3–5 sequence is common currency in musical literature, and the pitch structure of the 'Fate' chord can be isolated in many other works, such as Bach's *Kreuzstab* Cantata, Schumann's *Vogel als Prophet* or Richard Strauss's *Die Frau ohne Schatten*. The fascination of Zemlinsky's symbols lies in their very communal quality. Where Bach and Shostakovich unambiguously spell out their names as pitch material, where Schumann openly plays with the name of Pauline d'Abegg and Josef Suk infuses his later music with a clearly identified 'Death' motif,

---

family life: 'On the thirteenth day of a month, my mother, [. . .] who was otherwise particularly intelligent and enlightened, never left the house on principle. Also on Fridays. To break a mirror was a particular mishap, which unavoidably caused seven years of bad luck. When smoking, if you offered to light someone's cigarette, then only ever with one match for two people, never a third (Greissle-Schönberg, *Arnold Schönberg und sein Wiener Kreis. Erinnerung eines Enkels* (Vienna, 1998), 41).

Zemlinsky's references remain enigmatic and ambiguous; they easily lose themselves in the crowd. Like Schoenberg, he will have been satisfied that 'those in the know can understand'; indeed he implied as much himself when he revealed to Alma that one of her motifs had been 'worked into' the score of *The Triumph of Time*, but 'imperceptibly, just for us'.

Over half a century after Zemlinsky's death, the Alexander-Zemlinsky-Fonds, inaugurated by his widow to administrate the estate, commissioned the Czech sculptor Josef Symon to create a monument for his grave in the Vienna Zentralfriedhof. Symon, who had no particularly intimate knowledge of Zemlinsky's art, can scarcely have known of the symbols beneath its surface. When the monument was unveiled, in 1994, it was greeted as a considerable improvement on the plain wooden cross that had so far marked the spot.*But by some strange quirk of fate, Symon had taken his information from an out-dated reference work, and chiselled '1872' into the stone as the year of birth instead of 1871: Zemlinsky's 'fortune' remained 'hidden from others'. (The 'error' was later corrected.) And as the artist explained, he had chosen the five man-high stone figures to represent the five geographical stations of Zemlinsky's career: Vienna, Prague, Berlin, Vienna, New York. Five figures symmetrically arrayed, each with five asymmetrical facets.

In Zemlinsky's view of the world there was indeed no room for coincidence.[†]

---

* See plate 28.
[†] Cf. Louise Zemlinsky, in a posthumously published interview: 'There are no coincidences. Zemlinsky said that to me time and again, and now I see it myself' (Burkhard Laugwitz, '"Meine Zeit kommt nach meine Tod". Begegnung mit Louise Zemlinsky', *Das Orchester*, v/1993, 547–50).

VI

Prague 1911–1918

previous page:
Alexander Zemlinsky
caricature by Rudolf Herrmann
first published in *Der Merker*, 1910, II

The Musical Director

While Muslims, Christians and Jews co-existed peacefully in Bosnia under Ottoman rule for over three hundred years, in Bohemia the Habsburgs never sought or achieved any comparable symbiosis. The Czech Hussites and German* Catholics of Prague lived side by side in a dual class system, united only by a common federal and municipal government. The power and wealth of the region lay entirely in German hands, indeed under the Austrian monarchy (i.e. from 1526) the Slavs of Bohemia and Moravia – save for a handful of intellectuals – were reduced to a people of peasants and labourers. In Prague there was also a large and influential community of Ashkenazic Jews, one of the oldest and most resilient in Europe.

Opposition to Metternich's oppressive regime led in many regions of the Habsburg Empire to unrest and revolution. At Whitsun 1848 the Repeal Club of Bohemia proclaimed an uprising of Czech nationalists. Within a few days the revolt was quashed by military force, and for a time the German nobility retained control. Gradually, however, with the emergence of pan-Slavism, and as an outcome of strictures imposed on Austria with the *Ausgleich*, the balance of power began to shift. A reform of the suffrage laws in 1882 caused the Germans to lose their parliamentary majority, and eight years later, with the rise of the ultra-nationalist Young Czech party, Bohemia became effectively autonomous. Movement of population from rural areas into the city reflected this change of emphasis: where the census of 1856 recorded 50,000 Czechs and 73,000 Germans in Prague, by 1882 there were 122,000 Czechs and 33,000 Germans. When Zemlinsky arrived, thirty years later, Czech outnumbered German by twelve to one, and of 35,000 non-Czechs living in the city, 25,000 were Jews.[1]

Music-theatre, like every other cultural institution, had always been administrated and financed by the German ruling classes. The Nostitzsches Nationaltheater, opened in 1783, was Prague's first permanent opera house. It was here that Mozart gave the world premières of *Don Giovanni* and *La Clemenza di Tito*, and at the Ständetheater (Estates Theatre, or Stavovské Divadlo),[†] as the building was renamed in 1798, the Musical Director from

---

* The term 'German' in this context refers to German native speakers, regardless of their nationality.
† Presentday Czech equivalent names are included in parentheses.

1813 to 1816 was Carl Maria von Weber. Not until 1862, with the Provincial Theatre (Prozatímní Divadlo), did the Czechs acquire an opera house of their own.* In 1881, at a time when monumental state opera houses were being erected in every autonomous capital of the former Habsburg Empire,† the house was expanded. Under its new name, National Theatre (Národní Divadlo), prominently situated on the bank of the Vltava, it stood – as it stands today – as a monument to the victory of pan-Slavism.

Anxious to avoid cultural eclipse, members of the German community formed a consortium and applied to parliament for a subsidy of 500,000 fl. with which to build their own new theatre. The application was rejected. In April 1884 the executive committee therefore launched an appeal for private sponsorship, supporting the action with lotteries, charity concerts and fund-raising balls. Donations poured in from all over Germany and Austria, even from the New World, and by the following summer sufficient funds had been collected to sign a contract with the famous firm of Viennese theatre architects, Helmer and Fellner. Construction work began in March 1885.

The Neues Deutsches Theater (henceforth referred to as NDT), situated a few hundred yards north-east of the National Museum on the Königliche Weinberge (Wilsonova), opened its doors on 5 January 1888 with a festive per-formance of *Die Meistersinger von Nürnberg*. As in most nineteenth-century theatres, backstage facilities and rehearsal rooms were cramped and dingy. The dressing rooms were damp, and the architects had forgotten to provide for a rehearsal area; the main stage, though generously proportioned, was shallow, the proscenium arch inordinately narrow, backdrop changes were hampered by lack of overhead space, and the understage area was too small to permit the use of traps or special effects. The entrance lobbies and foyers, on the other hand, were spacious and lavishly decorated, and the acoustic was superb. With 1,900 seats – 100 more than the Vienna Hofoper and 400 more than the Národní Divadlo – the NDT boasted one of Europe's most capacious auditoriums.

For the first twenty-five years of its existence, the company was directed by Angelo Neumann. A professional to his fingertips, he could look back on years of experience as singer, stage director, *intendant* and impresario. His Wagnerian touring company had taken the *Ring* to every major European city, and having purchased the entire Bayreuth equipment store in 1882, he brought with him personal assets that proved of immense value to his new theatre. Thanks to Neumann's ear for young talent, the NDT boasted a fine ensemble of singers

---

* Performances of works in Czech, such as the operas of František Škroup, were given at the Ständetheater, but were abandoned after 1860 due to lack of public interest.
† The Belgrade National Theater was founded in 1868, the Romanian Opera, Bucharest, in 1877 and the Royal Hungarian Opera, Budapest, in 1884. In Sofia the Dramatic Opera Company was inaugurated in 1891, and the National Theatre in Zagreb, designed – like the Neues Deutsches Theater in Prague – by the architects Helmer and Fellner, was opened in 1895.

and a distinguished lineage of Musical Directors: Gustav Mahler (1885–86), Karl Muck (1886–92), Franz Schalk (1895–98) and Leo Blech (1898–1906).* Yet Neumann was also renowned for his uncompromising behaviour, and towards the end of his career he grew churlish and unpredictable. Both Bodanzky and Klemperer, who joined the NDT in 1907, found his style of leadership intolerable and were swift to seek positions elsewhere. After Bodanzky's departure for Mannheim in 1909 and Klemperer's resignation the following year, no successor was appointed. For lack of a guiding hand, the musical apparatus fell into disarray.

Neumann died unexpectedly after a brief illness on 20 December 1910. His position was advertised in the German press for three months, but not until April 1911 did the governing board nominate a successor. Their choice fell on Heinrich Teweles, who had worked at the NDT as dramaturg from 1887 to 1900, and subsequently as chief editor of an influential German-language newspaper, the *Prager Presse*. Teweles was a writer of modest talent and a man of conservative disposition; his conciliatory style of leadership proved quite the opposite of his predecessor's. Having observed Neumann's final years from close hand, moreover, he was aware of the urgent need for an authoritative and experienced musical director.

Zemlinsky was an obvious candidate. Teweles would scarcely have been in a position to approach him until shortly before the close of the Volksoper season, hence there was no time for the customary formality of a guest appearance; indeed the governors must have considered themselves fortunate at such short notice to have won his services at all.† As it was, his Munich contract ran until early September, and Teweles was obliged to open, on 4 August, with a stopgap repertoire of operetta, ballet and *Spieloper*.

In the eyes of the public, the NDT was far more than a mere opera house. It served, according to the statutes, as 'a fortress of the German spirit on hotly disputed territory, a bastion of German poetry, language, manners and customs in an imperilled frontier region'.[2] On occasion the theatre was transformed into a concert hall and was even used, for a brief, experimental period, for film shows; sometimes the premises were also made available for charity balls, prize-giving ceremonies, gymnastic displays and political rallies. Apart from an ensemble of 34 singers, a chorus of 62, a ballet company of 21 dancers and 16 *élèves*, and an orchestra of 60, Teweles inherited from Neumann a sizeable company of actors, 30 in all, whose repertoire extended from Shakespeare, Goethe and Schiller to Strindberg, Schnitzler and Wedekind.

---

* All Neumann's chief conductors were young and relatively inexperienced: on taking office, Mahler was twenty-five, Muck twenty-seven, Schalk thirty-two, Blech twenty-eight and Bodanzky thirty.
† Zemlinsky's engagement was announced in the German-language newspaper *Bohemia* on 22 April.

In contrast to the Národní Divadlo, the NDT was financed almost entirely by private enterprise. There were enough wealthy German industrialists in Prague to underwrite the annual budget several times over, and, considering the tiny segment of urban population from which the theatre drew its audiences, ticket sales were remarkably high. But the books had to be balanced, the public had to be given what it wanted, and any desire to remain up to date had to be offset against the high cost of royalties for new music. Due to the extortionate demands of Strauss's publishers, for instance, the first Prague performance of *Der Rosenkavalier* was given not at the NDT but at the publicly subsidized Národní Divadlo, in Czech, and although Teweles did eventually succeed in staging new works by Blech, Kienzl, Korngold, Schillings, Strauss, Weingartner and Wolf-Ferrari, he was obliged to balance novelties sparingly against the operettas, light operas and popular classics (whether sung or spoken) on which his box office depended. Whereas the Národní Divadlo frequently performed works by Austrian and German composers, no music by Czech composers was performed at the NDT until after the First World War, and even then only on Zemlinsky's personal initiative.

Dramatis personae

Beyond the confines of the NDT, Zemlinsky's artistic contacts in Prague were less multifarious than those of his Vienna years, and his circle of friends was drawn almost exclusively from the German–Jewish sector of the population. After sixteen years of residence, his command of Czech was still negligible.* Despite his part-Slovakian ancestry, despite his friendly relations with Czech officialdom, and despite his championing of Smetana and Dvořák, Suk and Janáček, he never cast off his Viennese roots.

Ida Zemlinsky presumably had to attend to the domestic side of moving house largely on her own. The family settled into a spacious apartment at Havlíčekgasse (Havlíčkova) 9, directly opposite the Central Railway Station (Masarykovo nádraží) and only ten minutes' walk across the Stadtpark† to the NDT. They remained at this conveniently central address until their departure for Berlin in 1927.

It cannot have taken long for Zemlinsky to make the acquaintance of his neighbours at Havlíčekgasse 11 (Palác Ferona), Rudolf and Albine Werfel. In September 1911, their son Franz Werfel was called up for a year of obligatory military service at the fortress of Hradčany, but as a passionate opera-goer he missed no opportunity to attend performances at the NDT. Ten years later he recalled:

---

* Louise Zemlinsky recalled that her husband never even learned enough Czech to pay for a tram ticket (conversation with Alfred Clayton, *ACl*, 237).
† A large area of the former Stadtpark is today occupied by the main-line railway station (Wilsonovo nádraží).

The years I spent in Prague are distant, the person I once was is a stranger to me, most experiences have grown unreal, forgotten . . . but amongst the unlost realities, the hours during which I heard Zemlinsky making music shine out with uncloudable radiance. [. . .] *Tristan*, *Carmen*, *Otello*, *Figaro* and that incomparable feast: *Così fan tutte* – this and so much more: immutable kernels of gratitude![3]

First personal contact between Werfel and Zemlinsky appears to have been made in Vienna, through Alma Mahler, rather than in Prague. Though Zemlinsky's idealized love for Alma remained undiminished, his attitude towards Werfel, who married her in 1921, was marred by neither envy nor bitterness. Their friendship, based on a deep sense of mutual admiration, lasted a lifetime. Zemlinsky also became a good friend of Werfel's sister Hanna and her husband (as from March 1917), the paper manufacturer Herbert von Fuchs-Robettin.

Hermann Grab (1903–1949), widely considered the most talented of the younger 'Prague Circle' of writers, studied music, philosophy and law. His book *Der Stadtpark*,[4] a Proust-inspired tale of a childhood in Prague, won the approval of Adorno and Thomas Mann. For a brief period Grab took harmony lessons with Zemlinsky, so brief in fact that in 1921, when his teacher recommended him to Schoenberg for further study, he had progressed 'no further than 7th chords'.[5] In 1932, honouring Zemlinsky on his (official) sixtieth birthday, Grab wrote:

When suddenly the small, nervous figure appeared from around a corner, it left you standing, for you found yourself confronted with the spirit of music incarnate. And those who later had the good fortune to meet him personally found all their expectations fulfilled.[6]

In 1939 Grab emigrated to New York, where he made his name as a specialist for early keyboard instruments. His last novel, *Hochzeit in Brooklyn*, was published posthumously in 1957.

Contact with other men of letters is sparsely documented. Although on good terms with Max Brod, Zemlinsky does not appear to have made the acquaintance of Franz Kafka, nor is there any record of contact with other prominent German writers in Prague, such as Willy Haas and Ernst Pollak, or with members of Werfel's 'Café Arco' circle. Despite the dwindling population of non-Czechs in Prague, the city boasted no fewer than five German-language newspapers. Since, as in Vienna, free exchange with the leading music critics was a matter of course, Zemlinsky soon made contact with Erich Steinhard (from 1920 chief editor of *Der Auftakt*), Felix Adler (chief critic of *Bohemia*) and Erich Rychnovsky (*Prager Tagblatt*). Though Steinhard later grew critical of the NDT and, implicitly, of its musical director, Adler and Rychnovsky remained staunch supporters.

Czech opera-goers seldom visited the NDT, and it was equally rare for

Germans to attend performances at the Národní Divadlo. Among professional musicians, however, segregationist mentality was deplored. At the NDT it was common practice, for instance, to hire extra players from the Czech orchestras, and vice versa. Zemlinsky's contact with his Czech colleagues was invariably cordial, and with the Chief Conductor of the Národní Divadlo, Karel Kovařovic, and his successor, Otakar Ostrčil, he entered into a spirit of friendly rivalry.* Likewise, his letters to the Principal Conductor of the Czech Philharmonic, Václav Tálich, bear witness to an enduring and heartfelt friendship, later reflected in frequent guest appearances with the orchestra.

It was within the NDT itself, however, that Zemlinsky formed his closest bonds. Under his leadership, the opera ensemble became one of the finest and most closely knit in Europe. International stars were beyond the theatre's budget but also foreign to the artistic creed. Experience of working with Zemlinsky provided many young singers – including Robert Burg, Martha Fuchs, Maria Müller and Friedrich Schorr – with a solid basis on which to launch distinguished careers. Nevertheless, some of the finest soloists at the NDT never attained the recognition they deserved.

Hedwig von Debicka (1888–1970) sang at the NDT from 1911 to 1914. With her agile technique and wide range, she excelled not only in coloratura roles, such as the Queen of the Night (*Die Zauberflöte*) and Constanze (*Entführung*), but also in the lyric-spinto repertoire, including Mimi (*La bohème*) and Desdemona (*Otello*). In the original version of *Ariadne auf Naxos*, performed at the NDT only six weeks after the world première in Stuttgart, Zemlinsky entrusted her with the exceptionally demanding role of Zerbinetta.† After leaving Prague, she sang in Vienna and, from 1926, in Berlin. In 1916 she married Pietro von Stermich, a conductor of Dalmatian descent, who joined the NDT in 1911 as Zemlinsky's second-in-command, taking charge primarily of the Italian repertoire. Later he conducted at the Vienna Volksoper and, from 1922, in Poznań.

Tilly de Garmo (1888–1990) joined the NDT in 1923; the following year she married the conductor Fritz Zweig. In Prague she sang the Infanta in Zemlinsky's *Der Zwerg*, the soprano part in the world première of the Lyric Symphony and the solo vocal part in the Three Fragments from Berg's *Wozzeck*. Her operatic repertoire included Despina (*Così*), Eva (*Meistersinger*) and Sophie (*Rosenkavalier*). She sang at the Staatsoper Berlin from 1926, but left Nazi Germany in 1934 and returned with Zweig to Prague. They fled to Paris in 1938 and emigrated to the US in 1940.

* In February 1926, Ostrčil was invited to conduct a concert at the NDT, an unprecedentedly bold step in the move towards Czech–German integration.
† The original version of Zerbinetta's aria, 'Grossmächtige Prinzessin', is a whole tone higher and almost twice as long as the revised version of 1916.

The Hungarian-born baritone Max Klein (1887–?), who joined the NDT in 1918, studied in Vienna and came to Prague via Leipzig and the Volksoper. At the NDT he appeared in several leading roles, notably Don Giovanni, Papageno (*Die Zauberflöte*), Wolfram (*Tannhäuser*), Posa (*Don Carlos*) and Marcello (*La bohème*). His greatest talent, however, was as a lieder singer. In 1918 he toured Bohemia and Moravia with Zemlinsky as accompanist; together, in 1920, they performed Schubert's *Schwanengesang* at the NDT. Klein's active career was brief, and from 1925 to 1938 he gave voice lessons in Vienna. After the *Anschluss* he emigrated to the US.

Having worked briefly with Zemlinsky at the Volksoper, Schoenberg's Czech-born cousin Hans Nachod (1883–1965) was engaged in Mainz and Kiel before joining the NDT ensemble in 1915. In Prague he sang most of the Wagnerian heldentenor roles, as well as Florestan (*Fidelio*), Don José (*Carmen*), Rhadames (*Aida*) and Turiddu (*Cavalleria rusticana*). He is best remembered, however, for Waldemar in Schoenberg's *Gurrelieder*, which he sang at the world première in Vienna (1913), as well as in Amsterdam and Prague (both in 1921). Of his *Lohengrin*, Rychnowsky wrote in 1916: 'Herr Nachod's vocal resources are considerable, but they are uneven, and one perceives that much of what he sings is left to chance.'[7] After a relatively brief career, he settled in Vienna. In 1938 he fled via Prague to London.

The baritone Heinrich Schönberg (1882–1941), Arnold Schoenberg's younger brother, sang at the NDT from 1913 to 1914 and from 1918 to 1932. Having studied in Vienna, he gained his first experience in small provincial theatres. In Prague he was entrusted with cameo or comprimario roles, such as the Notary in *Rosenkavalier*, Fifth Jew in *Salome* and Antonio in *Le nozze di Figaro*. Zemlinsky wrote of him to Schoenberg:

Of your brother I'm afraid I have nothing good to report. He is, I believe, hard-working and ambitious, but lacks all ability. Despite taking great pains, his enunciation is hopeless, and on stage he's always shit scared (*hat er immer die Hosen voll*). The voice has a frightful tremolo. – All things said and done, I have to exert my full influence to keep him on here.[8]

In 1917 Heinrich Schönberg married Bertha Ott, daughter of the Burgomaster of Salzburg. After the *Anschluss*, this marriage into a prominent Arian family exempted him from arrest and deportation. But when, after a series of unsuccessful operations, he died in 1941 of septicaemia, some people (notably his brother) were convinced that he had fallen victim to Nazi euthanasia.

The Latvian-born composer, conductor and musicologist Gerhard von Keussler (1874–1949), who had come to the city in 1906 as Conductor of the Männergesangverein, was one of the most respected figures in Prague musical life. Apart from conducting choral concerts at the NDT, he lectured on music history and aesthetics. In 1918 he was appointed Director of the Berlin

Singakademie and succeeded Hausegger as Conductor of the Berlin Philharmonic. In 1932 he emigrated to Australia, but returned to Berlin four years
later to teach composition at the Akademie der Künste.

Several of Schoenberg's composition pupils worked with Zemlinsky at the
NDT.* Karl Horwitz (1884–1925) joined the music staff in 1911 as a repetiteur
and stayed on until the outbreak of war in 1914. Initially he was a colleague of
the twenty-one-year-old Erich Kleiber, who left in 1912 to take up his first conducting post at Darmstadt. Subsequently Horwitz worked as a composer, but in
1924 he lost his hearing. With one substantial composition to his credit, the
symphonic poem *Vom Tode*, as well as two quartets and several song-cycles, he
died the following year, aged forty-one.

Like Horwitz, Heinrich Jalowetz (1882–1946) studied musicology with
Guido Adler while attending Schoenberg's composition class at the
Schwarzwald School. Prior to his engagement at the NDT (1916–24), he con-
ducted in Regensburg, Danzig and Stettin. He left the NDT in 1924 to become
Chief Conductor at the Volksoper and, the following year, successor to
Klemperer in Cologne, a post he retained until 1933. In 1938 he emigrated to
North Carolina.

Paul Pella (1892–1965, real name Morgenstern) was also a pupil of
Schoenberg's in Vienna. He joined the music staff of the NDT in 1919 as
operetta conductor, but was soon promoted to Second *Kapellmeister*. From
1922 he was Musical Director in Darmstadt, and from 1927 in Aachen, where
he conducted one of the earliest productions of *Wozzeck*. Anti-Semitic agitation
caused him to resign in 1932, and after a brief period in Berlin he emigrated to
Holland, where he survived the years of occupation in concealment. After the
war he was for three years Artistic Director of the Netherlands Opera in
Amsterdam, returned to Aachen in 1950 as Musical Director, but finally settled
in Holland, where in 1955 he founded the Opera Forum in Enschede. A
mainstay of his repertoire was *Kleider machen Leute*, which he conducted in
Darmstadt and Aachen.

Viktor Ullmann (1898–1944), Silesian-born son of an Austrian army captain, studied the piano with Eduard Steuermann and enrolled in Schoenberg's
composition seminar, where he was also taught by Hanns Eisler and Rudolf
Kolisch. In 1920 he settled in Prague, studied composition with Jalowetz, and
wrote for the musical journal *Der Auftakt*. He joined the music staff of the

---

* Webern worked at the NDT for a few weeks in January–February 1916, for the whole of the
1917–18 season and, again for a few weeks, in the autumn of 1920. He first came to Prague,
at Zemlinsky's instigation, in September 1911, but decided to follow Schoenberg to Berlin (his
contract was transferred to Horwitz). A few months later he again expressed interest in
working at the NDT, but Zemlinsky was unable to oblige. In the summer of 1913 he returned,
rented an apartment and transferred his household from Vienna, but suffered a nervous
collapse and withdrew from his contract two days before the season was due to begin.

NDT in 1921, where his first responsibilities included training the chorus for *Lohengrin* and the *Gurrelieder*. After the Zemlinsky era he conducted operetta at Aussig (Ústí nad Labem) and worked at the Zurich Schauspielhaus. From 1931 he gave up music and spent two years working in an anthroposophical bookshop in Stuttgart, then returned to Prague, where he came under the influence of Alois Hába. Between 1935 and 1941 he composed two operas, *Der Sturz des Antichrist* and *Der zerbrochene Krug*. Unable to flee from Nazi-occupied Czechoslovakia, in 1942 he was deported to Terezín, where he composed over twenty works, including the opera *Der Kaiser von Atlantis*. He perished in Auschwitz.

A singular and all but undocumented bond of friendship linked Zemlinsky with Georg Szell (1897–1970). As the composer–pianist prodigy György von Széll he made his Viennese début aged eleven; at sixteen he conducted the Vienna Philharmonic. After engagements at the Berlin Staatsoper and in Strasbourg, he came to the NDT for one season, 1919–20, making his début on 7 October with Meyerbeer's *L'africaine*.* A few weeks later, Zemlinsky confided to Alma:

Because Herr Szell accompanied Strauss on tour, and because he is smooth and self-confident, moves in high society, and knows how to get on with everyone but not to be on too intimate terms with anyone, there is much agitation in the press on his behalf. He is an inexperienced, capable, *cold-hearted* conductor, but endowed with an excellent memory. (All this, please, in confidence! Szell has a large repertoire of jokes, and otherwise I get on very well with him. I don't know what he says about me, but here I am entirely on his side and do everything possible to further his interests.)[9]

During the summer of 1922, while Zemlinsky was working on the score of the Lyric Symphony, he and Szell were neighbours in Bad Aussee ('A fantastic pianist,' he wrote to Schoenberg at the time, 'but what fees he demanded!').[10] When Zemlinsky left Prague, in 1927, Szell took over his conducting class at the Deutsche Akademie für Musik; two years later he was appointed Musical Director of the NDT, a position he retained until his emigration to the UK in 1937. Szell's interpretation of Zemlinsky's *Kreidekreis* at the NDT (1935) was praised as one his finest achievements.

Of the stage directors with whom Zemlinsky worked at the NDT, two deserve particular mention.

Fritz Bondy (1888–1980), Teweles's stepson and father of the writer François Bondy, worked at the NDT from 1913 to 1919, principally as a producer of spoken drama. He did however make one excursion into the field of opera, namely for the Prague première of *A Florentine Tragedy*. Later he travelled extensively, working in Vienna, Paris, Budapest and elsewhere, before

---

* Szell's Prague repertoire also included *Rigoletto* and *La traviata*.

settling in Switzerland. In post-war Zurich, under the pseudonym N. O. Scarpi, he was active for many years as novelist, raconteur and humorist.

One of the most universal talents at the NDT was Louis Laber (1889–1929). Born in the Ukraine, he studied voice in Italy and came to Prague in 1919. As tenor buffo he sang several principal roles, including Pedrillo (*Entführung*), Jaquino (*Fidelio*), David (*Meistersinger*), Mime (in the *Ring*) and Klaus-Narr in the *Gurrelieder*. Having made his début as stage director with *La bohème* in 1920, he collaborated with Zemlinsky on many important productions, including Puccini's *Trittico*, Korngold's *Die tote Stadt*, Schreker's *Der ferne Klang*, Reznicek's *Ritter Blaubart* and Hindemith's trilogy, *Sancta Susanna*, *Mörder, Hoffnung der Frauen* and *Das Nusch-Nuschi*. As from 1925, Laber also designed the sets and costumes for his own productions. He left the NDT, together with Zemlinsky, in 1927. After a season at Aussig with Ullmann, he was engaged as Chief Producer by the Finnish National Opera in Helsinki. Accused in the Finnish nationalist press of espionage, he was unable to renew his residence permit or obtain a passport for stateless persons. Publicly dishonoured, and threatened with deportation, he took his life on 26 December 1929 with an overdose of morphine.[11]

First Seasons in Prague

Zemlinsky arrived on 6 September 1911.[12] As was his way, he set to work at once, rehearsing and performing three mainstays of his repertoire, *Fidelio*, *Tannhäuser* and *Der Freischütz*, within just six weeks. None of the productions was new,* but thanks to his rapid and effective rehearsal technique the scores sounded fresh and revitalized. In a review of *Fidelio* headed 'Sensational success for Zemlinsky', Felix Adler wrote:

When he performs a work, he lets it speak for itself, thus creating it anew: an infinitely valuable aspect of Zemlinsky's approach. [. . . His] gestures are economical and decisive, intended for singers and orchestra alone, never calculated to impress the public. [. . .] His inherently intimate approach to music eschews all brutal show of strength. Never, not even in *fortissimo*, is the stage drowned by the orchestra. [. . .] One left the theatre convinced that the works of our masters are now in the best of hands.[13]

Rychnowsky's reaction was no less enthusiastic:

Zemlinsky is one of those artists who interpret a work for its own sake rather than for the sake of success. Not only did he restore order to those aspects of Beethoven which had been in disorder, he also infused the performance with something of his

* At Zemlinsky's instigation, important details of the staging of *Fidelio* were altered, and in place of the overture, as at the Volksoper, he substituted *Leonore* no. 3.

own, strong individuality, everywhere one sensed his invaluable sense of structural disposition.[14]

From now on, in the eyes of press and public, Zemlinsky could do no wrong. For the unaffected intensity of his approach, the impeccable ensemble between stage and pit – achieved in long hours of rehearsal – and the lucid, diaphanous sound of his orchestra, the critics found nothing but praise.

Teweles was relieved that his choice, made entirely on the recommendation of 'trustworthy friends' in Vienna, had proved so satisfactory. In his memoirs he recalls:

Already at his début Zemlinsky scored the greatest success. With him I had truly struck gold. [. . .] Whatever he presented was first class. [. . .] He not only won over the entire audience but the whole ensemble as well. Every singer insisted on rehearsing with him, as he understood better than anyone else how to elucidate the musical and dramatic aspects of a role.[15]

Louis Laber's recollections of Zemlinsky in rehearsal and performance present a vivid picture:

Were he not a musician, he could have become one the most talented character actors or stage directors of our time. From the very beginning, at the first piano rehearsal, he begins to mould the singer into the character he is to impersonate. He sings every phrase, acts out every scene, all with an astonishing intensity, strength of characterization, spirit, humour and range of colour. [. . .] At stage rehearsals, with his keen eye he helps and supports the production. He hears and sees a thousand things at once, and from the rostrum, during orchestral and dress rehearsals, loudly criticizes the actors' movements, the lighting and countless details on which the success or failure of a performance can hang. [. . .] Down in the pit, Zemlinsky re-enacts the whole opera, every role; he laughs, pulls a ferocious Alberich face, assumes the dignified stance of a Wotan, sculpts the graceful line of Papageno and Papagena, etc., etc.[16]

Every month Zemlinsky added a new work to his Prague repertoire: revivals of *Die Walküre*, *Die Zauberflöte* and *Lohengrin* (uncut), and new productions of *Le nozze di Figaro*,* Kienzl's *Der Kuhreigen* (three months after its world première in Vienna), *Tristan* (according to Adler, 'an interpretation of intimate subtlety')[17] and *Meistersinger*.

From the outset, Angelo Neumann had ensured that orchestral concerts should also be part of the NDT programme. These Philharmonic Concerts became a hallowed tradition and, for the Musical Director, a welcome relief

* Zemlinsky reinstated the recitatives, which had been replaced with spoken dialogue, accompanying them himself on a small upright piano. He also incorporated the recitative scene depicting Marzellina's lawsuit against Figaro in act III (the 'Gerichtsverhandlung') that Mahler had composed for the Vienna Hofoper in 1906.

from his duties in the pit. Zemlinsky's 1912 programmes were by Prague standards sensational. At Schoenberg's instigation, he opened his first concert, on 25 January, with Busoni's *Turandot*-Suite,* followed by the Beethoven Violin Concerto with Fritz Kreisler as soloist and, after the interval, Strauss's *Symphonia domestica*. Following the same principle – a famous soloist to fill the house, supported by a programme of unfamiliar or new works – the second concert (29 February) presented Schoenberg conducting Mahler's pot-pourri of Bach's Second and Third Orchestral Suites and his own *Pelleas und Melisande*, followed by Pablo Casals in Saint-Saëns[†] and Haydn. The Prague public was no less divided on the issue of *Pelleas* than audiences in Vienna or Berlin, and the performance was followed by thirty minutes of uproar. In contrast to the Viennese, however, the season-ticket holders in the stalls had the grace to hold their peace until the music was over.

The climax of the season followed on 28–30 March: a public rehearsal and two performances of Mahler's Eighth Symphony. With a team of soloists drawn entirely from the NDT (including the English tenor Alfred Piccaver) and as many choral singers as Prague could muster, the performance – after Munich and Vienna, the third in the work's history – was a triumph.[‡] Preparations for the event were overshadowed, however, by the last-minute withdrawal of a group of Czech participants. As Teweles recalls, 'The Arian choral societies refused to participate, because Mahler and I were Jews, and the Arians were more concerned with purity of race than with purity of intonation.'[18] This was not entirely true.[§] The actual reason for the fracas was that members of one Czech choir had objected to participating in a performance of a work with a German text. In future years Zemlinsky took pains to avoid such confrontations, but comparable situations did arise, and invariably they ended in disaster.

---

* Schoenberg had been hoping that Max Reinhardt would engage him as conductor for the production of Gozzi's *Turandot* with Busoni's incidental music, which opened at the Deutsches Theater, Berlin, on 26 October 1911 (in the event, Reinhardt chose Oskar Fried). 'Busoni's *Turandot* (really dreadful music, namely: none at all!)', he wrote to Zemlinsky; 'Busoni [. . .] has absolutely no talent for composition; these people who speak so wisely and brilliantly: unbelievable how little they have to say!' (*Web-Br*, 16 December 1911, 69). Zemlinsky's opinion, if scarcely less unflattering, was more circumspect: '*Turandot*: there's no music in it, but I expect it to be a very effective piece, and it should sound quite unusual' (*Web-Br*, January 1912, 73).
† Casals had originally expressed his wish to play the Dvořák Concerto; in line with NDT policy of not performing music by Czech composers, Teweles requested him to change the programme (cf. Jiři Vysloužil, 'Zemlinskys Prager Antrittsjahre', *AeSU*, 246).
‡ On 25 March Schoenberg gave a public reading in Prague of his essay 'Mahler' (later published in *Style and Idea*). Webern, who travelled up from Vienna to attend Zemlinsky's rehearsals, was invited to play the celesta – a kindly gesture, for the fee would have covered his travel expenses.
§ Teweles published his memoirs in Prague in 1927, at a time when political correctness was a *sine qua non*.

On this occasion, however, everything turned out for the best. The day was saved by Schreker and the 110 members of his Philharmonic Chorus, who had sung in the Vienna première under Bruno Walter shortly beforehand, on 14 March.* In response to Teweles's urgent appeal, they arrived in time to participate in the final rehearsals. Mahler's 'Veni Creator Spiritus', that 'confident shout by humanity to the skies for the creative vision that the world so desperately needs' (Deryck Cooke),[19] thus unexpectedly became an affirmation of brotherhood within a racial and cultural minority.

As the close of Zemlinsky's first season the Czech critic Zdeněk Nejedlý published a curt eulogy:

Alexander Zemlinsky was appointed First *Kapellmeister* at the German Theatre in Prague, and from otherwise paltry resources he has produced veritable feast days for anyone with a sense of artistic style. [. . .] A theatre in which everybody works. The people at our theatre do not work, they merely grumble.[20]

During this entire period Zemlinsky had scarcely found time for composition. He did, however, enjoy the pleasure of attending a new production of *Es war einmal . . .* in Mannheim, conducted by Bodanzky, which opened on 19 May.†

Es war einmal. . . was also the first novelty of the 1912–13 season at the NDT, in a production by Claus Pringsheim‡ which opened on 19 October and was given six times.§ Teweles recalls that it had been a struggle to persuade Zemlinsky to perform a work of his own at all; encouraged by the enthusiastic reception, however, he finally agreed to the long-delayed première of *Der Traumgörge* in the 1914–15 season.

Despite their success, Zemlinsky and Teweles were dissatisfied with overall musical standards, and the first season accordingly ended with a mass exodus of artists and technicians. Seventeen new singers and a new ballet director were hired, three new repetiteurs joined the music staff, and Paul Gerboth from the Volksoper was engaged as staff producer. The latter made his début on 7 December with Strauss's *Ariadne auf Naxos*, preceded by Molière's *Le bourgeois gentilhomme*. As at the world première in Stuttgart, the sets were built from designs by Ernst Stern; otherwise, according to Felix Adler, the NDT

---

* Zemlinsky had travelled to Vienna to hear the performance, accompanied by Karl Horwitz and Gerhard von Keussler.
† 'I am composing – "alterations",' he wrote to Schoenberg in January 1912, 'namely for *Es war einmal . . .* in Mannheim' (*Web-Br*, 74). The most substantial addition to the Mahler version, of which the performing materials were hired out to Mannheim, was an orchestral adaptation of the Princess's round-dance, used for the scene change before act 1. Zemlinsky himself conducted the second performance, on 21 May.
‡ On the programme, unusually, no producer was named. With his experience of the work in Vienna and Mannheim, Zemlinsky presumably took much of the responsibility for stage direction himself.
§ At the last performance, on 2 February 1913, the opera was coupled with *I Pagliacci*(!).

production was in every way superior, particularly with regard to musical precision: 'Truly,' he wrote, 'it felt as if one were attending a performance at a
court opera of the first rank.'[21]

Further highlights of the season were revivals of *Rheingold*, *Siegfried* and
Götterdämmerung, a gala performance of *Meistersinger* with Leo Slezak, and a
new production of *Salome*. The Philharmonic Concerts were less spectacular
than the previous season's, but by no means lacked interest. To a programme of
Weber, Mozart and Richard Strauss on 27 February 1913, Zemlinsky added
Korngold's Schauspiel-Ouvertüre op. 4 ('Now tell me honestly, Erich,' he asked
the sixteen-year-old, 'did you really orchestrate it yourself?').[22] On 3 March
followed Mahler's *Lied von der Erde*, Zemlinsky's first performance of a work
that was to become a hallmark of his concert repertoire. To celebrate Wagner's
hundredth birthday, on 22 May, he conducted a programme of excerpts from
Parsifal, seizing the opportunity to acquaint his orchestra and chorus with the
score before the ban on staged performances outside Bayreuth was lifted at the
end of the year. As *cul de lampe*, on 31 May, followed Beethoven's 'Choral'
Symphony.

On 29 January 1914, a programme that opened with Tchaikovsky's
'Pathétique' Symphony and closed with Strauss's *Tod und Verklärung* included
the world première of three of Schoenberg's orchestral Lieder op. 8. Public reaction was again hostile, and the composer refused to acknowledge his applause.
Schoenberg was so delighted with Zemlinsky's conducting, however, that he felt
moved to write to Alma about it:

You should go and hear how Zemlinsky makes music: a purer Mahler school than
the conducting of those who imitate Mahler more exactly! A search for content in
the form and for form in the content. Unaffected too. And never obtrudes. Since the
death of Mahler, he qualifies, I believe, as his true successor.[23]

Two performances of Mahler's Third Symphony followed, on 27 March and 5
April, and Zemlinsky wound up the concert season with Mendelssohn's *Elijah*.

The thirty-year Bayreuth monopoly on *Parsifal* elapsed on 1 January 1914,
and theatres the world over rushed to perform the work. Prague was no exception, and new productions were given simultaneously at the NDT and the
Národní Divadlo – or nearly simultaneously, for Teweles reverted to Neumann's
practice of beginning Wagner performances at 4 p.m., thus beating his Czech
colleagues to the post by an hour. The sets for Gerboth's production were
designed by Erwin Osen, a young artist from Vienna, whom Zemlinsky had met
in Munich the previous summer.*

---

* Erwin Dominik Osen (1891–1970; sometimes also known as 'Mime von Osen') gained his
first experience of theatre in the children's ballet of the Hofoper during the Mahler era. A fellow student and friend of Egon Schiele at the Vienna Academy, he was by all accounts a wayward and eccentric figure. In 1910 Schiele painted a series of nude portraits of him.

Firstly the most salient point [wrote Adler]: of the two thousand spectators, none seems to have felt that the work had in any sense been desecrated. [. . .] Erwin van Oosen [*sic*] is a radical modernist, violently opposed to kitsch or trumpery. His models are Roller and Klimt. [. . .] From a purely musical angle, the fact that the performance not only fulfilled every hope but also surpassed expectation – for that we have to thank Alexander von Zemlinsky.[24]

At the opposite end of the cultural spectrum, on 6 and 7 May the Prague public enjoyed the rare opportunity of experiencing Zemlinsky in operetta, with Max Pallenberg and Maria Jeritza in the Reinhardt productions of *The Mikado* and *La belle Hélène*. As final high point of the season, on 7 June, followed the first NDT production of *Der Rosenkavalier*, directed by Gerboth, using the obligatory sets and costumes by Alfred Roller.

Zemlinsky had concluded his first Prague season on 2 June 1912 with a performance of *Die Meistersinger*. Ten days later, in Berlin, his mother died. During the past decade Clara had spent most of her time with Mathilde and her children, and since neither family now lived in Vienna, mother and son had drifted apart. They had last seen each other in February, when Schoenberg conducted *Pelleas* (Clara travelled down to Prague for the event and stayed on for a few days). But there is no evidence that their relationship grew any closer, nor did Zemlinsky feel moved to write a new work in memory of her.

Since the summer of 1910, admittedly, there had been no time for composition at all. Mathilde was so upset by Clara's death that she suffered a nervous collapse,[25] and though Schoenberg was desperately short of money, he was obliged to take her to the seaside to recuperate. After the funeral, he and his family therefore travelled with the Zemlinskys to the popular resort of Karlshagen on the Baltic island of Usedom, where they spent July and part of August. Zemlinsky had brought with him a new libretto for *Malva*, and began to sketch music for it.* But the atmosphere was unconducive to work, he made little progress, and at the end of the summer the project was abandoned. His efforts, at least, were not entirely in vain: one striking idea was salvaged for the music to Shakespeare's *Cymbeline*, composed the following year, and two decades later a variant of the same motif found its way into act II of *Der König Kandaules*.[26]

The theatre season, which opened on 11 August, put paid to any further composition. Schoenberg was meanwhile organizing an ambitious orchestral concert in Vienna, with new works by Berg and Webern, the Chamber Symphony, Mahler's *Kindertotenlieder* and an orchestral version of Zemlinsky's

---

* The libretto is preserved in the Zemlinsky Collection (*LoC* 16/12A), where the author appears to be identified by the initials R.L. A sketch for a title page in Zemlinsky's pocket book (*LoC* 19/1), dated 'Carlshagen, July–August 1912', contains neither music nor text, but a name: Julius Hauptmann. Whether the page has any bearing on *Malva* is unclear.

Maeterlinck songs. When the programme was announced in the press, however, the Maeterlinck songs were not included. On Wednesday 5 March, less than four weeks before the concert, Zemlinsky wrote to query the omission. Schoenberg replied by return of post, assuring him that he wished 'at all cost' to perform the songs, and asking for the music within 'four to five days'.[27] The moment could scarcely have been less opportune, for Zemlinsky had not even begun the orchestration, and at the NDT he was in the midst of a Wagner cycle:

Friday	*Siegfried* (performance)
Saturday	*Götterdämmerung* (dress rehearsal)
Sunday	*Götterdämmerung* (performance)
Monday–Wednesday	*Meistersinger* (rehearsals with guest singers)
Thursday	*Meistersinger* (performance)

Nevertheless, on the Tuesday he wrote to tell Schoenberg that scores of three songs were on the way to Vienna, adding, 'I believe that they're very easy for the orchestra & will sound very well.'[28] The first song, intricately scored for large orchestra, was despatched four days later. None of these manuscripts betrays the least sign of haste; indeed the new versions include extra contrapuntal lines and in some cases new preludes or postludes.* For sheer speed and professionalism, the achievement was a *tour de force*.

The concert, which Zemlinsky did not attend, was given on 31 March at the Musikverein. Webern's Six Orchestral Pieces op. 6, which opened the programme, provoked laughter and loud-mouthed protest. The Maeterlinck songs were accepted without demur, but demonstrations of unparalleled hostility accompanied Schoenberg's Chamber Symphony. During Berg's Altenberg Songs pandemonium broke out, fists flew and the concert had to be abandoned. Together with the world première of Stravinsky's *The Rite of Spring* two months later in Paris, the event went down in music history as the scandal of the century. At face value Zemlinsky survived unscathed, but in the ensuing hubbub of police reports and court cases his art suffered a total eclipse: Schoenberg had stolen the show.

Some weeks before the close of the season, in early May 1913, Zemlinsky took advantage of a brief pause in his theatre schedule† to sketch out seventeen pages of short score for a new opera, *Der Meister von Prag*, based on a libretto by Karl von Levetzow. Preparations for the *Parsifal* concert must have disturbed his concentration, however, for the project was abandoned. Once the season was over, he took a few days' rest at Kitzbühel, then travelled to Munich

---

* Derrick Puffett published a detailed, if sometimes misinformed discussion of the differences between the orchestral and piano versions, 'Transcription and Recomposition: The Strange Case of Zemlinsky's Maeterlinck Songs', in C. Ayrey and M. Everist (eds.), *Analytical Strategies and Musical Interpretation* (Cambridge, 1996).
† The annual May Festival began with performances of *Rigoletto* and *Un ballo in maschera*, works Zemlinsky assigned, as usual, to his assistants.

for rehearsals of *The Mikado* with Max Reinhardt. The production opened on 11 July,* after which the baton was passed to an assistant and, with a sizeable fee in his pocket,[29] Zemlinsky rejoined his wife and daughter in their Tirolean refuge. 'We've been inundated with rain for the past five weeks,' he wrote to Schoenberg.[30] Country rambles were out of the question. Unable to relax, he began to compose. Between 18 and 20 July he wrote two new Maeterlinck songs; then, in a burst of creativity, before the ink had even dried on the paper,[†] he started on a new work, a monumental composition for string quartet.

String Quartet no. 2

During the previous summer at Karlshagen tension had arisen within the family circle, indeed to such an extent that by the end of the vacation Schoenberg and Zemlinsky were no longer on speaking terms. Shortly after returning to Berlin, Schoenberg wrote a letter of reconciliation:

Perhaps it would be as well if we were to avoid contact for a while. Maybe we shall soon calm down and resume friendly relations. That I did not say goodbye to you was perhaps odious. But believe me, if you had taken as much as one step, I would not have hesitated. [. . .] For that reason, I would like to say: my attitude to you remains as of old. I am grateful for everything you ever did for me. [. . .][31]

Zemlinsky replied:

My dear friend, I was reading Strindberg, utterly and deeply absorbed in the atmosphere of *Inferno*, shaken, distraught, apprehensive and extremely tense – when your letter arrived. You can imagine how I read it and how, in that particular state of mind, I reacted![32]

Whatever wrong had been done could completely be righted only with music. In the summer of 1913 Zemlinsky hastily sketched the outlines of a large-scale composition, which from the outset was conceived for Schoenberg and, ultimately, bore his name on the title page.[‡] After eight days he sent a brief report: 'It will have only one movement, i.e. four sections in one movement, and purports to be in F♯ minor.'[33]

The concept of a single-movement form, closely akin to that of Schoenberg's Chamber Symphony and First Quartet, was an unmistakable gesture of solidarity, as was the choice of F♯ minor, the key of Schoenberg's Second Quartet.

---

* The first night had to be interrupted when Pallenberg, who was singing the title role, walked off the stage, claiming to be indisposed. Zemlinsky had composed a brief entr'acte that was interpolated between acts II and III.
† The earliest dated sketch for the Second Quartet is inscribed '19.7.1913', i.e. one day prior to completion of the Maeterlinck Songs.
‡ The dedication was inadvertently omitted from the first-edition score. Although included in the second impression, it was again omitted from the title page of the miniature score, copyrighted in 1943.

Soon, however, it became clear that the work, running the gamut of grief and serenity, would exploit the same tonal polarity as the op. 5 Gesänge, D minor/ D major. Rather than abandoning his original plan, however, Zemlinsky integrated it into the final scheme. Thus the work opens in a subdominant area of D minor, but with a key signature of three sharps, and already in the fourth bar the harmony moves towards F♯ minor (EX. 48A). Material from another preliminary sketch, a Mahlerian march in F♯ major with dotted rhythms and trills, was adapted to its new surroundings (between 10 and 14) in a tonally ambivalent region between D minor and G♭ major. Though destabilized by whole-tone harmony, the finale (*Allegro molto*, 101⁻³) opens with sixty bars of F♯ major, and the key also predominates in several later passages. Less direct evidence of the F♯ minor origin can also be detected in the Lydian D major of the second subject group (EX. 48B) and the D minor/E♭ minor duality of the scherzo.

On 9 August the new season opened at the NDT, and work on the Quartet had to be interrupted. During the winter, such time as was available for creative work was spent on the incidental music to Shakespeare's *Cymbeline*, commissioned by the Nationaltheater in Mannheim. Zemlinsky expected to finish the Quartet by the following summer, but he continued to revise it until March 1915. Score and parts were published the following year by Universal Edition, bearing the opus number 15.

With its epic proportions (1,221 bars), this was the most ambitious instrumental composition that he ever wrote. In the monolithic tradition of Beethoven's op. 131, it stands beside Hugo Wolf's D minor Quartet, Schoenberg's op. 7, Josef Suk's op. 31 and Elliott Carter's First Quartet, and in its day was reputed to be the most demanding work in the entire repertoire.[34] After the world première, given by the Rosé Quartet on 9 April 1918, it was taken up the Feist Quartet (whose rehearsals were supervised by Webern), and during the early 1920s performances were also given by the Amar Quartet. There, for half a century, the case rested. During the 1970s the work was disinterred by the LaSalle Quartet, whose recorded interpretation, issued in 1978, can be regarded as authoritative.

As much a wordless music-drama as a work of 'absolute music', the Second Quartet is the composer's personal *Inferno*, a tormented account of tormented relationships. Zemlinsky hinted darkly about the programmatical content in a letter to Alma –

Perhaps it will make a certain impression on you. Particularly if you know which period of my life finds expression in it. (But perhaps also none at all.)[35]

– but a programme in the conventional sense probably never existed.* He appears to have drawn inspiration from episodes in the lives of those closest to

---

* Later correspondence with Schoenberg about op. 15 is concerned entirely with practical questions. Zemlinsky was unable to attend the world première, which was evidently marred

him, reliving above all the horrors of the Gerstl affair, and using the quartet medium to orchestrate the interaction of those involved.* In contrast to Strindberg's novel, which ends with a section entitled 'Jacob Wrestles', the final bars of the Quartet speak of peace and reconciliation. But 'shaken, distraught, apprehensive and extremely tense' as Zemlinsky found himself, no words could more fittingly outline the opening of his secret programme than those written by Schoenberg in the autumn of 1912, also under the shadow of Strindberg's *Inferno*, for *Die Jakobsleiter*:

Der unerträgliche Druck . . . ! Die schwere Last . . . ! Welche schreckliche Schmerzen . . . ! Brennende Sehnsucht . . . ! Heisse Begierden . . . ! [. . .] Mord, Raub, Blut, Wunden . . . ! Besitz, Schönheit, süsses Behagen . . . ! Heitere Tatkraft und glückliches Wirken . . . ! Ein Werk steht da, ein Kind kam zur Welt, ein Weib küsst, ein Mann jauchzt . . . und wird wieder stumpf . . . und sinkt zurück; und ächzt weiter, und stirbt, wird begraben, vergessen . . .

The intolerable pressure . . . ! The heavy burden . . . ! What dreadful pains . . . ! Burning desire . . . ! [. . .] Murder, robbery, blood, wounds . . . ! Possession, beauty, sweet contentment . . . ! Buoyant creativity and fortunate issue . . . ! A work is completed, a child is born, a woman kisses, a man rejoices . . . and grows numb once more . . . and sinks back . . .

While stretching traditional concepts of motivic and structural relationship to their furthest limits, the Second Quartet respects tradition; its polyphony arises as much from the interplay of human emotions as from variative development; its structural divisions serve not only to outline a symphonic architecture but also to raise and lower the curtain on an imaginary stage. The discourse progresses jaggedly, even violently. Moods of acquiescence or apathy erupt with little forewarning into hysteria or exaltation, sink, collapse and burst forth anew. Kaleidoscopic changes of instrumental grouping depict constantly changing relationships between the participants: one voice moves alone, in isolation; two voices move rapidly and independently, 'without consideration' for the others;[36] individual figures oppose and harangue, rejoice and bewail. The dominant voice is often that of the cello, which runs hysterically through the registers, raises its voice as if to shout the others down, asserts itself as melody

---

by slow tempi and an overall lack of flexibility (*Web-Br*, 15 April 1918, 193). In 1920, when the work was scheduled for performance in concerts of Schoenberg's *Verein für musikalische Privataufführungen*, he therefore took the unusual step of sending metronome marks. Since these are not included in the published score, they are listed here: Opening ♩ = 72; 2 ♩ = 100; Heftig bewegt (p. 5) ♩ = 138; 16 ♩ between 84 and 88; 17 ♩ = 60; 20 ♩ = 72; 32 ♪ = 52; 46 ♪ = 126; 101⁴ ♩. = 72 (*Web-Br*, c. February 1920, 214.)

* Writing to Schoenberg after the world première, Zemlinsky remarked, 'Incidentally, Frau Mahler appears to have taken my Quartet as a personal affront. She hasn't written me a single word' (*Web-Br*, 15 April 1918, 194). There is little to suggest, however, that Alma was in any sense part of Zemlinsky's secret programme.

and bass line at once, obdurately insists on pedal points that restrict the freedom of harmonic movement. At such moments, the personality of the dedicatee – himself a cellist – rises unambiguously to the surface; at others, fully integrated, the cello joins in passages of homophony. Such moments of unanimity, however, are rare. The argument is preponderantly polyphonic, and in several sections metric uniformity and harmonic alignment are further obscured by polyrhythm:

EX. 47   op. 15, 138⁺⁴

In his survey of Zemlinsky's quartets, written in 1974, Rudolf Stephan expressed the fear that, in performance, op. 15 would suffer from an imbalance between form and content. While acknowledging the work's originality, he also voiced disappointment – common at the time – that the composer had not found the courage to cross the threshold of tonality.[37] Horst Weber, writing two years later, had the benefit of knowing the LaSalle Quartet interpretation, which revealed the full depth of the work's expressive power and offered ample confirmation of its formal coherence. In allotting op. 15 pride of place in his monograph on Zemlinsky,[38] Weber was the first to draw attention to its technical refinement and – no longer handicapped by that post-war aesthetic which found merit only in the absolutely progressive – to place the work within an accurate historical context.* Regrettably, by attempting to demonstrate that every theme followed a pattern of 'proposition, confirmation, renewed proposition and challenge', he forced the melodic material into an analytical straitjacket, and by claiming that 'the composition unambiguously supplants sonata form with a primary formal scheme of alternating sections of exposition and development',[39] he imposed objective, symmetrical order on a structure that is inherently subjective and asymmetric.

Werner Loll, in his study of Zemlinsky's chamber music,[40] has subjected the work to an exhaustive structural and harmonic examination (including a detailed investigation of the sketches), reinforcing his arguments with facsimiles, tables and musical examples, and concludes with an illuminating comparison of Zemlinsky's variative processes with those of Max Reger. Despite the opacity of his neo-Dahlhausian *Wissenschaftsdeutsch* (a stumbling-block even to the most intrepid), his analysis reveals the strength and beauty of Zemlinsky's musical logic.

At first hearing, the symphonic outline of op. 15 is readily apparent even to an unschooled ear. Stephan and Weber base their formal analyses on the assumption that this traditional outer shell accommodates comparably traditional thematic material, developed along comparably traditional lines. Loll, in contrast, while acknowledging the four-movement form, draws attention to the ambiguity of Zemlinsky's variative technique:

The discrepancies [between Stephan and Weber] can evidently be explained, above all, by their divergent opinions as to which passages can be considered thematic, in the sense of exposition, or reciprocal, in the sense of development.[41]

He therefore offers several additional interpretations of the form – as single-movement sonata, nine-movement suite and open-ended cycle – each of which, he stresses, should be considered complementary rather than exclusive (his outlines are set out besides those of Stephan and Weber in the diagram on pp. 236–7).

No attempt to analyse op. 15 from the standpoint of sonata form can entirely account for its formal complexity. While fundamentally respecting the ideal of symphonic unity, Zemlinsky expresses his vision in the form of a free stream of consciousness, logically ordered, as in the dream sequence of *Der Traumgörge*, but ultimately intuitive, motivically organic, but open-ended and all but devoid of recapitulation. His concept of musical logic *per se* had scarcely changed since 1901, when he expounded his principles, in their simplest form, to Alma:

* Weber's extensive and well-informed sleeve-notes for the LaSalle recordings of Zemlinsky's four quartets count as a significant contribution to the literature on this subject, and one of the few so far to have been published in English. Of 124 pages of text in his study *Alexander Zemlinsky* (Vienna, 1977), ten are devoted to the Second Quartet.

EX. 48

EX. 48

Formulate a clear plan [. . .] then isolate the main idea. [. . .] Decide which motifs dominate. Then ascertain where the mood – i.e. key, tempo, rhythm, melody – *really* has to change.

Once a mood has changed, and with it the balance between main and subsidiary ideas, there is no return. Each new statement of the 'motto' (to adopt the terminology of Stephan and Loll) depicts a new state of awareness and heralds a turning-point in the drama. And since this 'motto' is nothing less than the 'Self' motif, these changes of mood, colour and affect can be understood as personal commentaries, inflexions of a narrator's voice that modulates as the narrative progresses.

As an adjunct to the formal analyses of Stephan, Weber and Loll, EX. 48 outlines the stream-of-consciousness developmental processes of the Second Quartet in the form of a genealogical tree of motifs. For the sake of clarity, only the two principal lines are followed, both of which stem from the 'motto'. EXX. 48C–K trace the evolution of the 'Self' motif; EXX. 48B and M–S follow the separate development of its opening two-note particle, D–E.

In EXX. 48C and 48D, the 2–3–5 components of the 'Self' motif are expanded by a fourth pitch to generate the pentatonic cells F–C–D–G and D–E–G–A. As discussed in part V, these are derived from transpositions of the 'Mathilde' theme, A–H–D–E. The origin of EX. 48G, the opening theme of the scherzo, is ambiguous: on the one hand, its contour corresponds to the variant of the 'Self' motif employed in Psalm 23 (EX. 39B); on the other, its pitch material is again related to the 'Mathilde' theme. Whatever their origin, all three derivates symbolize family bonds. The homophony of EXX. 48C and 48S, etched against predominantly polyphonic surroundings, speaks of consensus, unity, solidarity; EX. 48D, on the other hand, played by the first violin unaccompanied, presents the 'Mathilde' theme in isolation.

By interverting the 'World' motif and lowering the second note by an octave, Zemlinsky arrives at the first three pitches of EX. 48E, G♭–A♭–E♭. Arrayed sequentially, this new idea first appears as transition to the scherzo, a descent into the depths, which sets the scene for the ensuing *Totentanz*. Split into a spiky dialogue of falling 7ths and rising dyads, the motif provides the substance of the second scherzo theme, EX. 48F. A further variant, EX. 48H (later marked 'with vulgar, trivial expression'), multiplies the falling minor 7th with a 7th chord. In EX. 48J the motif recurs vehemently in the viola, *forte sul ponticello*, shadowing the 'violent' reaction (EX. 50) of the violins. In the closing bars of the work the motif is inverted (EX. 48K) and rises serenely into the heights. After thirteen bars of idyllic repose, this final leap of a major 9th, E–F♯ – fourteen semitones – presents a unity of affect and number.

Just as the 'Mathilde' theme grows organically from the 'Self' motif, the Lydian sweetness of EX. 48B emerges almost imperceptibly from the first reprise of the 'motto', at 14. Initially the *Adagio* (EX. 48M) recaptures this spirit of tranquillity, superimposing the 'Self' motif (first violin), now in a D major context, upon a chromatically altered variant of the Lydian theme (viola) and an open 5th, D–A, in the cello. Five bars later, a varied repetition of this threefold constellation (EX. 48N) reveals a latent instability: the line of the viola is further disfigured, causing the harmony to veer momentarily towards E♭ minor and forcing the cello to abandon its bucolic D major bourdon. From this point the seismic curve of the *Adagio* begins to rise. The effect of this one chromatic displacement (the F♮ of the viola in EX. 48M) is comparable to that meteorologists' hypothetical fluttering of a butterfly's wings which, by chain reaction, ultimately unleashes a typhoon. Gradually widening the amplitude of seismic vibration, the *Adagio* grows from a warm, sonorous opening to a climax of protracted frenzy.

The disturbance is more than local: with an explosive *pizzicato*, the cello carries over the nervous energy of the *Adagio* into the scherzo, taking the incident of the parallel 5ths (EX. 48P) as a pretext for renewed conflict. In every theme of this lineage, Schoenberg stands revealed. His initials are embedded in the parallel 5ths, D–A̲ and E♭(=S̲)–B♭; the same letters head the opening segments of the third scherzo theme, EX. 48Q, and the ensuing *glissando* leap encompasses thirteen semitones. From here it is but a small step to the 'Siegfried' motif, outlined by EX. 48R, with its implication of a hero struggling against destiny: 'Jacob Wrestles'.

Both Stephan and Loll identify the *Drehfigur* which succeeds the first statement of the 'motto' (first violin) as the first subject of a sonata allegro:

EX. 49A   Zemlinsky: op. 15, bars 11–13

Yet, despite its obvious kinship with the principal *Drehfigur* themes of Schoenberg's op. 10 –

rehearsal number*	Stephan single-movement form	Weber single-movement ↔ four-movement sonata form		Loll single-movement form	four-movement sonata form	nine-section cyclic form
opening	Motto		I Opening Allegro	Motto	I 1st movement	Motto
1	1st subject ⎫	1st subject group		Exposition		1 Opening Allegro
6²	2nd subject ⎬ Exposition	Development (I)				
11	3rd subject + transition ⎭		II Slow Movement			
14	Motto	2nd subject group (Variations)				Motto
16						2 Andante (arch form)
17	Andante ⎫ 2nd subject					
20	Andante mosso (figural variation) ⎬ group					3 Variations I
24	Allegretto (Codetta)			Motto		Motto
31¹						
32	Slow movement = central development section	Adagio-development (II)		Development section I (in two parts)	II Adagio	4 Adagio

Rehearsal no.*					
46	Scherzo and Trio	Variations	III Scherzo and Trio	III Scherzo	5 Variations II
56		Scherzo-development (III) [Trio]			6 Scherzo
78				[Trio] [Scherzo reprise]	
83					
90⁶	Motto (condensed reprise)	Reprise (abbreviated)	IV Finale		
92			Motto	Transition to …	Motto
100		Development section (IV)	Reprise I (condensed)		7 Andante
100⁵	Finale: Rondo in free form (exposition with development character)		Development section II	IV Finale	8 Finale
132	Coda: condensed reprise of 1st section	Coda			
134			Motto		Motto
135⁴			Reprise II		9 Andante (Coda)

Zemlinsky: Second Quartet op. 15
Formal Analyses by Rudolf Stephan, Horst Weber and Werner Loll

* Rehearsal numbers correspond to the Universal Edition study score, Philharmonia no. 66 (Vienna, 1916)

EX. 49B   Schoenberg: Second Quartet op. 10
(I) first movement (opening); (II) third movement (opening)

– the idea is given substantially less prominence during the further course of the argument than the terminology would imply. Its underlying harmony, however – the 'Fate' chord surrounded by a plethora of auxiliary notes – plays as significant a role in the drama as the 'Self' motif. In its simpler, four-note form, the chord overshadows the entire 'theme and variations' episode (20 to 30); with the auxiliary notes B♭ and C, it underpins much of the impassioned cello/viola duet in the *Adagio* (39^{-1} to 40) and insinuates itself into the third scherzo theme (EX. 48Q). Once again, shortly before the coda (135^3 to 136), the chord, now reunited with its original *Drehfigur*, plunges the stage into darkness. In two brief episodes (at 92 and 136^3), the minor triad of the 'Fate' chord shifts to the major, signifying, as in Mahler, progress from darkness to light. In this simple metamorphosis lies the crux of the entire drama.

As the drama of the opening abates ('grows numb once more . . . and sinks back . . .), there follows a section of 25 bars, marked 'Ruhig', in which the predominant idea is formed from a dotted ostinato in the viola, later doubled in octaves by violin II; high above, violin I meanders through a long melody, and far below the cello wends its own chromatic way. Vague and distorted as the image may be, the dotted figure mirrors an idea from Strauss's *Elektra*:

EX. 50A   Zemlinsky: op. 15, 5^{-2}

1 The Sephardic Synagogue in Vienna, watercolour *c.*1890: Franz Reinhold.

2 Adolf von Zemlinszky, *c.*1864.

3 Clara Semo, *c.*1870.

4 At two years of age, with a relative (? Bianca Semo), 1873.

5 In Berlin, 1898.
6 With a lady friend (probably Ida Guttmann) at the Volksoper, 1905.
7 Mathilde Schoenberg and Clara Semo in Berlin, c.1912.
8 With Schoenberg in Prague, 1912.

9 Rehearsing at the Lucerna in Prague, date unknown.
10 In Berlin, 1932.
11 With Brecht and Weill, Berlin 1931.

12 Louise Zemlinsky
in Vienna, c.1935.

13 Hansi Zemlinsky
in New York, 1946.

14 Louise Zemlinsky,
self-portrait 1964.

15 Mathilde Schoenberg, 1907: Richard Gerstl
16 Self-portrait, 1908: Richard Gerstl.
17 Zemlinsky, 1908: Richard Gerstl.
18 Couple in a field (?Edward Clarke Rice and his wife Melanie), 1908: Richard Gerstl

19 *Sarema*, blocking sketch for act ii, scene 1,
Munich Hofoper, 1897

20 Selma Kurz and Erik Schmedes
in *Es war einmal . . .* , Vienna Hofoper, 1901

21 Alfred Roller: Set design for *Der Traumgörge*
act i, Vienna Hofoper, 1907

22 *Eine florentinische Tragödie*, vocal score,
Universal Edition, Vienna, 1917

23 Costume design for *Der Zwerg*, Cologne 1922: August Haag
24 *Der König Kandaules* at the Volksoper, Vienna, 1997
25 *Der Kreidekreis* at the Staatsoper, Berlin, 1934

26 The house in Grinzing
(Kaasgrabengasse 24)

27 The house at Larchmont
(81 Willow Avenue)

28 Zemlinsky memorial,
Zentralfriedhof Vienna, 1996:
Josef Symon

EX. 50B   Strauss: *Elektra*, 126ᵃ

It is the first entrance of Orestes, who stands and stares, aghast, at the 'fearful eyes' and 'hollow cheeks' of his own sister – in the context of the family relationships that fuel the dramatic fires of op. 15, a connection that appears not altogether irrelevant.

Despite the striking diversity of their analyses, Loll, Stephan and Weber all agree that the scherzo, which begins at 46, is followed by a trio (at 78). The sudden change of musical character at this point – from jagged semiquaver motion to smooth cantilena, from polyphony to homophony, from restless activity to quiet repose – does indeed indicate a new section of classical trio character. But this wellnigh ostentatious planting of a 'trio' flag is supported neither by statistics nor by thematic analysis (nor is it included in the score). Zemlinsky's 'trio' is an ingenious illusion: it occupies only 42 bars, as opposed to 383 bars of scherzo-related material, and of these bars, 5 (from 80) are themselves given over to a reminiscence of the scherzo. Although the *pp* entrance of the upper voices creates the impression of an entirely new idea, the melodic outline (ex. 48s) originates in the homophonous 'variations' theme (ex. 48c), while its intervals – a pair of 4ths, a semitone apart – are drawn from the third scherzo theme (EX. 48Q, itself derived from the parallel 5ths of the cello, EX. 48P). From the standpoint of music-drama, the 'trio' introduces a new, warm-hearted character, whose presence momentarily dispels the nightmarish atmosphere of the *Totentanz*.

A more pervasive, more ominous figure is impersonated by the dotted hemiola rhythm, first introduced as a muffled heartbeat, shortly before the *Adagio* (at 28⁻⁴):

EX. 51

Having disappeared for 570 bars, the figure returns almost fortuitously in a subsidiary voice (viola at 98) and within a duple-metre context. Rapidly becoming the centre of attention, it then provides the backbone of the finale's hemiola-dominated main theme (*Feurig*, 101). In a 60-bar diminuendo (109 to 115), the 'heartbeat' subsides from *ff* to *ppp*. A brief silence; then the cello, in quasi-recitative, softly recalls the hemiola theme. The violins counter with a violent expostulation (EX. 48J) in 'heartbeat' rhythm. This same wild gesture, harmonically expanded and melodically wider spun, recurs in act II of *Wozzeck*:

EX. 52   (A) Zemlinsky: op. 15; (B) Berg: *Wozzeck*, act II, 95[1]

It is the moment where Wozzeck enters Marie's room, surprising her while admiring a pair of ear-rings given to her by her lover. With hindsight, the passage in op. 15 could be interpreted as depicting a comparably compromising situation and a comparable moment of 'being caught unawares'.

At 132[3], with no evident motivation, the viola launches into a *fff* ostinato of octave Ds, grinding out the 'heartbeat' rhythm over and over, as if in a frenzy. The other three voices answer as one, with a strident reprise of the 'variations' theme (EX. 48C). To this new conflict, the music can offer no solution: the viola breaks off unexpectedly, as if exhausted, and the other voices tail off in a diminuendo. The 'Self' motif re-enters (in the sketches this final return of the motto is marked 'in soft lamentation')[42] to restore concord. Now that the group has been reunited and the 'heartbeat' rhythm laid to rest, the stage is set for a final scene of reconciliation.

A Florentine Tragedy

Only two days after completing the fair copy of the Second Quartet, Zemlinsky began work on his new opera. Structurally the scores are similar, their single-movement forms divided into clearly differentiated symphonic sections. Common to both works is a scenario of infidelity, violent death (suicide on the one hand, murder on the other) and rapprochement. Yet while the Second Quartet recalls crisis-ridden years in the form of a secret diary, *A Florentine Tragedy* avoids self-portrayal altogether. And where every bar of the quartet bears witness to deep-seated personal involvement, the opera, despite its vivid vocabulary of musical Expressionism, is a model of objectivity. In this respect, text and music are ideally matched. 'We live in an age when unnecessary things are our only necessities,' wrote Wilde.[43] His play wilfully juxtaposes affects (love and hate, beauty and ugliness, youth and old age) and archetypes (noble and commoner, Catholic and Jew), inviting the spectator to witness their violent interaction as if in a wrestling match. Bloodthirsty yet bloodless, the drama is synthetic: a study of human relationships *in vitro*.

Ever since Alma had taunted Zemlinsky with his physical ugliness, he had been searching for a theatrical remedy with which to cauterize the wound. In 1909 he asked Schreker to write a libretto for him on the 'tragedy of the ugly man'. The outcome was *Die Gezeichneten*, the perverse tale of Alviano, a hunchbacked Genoese nobleman, Tamare, his vigorous young rival, and Carlotta, the painter whom they both love. Already while writing the libretto, however, Schreker found musical ideas 'taking firm shape and form' within him. He therefore asked Zemlinsky to relinquish his rights to the text, and composed the music himself. In 1911 he offered Zemlinsky a new libretto, *Der rote Tod*, inspired by Edgar Allan Poe's *Mask of the Red Death*. In certain aspects – a doom-laden atmosphere of Gothic horror, a setting in seven rooms of seven colours – the story was a precursor of Maeterlinck's *Ariane et Barbe-bleue*. It could have afforded magnificent opportunities for orchestral tone-painting, indeed Zemlinsky considered the libretto 'very original'.[44] Nevertheless, he turned instead to *Malva*, magnetically drawn to the symbol of the eternal triangle.

In 1913, at Schoenberg's suggestion, he read *Merlins Geburt*, a mystery play from a cycle of eight Holy Grail dramas by Eduard Stucken. Though discouraged by Marie Pappenheim, Schoenberg had himself expressed interest in setting it to music, and hesitated only on account of two scenes with numerous subsidiary characters, which did not appeal to his sense of theatre.[45] Zemlinsky read the play through: 'Much I like, some things not at all,' he wrote.[46]

Guest appearances of the Ballets Russes at the NDT in January 1913 and February 1914 brought Zemlinsky into contact with Diaghilev. Always on the look-out for collaborators of distinction, and lured by the prospect of a ballet to a text by Hofmannsthal, the great impresario expressed a keen interest in *The Triumph of Time*. In the spring of 1914 Zemlinsky therefore contacted Hofmannsthal – not directly, but via Alma – to propose revising act 1 (*The Crystal Heart*) as an independent dance-drama. 'I'm rather keen on the idea,' he told Schoenberg, '& am already making sketches.'[47] Alma duly contacted the poet, took him for a stroll and broached the subject with as much tact as she could muster. Unable to obtain his assent, she wrote to Zemlinsky, explaining that since 1901 Hofmannsthal had gathered 'new experiences in theatre' and no longer considered his work worth reviving.* As he wrote to Alma, it was a stunning blow:

I took an imaginary 'stroll' with him myself and heard him say the following: 'At present I am partner in such a solid firm, and business conditions are so secure, that any attempt on my part to make other contacts would be frowned upon. Z. may be an artist of esteem, but for the time being I am quite satisfied with my esteemed R[ichard] St[rauss]. I live quietly and with a clean conscience, and am making a healthy profit – rewriting the works of others.'[48]

The time had come to show the world what he was really worth. If Hofmannsthal considered it beneath his dignity to collaborate with a mere Zemlinsky, then he would work with an author of even greater renown. Levetzow and Stucken were all well and good, but Diaghilev had reminded him that only a big name would draw a crowd. With a setting of Oscar Wilde, Strauss had caused a furore; why should he not follow suit, with *A Florentine Tragedy*?

Cast

Guido Bardi, Prince of Florence (ten); Simone, a merchant (bar); Bianca, his wife (sop). Sixteenth-century Florence, in Simone's house, [towards evening].

Synopsis and formal outline

	Prelude
Simone, returning from a journey, surprises Bianca with Guido.	1 Allegro *Slow introduction* (1^{-10})
Feigning disregard, he welcomes the handsome young Prince as a client. After a brusque exchange with Bianca, he displays his wares.	*Exposition:* *1st subject group* (6^2)
First he unrolls a bolt of richly embroidered Luccan damask,	*2nd subject group* (23)
for which Guido coolly offers more than twice the asking price;	*Development* (27^{-5})
then he brings out his masterpiece, an ornate Venetian robe of state.	*Arioso* (28^{-2})
Guido agrees to buy it, regardless of the cost,	*Recapitulation* (37^{-2})
indeed he proposes, as if in jest, to purchase the entire stock – in exchange for Bianca.	*Coda* (45^{-5})

* At that very time, in May 1914, Diaghilev mounted the world première of Strauss's ballet *Die Josephslegende*, to a scenario by Hofmannsthal and Harry Graf Kessler.

The merchant orders his wife to spin – 'spin some robe which [. . .] might serve to wrap a dead man'. The distaff is worn; she refuses.	II Andante *Rondo*/1 (45^3)
Simone strikes up a conversation about malpractices in foreign trade,	*Trio* I (53^{-2})
but Guido feigns boredom. Bianca scolds her husband for his lack of refinement,	*Rondo*/2 (54^4)
whereupon he turns the conversation to foreign affairs. Again, Guido shows no interest.	*Trio* II (57^5)
Within his four walls, mutters the merchant, stands 'that mighty stage whereon kings die'. He withdraws into an adjoining room.	*Rondo*/3 (59^4)
'Oh, would that death might take him', whispers Bianca.	*Coda* (64^{-1})

Simone, returning, overhears her. He speaks of death, tainted morals and old age.	III Arioso (67^{-3})

Pointing to Guido's lute, he entreats him to play,	IV Scherzo (71^4)
for music 'can draw poor souls from prison-houses'.	*Trio* I (81)
'Your lute I know is chaste,' he adds sardonically.	*Scherzo* (86)
The Prince, content 'with the low music of Bianca's voice', declines.	*Trio* II (91^5)
Simone offers to drink wine with him,	*Scherzo* (98^{-4})
but starts back at the sight of a blood-red stain on the tablecloth.	*Trio* III (102^{-5})
He fills two glasses for the lovers,	*Scherzo* (106^{-3})
and Guido drinks a toast to Bianca,	*Trio* IV (108^{-1})
rapturously extolling the sweetness of the wine.	*Scherzo* (110^{-1})
Rejecting Guido's company, Simone withdraws into the garden.	Transition (112^{-3})

The lovers' discourse grows passionate: they seal their bond with a kiss.	V Arioso and Duet (116^{-5})

Simone re-enters, and Guido takes his leave. Bianca fetches a torch, while Simone brings the Prince his cloak and sword.	*Transition* (126A⁻²)

Transition ($126A^{-2}$) is to the right of the first paragraph.

Simone re-enters, and Guido takes his leave. Bianca fetches a torch, while Simone brings the Prince his cloak and sword. | *Transition* ($126A^{-2}$)

Comparing the shining poniard with his own rusty blade, his tone grows menacing. They fight. Simone is wounded, but rallies, disarms the Prince, hurls him to the floor and strangles him. Then he turns to his wife. | VI Finale (129^2)

- -

Bianca kneels before him: 'Why did you not tell me you were so strong?' 'Why did you not tell me you were beautiful?' He kisses her on the mouth. | *Postlude* (150^4)

Wilde began work on his play in 1893, conceiving it as one of a trio on 'love's cross-purposes',[49] and continued during a visit to Italy the following spring. Soon after his arrest, in April 1895, the manuscript was stolen from his study. Later a copy was found among his posthumous papers, but it lacked the opening love scene for Guido and Bianca. At the world première, on 12 January 1906 in Berlin, Max Reinhardt filled the gap with a serenade sung by Guido, while the first London production, on 10 June 1906, used a substitute scene written by Thomas Sturge Moore.* Puccini, who read the play at the time, found it 'beautiful, inspired, strong and tragic, [. . .] a rival to *Salome* but more human, more real'[50] and expressed an interest in setting it to music. Six years later he even considered expanding it into two acts, but was dissuaded by his publisher, Tito Ricordi.[51] In search of material for 'a passionate Italian tale with women and monks', Busoni read the play in 1913, but finding Wilde's ending to be 'based on a joke' he concluded that 'the play resists music, mine at least'.[52]

Behind the neo-Shakespearean surface of polished blank verse, the reader catches occasional glimpses of Wilde's own, precarious situation. For him, commerce had become the unavoidable concomitant of lust, and in exchange for Bianca's caresses Guido falls victim to sexual blackmail. The Prince's extravagance, hedonism and egocentricity serve to identify him with Wilde's lover, Bosie (Lord Alfred Douglas), and Simone's description of Guido's family as 'a garden full of weeds'† can be read as a slur on Bosie's father, the Marquis of Queensberry.

Once Simone has entered, he dominates the stage. Nothing would prevent him killing his victims outright, but before administering the *coup de grâce* he chooses to indulge in a sadistic game. This forcibly subdued brutality of a cuckolded husband, which eventually erupts into violence, places Simone close to

* Zemlinsky's request to Max Meyerfeld to write an opening scene was met with refusal.
† The line is not included in Zemlinsky's libretto.

the fisherman Vasilli in *Malva* and to Alviano in *Die Gezeichneten*, indeed the triangular disposition of the three plots is all but identical: a young man, handsome and sensuous, pitted against an older, uglier rival; between them, in whatever shape or form, the *Ewigweibliche*.* Yet the sophistication of Wilde's language, diametrically opposed to the coarseness of Gorky, offered Zemlinsky the more appropriate vehicle for musical refinement. For him, the play's most glaring defect – the dramaturgical imbalance between Simone and the other characters – will have been amply compensated by the colour and imagination of the writing. Its subtleties, such as Wilde's minute description of the brooch on the Venetian robe of state, will scarcely have escaped his sense of structural finesse. Here, namely, Wilde condenses the whole drama into an allegoric picture:

Upon one side / a slim and horned satyr leaps in gold / to catch some nymph of silver. Upon the other / stands Silence with a crystal in her hand, / no bigger than the smallest ear of corn.

The death-ridden atmosphere of the play may have stirred memories of the Gerstl affair, but Zemlinsky also appreciated its pertinence to Alma's love affair with Walter Gropius in 1910, which had seriously aggravated Mahler's heart condition and almost certainly exacerbated his final illness. When Alma attended the première of the Vienna production, she was duly outraged. In reply to her letter of protest, Zemlinsky outlined the story as he understood it and, without mentioning names, pointed an accusing finger:

The treachery of fate drives two people apart. The husband's passion for his work leads him to overlook his wife's beauty, while the woman at his side, finding herself cheated of her youth and physical appeal, becomes a slave to apathy, dejection and open hatred. To bring the two back to reality, a terrible catastrophe is called for. This is a real tragedy, because one life has to be sacrificed to save two others. And you, of all people, have failed to understand that?! [. . .] 'Why did you not tell me you were so – weak?'[53]

Although the four-movement structure of *A Florentine Tragedy* – allegro, andante, scherzo and finale – is readily discernible to the unaided ear, as with the Second Quartet, classical analysis cannot entirely account for its formal complexity. In the allegro, variative processes blur the distinctions between exposition and development, and the ternary D♭ major episode of the state robe (the arioso of the formal plan on p. 242), though organically integrated into the structure, scarcely corresponds to any standard element of sonata

---

* Bianca's very name, which signifies nothing more than a woman with a fair complexion, is symptomatic of Wilde's indeterminate characterization. In this spirit of physical and spiritual anonymity, a textual alteration in the Prague production of 1917 changed the colour of her hair from black to blond (instead of 'deines Haares Mitternacht' at 117[4], Guido sang 'deines Haares gold'ne Pracht').

form.* Similarly, the andante (Simone's spinning song) is only an approximation of a rondo: the ostinato bass line that supports the opening cantilena reappears sporadically in the trio sections, implying variation form, and the semitonal sigh that initially accompanies the cantilena evolves by stages into a theme in its own right, which ultimately supplants all other motivic shapes. Both scherzo and finale correspond more closely to classical models, but here, too, motivic cross-references transcend sectional divisions. The technical challenge of setting Wilde's text to music lay in mirroring the artifice and richness of the literary style while creating and subliminally maintaining an atmosphere of impending disaster. In this sense, Zemlinsky's score is an object lesson in the art of subjugating the more extravagant and even blood-curdling aspects of musical Expressionism to the fundamental disciplines of logic and clarity. As in *Der Traumgörge*, larger-scale forms remain subservient to the seismic curve of dramatic dialogue; motifs are constantly varied and reshaped according to the mood and tempo of the action. The genealogy of the convulsive double-motif that accompanies Simone's first entrance (EX. 53A), for instance, could be charted through several intermediate stages, from its origins in the opening bars of the prelude (EX. 53B) to its final stage of development, in the finale (EX. 53C):

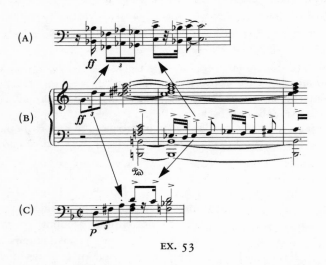

EX. 53

The inner shell of D minor symphonic form is enclosed within an asymmetrically proportioned A♭ major framework. Contrary to expectation, the orchestral prelude, ostensibly conceived as a wordless ersatz for Wilde's missing love

---

* Hans-Ulrich Fuss (in 'Zemlinskys *Eine florentinische Tragödie*', *Musica*, 1985, 15–22) sees the first 'movement' as a rondo. While the episodes of the Luccan damask and the robe of state could well be understood as representing the first and second episodes of classical rondo form, the lack of any identifiable refrain makes his hypothesis untenable.

scene, proves to be dramatically ambivalent. In the spirit of the upsurging semi-quaver motif of Strauss's *Don Juan* or the opening horn figure of *Der Rosen-kavalier*, the trumpet fanfare of EX. 52B can be understood as a phallic symbol, and the orchestral *furioso* as conveying the ecstasy of coitus. Yet the ensuing music (*Rauschend*, at C⁻³) is later identified not with Guido but with Simone, and returns verbatim in the scene of the Luccan damask, epitome of his pride and joy. Not until the final kiss are its rights of ownership clarified: the D minor of Guido's murder moves – as in the Second Quartet – to the D major of reconciliation; Simone eyes are at last opened to the beauty of his wife, and the ecstatically winding love motif, first heard in the fourth bar of the prelude, rises softly through D minor and A♭ minor to purest A♭ major (with F♭ and B♭♭ cutting sweetly into the chord like love bites). All that had been stolen, the smallest motif, the subtlest harmonic inflexion, everything formerly associated with Guido, is now again in possession of Simone. Only as the bass line passes through A minor, the key of death, does the radiant A♭ major of his victory suffer a momentary discoloration.

Inspired by Wilde's rich imagery, Zemlinsky conjures up a superabundance of orchestral colours. In the episodes of the Luccan damask and the state robe, in the wild abandon of the scherzo and the unrelenting fury of the murder scene, Simone is pitted against a deluge of orchestral sound. At the world première in Stuttgart, conducted by Max von Schillings, the over-dominant orchestra caused unfavourable comment; for Prague, where the composer himself conducted, the score was accordingly subjected to careful pruning. In Zemlinsky's hands, as Felix Adler remarked, 'everything was made transparent';[54] later interpreters have often struggled in vain to maintain an acceptable balance between stage and pit.*

Already at the world première, the influence of Strauss on Zemlinsky's orchestral technique, declamatory style and dramatic timing provoked non-adverse critical comment. *A Florentine Tragedy* is his most overtly Straussian score and stands as close to *Salome* and *Elektra* as *Die Seejungfrau* to *Ein Heldenleben*. As before, his intention was to create a work of similar impact but superior workmanship: unlike Strauss, he upheld the ideal of total thematicism. But for a few suggestive details, such as the whirring of the distaff in the spinning song (non-illustrative, in that Bianca refuses to spin) or the mandolin chords for Guido's lute (non-illustrative, in that Guido refuses to play), he also avoids pictorial illustration. More evident, if only in the iridescent orchestration of the love music (particularly the slow, dreamlike section of the prelude, from M²), is a certain proximity to Schreker. Inability to distinguish between cause and effect have prompted some more recent critics also to detect the influence of Korngold.

---

* Zemlinsky's orchestral material, which include copious alterations, is preserved in the archive of the Národní Divadlo.

Influenced as Zemlinsky may have been by certain of his contemporaries, his score was itself influential. Berg, for one, knew it well. The obscene gesture of the solo violin at the moment of Guido's last gasp, slithering down the 'Fate' chord from a high G♯ to a low D, is quoted verbatim, if parodistically, in Wozzeck (act II, solo viola at 230). Likewise the whining 5ths of two violas *sul ponticello* and the ensuing high *pizzicatos* that represent Simone's thought 'that like an adder creeps from point to point, that like a madman crawls from cell to cell' (at 114), contribute to Berg's depiction of the snivelling Captain (act II, 200²) and of Wozzeck's derangement (act I, 225⁻²).

The short score of A Florentine Tragedy was completed in nine weeks, but nearly two years passed before the opera was performed. With his lack of commercial sense, Zemlinsky had neglected the question of copyright. Due to the vagaries of wartime, contact with Robert Ross, the executor of Wilde's literary estate, was impossible, and further difficulties were caused by the translator, Max Meyerfeld, who refused to concede exclusive rights.* Once Universal Edition had established a sound legal base for the new work, however, four productions followed in quick succession. At the world première in Stuttgart, Zemlinsky found the singers mediocre and Schillings's conducting 'dreadfully clumsy'; on 4 March 1917 he himself conducted the opera in Prague, staged by Fritz Bondy and with Hans Nachod in the role of Guido. Later that year the work was given at the Vienna Hofoper (a production Zemlinsky considered execrable) and in Graz.

Despite the shortcomings of the Stuttgart production and the apathetic reaction of a meagre audience, the critic of the *Schwäbische Merkur* proclaimed the work a masterpiece:

With A Florentine Tragedy the stage has won a work that is captivating, powerful, inwardly stimulating and enchantingly beautiful; a work whose like has not been written since *Salome*. [. . .] Compared with the mere surrogates and fumbling efforts of beginners, of which we hear more than our fair share, this masterpiece demonstrates how deeply such music can move us, how sorely it is needed.⁵⁵

Schoenberg, who heard the opera in Prague, wrote to Alma of a *'very fine'* première of 'a very significant work',⁵⁶ and Werfel, who evidently attended the Viennese première with her, wrote (with characteristic hyperbole):

In Zemlinsky's opera A Florentine Tragedy I found one particularly inspired idea – besides a hundred other powerful moments of beauty – which [. . .] appears not to have been composed (assembled), but whose origin is seemingly primordial. It is the

* For the event of Meyerfeld withholding the rights altogether, an alternative translation was prepared by Marie Pappenheim. In 1929, despite protests by Zemlinsky and Universal Edition, Meyerfeld made his translation available to the Swiss composer Richard Flury, whose score was performed the same year in Biel-Solothurn.

eruption of love to the words (I quote from memory): 'Your image will be with me always', that phrase which so wonderfully swells up to dominate the opera's matchless prelude. [. . .] These bars have followed me for years, their rising strain accompanies many a sensation of joy and strength. One thing is clear: the man who put these notes to paper has a soul of fire, [. . .] he emanates from the innermost heart of music.[57]

Productions followed in Leipzig (1922), Aachen (1924), Schwerin (1925), Freiburg (1927) and Brno (1928). For fifty years the opera then vanished from the stage* – a far cry from the spectacular international success of *Salome*. Fame and fortune proved as elusive as ever.

* Mention should be made of one intermediate revival: Luc Balmer's studio performance for Radio Berne in 1954. The prelude was also sporadically performed as a concert piece.

2

Prague in Wartime

On 19 September 1914, seven weeks after the outbreak of war, Zemlinsky participated in a 'Patriotic Concert' at the NDT. He opened the programme with Weber's *Jubel* overture, then followed poetry readings, choral music and lieder (including the two Liliencron songs from his op. 8),* and the event concluded with Schiller's *Lied der Glocke*, staged by Parcival de Vry (Technical Director of the NDT) as a series of *tableaux vivants*.† At face value the programme was a model of political correctness; beneath the surface, the choice of works reflected an ambivalent if not subversive attitude. *Jubel*, dedicated to Friedrich August I of Saxony on the occasion of his fiftieth jubilee, ends with a bombastic rendering of the patriotic song *Heil dir im Siegerkranz*. To the cosmopolitan public of the NDT, however, the melody will have been more familiar under its original title: *God Save the King*. And those who read the militaristic texts of Zemlinsky's op. 8 will scarcely have overlooked their critical message: *Mit Trommeln und Pfeifen* is the lament of a deserter on his way to the gallows; *Tod in Aehren* poignantly depicts the death of a common soldier.

Later that year, in Vienna, Zemlinsky's Maeterlinck songs were published as 'Sechs Gesänge op. 13': the poet, as citizen of an enemy nation, remained unnamed.‡ At the NDT, revivals of *Orpheus in the Underworld* (4 October 1914) and *The Tales of Hoffmann* (24 January 1915) were billed under the name of 'Jakob Offenbach'. But already on 18 April, with Auber's *Fra Diavolo*, the ban on French music was surreptitiously lifted; on 7 November, with a new production of *Djamileh*, Bizet re-entered the repertoire, and *Carmen*, revived two weeks later, remained a popular favourite throughout the war. Initially, the programme for 1914–15 had also included operas by Leoncavallo, Mascagni and Verdi, but after Italy's declaration of war on Austro-Hungary (23 May 1915), Italian music was also forbidden. In Prague, this ban too was soon lifted: on 18 October 1915 the NDT revived *La bohème*, followed by *Otello* (9 December, with Leo Slezak, conducted by Zemlinsky), *Il trovatore* (28 January 1916), *Un ballo in maschera* (31 January) and *Tosca* (4 February).

---

* The group included two Loewe ballads, Schubert's *Gebet während der Schlacht* and Wolf's *Der Tambour*.
† The concert was repeated six days later.
‡ Maeterlinck published several articles in French newspapers, decrying the execution of Belgian civilians by German soldiers. Universal Edition has never rectified the omission of his name from the title page of the 'Sechs Gesänge'.

Otello in war-time Prague: for Werfel the occasion remained an 'unlost reality', and for the twelve-year-old Hermann Grab the performance came to symbolize the urge for normality in a time of barbarism and meaningless carnage. In 1937 he could still recall the occasion in detail:

Why should the theatre be heated, why should it be lit up? We sit in the auditorium shivering in our winter coats, our pockets full of corn bread, and hear Slezak as Othello. We go wild with delight. When we leave the house after the performance, the streets are dark. An isolated droshky stands by the roadside. Slowly we walk home. A little paperboy rushes up to us: 'Special issue! 3000 Russians fallen in East Galicia!' The paper is duly bought and skimmed through – then the conversation returns to Slezak and Othello.[1]

As far as the Czechs were concerned, this was not their war. And for the Germans in Prague, as Zemlinsky reported to Schoenberg, the situation was far from easy:

The people here are in a most curious frame of mind: the Czechs are depressed and reluctant, cheered by every piece of bad news; the Germans are depressed as well, because they feel themselves to be on enemy territory. The Czechs console themselves with the thought that the Russians will soon be arriving![2]

When war broke out, Zemlinsky was on vacation at Sellin on the isle of Rügen. To break a return journey made arduous by the lack of civilian transport, he overnighted with the Schoenbergs in Berlin before travelling on to Prague. Shortly after arrival he noted, not without an undertone of apprehension, that the authorities were recruiting 'smaller, weaker men, [. . .] particularly Germans and Jews', while 'those with the slightest sign of corpulence' were being passed over.[3] Initially exempted from military service, he contributed to the war effort by holding the fort at the NDT.

Many artists were unable to reach Prague in time for the new season; others, having been called up for army service, never returned. At first the repertoire had to be limited to operetta and comedy, but even light entertainment failed to draw a crowd. The financial situation grew critical, and since an application for government subsidy was rejected, salaries were reduced and paid out on a weekly or even daily basis. Replacements had to be found for several leading soloists; chorus and orchestra were decimated; the stage crew reduced to four. Teweles, though obliged to shelve several important projects – notably the world première of *Der Traumgörge* – contrived to fill the gaps in his ensemble, and presented a well-contrasted programme.

Zemlinsky's versatility stood him in good stead. Apart from conducting most of the opera performances, he made frequent appearances as a pianist (a performance of Strauss's *Enoch Arden*, given to a full house, brought him a profit of 600 Kč),[4] took over the direction of the Prager Männergesangsverein from Keussler, and even tried his hand at stage direction. As he wrote proudly to

Schoenberg, *The Barber of Baghdad*, which he produced and conducted in February 1915, 'turned out to be one of our best productions'.[5] In view of the shortage of stage personnel, the number of orchestral concerts was doubled, and Zemlinsky made a virtue of necessity by programming a complete cycle of Beethoven symphonies.

In Mannheim the Nationaltheater announced plans for the 1915–16 season, which included new productions of *Kleider machen Leute* and Shakespeare's *Cymbeline** with incidental music by Zemlinsky. The greater part of the latter had been composed and orchestrated in the autumn of 1913, and only Cloten's 'Hark, hark, the lark' still had to be written.[†] Time was short. As it happened, Shakespeare's poem corresponded both in mood and metre to Gregorovius's *Blaues Sternlein*, which Zemlinsky had set to music in 1898. He therefore adjusted the scansion of the op. 6 song to fit the new text, decked out the piano part with a filigree mantle of orchestral bird calls, extended the prelude by two bars and reharmonized the close. In an effort to bring his urbane Tonkünstler-verein manner in line with the brooding, post-Romantic style of his more recent work, he crammed perhaps more detail into the slender lied than it could properly support.

In the prelude, two *espressivo* themes of leitmotif character are woven into a vivid tapestry of martial fanfares, impassioned climaxes, enigmatic echoes and abrupt silences. The first theme, associated with the figure of Posthumous, seems to have been overheard from Berg's Quartet op. 3 (composed in 1910) –

EX. 54   (A) Zemlinsky: *Cymbeline*; (B) Berg: Quartet op. 3,
second movement, bars 5–6

– while the second theme, associated in the *Malva* sketches of 1912 with the fisherman Vassili, represents the sphere of Imogen. The F♯ minor introduction to her scene with Pisanio, in which she bewails her husband's departure for Italy

---

* The titles were listed under *Novitäten* ('Novelties') in the *Deutsches Bühnenjahrbuch*, 1915. Most earlier productions of *Cymbeline* had been based on textual adaptations, such as *Imogen*, performed in Leipzig and Bremen during the 1880s with incidental music by Schumann's friend Albert Dietrich.
† During the war, manuscript paper grew scarce. For the items composed in 1913, Zemlinsky used 24-stave score paper, but for the last five pages of Cloten's song he had to resort to 14-stave paper of a format normally used for copying orchestral parts.

(I/iii), revisits the desolate landscape, high on unaccompanied violins, of the 'Mathilde in solitude' episode of the Second Quartet.* The cortège preceding act IV exploits the morose quality of the Phrygian mode, distantly recalling the *Pelléas* music of Fauré, while the introduction to act V paints a battlefield scene of barbaric splendour, in much the same vein as the Shakespearean film scores composed thirty years later by William Walton. Perhaps the most striking sections of this uneven work are the spoken settings of 'Fear no more the heat o' th' sun' and the 'solemn music' prescribed by Shakespeare for the scene in which the murdered Sicilius Leonatus and his family appear to Posthumous in a dream.

The *Cymbeline* music is as extravagantly orchestrated as the Shakespeare scores composed for Max Reinhardt by Humperdinck,[†] with triple wind, harp, harmonium, celesta, and a substantial array of offstage wind and brass. The manuscript was delivered to Mannheim in February 1915,[6] but the National-theater, decimated like every other theatre in Germany, was unable to stage so ambitious a project. Nor can it have been considered the appropriate moment to mount a play whose principal theme was the heroism of the ancient Britons. In December 1914, furthermore, Bodanzky had announced his departure for New York, and without his support the project was doomed.

For Zemlinsky there remained a generous fee (600 marks)[7] and a vacant opus number, which he soon filled with the published score of Psalm 23. Eighty years passed before the *Cymbeline* music was heard. In consideration of an event so long postponed, those who attended the first performances[‡] could well have murmured the line from Posthumous's dream in which Jupiter, the *deus ex machina*, reveals that, in the eyes of the gods, human destiny is but a vexatious game:

Whom best I love I cross; to make my gift, the more delay'd, delighted.[8]

Despite the energy with which Zemlinsky approached his duties, he was painfully aware that Prague, from an artistic standpoint, was an enclave of provincialism; despite the euphoria with which his achievements at the NDT were greeted by press and public alike, he knew that he was capable of greater things. Already in the spring of 1914 he investigated the possibility of moving to Brunswick,[9] and only weeks later a Berlin agent advised him to apply for the post of Conductor of the Gürzenich Concerts in Cologne. Since the latter

* The first four notes, F♯–C♯–A–E, can be read as a transposed interversion of the 'Mathilde' motif.
† Between 1906 and 1908, Humperdinck collaborated with Reinhardt at the Deutsches Theater, Berlin, on four Shakespeare productions: *The Merchant of Venice*, *A Winter's Tale*, *The Tempest* and *As You Like It*.
‡ A suite from the incidental music to *Cymbeline* was performed at Hamburg on 15 September 1996 and at Cologne on 18 March 1997.

was a position of some prestige, he approached Alma for a recommendation:

You help so many people, have such a felicitous touch, and certainly do so gladly. Therefore I ask you: are you well connected with any influential personality in Cologne, whose attention you could draw to my particular merits? E.g. that I was partly a pupil of Brahms, that I am in fact entirely a pupil of Mahler's, that I am a true musician, etc.[10]

Schoenberg did his best to persuade Zemlinsky to stay in Prague:

I can understand your impatience: your director is an ass, the public is small, and at present the international impact is negligible. I can understand that you want to perform things as they should be performed. But you would be amazed at the low standards in the leading theatres. I am sure that your impact would be greater, but it seems that the public takes not the least interest in quality. In this respect, it scarcely matters where you are, provided that working conditions are acceptable.[11]

Shortly after the announcement of Bodanzky's departure for America, Carl Hagemann offered Zemlinsky the position of First *Kapellmeister* at Mannheim. Considering that the Nationaltheater was second in rank only to the court operas in Berlin, Dresden and Munich, this was as attractive a prospect in wartime as it had been a few years before. But from a theatre of such stature Zemlinsky naturally expected commensurate payment, and accordingly he tendered a demand for an annual salary of 14,000 marks. He heard nothing more.[12] In his place, Hagemann engaged a conductor willing to accept a more moderate fee, a man fifteen years Zemlinsky's junior, talented, but with a shaky stick technique and little operatic experience: Wilhelm Furtwängler.

Zemlinsky wrote to Alma:

If I must be condemned to waste all my talent and ability in Prague (and with the best will in the world, these are qualities I cannot deny) [. . .], and if I can find nobody who still believes in me and is glad to lend me a helping hand – even if I am not looking for anyone – even my best friends will forget me – *you* included! But in the course of time I have learned to swallow the bitterest of pills, and in a certain sense they have done me good. I have grown hardened, have developed a protective shield against all forms of disappointment. Meanwhile, to be sure, life runs its course.[13]

Apart from their illicit excursions into French and Italian repertoire, Teweles and Zemlinsky concentrated their efforts on the great Austro-German composers. Having opened the first wartime season with *Fidelio** and a concert version of *Egmont* with Beethoven's incidental music, they continued with operas by Cornelius, Mozart, Nicolai, Wagner and Weber; in concert, the Beethoven symphonies were complemented by lieder and keyboard music by

---

* Zemlinsky reverted to Mahler's practice of beginning with the E major *Fidelio* overture and interpolating *Leonore* no. 3 before the final scene.

Bach, Brahms, Schubert and Hugo Wolf; the 'Eroica' Symphony was preceded by *The Creation*, the 'Choral' Symphony (for which Zemlinsky adopted the orchestral retouchings of Mahler) by Mozart's G minor symphony (K. 550). As a memorial to Carl Goldmark, the doyen of Viennese composers, who had died on 2 January 1915, Zemlinsky performed several of his lieder and orchestral works, and finished the season with a new production of *Das Heimchen am Herd* (*The Cricket on the Hearth*), a score that in its day had exerted a seminal influence on the *fin-de-siècle* cult of folk-tale opera.

Four days after the Goldmark première, on 16 June, Zemlinsky received an ominous letter from the recruiting office. Schoenberg did his best to console him: 'I'm certain you're too weak';[14] 'I shouldn't think they'll take you, your constitution is far too sickly.'[15] The summer was spent at Königswart (Lázně Kynžvart) near Marienbad, orchestrating *A Florentine Tragedy* and awaiting the fateful confrontation with the MO. Early in September the verdict was passed: unsuitable.

During the 1915–16 season, Webern obtained a dispensation from his garrison commander at Leoben to rejoin the music staff of the NDT. In January 1916 he assisted Zemlinsky in rehearsals of Schumann's Scenes from Goethe's *Faust*.[16] But after only a few weeks, his conscience troubled by the news that Schoenberg himself had been forced into uniform while 'Lehár, that pig, was released at once',[17] he returned to active service.

As the war progressed, Zemlinsky made a point of performing music by twentieth-century Austrian composers. In concert, he conducted Mahler's Fourth Symphony and the *Kindertotenlieder*, Reznicek's *Donna Diana* overture and Schoenberg's 'Song of the Wood-dove' from the *Gurrelieder* (in a version for reduced orchestra, specially prepared by Webern); classical symphonic programmes were interspersed with lieder by Rudolf von Prochazka, Heinrich Rietzsch and Schreker, which he himself accompanied at the piano. The operatic repertoire, though largely confined to standard works, included an exquisite new production of *Così fan tutte* (also partly assisted by Webern) and, as sole novelty, *Mona Lisa* by Max von Schillings. The most spectacular event of the 1915–16 season, however, was a series of performances of Strauss's *Alpensinfonie*, an organizational *tour de force* of which Teweles was particularly proud:

As a matter of principle, I took care to fulfil the composer's every demand. Eighteen first violins! In the conductor's opinion, sixteen would have done just as well. But a symphony demands no less careful a production than a theatrical work. [. . .] The *Alpensinfonie* was presented as a special event and that was exactly what it was: it was performed on its own* and filled three houses in succession.[18]

---

* A slip of memory: the first performance was preceded by the 'Eroica' Symphony, the second by Beethoven's Fifth Symphony and the *Lied der Waldtaube*, the third by Reznicek's *Donna*

Zemlinsky, who took no less flattering a view of Strauss's new symphonic poem than he had of *Ein Heldenleben*,* endorsed Paul Bekker's opinion that 'from this art I believe we can expect nothing more than the aura of a diverting game'.[19] A work far closer to his heart, and one that still awaited its world première, was Schoenberg's op. 9B, the orchestral version of the Chamber Symphony. Although protests were expected from the public, a performance was scheduled for 27 January 1916. Schoenberg pointed out, however, that he had experienced enough fiascos in Prague, not only at the NDT, but also at the Rudolfinum, where a performance of *Pierrot lunaire* in February 1913, only a few weeks before the 'scandal concert' in Vienna, had been disturbed by violent protest from a large section of the public.

Delighted as I am that you intend to perform my Chamber Symphony [he wrote], and much as I would wish to hear the work in performance at last, [. . .] I would ask you to refrain from doing so until the war is over.[20]

For op. 9B Zemlinsky substituted the 'Song of the Wood-dove'. And when the Chamber Symphony was next performed, two years later in Vienna, it was given before an invited audience.

The season closed with revivals of *Rheingold* and, as omen of future developments in the theatre of war, *Die Götterdämmerung*.

In the autumn of 1916 Heinrich Jalowetz joined the music staff as *Kapellmeister der Oper*. Initially his presence caused friction, particularly when it transpired that he had applied for the musical directorship in Frankfurt, a post on which Zemlinsky had also set his sights.

Jalowetz would take the job for 4000 marks [Zemlinsky wrote to Schoenberg], while I've been offered 10 to 12. That apart, I know from experience that he'd slip one year's salary into his agent's pocket, etc. What do you think? Here I am, valiantly slaving away making music, still convinced that talent, energy, seriousness & idealism are better qualities than a big mouth, money & connections. I'm gradually taking over the role of 'uncle' who brings along goodies for *everyone*, only to be given a sop in return. *Nobody* thinks of me, *nobody* gives me a helping hand. [. . .] Today I made a final attempt to get away from here. It's the last time. After that – resignation.[21]

In this case his grumbling was unjust. Jalowetz proved a willing helper and a reliable friend, well qualified to share the irksome burdens of musical directorship. Five years later he concluded a biographical sketch of Zemlinsky with quiet-spoken words of appreciation and respect:

Diana overture and Fidelio Finke's *Frühling* (five songs with orchestra, world première, conducted by the composer).

* Webern, who attended one of the performances, wrote to Schoenberg: 'I can't help thinking of those kitsch pictures which cover an entire wall, the sort you can see in museums!' (Hans and Rosaleen Moldenhauer, *Anton von Webern, Chronik seines Lebens und Werkes* (Zurich, 1980), 194).

To the many young conductors who have enjoyed the privilege of working under him and with him in the theatre, he is a model of professionalism and leadership.[22]

On 17 September 1916 Zemlinsky conducted the world première of Weingartner's opera *Kain und Abel*. Determined as he was to overlook his disgraceful treatment at the Hofoper, he prepared the work with customary care and diligence. Nevertheless, the débâcle of *Der Traumgörge* remained unforgotten, and secretly he must have smiled when Weingartner's work was taken out of the repertoire after only three performances. Korngold, meanwhile, with his sure instinct for ingratiating himself, had unearthed an early one-act play by Teweles, *Der Ring des Polykrates*, and set it to music as a companion piece to *Violanta*, his contribution to the current vogue for Renaissance cloak-and-dagger opera. Bruno Walter gave the double-bill a lustrous première in Munich on 16 April, and on 16 November Zemlinsky followed suit in Prague. The two works met with 'superficial success'[23] but were given only four times. On 1 January 1917 followed the revised, two-act version of *Ariadne auf Naxos*. The opera was warmly received, but due to the large cast and the exceptional demands made on the orchestra, which precluded the use of players borrowed from the Národní Divadlo or elsewhere, it was given only three times. *Ariadne* nevertheless remained one of Zemlinsky's favourite scores, and he ensured that it was reintroduced into the repertoire as soon as circumstances were more propitious.

On 4 March followed the Prague première of *A Florentine Tragedy*. Despite enthusiastic notices by Adler and Rychnowsky, the public remained indifferent. To keep the work in the repertoire, Teweles devised the weirdest of couplings. At the première, Zemlinsky's work was followed, appropriately enough, by another contemporary Austrian opera, Bittner's *Das höllisch Gold*. Later, however, it served as a curtain-raiser to *Hänsel und Gretel* or *The Barber of Seville*; and on 2 May Teweles assembled a grotesque triple-bill of Zemlinsky, Wolf-Ferrari and Leo Fall.

On 29 November 1916, to make amends for the cancellation of Schoenberg's Chamber Symphony, Zemlinsky gave the world première of the string-orchestra version of *Verklärte Nacht*. The work scored a resounding success, as did *Pelleas und Melisande*, which he reintroduced to Prague on 28 February 1918.* Other major scores new to his repertoire were the Verdi *Requiem*, Bruckner's Ninth Symphony and Mahler's Second.[24] As the war drew to a close, Massenet's *Manon* and Puccini's *La fanciulla del West* were added to the operatic repertoire (both conducted by Jalowetz), and with a performance of *La Mer*[25] Zemlinsky ventured into the *terra nova* of Debussy (he retained his preference for Dukas, however, whose *L'apprenti sorcier* followed later that

---

* At an introductory lecture by Felix Adler on 24 February, excerpts from the work were performed on two pianos by Jalowetz and Webern.

year).[26] Thanks to Teweles's careful management, the budget allowed for three complete *Ring* cycles and the appearance of internationally accredited soloists, such as Bronislav Hubermann.[27] The seventh anniversary of Mahler's death was celebrated belatedly, in a concert on 8 June 1918, with *Das klagende Lied* and *Das Lied von der Erde*.

Since 1909, when Zemlinsky had asked Schreker to write 'the drama of an ugly man', his creative life had centred on the search for viable librettos. The Viennese première of *A Florentine Tragedy* on 27 April 1917 occasioned an unexpected revival of contact between the two composers: Schreker wrote to express his appreciation of the new work,[28] and Zemlinsky replied that Reichenberger's reading of the score had completely misrepresented his intentions. In 1914, the NDT had undertaken to perform *Der ferne Klang*, but at a time when depletion of the chorus made even *Tannhäuser* and *Lohengrin* unperformable, the production of so large and demanding a score was out of the question. Apologizing for the postponement, Zemlinsky suddenly changed the subject: '*Why don't you write a libretto for me*! [. . .] I have a fine subject to propose to you, terrifically interesting. But I would also gladly compose something of your own choosing.'[29] Schreker must have pleaded lack of time (he was himself working on a new opera, *Das Spielwerk und die Prinzessin*), but Zemlinsky was not easily dissuaded. Later that spring he suggested a libretto based on Selma Lagerlöf's novel *Herr Arnes penninger* (*Herr Arne's Treasure*, published in 1904), an idiosyncratic combination of detective novel, ghost story and historical romance. 'Right now, I am burning to compose something,' he wrote.[30] Schreker read the book and sketched out a brief scenario. He was a fast worker, and could have produced a libretto in a matter of weeks. But his own work took priority, and Zemlinsky was obliged to 'burn' without him.

He had already offered to send Schreker a copy of his own draft scenario. Left to his own devices, and anxious to start on the project at once, he decided to write the libretto himself. Before the summer was over, he had completed the text and sketched out the music for the opening scene.* In the autumn, however, the project experienced an unexpected setback: on 17 October, Max Reinhardt presented a new play by Gerhart Hauptmann entitled *Winterballade* – a free dramatic adaptation of *Herr Arnes penninger*. There was little point in competing with one of the greatest writers of his time. At first Zemlinsky contemplated writing to Hauptmann,† perhaps with a view to transforming his play

---

* Cf. letter to Schoenberg, dated 27 August 1917: 'I myself have written a complete libretto (no *more* but also no less than that) & also composed the scenic prelude' (*Web-Br*, 171). The manuscript libretto is preserved in the Zemlinsky Collection (*LoC* 28/15) but, apart from a few marginal jottings in the text, no music survives.

† In an undated letter to Emil Hertzka, managing director of Universal Edition, he asked to be given Hauptmann's address.

into an opera libretto, but by the end of the year the idea had been abandoned.

At the beginning of the 1917–18 season Webern rejoined the music staff of the NDT, this time as chorusmaster. With a roster of seven conductors and repetiteurs, his presence was scarcely necessary, yet Zemlinsky, the 'uncle who provided goodies for *everyone*', cosseted him like a delicate child. Even if his charge was capable of standing on his own feet, Zemlinsky insisted on personally supervising preparations for his first public appearance. Lortzing's *Zar und Zimmermann* was well chosen, being neither insultingly easy nor dauntingly difficult to conduct, and the production, by Paul Gerboth (with Friedrich Schorr in the role of Tsar Peter) was greeted enthusiastically. Zemlinsky led the rehearsals and conducted the première on 13 January 1918 himself; Webern then stepped in for four repertoire performances. As Webern worked alongside Zemlinsky and Jalowetz at the NDT, his comparative lack of experience engendered in him a sense of inferiority; furthermore he pined for Vienna and for Schoenberg, to whom he felt an even stronger bond of allegiance than to Zemlinsky. At the end of the season he returned to Vienna. 'I deeply regret his leaving,' Zemlinsky wrote to Schoenberg, 'but I believe he is right in deciding to abandon theatre altogether.'[31]

Georg Klaren
caricature by Alban Berg[32]

In the winter or spring of 1918, a young writer named Georg Klaren, prompted presumably by the success of *A Florentine Tragedy* in Vienna, sent Zemlinsky a sample of his work and proposed collaboration. Finding 'much good material'[33] in Klaren's work, Zemlinsky proposed three alternative subjects: Keller's *Romeo und Julia auf dem Dorfe*, Balzac's *La peau de chagrin* or Oscar Wilde's *The Birthday of the Infanta*.* At the time, Klaren was working on a biography

---

* In March 1918 Zemlinsky also briefly considered a libretto by Feld and Levetzow entitled *Die heilige Ente*, the comic fable of a Mandarin, manipulated by the gods, who finds the path to love and enlightenment. Set to music by Hans Gál and first performed at Düsseldorf in 1923 under Georg Szell, the piece later enjoyed considerable success.

of the sexual pathologist Otto Weininger,* whose spectacular suicide in 1903 had caused a stir in literary and psychoanalytical circles, and whose dissertation *Geschlecht und Charakter* (*Gender and Character*), published a few months after his death, had for years been the talk of the Vienna coffee-houses. Klaren, who was himself well versed in sexual pathology and Freudian analytical theory, found Zemlinsky's taste in operatic subjects psychologically revealing. Identifying Simone in *A Florentine Tragedy* as the composer's ego, he detected 'a willingness to [. . .] enthuse in an orgy of masochism'; the closing scene hence affirmed Weininger's theories of female domination:

It is Bianca who holds the torch, and all that matters is to die at her feet, to see the woman as a demonic force, as sovereign.[34]

Zemlinsky's enthusiasm for Keller, he explained, was 'the longing for a peaceful idyll, for naïve primitivity, a longing that besets all decadents.'[35] And in *La peau de chagrin*, he continued,

this search for an idyll is combined with that desire – familiar to every passive individual – for brute strength, expressed in erotic terms: the sadism of a Don Juan, [. . .] of the archetypal lady-killer, who stands beyond Good and Evil.[36]

Klaren's diagnosis of Zemlinsky's nervous condition as hypersensitive passivity, coupled with a hyperactive sexuality bordering on the perverse, was not as wayward as it must then have appeared. And considering that he knew Zemlinsky only from afar, his insights into the man as public figure and creative artist were remarkably accurate:

To see Zemlinsky conduct – and I stress: to *see* – is to becomes aware of movements that have been described as nervous spasms. It seems unimaginable that such a man could impose his iron will upon an orchestra. But one *hears* and knows that this is the case. [. . .] What do people usually mean when they talk of 'nervous' people? – neurasthenics, it would appear. But neurasthenia signifies weakness of the nerves; when energies are mobilized that demand more than any healthy nerves could achieve, can one speak of weak nerves?

He is the seeker whose head projects into a *new* era, but who cannot entirely raise his body up after him, whose *past* shackles him to a *present* which stands in opposition to his psychological constitution; the resultant suffering makes an artist of him.[37]

The first of four projected scenes for Klaren's adaptation of *La peau de chagrin* (initially entitled *Das Chagrinleder*, but later changed to *Raphael*) arrived in May.† Zemlinsky set to work on the music at once – composition, he

---

* Georg Klaren, *Otto Weininger. Der Mensch, sein Werk und sein Leben* (Vienna, 1924). The book was completed in 1919.
† The plot: Raphael uses the magic power of his chagrin leather to win the affection of the courtesan Fedora. Soon, however, he grows disgusted at her sycophantic behaviour, insults her,

told Schoenberg, was 'the best & only narcotic against the terrible misery'[38] of war – and when the season ended, he withdrew, as in 1917, to the idyllic resort of Spindelmühle (Špindlerův Mlýn) in the Giant Mountains. There he worked 'almost as in old times, several pages every day'. Work continued in the summer of 1919, but this project, like so many others, was ultimately abandoned, probably because Klaren had meanwhile delivered a new libretto, *Der Zwerg*, which was closer to his heart.

With a performance of *Die Meistersinger*, on 19 June 1918, Zemlinsky took leave of the NDT for the summer. Eight weeks later, when he returned to rehearse Eugen d'Albert's *Die toten Augen*, his name was no longer officially 'von Zemlinsky' but simply 'Zemlinsky',* Teweles had resigned,† Prague was on the point of being proclaimed capital city of the Republic of Czechoslovakia, and the Austrian Empire was in its final stages of collapse. Seven years in Prague had brought forth only two larger-scale works – masterworks, admittedly, but the tip of an iceberg of frustration and failure. Zemlinsky's chagrin leather was shrinking; life was 'running its course'.

---

and murders her protector in a duel. Of the few surviving sketches, the first idea, dated 'May 1918', refers back to the 'trio' theme of the Second Quartet, while also providing an initial impetus for the Lyric Symphony:

* As from 7 December 1918, when Zemlinsky premièred a new production of Weber's *Oberon*, his name was printed on NDT programmes without the 'von'.
† Teweles was unwilling to bear any further responsibility for the NDT. His wife had died shortly after the outbreak of war, and he had lost his savings, most of which were invested in war bonds.

VII

Lieder (II)

previous page:
The Music-giant
cartoon by Emil Weiss(?)
first published in *Montagsblatt*, 31 May 1926

I would kneel at your feet eternally, kiss the hem of your robe, worship you like a saint. [. . .] After you, there is nothing![1]

With these effusive, ominous words Zemlinsky had once poured out his love to Alma, his 'sovereign', his 'demonic force'. Andersen's tale of *The Little Mermaid* relived the heartbreak, Dehmel's *Maiblumen* mourned the fall. In the early summer of 1903, perhaps still in search of ideas for a 'Symphony of Death', he composed a setting of *Es war ein alter König*, a laconic parable by Heine that tells of an old king, his young queen, and a handsome page-boy:

Sie mussten beide sterben, / Sie hatten sich viel zu lieb.

The two both had to perish, / Their love was far too strong.

Other songs dating from the same year are lost,* and even the Heine setting survives almost by chance. Eighteen years later, Zemlinsky, himself now the 'old king', prepared a slightly revised version as a Christmas present for his 'young queen' Luise – but that is another story.

Of the relatively few lieder composed between 1901 and 1916, many have personal backgrounds; each has an individual physiognomy. Some, notably *Es war ein alter König*, are prophetic of future developments; others, such as the Two Ballads of 1907 and the Four Songs of 1916 follow experimental paths that ultimately led nowhere. Many are terse and enigmatic, almost wilfully obscure; accompaniments often sound like the bare bones of an imaginary orchestral score; motivic relationships are as often implicit as explicit.

Es war ein alter König opens with that 7th chord Alma had so relished in *Selige Stunde*. But the song also treads fresh ground, if warily, abandoning the chromatically flowing, post-*Tristan*esque harmonies of *Maiblumen* for a leaner, more angular style. In the revised version, greater familiarity with the idiom enabled Zemlinsky to work into the harmonic argument an approximation of Wagner's *Tristan* chords.

Über eine Wiege was composed for a soirée of the Ansorge Verein (10 April 1904) in honour of the poet Detlev von Liliencron. With the economy of a Japanese woodcut, the poem depicts a silent tragedy: a cradle in the sunshine,

---

* In a letter to Schoenberg dated 12 January (*Web-Br*, 35), Zemlinsky mentions 'a few lieder for Fräulein [Gabriele] Kunwald'.

a hovering blue butterfly, a bird perched on the hand of a dead child. Zemlinsky gently colours the picture with fluttering piano figurations, etched against a calmly expressive vocal line, the sunlight orange of D major tinged with the purple of E♭ minor and the black of A minor. Throughout the closing strophe a low D chimes softly like a distant bell. With a grief-stricken shift to C major the structure subsides; the bell resumes its tolling.

In the summer of 1905, while holidaying at Sekirn in Carinthia, Zemlinsky composed his *Schlummerlied* (lullaby), to words by Richard Beer-Hofmann.[*] The first draft, in a sketchbook for *Der Traumgörge*, was written on 5 July, just one day before completing act II of the opera. Although the fair copy bears no dedication,[†] the song was presumably conceived for Alma, now mother of two children,[‡] whom Zemlinsky visited at Maiernigg a few days later. In contrast to the nursery-rhyme dreams of Görge, lulled to sleep by his mother's shade, Beer-Hofmann's lullaby is much of this world, bleak and pessimistic:

Dunkel verborgen die Wege hier sind, / dir und mir und uns allen, mein Kind. / Blinde nur sind wir und gehen allein, / keine kann keinem Gefährte hier sein.

Dark, my dear child, and concealed lies the way, / you and I and we all are astray. / Lone is the passage, and we cannot see, / none for another companion can be.

The song, a study in tonal ambiguity and slowly changing shades of one soft colour, stands at a far remove from the broadly conceived architectural harmony and wide colour range of *Der Traumgörge*. A monotonous anapaestic rhythm permeates the score (the opening bars also imply 4ths harmony, but the idea remains largely unexploited); voices fan out chromatically, but soon return, as if tethered, to their starting-point; chord progressions arouse expectations that remain unfulfilled.

In the spring of 1907 Schoenberg and Zemlinsky participated in a contest sponsored by the Berlin periodical *Die Woche*. Candidates were required to submit settings of texts from an anthology of modern German ballads, published in a special number of the same journal some months previously.[2] Both composers chose the poems *Jane Grey* by Heinrich Amann and *Der verlorene Haufen* ('The Lost Brigade') by Viktor Klemperer.[§] Whatever they may have hoped for, they were disappointed: the prizes went to composers of little or no

---

[*] The text is taken from *Schlaflied für Mirjam*; of the original four verses, Zemlinsky set only the second. Beer-Hofmann's poem, first published in *Pan*, vol. 1, no. 2 (Berlin, 1898), enjoyed considerable popularity: in 1912 it was recorded by the celebrated actor Alexander Mossi, and reprints were published until well into the 1920s.

[†] The initials 'M.O.', which head the first draft, may indicate an intended dedication.

[‡] Her first daughter, Maria (Putzi), was born on 3 November 1902 and died of diphtheria in June 1907; her second child, Anna (Gucki), for whom the lullaby was probably intended, was born on 15 June 1904.

[§] As was customary, entries were handed in anonymously, with a motto on the title page to

repute, Hans Hermann, Heinrich Eckl and Gustav Lazarus, and when the adjudicators selected settings of the Amann and Klemperer texts for publication, Schoenberg and Zemlinsky were again passed over, this time in favour of Philip Rödelberger and Hugo Kaun.*

Considering that their ballads were composed almost simultaneously in adjoining apartments, and that they even share the same key (D minor), it may seem surprising that the pieces themselves have so little in common – nothing but an atmosphere of gloom and dismay to accompany Jane Grey's walk to the scaffold, and a stylized vocabulary of fanfares and drum-rolls to invoke the spirit of the desperadoes of *Der verlorene Haufen*. Schoenberg distributes his motivic argument equally between singer and piano, as if in a purely instrumental composition, while Zemlinsky's accompaniment supports and complements the voice, as if in an operatic aria. Schoenberg sets *Der verlorene Haufen* in compound metre and scans *Jane Grey* with preponderantly weak-beat entries, while Zemlinsky prefers simple metre and up-beat or strong-beat entries.[3] Compared even with *Der Traumgörge*, the harmonic style of his Two Ballads is exceptionally bold and experimental. *Jane Grey*, a study in chromaticism, often uses functional chords to non-functional end; *Der verlorene Haufen*, which has an exceptionally demanding piano part, experiments with 4th chord harmonies, sprung rhythms and stark, coarse-grained sonorities, arriving at a hybrid style that occasionally anticipates middle-period Shostakovich. But Schoenberg is considerably bolder, combining elements of 4th chord, whole-tone and augmented-triad harmony to novel and disquieting effect. From his Two Ballads (published in 1920 as op. 12)[†] it was but a small step to the full emancipation of the dissonance. As for Zemlinsky, the Two Ballads number among his most substantial lieder[‡] and make a powerful impression in the concert hall. Yet there is no evidence that they were ever

---

identify their authorship. Zemlinsky chose as motto a particularly intriguing 4ths chord from *Der verlorene Haufen*:

* Hugo Kaun (1863–1932) was a composer of some stature, with a sizeable *œuvre* of symphonic music and chamber works to his credit. During a period in the US, from 1884 to 1901, some of his orchestral music was performed by the Thomas Orchestra in Chicago.
† *Jane Grey* was performed at a concert of Schoenberg's Verein für musikalische Privataufführungen on 23 October 1920 (whether this was the first performance is unclear).
‡ Since bar numbers provide unrepresentative statistics, the proportions of the ballads are better expressed by timings. Schoenberg's Two Ballads (in the Vanni–Optoff–Gould recording of 1968/71) last respectively 6'45" and 5'07", and Zemlinsky's (Andreas Schmidt–Garben, recorded in 1993) 4'51" and 5'04". The longest of Schoenberg's lieder are the Gesänge op. 1 (in the Gramm–Gould version of 1965 respectively 5'55" and 8'45"); Zemlinsky's most extensive is the *Turmwächterlied* op. 8 no. 1 (7'23" in the Schmidt–Garben recording of 1988).

performed during his lifetime (they were not published until 1995), and once the result of the contest had been announced, he seems to have taken no further interest in them. Perhaps he realized that he had entered into competition not as much with the Eckls and Rödelbergers of the musical world as with Schoenberg himself. 'Was machst denn du?' sings Strapinski in the 'Schneiderlein' song, composed only a few weeks later. 'What are you doing? Are you awake?' For him, as he soon must have realized, this was the wrong way. To follow Schoenberg along the road to atonality would be to abandon everything in which he believed: the expressive, colouristic and symbolic qualities of key, the divine order of musical number.

Later that year the rift widened. Between 2 and 14 December Zemlinsky composed a cycle of Five Songs to texts by Dehmel, fever-pitched poems of love, betrayal and death; three days after their completion, on 17 December, Schoenberg composed the first of his Two Lieder op. 14, to a poem from *Das Jahr der Seele* by Stefan George, *Ich darf nicht dankend an dir niedersinken*, a dialogue between a disconsolate lover and his own grief. The choice of texts, on both sides, was scarcely coincidental.

In 1890 Stefan George made the acquaintance of a young lady named Ida Coblenz. She played the piano in the living room of her family home at Bingen, while he sat and contemplated the ancestral portraits on the wall; they took long walks together in the mountainous Rhineland countryside; he wrote poetry for her. The eighth poem of his *Book of the Hanging Gardens*, written *c.*1893, opens with this surprising confession:

Wenn ich heut nicht deinen leib berühre / wird der faden meiner seele reissen / wie zu sehr gespannte sehne.

If today I do not touch your body, / then a thread will sever in my being / like an over-tautened sinew.

Ida Coblenz was the only woman to whom George ever felt physically attracted. In 1891, during a stay in Vienna, the twenty-three-year-old poet had met the seventeen-year-old Hugo von Hofmannsthal in Café Griensteidl. During the ensuing weeks he bombarded the young 'Loris' with attentions – both literary and amatory – but in vain. After a skirmish of letters, he left Vienna disappointed and insulted; Hofmannsthal wrote meanwhile of a 'seducer' who could 'kill without touching'.[4] Having returned to Bingen, George turned to Ida Coblenz for sympathy, but in April 1895 she married a businessman and moved away from the area. After only a few weeks, her marriage foundered. In the summer she wrote to Dehmel, who was then literary editor of *Pan*, reprimanding him for ignoring George's latest works; on 5 August he replied, pleading ignorance. Shortly afterwards he and Ida Coblenz met for the first time. Several phases of their turbulent relationship are recorded in *Zwei Menschen*, Dehmel's novel in verse form, which opens with the poem for which he is best remembered, *Verklärte Nacht*. The following year, when the unsuspecting George called on Ida at the family home in Bingen, he chanced upon Dehmel, who happened to be visiting at the same time. That was the end. In *Das Jahr der Seele* he charted the passage of a soul from an autumn of discontent through a winter of grief to a new strength, engendered by the rays of the summer sun.

In the verses with which George learned to come to terms with his isolation, Schoenberg too found consolation and new hope.

Zemlinsky, in contrast, returned to Dehmel's searing eroticism. Not since before meeting Alma, in 1898, had he taken any creative interest in this literature. At so sensitive a time, this renewed involvement must have struck Schoenberg as bordering on the perverse.* Only three of Zemlinsky's Five Songs survive in fair copy and, although they were probably known to his inner circle of friends and pupils, there is no record of them having been performed in public. Several of the texts refer to boats and journeys over water, alluding to, or perhaps even condoning, Mathilde's clandestine lakeside romance of the previous summer. Common to all five is a volatile mixture of passion and *Angst*.

In contrast to the bold, disjunctive voice-leading and 4th chord harmonies of the Two Ballads, the Five Songs concentrate on linear motion and a harmony saturated with 3rds, 7ths and 9ths. The brevity of the poems also allows Zemlinsky to revert to his technique of moulding a single motif or pattern to the seismic curve of the text. *Vorspiel* and *Auf See* end indeterminately, like the *Schlummerlied*, but now in areas further remote from the tonic. *Letzte Bitte*, with its homophonous accompaniment of 6th and 7th chords, *Stromüber*, built from two variants of a 'Dies irae' *Drehfigur*, and *Auf See*, notable for its mesmeric patterns of 7ths and 9ths, establish a specifically Secessionist vocabulary of extended tonality. Both the harmony and texture of the canonic scale figures at the climax of *Stromüber* were directly recalled by Berg in his Piano Sonata, composed the following year (EX. 56).

Ansturm ('Assault') envelopes the *Drehfigur* of the Clarinet Trio in triadic harmony, and creates by purely rhythmic means an atmosphere of steadily mounting tension (EX. 57).

A comparison with Alma Mahler's setting of the same poem (the third of her Four Lieder, published in 1915) makes an interesting study. Where for Zemlinsky one idea and one tempo suffice, Alma divides the text into seven sections of varying tempo and character. Zemlinsky builds to a powerful climax at the words 'dann bebst du' ('then you tremble'), while Alma sets these words *piano* as quasi-recitative, and illustrates them with a frilly passage of broken-

* Two of the poems, *Ansturm* and *Stromüber*, were actually written before Dehmel met Ida Coblenz, and published in 1891–3. The other three, taken from the anthology *Weib und Welt*, were published in 1896.

EX. 56   (A) Zemlinsky: *Stromüber*, bars 32–3 (original key: D minor);
(B) Berg: Piano Sonata op. 1, bars 89–90

EX. 57

O spurn me not, if all my craving clamorously breaks from its confines.

chord figuration. On the one hand, the syncopated heterophony of Zemlinsky's setting pays homage to the Romantic tradition in which he was steeped;* on the other, it serves to articulate the neurosis of the society in which he lived; thus this one brief song exactly defines his place in musical history. Alma flits deftly from one style to another – an echo of Richard Strauss, a smattering of Reger, a touch of Bruckner, a dab of the ultra-modern – but nowhere does her work give any evidence of a considered artistic concept or an individual creative personality. She presents the poem like a string of coloured beads, some rounded and shiny, others misshapen and dull; Zemlinsky declaims the text with a 'soul of fire'.

Were it not for musicians – notably Debussy, Dukas and Fauré – Maurice Maeterlinck would today be considered little more than an interesting historical figure. As it is, no critical or complete edition of his works has ever been published, paperback editions are rare, and the lesser-known dramas and essays have been out of print for decades. His plays, though often studied in university literature courses, are rarely staged; his verse is all but forgotten. In its day it was both praised and pilloried: on the strength of the *Serres chaudes* (1889), Mirbeau pronounced Maeterlinck a Belgian Shakespeare; Tolstoy read the Quinze Chansons (1896), stripped them of their Symbolist clothing and, as in the tale of the emperor's new clothes, uncovered their nakedness. Writing of these poems in 1912, the American critic Edward Thomas wrote that 'Maeterlinck writes in colourless water and depends upon nothing in time or space save words.'[5] This very indeterminacy, which leaves so much room for personalized interpretation, should by rights have appealed to French composers of *mélodies*. But where many delighted in Baudelaire and Mallarmé, Rimbaud and Verlaine, only few – notably Chausson and Lili Boulanger – were drawn to Maeterlinck. His Quinze Chansons emulate the artlessness of folksong, evoke images of Celtic mystery and awaken in the reader a deceptive, atavistic sense of familiarity. But there is also much that baffles and perplexes. As to their interpretation, Maeterlinck offers no clue. Like Salvador Dalí, he seems to say, 'If you can find no meaning, there is none.'

Of the genesis of Zemlinsky's Four Maeterlinck Songs little is known other than that he composed them in the summer of 1910 at Bad Ischl, evidently as a diversion from correcting orchestral material for *Kleider machen Leute*. Far from being mere reflections in the 'colourless water' of the verse, these songs are arguably the finest he ever composed, and the only works of his which, during fifty years of oblivion and silence, were still occasionally remembered and

---

* Syncopated heterophony originates in the pianism of the Romantic virtuosi (e.g. in variation 5 of Mendelssohn's *Variations sérieuses*). Eventually it becomes a linear/harmonic technique in its own right (cf. bars 53–9 of Brahms's *Academic Festival* overture).

performed. They stand emotionally and technically aloof, a challenge to interpreter, biographer and analyst* alike.

The opening phrase of *Die drei Schwestern*, a more puzzling poem than
most, is identical in pitch and rhythm to that of *O Blätter, dürre Blätter* (op. 5/1
no. 3). Perhaps this slender link to the real world can throw some light on
Zemlinsky's interpretation of the poem; but perhaps he chose not to interpret it
at all.[†] *Die Mädchen mit den verbunden Augen* outlines in a few words the fate
of the captive princesses in *Ariane et Barbe-bleue*. Parenthetical interjections –
'Take off the golden blindfold!' – are articulated by abrupt changes of tempo,
and the words 'Leben gegrüsst' ('greeted life') are set to an augmented variant
of the 'World' motif,[‡] encapsulated within the fourteen semitones of a falling
major 9th. Congruently, in the *Lied der Jungfrau* (taken from act II of *Sœur
Béatrice*, published in 1896), the words 'verirrt sich die Liebe' ('if love should
stray') encircle the major 9th – now rising – within a twofold variant of the
'World' motif (original and interversion). *Und kehrt er einst heim* is a dialogue
in which a woman, on the point of leaving her husband, instructs her serving
maid how to break the news to him. In her parting words, Zemlinsky alludes
to a love motif from the *Gurrelieder*.[§]

EX. 58   (A) Schoenberg: *Gurrelieder*; (B) Zemlinsky: *Und kehrt er einst heim*

[Say,] for fear that he weeps, a smile was on my lips.

After the death of Mahler, contact with Alma appears to have broken off. It was
re-established, but only briefly, in the summer or autumn of 1912, when she
wrote to demand the return of her copy of Casanova's *Memoirs*(!). She did not
trouble to attend Zemlinsky's performance of Mahler's Eighth Symphony in
Prague nor write to condole him on the death of his mother; when in Vienna,

---

* Helpful analytical comment can be found in Neuwirth and Kneif, *TiU*, 111–19 and 137–44.
† In the orchestral version the triumphant tonefall of the last verse is negated by the hysteria
of the two-bar postlude, creating an antithesis that Schoenberg considered over-abrupt (*Web-
Br*, 13 March 1913, 90).
‡ Cf. ex. 60.
§ The phrase, sung by Tove, first appears to the words 'So lass uns die goldene Schale leeren
ihm, dem mächtig verschönenden Tod' ('So let us drain the golden goblet to him, the great
beautifier, death') at the climax of the love scene (69²).

he therefore ignored her. No doubt the news of her stormy affair with Oskar Kokoschka had travelled as far as Prague, and for a long time there was no further contact. Quite unexpectedly, in the summer of 1913, she wrote to express her appreciation of one of his Maeterlinck songs. He replied at once:

I was absolutely thrilled to hear from you again! Particularly that a little song of mine is plaguing you. As soon as I return to Prague, in about ten days, I shall send you *copies of all four.* I would be delighted if you also take some pleasure in the others. Take a good look at *Und kehrt er einst heim.*[6]

'Take a good look': years before he had written similarly about the piano piece entitled *Liebe*,[7] indirectly drawing her attention to its hidden message. Doubtless he recognized the relevance of this song to her affair with Gropius in the summer of 1910; indeed the date of composition suggests that the news of her escapade may have reached him at the very time of its genesis.

As it happened, he had just added a further two Maeterlinck songs to the cycle, both of them depicting situations of marital infidelity. *Als ihr Geliebter schied*, from act III/iii of *Aglavaine et Sélysette*, is sung offstage from a tower overlooking the sea. Maeterlinck's towers are often places of seduction, betrayal and *crime passionnelle*. The tower of *Aglavaine et Sélysette* is no exception: tormented by her husband's love for Aglavaine, Sélysette leans from the tower window and falls to her death. Read out of context, the poem offers the reader no hint of this dramatic background. As such, it incurred the particular displeasure of Tolstoy: 'Who went out? Who came in? Who is speaking? Who died?'[8] Zemlinsky's music is correspondingly obtuse. The 'World' motif abounds here, also disfigured reminiscences of the *Gurrelieder* motif of ex. 57.*
A harmony of smoothly flowing, non-functional triads passes three times through the flattened 7th chord of D minor; the closing bars allude briefly to the 'Fate' chord. The cycle ends with the ninth of the Quinze Chansons, *Sie kam zum Schloss gegangen*. Both Maeterlinck and Zemlinsky return here to *terra firma*, with an intelligible story-line and a melodious, ballad-like piece in D major. As if turning full circle from the Heine setting of 1903, the old king takes leave of his young queen as she sets off into a new life with another man.† His agonized question, 'Wohin gehst du?', remains unanswered. Silently the lovers embrace and hurry off into the twilight. The 'unfulfilled' D octave of *Der Traumgörge* vibrates softly in the bass.

When the Maeterlinck Songs were published, in 1914, Universal Edition insisted on the downward transposition of the first two, bringing their soprano

---

* The relationship is particularly clear in bars 21–2 ('[war ein] anderer daheim').
† Several commentators, drawning attention to the ambiguity of the unidentified 'sie' ('elle') of the poem, identify the figure as death, *la mort*. This may or may not have been the poet's intention, but it was a subtlety of which Zemlinsky, who understood scarcely a word of French, can scarcely have been aware.

tessitura in line with the mezzo range of the other four. The editorial incursion is regrettable,* for it obliterates the internal cyclic structure and obscures the external tonal relationships, on the one hand to the Gesänge op. 5, on the other to the Second Quartet. Schoenberg, familiar with the songs in their original keys from the orchestral version, remarked that he found the transpositions 'disturbing'.[9] Webern, who knew them equally well, wrote simple words of appreciation:

'Und kehrt er einst heim . . .' the passage: '[Say,] for fear that he weeps, a smile was on my lips.' Indescribable. Or in the last one: 'Where are you going . . . take care in the light of dusk.' My God, how beautiful it all is.[10]

Three years later, preparing Zemlinsky's Four Songs (1916) for their first performance in Prague, Webern's enthusiasm knew no bounds:

I am still utterly overcome by the deep, shattering experience of your lieder. While rehearsing them with Fräulein Mihacsek,† I was in a continual state of ecstasy. The miracles of these structures still resonate incessantly within me.[11]

These songs, the sole fruit of an otherwise barren year, combine three Hofmannsthal poems, of strikingly diverse subject matter, content and proportion, with a German translation of Baudelaire. From a literary standpoint, the group nostalgically re-examines the 'sickly but delicate nerves' of the later 1890s. Musically speaking, they strike out valiantly in new directions, but offer no longer-term solutions. Webern's enthusiasm was presumably motivated by their extreme concentration of motivic activity, combined with an uncommonly clear focus on the poetry. After Hofmannsthal's rebuff of two years previously, Zemlinsky made no attempt to publish them.

Noch spür ich ihren Atem, a poem in *terza rima*, is concerned with transience – the continual presence in a child of its forebears, and in the adult of a child.‡ 'Everything glides and slips away,' writes Hofmannsthal, and transience constitutes a threat to the individual's very identity – a thought that for him is 'much too dreadful even to bewail'. Zemlinsky reads the text with a different inflexion: the thought is dreadful, but preordained; what is preordained must

---

* At a time when the lied was rapidly becoming the exclusive domain of professional singers, such a concession to the requirements of amateur singers was scarcely necessary.
† The Four Songs (1916) were first performed on 19 November 1922 in a concert of the Prague Verein für musikalische Privataufführungen by Felicie Hüni-Mihacsek (soprano) and Eduard Steuermann (piano). At a performance on 10 March 1923, in a concert of the Deutscher Literarisch-künstlerischer Verein, the programme also included Seven Songs by Viktor Ullmann, who was making his Prague début as a composer.
‡ Cf. Horst Weber, 'Noch spür ich ihren Atem auf den Wangen', *AeSU*, 189–96. The first line of text includes an ambiguity most German commentators have overlooked: 'ihren' can mean either 'her' or 'their'. In the context of poem as a whole, the erotic implication of the reading 'Her breath on my cheeks' seems less plausible than that of 'their breath', i.e. the breath of the poet's ancestors.

be accepted, not lamented. Hence his vocal inflexion on 'Klage', the operative word, which stands at the very middle point of the song, is passive and unemphatic. Of greater significance to him is the concept of time that 'glides'. To translate the idea into sound, he uses a vocabulary of unisons, octaves, major and minor 2nds, primordial cells that beget a complete family of related scale figures, in which each member resembles the other, but with slightly varied individual contours. Some live longer, some die young, others are born disfigured:

EX. 59 *Noch spür ich ihren Atem*, bars 1–9 (melodic outline of the piano part)*

Hörtest du denn nicht hinein is the fugitive vision of a serenader. Crushed between the dark oppression of night and the over-bright oppression of day, he sings, as best he can, an ecstatic, five-word hymn to the 'demonic force':

Liebste du, mein Alles du!

Dearest one, you my all!

As if to contradict this self-abasement before the beloved, expressed in extremes of vocal tessitura, the song reaches its soft climax – a bar of C major with *sixte ajoutée* – at the word 'ich'. A stammering triplet figure, underpinned by pitches associated with the 'Fate' chord, provides a single-bar introduction and a three-bar coda. Where at the outset some semblance of musical order is imposed on this chaos of emotions, at the close an open-pedal effect implies total loss of control. The last word, swathed as if in the dissonant jangling of an Aeolian harp, is the flattened 7th, Zemlinsky's chord of unfulfilment.

Die Beiden is the *Tristan*-inspired sonnet of a lovers' assignation and their trembling attempt to share a goblet of wine.† Zemlinsky approaches the text scenically, even to the extent of including an expansive interlude in which the man

---

* Octave doublings have been omitted. In the printed edition (*Posthumous Songs* (Munich, 1995)), bar 4, the middle note in the piano left hand (here the first entry in the bass clef) should be F♮, not A.
† Schoenberg composed two settings of the text, shortly after its publication, in 1898, at the time of his burgeoning love for Mathilde. Zemlinsky's use of the minor 9th in the last verse of his setting (at the words 'denn beide bebten sie *so sehr*, dass keine Hand *die an*dre fand') could be interpreted as an allusion to these events.

dismounts from his horse to greet his beloved. The woman's 'light and confident' gait, the pounding of horse's hoofs, the trembling of hands: everything is conveyed by varying the articulation, intensity and register of a single dotted rhythm.

Debussy's *Harmonies du soir* and Zemlinsky's *Harmonie des Abends*: separated by three decades of time and five hundred miles of space, these two pieces palpably demonstrate Hofmannsthal's concept of transience. Even if by 1916 the Parisian salon of the later 1880s might have lost much of its perfume, traces still linger. But the languorous Hispanic arabesque has given way to a Bohemian *Naturlaut,* after Klimt the veiled luxuriance of a Moreau is clarified and intensified, and after the Strauss of *Salome* and *Elektra* the latent violence of the *belle époque* has risen to the surface. Debussy's languorous intimation of a *valse mélancholique* gives way to a lugubrious slow waltz, whose next of kin is the *Valse de Chopin* of *Pierrot*. In this music Zemlinsky also relives his own past. Disfiguring and inverting the sentimental 'Du-i-du' motif of *Die Fledermaus*,* he symbolically reviews the setbacks and intrigues that accompanied his Viennese career; quoting a progression from his own Maeterlinck Songs, he reiterates Ariane's longing for the light of day:

EX. 60   (A) *Die Mädchen mit den verbunden Augen* (original key), bars 19–20
(B) *Harmonie des Abends*, bars 61–6

[The girls with blindfolded eyes] greeted life.
[like a heart] that is troubled when the day grows dark

---

* I.e. the rhythmic and melodic figures in the piano accompaniment from bar 40 *et seq.*

Whether Hofmannsthal shudders at the thought of his own transience or bombastically celebrates the *Triumph of Time*, his view of time is retrospective. The music of *Harmonie des Abends* similarly seems to ignore or even deny the future. Yet this music did live on, if at first silently. In 1940, Viktor Ullmann composed a cycle of Three Sonnets from the Portuguese op. 29, settings of Elizabeth Barrett Browning translated by Rilke into German. His manuscript bears the dedication: 'For Alexander Zemlinsky in unbounded loyalty'* – an idealized gesture, for communication between Nazi-occupied Prague and New York was wellnigh impossible. The first song, *Briefe, nun mein!*, rekindles the spiralling, flickering flame of the 'languishing round-dance' ('langoureux vertige') with which *Harmonie des Abends* closes:

EX 61A Zemlinsky: *Harmonie des Abends* (bars 103–7)

EX 61B Ullmann: *Briefe nun mein* op. 29 no. 1 (opening)

Ullmann's composition was 'the memory of a memory',[12] yet its message, the thrill of rediscovery, proved to be prophetic:

My letters! all dead paper, mute and white! / And yet they seem alive and quivering

*'Für Alexander Zemlinsky in unverjährbarer Treue'.

/ Against my tremulous hands which loose the string / And let them drop down on my knee tonight.[13]

Much of Ullmann's 'dead paper' miraculously survived the Holocaust; after decades of oblivion, many a work of Zemlinsky's is today 'alive and quivering'.

VIII

Prague 1918–1927

previous page:
Alexander Zemlinsky Conducts the Czech Philharmonic
ink drawing by Dr Desiderius
(during a performance of Mahler's Sixth Symphony on 23 February 1927)
first published in *Prager Presse*, 6 March 1927
The artist (real name Hugo Boettinger) was a close friend of the composer Josef Suk

Under Czech Rule

The NDT reopened after the summer recess on 11 August 1918, with *Hannerl or Das Dreimädlerhaus part II*, an operetta pastiche to music by Schubert. A week later Franz Josef's birthday was celebrated with a gala performance of Hugo Wolf's *Der Corregidor*, and on 7 September Zemlinsky gave the Czech première of Eugen d'Albert's *Die toten Augen* (Rychnowsky wrote of the 'captivating precision and sonic beauty' of his conducting).[1] Where *Der Corregidor* assiduously paraphrases Alarcón's light-hearted tale of a foolish miller and his beautiful young wife, *Die toten Augen* explores the same antithesis of ugliness and beauty in a context of violence and self-destruction.* Like Schreker's *Die Gezeichneten*, premièred earlier the same year in Frankfurt, this was an opera much in tune with the times.

Nostalgic Austrian kitsch of the *Dreimädlerhaus* variety could still draw a crowd, but the glorious *Dreikaiserbund* of 1873 was no more. Franz Josef had died of old age, Alexander II and his heirs had been slain by Bolsheviks at Yekaterinburg, and Wilhelm II forced into abdication and exile. Like Alarcón's foppish *corregidor*, the Austrian civil servants in Prague had been replaced by representatives of a new democracy. And like Myrtocle, the heroine of *Die toten Augen*, many Germans living in Bohemia sought escape from the ugliness of their situation, figuratively speaking, in blindness. To speak German on the street was to run the risk of verbal or even physical abuse. To sing František Škroup's *Kde domov můj* had been a treasonable offence; now the song was the Czech national anthem.

On June 3 1918 Czechoslovakia was recognized as an Allied power, with frontiers agreed between the US government and the Czech president designate, Tomáš Masaryk. On 28 October, a national committee (Národní výbor) took control of the country. Writing to Schoenberg the following week, Zemlinsky outlined a bleak scenario:

The 'Národní výbor' is amazingly well organized. At present, order and security reign supreme. How things might look tomorrow – is another matter! [. . .] Even if 'tolerated', the German community will collapse, & with it, naturally, the theatre.

---

* The plot in brief: the Roman Arcesius is wise but ugly, his wife Myrtocle beautiful but blind. Having miraculously regained her sight, she falls into the arms of a handsome soldier, whom she assumes to be her husband. Arcesius slays him, and Myrtocle, having witnessed the ugliness of the world, blinds herself anew by staring into the sun. The opera was first performed at Dresden on 5 March 1916.

Perhaps very soon. And then?!? All things told, it is dreadful! The end, just as I fore-saw it, but more wretched by far. I weep, too, for my poor Vienna. [. . .] At present art appears ridiculous, i.e. having to produce it. I haven't worked for weeks.[2]

Yet Masaryk, though an ardent nationalist, was no fanatic. Prepared to risk unpopularity in pursuit of truth and justice,* he had in 1899 successfully defended Jews in a ritual-murder trial. He was well travelled, fluent in English, German, French and Russian, and passionately fond of music.† Before the war he had spoken of the Germans in Bohemia as 'immigrants and colonialists',[3] but now, with nationalist feeling running high, he refused to countenance the persecution, expulsion or dispossession of any non-Czech minority. 'In order to coexist,' he observed, 'peoples must not necessarily love each other.'[4]

Masaryk formally took office on 21 December. Two days later Zemlinsky conducted *Fidelio* at the NDT in his presence, with the veteran Erik Schmedes as Florestan; the following March, to honour the President of the Republic on his sixty-ninth birthday, the NDT presented a gala performance of *Parsifal*. As the judicious choice of works indicates, these were no empty gestures. The Estates Theater, used for rehearsals and smaller-scale productions, had immedi-ately been appropriated by the Czech authorities, but thanks to Masaryk's per-sonal protection, the future of the NDT itself was safeguarded.

Already in the autumn of 1916 Teweles had nominated the Viennese actor Leopold Kramer as his possible successor,[5] and shortly before tendering his res-ignation he proposed upgrading Zemlinsky's status from First *Kapellmeister* to *Opernchef*, giving him full rights of artistic co-determination. At the beginning of the 1918–19 season the board of governors accepted both these proposals.

Like Teweles, the new Director of the NDT, Leopold Kramer (1869–1942), was born in Prague. His father sent him to Vienna as apprentice to a firm of merchant bankers, but secretly he took lessons in stagecraft and made his acting début, aged twenty-five, in Schiller's *Die Karlsschüler*. Having gained experi-ence at Olmütz (Olomouc), Halle and Gmunden, he returned to Vienna in 1896 to join the ensemble of the Deutsches Volkstheater. Tall and handsome, he cut an impressive figure on stage. Though often typecast as young hero in the modern dramas of Bahr or Schnitzler, he also excelled in the classics, proved an adept comedian and, later in his career, a skilful stage director.

Kramer may have been a popular figure on the Viennese stage, but he had little knowledge or deeper understanding of serious music. For Zemlinsky, who saw him as little more than a boulevard comedian, the prospect of

---

* As editor of a Czech periodical, Masaryk proved, after a heated debate, that two allegedly medieval poems (the so-called Grünberger und Königinhofer manuscripts), regarded as Slavic counterparts of the *Nibelungenlied*, were in fact nineteenth-century forgeries.

† Masaryk's wife, Charlotte Garrigue, had studied music in Leipzig. His son, Jan Masaryk, was not only a distinguished politician but also a pianist and composer (in 1942 he recorded his Songs of Lidice with the Czech soprano Jarmila Novotná for RCA).

collaboration was unconscionable. In the summer of 1918, before the engagement was officially announced, he redoubled his efforts to leave Prague. '*Help me to return to Vienna!*' he wrote imploringly to Alma; 'I must get away from here at all costs,' he told Schoenberg,[6] and in August he attempted to contact the new Director of the Vienna Opera, Leopold von Andrian. But his efforts were fruitless. Alma did nothing,* and in the aftermath of the Austrian November Revolution, Andrian resigned after only two months in office, to be replaced by Richard Strauss and Franz Schalk. Bowing to destiny, and somewhat strengthened by his new contractual powers, Zemlinsky did his best to adjust to the situation. Initially coloured by deep suspicion,† his icy working relationship with Kramer gradually melted into friendship. Kramer's wife, the actress and operetta soubrette Pepi Glöckner, must also have helped to smooth the way. As much, at least, is implied in her warm-hearted farewell address to Zemlinsky, written in 1927:

Drum zürne meinem Manne nicht / wenn er Dir heut just fehle: / Als Frau und auch als Wienerin / steh näher ich Deiner Seele.

My husband do not scorn because / today he can't salute you: / a woman, and with Viennese charm, / I'm sure will better suit you.‡

Hostility from without left no room for squabbles within the theatre. Anyway, there were more urgent problems to attend to. Just as in Germany and Austria, anti-Semitism was rampant. For the war and, above all, for the humiliating and financially crippling conditions under which peace had been negotiated, the blame was primarily laid on international Jewry. Some Czech newspapers went as far as to urge that all German property be confiscated and to demand that 'all Jewish and half-Jewish leaders should – in the literal sense of the word – be wiped out'.[7] On 16 November 1920 a mob descended on the Jewish quarter of Prague and stormed the old Rathaus. Kafka, who experienced the demonstration at close hand, wrote to his friend Milena Jesenská:§

I have been out on the streets every afternoon, bathing in anti-Semitic hate. On one

---

* Zemlinsky's next letter to her, written on 30 January 1919, began: 'My dear, highly esteemed friend – if that is what you still are' (*AZ–AMW*, 109).
† On 22 April 1921 Zemlinsky wrote to Schoenberg, 'As for Kramer, that viper, that envious, vain, hollow comedian, I can bear it no longer. [. . .] The greater my success and the more I am in demand, the more envious and perfidious he becomes, & at my cost he does everything possible to make his director's halo shine more brightly' (*Web-Br*, 224).
‡ Presumably this poem was written to be read at Zemlinsky's farewell party on 24 June 1927.
§ Milena Jesenská, daughter of a Czech dental surgeon, was married, if unhappily, to the writer Ernst Pollak. The story of her love affair with Pollak, whom she met in 1914, exemplifies the tension between Czechs and German Jews: in an attempt to terminate the relationship, her father committed her to a mental home, which she was able to leave only when she came of age in 1917.

occasion I heard someone describe the Jews as 'prašivé plemeno' [a race of dirty rats]. Where people are so detested, surely the obvious thing to do is to leave? (For that, Zionism or racial solidarity is quite unnecessary.) The heroism of those resolved to stay is comparable to that of the cockroaches in the bathroom that refuse to be stamped out.[8]

On the evening of 18 November, taking illegal orders from a city councillor, an infantry battalion from the suburb of Smíchov marched on the NDT. The theatre was full, and only a hasty telephone call from a police commissioner prevented an ugly incident. During act II of *Tosca* the lights went up and the audience was requested to leave. By the time the troops arrived, the house was in darkness. Meeting with no resistance, they stormed the building and raised the Czech flag. Two days later the confiscation of the NDT was officially ratified. Months of repossession negotiations followed, but to no avail. Until the Nazi invasion of Bohemia in 1939, the house remained government property; indeed a resolution was passed in parliament justifying the deed as 'retribution for cultural injustice and acts of violence against Czech minorities'.[9]

Pragmatism ultimately triumphed over prejudice. In the 'live and let live' spirit of medieval Spain, the new regime eventually came to a working agreement with the German minority,* and as from April 1921, in lieu of indemnity payments, the NDT's annual subsidy was raised from 273,000 to 823,000 Kč[10] – a satisfactory compromise all round. Meanwhile a conflict of far greater implication had arisen. For some months the authority of Masaryk's Socialist–Liberal coalition came under attack from Communist revolutionaries, and in December 1920 the army was called out to quell a strike of over a million workers. But here, too, common sense finally prevailed. For the first time in over a thousand years Czechs held control of their own country, a responsibility that was not taken lightly. Already in November 1918, Zemlinsky had remarked on the changing wind of fortune:

Many Viennese industrialists have already bought up property in Prague & are moving their businesses here!!! All are turning towards Czechoslovakia! Jews & Germans, but Jews above all![11]

While the German mark and the newly introduced Austrian schilling spiralled and galloped, the Czech crown remained stable. Prague became something of an Eldorado.

With Zemlinsky as *Opernchef* the NDT progressed artistically on all fronts. New works were given less frequently than during the Teweles era, but chosen with greater discrimination. Repertoire works were performed to the most exacting standards of ensemble theatre, while the growing strength of Czech

---

* Between 1918 and 1920, four thousand Bohemian Jews emigrated to Palestine (cf. *Tan*, 1/4).

currency enabled Kramer to engage artists of international standing when required. Every effort was also made to keep abreast of new international trends and standards of production and design.

Dissatisfaction with the outmoded style of Gerboth's *Ring* prompted Kramer to present a new production by Franz Ludwig Hörth, from the Staatsoper in Dresden. Before rehearsals began, new stage equipment was installed, including a cyclorama, high-voltage lighting, a 2000-volt *laterna magica* projector and a gigantic mobile canvas for water effects. Hörth made full use of these facilities, and on the opening night of *Rheingold*, 16 May 1923, the public was astonished to see the cramped stage of the NDT opening on to endless vistas of mountains, rivers and moonlit landscapes.[12] Other productions reflected the opposite trend to *Neue Sachlichkeit*, that art of reduction and formalism which later reached its theatrical zenith in the experimental productions of the Berlin Krolloper. Experiments in new techniques were the order of the day. In Laber's *Orfeo* production of 1925, for instance, the choral scenes were portrayed by means of eurhythmic dance, performed by members of the Dalcroze School, while the chorus itself stood in rank and file to the left and right.*

Though Zemlinsky still preferred German to Italian repertoire, he conducted *Aida* and *Il trittico* with evident enjoyment, and even tried his hand, for two performances, at *Manon Lescaut*. Of contemporary works he introduced Schreker's *Der ferne Klang* and *Der Schatzgräber*, Korngold's *Die tote Stadt*, Reznicek's *Ritter Blaubart*, Hindemith's triptych of one-act operas and the revised version of *Kleider machen Leute*. In October–November 1921 he consolidated his stature as a Mozart interpreter with a cycle of the five great operas,[†] and the following summer he and Jalowetz shared the honours in a forty-day Wagner retrospective, which included the *Ring*, *Der fliegende Holländer*, *Tannhäuser*, *Lohengrin*, *Tristan*, *Die Meistersinger* and *Parsifal*.[‡] Richard Strauss remained a popular favourite, with revivals of all pre-war productions and, in January 1921, a further series of *Alpensinfonie* performances; *Ariadne* returned in a new production by Laber (1924), and the repertoire was extended to include *Elektra* and *Intermezzo*. On 24 January 1921, travelling

---

* Emile Jacques-Dalcroze (1865–1950) studied composition with Bruckner and Robert Fuchs. During the 1890s he developed a technique of 'rhythmical gymnastics' or eurhythmics, which exerted considerable influence on modern dance. In 1910 he opened a School of Music and Rhythm in Hellerau near Dresden, whose pupils participated in the NDT production.

† It was probably at this time that Stravinsky heard *Figaro* at the NDT, prompting his much-quoted remark that Zemlinsky was 'the all-round conductor who achieved the most consistently high standards [. . .]. I remember a performance of *The Marriage of Figaro* by him in Prague as the most satisfying operatic experience of my life' ('On Conductors and Conducting', *Show*, August 1964, 107; also in *Themes and Conclusions* (London, 1972), 225).

‡ Zemlinsky conducted half the cycle, entrusting the *Ring* and *Der fliegende Holländer* to Jalowetz.

from Vienna to Berlin, Strauss made a brief stop in Prague to conduct a performance of *Salome*. As he wrote to his wife a few days later:

Things are going very well for me. In Prague, after a *Salome* prepared in exemplary fashion by Zemlinsky, the success was sensational. [. . . In Berlin] the première of *Die Gezeichneten** was a great success – for me! Even [the critic Adolf] Weissmann wrote that, compared to this, Strauss is really something else![13]

Delighted with the high standards of the NDT, he returned in June 1921 to conduct *Elektra*, *Der Rosenkavalier*, a repeat of *Salome* and a programme of Mozart's 'Jupiter' Symphony and his own *Don Juan* and *Till Eulenspiegel*.[†] In return for Zemlinsky's devotion, he accepted *Der Zwerg* for production at the Vienna Staatsoper – where it was poorly staged and conducted (by Karl Alwin) with little spirit or understanding. Accused in the press of having neglected the works of living composers other than his own, Strauss asked:

Is it my fault if composers write nothing but flops? Despite continuous sabotage by Schalk, I still considered it my duty not to withhold from the public those works which were a little better, at least the ones by Viennese composers: Kienzl, Zemlinsky, Schmidt, Bittner, Schreker (Schalk agreed only to Korngold). [. . .] Enough of such nauseating matters . . .[14]

In the interim, relations with the Korngolds had cooled appreciably,[‡] but Zemlinsky still encouraged and supported his former pupil. On 3 March 1920, 'little' Korngold conducted a concert of his own works, prefaced – as if alluding to a paternal relationship even more troubled than his own – by a Symphony in G by Leopold Mozart. Later that same year, with the simultaneous world premières in Hamburg and Cologne of *Die tote Stadt*, he reached the zenith of his career. Naturally the new opera was also staged at the NDT (it opened on 4 February 1922), and naturally the twenty-four-year-old composer was present to acknowledge the applause. But as with *Violanta*, the public saw through the glitter, and the work soon vanished from the repertoire.

---

* I.e. the Berlin première, conducted by Fritz Stiedry, on 5 January.
† On 14 June he also conducted the Czech première of *Die Josephslegende* at the Národní Divadlo.
‡ In his review of the Vienna production of *A Florentine Tragedy*, Julius Korngold quoted from the play – 'I have heard that by the simple fingering of a string, or delicate breath breathed along hollowed reeds, or blown into cold mouths of cunning bronze, those who are curious [i.e. skilful] in this art can draw poor souls from prison-houses', and added, 'Zemlinsky is a master in this art.' But his concluding remark was sphinx-like: 'Let us not quibble with a composer who is found wanting only where music itself must be found wanting' (*Neue Freie Presse*, 29 April 1917, reprinted in *Deutsches Opernschaffen der Gegenwart* (Vienna, 1922), 252–3). The friendship, such as it was, came to an abrupt end when Korngold demanded the return of a grand piano that he had lent Zemlinsky in exchange for his treasured Bösendorfer. 'I sent him a letter that will not turn up amongst his posthumous papers,' wrote Zemlinsky to Schoenberg, '& placed the piano "at his disposal"' (*Web-Br*, c. August 1918, 200). In the event, he received as replacement a 'magnificent concert piano' from an unnamed benefactor (*Web-Br*, 19 January 1920, 221).

On 9 December 1923 Otto Klemperer conducted a concert of Haydn and Bruckner (Eighth Symphony), his first appearance at the NDT since 1909.* Since leaving Prague, he had conducted at Strasbourg, Hamburg and Cologne, experiencing triumphs and setbacks in equal measure. By now he was considered one of the most powerful musical personalities of his generation. Felix Adler wrote of the 'almost Mahlerian luminosity' of his Bruckner, observing that with his strictly architectural approach 'complaints about formal coherence [. . .] vanished into thin air'.[15]

As ever, the NDT also catered for simpler tastes. Kramer viewed the theatre primarily as a place of entertainment, a standpoint supported by the stringencies of his budget and, as the Roaring Twenties gained momentum, one much in accord with the *Zeitgeist*. The blindness of Myrtocle was widespread now: people went to the theatre to escape the drabness of reality, to close their eyes to depression, hunger and unemployment, the threat of Fascism to the right and Communism to the left. Kramer was repeatedly attacked in the press for the preponderance of light entertainment in his programmes, but that was what most of his season-ticket holders actually wanted. Even Zemlinsky still occasionally presided over an evening of operetta – *Die Fledermaus*, *Boccaccio* or *Der Opernball* – showing that he had lost none of his old Carltheater sparkle.

After the official cessation of hostilities, he opened the first Philharmonic Concert, on 28 November 1918, with a work that represented the long-standing cultural entente between Austria and Bohemia: Mozart's 'Prague' Symphony. Not least because Mahler's background stood as a comparable symbol of reconciliation and integration, his music enjoyed undiminished popularity both in Czech and German circles. During the first five post-war seasons, Zemlinsky conducted the First, Third, Seventh, Eighth and Ninth Symphonies, *Das klagende Lied* and *Das Lied von der Erde*; in May 1923 he performed the Third and the Eighth on two evenings in succession, with a repeat performance of the latter a fortnight later. His contemporary concert repertoire included Bartók, Dukas, Pfitzner, Ravel, Schillings, Stravinsky, Webern and music by two of his own pupils, Fidelio Finke (the symphonic poem *Pan*) and Hans Krása (four Morgenstern songs, sung by Max Klein). But apart from the Maeterlinck Songs (included in the same concert as the Krása songs) and Psalm 23 (performed a few weeks later), his own music was conspicuously absent. Concertos were rare on his programmes and served primarily as a platform for younger artists: the twenty-three-year-old Eduard Steuermann in Bartók's Rhapsody op. 1, for instance, the eighteen-year-old Rudolf Serkin in Schumann, or the five-year-old Wolfgang Schneiderhan, making his Prague début in 1920 with the Beethoven Violin Concerto.

* Despite Klemperer's reputation, the concert was 'very poorly attended' (*Web-Br*, c.1923/24, 258).

Without doubt the most spectacular of Zemlinsky's post-war concerts was the Czech première of the *Gurrelieder* on 9 June 1921. Adler witnessed its genesis at close hand:

For weeks and months, rehearsals have been going on in every hall in Prague in which singing in German is permitted; under Zemlinsky's supreme command, every conductor in the house has taken sectional rehearsals, in every corner of the theatre, even the foyer and the ballet studio. [. . .] Zemlinsky works in the Urania with the soloists and an orchestra that fills the entire hall, while late in the evening the chorus stands at his disposal in the Drei-Reiter-Saal. And so work goes on, from morning to night, with untiring persistence, unflagging enthusiasm.[16]

Schoenberg, unaccountably, did not attend either of the two performances. Amidst the jubilation his absence sounded a sour note, but Zemlinsky bombarded him with euphoric letters and telegrams, countersigned by participants, relatives and friends. Despite his heartfelt enthusiasm, however, as former teacher he could not suppress a mild grumble about the orchestration:

The soloists could be clearly heard at all times, *all* the choirs too. The dynamics have to be observed with absolute precision, of course, and sometimes reduced by half.[17]

In September 1919 a wealthy young pupil of Ostrčil's named Vladislav Žak (1894–1977) founded a new orchestra, sometimes referred to as the Bohemian Philharmonic (or, confusingly, the 'Sächsische' orchestra). Only a few weeks after the confiscation of the NDT, in January 1921, Zemlinsky was invited to conduct a programme of Mozart and Mahler with this orchestra in Brno and Prague. A further series, in April, was devoted to Mahler's Fifth, a work that he scarcely knew. 'I studied it on my own for four days,' he told Schoenberg, 'but towards the end I thought my head was bursting. Then I had to prepare it in just four rehearsals, but the orchestra was eager and enthusiastic.'[18] These concerts were the first in living memory at which Czech musicians had played under a German conductor. By the end of the year Žak was obliged to disband his orchestra* for lack of funds, but now that the ice was broken, Zemlinsky found himself a *persona grata* of Czech musical life. In July 1922 Tálich invited him to conduct the Czech Philharmonic.† His first concerts, two performances of Mahler's Sixth Symphony‡ and a programme of Smetana, Schubert and

* The Žak Orchestra also appeared in concert with Zemlinsky at the NDT, on 18 October, with Bach's D major Suite and Schubert's 'Great' C major Symphony.
† Cf. letter to Tálich, 12 July 1922 (Tálich archive, Beroun). From a letter to Kramer (dated merely 'Sunday'), it transpires that the invitation was originally for 6 October 1922. The postponement was evidently due to the fact that a performance of *Tristan* was scheduled at the NDT the previous evening. Zemlinsky suggested that he conduct Mahler's Fifth or Seventh Symphony, Strauss's *Symphonia domestica* preceded by a Beethoven symphony, or a classical programme including a Brahms symphony. The requested fee was 2000 Kč.
‡ From the programme notes for Zemlinsky's performances of the Sixth Symphony at the NDT and with the Czech Philharmonic it transpires that he invariably played the *Andante* before the *Scherzo*.

Beethoven, followed in April 1923. From then on until his emigration in 1938 he was the orchestra's regular guest.

In token of mutual respect, the NDT broke its ban on works of Czech origin. A guest appearance of the Raimund-Theater from Vienna brought Karel Čapek's play *The Macropoulos Affair* in November 1923, and the following March, in celebration of the Smetana's centenary, Zemlinsky conducted a new production of *Hubička* (*The Kiss*, sung in German).* Both at home and abroad he began to assume the role of special envoy for Czech music. In later years he was to record works by Dvořák, Fibich, Smetana and Weinberger, and in Germany he introduced several unfamiliar scores by Czech composers, notably Janáček's Glagolithic Mass and Lachian Dances, Novák's Serenade in G and Suk's *Asrael* Symphony.

Despite abiding political differences, most leading figures in Czech culture politics had long since made their peace with the (German)–Jewish minority. In November 1918, for instance, the NDT came under the nominal direction of a Czech *Intendant*, Anton Němec, whose influence, contrary to expectation, proved entirely beneficial. And in 1920, thanks to an annual government subsidy of 250,000 Kč, the German community was able to open a new college of music, the Deutsche Akademie für Musik und darstellende Kunst.[19] Zemlinsky, who was appointed Rector, held masterclasses in composition and conducting.[†] Teaching cost valuable time, however, and he was obliged to accept a paltry 100 Kč a month ('scandalous, outrageous, a humiliation', he complained to Kramer).[20] Of his composition pupils, Krása proved the most successful, with performances in Paris and Zurich; several of his works were published by Universal Edition, and in 1933 his opera *Verlobung im Traum* was premièred by Szell at the NDT. Thirteen students 'full of enthusiasm & – with little talent'[21] enrolled in the conducting class. The most successful were Adolf Singer (1908–1980) and Peter Herman Adler (1905–1988). Singer, who joined the staff of the NDT in 1926, later emigrated to Palestine, where in 1947 he founded the Israel National Opera; Adler conducted in Bremen and Kiev before emigrating to the USA in 1939, where he was appointed Director of the NBC Opera Company and later Artistic Director of WNET (National Educational Television). In conversation with Hans Heinsheimer, he recalled:

Zemlinsky's conducting class at the small but excellent German conservatoire in Prague was something very new. For him, tuition was founded less on technical details and the tricks taught today than on discussing scores. In the operatic field, the enormous impression made on him by Mahler was crucial. [. . .] 'The better you

---

* On the same evening, as a gesture of 'pragmatic culture-politics', the Národní Divadlo presented a new production of *Tannhäuser* (*Prager Tagblatt*, 21 March 1924; quoted in *Tan* B5).

† Other professors were Henri Marteau (violin) and Conrad Ansorge (piano).

know the music,' he would always tell us, 'the better a conductor you will be. That's what everything depends upon.'[22]

Classes, as Zemlinsky's widow remembered, often began at eight o'clock in the morning, so that he could arrive at the NDT in time for rehearsal at ten. But just as Schoenberg had learned primarily by observation, many a young Czech musician learned simply by watching Zemlinsky on the rostrum of the NDT or at the Rudolfinum: Karel Ančerl, for instance, who was appointed Chief Conductor of the Czech Philharmonic in 1950, or Rafael Kubelik, who in later years still vividly recalled the concentration and rapt intensity of his Mahler.[23]

In the autumn of 1920, Webern returned to the NDT, encouraged by the prospect of teaching at the Akademie. 'I promise not to disappoint you again, I shall stay the course,' he assured Zemlinsky.[24] But it was not to be. Travel permits and visas were expensive and hard to obtain, and he was obliged to leave his wife and children behind in Mödling. Negotiations for the promised post at the Akademie, which for him would have been a financial necessity, fell through at the last minute. By mid-October he was back in Vienna.*

Webern's connection with Prague was not entirely severed, however, for as an active member of Schoenberg's Verein für musikalische Privataufführungen (Society for Private Musical Performances), he continued for several years to contribute to musical life in the city. In March 1920, the *Verein* gave four concerts at the Prague Mozarteum. Somewhat wary after the fracas that had accompanied *Pierrot* in 1913, Schoenberg selected programmes that covered a wide spectrum of contemporary styles, while avoiding anything that might provoke a further scandal.† The success of these concerts prompted Zemlinsky, Finke and Tálich to propose the founding of a similar society on the basis of Czech–German collaboration. As it transpired, the political climate was not yet clement, and the idea had to be shelved. The following year *Pierrot* was given a further hearing, this time conducted by Erwin Stein.‡ Jalowetz prefaced the performance with a lecture in which he outlined the principles of the Vienna *Verein* and stressed the necessity for hearing difficult works several times before passing judgement. His words fell on receptive ears: this time *Pierrot* was received with enthusiasm.

Once the political clouds had begun to lift, it became possible to revive the

---

* Cf. Hans and Rosaleen Moldenhauer, *Anton von Webern, Chronik seines Lebens und Werkes* (Zurich, 1980), 212–13. A further reason for Webern's leaving Prague, cited by the Moldenhauers without naming a source, was that his activities at the NDT were restricted because 'the Czechs demanded use of the theatre for three days of the week'.
† The concerts included music by Bartók, Berg, Debussy, Novák, Ravel, Reger, Satie, Scriabin, Stravinsky, Suk, Szymanowski and Zemlinsky (the Second Quartet). Of his own music, Schoenberg's chose the Piano Pieces op. 11 and Orchestral Pieces op. 16 in a version for chamber ensemble.
‡ Zemlinsky had originally intended to conduct this concert himself, with a repeat performance in Brno the following day (*Web-Br*, 19 January 1921, 221).

idea of a Prague *Verein*. The initiative was taken by a civil servant and amateur musician named Georg Alter, who organized and administrated the venture single-handed. At a founders' meeting on 23 April 1922 Schoenberg was elected Honorary President and Zemlinsky Chairman; with 230 members, the new *Verein* was substantially larger than its parent body, and whereas in Vienna most of the members were themselves professional musicians, in Prague the public consisted largely of amateurs.[25]

Two 'propaganda concerts' were given on 25 and 26 May, the first an intriguing coupling of *Pierrot lunaire* and Debussy's Cello Sonata (subtitled 'Pierrot fâché avec la lune'), the second a programme of Reger, Novák, Bartók, Berg, Webern, Stravinsky and Milhaud. In the regular concert series, which opened in October, several of these works were repeated. While in Vienna it was part of the *Verein* policy to repeat every work at least once, in Prague many members objected to this practice. With unaccustomed bluntness, Zemlinsky passed on the complaint to Schoenberg:

Particularly the Milhaud [*Le bœuf sur le toit*], which is after all insignificant, was found superfluous. [. . .] Likewise, it is impossible to include Reger in every concert. This caused displeasure too. After all, things are different here. In Vienna you have a concert every week, but we have a maximum of one a month! For our members these concerts are not cheap, & they would like to get to know as much music as possible. [. . .] Finally, vocal works must be included too.[26]

Sensitive as ever to adverse criticism, Schoenberg replied by return of post, justifying his policy with elaborate statistics, praising Milhaud as 'the most significant representative of the current trend in all Latin countries: polytonality' and defending Reger 'because he is already dead and one still has no clear picture of him'.[27] Milhaud, in his opinion, was very talented. 'Whether I like him', he added, 'is immaterial.' His intention in founding the *Verein* had been not only to create a secure platform for his own music and that of his Viennese allies, but also to keep himself informed of trends and developments abroad.

Membership of the Prague *Verein* had meanwhile risen to four hundred. Yet the venture proved short-lived. When Jalowetz returned to Vienna in 1923, his place on the committee was taken by the journalist Erich Steinhard, who also sat on the Czech committee of the International Society for Contemporary Music (ISCM). In December 1923, largely through his influence, the *Verein* subsidy was reassigned to the ISCM. That was its death knell. Three further concerts were given in April–May 1924, but two of these were devoted entirely to Prague composers, and the third was in effect an ISCM matinee. Zemlinsky, who had played little more than a figurehead role, saw little reason to keep the venture alive.* Schoenberg's vision of a *jeu sans frontières* was rapidly

---

* He never actively participated in the concerts, nor did he attend them all. The *Verein* did serve as a platform for two of his more recent works, however: the Four Songs of 1916

fading,* and despite the later efforts of Webern and Erwin Stein to revive activities, the *Verein* died a natural death.

'Bin ich kein Wiener?'†

In November 1916 Zemlinsky was approached by the orchestra of the Volksoper with a view to resuming his concert series of 1909. 'At last I have the prospect of conducting in Vienna again!' he enthused to Schoenberg[28] – there were even plans to perform the *Gurrelieder*. But the vicissitudes of war put a stop to all such fine ideas, and he did not conduct again in Vienna until February 1919, when the concert agent Hugo Heller engaged him for a series of performances of *Das Lied von der Erde* at the Konzerthaus with the Tonkünstler-Orchester.‡ His plain-language account of the event in a letter to Alma indicates that the war had done nothing to banish *Schlamperei* and intrigue from Viennese musical life:

For once in a while I come to Vienna, where some scoundrel of an agent pulls a fast one on me, I do one of the *hardest* pieces, with an orchestra I don't know, in two rehearsals!!!! of which the second is the 1st with the singers, who have never sung it before and *don't have time to finish their songs*, because they have commitments at the Opera. Against my better judgement I perform the piece on two rehearsals so as not to cancel, i.e. to avoid the risk of being accused in certain quarters of being incapable of working quickly; I bring it off all the same, and the impression is no bad one, in fact for experts the second performance is good – but not to my advantage, on the contrary: insiders sneer at me for having gone through with the performance despite the lack of rehearsal, etc. Positions are becoming vacant, and everyone should know and does know that my heart has always been in Vienna and that I long to regain a footing – but nobody thinks of me, or those who do just say: 'Zemlinsky has it made for him in Prague, has a good job, *is earning plenty of money*', etc. Doesn't it make you sick?![29]

In 1910, in an article entitled 'Die Jungwiener Tondichter' ('The Composers of Jung-Wien'), Richard Specht had published biographical outlines of several Viennese composers,[30] with Zemlinsky and Schoenberg heading the list. In 1921 he published a similar article, 'Neue Musik in Wien' ('New Music in

----

(performed on 19 and 20 November 1922) and the Second Quartet (28 November 1923), played by the Amar Quartet.
* The penultimate *Verein* concert, a piano recital by Erwin Schulhoff, with the Ninth and Tenth Sonatas of Scriabin, the op. 66 Sonata of Cyril Scott and Schulhoff's own Third Sonata, did succeed in recapturing something of Schoenberg's vision.
† 'Am I not Viennese?' These words served in 1992 as title for a Zemlinsky exhibition in the archive of the Gesellschaft der Musikfreunde in Wien, organized and catalogued by Otto Biba.
‡ The concerts, with Georg Maikl (tenor) and Hans Duhan (baritone), were originally scheduled for November 1918. At the third concert, Schreker's Philharmonic Chorus joined forces with Zemlinsky to sing his Psalm 23.

Vienna').[31] Now he wrote more quizzically of Schoenberg and disparagingly of Berg, Webern and Hauer, but approvingly of Bittner, Korngold, Marx, Prohaska, Schmidt, Schreker, Weigl and Wellesz, and encouragingly of several younger talents, including Hans Gál, Wilhelm Grosz, Hugo Kauder, Walter Klein, Robert Konta, Egon Lustgarten, Felix Petyrek, Josef Rosenstock and Georg Széll (*sic*). But of Zemlinsky, his former teacher, no word: here too, *Schlamperei* and intrigue. Writing to Specht, Zemlinsky again vented his frustration:

Every name is included. Even some that one is hearing for the first time (and that one is probably also hearing for the last time). The only name that is missing is mine. Never in my life have I ever complained about such things. Today is the first time. I do not understand the reason for this insult. Am I not Viennese? The most genuine in every respect? Is the fact of my having been overlooked in such a situation not itself proof that I am genuinely Viennese?[32]

In 1920 the Viennese publisher E. P. Tal brought out Wellesz's monograph on Schoenberg, the first in a projected series of composer biographies that was to include studies of Debussy, Reger, Joseph Marx and Zemlinsky. Berg wrote excitedly to Schoenberg, expressing the hope that he would be entrusted with the Zemlinsky project:

I have a great many things to say about this music that has grown so dear to me. [. . .] For it *has* to be said once and for all, that here, living inconspicuously, is one of the few masters, worth more than all the officially accredited 'masters', Pfitzner, Schreker, and the whole German and Nordic lot.[33]

Originally he intended to publish a preparatory essay on Zemlinsky in *Anbruch*[34] – but neither this idea nor the plan for a monograph ever came to fruition.

Recognition came instead from Prague, with a special number of *Der Auftakt* to honour Zemlinsky on his fiftieth birthday. An introductory eulogy by Werfel ('even the twitch of his shoulder when he raises the baton is music, an upbeat spark that kindles fire') was followed by essays on various aspects of the man and his music. Jalowetz provided a biographical outline (almost as revealing for its omissions as its inclusions), Klaren wrote on 'Zemlinsky from a psychological standpoint' and Steinhard sang the praises of the conductor. His compositions were evaluated by Rudolf Stephan Hoffmann (opera), Robert Konta (lieder) and Fidelio Finke (chamber music), while the Viennese critic Robert Fleischmann endeavoured to place his art in a historical perspective (the result: a jumble of platitudes and non sequiturs). Louis Laber and Max Klein contributed heartfelt tributes to their *Opernchef*, and Paul Stefan remembered the *temps perdu* of Zemlinsky and the *Vereinigung* in pre-war Vienna. Three famous composers had the last word: Korngold wrote touchingly of his gratitude, Schreker expressed condescending admiration ('Prague can be proud of him'), and Schoenberg, who concentrated on the problematic aspects of 'drama of the soul', concluded with the Sibylline remark, 'Zemlinsky can wait.'

While prospects of returning to Vienna remained as dim as ever, Berlin was full of opportunity. In the spring of 1923, *Bohemia* reported that Zemlinsky had been offered the artistic directorship of the Deutsches Opernhaus in Berlin-Charlottenburg.[35] The post was not unattractive, for it offered full control of the theatre and a special brief for reforming the musical apparatus. The NDT contract was up for renewal, however, and already in January Kramer began pressing him to sign. Pleading for time, he continued to negotiate with Charlottenburg until April, but in May he finally signed up again in Prague, with improved conditions.[36] The following month he was again in Berlin, this time to participate in an Austrian Music Week. Pella conducted two performances of Mahler's 'Symphony of a Thousand' and Jalowetz three of the *Gurrelieder*. At a further concert, on 5 June, Webern conducted orchestral songs by Bittner, two pieces from Berg's op. 6 and his own Passacaglia op. 1; Steuermann played the Schoenberg Chamber Symphony in his arrangement for piano solo and Zemlinsky conducted his Maeterlinck songs, which met, according to Jalowetz, with 'wellnigh *sensational* success'.[37] Berg also noted that 'Zemlinsky enjoyed the greatest success of the evening', but added ruefully:

[He] rehearsed for two hours in the morning, so that [. . .] there was barely time to read through my two pieces.[38]

Max von Schillings had abandoned his conducting career in 1919 and taken over as Director of the Berlin Staatsoper. Things had not gone well for him, he had shown little artistic initiative, and complaints about declining standards eventually led to harassment from the press and the Ministry of Culture. In April 1923 Furtwängler resigned his position as Conductor of the Staatskapelle Concerts in protest, and six weeks later the *Generalmusikdirektor* of the Staatsoper, Leo Blech, followed suit. In search of successors for both posts, Schillings approached Klemperer, Bruno Walter and Zemlinsky.* Under normal circumstances, these were positions that no musician of repute would refuse. But circumstances were far from normal: the prospect of working under an *Intendant* who was likely to be dismissed at any moment was itself unattractive, and, more to the point, hyperinflation was raging. Klemperer enjoyed the support of the Ministry, but he demanded an irredeemable ten-year contract and other conditions that could not be fulfilled. Zemlinsky's demands, as he reported to Schoenberg, were almost as excessive. Fearing that by the autumn a contract signed in the summer would already be worthless,† he insisted on a salary at

---

* Cf. Heyworth, *Otto Klemperer, His Life and Times*, I (Cambridge–London, 1983), 179–80. Blech had meanwhile taken the appointment as Artistic Director of the Charlottenburg Opera that had been offered to Zemlinsky earlier that year.

† By mid-1923 the German mark was losing value literally by the minute. A loaf of bread sold

least equal to what he was earning at the NDT. But, at a time when a whole family in Germany could subsist for several weeks on 100 Czech crowns, his demand was utopian. Had he but realized what was at stake, he might for once have thrown caution to the winds. But he played the wrong cards and lost: the job of Principal Conductor at Germany's leading opera house went to one of his former assistants, Erich Kleiber.

It was the worst miscalculation of his career.

---

in the morning for 20,000 marks cost 5,000,000 by nightfall; restaurant prices rose while customers were still dining. On 15 November, when the collapse came, one pound sterling was worth 43 billion marks.

2

Luise

One day in 1914 (or according to a conflicting account 1915),[1] Hanna Sachsel brought her daughter Luise* to audition at the NDT, evidently with the intention of enrolling her in the extra-chorus of the opera. She was a bright young girl, showed great talent as a painter and was blessed with a strong mezzo-soprano voice. At fourteen (or fifteen) she was not only uncommonly intelligent but also attractive, slightly built, with light brown hair, and grey eyes that could crease into a captivating smile.

Friends of my mother said I'd do better as a singer [she recalled], that a girl couldn't make a career as a painter. They advised my mother to take me to Zemlinsky, as he was known for talking people out of singing. [. . .] He told my mother that I had a very lovely voice and that I absolutely must take singing lessons. He wanted to hear me in a year, and recommended me to a new teacher. When he heard me a year later, he told me he was disappointed and would teach me himself. He had taken voice lessons from a well-known singing teacher, to whom he had given music lessons.[†] And so I studied voice with Zemlinsky.[2]

In 1918 she also enrolled in the class of Franz Thiele at the Prague Academy of Art. The report at the end of her first year was excellent: punctuality, diligence, discipline and achievement – all first rate. But her second-year report, dated 6 July 1920, was less satisfactory: achievement still 'good' and discipline 'impeccable', but diligence only 'adequate' and punctuality 'irregular'.[3] Why the deterioration? Perhaps because her father had died that year, aged fifty-two; perhaps also because the relationship with her voice teacher, twenty-nine years her senior, had grown from friendship to love – passionate love.

In contrast to Alma, who put the more impressive mementoes of her love life on display, like trophies, Luise was a model of reticence and discretion. And where Helene Berg made a point of publishing even the most intimate of her husband's love letters, Luise destroyed all hers. It was a relationship of slavish devotion,[‡] and a love she was prepared to share with no one, least of all with posterity.

---

* As Zemlinsky invariably used the Czech orthography (often in the diminutive form 'Luiserl'), it is retained here. From 1926, when she sang at the Vienna Volksoper, she Germanized the spelling ('Louise'). The change is implemented from part IX onwards.
† This may have been Eduard Gärtner.
‡ 'I had the role of my husband's devoted slave. That was customary in those days – women were "second class"' (Burkhard Laugwitz, '"Meine Zeit kommt nach meine Tod". Begegnung mit Louise Zemlinsky', *Das Orchester*, V/1993, 547–50; the last two words in English).

Her father, Ludwig Sachsel, was born in 1867 in Neubydzow (Nový Bydžov, fifty miles north-east of Prague) and served at Lemberg (Lwow) as a lieutenant in the 57th Infantry Regiment of the Prince of Sachsen-Coburg-Saalfeld.* Taken ill during manoeuvres, he was obliged to enter a reserve battalion and in 1904 to retire from military service altogether. In 1899 he married a girl from his home town, the twenty-four-year-old Hanna (or Johanna) Mayer. Finding employment with his grandfather's firm of linseed refineries, a flourishing concern with plants all over Central Europe, he and his wife settled in the Galician town of Podwoloczyska (Volochysk in the Ukraine, a hundred miles south-east of Lwow). Luise was born there on 4 June 1900, and a brother, Otto, followed on 27 April 1901. Two months after his birth the family returned to Nový Bydžov, where the children grew up and completed their regular schooling. Later they moved to Prague and settled in the fashionable district of Karlín.[4]

During her first years with Zemlinsky, the daily routine, as Luise later described it, was straightforward, if not monotonous. After breakfast she would collect him from the Havlíčekgasse; together they would walk to the Akademie or through the park to the theatre. Once the morning rehearsal was over, she would see him home. That, on the face of it, was all.

On one occasion, during her second year at art school, he let her paint his portrait.[†] 'But I don't have much time,' he said. 'You'll have to make do with forty-five minutes.'[5] Just as in his sittings for Gerstl and Schönberg, he removed his glasses, something he was loath to do for photographers. Offset by the stern symmetry of the facial muscles, the firm line of the nose, the magisterial downward turn of the lip, the severity of the chin, his eyes betray nothing of the intimate bond between subject and artist. Yet the outline is soft and vague, the black and white of shirt and jacket cross-fades into an aureole of pastel shades, ranging from pale peach-blossom to bluish-green: through Luise's eyes, we see Zemlinsky as a holy man.

Her language of light corresponds approximately to the 'cosmological circle' of colour as defined by Rudolf Steiner: green (here mixed with blue) presents an inanimate picture of life, peach-blossom a living picture of the spirit, white a spiritual picture of the mind, and black a mental picture of the inanimate.[6] She may have learned of Steiner's anthroposophical art theories at the Prague Academy or even during her schooldays. Later she attended lectures at Steiner's study centre, the Goetheanum in Dornach, near Basle. Among her posthumous

---

* The Sachsel family, which was large (Ludwig was one of seven brothers) and of pure Ashkenazic origin, had lived in Neubydzow since the 1790s. Louise Zemlinsky gave conflicting accounts of her family background. In the interests of reliability, the information given here is based on documents – passports, certificates of birth, marriage and death, etc. – from *NLZ*. Further details were clarified with the help of Friederike Zeitlhofer (office of the Austrian Cultural Institute in New York), Silvia Kargl (Alexander Zemlinsky Fonds) and Arnold Greissle-Schönberg.

† See book jacket.

papers survives a treasured souvenir of that occasion, a signed photograph of Steiner, dated February 1924, with the following handwritten inscription:

Suche in der Welt nach allen Seiten, und du findest dich. Suche in dir nach allen Tiefen, und du findest die Welt.

Search every corner of the world, and you will find *yourself*. Search every recess of yourself, and you will find the *world*.

The Dwarf

Oscar Wilde, in his heyday, held a diametrically opposing view: 'Whoever observes himself', he would say, 'arrests his development'.[7] Only after his downfall did he come to 'search every recess' of himself, a process he related after his release from gaol in the form of a grim parable:

A man saw a being, which hid its face from him, and he said, 'I will compel it to show its face.' It fled as he pursued, and he lost it, and his life went on. At last his pleasure drew him into a long room, where tables were spread for many, and in a mirror he saw the being whom he had pursued in youth. 'This time you shall not escape me,' he said, but the being did not try to escape, and hid its face no more. 'Look!' it cried, 'and now you will know that we cannot see each other again, for this is the face of your own soul, and it is horrible.'[8]

A room decked out with festive tables, and within it a mirror that opens the beholder's eyes to self-knowledge: this was the image that inspired Georg Klaren to offer Zemlinsky his operatic adaptation of Wilde's *The Birthday of the Infanta*.

Cast

Donna Clara, Infanta of Spain (sop); Ghita, her favourite lady-in-waiting (sop); Don Estoban, major-domo (high bass); the Dwarf (ten); three ladies-in-waiting (sop); two girls (sop). The Infanta's playmates, court ladies (female voices); an elderly lady-in-waiting, lackeys, Moorish slaves, commoners (silent).

Synopsis

A loggia in Moorish style, leading to a garden; stage left a throne on a dais Preparations are in full swing for the Infanta's birthday party. While she and her retinue play and sing in the garden, Ghita and the other ladies-in-waiting, supervised by Don Estoban, deck the room with flowers. Tiring of their round-dance, the Infanta and her friends invade the loggia and inquisitively ogle the presents. The exasperated Estoban ejects the girls, and the servants restore order, making sure that all the mirrors are covered. As the ceremony begins, commoners file past with gifts, to the sound of fanfares and courtly dance music. Moorish litter-bearers enter with a present from the Sultan, a dwarf dressed as a cavalier. With a stiff bow, the little fellow takes up his guitar and breaks into a melancholy love song. Dismissing her sniggering companions, the Infanta begins to woo his affection. 'Now I know that I love!' he finally exclaims. She flees his embrace, but on the dance floor she gives him a white rose from her hair, which he smothers with kisses. Ghita attempts to let him see his reflection in her hand mirror, but realizing that he is unaware of his hideous appearance, flees in dismay. Patiently awaiting the return of his beloved, the Dwarf climbs the dais to kiss her stool, thereby involuntarily loosening the cover from the largest mirror. Confronted by a repulsive monster, he screams out in horror. When he realizes that the reflection is his own, he collapses, broken-hearted. The Infanta returns. 'Tell me that I am handsome, tell me that you love me,' he begs her. Petulantly she dances off. Ghita hands him the white rose. He kisses it and dies.

Franz Werfel had strong ideas on the art of writing for the operatic stage (more the pity that he himself never did so).* Ideally, he felt, an opera must be a drama not of words but of deeds, and he decried the vogue for 'literature opera' on grounds of verbosity and insincerity:

Even the craziest nonsense in a Donizetti libretto is not as foolish as the text of *Salome*, which offers the musician mere ornament and chilly effusiveness. The librettists of olden times were less concerned to devise powerful dramatic moments than to establish *situations for music*. What did they care for literature, for words?[9]

Hence a libretto, in his view, should be no more than a 'mask for music'. Before writing his tribute to Zemlinsky for *Der Auftakt*, he read through Alma's vocal score of *Der Zwerg*. The work, as yet unheard, made an uncertain impression on him. Klaren's concept of an opera about a 'man who knows nothing of his ugliness' struck him as lacking dramatic substance, but in offering the composer inherently musical situations the libretto did at least conform to 'operatic law': it was a true 'mask for music'.† Klaren, interpreting the compliment as backhanded, pointed out that Maeterlinck, d'Annunzio and Hofmannsthal had never considered their librettos subservient to music, nor had Puccini ever 'wasted his seductive melodies on librettos that were merely a mask'.[10] Nevertheless, he readily admitted that *The Birthday of the Infanta* had served as a mouthpiece for his own views on sexuality and sexual psychology. By offsetting the Dwarf against the synthetic society of the Infanta and her retinue, he had first thought to create a bridge between Wilde's stylized impressions of Spanish courtly life and his own view of post-war Central European society:

My initial concept was of a play for which the ideal stage designer would have been Velázquez: sumptuous courtly surroundings, peopled with over-refined, decadent,

---

* The nearest that Werfel ever came to writing an original libretto was *Die Zwingburg*, a scenic cantata for Ernst Krenek (1922), but even this was only the revision of a text by another writer.
† The programme book for the first production of *Der Zwerg*, in Cologne, included a reprint of Werfel's essay from *Der Auftakt*.

not to say tainted characters – a fashionable crowd, who today would go into raptures over Tagore and dress only in batik – and to confront them with the Dwarf as
a disfigured but unsullied child of nature.[11]

In the event, this projected satire on *décadence** was reconfigured to become an
essay on sexual pathology:

A man comes into contact with his fellow men, unaware that he is *different*, [. . .]
and is destroyed by a woman who, instead of seeking his *innermost* depths, does not
tell him *how* he differs, but simply plays with him.[12]

The Dwarf became a neurotic with masochistic tendencies, the Infanta a
nascent *femme fatale*, their confrontation an exposition of the theories of
Klaren's idol, Otto Weininger.

Weininger's fame rested on his dissertation, *Geschlecht und Charakter*
('Gender and Character'), which testified to the twenty-two-year-old author's
prodigious grasp of classical literature, physiology, anthropology and psychoanalytical theory. He hypothesized a universal bisexuality, according to which
sexual predisposition was measured on a sliding scale ranging from theoretical extremes of pure masculinity (**M**) to pure femininity (**W**). Though his
academic methods appeared erudite, in fact he misused science as a pretext
for voicing exorbitant personal opinions and tendentious hypotheses. Himself
a homosexual, his views were aggressively misogynist; himself a Jew, he
decried the Jews as lacking 'depth, ardour and capacity for enthusiasm'; in a
race he considered the very 'antipodes of heroes' he detected a 'lack of
inner dignity'.[13] When his book was published, in the spring of 1903, it
aroused interest only in professional circles, and then only because of alleged
plagiarism.[†]

A few months later, Weininger rented a room near the Schottentor, at
Schwarzspanierstrasse 15, the house in which Beethoven had died. There,
during the night of 3 October, he shot himself in the chest.

Here was another real-life 'tragedy of the ugly man'. Stefan Zweig recalled
that Weininger usually looked as if he had just emerged from 'a thirty-hour
train journey, dirty, tired, unkempt, his stance contorted and self-conscious, as
if pressing himself against an invisible wall',[14] and others close to him considered self-deprecation to have been the principal cause of his suicide.

Whatever its true background, the effect of this tragedy was a sudden surge

---

* Janáček's *The Excursion of Mr Brouček to the Moon*, composed in 1908, is based on this
very idea. The work received its first performance at the Národní Divadlo in Prague in April
1920, i.e. while Zemlinsky was working on *Der Zwerg*.
† Wilhelm Fliess accused Freud, not without justification, of having passed on his still incomplete research findings on bisexuality to Weininger. Although Freud alleged that he had urged
Weininger 'not to publish such nonsense', he later admitted that the author was 'a burglar with
a key he had found' (Peter Gay, *Freud. A Life for Our Time* (London, 1988), 155).

of interest in the author and his work. *Geschlecht und Charakter* became a bestseller, and Weininger's concept of **M–W** sexuality remained, well into the 1920s, a favourite topic of coffee-house debate. Arthur Schnitzler and Karl Kraus wrote admiringly; Strindberg proclaimed the suicide an act of heroism, and Schoenberg, in the foreword to his *Harmonielehre*, saluted Weininger, together with Strindberg and Maeterlinck, as one of the great 'free thinkers' of the age.* The philosopher Oswald Spengler found his death 'as the outcome of a mystically experienced inner conflict between Good and Evil, one of the most sublime moments of latter-day religiosity',[15] and Klaren himself, writing of 'a true philosopher's death, comparable to those of antiquity', explained that Weininger had shot himself in the heart rather than the head 'so as not to destroy the domain of the soul'.[16]

Three weeks after the première of *Der Zwerg*, Klaren published an article in the *Kölnische Zeitung* explaining how he had superimposed Weininger on Wilde:

The Dwarf is intended primarily [. . .] to represent an abstract idea: the confrontation of *every* man with *every* woman; his ugliness should be interpreted in a wider context, as representing that sense of inferiority which – as Weininger teaches – [. . .] overcomes every eroticist when confronted by the object of his idolization, his lack of self-knowledge; likewise the fact that only a woman who loves can teach us that self-knowledge.[17]

One important aspect of the libretto, on which he did not elaborate, was that several attributes of the title figure had been modified to correspond to those of Zemlinsky himself. Wilde's Dwarf is the son of a charcoal-burner from the cork woods surrounding the palace grounds; Klaren's is a cavalier from the Orient, allegedly of noble birth, and a present from the Sultan: clear allusions to Zemlinsky's Jewish–Muslim background, the family's fictitious *Adelsprädikat* and part-Turkish origin. This Dwarf, furthermore, is no 'ugly and useless child' as in the short story, but a composer:

Ein Ruf als Sänger eilt ihm voran aus fernem Land.

From far-off lands his fame as singer goes before him.

The Infanta was correspondingly adapted to her new surroundings. Where in Wilde she is a girl of twelve, in Klaren she is six years older, already a young woman, but still 'endowed with all the cruel whims of puberty'.

Not yet an adult and no longer a child [. . .], her cruelty is depicted as a tendency to sadism or a remainder of that nonchalance with which a little girl inquisitively destroys her doll, at any rate inborn and natural rather than pathological or

* But only in the first edition of 1911.

synthetic. [. . .] In contrast to Ghita, whose feelings are purely maternal, she is, in Weininger's terminology, the harlot* *in nuce.*[18]

Whether by accident or design, the Infanta thus acquired many negative traits of Alma (had not Zemlinsky himself once reprimanded her for demanding 'the comforts of courtesans'?). Ghita, for whom there is no direct equivalent in Wilde, was presumably incorporated to represent Weininger's 'mother' principle. Considering how tautly Klaren drew the net of personal allusions around his characters, it seems legitimate to see in her an idealized portrait of Ida Zemlinsky; even the names have a similar ring.

With the death of the Dwarf, Klaren parts company from Zemlinsky and his circle to relive and perhaps even motivate the agony of Weininger's last hours. The suicide is presented as a martyrdom, a self-transfiguration:

At the close, an eroticist like the Dwarf, whose intellectualism is so far remote from carnal desire, simply *has* to die, just as Tristan *had* to die. This is why I made no superficial effort to motivate his death. In Wilde he dies of a broken heart; for me as librettist it would have been a cheap effect to let the Dwarf, in the depths of despair, strike out at the mirror and bleed to death – but this was unnecessary. He dies simply because he loved, because with *such* a love he cannot live.[19]

Faced with a libretto teeming with psychopathological associations, Zemlinsky reacted like a true 'child of nature'. As in *The Triumph of Time*, he sought to compensate for conceptual obscurity with clear forms and lucid sonorities. Not that Klaren's text itself is obscure – true to his subtitle 'a tragic folk tale for music', the vocabulary and syntax are largely straightforward – but on two crucial issues his libretto appears confused. This Dwarf is no hillbilly, as in Wilde, but a young man of good family: why then, critics asked, had he never before looked in a mirror? And what exactly was the significance of the white rose? In Wilde's plant symbol Klaren perceived an exalted philosophy:

The white rose symbolizes the supernatural love of a man redeemed from woman through her. When the Dwarf, dying, presses it to his lips, his desire is fulfilled, just as sexual love is fulfilled in physical union, and although, unlike Isolde, the Infanta does not die, in death he is thus united with her.[20]

Zemlinsky scarcely shared this Wagnerian vision of redemption, nor does his score, for all its pathos, conclude with anything approaching a *Liebestod*. For

---

* In Weininger's terminology, a harlot (*Dirne*) is any woman who 'embodies the principle of recklessness. In contrast to a mother, she makes no provision for the future; she, not the mother, is the good dancer, only she demands entertainment, high society, shopping sprees and pleasure palaces, seaside resorts and spa towns, theatres and concerts, constantly changing attire and precious stones; money spent in handfuls, luxury in place of mere comfort, turmoil in place of quiet; not for her the easy chair amidst a circle of grandchildren and great-grandchildren: she lives to be carried triumphantly through the world on the throne of a beautiful body' (Weininger, *Geschlecht und Charakter. Eine prinzipielle Untersuchung* (Vienna, 1903; *rp*, Munich, 1980), 309).

him, the symbol may have awakened memories of the red roses that had once adorned Alma's photograph on his writing desk. But the Infanta's white rose he saw primarily as a symbol of chastity* – a more conventional interpretation, but one that clarified rather than contradicted Klaren's. On the all-important question of the mirror their views differed more radically. Since Klaren interpreted the Dwarf's fear of his own reflection as an indication of sexual inferiority, his hero became a mirror image of Alviano, the perverted hero of *Die Gezeichneten*; Zemlinsky, in contrast, saw the mirror as reflecting only physical ugliness. Questioned on this very point, he explained:

In Schreker it is a case of conscious disfigurement, while my Dwarf seeks his fortune in fairy-tale-like ignorance of his deformity, and thus becomes tragic.[21]

The soul of his Dwarf is untainted. Pathetically clutching his white rose, symbol of the unattainable, he dies – as Görge lived – incapable of fulfilling his dream.

Zemlinsky himself had loved, only to be rejected for being poor, ugly and of undesirable racial background; now he himself was loved – worshipped indeed – and by one of his own kind. Luise could not rival Alma's charisma, but she was blessed with strength of character, good looks, intelligence and talent. She entered Zemlinsky's life as an antidote to eighteen years of humiliation. *Der Zwerg*, composed during the first months of a relationship that was to endure half a century beyond the grave, became for him a coffin – to borrow the imagery of *Dichterliebe* – in which all his love and pain were laid to rest. At the moment when the Dwarf sings, 'Now I know that I love!', he wrote into his autograph full score the place and date of composition: 'Liebwerda i.B.,† 3 August $\overline{20}$'. Normally he would date only the closing bar of his manuscripts, sometimes also the opening. There seems little doubt that this entry *in medias res* can be read as a message to the *ferne Geliebte*.

He also wrote twice to Alma that summer, hoping to arrange a meeting. But their letters and telegrams crossed or went astray, and back in Prague he wrote again, more wistfully, to postpone the rendezvous indefinitely:

Once again I shall have to wait a long time for a proper heart-to-heart, for a chance to talk of what moves us, what oppresses us, etc. – me, at least. I am in great *need* of it, and often.[22]

Der Zwerg is the only opera of Zemlinsky's to use anything approaching Wagnerian leitmotiv technique. Compared to the tautly organized symphonic architecture of *A Florentine Tragedy*, the structure is more flexible, a combination of dance suite and operatic *scena*, through-composed recitative, number

---

* On the dance floor the Dwarf kisses the rose. Klaren complained (in his *Kölnische Zeitung* article) that Zemlinsky had omitted two crucial words from his libretto, thus giving the false impression that the Dwarf kisses the Infanta (page 123 of the vocal score: 'Und er küsst sie vor allen Leuten'; original libretto: 'Und er küsst sie, die Rose, vor allen Leuten').
† I.e. 'in Böhmen' (in Bohemia).

opera and arioso.* Deliberately breaking with Fuchsian principles of developing variation, the score also finds room for extended passages of literal repetition, a first intimation of the neo-classicism that was to follow. Despite the Expressionist outer shell – opulent orchestral textures, extremes of register and dynamics, hysterical outbursts and overpowering climaxes – the melodic material itself is largely retrospective, much of it being adapted from works directly connected with Alma. A seminal role is taken by the third Dehmel Fantasy, *Liebe*, composed in 1898 (EX. 63A).† Its outline is visible in the whole-tone swell of Ghita's theme (EX. 63B, pages 7 and 9),‡ and a figure derived from its first four notes accompanies the banter of the three ladies-in-waiting (EX. 63C, page 7). When the Infanta skittishly warns the Dwarf, 'If you love me, you must be very handsome', the melody finally appears in its original guise (EX. 63D, page 104); from here on it plays a central role, the embodiment of Dehmel's ecstatic 'You and the world, at one, reposed in me'.§ As the Dwarf climbs the dais to kiss the Infanta's stool, the *Liebe* theme accompanies him, *dolcissimo* on solo strings. Once the mirror has been unveiled, it never returns.

In the opening bars Zemlinsky introduces two four-note motifs, one associated exclusively with the Infanta, the other verbally identified by her ladies-in-waiting as a symbol of 'birthday':

EX. 62

The birthday table of our most gracious Infanta.

These 28 introductory bars (14+14) suffice to establish a surface of bustling joviality and good humour; subliminally they address wider issues. The 'Birthday' motif, an unvarying, timeless symbol, consists of a threefold asymmetrical

---

* Zemlinsky himself described the score as 'continually flowing music, which is by no means modern in the atonal sense; it has no arias as in Italian opera, but the Dwarf sings a three-verse song, for instance, which could [. . .] be performed independently of the rest' (unnamed author (identified as '–n'), 'Zemlinsky über seinen "Zwerg"', *Komödie*, November 1923).
† Rudolf Stephan Hoffmann drew attention to this in his essay 'Zemlinskys Opern' (*AT*, 213).
‡ Page numbers correspond to the vocal score by Heinrich Jalowetz (Vienna, 1921; UE 6630).
§ When the Dwarf takes up the strain (pages 105–6), Zemlinsky also quotes from the second phrase of *Liebe*.

rotation of the 'World' motif; the Infanta's motif is based on a mordent, an ornament that turns back on itself, hence also unvarying, but in the sense of being incapable of further development. In fandango rhythm, the mordent motif flits gracefully across the dance floor (cf. EX. 64C); as the Infanta trips daintily away from the scene of tragedy, the figure, now a delicate flourish on the celesta (page 164), seems to suggest the rustle of crinolines.

Each verse of the Dwarf's courtly love song concludes with the major–minor alteration of the *Liebe* theme. It also pervades the motif of 'Love and Death', EX. 63E, first heard on muted strings 'tenderly and dreamily' during the presentation ceremony (page 64). The implications of this motif are far wider than that 'sense of inferiority' envisaged by Klaren. Shifting from the sunlit radiance of A major to the bitterness of F minor, from the warmth of A♭ major to the deathly chill of A minor, these few chords summarize the entire tragedy. As Ghita takes the broken little man into her arms (page 163), it is this theme that provides the opera's shattering climax.

EX. 63   (A) op. 9, no. 3 (*Liebe*), opening bars; (B–C): *Der Zwerg*, 10³; 12²

EX. 63   (D–E) *Der Zwerg*, 159^2; 93^{-1}

A further group of themes originates, if indirectly, in the principal motif of *Die Seejungfrau* (cf. ex. 19):

EX. 64   (A–C) *Der Zwerg* 57^{-1}; 87^5; 186^3

EX. 64A, the Dwarf's central motif, is assembled from the same components as the Mermaid's 'Home' theme, a pivoting 4th (here a 4th and a 5th) and a descending scale figure of three or four notes. EX. 64B, almost invariably coloured by the dark timbre of the cor anglais, represents the Dwarf as a 'whim of cruel Nature'. The semitone nuance of the *Liebe* theme is present here too, accentuated by a shift from D minor to B♭ minor, the key of tragedy. EX. 64C depicts the Dwarf dancing with the Infanta, his line now graced by her characteristic mordent. The chromatic falling sequence in bars 4–6 of this 'Spanish Dance' also links the theme to EX. 65B, one of a further group of interrelated Dwarf motifs:

EX. 65   (A) *Der Zwerg* 56^{-2}; (B) 58^2 and 58^7; (C) 229^4

These are built from the same basic components as EX. 64, but inverted and assembled in reverse order. EX. 65A represents the Dwarf as others see him: a monster. Snarling trombone *glissandos*, sinister *sul ponticello* slides, frog-like hops – he is spared nothing. An instant later, the same idea, now an elegant violin solo (EX. 65B), represents the Dwarf as he sees himself: a cavalier. The second strain of this new theme is initially presented as a mirror image of the first (no exact correlate, but a free inversion, recognizable as such even to the unschooled ear). Zemlinsky uses this device to encompass three dualities: object and mirror image, ugliness and grace, man and God (pages 49–50, 60–61 and 68).

With soaring vocal lines, coruscating orchestral colours, episodes of intense calm and outbursts of searing intensity, the Infanta's confrontation with the Dwarf creates the perfect illusion of a love duet. For sheer beauty these pages stand unrivalled in Zemlinsky's *œuvre*. Nevertheless they contain a disruptive element, a persistent reminder of the Dwarf's ugliness. The Infanta sings of her 'radiant hero' (page 93), her 'Adonis' (page 96), but frog hops in horns and trumpets interrupt the song. The Dwarf grows more fervent, his *Liebe* theme now glowing in C major (page 111), but the line is disfigured by a hobbling *col legno* of cellos and basses. His final, desperate attempt to kiss her unleashes an orchestral paroxysm of hideous anguish.

Klaren handles the ensuing scene, in which Ghita attempts to open the Dwarf's eyes to reality, with an awkward mixture of *naïveté* and pathos. Ignoring his librettist's invitation to Wagnerize, Zemlinsky underpins the first section with a fast-moving chaconne on a two-bar ground. This device, which he had never used before, serves to hold the dialogue within the bounds of E minor and G minor. 'My soul is in a prison-house,' complains Simone in *A Florentine Tragedy*; the Dwarf's soul is likewise incapable of escape – but from illusion, not reality. Incessant movement from the one key to the other depicts him nervously pacing up and down the confines of his mind. On to the wall of his prison cell the orchestra projects reminiscences of past encounters with his *alter ego*, each episode interwoven with EX. 65C, a new motif variant that portrays him through Ghita's eyes: neither monster nor cavalier, but a living tragedy.

The Dwarf's duel with his own mirror image draws on much the same Grand Guignol vocabulary as the murder scene of *A Florentine Tragedy*, assembling all salient themes and motifs in a powerful *stretta*. The orchestration is as incisive and brilliant as ever but, as elsewhere in this remarkable score, textures are leaner, proportions more economical.*

Zemlinsky almost certainly knew Schreker's ballet *Der Geburtstag der Infantin*, commissioned by the sisters Elsa and Grete Wiesenthal and performed by them in June 1908.† Although the music of *Der Zwerg* has nothing in common with that work, both composers were clearly as attracted to the decorative framework of Wilde's tale as to the tragedy itself. At face value, *Der Zwerg* contains elements both of *tragédie lyrique* and *comédie-ballet*, is almost as much an entertainment as a psychoanalytical case study. Almost a third of the opera

---

* It would be tempting to draw a parallel between the Dwarf's moment of recognition (page 146) and the scene where Wozzeck throws his bloodstained knife into the water (*Wozzeck* act III/iv, 255–60): the gesture of tumbling (253 in *Der Zwerg*) and the ensuing low brass chords (254¹ *et seq.*) are strikingly similar. Yet Berg neither read a score of *Der Zwerg* nor heard it performed until October 1923, over a year after completing his score. Nor can there have been there any direct cross-fertilization in the opposite direction, for Zemlinsky did not see a score of *Wozzeck* until January 1923.
† In 1926 he requested a score of Schreker's suite from the publisher (letter to Universal Edition, 30 November), with the alleged intention of performing the work.

is given over to embellishment: the servants deck and redeck the table with presents, the Infanta's friends adorn and readorn her with flowers. The ball game in the garden (a scenic reminiscence of the *Jugendstil* episode in act 1 of *Es war einmal . . .*), the rough-and-tumble in the loggia, the presentation ceremony itself: these scenes constitute an engaging and liberally proportioned divertimento. This extravagant use of stage time is intentional, for it serves to maximize the dramatic contrast. 'Wir tanzen und spielen,' ('We dance and play,') sang Görge and Gertrud, and a solo violin reached towards the sky. In a sense, *Der Zwerg* takes over where that music left off. But as the drama unfolds, the world of dreams becomes a mental torture-chamber. Görge's Princess had once opened up alluring vistas of 'the world, the wonder-world'. Now, at the height of the Dwarf's agony, her passionate 'World' theme reappears, talisman-like (page 157, 272³–273³), as bringer of evil tidings.

Lacht alle Schöpfung? Lachtest du mit?
Is all Creation laughing? Would you laugh too?

– asks the Dwarf.

Ich lieb dich aus Mitleid und Ekel.
I love you out of pity and disgust.

– is the devastating reply.

In private, Zemlinsky had often been the object of Alma's 'pity and disgust'; in public, he found himself at the mercy of every satirical columnist and caricaturist in the land. To compose an opera on so sensitive a theme as his own physical appearance seemed a particularly distressing form of self-abasement. Already while he was working on the first sketches, in the summer of 1919, his friends tried to dissuade him. 'The libretto suits me uncommonly well,' he wrote defiantly to Hertzka, 'therefore I am persevering with it, despite all objections'.[23] Whatever its deficiencies, for him the work was an ideal combination of 'imagination of the eye' and 'drama of the soul'. Composing *Der Zwerg* was an Orphic ritual of self-destruction and self-purification. Only music could free him from the prison-house of his soul.

Most of the short score was composed within a matter of weeks in the summer of 1919.[24] During the ensuing season at the NDT – with new productions of *Meistersinger* on 7 September and *Rheingold* on 7 December, interspersed with revivals of *Fidelio*, *Aida*, *Don Giovanni*, *Die toten Augen* and *Die Walküre* – progress was inevitably slower. Nevertheless, by Christmas the music was finished.[25] The following 20 June Zemlinsky started to orchestrate, and once the curtain had fallen on his last performance of *Meistersinger* (18 July), the summer was free for creative work.* At Bad Liebwerda, in the clean air of the Iser Mountains, he completed all but the last fifty pages of his intricate full score.[26] Back in Prague he toiled away at the closing scene, mostly late at night, while Jalowetz delivered pages of vocal score to the engraver as and when they were ready.[27] The final double-bar was signed on 4 January 1921; by mid-March the vocal score was already in print.

It was Zemlinsky's fondest hope that *Der Zwerg* would be premièred at the Vienna Staatsoper. Alma was therefore among the first to receive a complimentary copy (she is reported to have 'liked it immensely'), accompanied by instructions to contact Schalk and exercise her powers of persuasion.† But Hertzka prudently also sent copies to other major opera houses, and by mid-April Bodanzky in New York, Ludwig Rottenburg in Frankfurt and Egon Pollak‡ in Hamburg had expressed interest in the work. Then, on 2 May Zemlinsky wrote excitedly to Hertzka:

Today I received a telegram from Klemperer in Cologne, which reads as follows: HAVE READ YOUR OPERA ZWERG WITH GREAT ENJOYMENT. COLOGNE IS PREPARED TO ACCEPT SOLE RIGHTS FOR WORLD PREMIÈRE. WILL YOU PLACE YOUR WORK IN OUR HANDS. KLEMPERER. What to do? This is my opinion: Cologne strikes me, musically speaking, as a little off the beaten track. Perhaps the public is also too insipid. On the other hand, Klemperer would be my guarantee of first-rate musical presentation. If they also have a good singer for the principal role, one should not hesitate. What do you think?[28]

The Cologne ensemble happened to boast a dramatic tenor, Karl Schröder,§ who commanded the necessary range, power and stage sense. Since Schalk had still made no concrete offer, Klemperer got his way, and the première was scheduled for early November. In mid-September, however, Schröder applied for leave of absence for *Die tote Stadt* in New York.¶ Klemperer wrote to inform Zemlinsky that the production would have to be postponed until February;[29] in the event, it was delayed until May.

Zemlinsky and Ida attended the final rehearsals as guests of the Cologne Theatre Commission. Their few days in the Rhineland were convivial ('The

---

* Or very nearly: at the end of August, he gave three concerts with the NDT orchestra in Reichenberg.

† Before taking a decision, Schalk and Strauss attended a performance of *Kleider machen Leute* in Prague on 16 June 1922.

‡ Pollak had conducted the Hamburg world première of *Die tote Stadt*.

§ After engagements at Bremen and Elberfeld, and occasional appearances at Bayreuth, Karl Schröder (1886–1923) joined the Cologne opera ensemble in 1913. Apart from Paul in *Die tote Stadt*, his repertoire included Parsifal, Lohengrin, Bacchus (*Ariadne auf Naxos*) and the Emperor (*Die Frau ohne Schatten*).

¶ The première took place on 19 November, with Maria Jeritza in the role of Marietta and Bodanzky as conductor. For reasons unknown, Schröder did not participate: the role of Paul was sung by Johannes Sembrach.

grub is good here,' he reported to Schoenberg),[30] and the music was excellent. 'Klemperer is a *somebody*,' he had assured Hertzka.[31] Results bore him out. 'Klemperer magnificent,' he wrote to Schoenberg after the dress rehearsal,[32] and he was also impressed by the young man in charge of piano rehearsals, Hans Wilhelm Steinberg.[33] As the première drew near, a group of friends from Prague, including Jalowetz and Keussler, Adler and Rychnovsky, the photographer Otto Schlosser and the music-dealer Josef Taubeles, made their way to Cologne, prompting the critic Paul Hiller to remark that so much 'well-intentioned propaganda' served if anything to cast a dubious light on the occasion.[34]

Zemlinsky's fears of a tepid public reaction proved unfounded: the first night was a complete success.* Klaren's metaphors were found baffling, however, and the critics devoted almost as much column space to psychoanalysis as to music. For Zemlinsky their approval was unanimous. '[He] is [. . .] as much a master of technique and form in small details as in larger scenes,' wrote the *Kölnische Zeitung*,[35] and the *Kölnische Volkszeitung* considered the opera 'in terms of artistic refinement' to have 'surpassed almost every modern work that in recent years has graced the Cologne stage'.[36] Even if, according to Hiller, the opera was not as 'sensationally significant' as the composer's friends would have it –

one can at least report that the première was altogether a great success, and that, hand in hand with his chief protagonists, Zemlinsky, whose presence had been made known to the public, was able to take endless curtain calls.[37]

Having kept a watchful eye on the proceedings, Strauss and Schalk[†] at last decided to accept the work for Vienna. A production was scheduled for the second half of the 1922–23 season,[‡] ideally cast with the Norwegian tenor Karl Aagard Oestvig[§] in the title role and the twenty-two-year-old Maria Rajdl (his wife) as Infanta. The contract with Universal Edition was not ratified until March 1923, however, and the postponement of another production (*Manon Lescaut* with Lotte Lehmann) caused rehearsals to be deferred until the autumn. Of the dress rehearsal, which took place on 22 November, Berg sent a lively if depressing account to his wife:

The performance is second rate. Even Oestvig, the best of all, has not yet grown into his part. But R[ajdl] and the smaller parts are third rate.[¶] The female chorus sounds

* Coupled with Stravinsky's *Petrushka*; both works were produced by Felix Dahn and designed by Teo Otto.
† Strauss wrote to Klemperer on 30 May 1922, congratulating him on his success. (See Peter Heyworth, *Otto Klemperer, His Life and Times*, vol. I: *1885–1933* (Cambridge, 1983), 162.)
‡ Coupled with *Gianni Schicchi*.
§ Oestvig (1889–1968) sang from 1914 to 1919 at Stuttgart, where he participated in the world première of Schillings's *Mona Lisa*; in Vienna he created the role of Emperor in *Die Frau ohne Schatten*. He joined the ensemble of the Städtische Oper, Berlin, in 1926.
¶ Zemlinsky's opinion of the two protagonists was evidently higher, for he engaged them both for the Prague production of his opera in 1926.

meagre (inaudible), making the whole opening section rather tedious. Production, stage direction and sets (Roller)* are poor, in my opinion. Disregarding all this, as well as the inflexible conducting (Alwin), there really is still plenty to be enjoyed to the full, thanks to the unendingly sweet, surging melody! The music, by the way (due to the complex polyphony) is not all that easy to understand. [. . .] Almschi is in utter despair about the performance too, finds it poor, hence tiresome, and is prophesying a fiasco.[38]

On the strength of what he had heard, Berg saw little chance for the work's success:

It contains much that is undramatic, and the dramatic scenes, on the other hand (such as the first entry of the Dwarf) are so agonizingly tragic that one can scarcely bear it. What a shame for the glorious music.[39]

After the rehearsal Zemlinsky dined with Schoenberg, Berg, Webern and the Greissles at the Opera restaurant (he was in such a nervous condition that he burned a hole in the tablecloth with his cigar).[40] He knew only too well that his future in Vienna hung on this one production; alas, there seemed little hope of its succeeding. At the première, however, Berg's impression was more positive:

It was *appreciably* better than at the dress rehearsal, and accordingly a very great success. I was sitting with Webern behind a pillar, and benefited much more from reading the vocal score than from sitting in the stalls.[41]

Even those critics who counted as Zemlinsky's supporters summoned up little enthusiasm for his latest work. Julius Korngold studiously avoided passing judgement at all, confining his remarks to description and analysis.[42] But in essence his unspoken verdict concurred with that of Elsa Bienenfeld:

I can think of no one whose heart beats more passionately for his art, no one who serves his art with greater selflessness. With all his strength, and with more than strength, he seeks the divine spark, [. . .] even if his strength fails him, even if his wings prove too weak to carry him. Of all artists currently active, he is in truth the most tragic.[43]

Other reviews were more hostile. One critic dismissed the work as a 'laboratory opera',[44] another found it merely impractical – 'too little for a whole evening, too much to be taken in without an interval'.[45]

   Der Zwerg fared poorly in Karlsruhe,[†] better in Prague,[‡] but disastrously at the Städtische Oper in Berlin-Charlottenburg,[§] where, despite perfectly accept-

---

* Roller's name was not included on the programme: presumably his sets had been culled, as in the ill-fated *Traumgörge* production, from productions no longer in the repertoire.
† Première on 11 March 1924, coupled with Korngold's *Der Ring des Polykrates*.
‡ Première on 25 May 1926, coupled with Korngold's *Violanta*.
§ Première on 22 September 1926; coupled with a ballet entitled *Der letzte Faun*.

able box-office returns, Bruno Walter removed the work from the repertoire after only two performances. Plans for a production with the celebrated helden-tenor Fritz Windgassen at Stuttgart in 1930 foundered on the tessitura, which he found too high; similar problems thwarted Pella's intention of staging the work in Aachen. Other theatres, including Freiburg, Danzig and Olomouc, expressed interest in the work, but failed to follow it up.

Apart from purely technical or administrative obstacles, the opera was no longer in tune with the *Zeitgeist*. The Roaring Twenties were not conducive to soul-searching: in a time of severe collective crisis, the tragedy of the individual paled into insignificance.

Lyric Symphony

After two years of playing Dulcinea to Zemlinsky's Quixote, Luise tired of the role.[46] Having graduated from the Academy of Art in the summer of 1921, she was accepted for the class of Irene Schlemmer-Ambros at the Akademie für Musik und darstellende Kunst (Academy of Music and Performing Arts) in Vienna. The news probably reached Zemlinsky in June – the scenario, admittedly, is hypothetical – while he was orchestrating *Der Zwerg* in Bad Liebwerda. Perhaps his enigmatic marginalia in the score, beneath the words 'Now I know that I love!', should hence be read as an expression of despair rather than joy.

In describing the Infanta's retinue as 'a fashionable crowd, who today would go into raptures over Tagore', Klaren had sought to ridicule the escapist fringe of a society over-saturated with its own culture. Writing in the early summer of 1922, he could scarcely have known that Zemlinsky had just started work on a vocal symphony intended to relive his experiences with Luise – 'something like *Das Lied von der Erde*', as he described it to Hertzka[47] – to verses by Rabindranath Tagore.

Gitanjali, A Lyric Offering, published in English in 1912, had made Tagore famous in Europe almost overnight. The book was reprinted ten times within a year; Ezra Pound, Saint-John Perse and Gerhart Hautpmann were numbered among its admirers, Gide, Jiménez and Pasternak among its translators. Nobody was surprised when, in 1913, 'because of his profoundly sensitive, fresh and beautiful verse, by which, with consummate skill, he has made his poetic thought, expressed in his own English words, a part of the literature of the West',[48] he was awarded the Nobel Prize for Literature.

In time it became clear that this integrative judgement was premature. While not sharing Gandhi's disdain for everything Western, long visits to Europe and the US made Tagore increasingly aware of rifts and differences between cultures and continents. Liking ever less of what he saw, and giving polite but firm voice to that dislike, he began to lose the sympathy of influential patrons. In Austria and Germany some intellectuals grew suspicious of such popularity – Rilke, for instance, who had himself initially planned to translate *Gitanjali* – while others, notably Kafka, Thomas Mann and Spengler, expressed outright disdain. This could explain why the German editions of his works were prepared not by prominent men of letters, as in other countries, but by professional translators. *Gitanjali* and two further anthologies, *The Crescent Moon* and *The Gardener*, were published in Munich in 1914, stylishly translated by Hans Effenberger; Hedwig Lachmann's translation of *The Post Office* (Tagore's most popular play) followed in 1918, and 1921 saw the publication of a handsome eight-volume edition of collected works, nicely timed to coincide with the poet's first European tour.*

Since most translators worked from Tagore's own English texts, much of the flavour of his original Bengali was lost.† In German, nevertheless, his verse reads surprisingly well, sometimes indeed better than in English. For a poorly structured line such as, 'Let love melt into memory and pain into songs', Effenberger finds rhythmic poise and alliterative definition:

Lass Liebe in Erinn'rung schmelzen und Schmerz in Lieder.

With syntactical elegance he transforms the platitudinous 'You are my own, my own' (the climactic phrase that Berg later quoted in his Lyric Suite) into the distinctive

Du bist mein Eigen, mein Eigen.‡

Zemlinsky appears to have been drawn less to the religious fervour of this poetry than to its erotically charged mysticism: the refined but explicit symbolism of the poet's flute with its 'keen call' and 'vanishing strain', the young girl's chain of rubies, crushed beneath the wheels of the prince's chariot to leave 'a red stain upon the dust'. Heavily perfumed, rich in arabesque and metaphor, this was a style familiar to him from Wilde and Baudelaire, a language that was pure music.

Tagore's European tour, which began in April 1921, was an unqualified success. Having been fêted and acclaimed in France, Germany, Austria, Switzerland, Denmark and Sweden, he spent four days in Prague (18–21 June) lecturing on Buddhism and Indian literature at the Charles University. On the eve of his departure he also gave a poetry reading, of which Janáček has left a vivid eye-witness account:§

* Publication was delayed until the late autumn, however, by which time Tagore had returned to India.
† A notable exception was the Czech edition, translated by Vincenc Lesny, professor of Indology at the Charles University.
‡ The standard translation would be 'Du bist mir eigen.' By using the substantive *Eigen*, Effenberger stresses the aspect of ownership or possession; a (literal) retranslation would be 'You are my property.'
§ First published the following day, 22 June 1921, in *Lidové Noviny*. In 1922 Janáček

It seemed as if a white sacred flame flared up suddenly over the thousands and thousands of heads of the men and women present . . . but Tagore did not speak. He sang – his voice sounded like a nightingale's song – smooth, simple, without any clash of consonants. [. . .] On his face you could trace indescribable grief. He spoke to us in his native language – we did not understand – but from the sound of his words, from the melodies of his poetry I could recognize and feel the bitter pain of his soul.

That evening Zemlinsky delegated a performance of *Siegfried* to Jalowetz (it was the first time that he had missed a *Ring* performance). Perhaps he had received a presidential invitation to the reading, for Tagore was an official guest of the Czech government; perhaps he was even introduced to the poet – nothing is certain. It is certain only that a meeting took place in the autumn of 1926, during Tagore's second visit to Prague, when on the eve of his departure (13 October) the NDT gave a soirée in his honour. After a welcoming speech by Kramer, Zemlinsky conducted the *Air* from Bach's Suite in D; readings of poetry and prose were followed by the finale of the Lyric Symphony, and the evening ended with a staged performance of *The Post Office*.* This was not the first time that Tagore had heard his verses set by a Western composer.† Even if the results might have struck him as bizarre, his ear was always open:

Our melodies are intended for the solitary individual; European music is for the multitude. Our music removes us from the domain of everyday joys and sorrows to a region devoid of company, as aloof as the universe; the music of Europe revels in the perpetual oscillations of the human condition.[49]

Shortly before his first visit to Prague, Tagore had travelled to Paris by aeroplane. Before boarding, he was asked whether this was his first flight. He smiled. 'The first of its kind,' he replied.[50] In the spiritual and sensual dimensions he was a seasoned aviator. And when lovers take wing, as he wrote –

Duration is measured by intensity of feeling; the emotions of the moment seem endless. [. . .] Moments become hours and hours moments, as if in a dream. And then it seems to me that the subdivisions of time and space are figments of my mind. Each atom is immeasurable and each moment infinite.[51]

---

composed his remarkable setting of *The Wandering Madman* (from *The Gardener*) for soprano solo and male-voice chorus.
* In their 'Chronicle of Eighty Years', Prabhaktumar Mukhopadhyaya and Kshitis Roy give a delightfully jumbled account of the event: '[Tagore] attends a Bach recital at the New German Theatre and also a performance of the Czech version of *The Post Office*. Zemlinsky sings a few Tagore lyrics translated into Czech and set to Western music' (*Rabindranath Tagore, A Centenary Volume* (Sahitya Akademi, New Delhi, 1961), 486).
† Already in 1914, Louis Durey, the least remembered member of *Les Six*, set three poems from *Gitanjali* for voice and piano, in a style self-avowedly influenced by Schoenberg's *Buch der hängenden Gärten*. In 1920 Universal Edition published Szymanowski's Four Songs op. 41 to poems from *The Gardener*, with dual German/Polish texts by Effenberger and Jaroslav Iwaszkiewicz. Three of these, *The Young Prince* (I and II) and *The Last Song*, are textually identical to the second and sixth song of the Lyric Symphony.

Alma had inspired Zemlinsky to music that was 'more yearning, more turbulent, more pessimistic'. With Luise at his side, his art acquired a new fundament (*Grundton*) which he himself described as 'deeply serious, yearning but unsensual'.[52] The overpowering, sometimes hysterical intensity of *Der Zwerg* was built on a *Grundton* of passive contemplation, a foetal state, so to speak, to which at irregular intervals the music returns. The Lyric Symphony goes further, with a seismographic curve that plunges from peaks of frenzied activity, at which the experience of hours seems compressed into moments, to troughs of intense calm, where 'moments become hours'. None of his works runs a wider gamut of emotion, none so utterly consumes its reserves of nervous energy.

The poems, taken from *The Gardener** and sung alternately by baritone and soprano, disjunctively outline a love drama, from the first stirrings of desire to the agony of farewell – a *via crucis* in seven stations. The number 7, which Zemlinsky explicitly included in the subtitle ('Symphonie in sieben Gesängen'), invokes the image of perfection or completion, a pre-echo of the baritone's words in the closing song: 'Let it not be a death but completeness.' The death of love implies a rebirth, and in these seven movements the wheel of fate turns full circle:

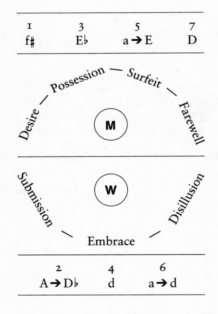

In *Der Zwerg* Zemlinsky translates the concept of 'completeness' into sound in the form of a threefold rotation of the 'World' motif (EX. 62B). The same

---

* Poems 5, 7, 30, 29, 48, 51 and 61 (*Collected Poems and Plays of Rabindranath Tagore* (London, 1936)).

figure, now in *adagio* tempo, plays a significant role in the finale of the Lyric Symphony (for instance in EX. 66D, bars 2–4). Each of the **M** movements introduces material of programmatic character, to which Zemlinsky applies 'a kind of leitmotivic treatment', as he himself described it. These ideas recur throughout the work, in ever changing constellations, like characters in a drama:[53]

EX. 66   (A) I, bars 2–5; (B) III, 57³; (C) V, opening bars; (D) VII, 110⁻¹

The themes and motifs of the **W** movements, in contrast, are not included in this global scheme. Indeed, as the story reaches its conclusion, in the sixth movement, the **W** element is completely suppressed. Zemlinsky assembles the movement from fragments of **M** material, interspersed with seemingly athematic phrases of quasi-recitative. **W** is reduced to a figment of **M**, a process that tacitly endorses the sexist theories of Weininger:

The relationship between man and woman differs in nothing from that between *subject* and *object*.

Man is form, woman is matter, [. . .] matter that can assume any given form.

A woman has no awareness of her own, only an awareness bestowed upon her by a man; she lives uncognizantly, the man cognizantly.[54]

The opening bars (marked 'with solemn and passionate expression') show the influence of an idea originally conceived for 'Raphael' (see p. 261), an articulation of that 'desire of every passive individual for brute strength' of which Klaren had once written. Having made extensive use in *Der Zwerg* of a motif dating from 1898, Zemlinsky returns here, in the third bar, to an even earlier idea, the 'Circassian' syncopation of *Sarema*, symbol of masculine obduracy and resilience. The rhythm pulsates at its fiercest during the transition to the third movement, but also appears in less unequivocal forms, gently entwining itself around the voice ('I forget, I ever forget, that I have no wings to fly'), and (in augmentation) contributing an element of rhythmic pliancy to the first movement's second-subject group. There is no place for Circassian fire in the trance-like *scène d'amour* of the third and fourth movements; all the more arresting then is its sudden rekindling in the fifth movement, to the words 'Open the doors, make room for the morning light', all the more moving the *cul de lampe* of the finale, where the once proud figure is reduced to a faltering hemiola.

Although Luise later often drew attention to the private, autobiographical aspects of the work, the Lyric Symphony goes further than any of Zemlinsky's operas to reinforce Tagore's observation that 'European music is for the multitude.' In the concert hall, liberated from all conventions of theatre, the Dwarf's mirror is turned to the audience, inviting all to share in the composer's personal experience. As a token of this universality, the 'Self' motif is inverted in the fifth song (EX. 66C), transforming it into Beethoven's 'Es muss sein' motif, his 'decision taken with a heavy heart' in the Quartet op. 135. 'Beethoven's pursed lip'[55] lends itself well to the rage and bitterness of the situation, but perhaps this motivic *coup de main* can also be interpreted, in Zemlinsky's most universal work, as a gesture of homage to that most universal of all Western composers.

As in the Second Quartet, the tonal centre of the Symphony moves by stages from the F♯ minor of suffering to the D major of enlightenment. But where the Quartet ends conclusively and in a context of undisturbed diatonicism, the Symphony's closing bars are open-ended, fading away on a pan-diatonic chord with a Lydian G♯. The 'Wanderer' key of D minor appears frequently in every movement, a constant point of reference. But at the epicentre, in the fourth movement, functional harmony is momentarily suspended, the chromaticism of the 'Wanderer' enmeshed in a net of pentatonic clusters, the 'Fate' chord immobile in the lovers' embrace. For bars at a time nothing moves. The keys of the intermediate movements are chosen as much from the standpoint of structural cohesion as of symbolic significance. The second, in blue-skied A major with two trio-like episodes in the 'mystic' key (Ullmann) of Db major, approximates, as Zemlinsky wrote,[56] to the scherzo of a traditional symphony. Tonally a relative-major pendant to the minor-key first movement, it is separated by a tritone from the *Adagio*, which vacillates between the Eb minor of 'crisis' and the Eb major of 'transfiguration'. Movements five and six constitute a diptych in A minor: the baritone, in his song of liberation, strives towards the dominant (EX. 66c); the soprano, shattered by her failure to 'embrace her dream', moves towards the subdominant minor, though her song is underpinned by an unremitting pedal on the dominant, E. Her parting words trigger off a violent orchestral outburst, which juxtaposes in flashback technique the leitmotivs associated with 'desire', 'possession' and 'surfeit', underpinned for 13 bars by the 'Fate' chord in A minor. Finally the bass line descends from E to D, ushering in the new tonic, D major, but initially in a minor-key context and with a flattened 7th, symbol of frustration and disappointment.

Even if Zemlinsky himself declared the Lyric Symphony to be 'something along the lines of *Das Lied von der Erde*', the similarities are skin deep. The form of Mahler's work is linear, Zemlinsky's is circular; Mahler divides his work into six clearly separated movements, Zemlinsky prefers a through-composed, operatic structure. As if to emphasize this fusion of opera and symphony, his moments of supreme climax – the consummation (at the close of the second song) and the dismissal (before the seventh) – are placed symmetrically, like scene changes, within passages of transition. In their approach to orchestral sonority the two composers differ most radically. Where Mahler's ideal is of sharp-edged clarity, for Zemlinsky clarity is often subservient to emotional pluralism. The scoring is often denser and, if performed with anything less than exquisite care, less diaphanous than in any other of his works. Images such as 'the sunny haze of the languid hours' (1/29–31[-2]), 'wind sighing through the leaves' (69[-1]), 'the mist of heavy incense' (86[4]–87) and even 'silence' (117) are evoked with delicacy and imagination; particularly the fourth song draws on a finely graded palette of half-tones. But often the singers are engulfed in a dark forest of orchestral filigree work. In performance the score requires Mozartian grace and precision. For all its abandon, this music reveals its true beauty and power only if performed with discipline and cool-headed restraint.

Originally the première of the Lyric Symphony was scheduled for 5 June 1923, as part of the Austrian Music Week in Berlin;[57] in the event, it was delayed by 364 days. The orchestral parts were not ready, and although

Zemlinsky had evidently taken the bulky autograph score to Berlin with him in his hand luggage, he returned it to Prague by post. It never arrived – that is, it did arrive, but not until December.* Universal Edition's copyists set to work at once, but it proved impossible to schedule a performance before the summer. By one of those 'coincidences', the première was given on Luise's birthday, 4 June. Having made plans to leave Prague a few days beforehand, she informed him that she would be unable to attend. He was greatly disturbed. Several times he recounted to her the story of Wagner performing *Siegfried Idyll* for his wife on the morning of their son's first birthday. 'What do you think of that?' he asked; she had no idea. Only when she finally heard the work, many years later, did she understand what he had been driving at: it was she of whom the baritone sings, 'I have caught you and wrapt you, my love, in the net of my music.' She was the unnamed dedicatee of his orchestral masterpiece.[58]

* Arnošt Mahler, who recounts the story as an authenticated anecdote, adds that Zemlinsky was in despair, declaring that it would be impossible to rewrite the score from memory ('Alexander Zemlinsky. Das Porträt eines grossen Musikers', *TiU*, 18).

3

The Spirit of the ISCM

On the initiative of Rudolf Réti, Egon Wellesz and Paul Stefan, the ISCM was inaugurated with a festival of chamber music at Salzburg in the summer of 1922. A constitution was drawn up in London the following January under the presidency of Edward J. Dent, at which it was decided to hold separate festivals of chamber and orchestral music on an annual basis, each hosted by a different country, with programmes selected by national subcommittees, and progressive and conservative composers placed side by side. This alliance of old and new proved a source of constant friction, but the spirit of the early festivals was buoyant, fired by the conviction that an international musical society would do much to support the League of Nations (founded in 1920) in its mandate for 'respecting and preserving against external aggression the territorial integrity and existing political independence of all the members'.[1] In a united Europe, so the theory, there would be no war.

The third orchestral ISCM Festival was held in Prague from 31 May to 6 June 1924,[*] with three concerts at the Rudolfinum and two at the NDT. In order to accommodate all the works selected by the subcommittees, the programmes were long and poorly balanced. On 31 May the Czechs presented Ostrčil's Sinfonietta, the Austrians Karl Horwitz's symphony *Vom Tode*, the Swiss Bloch's Psalm 22 and Honegger's *Pacific 231*, the Italians Vittorio Rieti's Concerto for wind quintet and orchestra, and the French the Bacchanale from Florent Schmitt's *Antoine et Cléopâtre*.[†] Zemlinsky was unable to attend the second concert, on 1 June,[‡] but presumably heard the dress rehearsal, since the programme included an important new work by his friend Josef Suk, *Zrání* (*The Ripening*). He seems also to have taken pleasure in Malipiero's *Impressioni dal vero* (flanked by Szymanowski and Roussel), for two years later he himself conducted the work at the NDT. Whether he found time for the concert on 2 June, with works by Erdmann, Prokofiev, Stravinsky and Bax, is uncertain. For one thing, the programme (apart from *The Song of the Nightingale*) will have been less to his taste; for another, he was busy preparing

[*] Zemlinsky attended the 1923 ISCM Chamber Music Festival in Salzburg, in the company of Berg and Jalowetz.
[†] On the same day, the German community in Prague contributed a matinée concert, with lieder by Bruno Weigl and Viktor Ullmann, a piano trio by Fidelio Finke and Erwin Schulhoff's Fourth Piano Sonata.
[‡] He was conducting Verdi's *Otello* at the NDT.

his own contributions to the Festival, the world première of the Lyric Symphony on 4 June and, two days later, of Schoenberg's *Erwartung*.

Felix Adler was diplomatic in his praise of Zemlinsky's new work, which, for all its mastery, must have struck many a Festival visitor as a relic of the past:

Like Suk's *Zrani*, the Lyric Symphony is a work of maturity, drawn from a source of rich experience, sublimated by the perfection of an art whose roots are planted in firm soil. As such, it has long outgrown that experimentalism which is the hallmark of those younger composers who are still feeling their way.[2]

Paradoxically, the warmest welcome came from a leading 'younger composer', Alban Berg. It was probably during his 1924 visit to Prague that he first met Werfel's sister, Hanna von Fuchs-Robettin, with whom he soon became involved in a passionate love affair. Whatever the exact circumstances of his visit (which is only sparsely documented), when Berg wrote to Zemlinsky later in the month of his 'profound enthusiasm' for the Lyric Symphony, he was still clearly under the spell of Prague. His letter reads ambiguously, as if addressed to someone in whom he knew he could confide, and Tagore's innocuous word 'lyric' acquires a secret meaning, as if the concepts of symphony and sweetheart had become interchangeable:*

[Even if] now at last I believe that I really know your Lyric Symphony, in ten years time [I will] be forced to admit that today I have only an *inkling* of the score's boundless beauties. But this can do nothing whatsoever to diminish my love, which – as it affects me in a *particularly personal* way – is that true love which overcomes me only in the case of a small, select body of music.

[. . .] Freed from all the secondary considerations, limitations and obstacles that have to be surmounted in works of other genres [. . .], with the Lyric Symphony (never before was a title so unambiguous & at once so meaningful) a musical [child] is born – one that contains not one note too many, nor indeed one too few.[3]

With *Erwartung*† the ISCM could hardly claim to be promoting 'new music', for the score was fifteen years old. Even if its Expressionist aesthetic was outmoded, this was still the newest, boldest and most demanding work on the programme. Yet many of the critics virtually disregarded the score and wrote only of the achievement of performing it: heroes of the day were the soprano Marie Gutheil-Schoder, the NDT orchestra and, of course, its conductor. It was left to Zemlinsky himself to deflect his hard-earned glory on to the music:

* Since the final version is lost, *Web-Br* reproduces the preliminary draft of Berg's letter. The 'ten years' of the opening sentence was no arbitrary figure, for 10 was Hanna Fuchs-Robettin's secret number.
† Schoenberg's monodrama was coupled with Ravel's *Die spanische Stunde* (i.e. *L'heure espagnole*), conducted by Erich Steckel; both works were directed by Louis Laber, with set designs by Hans Piperger. There had been a plan to couple *Erwartung* with Krenek's *Die Zwingburg* (cf. unpublished letter from Krenek to Alma Mahler, 7 October 1922, *vP/D*), but the idea was evidently rejected as being out of line with ISCM policy.

At the Prague ISCM Festival in the summer of 1924 I conducted the first performance of a stage work by Schoenberg, the monodrama *Erwartung*. At the première
it made a profound impression and was a great success. Since then, however, no
other theatre has taken it into the repertoire. Considering that every new work of
Schoenberg's is greeted as a major sensation, this reticence is all the more surprising. The only explanation I can find lies in the work's allegedly 'almost insuperable
difficulties'. This opinion, I hasten to add, is unfounded. At first reading, certainly,
the score appears to present an exceptional challenge. But experience has shown
that if two artists – a singer and a conductor – convinced of the high quality of this
music, are prepared to work until they have entirely mastered it, the greatest problems can be surmounted; a conductor – but no conductor who, taking orders from
his superiors, rehearses apathetically, exchanging ribaldries with the orchestra – and
a singer with a beautiful voice (it is essential that the role be sung beautifully) and
powerful dramatic flair. Once these requirements have been fulfilled, the greatest
difficulties have already been overcome. The orchestral writing is no more difficult
than that of other contemporary works, and the score has one great advantage: it is
superbly orchestrated, almost everything sounds of its own accord.

I organized my orchestral rehearsals as follows: first I divided the orchestra into
very small groups, which rehearsed separately, [. . .] then full strings and harp; full
wind and percussion; finally full orchestra without the soloist. After that, two so-
called sitzprobes (voice and orchestra) sufficed before the actual stage/orchestra
rehearsals began. Since the work lasts only half an hour, much could be achieved
during the customary three-hour sessions, so that it was possible in three such stage
rehearsals to achieve an absolutely clear and convincing realization of the score. To
alleviate certain problems of intonation for the singer, I had a harmonium recessed
into the stage, near the area where she was acting; from time to time, without disturbing the audience in the least, this was used to give her a 'note'. Thus we managed to perform the work at a level which betrayed nothing of its difficulties.[4]

Zemlinsky took altogether fourteen orchestral rehearsals for *Erwartung*, not to
mention innumerable sessions with Gutheil-Schoder at the piano and on stage:
some indication of the selflessness, professionalism and infectious enthusiasm
with which he approached every aspect of his art.

String Quartet no. 3

Since the fateful summer of 1908 a cloud had hovered permanently over the
Schoenberg household. Alma, aware of the crisis, considered it expedient to ignore
Mathilde altogether, a course of action to which Schoenberg vociferously objected:

My wife is at least as intelligent as [Bruno] Walter's (I give you my word: she is more
intelligent, indeed one of the most intelligent women I know!). [. . .] I am firmly convinced that upon closer acquaintance you would summon up greater sympathy for
her than for most other women. For one can really make conversation with her, due
to her remarkable astuteness, her rare tact and sense of comportment. To be sure:
she is no outgoing person. Due to modesty, a kind of shyness.[5]

A few months later he wrote to Alma in praise of Mathilde's musical talent, stressing that she sang Mahler lieder to his accompaniment '*very often*', and that she knew them all by heart.[6] More often, however, there was talk of ill-health, weak nerves, of an inability to cope with the daily round. As time passed, Mathilde withdrew ever further into her inner self. Salka Viertel, who met her around 1920, recalls 'a frail, sick-looking woman who sat silently in the corner of the couch, always wrapped in a shawl',[7] and Luise remembered her only as 'the silent woman'.

In July 1923 Schoenberg wrote to Zemlinsky expressing his sympathy for Ida, who was convalescing after a hysterectomy operation, and adding almost as an aside that Mathilde was 'not at all well'.[8] In early September her doctor diagnosed an infection of the gall bladder and liver. During the following weeks her condition deteriorated rapidly, obliging the Schoenbergs to curtail their holiday on the Traunsee and return to Vienna.[9] On arrival, on 20 September, Mathilde was taken to the Sanatorium Auerspergstrasse, where a more thorough examination revealed a malignant tumour of the adrenal gland.[10] She died in hospital four weeks later, on 18 October 1923. Zemlinsky was too shattered even to attend the funeral.

Soon after her death, Schoenberg completed a long poem, *Requiem*, that he had begun two years earlier. 'Let it be a monument', he wrote –

that for many hundred years the name of Mathilde be spoken with all the admiration due to a woman who, like her, had the capacity for arousing such great love.[11]

Even if his words were chosen with great care, their message was ambivalent. In the poem itself he addressed the question of his wife's capacity for 'great love' – and the disastrous consequences of that capacity – more directly:

Nun lieben wir dich, Totes, / mehr als das Leben; / nun bist du uns rätselhafter / als deine Widersprüche uns waren, / die wir selten lieben, meistens nur hassen konnten, / weil du selten Liebe, meistens Hass verdientest – / soweit wir's begriffen.

We love you now, departed spirit, / more than life itself; / your riddles now perplex us / more than the incongruities of your life, / which we could love but rarely, and often hated, / because love you deserved but rarely, and hate often / – as we understood it.[12]

The text of *Requiem* was published in 1925, but without a dedication. Although Schoenberg had originally declared his intention of creating a work that would stand as a monument to his wife, no music was ever composed.

After twenty-two years of marriage he found life as a widower intolerable. 'Perhaps I shall move into a hotel for a few days,' he told Zemlinsky.[13] Instead, he invited Trudi and her family to move into his apartment in the Bernhardgasse, from which he had summarily ejected them two years before. Arnold

Greissle-Schönberg describes the situation during the weeks that followed:

Not only did he smoke like a chimney, about sixty cigarettes a day, he also drank a good deal of schnapps and three litres of coffee a day, and even started taking Pantopon (concentrated opium tablets). My mother was afraid he would kill himself.[14]

Eight weeks after completing *Requiem*, Schoenberg invited the members of the Kolisch Quartet, Marie Pappenheim and a few other close friends to a New Year's Eve party. The tone was subdued, for the shadow of bereavement still lingered in the house. But among the guests was a newcomer to the circle, Kolisch's twenty-five-year-old sister Gertrud. 'With her dry, somewhat pert humour,' writes Stuckenschmidt, 'she quickly won [Schoenberg's] affection.'[15] A few days after the funeral he had written to Zemlinsky, 'I seem to need some-one who at the right time can tell me that I am in the wrong, even if I am in the right.'[16] In Gertrud Kolisch he found such a partner. Not until the following 21 August, however, did he inform Zemlinsky of his engagement. The wedding was celebrated in Mödling soon after, just two weeks before Schoenberg's fiftieth birthday and only ten months after Mathilde's death.

By remarrying within the statutory twelve-month period of mourning, Schoenberg had flouted the requirements of convention; instead of fulfilling his vow to compose a Requiem for his dead wife,* he had written a wind quintet for his baby grandson Arnold. From now on he began to suppress all memory of Mathilde, and the very mention of Gerstl would drive him into a rage. Though in later years he invariably spoke of Zemlinsky with respect and affec-tion, in Gertrud's presence the name of Mathilde was anathema.[17]

Zemlinsky's Third Quartet was conceived partly as a substitute for the promised Requiem and partly as a reaction to events following his sister's death. Work began on the score on the very day on which Schoenberg wrote to announce his remarriage, 21 August,† and continued at fever pitch, with the first movement completed in three days and the final double-bar‡ signed only three weeks later, on 13 September.

Modestly proportioned and conventional in its four-movement outline (*Allegretto*, *Theme and Variations*, *Romance* and *Burlesque*), the op. 19 Quartet betrays at first hearing little of the emotional upheaval that accompanied its genesis. Masked by a wide range of colours and special effects, the work assumes a pose of gentle sarcasm, much in the spirit of the scene with the

* Schoenberg's draft dedication to the *Requiem* begins: 'Mathilde, I have vowed to erect a monument to your memory.'
† Zemlinsky had originally set this period of his vacation aside to write an essay for Schoen-berg's fiftieth birthday.
‡ Actually the closing bar of the third movement, which was the last to be written.

villagers in the epilogue of *Der Traumgörge*, and teases the ear, particularly in the finale, with sonic brilliance and rhythmic energy. In contrast to the full-blooded emotionalism of op. 15 or the wide-screen orchestral panorama of the Lyric Symphony, this music does not readily draw the listener in, let alone invite him or her to share in the experiences of which, indirectly, it seems to speak. A critic at Siena in 1928 caused a stir when he discerned in it a mood 'wavering between tragic earnestness and bloody (*blutige*) irony'.[18] His insight is shared neither by Weber, who writes of an 'almost playful tone' and 'a certain emotional reserve',[19] nor by Stephan, who senses 'a spirit, albeit well-differentiated, of *Spielmusik*'.[20] Adorno, who considered op. 19 the finest of all Zemlinsky's chamber works, summarizes his largely technical appraisal with a characteristically cryptic insight:

With self-critical circumspection, the work creates an impression of tenuousness, avoiding all extremes of self-assertion: personally formulated impersonality.[21]

Op. 19 represents a complete break with the Secessionism of *fin-de-siècle* Vienna and a withdrawal from that *Tristan*-inspired world of ecstasy which, since the death of Brahms, had been Zemlinsky's natural artistic habitat. Apart from the personal calamity of Mathilde's death and the collapse of a friendship that had endured for thirty years, the change was catalysed principally by the spirit of the ISCM, which opened his mind to new styles and ideas, many of them far removed from Schoenberg and his school. By no means, however, does op. 19 signify a final burning of boats. As in Nielsen's *Sinfonia semplice*, of which the work is an almost exact contemporary,* avant-garde techniques are adopted less for the sake of moving with the times than as an ironic form of protest. The variable metre of a Stravinsky, the *Neue Sachklichkeit* of a Hindemith: these and much else are paraded as if through a hall of mirrors, distorted, blurred and gently derided.

Thereby Zemlinsky arrives at a new, individual language. His textures have grown linear, his periodic structures asymmetrical, and with the principle of 'delayed resolution' carried to its furthest extreme, key centres cross-fade, overlap and vanish with bewildering rapidity. Yet behind this show of modernism op. 19 reveals the same experienced hand that crafted the Clarinet Trio or the Second Quartet. As ever, the entire fabric evolves from the pitches and rhythms of the opening bars, exploiting a minimum of thematic material to maximum effect. The opening theme itself is a quotation from the Lyric Symphony (EX. 67)

'Vergiss diese Nacht' – 'Forget this night, when the night is no more': the idea itself is pure **W**, the 'seemingly athematic' melody of a woman scorned and rejected. Its relevance in this context is self-evident, as is the complete absence in all four movements of the 'Mathilde' theme itself. The second subject, a

---

* Nielsen composed the *Sinfonia semplice* (Sixth Symphony) between October 1924 and December 1925.

EX. 67   (A) String Quartet op. 19, opening bars; (B) Lyric Symphony, VI/98⁻¹;
(C) op. 19, bars 12–14

Commentary   A scale figure, a perfect 4th, a *Drehfigur* and a dotted rhythm: for years Zemlinsky had been using these same musical building bricks. Here the *Drehfigur* of the viola (bars 1–2, combined with its mirror image in the cello) can be identified as the origin of every subsequent idea. The first phrase includes eleven of the twelve semitones (with a few repetitions), and the twelfth semitone, E♮, follows in bar 3 as the resolution of the extended D♯ leading note in violin I. Zemlinsky had presented comparable chromatic arrays in the Gesänge op. 7 but, as then, nothing in this passage presages serial technique. After momentary hints of B major and B♭ minor, the principal key, C major, appears towards the end of bar 2. Even so, the tonic is masked by the 'blue' note [22] D♯, and by the time it has resolved, the other voices have already moved towards E minor and D♭ major.

wide-spanned theme characterized by double-dotted rhythms, introduces an opposing **M** element, accentuated in the development section by a long passage of 'Circassian' syncopation. **W–M** contrast is further underlined by divergent tonal orientation: **W** sets out from a home base of implied C major with a tendency towards the subdominant, F major, and thence further into the flat keys; **M** is rooted in D minor, moves into sharp-key territory and, by the end of the development section, has penetrated as far as the G♯ pedal of an implied C♯ minor. Far from resolving this confrontation, the movement ends incoherently with a nervous burst of **M** rhythms centred on a C major 7th chord.

In February 1923 Schoenberg called together his inner circle and read them an essay on the technique of composition with twelve notes. Upon this historic event the second movement of op. 19, a theme with seven variations, casts a sardonic eye. As Zemlinsky understood it, Schoenberg had introduced a new currency into music, whose common coin was the semitone. Using the serialist's 'trick' of octave displacement, he takes the semitonal *Drehfigur* from the first movement and transforms it into a theme:

EX. 68   op. 19, II/opening bars*

The mystery of these bars (implied by the tempo marking, *Geheimnisvoll*) is not verbal, as in the first movement, but numerical: by constructing a theme of 2×14 pitches, with leaps of thirteen semitones (B♮–C in bar 1) and of a minor 13th (B♭–G♭ in bar 2), Zemlinsky juxtaposes his secret number with that of Schoenberg. Number symbolism also determines the overall structure:

Theme   8 (4+4) bars
Var. I   9 bars
Var. II   8 (4+4) bars
Var. III   9 bars
Var. IV   8 (4+4) bars
Var. V   9 bars
Var. VI   22 (14+8) bars
Var. VII   22 (14+8) bars
[Coda]   4 bars

In a formal analysis written by Jalowetz for the Universal Edition study score, the movement is described as –

a new type of variation form. The melodic material is strictly preserved in the first variations, and the structure and character of the various elements are preserved throughout; yet in none of the variations does the number of bars correspond to that of the theme.

As shown in the table above, Jalowetz's latter allegation is not entirely accurate: there are two variations of 8 bars, three of 9 bars and two of 22 bars. The

* In the published score the last melody note in bar 2 lacks the necessary ♮.

significance of the number 14 in the bipartite variations VI and VII is clear enough, while the number 22 presumably refers to the fact that Mathilde died on her twenty-second wedding anniversary.

The novelty of this movement lies less in its numerical mysteries, however, than in its idiosyncratic use of variation form. Given a theme with little melody and even less harmony, the variations are obliged to fall back on their own resources. Each elaborates on material introduced in the preceding variation, while the theme itself gradually loses relevance. By variation III it has all but disappeared, and when it returns, in the second part of variation VII, the supercilious undertone of its first appearance has changed to a mood of sorrow. Only in the brief coda does the *misterioso* of the opening return, as if to extinguish the few lights still left burning.

Both the title and form of the finale imply a link with the *Rondo-Burlesque* of Mahler's Ninth Symphony, with its sarcastic dedication to his fellow composers ('my brothers in Apollo'). Although the cello's opening invitation to fugal discourse is ignored, the spirit of daredevil virtuosity proves infectious. Where the first and second movements were addressed respectively to Mathilde and Schoenberg, the addressee of this movement is clearly Zemlinsky himself, with the 'Self' motif presented in every conceivable variant and every appropriate key. Only during the first rondo episode, a lopsided Spanish dance with a mischievously false bass, does the motif recede. In its place Zemlinsky introduces his *alter ego*, the Dwarf, complete with disfiguring *glissando* and grotesque leaps:

EX. 69   op. 19, IV/41–53

In the central episode of the *Rondo*, a parodistic minuet, the 'Self' motif assumes the role of universal dancing partner, a counter-subject to all comers. In the coda the dance then reaches its climax; 'World' and 'Self' are caught up in a whirlwind, spinning frenetically towards the final double-bar:

EX. 70   op. 19, IV/248–51

Seeking refuge in a tonal centre that never was, unison Cs restore some semblance of order.

Between the mordant sarcasm of the *Variations* and the vertiginous energy
of the *Burlesque*, the *Romance* (which was composed last) offers a measure of
lyric relief. To a mildly dissonant accompaniment of parallel 5ths and 2nds, the
viola expounds a long melody, characterized by syncopations and leaps spanning or exceeding the octave. Spinning the melody further, violin 1 alludes to a
phrase from the Lyric Symphony originally associated with the words 'Speak to
me, my love!' (EX. 71).

Apart from thematic resemblances, this passage also explores the parallel-
2nds harmony to which the corollary section of the Lyric Symphony owes its
distinctive colour. Note-heads nestle side by side, as if in intimate embrace: a
rare example in Zemlinsky's art of 'eye music'. The mood grows impassioned,
with melodic leaps of over two octaves in the cello and violin 1 (Berg recalls
them in spirit, if not in letter, in the *Trio ecstatico* of the *Lyric Suite*), but the
ecstasy abates, and the viola resumes its wide-spun melody. The harmony is
more dissonant now, the accompaniment *ohne Ausdruck* and reduced to *ppp*.
As semiquaver movement slows to quavers, romantic spirit freezes into a posture
of grief. The viola alludes to the 'descent into the depths' of op. 15 (EX. 48E),
as if heralding the new *Totentanz* of the finale.

After his alarming experience with the score of the Lyric Symphony, Zemlinsky
retained the original manuscript of op. 19 in Prague and sent only a copy to
Vienna.* Friedrich Buxbaum's Wiener Streichquartett started rehearsals at once
and premièred the work in Leipzig on 24 October 1924, only a matter of weeks
after the work's completion. The final rehearsals (in Vienna) were attended by
Webern and Berg. 'What unimaginable richness, what beauty, what sonic effects –

---

* Preserved in the Stadt- und Landesbibliothek der Stadt Wien.

EX. 71 (A) Lyric Symphony, IV/76[3]; (B) op. 19, III/13-15

all overwhelming,' wrote Webern,[23] and shortly afterwards, when Zemlinsky asked him to rehearse the work with the Sedlak–Winkler Quartet for performances in Vienna and Prague, he accepted with alacrity.[24] Berg also wrote enthusiastically,* and as Austrian representative on the selection committee he later succeeded in programming op. 19 for the 1928 ISCM Festival in Siena, though not without resistance from his Czech, Italian, Spanish and Swiss colleagues. Of the meeting, which was held in Zurich, he reported with fine irony to Schoenberg:[†]

Apparently not all the gentlemen of the jury were aware that Zemlinsky's quartet writing isn't much worse than that of, say, Bridge, that his powers of invention aren't that much poorer than, say, Bloch, and that he is scarcely less modern than, say, Alfano – and that it is a scandal of the first order that he has never been performed by the ISCM.[‡][25]

---

* The letter is lost (for Zemlinsky's reply cf. *Web-Br*, 310).
† After an altercation with Dent at Venice in 1925, Schoenberg had by this time severed relations with the ISCM.
‡ Berg seems to have forgotten that the Lyric Symphony was performed at an ISCM concert.

The Siena performance, given on 11 September 1928 by the Kolisch Quartet, did much to further Zemlinsky's international reputation. Among those who heard it on that occasion was the redoubtable Cobbett. In the 1929 edition of his *Cyclopedic Survey of Chamber Music* he supplemented Hugo Leichtentritt's faint praise of the work with an editorial gloss:

It is only fair to this clever composer to add that on the occasion of its first performance in Vienna it was encored and was presumably to the taste of an audience traditionally associated with music of a different nature. Time will doubtless bring back the Viennese to the more joyous feelings natural to them, which have for so long been viewed with sympathy and delight by the music-lovers of the world. The gaiety of such a nation as the Austrians cannot be eclipsed for long.[26]

Last Seasons in Prague

Zemlinsky returned from his 1924 summer vacation in Alt-Aussee to an opera season that was, by NDT standards, unusually lacklustre. Apart from paying his customary respects to Mozart and Wagner, he conducted *Fidelio*, *Der Opernball*, *The Kiss*, Laber's Dalcroze-inspired production of *Orfeo* and new productions of *Ariadne* and *Intermezzo*, but was happy to delegate *Carmen*, *La dame blanche*, *Le prophète* and Bittner's *Das Rosengärtlein* to younger colleagues. For him the highlight of the season was Laber's beautifully designed *Ariane et Barbe-bleue*, premièred in the presence of the composer on 20 May as a fringe contribution to the 1925 ISCM Festival. According to Rychnowsky, Zemlinsky conducted with 'radiant luminance'; the work itself, in his view, was 'an interesting discovery, nothing more'.[27] As at the Volksoper in 1908, it was given just three times.

The NDT public had grown fickle. Anxious not to overstep his budget, Kramer capitulated ever further to popular taste, filling the playbill with operettas and cheap revues, and thereby invoking the displeasure of the critics. While Adler and Rychnowsky expressed their censure only indirectly, in the editorial columns of *Der Auftakt* Steinhard used the opportunity to launch a prolonged and concerted attack. The headlines speak for themselves: 'Signs of decline at the Prague German theatre', 'Aimlessness of Prague opera management', 'Bulletin of a theatre's painful convalescence'.[28] Even if Steinhard's campaign was motivated less by a sense of artistic responsibility than by journalistic zeal, it had to be admitted that Kramer and Zemlinsky had lost much of their former dynamism. And once the seed of discontent had been sown, it was only a matter of time before it burgeoned. Kramer's resignation, on 16 December 1926, and Zemlinsky's departure to Berlin, announced three days later, were the logical outcome.

Whatever Steinhard's ulterior motive, his accusations goaded Kramer into action, and in the 1926–27 season the NDT surpassed itself. Apart from a wide choice of popular repertoire (*Tiefland, Fidelio, Carmen, Die Königin von Saba, La juive* (with Leo Slezak), *Der Evangelimann, Figaro* and *Don Giovanni, Tosca* (with Jan Kiepura), *Madama Butterfly, La fanciulla del West* and *Il trittico, The Barber of Seville, The Bartered Bride, Ariadne auf Naxos, Der Rosenkavalier, Eugene Onegin, Aida, La forza del destino, Rigoletto* and *Il trovatore, Der Freischütz, Lohengrin, Meistersinger, Parsifal, Tannhäuser, Tristan* and two complete *Ring* cycles), the bill of fare included revivals of *Der Zwerg* and *Violanta*, seventeen operettas* and several ballet programmes, including a double-bill of Bartók's *The Miraculous Mandarin* and Dohnányi's *Der Schleier der Pierrette*. Time and money were still found for three ambitious new productions, *Cardillac, Jenůfa* and *Jonny spielt auf* – and this in a theatre allegedly showing 'signs of decline'!†

The advent of Hans Wilhelm Steinberg in the autumn of 1925 caused a considerable stir. After the termination of Klemperer's contract in Cologne, he had stayed on, but disagreements with the new regime prompted him to resign in mid-season. Stranded in Berlin and almost penniless, he appealed to Zemlinsky for help. Recalling his excellent work on *Der Zwerg*, Zemlinsky invited him to conduct *Aida* at the NDT on 18 June 1925, with Slezak as Rhadames. As Adler reported, the performance made a powerful impression:

[Steinberg] belongs to Otto Klemperer's circle, which is in itself a recommendation. His conducting recalls Klemperer in gesture and stance, indeed to such a degree that one could imagine one was watching the original. [. . .] No doubt his wish to be engaged as Zemlinsky's partner will be fulfilled.[29]

On 25 October, when Steinberg made his official debut with *Der Zigeuner-baron*, Max Brod was no less enthusiastic:

Zemlinsky's *Fledermaus* remains unforgettable. And on Sunday *Kapellmeister* Steinberg delivered a comparably fine-tuned performance of *Der Zigeunerbaron*. All the sparkle, tension and excitement of this music, with its characteristically Danubian dash of Tokay, came across with redoubled vitality.[30]

* *Sonja* (Leo Ascher), *Adieu Mimi* (Benatzky), *Oscar lass dich nicht verführen* (Ralph Erwin), *Vierzehn Tage Arrest* (Edmund Eysler), *Der liebe Augustin* (Leo Fall), *Das Schwalbennest* (Bruno von Granichstaedten), *Pillen, Krach und Karokönig* and *Miss Chocolate* (Bernhard Grün), *Die Zirkusprinzessin* and *Ein Herbstmanöver* (Kálmán), *Glück in der Liebe* (Michael Krausz), *Paganini* (Lehár), *Ich und Du* (Lamberto Pavanelli), *Prinzessin Turandot* (Georg Pittrich), *Alexandra* (Albert Szirmai), *Die Fledermaus* and *Wiener Blut* (Johann Strauss) and *Der Vogelhändler* (Zeller).

† During the same season, the Národní Divadlo staged seven new productions: *The Makropoulos Affair, The Brothers Karamazov* (Otakar Jeremiáš), *Turandot, L'enfant et les sortilèges, Sadko, Schwanda the Bagpiper*, and the Prague première of *Wozzeck*, conducted by Ostrčil. *Wozzeck* opened on 11 November 1926 but was withdrawn after three performances due to protest from anti-Semitic members of the Prague City Council, who were evidently unaware that neither Berg nor Büchner were Jews.

His musicianship was impeccable, if coarser grained than Zemlinsky's, and his memory astonishing. Within six weeks of arrival he had conducted repertoire performances of *Carmen*, *Die Zauberflöte*, *La bohème*, *Madama Butterfly*, *Der Rosenkavalier*, *Il trovatore*, *Rigoletto*, *Lohengrin*, *Das Rheingold* and *Siegfried* – all by heart. Above all, he possessed a rostrum glamour of the kind that Zemlinsky consciously avoided.* Adler sometimes complained of Steinberg's tendency to sensationalism and 'conspicuous self-assertion',[31] but from the outset he was the public's darling. The press delighted in playing off the two maestros against each other, and although they remained on friendly terms, the working atmosphere inevitably suffered. As for the board of directors, their preference was clear: no sooner had Zemlinsky resigned than Steinberg was appointed his successor.†

From 15 to 20 May 1925 the ISCM returned to Prague, with three programmes that manifested even less sense of form than those of the previous year. Dent's personal taste was reflected in the opening item, the Sarabande from Busoni's *Doktor Faust*, performed only a week before the world première of the completed opera in Dresden. Between three masterpieces, Vaughan Williams's 'Pastoral' Symphony, Krenek's Concerto grosso no. 2 and Bartók's Dance Suite, the two succeeding concerts offered a jumble of good and less good, modern and less modern.‡ The ISCM Chamber Music Festival was held later that summer, from 3 to 8 September, in Venice. Zemlinsky interrupted his vacation in Alt-Aussee for a brief excursion across the Alps, but only to sun himself on the Lido, take a gondola ride past the Villa Mahler (Alma was not there), and make a dinner appointment with Anna Mahler (who failed to show up). By the time the Festival started he had long since left, and on 7 September, while in Venice Schoenberg was conducting his Serenade op. 24, Zemlinsky was back in Prague, conducting *Ariane et Barbe-bleue*.

---

* According to the critic Paul Nettl, 'Zemlinsky demanded the utmost from his orchestra, whereby the manner in which he bared his musician's soul was wellnigh exhibitionistic. He consumed himself when conducting' (*Reichenberger Zeitung*, 2 June 1927, archive of the Czech Philharmonic).

† '[He] has shown that a reform of the operatic repertoire [. . .] is possible', wrote Steinhard in the autumn of 1927. 'We will have to acknowledge him as the saviour of the German opera in Prague' ('Tagebuch', *Der Auftakt*, 1927, 332). Soon afterwards, however, Steinberg announced his engagement as *Generalmusikdirektor* in Frankfurt, a post he occupied until 1933.

‡ Apart from those mentioned above, the composers represented were Fidelio Finke, Heinrich Kaminski, Rudolf Karel, György Kósa, Gian Francesco Malipiero, Roland Manuel, Bohuslav Martinů, Darius Milhaud, Vitežslav Novák, Paul A. Pisk, Rudolf Réti, Vittorio Rieti and Ernst Toch. Stravinsky's Symphonies of Wind Instruments was announced for the third concert but not performed. Berg's verdict on the concerts was devastating: 'Works ranging from the very mediocre to the utterly worthless' (Bernard Grun (ed. and trans.), *Alban Berg. Letters to His Wife* (London–New York, 1971), 16 May 1925, 536); 'Yesterday's concert was hideous, Réti a scandal!' (ibid., 18 May 1925, 538).

Fired by the spirit of the ISCM, Zemlinsky made an effort to transform the NDT itself into a year-round festival of contemporary music. Though unable to realize more than a handful of his operatic projects (the failure of his plan to stage *Wozzeck* at the NDT was the bitterest of many disappointments), he still retained control of the orchestral concerts. But here too, public apathy and inertia upset his plans. A programme of Ullmann, Schulhoff and Schimmerling* on 25 March 1925 met with approval, if only because all three composers were Prague-born, and on 19 April Berg's *Wozzeck* Fragments, flanked by Beethoven's and Mahler's First Symphonies, were well received (Rychnowsky wrote of music that 'emanated from secret shafts of the dark subconscious').† Bartók's Orchestral Pieces op. 12 and the Symphonic Fragments from Debussy's *Martyre du S. Sébastien* (on 19 January 1926) were heard only unwillingly by an audience that had come primarily to hear Hubermann in Mozart and Beethoven. No contemporary choral work since Mahler's Eighth Symphony and Schoenberg's *Gurrelieder* made a profounder impression, according to Adler, than Honegger's *Le roi David*, performed in February 1926,[32] but the house was well sold only because of the relatives and friends who always attended choral concerts, and a programme of orchestral music by Honegger, Malipiero, Milhaud and Brahms played a few weeks later to an almost empty house. Crisis meetings were called, and a motion was tabled to abolish the Symphonic Concerts altogether. In the event their number was drastically reduced, and during Zemlinsky's last season the only contemporary works in his programmes were the preludes to Pfitzner's *Palestrina*, Kurt Weill's *Quodlibet* and Manuel de Falla's *Nights in the Gardens of Spain*.[33]

News was meanwhile spreading beyond Prague of Zemlinsky's prowess on the rostrum. Even if appearances in Vienna were still few and far between, he began to establish an international reputation, with two concerts at the Augusteo in Rome (January 1924) and an invitation to conduct the Orquestra Pau Casals in Barcelona (March 1926). True to form, he introduced himself to Catalonia with music from Bohemia (Dvořák and Smetana), Viennese classics (Mozart, Beethoven, Schubert, Reznicek and Goldmark) and ISCM favourites (Bartók, Malipiero and Stravinsky). Leaving Steinberg as a willing deputy at the NDT, he then set out with Hermann Grab as travelling companion to visit the land of his forefathers, taking in Madrid, Toledo, Seville and Granada. At the end of March he hastened back to Prague for the Easter-week revival of *Parsifal*.

Apart from a few such interludes, these last Prague years were the most sunless of Zemlinsky's career. With the death of his sister, the breakdown of his

---

* Hans Schimmerling (dates unknown) was on the conducting staff of the NDT during the season 1924–25.
† Berg heard of the event only after it had taken place. To make amends, Zemlinsky repeated the performance four weeks later, as a curtain-raiser to *Ariane et Barbe-bleue*.

friendship with Schoenberg and the absence of Luise, life had grown bleak. As he wrote to Alma in 1925:

It is simply too dreadful how I am tied up here (perhaps also partly of my own doing) and how, as year follows year, I feel ever more wretched. I certainly lack the courage to take risks, perhaps to subsist for a year without my relatively high income, to do without certain comforts, etc. You will surely understand that I have no desire to combat the prejudice that is poisoning my reputation, particularly in Vienna. I am certain that any rewards I would reap from such a victory would be quite disproportionate to the setbacks I would be bound to experience.[34]

Mahler's Tenth

Even if Zemlinsky was no longer able to arouse enthusiasm for contemporary music, the Prague public still shared his love of Mahler. Between 1924 and 1927 he performed the First and Second Symphonies at the NDT, and the Sixth and Ninth (with the Czech Philharmonic) at the Rudolfinum; for his farewell concert at the NDT, on 13 May 1927, he chose the Seventh; and since he had introduced himself to Prague in 1912 with the Eighth, he took his leave on 1 June with the same work.*

Zemlinsky also introduced the *Adagio* and *Purgatorio* from the Tenth Symphony to Prague, two months after the world première in Vienna,† at a special concert for the Democratic Freedom Party on 11 December 1924. Since Mahler had instructed his New York lawyer that the manuscript should be destroyed after his death, the ethical question of performing or publishing the surviving torso became a topic of heated debate. When Klemperer conducted the work on 28 December in Berlin,‡ critical opinion was largely adverse; in Prague the consensus was more positive.

Confronted with music of such high stature [wrote Steinhard], one must readily admit that it would be a mistake to deprive the world, merely for formal reasons, of so incommensurable an art work. [. . .] Under the impression of Zemlinsky's powerful performance, the audience was deeply moved.[35]

Zemlinsky came to play an active role in this controversial resurrection. After Mahler's death, Alma had put the manuscript on display in her vitrine,

---

* The concert was promoted not by the Czech Philharmonic, but by the 'Gau Prag des Sängerbundes der Sudetendeutschen', i.e. the blanket organization of German-speaking choral societies in Prague. All seven soloists were members of the NDT ensemble, and the only reason for engaging the Czech Philharmonic rather than the orchestra of the NDT (as transpires from press reports) was that the latter had demanded too high a fee.
† Conducted by Schalk on 12 October at the Staatsoper, preceded by Gluck's overture to *Iphigénie en Aulide* and followed by Mahler's Fourth Symphony.
‡ Klemperer also performed the *Adagio* and *Purgatorio* – though against his better judgement – in London, on 24 April 1961.

open at the final page, with its heartrending inscription: 'Für dich leben, für dich sterben' ('To live for you, to die for you'). In the winter of 1922–23 she showed the score to her son-in-law Ernst Krenek,* in the hope that he would complete it. The first two movements, he told her, were performable almost as they stood. As for the rest:

It was quite clear that nothing could be deduced from these sketches that could remotely satisfy the requirements of a public performance. It would have taken the shameless audacity of an unutterable barbarian even to attempt to orchestrate these impassioned scribblings. [. . .] After some altercation Alma consented, consoling herself with the thought that two movements of the Tenth Symphony would yield more profit than none at all.[36]

Once the fair copy of the *Adagio* and *Purgatorio* was complete, Alma sent it for an expert opinion to Schalk (Krenek remembered him as 'a malevolent goat [. . .] sceptical and haughty').[37] On 15 February 1923 he replied to the effect that he considered the *Adagio* to be only a preliminary version, and that Mahler would later have revised and reworked it; the *Purgatorio* he considered quite unsuitable for performance.[38] Evidently Alma brought her persuasive powers to bear on him, however, for later he agreed to perform both movements at a Staatsoper concert in January or early February 1924. Berg, who knew the score from a private performance at the piano in Alma's house on 25 November 1923,[39] later checked through Krenek's transcription and drew up a detailed list of errors and omissions. Zemlinsky, who probably also saw the score at the same time (he was in Vienna for *Der Zwerg*), decided to couple it with the projected world première of his Lyric Symphony the following 18 February.[40] All was arranged, when Schalk, still dissatisfied with Krenek's scoring of the *Purgatorio*, postponed his performance until the autumn. Obliged to follow suit, Zemlinsky therefore also had to defer the première of the Lyric Symphony. Alma was anxious to arrange for the entire short score to be published in facsimile, but she had entrusted Schalk with the manuscript of the *Purgatorio* which he had taken with him on holiday. On 14 August 1924 he wrote to her from St Moritz:

Particularly this movement, as you know, has given me quite a headache & I have now produced a new version of the score, which I would like to show you as soon as possible & in person. – Certain elements of Krenek's arrangement have of course been retained.[41]

When Zemlinsky came to prepare the work for performance, he made several retouchings to the scoring of the *Adagio*. At the request of Universal Edition, he incorporated these into the published score (the task took him ten hours),[42] but before doing so he wrote to Alma, requesting that

---

* Krenek's liaison with Anna Mahler dated back to 1920; they married in 1923 and divorced in 1925.

for the sake of honesty, a brief foreword should be included, explaining that changes have been made, because etc. etc.[43]

Deryck Cooke asserts (quite rightly) that these retouchings were 'unstylish and indeed unnecessary'.[44] As was evident from Mahler's alterations to the scoring of *Es war einmal . . .* and *Der Traumgörge*, and as again became apparent in the orchestration of the allegedly 'Mahlerian' Lyric Symphony, Zemlinsky's concept of orchestral sound differed substantially from Mahler's. When the score of the Tenth Symphony finally appeared in print,* it transpired that his plea for 'honesty' had been ignored: no explanatory foreword was included, nor had Universal Edition taken any heed of Berg's errata list: Viennese *Schlamperei* yet again. After a few further performances,† Zemlinsky quietly dropped the work from his repertoire.

The Return of Luise

Having completed her studies, Luise set out in the spring of 1924 to seek fame and fortune as a singer. Back in Prague, she informed Zemlinsky that she intended to audition for the NDT; his response was discouraging. Not to be deterred, she sang for Kramer and was promptly engaged. A performance of *Die Meistersinger*, scheduled for 29 September, was postponed at short notice, and *Tannhäuser* given in its place. Luise happened to have studied the role of Venus at the Akademie and, since no other mezzo was available, she was asked to fill the breach. She did well, and Zemlinsky made amends for his former gruffness with a written assurance that in future performances of the work she would replace the NDT's *prima donna assoluta*, Susanne Jicha.‡[45] In theatre, such promises are made to be broken. That apart, Jicha was a star, and Luise a novice. In the light of their continuing liaison, Zemlinsky was concerned that preferential treatment might harm her career. If she were to play Venus in Prague, then for him alone – and in private. During two seasons at the NDT she was entrusted with only three further roles: Second Lady (*Die Zauberflöte*), Second Norn (*Götterdämmerung*) and Third Lady-in-waiting (*Der Zwerg*).§

In the spring of 1926 she therefore auditioned for an agent from Vienna,¶

* The study score was first published by A.M.P. in 1951.
† Zemlinsky's last chronicled performance was at a Workers' Concert with the Vienna Symphony Orchestra on 14 February 1926; it was followed by Psalm 23.
‡ Susanne Jicha (1889–1932), a pupil of Lilli Lehmann, had sung at the NDT, with a few brief interruptions, since 1911. Her repertoire included mezzo roles, such as Fricka, Brangäne and the Composer (*Ariadne auf Naxos*), but also Brünnhilde, Isolde, Donna Anna and Elektra, as well as the principal role in *Ariane et Barbe-bleue*. In 1926 she married Hans Wilhelm Steinberg.
§ Her vocal score of *Der Zwerg* is preserved in *MolA*.
¶ Louise Zemlinsky later asserted that she also sang Ulrica (in *Un ballo in maschera*), implying

with Kramer and Zemlinsky listening in. 'Director Kramer wanted to give me a fantastic [new] contract,' she recalled, 'but Zemlinsky said he would not allow it.'[46] The agent was impressed, however, and she was engaged for the following season at the Volksoper. Here too she made her début as Venus, but she arrived late, missing several performances, and did not take the stage until 18 December. Somehow she had arranged for a critic to attend the performance, and the following day a few glowing lines about her appeared in one of the daily papers (the press cutting became one of her most treasured mementoes). On 28 December she sang the subsidiary role of Berthalda in a new production by Rainer Simons of Lortzing's *Undine*.* Normally the Viennese press would have given full coverage to any new production at the Volksoper, but on the day following the première, 29 December, the death was announced of Rilke, and every arts column in Europe was taken up with eulogies and obituary notices. Of the two Viennese papers that did find space for *Undine*, the *Wiener Zeitung* singled out Luise as being 'exceptionally gifted'.[47]

Undine was repeated on New Year's Day 1927, but Luise did not partici-pate;[†] indeed she never sang in public again. Before her career had properly started, it was already over. 'I gave up singing for the sake of my husband,'[48] she later explained, not without a hint of pride. Only shortly before her death did she reveal to a close friend in New York that there was more to this abrupt end of a promising career than mere devotion. She had discovered that she was pregnant; anxious to avoid a scandal, Zemlinsky insisted on abortion.

Four Barren Years

Inspiration flowed sparely now. Zemlinsky must soon have realized that the modernism to which he had broken through in the Third Quartet, if used only as a weapon of parody or sarcasm, was ultimately a tool of self-destruction. Vitriolic humour was not enough. If he was to expand the dramatic and expres-sive possibilities of his new language, it required a more solid basis.

The Zemlinskys spent the summer of 1925 at Alt-Aussee, where they were joined by Marie Pappenheim, Schoenberg's sister Ottilie and his new mother-in-law, Henrietta Kolisch.[‡] Pappenheim had written a comedy in two acts with spoken dialogue (*Der Graf von Gleim*), based on a plot not unlike that of

---

that this was an NDT performance (cf. Burkhard Laugwitz, '"Meine Zeit kommt nach meine Tod". Begegnung mit Louise Zemlinsky', *Das Orchester*, v/1993, 547–50). During this period, however, the work was not in the repertoire. Presumably she sang Ulrica's act 1 aria at her audi-tion for the agent from Vienna.

* Simons was working his way through a whole cycle of Lortzing at the Volksoper.

† Berthalda was sung by Ada Hecht.

‡ Weber surmises that it was Mrs Kolisch who added her signature ('Mama') and a brief note to a postcard from Zemlinsky to Schoenberg dated 13 August 1925 (*Web-Br*, 271).

Smetana's *The Two Widows*. For a few days Zemlinsky occupied himself with this project, rewriting the text and composing thirty-three pages of sketches; then he dropped it.*

In April 1926 Hertzka sent him half-a-dozen librettos by various authors. One of these, by Hans Heinz Ewers, librettist of *Die toten Augen*, was entitled *Das Rosenfest der rheinischen Nonnen*, a drama of romance, guilt and salvation, set against the jovial background of a wine festival in a Dominican convent on the Lower Rhine. Like Puccini's *Suor Angelica*, the drama ended with a miracle of beatification; in other respects too, Ewers proved himself no less eclectic, contriving to incorporate into a few scenes the legend of Tannhäuser, St Francis's *Hymn to the Sun*, imagery from heathen nature worship, Catholic mysticism and much else. 'I already knew the libretto by Ewers,' Zemlinsky told Hertzka dismissively. 'He sent it to me a long time ago & I wrote to him about it.'[49] Within six days the whole package was on its way back to Vienna.

He had in fact just completed a monastic drama of his own: *Der heilige Vitalis*, an opera in three acts with extensive crowd scenes and complex ensembles.† In view of the continuing success of *Kleider machen Leute*, he had opted once again for a project based on Gottfried Keller.‡ Set in eighth-century Alexandria, his libretto tells the tale of Vitalis, a monk 'who had taken it upon himself to persuade fallen women of their sinful ways and lead them back on to the path of virtue'. His methods are unconventional but effective: having made an assignation with his chosen victim, he spends the night with her, but repulsing every desire of the flesh, withdraws to a corner of the room and kneels until dawn in silent prayer. The ploy is often successful, but his brethren know nothing of it, and since he makes no effort to cover his tracks, indeed brags openly of his nocturnal exploits, Vitalis is decried as a disgrace to holy orders. The first part of the legend tells of his efforts to save the soul of the most notorious courtesan of Alexandria.§ Though feigning tearful compliance, she counters his prayers and pious exhortations with guile and seductive charm. Faced with so formidable an adversary, Vitalis commits cardinal sin: lacking money for further visits, he plunders the chapel collecting box, and when a burly centurion tries to bar his way into the courtesan's house, he fells him with a spear. Soon after his release from prison, a young lady named Iole enters the story.¶ From her father's house on the opposite side of the road she has been observing the monk's antics; curiosity has led to pity, and pity to love. With a substantial

---

* Further details in Ernst Hilmar, 'Text und Musik in einem Opernfragment Zemlinskys', *AeSU*, 279–83.
† A synopsis of the plot and two typed versions of the libretto are preserved in the Zemlinsky Collection at the Library of Congress.
‡ Keller's novella *Der schlimm-heilige Vitalis* ('The Sinful Saint Vitalis') is the fifth of the *Seven Legends*, first published in 1872.
§ In Keller the character is unnamed; Zemlinsky calls her Fulvia.
¶ In Zemlinsky's libretto Iole is already introduced in the opening scene.

bribe she buys the courtesan off the premises;* posing as a novice in the arts of Venus, she takes her place. Vitalis spends many hours with Iole, preaching the gospel of chastity and humility, but ultimately it is she who triumphs. His monk's habit is cast into the fire; dressed in secular finery, he leaves the house of ill-repute hand in hand with his new bride.

It takes little fantasy to see Vitalis, the lecher with a heart of gold, as a self-portrait of the composer, Keller's sexually athletic *magna peccatrix* as an exaggerated picture of Alma, and the drunken louts who frequent her premises as the lovers and suitors who, since Mahler's death, had joined her in a round-dance of marriage and divorce, pregnancy, childbirth and abortion. The pure-minded Iole, who takes it upon herself 'to transform a valiant martyr into an even better spouse', would then be Luise, and in this context even Iole's father,† a prosperous widower, art collector and amateur poet, translates credibly as Hanna, Luise's widowed mother.

Surviving typescripts of the libretto reveal fine command of stagecraft and resourceful use of language. But the drama unfolds stiffly, in an outmoded style ill attuned to the linear, neo-classical texture of the music. Zemlinsky takes a surprisingly strait-laced view of the legend, weighing down Keller's impish humour with a mantle of religious sentiment. A saccharine 'Hymn to the Virgin', for instance, serves to transform the satirical scene of the pilfered collecting box into a miracle of divine grace (EX. 72).

Work on the short score progressed during the summer of 1926, spent at the Belgian resort of Knokke, and probably also the following summer at Unterach on the Attersee. In due course the *Vitalis* portfolio grew to over 240 pages, but by the end of 1927 the project had died a natural death. In the winter of 1930 Zemlinsky announced that he was working on a *heitere Legende* (merry legend) for orchestra, indeed by March it was allegedly 'all but complete'. Perhaps he was thinking of salvaging the best material from *Vitalis*, which he had subtitled 'a holy legend', for a symphonic poem.[50] Of such a score, however, no material has survived. Asked why the *Vitalis* project was never finished, Luise replied, 'For moral reasons.'[51]

Contact with Schoenberg was sporadic now, and loyalty to Schoenberg had also prompted Webern to keep his distance. In Berg, however, Zemlinsky found an ever closer ally, not only in artistic questions but also in confidences of a more intimate nature. In November 1926 Berg asked Zemlinsky to accept the dedication of his Lyric Suite. Well aware that this was a dedication by proxy, and that discretion prevented all mention of the *ferne Geliebte* to whom the work was actually addressed, Zemlinsky wrote to thank him, adding that the epithet

---

* In Zemlinsky's version of the story, Iole persuades Fulvia to let her use the house just for one night.
† Zemlinsky calls him Kaphis.

EX. 72   *Der heilige Vitalis*, scene iv

Maria, queen of heaven, hard is my role, unequal the task*

'lyric' particularly whetted his appetite to see and hear the new score. Since he was unable to attend the world première in Vienna on 8 January 1927, the Kolisch Quartet gave a private performance for his benefit nine days later in Prague, attended by Felix Adler, Peter Herman Adler, Georg Alter, Otto Schlosser, Viktor Ullmann and other close friends.[†]

I consider it to be quite exceptionally inspired & fabulously well written [wrote Zemlinsky. [. . .] The quotation [from the Lyric Symphony] in the 4th movement was a delightful surprise. I am truly proud to be the dedicatee of this magnificent work.[52]

On 22 July 1927, while on holiday at Unterach, Zemlinsky started work on a fourth string quartet. By the time he returned to Prague, towards the end of August, he had completed the first two movements (*Andante–Vivace* and *Adagio*), 179 bars of a ternary-form intermezzo (*Allegro molto*), 28 bars of a *Theme and Variations*, 64 bars of an *Allegro moderato e appassionato* and 86 bars of the finale (*Allegro con fuoco*). With its six-movement cyclic outline – though quite unlike that of the Lyric Suite – the work may have been intended

---

* In the manuscript libretto the third line reads: 'Gross mein Gewinn' ('Great is my gain').
† Weber has established that the performance was given in the apartment of Otto Schlosser (*Web-Br*, 323).

as a homage to Berg. Yet the first movement also quotes from the American Civil War song *Yankee Doodle* (modified to incorporate the 'World' motif), implying that the work was addressed to a friend or friends over the ocean:

EX. 73   Two Movements for String Quartet (1927), I, bars 23–7 and 174–5

The most likely dedicatee in America would have been Bodanzky. Every year, once the 'Met' had closed for the summer recess, he would make his way to Europe to hold auditions, meet with composers and impresarios, and catch up with his friends in Vienna. As Musical Director of the Society of the Friends of Music in New York he had recently introduced two of Zemlinsky's compositions to America: the Maeterlinck Songs on 24 February 1924, with Madame Cahier (Jane Walker) as soloist, and Psalm 23 on 13 February 1927. And on at least one occasion (documented by a seaside snapshot), he spent part of his summer holiday with the Zemlinskys. Clearly their friendship had remained very much alive.

As the summer of 1927 drew to its close, with the move to Berlin now imminent, Zemlinsky was obliged to set creative work aside, leaving the new quartet unfinished. Not until 1994 were the surviving Two Movements for String Quartet (1927) published and performed. The first, an expressive *Andante* introduction followed by a toccata-like *Vivace*, approaches the virtuoso spirit of the finale of the Third Quartet. With a mixture of humour and grim determination, the four players are led through an assault course of changing metres and shifting accents, a *perpetuum mobile* of semiquavers that pauses only for a reprise of the *Andante*. The *Adagio misterioso* is cast in free rondo form, with more agitated sections of *più mosso* and a puppet-like *tempo di minuetto*. In a context of unprecedentedly dissonant homophony and predominantly low tessitura, disjunct phrases and tortuous polyphonic lines collide, subside and dissolve. Never before had Zemlinsky's music descended to such depths of gloom. Taken together, these fragments of an unfinished drama present a strongly contrasted diptych of light and darkness, action and contemplation.*

Changing Trains

Although Zemlinsky had proved that he was no conservative, he viewed the concept of composition with twelve notes with considerable scepticism. Schoenberg did his best to explain the basic principles to him:

Do you still remember asking me recently about the technique of composition with twelve tones? This is how the first movement of my Suite [op. 29] begins: four six-note chords, I–IV–V–I.[53]

As demonstration of the new technical possibilities, he included an annotated copy of the opening bars. Zemlinsky replied:

It is very kind of you to send me this brief instruction manual. But – despite all my efforts – I seem not to have grasped it. [. . .] I do not understand how you can speak of IV or V when the music is not based on a diatonic scale. If the scale is chromatic, surely if you take E♭ as I, then IV would be G♭ and V would be G[♮]?!54

Some years later Schoenberg came across a draft copy of his original letter, to which he added the following comment:

At the time I was unaware that the question was malicious, and merely considered it remarkably stupid. Today I know that people like Z. act stupid if they want to get away with annoying someone (and unnecessarily so!!). Fortunately it has always taken me a considerable time to apprehend such malice.[55]

The 1924 *Festschrift* for Schoenberg included two essays by Hanns Eisler: a penetrating study of 'the musical reactionary'[†] and a selection of amusing anecdotes. Eisler had studied with Schoenberg from 1919 to 1923, was one of his most promising pupils and one of whom he was particularly fond. Zemlinsky probably heard his prize-winning First Piano Sonata when Steuermann gave its first performance at a Prague *Verein* concert on 10 April 1923,[‡] and if the two composers did not meet on that occasion (or during one of Zemlinsky's trips to Vienna), they will certainly have met when Eisler accompanied Berg to Prague for the 1925 ISCM Festival.[56] By this time Eisler had composed several works

---

using serial technique, notably the song-cycle *Palmström* ('five studies on twelve-note series') for *Sprechstimme*, flute, clarinet, violin and cello, written at Schoenberg's request to be performed with *Pierrot lunaire*. But now he was in the throes of an artistic and social revolution. Despite his unbounded admiration for Schoenberg, he felt compelled to renounce his teacher's aesthetic as bourgeois élitist. In 1926, following the dictates of conscience, he joined the German Communist Party. At some point during this period of ideological gestation, he and Zemlinsky met on a railway journey.* The gist of their conversation can be gleaned from a curt note from Schoenberg to Zemlinsky, dated 3 March 1926:

I would be very grateful if you would reply to the following. Please enter your answers directly opposite the questions.
  I Did Mr E. say that he is turning away from all this modern stuff?
  II That he did not understand twelve-tone music?
  III That he did not consider it music at all?
  This is what you told me at the time, and as E. denies it, I would like to get to the truth.[57]

Eisler had committed the unforgivable sin of criticizing Schoenberg to an outsider (as Zemlinsky was now considered). Not until teacher and pupil met up again in Hollywood, refugees from Nazi Germany, were they reconciled. Later still, in 1950, Eisler looked back almost remorsefully on what he had done:

I broke with him. I did so in a crude manner. Ungrateful, recalcitrant, irritable, scornful of his bourgeois conformism, I parted from him in anger. His attitude towards me remained one of generosity.[58]

For the time being the break was irreparable, and in 1927 Eisler exacerbated the situation by condemning *Die Jakobsleiter* as an 'escape into mysticism', a comment all the more wounding for its direct connection with Strauss and his ballet *Schlagobers* (1921–22), which he condemned as an 'escape into frivolity'. Both composers, according to Eisler, had failed to adjust their outlook to the changing situation:

During the post-war years almost every art form brought forth a number of truly revolutionary artists, whose works drew true consequences from the social situation. *In music this did not and does not exist.* [. . .] More than any other art form, contemporary music lives in a world of its own and can be kept alive only synthetically. [. . .] Despite all its technical finesse, it has reached a point of stagnation, because it lacks ideas and lacks a lobby. An art that loses its lobby loses itself.[59]

---

* Weber suggests that they travelled to Vienna together after the 1925 ISCM Festival in Venice (*Web-Br*, 271). Eisler's Duo op. 7 for violin and cello was performed at the Festival on 4 September, and since Zemlinsky had to be in Prague for *Ariane et Barbe-bleue* three days later, they might conceivably have boarded a train to Vienna immediately after the concert.

New ideas began to gestate in Zemlinsky's artistic and social conscience. In 1927 he signed a petition for the retrial of Saccho and Vanzetti, Italian anarchists sentenced to death by the Massachusetts Superior Court.* Freed from the *l'art pour l'art* mentality of Secessionist Vienna – and perhaps with the young Eisler to guide him on his way – he found the strength to surmount the creative crisis that for several years had been hampering his artistic development. Like Myrtocle, his eyes had at last been opened.

Every German choral society in the city, soloists from the NDT and the Czech Philharmonic, reinforced by players from the NDT, came together on 1 June 1927 to take their leave of Zemlinsky with a performance of Mahler's 'Symphony of a Thousand'. Zdeněk Nejedlý underlined the significance of the occasion 'for the entire musical world in Prague, regardless of nationality':[†]

Compared to the capricious Kovařovic, Zemlinsky has always conducted with an architectural logic and sheer purity of technique that left nothing to chance. [. . .] Particularly Mozart and Beethoven were revealed to us in a new light. [. . .] With his choice of repertoire, Zemlinsky also opened new paths. At a time when all attention was focused on the dazzling figure of Richard Strauss, we were made aware of a more neglected master, Gustav Mahler; later our attention was also drawn to his followers, with Schoenberg as their leader. In these respects, Zemlinsky has been our mainstay and our guide.[60]

Taking leave of Zemlinsky with his customary warmth and respect, Felix Adler scoffed at those whose allegiance had wavered:

It does credit to Zemlinsky that he would rather make enemies than friends, that he never associated with cliques and 'know-alls', that his attitude has always been selfless, and that in awareness of his mission he has presented his audience not with 'lollipops' but with music that was in real need of propagation. [. . .] Those well disposed towards him were always aware of this; those who disagreed will realize what they have lost only when he is no longer with us.[61]

---

* According to Louise Zemlinsky, this was one of the few occasions on which Zemlinsky engaged in anything approaching political activity (*ACl*, 318).
† Literal translation kindly provided by Luboš Kohoutek.

IX

Berlin 1927–1933

previous page:
Zemlinsky, summoned to Berlin, will be leaving Prague next year
artist unidentified
first published in *Montagsblatt* (Prague), 26 April 1926

I

At the Krolloper

Empty bookshelves and bare floorboards, the grand piano a legless, blanketed torso, packing cases, removal men, last-minute well-wishers and inquisitive neighbours: Zemlinsky was moving house. For sixteen years the apartment in the Havlíčekgasse had offered him and his family a safe haven. He could scarcely have foreseen that in the next thirteen years his address would change a further ten times* – and not always of his own volition.

On 30 August 1927, one day before the move, the postman delivered a package from Vienna containing the engraved study score of Berg's Lyric Suite, fresh from the press and with a handwritten dedication from the composer. Before the day was out, despite the hubbub of removal, Zemlinsky had hastily scribbled a note of thanks.[1] Berg now all but replaced Schoenberg in his affections. Admittedly they lived too far apart for regular contact, but when they did meet, in Vienna or Berlin, Zemlinsky positively revelled in his colleague's unfailing courtesy and natural warmth.[2]

Kramer's resignation and Zemlinsky's move to Berlin signified the end of an era in the history of theatre in Prague. With them almost half the NDT ensemble decided to leave, some for engagements in Germany, others for freelance careers. Two mainstays of the production team, Laber and Ullmann, rather than remaining at the NDT under the new regime, took engagements at the insignificant Stadttheater in Aussig; two others, Zemlinsky's musical assistant Artur Feinsinger and his pupil Hans Krása, joined the music staff of the Krolloper.[†] Of the NDT ensemble, Klemperer hired Klara Kwartin, who had sung first soprano in Zemlinsky's farewell performance of Mahler's Eighth,[‡] and in 1929 followed a singer who had made her sensational début at the Národní Divadlo, aged twenty-two, as Violetta in *La traviata*: Jarmila Novotná, a vivacious and attractive young lady, whom Zemlinsky evidently admired not only on account of her artistry.

* During his four years at the Krolloper, Zemlinsky moved house as many times. His addresses, as cited in the annual editions of the *Deutsches Bühnenjahrbuch*, were: In den Zelten 17 (1928); Tile-Wardenberg-Str. 29 (1929); Pariser Str. 19 (1930); Landshuter Str. 26 (1931). He retained the latter address until September 1933.
† Krása returned to Prague after only a few months.
‡ Where in present-day performances the first soprano part in the 'Symphony of a Thousand' is usually sung by a dramatic voice, Kwartin was a high coloratura soprano. She sang at the NDT from 1924 to 1927, where her roles included Zerbinetta (*Ariadne auf Naxos*), Gilda (*Rigoletto*) and Konstanze (*Entführung*).

On the morning of 1 September, while the Zemlinskys were rattling northwards in the train to Berlin, Klemperer was taking his first rehearsal for Stravinsky's *Oedipus rex* at the Kroll. During the lunch break, he and the remaining members of his production team – dramaturg Hans Curjel, Second *Kapellmeister* Fritz Zweig and designer Ewald Duelberg – convened for an informal briefing at a restaurant near the Staatsoper Unter den Linden.[3]

Then, as now, Berlin housed three full-time opera companies. Since the end of World War I, the theatre scene in the city, both private and state-subsidized, had undergone many changes. Under the direction of Max von Schillings, the Lindenoper, with 1,200 seats, had been annexed to the Krolloper on the Platz der Republik, which seated 2,100, the former retaining its status as a temple of culture, the latter as a place of lighter entertainment. Since 1912, the Deutsche Oper in Charlottenburg (later renamed Städtische Oper), with 2,300 seats, had entered into friendly rivalry with the Staatsoper, much in the spirit of the Volksoper in Vienna.* In 1925, to end the two-year interregnum in Charlottenburg following the departure of Leo Blech, Heinz Tietjen was appointed *Intendant* of the Städtische Oper and Bruno Walter his Musical Director. The following year, in the interests of artistic co-ordination, the authorities appointed Tietjen *General-Intendant* in charge of the Staatsschauspiel at the Schiller Theater and all three opera houses. With standard repertoire now well covered by the Lindenoper and the Städtische Oper, Leo Kestenberg, Artistic Adviser at the Prussian Ministry of Culture, proposed that the Kroll might in future be used as a centre for experimental music-theatre, run on a largely independent basis.†

The idea soon became reality, and on 22 September 1926 Klemperer's appointment as Director was announced in the press. Ten weeks later, in early December, he was in Prague to conduct the Czech Philharmonic. It was presumably at this time that he finalized negotiations with Zemlinsky, for shortly afterwards, on 19 December, *Bohemia* announced the resignation of the NDT's *Opernchef* and his engagement as First *Kapellmeister* in Berlin.[4]

'I can only be the master!' he had once protested to Alma.[5] If only he had accepted Schillings's offer in 1923, he would by now have indeed been the master of Germany's leading opera house. But now he had accepted a position subservient to a younger colleague. After twenty-six years of musical directorship in theatres great and small (disregarding his few months under Mahler at

---

* Opera, operetta and musical comedy were also presented at the Theater des Westens, the Kurfürstenoper, the Apollo-Theater and the Metropoltheater.

† For a comprehensive history of the Krolloper the reader is referred to Peter Heyworth's *Otto Klemperer, His Life and Times*, vol. I: *1885–1933* (Cambridge, 1983). Heyworth stresses that, in official terminology, the Kroll was run 'on as independent a basis as possible' (242). As later became apparent, this vague formulation provided a fatal loophole, which left the theatre open to wilful intervention by Tietjen and higher officials at the Ministry of Culture.

the Vienna Hofoper), he must have found it difficult to adjust to the new status. Klemperer valued him as a stabilizing influence, as an older friend to whom one could turn for counsel. Others saw in him the experienced artisan, whose performances, if less than world class, always ran without a hitch. His Prague audiences knew him to be capable of far greater things. But in Berlin, approaching his sixtieth birthday, he found himself surrounded by a galaxy of stars – Furtwängler, Kleiber, Klemperer, Szell, Toscanini* and Walter – and faced with the challenge of projecting his distinct but sensitive artistic profile on a public that scarcely knew him. In an oft-quoted letter to Alma (evidently the last he ever sent her), he described his predicament:

Certainly I lack that *je ne sais quoi* that one needs – today more than ever – to make one's way. In such a crush it's no use just having elbows, one also has to know how to use them.[6]

Kestenberg's concept for the Kroll was imaginative, yet soon it transpired that it had been implemented with undue haste and with little regard for practical considerations. Under Klemperer's leadership the Theater am Platz der Republik established itself as a shrine of the avant-garde and a magnet to left-wing intellectuals. But even if Adorno, Ernst Bloch and Walter Benjamin, together with their many followers and sympathizers, were quick to accept the Kroll as a new spiritual home, they alone could scarcely fill the house. The original aim, as outlined by the stage designer Wilhelm Reinking, had been –

to create a theatre that would present extended series of operas in musically exemplary fashion and with meticulously prepared stage productions. If each opera ran for several months, it would be possible to make unusually lengthy production periods available for each new work.

The disadvantage of such a system, he explained, was that –

contemporary music inevitably failed to pull its weight. Stravinsky's *Oedipus rex* ran for eleven performances, Hindemith's *Cardillac* for nineteen, and Schoenberg's *Erwartung* for four, with only tolerably well-sold houses.[7]

Klemperer found himself largely at the mercy of the Volksbühne, a private organization of season-ticket holders with a membership of *Bildungsbürger*: solid, middle-class citizens with a healthy appetite for middle-of-the-road performances of the standard classics. Not for them the challenge of modern scores, innovative productions or experimental stage design.

While the Kroll's programme was scarcely designed to appeal to the masses, some members of the company found Klemperer over-conservative, impractical

* Although he appeared frequently as guest conductor, Toscanini never occupied a permanent position in Berlin.

and, like Mahler, lacking in 'imagination of the eye'. His intention, wrote the producer Arthur Maria Rabenalt, was 'nothing more – as he himself admitted – than to make "good operatic theatre"'. But the Kroll, in Rabenalt's view, fell far short of that goal:

The singers received no additional physical, gymnastic or dance training, which at the time was already an optional or obligatory feature of the more creative provincial opera houses in Gera, Würzburg, Darmstadt, etc. [. . .] All well-intentioned stimuli remained conceptually vague; though intellectually formulated, they lacked the conviction of graphic representation. [. . .] The Krolloper was a gathering point for modernism of every colour and shade. Duelberg stood beside Chirico, Schlemmer beside Teo Otto, Neher beside Reinking and Moholy-Nagy. Who could count the names or co-ordinate the incoherent temperaments?

'Nirgends brennen wir genauer,' wrote Ernst Bloch proudly of the Kroll – 'Nowhere do we burn more accurately.' But this was at best an ideological or conceptual accuracy; at a practical level, in management and administration, Klemperer's team was often found wanting.

Fidelio opened the first season on 19 November 1927, with abstract, starkly geometrical sets by Duelberg, and Klemperer not only as conductor but also as director. Zemlinsky followed eight days later with Smetana's *The Kiss*, directed by Rudolf Schulz-Dornburg and designed by Teo Otto. Critical opinion on the new opera company polarized immediately, with vociferous acclaim from the liberal and socialist press, and indignant disapproval from the Nazi-dominated conservatives (a pattern that on subsequent occasions repeated itself with monotonous regularity). The only reviews free of political bias appeared, paradoxically, in the communist weekly *Die rote Fahne* (*The Red Flag*), where behind the signature 'H.E.' it was not difficult to identify the critic as Hanns Eisler. Of *Fidelio* he wrote:

Klemperer tolerates no stars on his stage, and quite rightly too, but this is no excuse for dispensing with beautiful voices. [. . .] Generally speaking, the impression was of an excellently rehearsed ensemble from the provinces. [. . .] For Klemperer it was a great success and, as far as his conducting was concerned, justifiably so. But in future he himself should not take charge of the stage direction. He would be well advised to engage a competent producer.[8]

Reviewing *The Kiss*, Eisler reiterated his censure of Klemperer's hand-picked ensemble; for Zemlinsky, however, he had nothing but praise:

An absolutely wonderful musician, perhaps one of the best currently in Berlin. The performance was excellently prepared. Such music-making, refined, clean and noble, has not been heard in this city, this city of conductors, for a long time. The singers were perfectly adequate, but no more than that. [. . .] A producer is always obliged to make the best of things, which the talented Schulz-Dornburg managed well. The same goes for the designs by Otto Teo [*sic*], passable specimens of conventional theatre. It was Zemlinsky's outstanding achievement, however, that made the performance so enjoyable and refreshing.[9]

During his four seasons at the Krolloper, Zemlinsky was entrusted largely with exotica: two intricate ensemble works (*Il trittico* and *Louise*), two Czech operas (*The Kiss* and *The Bartered Bride*), two Italian scores less than ideally suited to his temperament (*Rigoletto* and *Madama Butterfly*), and a curious *tricolor* of Ibert, Milhaud and Ravel.* Of the repertoire that showed him at his best he conducted only *Les contes d'Hoffmann*, *Die Fledermaus*, *Der Freischütz*, *Salome* and *Erwartung*.

The press treated him with respect, but not with the adulation he had come to expect in Prague. Adolf Weissmann enthused over his Offenbach, Oscar Bie wrote of his *Butterfly* that he had 'rarely achieved anything more beautiful',[10] and even the right-wing radical Paul Zschorlich, one of the Kroll's most embittered adversaries, expressed unreserved approval. In Berlin, however, respect was not enough. Zemlinsky was too proud to bow to the laws of the urban jungle, too humble to test his strength against younger colleagues. As a result, he never advanced beyond a safe vantage point at the perimeter of the artistic fray. In a double-bill of *Erwartung* and *Die glückliche Hand* he alternated on the rostrum with Klemperer. Reviewing the production for the *B.Z. am Mittag*, Stuckenschmidt inadvertently pointed to the fundamental difference between the two artists: discipline, energy and the inner fire of a musical aristocrat on the one hand; compulsive vision, sure instinct and the authority of a born leader on the other:

Zemlinsky [in *Erwartung* . . .] proves himself once again to be a master of intensive rehearsal, a musician of high intellect. [. . .] The most powerful impression is made by Klemperer [in *Die glückliche Hand*], who with miraculous empathy tames the performance to his will. Rarely has one heard him conduct with greater intensity.[11]

Curjel recalls that Zemlinsky returned only unwillingly to *Erwartung*, and that he often interrupted the piano rehearsals with pessimistic remarks about the difficulties of the soprano part. In Prague, he recounted, a harmonium had been recessed into the stage to help Gutheil-Schoder find her notes. But Moje Forbach, his soloist at the Kroll, had perfect pitch and needed no such support.[12] Proud as she was of having mastered the role, she nevertheless recalled with dismay how the composer came backstage at an orchestral rehearsal and literally terrorized her into repeating the whole piece. Schoenberg could summon up little enthusiasm for the sets of *Die glückliche Hand* by the *enfant terrible* Oskar Schlemmer. Indeed, he walked out of the pre-dress rehearsal in a

* The Cio-Cio-San in Zemlinsky's *Butterfly*, Marie in *The Bartered Bride* and Concepción in *L'heure espagnole* was Jarmila Novotná.

rage, protesting that the production had been inadequately prepared. After an extra lighting rehearsal that ran until 4 a.m. on the day of the première, the Kroll did succeed, at least on the first night, in 'burning more accurately'.

The third performance of *Erwartung*, on 20 September 1930, was given under the bizarrest of circumstances. At the General Election, held five days previously, the Nazis had made massive gains; as a direct result, the Kroll was finding itself the object of increasingly critical scrutiny. Rehearsals were under way for a controversial modern-dress production of *The Barber of Seville* by Rabenalt, conducted by Zweig and with sets by Reinking. As Heyworth recounts, Tietjen appeared unannounced at the dress rehearsal:

As soon as Count Almaviva made his entry in a blazer and Oxford bags Reinking observed the usually impassive *Intendant* nervously drumming his fingers on the balustrade of his box. When Figaro raised the shutters of his barber's shop to reveal two massively bosomed and elaborately coiffed wax customers Tietjen leapt to his feet, shouted 'curtain' and stormed out of the auditorium.[13]

The première was postponed by several weeks. To avoid turning the first-night audience away, with the ill-feeling and loss of revenue that this would entail, it was decided to revive *Erwartung* – but with no supporting programme and, inevitably, no rehearsal. *Die glückliche Hand* had been taken out of the repertoire after three performances, and due to Zemlinsky's indisposition *Erwartung* had been given only twice, months before.* In an age when telephones were still rare, it must also have been difficult to notify all twenty-five or thirty additional musicians needed for *Erwartung* of the change of programme. Whether the orchestra was in fact complete, and how accurately the Kroll 'burned' that night is not on record, nor has anyone chronicled the calumnies of a first-night audience that came to hear two hours of Rossini and was instead presented with thirty minutes of Schoenberg. At the NDT under Teweles or Kramer, at the Volksoper under Simons, even at Müller's Carltheater, such chaos would have been unthinkable.

For the first time in sixteen years Zemlinsky was living in close proximity to his former brother-in-law. Soon after moving house, on his fifty-sixth birthday, he arranged to visit Schoenberg at his apartment in the Kantstrasse. The invitation was for afternoon tea, but Zemlinsky was delayed, and by the time he arrived Schoenberg had left to hear the Kolisch Quartet on a friend's radio. 'Evidently we have no time in common,' wrote Schoenberg.

As the apsides of our orbits are clearly difficult to calculate, perhaps Einstein could help out, and by taking account of the passage of time we could establish the theoretically optimum point in time and space for a meeting. So: what shall we do? I really would like to see you![14]

* The third performance of *Die glückliche Hand* was coupled with Milhaud's *Le pauvre matelot*, conducted by Zweig.

For all his joviality, contact remained sporadic. In 1928 he nominated Zemlinsky for membership of the Akademie der Künste, but the motion was not carried. He was clearly anxious to repay something of his old debt of gratitude, and it was probably on his recommendation that Zemlinsky was invited to direct the choral class at the Akademie, enabling him, if only with student forces, to introduce several new works to Berlin, notably Janáček's Glagolithic Mass and Kodály's *Psalmus Hungaricus*.*

Between duties at the Kroll, classes at the Akademie and a steadily increasing round of international guest appearances, Zemlinsky scarcely found time for private tuition. He did make at least one exception, however, for Jan Meyerowitz, a talented teenager from Breslau.† 'It was not easy to gain access to Zemlinsky,' Meyerowitz recalled, but –

as a teacher [he] was incomparable: he was noted for his intuitive ability to uncover in his pupils thought processes of which they were themselves unaware, to elucidate these and turn them in the right direction. No wonder that Schoenberg's talent, fostered by such a friend, had developed so rapidly.

Those who could benefit from his sporadic availability were best off. He would not accept Schoenberg's more recent theories, which, to their mutual regret, had caused something of a personal rift between the two men, but in public this discrepancy remained unnoticed [. . .] As to Schoenberg's personal qualities and his behaviour towards others, opinion was divided, then as now. Zemlinsky described him as a 'seducer' (*Herzensdieb*), whose powerful and charming personality had an irresistible effect on many people; others spoke of him as a 'lousy trickster' (*Zwiderwurzen*).¹⁵

By far the most spectacular of the productions conducted by Zemlinsky at the Kroll was *Les contes d'Hoffmann*, with eye-catching sets by the great Bauhaus artist László Moholy-Nagy, and a boldly modernistic production by Ernst Legal. 'For the first time,' enthused Bloch (in a verbless German then *en vogue*), 'a reversal of the new simplicity':

Astonishing beauty already in the prologue: a sort of bar table, steel chairs glinting in the dark, a staircase leading upwards, in the bar rowdy students, with Lindhorst blazing and terrible on a dais. The first act in Spalanzani's laboratory a surrealist picture after the manner of [James] Ensor, with electric uteri suspended in mid-air and galvanized corpses as chorus. The second act in the open air with Olympia's

---

* From Zemlinsky's correspondence with Universal Edition, it transpires that he also contemplated performing Delius's *Songs of Sunset* and Szymanowski's *Stabat Mater*.
† Meyerowitz (1913–1998) left Germany in 1933 to study in Italy. Arrested by the Nazis on rejoining his mother in 1938, he succeeded in fleeing via Belgium to France, where he was temporarily interned. Having become an American citizen in 1951, he later settled in Labaroche (Alsace). Though known primarily as a composer, conductor and musicologist, he is also remembered for his book *Der echte jüdische Witz* ('Genuine Jewish Humour'), published in 1997.

terrace and Venice doubling as brothel and as scene of one of the first detective stories in opera. The third act, Krespel's home, cramped by contrast: a funnel to the underworld, or rather a modern penthouse, its roots likewise severed from the earth.[16]

The production was a milestone in the history of stage design, but also grist to the mill of the Nazi press. Under the circumstances, it was a miracle that the critics even spared a thought for the performers.

Here, in this experiment for the eye [wrote Weissmann], Alexander v. Zemlinsky, otherwise far too little recognized, stakes a full claim for the music, with conducting that is firm yet supple. This impression was also confirmed by the warm-hearted applause that greeted him before the third act.[17]

Oskar Bie and the petulant Zschorlich wrote in similar vein; Zemlinsky himself reserved comment, at least in public, until he thought himself out of earshot. During rehearsals for *Das Lied von der Erde* with the Czech Philharmonic (on 3 January 1930, coupled with Mozart's 'Prague' Symphony), he spoke to a Prague critic of the new *Bartered Bride*, that he had just premièred at the Kroll, as a production that neither uprooted the action (as in *Hoffmann*) nor filled the stage (as in Duelberg's sets) with abstract patterns of oblongs and squares. 'Just imagine,' he enthused (verblessly) to the reporter:

Spontaneous applause for the opening chorus, and a simple, indeed extremely simple style of production. Reality in modern clothing, but no cubic or cubist effects, no mind-boggling enigmas of a geometry run wild. [. . .] A unison call, so to speak: back to the *music*![18]

Leningrad

With only three premières per season and no further repertoire performances to attend to, Zemlinsky's duties at the Kroll were comparatively light. Moreover, in his first engagement at a state-subsidized theatre (again with the exception of the Vienna Hofoper), even as second-in-command his earnings far outstripped his salary as *Opernchef* in Prague. Soon he began to expand his activities as guest conductor, in Barcelona, Brno, Paris, Rome, Warsaw and elsewhere; he also appeared sporadically in Vienna, where the Konzerthaus (under Botstiber's direction) and the newly formed RAVAG (Austrian Radio) offered new artistic stimuli; Tálich continued to invite him to Prague, and before Stalin rang down the Iron Curtain in 1936, he paid several visits to the USSR.

His first trip to Russia, in 1928, took him to Leningrad for two Verdi *Requiems* (1 and 8 February) and an *Alpensinfonie* (4 February, coupled with the *Freischütz* overture and Mendelssohn's Violin Concerto).* Ninety minutes

* Information kindly supplied by Ella Machrova, Dramaturg at the Mariinsky Theatre.

before the second performance of the Verdi he dashed off a letter to Klara Kwartin in Berlin:

The *Requiem* [. . .] was so successful that the following day I was invited to conduct a concert in Moscow on the 12th.* [. . .] The hotel is very comfortable & there's good theatre here too. And what I had been so afraid of: lousy food, is not the case, on the contrary, I wouldn't know where to eat better in Berlin.[19]

He was delighted to meet up with Laber, who had travelled three days and nights from Aussig to join him, the Glazunov Quartet promised to perform his Third Quartet, and he probably also met Boris Asaf'yev, an influential personality in the city's musical life and guiding spirit of the ACM, Soviet Russia's equivalent to the ISCM.[20] Above all, he returned home with a new contract in his pocket: the musical directorship of the Leningrad State Opera.[†]

He must have considered his future in Russia assured, for in the *Deutsches Musiker-Lexikon*, published in the spring of 1929, the engagement was made public (presumably there were also press releases to the same effect).[21] Artistically speaking, this would have been far more satisfying a position than at the Kroll, and not only because of its higher rank. Under the ministerial leadership of Anatoly Lunacharsky the avant-garde in Soviet Russia was as buoyant as anywhere in the West. Politically too, Zemlinsky could see for himself that the Bolshevik government was no band of criminals (though often portrayed as such in the German press), and that the people were not dying of hunger. Nevertheless, considerations of a more practical nature ultimately persuaded him to reject the offer.[‡] Ida was critically ill; there was a danger of losing contact with major musical centres in the West; outside the Soviet Union the rouble was almost worthless; above all, the contract itself was initially for only one season, with no guarantee that it would be renewed.[22]

'Nicht diese Töne . . .'

Of Zemlinsky's later guest appearances with the Czech Philharmonic, over half were dedicated to the music of Mahler. In November 1929 he repeated his D minor 'coincidence' of Bach's Concerto for three pianos, coupled this time with Mahler's Third Symphony; in January 1930 the distinguished Czech mezzo Marta Krásová joined him in *Das Lied von der Erde*; and in May 1931, in commemoration of the twentieth anniversary of Mahler's death, he conducted the Fifth Symphony, substituted at his request for the *Alpensinfonie*. In October

* In Moscow Zemlinsky evidently gave a concert performance of *Fidelio* (mentioned in a brief article about his activities in Russia published in *Die Musik*, xxiv/8, May 1932).
† The former Mariinsky Theatre, officially known at the time as the Gosudarstvennïy Akademicheskiy Teatr Operï i Baleta (State Academic Theatre of Opera and Ballet).
‡ From 1933 to 1936 the position in Leningrad was occupied by Zemlinsky's friend and colleague Fritz Stiedry.

1929, between the Fourth Brandenburg Concerto, Suk's Meditation on the St Wenceslas Chorale and the 'Eroica', Zemlinsky conducted the Prague première of Kurt Weill's *Kleine Dreigroschenmusik*, commissioned by Klemperer and premièred by him at the Kroll the previous February. Where Berlin had thrilled to the jazzy rhythms and bawdy implications of the 'Anstatt-dass-Song' and the 'Zuhälter-Ballade', Prague was outraged. *Autres pays, autres moeurs*: exporting Roaring Twenties culture to Czechoslovakia was an experiment that Zemlinsky never repeated.

Due to the agitation of the Nazis, and particularly their vociferous demands for *Lebensraum*, relations between the two countries were anyway on a knife edge. To honour Masaryk on his eightieth birthday, the Deutsche Männergesangverein of Prague had hired the Lucerna for 21 May 1930 (over a fortnight after the event) to perform the 'Choral' Symphony with a multi-national quartet of soloists and the Czech Philharmonic conducted by Zemlinsky. Before rehearsals even started, leading articles appeared in *Národ*, *Právo Lidu* and *Národní listy* decrying the idea of singing Schiller in German as a dishonour to Masaryk and 'an insult to the entire nation'. In recent months German films had been banned; on the streets of Prague there were anti-German demonstrations, and even in the musical world the sabres of chauvinism had begun to rattle. Steinberg had queered his pitch during the previous season: when Walter von Stolzing had fallen ill shortly before an NDT gala performance of *Meistersinger*, he had engaged a tenor from London named Bolland, singing in English, in preference to Richard Kubla from the Národní Divadlo, who was on the spot but knew the role only in Czech.* For a performance of the Maeterlinck Songs by the Czech Philharmonic, the conductor Adolf Heller† was required to adapt the vocal line to Maeterlinck's original French text. Animosity was running high; nerves were wearing thin. Anticipating further trouble, the committee of the Männergesangverein informed Zemlinsky that even if the chorus were to sing Schiller in the original, his soloists must yield to patriotic pressure and sing in Czech. Fearing that resistance could jeopardize his future as a guest conductor in Czechoslovakia, he assented.

The dress rehearsal was held in public. After the first three movements and the orchestral introduction to the fourth, which passed without incident, the bass soloist, Josef Schwarz (a bilingual, Prague-born member of the NDT ensemble), stood up to sing his recitative: 'O Freunde, nicht diese Töne!'

---

* To appease his critics, Steinberg subsequently conducted the 'Choral' Symphony at the Rudolfinum with the finale sung in Czech.
† Born in Prague, Adolf Heller (1901–1954) studied composition with Foerster and Novák and conducting with Tálich. He was engaged at the NDT from 1921 to 1924. After one season in Königsberg and three as Musical Director in Gablonz (Jablonec), he succeeded Zemlinsky as Conductor of the Deutsche Männergesangverein in Prague. He later emigrated to the USA, where he was appointed Director of the Chicago Conservatory (1939–42) and later of the Opera Reading Club in Hollywood.

Zemlinsky tapped his baton and in a stage whisper instructed him to sing in Czech, as agreed. The rehearsal continued: 'Radosti ty jiskro Boží.' An interjection from the chorus: 'Dieses Stichwort kennen wir nicht' ('We don't know that cue'); uproar. After much heated debate, a compromise was reached: the soprano and contralto, Novotná and Krásová,* would sing in Czech, the tenor Josip Rijavec† in French, Schwarz and the chorus in German.‡ Before the concert, the largely German-speaking audience was surprised to discover that their programmes were printed in Czech, with only a brief synopsis in erratic German. Even more surprising was the inclusion, on a separate sheet, of a lengthy statement by Zemlinsky, the gist of which was as follows:

[. . .] I have had no influence whatsoever upon the decision concerning the language to be sung in this performance. [. . .] I am an artist, not a politician, and am glad to leave such decisions to politicians. [. . .] During my fifteen years of artistic activity in Prague I always strove for harmonic collaboration between the two nations in the field of culture. [. . .] My catchword is not 'Deutschland über alles' ('Germany reigns supreme'). The guiding light of my artistic career has always been and always will be the catchword: 'Die Kunst über alles' ('Art reigns supreme').[23]

'Freude . . . radosti . . . joie . . . allegria' (*Prager Tagblatt*, 22 March 1930)
Original caption: 'Zemlinsky: "At least *I* remain speechless, thank heaven."'

* As a member of the Národní Divadlo, Krásová had received permission to participate only on condition that she sang in Czech.
† Rijavec (later José Riavez; 1890–1958) was a native of Istria. A pupil of Graedener and Schreker, he sang at the NDT from 1934 to 1937 and was a regular guest at the Teatro Colón in Buenos Aires.
‡ Between dress rehearsal and performance, Rijavec thought better of his suggestion and sang in German.

As soon as he and Novotná returned to Berlin, Tietjen suspended them from their duties.* Once they had written open letters of apology, however, they were promptly reinstated.[24] A letter from the composer Jaromír Weinberger to the *Münchener Neueste Nachrichten*, apologizing to the German people on behalf of his countrymen, also helped to pour oil on the troubled waters.†

'Be kind to me, oh, great dark city'

Ida had been in poor health since her operation in 1923. Under the strain of life in the metropolis she declined rapidly: the diagnosis was leukaemia. In mid-January 1929 complications arose and her condition grew critical. In hospital nothing could be done but to administer painkilling injections of morphine. Zemlinsky was rehearsing *Les contes d'Hoffmann* at the time, which in Legal's production concluded with the episode of Krespel and his daughter Antonia, stricken with a mysterious wasting disease. On stage at the Kroll the sinister Docteur Miracle gleefully clinked his flagons of medicine – 'Eh oui! je vous entend! Tout à l'heure! un instant,' enthused Bloch. 'Altogether the most eerie of operatic scenes and the most eerie of songs to go with it.'[25] A few blocks away, at the Charité, Ida was failing rapidly. She died on 29 January, aged forty-eight. The previous summer she had travelled with her husband to the ISCM Festival in Siena: the last few rays of light in an existence that had been singularly drab and sunless.

In the spring of 1929, Marie Pappenheim[26] drew Zemlinsky's attention to a handsomely designed anthology of poems by black American writers of the so-called 'Harlem Renaissance', recently published under the title *Afrika singt*.‡ Interspersed with vivid, jazz-inspired scenes from life in the great city, these poets sang of lynchings and racist terror, life in ghettos and on cotton plantations, dreams of a better future and an America with equal rights for all. Discussing the influence of this literature on European readers, the musicologist Malcolm S. Cole stresses that the book 'sent shockwaves through intellectual circles in Germany and Austria'.[27] Zemlinsky, too, was clearly enthralled, but less for the exotic flavour of the poetry than for the parallels he could draw with the European way of life. Langston Hughes's *Disillusion* will have awoken dim associations of his youth in the open ghetto of the Leopoldstadt, perhaps also of drab tenements in the poorer quarters of Prague and working-class hovels in Berlin. Even in translation, this was a language with subtle inner patterns of

---

* In reaction to further anti-German protests in Prague, in October 1930 Tietjen also postponed the Berlin premiere of Janáček's *From the House of the Dead*.
† Weinberger's *Schwanda the Bagpiper* was then in the repertoire of the Städtische Oper, a fact that had caused adverse comment in several German press reports of the Prague concert.
‡ Anna Nussbaum (ed.), *Afrika singt: Eine Auslese neuer Afro-Amerikanischer Lyrik* (Vienna–Leipzig, 1929).

light and shade, the voice of the suffering individual but also of a persecuted collective – and a far cry from the erotic mysticism of Tagore:

I would be simple again, / simple and clean / like the earth, / like the rain, / nor ever know, / dark Harlem, / the wild laughter / of your mirth / nor the salt tears / of your pain.[28]

In Countee Cullen's *A Brown Girl Dead* Zemlinsky found a touching obsequy for Ida:

With two roses on her breasts, / White candles at head and feet, / Dark Madonna of the grave she rests; / Lord Death has found her sweet.

On 28 April he sketched out a setting of the poem in E♭ minor, changing Cullen's 'dark Madonna' ('schwarze Madonna') to 'dark-brown girl' ('schwarzbraunes Mädel') to bring the image in line with the archetypal dark-skinned maiden of German folk poetry.* Between 4 and 12 May followed music to three texts by Langston Hughes: *Danse Africaine (Afrikanischer Tanz)*, *Song for a Dark Girl (Lied aus Dixieland)* and *Disillusion (Erkenntnis)*. Cullen wrote with a certain disdain of Hughes, the uncrowned king of the Harlem Renaissance, and a cosmopolitan intellectual with a Columbia University degree,† that he 'poetized the blues in his zeal to represent the Negro masses'.[29] But even if his self-styled 'studies in racial rhythms'[30] occasionally strike a synthetic note, his distinctive faculties of observation and expression made him more approachable to the European mind than most other American writers of his generation. Symptomatic of this rapport were his later music-theatre collaborations, notably with Kurt Weill (*Street Scene*, 1946) and Jan Meyerowitz (*The Barrier*, 1950). Hughes himself ascribed this empathy to the fact that his grandfather was Jewish. Indeed, to a Jew his description of 'Uncle Tom' will have sounded a familiar note:

Within – / the beaten pride. / Without – / the grinning face, / the low, obsequious double bow [31]

Towards the end of May Zemlinsky revised *Totes braunes Mädel* and *Afrikanischer Tanz*. The month of August found him in the role of merry

---

* As for instance in the *Wunderhorn* song *Es blies ein Jäger wohl in sein Horn* ('Wann werd ich mein schwarzbraunes Mädel doch krieg'n? Adé!'), the folk song *Ausmarch* ('Schwarzbraunes Mädel, du bleibst zu Haus') or Theodor Storm's poem *Im Volkston* ('Ein schwarzbraunes Mädel, so flink wie 'ne Katz'). In European etymology, a semantic link between the images of a 'black Madonna' and a 'brown girl' is found in the name of the mountain range Sierra Morena ('brown-girl mountains') of Andalusia, which in Roman times were known as 'montes mariani' (Mountains of the Virgin Mary).
† Many of the Harlem Renaissance writers had university degrees, often as sole black student in their class. Countee Cullen was himself a graduate of Harvard, Jean Toomer studied at the University of Wisconsin, and Frank Horne, a graduate of the College of the City of New York, made a distinguished career as an ophthalmologist.

widower (presumably with Louise as his travelling companion) at Juan-les-Pins on the Côte d'Azur. Under the unaccustomed heat of the Riviera sun he set another three poems from the collection (Jean Toomer's *Cotton Song*, Frank Horne's *Arabeske* and Langston Hughes's *Bad Man*), composed a new, expanded version of *Song for a Dark Girl*,* and with accustomed rapidity orchestrated the entire group. Before travelling on to Kreuzstein am Mondsee, near Salzburg, the full score, which he entitled Symphonische Gesänge (Symphonic Songs) op. 20, was complete.

On 14 August he wrote from his lakeside retreat to Hertzka, enquiring whether Universal Edition might be interested in 'a new opus'.[32] No reaction. A month later he wrote again from Berlin: 'Was my enquiry [. . .] so unwelcome that you have still not answered it?'[33] Hertzka replied:

I feel bound to say that new acquisitions, if not connected with the theatre market, are currently of no interest to us. We still have considerable losses to make good, after which we intend to concentrate on publications for the stage. Considering the severity of the prevailing economical and musical crisis, the publishing of serious music is an all but futile undertaking. Maybe the situation will improve, in which case we could again address the issue of publishing your new opus.

In thirty years, Zemlinsky had done much to promote new UE publications at home and abroad; since 1913, moreover, Hertzka had unhesitatingly accepted every new score of his as and when it was announced. Since publishing the Third Quartet, in the autumn of 1924, however, Hertzka had begun to concentrate his resources on the younger generation. Thanks to the wildfire success of Krenek's *Jonny spielt auf*, Weill's *Dreigroschenoper* and Max Brand's *Maschinist Hopkins*, income from royalties, hire fees and sheet-music sales was rising steadily. In a word, his protestations of a 'prevailing economical and musical crisis' were pure bluff. Schreker had been complaining bitterly to UE since 1926 that his interests were being neglected;[34] now it was Zemlinsky's turn. It was chastening to be fobbed off like an aspiring unknown with a few lines of boiler-plate prose. This was his first new 'opus' (time and again he stressed the word) in five years, and he was proud of it.

Twelve months later he again approached Hertzka about the Symphonic Songs. 'At any rate they are very beautiful,' he wrote, and slipping into the role of businessman, he proposed a deal:

Bodanzky has now *accepted* the work for his New York concerts & has asked me to contact you right away, so that you can negotiate a contract with him. [. . .] At the same time I would like to send the score to Director Krauss.† Do you think he

---

* The first version (German title *Lied aus Dixieland*), in 5/8 time throughout, encompasses only fourteen bars; the second uses a wider variety of metre and is over three times longer.
† Clemens Krauss was at the Vienna Staatsoper, where in 1930 he conducted the Austrian première of *Wozzeck*.

might be interested in something of the sort? Naturally I would prefer it if you were yourself to take a step in this direction. After all, you know me – – !

[PS] This season I have ten concerts in various cities – including Russia – & hope that UE will be well represented on my programmes.[35]

Bodanzky never conducted the Symphonic Songs; Krauss never even saw the score, and the only UE publication that Zemlinsky conducted in Russia was *Das Lied von der Erde*.* In May 1931 he did finally persuade Hertzka to acquire the rights to op. 20, but for several years the score simply lay on the shelf. Erwin Stein[†] wrote that he was delighted with it, that he would be approaching not only Krauss but also Furtwängler, and that he hoped there would be 'really plenty' of performances.[36] 'How do you want to do anything for my orchestral songs', replied Zemlinsky laconically, 'with only *one* copy of the score?'[37]

The delay was fatal. In 1929 Harlem Renaissance literature, indeed anything connected with or inspired by the blues, was the height of fashion. But by the time op. 20 was performed, art works of this genre had in Germany become the epitome of 'degeneracy'. The world première, on 8 April 1935, was given neither in Berlin nor Vienna, as hoped, but in Brno. And instead of a famous name, the conductor was Zemlinsky's old friend Jalowetz, himself a fugitive from Nazi Germany, forced to resign his post as Musical Director in Cologne.

Be kind to me, / oh, great dark city, / let me forget. / I will not come / to you again.[38]

There is little about the Symphonic Songs that could at face value be identified as 'symphonic': no readily identifiable sonata-form outline, as in the Second Quartet or the Lyric Symphony, no audible unity of themes and motifs, as in *Die Seejungfrau*. If in this context the term 'symphonic' signifies anything at all, then it implies an affinity with the Lyric Symphony: both works comprise seven songs, both are founded on a dualistic principle. Where the Lyric Symphony contrast elements of **M** and **W**, the antitheses of op. 20 are light and darkness, hope and despair, life and death (see diagram on p. 364).

Common to both works is the quality or affect of disillusion. Where in the Lyric Symphony this was the culminating stage in a process of approach and departure, in the Symphonic Songs *Disillusion* (i.e. the poem of that name)[‡] serves as asymmetrical axis to the whole cycle. Both structures relate, if perhaps

---

* Zemlinsky also planned to perform Schoenberg's First Chamber Symphony. It should be added that in 1930 Universal Edition published three works by younger composers to texts from *Afrika singt*: *Elend* for voice and piano by Edmund Nick (thirty-nine years old), eight *Afrika-Songs* op. 29 for low voice and chamber orchestra by Wilhelm Grosz (thirty-six) and six *Negerlieder* for medium voice and piano or orchestra by Kurt Pahlen (twenty-three).

† Stein had been on the editorial staff of Universal Edition since 1924.

‡ The original title of Langston Hughes's poem is *Disillusion*; Zemlinsky knew it as *Erkenntnis* ('insight' or 'cognition').

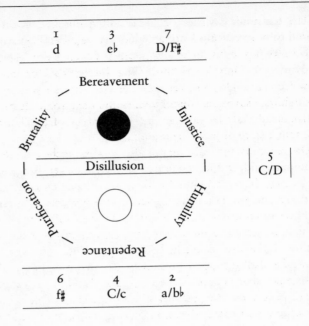

```
    1        3        7
    d        eb       D/F#
```

Bereavement

Brutality   Injustice

| Disillusion | | 5 |
| | C/D |

Humility

Purification

Repentance

```
    6        4        2
    f#       C/c      a/bb
```

1 *Lied aus Dixieland*   2 *Lied der Baumwollpacker*
3 *Totes braunes Mädel*   4 *Übler Bursche*   5 *Erkenntnis*
6 *Afrikanischer Tanz*   7 *Arabeske*

subconsciously, to Louise's portrait of 1919 with its Steiner-inspired 'cosmological circle' of colour.

Also common to both works is a scheme of tonal interrelationships flanked by D minor and Lydian D major. Where in the Gesänge op. 5 these two keys stand as dual symbols of grief and serenity, and in the Second Quartet progress from minor to major signifies a process of reconciliation, the Symphonic Songs extend only a slender promise of a better world. Central to the first and last poems of the cycle is the image of a lynched plantation worker. *Lied aus Dixieland* (in D minor) is a lament for the murdered man, *Arabeske* (in Lydian D major) a song of protest, but also of hope. Beneath the gallows tree a little Irish girl with red hair kisses a black baby:*

Grey eyes smile / into black eyes.

* Malcolm S. Cole points out that, due to a translator's error, the composers Erich Zeisl and Georg Grosz misinterpreted *Arabeske* as a jovial depiction of a black man swaying 'as in a hammock'. In describing the poem as depicting 'a shocking contrast', however, Cole himself overlooks its optimistic implication ('*Afrika singt*: Austro-German Echoes of the Harlem Renaissance', *Journal of the American Musical Society*, xxx/1 (spring 1977), 82).

The harmonic style of op. 20 is often obscure, and the skies clear only sporadically to reveal identifiable key centres. Zemlinsky often steers a course between two or even three keys, none of which is ever established as a tonic in its own right. Only in the third song, his epitaph for Ida, does the harmony grow from a single root, yet even here the key is never entirely defined: chromatic shifts, sharpened subdominants and pentatonic clusters (with the imagery of two heads side by side, as in the *Romance* of the Third Quartet) serve to maintain a state of permanent ambiguity.

Op. 20 calls for only marginally smaller orchestral forces than the Lyric Symphony; indeed the percussion section is larger. But whatever else the two works may have in common, their sound-worlds could scarcely be further apart: on the one hand the opulence of a perfumed garden, on the other the starkness of an urban skyline. Symptomatic of this new clarity is the reduction of the horn section from four to two; characteristic of the Afro-American connection is the use of pitched jazz drums (i.e. tomtoms) and a woodblock (*Arabeske* also includes a prominent part for mandolin). The orchestration is consistently sharp-edged and often reduced to barest essentials. All but twelve bars of *Erkenntnis*, for instance, are entrusted to an ensemble of oboe and four solo cellos, punctuated by a quartet of muted brass and woodblock; at the opening of *Lied aus Dixieland* the vocal line emerges from between imitative *a cappella* entries for solo woodwinds, and continues as counterpoint to a static oboe line, underpinned by a few soft chords. Even in the more robust songs, *Lied der Baumwollpacker* and *Übler Bursche*, Zemlinsky's scoring remains lucid, incisive and – in contrast to anything he had written since the turn of the century – utterly devoid of filigree work. The sonorities of *Arabeske* come close at times to late Janáček, notably in the gawky lines for E♭ clarinet and the distinctive timbre of piccolo and trombone four octaves apart.

In his Prague interview of January 1930 Zemlinsky stressed that 'modern music, too, is founded on common sense (*gutes Empfinden*)', and in contrast to Schreker he found kind words for Hindemith, Krenek and Weill.[39] In October 1932, interviewed by the *Neues Wiener Journal* on the occasion of his sixtieth birthday (*sic*), he outlined his views more precisely:

[In Austria] three composers strike me as being particularly distinguished in their respective fields: Berg, v. Webern (from the school of Schoenberg) and Krenek. [. . .] Of the German composers, Hindemith is in my opinion the most individual, the greatest, and can hence justifiably be described as the most outstanding. And Weill of course is an original figure who also ranks among the foremost.[40]

To a large extent op. 20 reflects the influence of these younger composers on Zemlinsky's own musical development. But even if he now scarcely gave a thought to the once immutable laws of Robert Fuchs, he never sacrificed his scrupulous technical control, never disavowed his instinctive feel for matching words to music or his ability (in Alma's words) to 'take a little theme as if into his hands, to mould it and transform it into countless variants'.[41] By applying variative technique to patterns instead of pitches, he evolved a new principle of intervallic asymmetry. *Lied aus Dixieland* presents a straightforward example:

EX. 74   *Lied aus Dixieland*, op. 20 no. 1, bars 38–42

Love is a naked shadow / on a gnarled and naked tree.

Commentary   Each figure in the upper voices adheres to one specific interval, respectively a major 3rd and a minor 3rd in the violins, and a semitone in the viola. The figures descend sequentially, but in irregular steps (here expressed in semitone units):

4 (2)	4 (2)	4 (2)
3 (1)	3 (2)	5 (2)
1 (2)	1 (3)	1 (2)

The sequence begins on an open 5ths chord, E♭–E♭–B♭, and ends, thanks to asymmetry, on a major triad, A♮–F♯–C♯. Bar 142 in act I/ii of *Wozzeck* (EX. 74A) may have provided an initial stimulus, with the difference that Berg's intervallic structure is strictly symmetrical. Had Zemlinsky maintained the symmetry of his pattern (EX.74B), he would have lost the tonal implications, the play of light and shade as the upper voices move in and out of phase with the supporting 'Fate' chord.

EX. 74A

EX. 74B

With op. 20 Zemlinsky concluded his painful process of artistic consolidation and established a fundament on which to build for the future. Looking back to the Roaring Twenties, Stefan Zweig noted with distaste that this was an era dedicated to the cult of youth. It was bad enough, he observed, if younger artists lacked experience and education: that would at least leave them impervious to tradition. 'But in the midst of this chaotic carnival,' he continued,

the most tragicomic drama of all was to observe how many an intellectual of the older generation, panic-stricken at the prospect of growing outmoded and no longer being considered 'up-to-the-minute', would hastily don a mask of synthetic primitivity, and with clumsily halting steps creep along some new path that clearly led nowhere.[42]

Even if his remarks were aimed principally at painters and writers, it would be only too easy to accuse Zemlinsky of such opportunism. His publishers were intent on remaining *à la mode*; of his operas only *Kleider machen Leute* still held the stage, and for masterly scores such as the Second Quartet or the Lyric Symphony nobody lifted a finger. The music itself silences such doubts.

Zemlinsky entered the 1930s not as some gaudily painted Aschenbach, hoping to seduce with synthetic youthfulness, but as an artist grown wise through disappointment, who could see how the world was turning and whose concern was to find a voice to which others would listen.

2

The Chalk Circle

Out of consideration for Ida's failing health, and until Hansi had completed her schooling, Zemlinsky had refrained from seeking a divorce. It was nevertheless an eventuality that he had actively considered. His treatment of Louise may have been less than exemplary, but his affection remained undiminished, and she was still utterly devoted to him. On 4 January 1930, little under a year after Ida's death, they married at a Berlin registry office.* Soon afterwards Hansi left for Vienna to make her way as a seamstress.[1]

As a wedding present, Zemlinsky decided to compose a new opera. It took little effort to find a subject appropriate to the occasion: Klabund's *Der Kreidekreis* (*The Chalk Circle*).† After a sensational world première at Meissen on 1 January 1925, the play had been running to packed houses all over Germany. Zemlinsky presumably saw the Prague production by Hans Demetz, with incidental music by Viktor Ullmann, which opened on the Kleine Bühne of the NDT two days after the world première.‡

Since the drama was clearly constructed and required neither ensembles nor choruses, it was relatively simple to adapt it to operatic requirements, a task that Zemlinsky shared with Louise during the spring of 1930.[2] Work on the short score began on 3 July 1930 $(3 + 7 + (1 + 9 + 3 + 0) = 23)$; act I was completed on 13 September, most of acts II and III followed during the summer of 1931, spent at Alt Aussee, and the final double bar was signed in Berlin on 8 October $(8 + 10 + (1 + 9 + 3 + 1) = 23)$, six days before Zemlinsky's sixtieth birthday. The orchestration was completed exactly one year later.

On the cover sheet of the short score,§ in bold pencilled lettering (not in Zemlinsky's hand), stands the title of a book: 'A. Rae, Metaphysik der Zahl' ('The Metaphysics of Number'): a slightly garbled reference to *Die Demaskierung der Zahl; ein Weg zum Erfolg* ('The Unmasking of Number; a Path to Success') by Alexander Raé, published in Berlin in 1932.¶

* Louise was baptized into the Protestant Church on 24 November 1930.
† Klabund (real name Alfred Henschke, 1890–1928). The *nom de plume* was a portmanteau word derived from *Klabautermann* (sprite, guiding spirit) and *Vagabund* (vagabond).
‡ Between January and June 1925 *Der Kreidekreis* was given over thirty times in Prague.
§ LoC, 22/1.
¶ Originally published by Glöckner Verlag (Berlin–Leipzig–Vienna). The Butler Library at Columbia University, New York, houses the only surviving copy in a public collection. Additional information in this copy (handwritten and rubber-stamped) reveals that Raé later transferred the copyright to New York, where under an address on West 98th Street he offered

Whatever the connection between book and opera, there can be no doubt that number played a crucial role in the genesis of *Der Kreidekreis*. The sketches reveal that the score was assembled with the help of an obscure system of numbered periods,* and instead of rehearsal numbers (which are more practical), Universal Edition marked up the published score with bar numbers, enabling Zemlinsky to check his calculations. Even if his system itself is obscure, the subtitle of Raé's book offers a clue to its purpose: 'a Path to Success'.

Cast†

Chang-Haitang (sop); Mrs Chang, her mother (alto); Chang-Ling, her brother (lyr bar); Tong, a procurer (buffo ten); Pao, a prince (ten); Ma, a mandarin (dram bar); Yü-pei, his wife of first rank (sop); Chao, clerk at court (bar); Chu-chu, chief judge (spoken); girl (sop); nanny (mezzo); two coolies (ten); soldier (bar). Child, court officials, policemen, soldiers, flower-maidens, master-of-ceremonies (silent).

Synopsis

I–1 *Tong's tea-house [in Nanking]* Unable to pay his taxes, the silkworm farmer Chang has hanged himself outside Ma's house. Notwithstanding the protests of her son Ling, the destitute Mrs Chang sells her daughter Haitang into prostitution.

I–2 *Another room in the tea-house* Prince Pao plays chess with Haitang. They talk of love, and on the paper wall Haitang draws a symbolic chalk circle. Bursting through the wall, the odious Ma musters Tong's new 'flower-maiden', and purchases her for a price that even Pao cannot outbid.

II–3 *Garden and veranda of Ma's house* The childless Yü-pei learns from Chao, her lover, that she is to forfeit both rank and inheritance to Haitang, who has given birth to a son. The beggared Ling, who has meanwhile joined an activist organization,

---

his services to readers as a consultant 'psycho-synthesizer and number analyst'. The content ranges from elevated discussion of number philosophy to tips for winning at the lottery. Zemlinsky may well have been impressed by Raé's analysis of the number 23:

2 + 3 = 5, 3 - 2 = 1, taken together: 5 + 1 = 6. The creative, constructive number 6 dominates. The outcome: 5 1 6. – Investigating 5 1 6 analytically: the centre of gravity is 1, i.e. strength of purpose. Adding and subtracting the flanking numbers (5 + 6 = 11, 6 - 5 = 1), the integer sum is 12, the product [i.e. the integer sum of (5 x 6) + 1] is 4. The future is overshadowed by the evil 4. Envy detracts from achievement and attempts to diminish its rewards. The harvested apple threatens to rot. After the wave-peak of success follows a trough, as if paying tribute to destiny. Nevertheless 23 has very many positive aspects (§26, 151).

* As for example in the scene for Yü-pei and the two coolies (III–5, beginning at bar 288): Zemlinsky numbers the first three phrases from 1 to 7, the next two from 1 to 8, then again five phrases from 1 to 7, but notes his intention of adding two extra bars. The closing bars of the opera (act III–7, beginning at bar 1555, or 1641 in the revised edition) are numbered from 1 to 6 and 1 to 8 (but the final, almost empty bar is *not* numbered).
† Orthography of names is here Anglicized.

comes to inform his sister of a plot to assassinate Ma. The oracle of the chalk circle persuades him to defer the execution.

II–4 *Room in Ma's house* Observing that Haitang has given her fur coat to a beggar, Yü-pei accuses her of ingratitude and infidelity. Ma protests that his new wife has made a better person of him. Yü-pei puts poison in his tea, and he falls dead. Haitang is arrested, and Yü-pei claims the child as her own.

III–5 *Courtroom* Since Yü-pei has bribed both judge and witnesses, Haitang is unable to defend her case. Yü-pei asserts that the mother of the child was not Ma's murderer. 'She speaks the truth,' exclaims Haitang, and Chu-chu passes sentence. A messenger arrives to proclaim the death of the Emperor and the accession of Pao to the throne. In the gallery Ling leaps to his feet: 'The new Emperor will be no better than the old,' he exclaims. He too is sentenced.

III–6 (Intermezzo) *Snowstorm landscape* Pao has summoned all condemned criminals and their judges to appear before him. Escorted on the road to Peking by two soldiers, Haitang bewails her misfortune.

III–7 *Imperial throne room* Pao pardons Ling and puts the two women to the test of the chalk circle. By refusing to fight over the child, Haitang proves herself to be the true mother. Yü-pei is inculpated by her own testimony; together with Chao and Chu-chu she is led away to be sentenced. Questioning Haitang about her first night in the tea-house, Pao reveals that he ravished her while she slept, and is hence father of her child. Praising the justice of the chalk circle, she ascends the throne at his side.

Klabund first drew attention to his talent in 1912 with Wedekind-inspired ballads published in Alfred Kerr's literary journal *Pan*. Shortly after the outbreak of the First World War he won wider acclaim with a volume of *Soldatenlieder* ('Soldier Songs'), but his enthusiasm for the Fatherland soon turned to disillusion, and in 1917 he published an open letter to Kaiser Wilhelm II in the *Neue Zürcher Zeitung*, urging abdication. Though later a regular contributor to *Die Weltbühne*, the influential left-wing journal of the Weimar Republic, Klabund remained politically neutral and committed to an ideal of non-violence. The Prussian authorities viewed him with mistrust, and under Nazi rule his books were banned. Had he lived to see Hitler rise to power in 1933, he would no doubt have joined his colleagues from *Die Weltbühne* behind barbed wire.*

Drawn to Oriental literature in 1915 by the martial verse of Li T'ai-Po, Klabund published several lyric anthologies from the Chinese, Japanese and Persian. *Der Kreidekreis* is based on *Hui-lan-chi*, written during the Yüan (Mongolian) Dynasty, i.e. between 1278 and 1368, by Li-Hsiang-tao.† Yüan

---

* Klabund suffered from a chronic tubercular condition, which was responsible for his early death at a clinic in Davos. His novel *Die Krankheit* (*The Illness*, 1917) was influential on Thomas Mann's *The Magic Mountain* (1924).
† Klabund worked from Stanislas Julien's French translation of 1832.

drama included song, dance and acrobatics, but also a kernel of social criticism, usually expressed in allegorical form. Ling's bitter attacks on the ruling classes, taken almost verbatim from the original, can scarcely be described as allegorical, however, indeed their vehemence threatens to sever the otherwise delicate fabric of dialogue.

For the greater part, Klabund brushes only a lacquer of Orientalism over his play. In his view it was no *chinoiserie*, and he insisted that 'it should be as if one were *dreaming* of China'. Through jasmine-tinted spectacles he shows his audience the depravity and corruption of German society in the Roaring Twenties. Even if concubinage was a traditional theme of art and literature in the Far East, the Nazis were quick to apprehend the topicality of Tong and his teahouse – far more seditious in their eyes than Ling's radical raving – and condemn the play as an attack on 'public morality'.

Brecht learned much from *The Chalk Circle*. Apart from appropriating the fable for his own *Caucasian Chalk Circle* (1944–5), he often emulated Klabund in choosing exotic settings for the revelation of home truths. Whether in the eighteenth-century Soho of *The Threepenny Opera* or the transatlantic urban jungles of *Happy End* and *Mahagonny*, he too delighted in propelling his audience from court house to whore house, from the mansions of the stinking rich to the hovels of the destitute. And where Klabund frees his heroine from the block by introducing the *deus ex machina* of the imperial courier, Brecht uses the same ploy to save his Macheath from the gallows. Both protagonists are rescued in the nick of time; both can thank their lucky stars.

For all its mass appeal, *The Chalk Circle* possesses a finesse and aesthetic sensibility altogether foreign to Brechtian theatre. Behind the outer shell of a drama about social injustice, Klabund depicts his heroine as the incarnation of art itself. Her purity emanates from another world. As the allegory shows, art can withstand prostitution, slander or dispossession, and suffers but does not die in captivity; put on trial, art seeks only the truth. But art also possesses a unique ability to orchestrate its own apotheosis. In a world determined by art, justice triumphs, the mighty are put down, the meek inherit the earth. For Zemlinsky no drama could have been more fitting.

As a wedding present the play proved less ideal. No doubt the choice was motivated primarily by the closing scene, in which Emperor and Empress unite in praise of the chalk circle, vying with each other in ecstatic expressions of endearment:

Mein Mondkind! Mein Sonnenkind! Mein Schmerzenskind! Mein Herzenskind!
[. . .] Dir werden alle Glocken Freude läuten! Dir werden alle Tage Glück bedeuten!

My moon child! My sun child! My child of pain! My child of my love!
[. . .] For you the joyful bells shall all resound! For you each day with fortune shall be crowned!

Like Haitang, Louise had entered the household as wife of second rank, softened her master's heart, and been promoted in reward to first rank. But there the likeness ended. Neither Chang's suicide, Tong's tea-house nor Yü-pei's poisoned sugar crystals presented appetizing parallels and, in the light of Louise's experience, the choice of a drama that hinged on the fate of a mother and child was less than felicitous. She herself later prepared an English translation of the libretto,* but let it be known that the play was not entirely to her taste. Klabund's intriguing language of symbols, familiar to her from her anthroposophical studies, must have helped redress the balance of sympathy. A circle, Klabund observes, is in fact a trinity of bounded area, unbounded area and perimeter. To expound its mysteries, Haitang draws a chalk circle on the wall:

PAO: The circle symbolizes the heavens' arc, the circle represents the ring that binds a married couple, joining heart-ring to heart-ring.
HAITANG: Beyond this circle lies the Void. Within this circle lies the Universe. How does the Void connect with the Universe? In the circle that rotates (*she draws spokes in the circle*), in the wheel that turns. [. . .] (*She rubs out the spokes.*) Look, the circle is empty again. Now, as I vainly twist and turn before it, it encircles me like a mirror.

In act II–5 the circle represents the dividing line between life and death. Taking the knife with which Ling plans to kill Ma, Haitang scratches a circle in the earth:

HAITANG: I shall throw the knife at the circle. The circle encloses his life. If the knife lands in the area within the circle, then the gods have pronounced sentence, and he must die. (*She hurls the knife. It lands exactly on the perimeter.*)

Finally, in act III–7, Pao's Solomonic scene of wisdom, the circle represents the millwheel of justice and – again – the wheel of fate.

Zemlinsky's 'Circle' theme consists of two mirrored segments. Each segment is subdivided into two parts, a rising sequence of 2nds and 5ths, and a falling asymmetrical pattern of 2nds and a 3rd. In its original guise the theme appears only once in each act (EX. 75).

Here a few elements of Zemlinsky's number system stand revealed: each phrase consists of five pitches (the fifth pitch of the first phrase also counts as the first pitch of the second phrase), and each segment occupies 14 crotchets. At each appearance of the theme, furthermore, the integer sum of the respective bar number – 842, 428 and 1238[†] – is also 14. To represent the knife landing on the perimeter of the circle (in act II), the theme is split across the bar-line.

---

* For the American première at Cincinatti on 12 May 1988.
[†] The numbering in act III applies only to the original version. Later print-runs of the vocal score included two orchestral interludes, added for the 1934 production at the Berlin Staatsoper, which defer the entry of the 'Circle' theme to bar 1326. Due to a printer's error, there is also a discrepancy of two bars between vocal and orchestral scores: in the unrevised orchestral score the 'Circle' theme enters at bar 1236.

EX. 75 *Der Kreidekreis*, (A) I–2, bar 842 and III–3, bar 1238;*
(B) II–1, bar 428 (with upbeat)

Unlike the chain of major 3rds with which Liszt draws a magic circle in the opening bars of his 'Faust' Symphony, or the regular pattern of 3rds with which Wagner forges his 'Ring' motif, the outline of Zemlinsky's circle is irregular. The musicologist Peter Revers offers a thought-provoking interpretation of this anomaly:

Two semantic resources seem to reside within the 'chalk circle' motif [. . .]: the elevated sphere of ritual itself, and the plane of human reactions and behavioural patterns which are the logical outcome of that ritual.[3]

With hindsight, this same principle of duality – the individual pitted against destiny, the 'Self' as mirror of the 'World' – and its musical representation in the form of contrasting 'semantic resources', can already be detected in Zemlinsky's earlier stage works. Particularly striking examples are the 'Görge' motif (EX. 25), Strapinski's 'transformation' motif (EX. 34) and the trumpet flourish that opens *A Florentine Tragedy* (EX. 53B). In *Der Kreidekreis* the symbols are further refined, bringing the concept into sharper focus.

Within a delicate Asiatic framework, and punctuated by a lithe dance rhythm, Haitang's charming 'Song of the Caged Bird' (at the close of act I–1) incorporates a similarly sophisticated system of ciphers and cross-references (EX. 76).

E♭ minor awakens memories of *Vöglein Schwermut* ('Little Bird of Melancholy'; op. 10 no. 3) and more specifically in this pentatonic context of *Totes braunes Mädel* ('A Brown Girl Dead') from op. 20. The melody itself, while anticipating the intervallic patterns of the 'Circle' theme (2nds and 5ths), follows the outline of the 'World' motif (E♭–D♭–B♭), with interversions in the

---

* Apart from the scoring, the presentation of the 'Circle' theme in acts I and III is identical. For the sake of formal clarity, its two halves (ex. 75a) are here printed in vertical alignment.

EX. 76   *Der Kreidekreis*, I–I, bar 561 *et seq.*

accompaniment figure (first and second bars) and the quaver figure of the second phrase (fourth and fifth bars). In the fifth bar the pentatonic pattern is broken to make way for the 'Fate' chord. The underlying jazz-inspired rhythmic pattern –

– can be traced back to the 3 + 3 + 2 formula first used in the Clarinet Trio of 1896 (cf. EX. 42).

Whether directly or indirectly, motivic particles from the 'Circle' theme serve as source material for every other theme and motif in the score. The music for Mrs Chang and Chang-Ling draws largely on the segment of 2nds and 5ths. Pao's music, in Lydian D major (EX. 77A), also evolves from this vocabulary. Vertically aligned, the pitches form a pandiatonic 5ths chord, D–A–E–B–F♯–C♯–G♯. By omitting two of the pitches (E and B), Zemlinsky arrives at a five-note array of 5ths, the 'Fortune' chord (EX. 77B), of the same provenance as the five-note 5ths chord of the 'Immortal Soul' in *Die Seejungfrau* (EX. 23) and the five 5ths that open *Kleider machen Leute* (EX. 32). Here too, the symbolism is purer: 'Fate' and 'Fortune' are separated by just one semitone, the alteration from F♮ to F♯.

Ma's villainy (EX. 77C), articulated in 'Circassian' rhythm, draws on the 'behavioural' segment of the 'Circle' theme, major and minor 2nds. Yü-pei's motif, notable for its 'unlucky' minor 9th (13 semitones), uses the same pitch material, but extended and disfigured. Her false witnesses, the nanny and the two coolies, present themselves with motifs of similar provenance, whereby the nanny's perfect 4ths imply loyalty led astray, and the perfect 5th in the coolies' theme credits even false witnesses with a spark of the divine.

EX. 77   (A) Pao; (B) 'Fortune' chord; (C) Ma as villain; (D) Yü-pei; (E) Nanny; (F) Coolies

Like an operetta or a musical comedy, *Der Kreidekreis* calls for concise musical forms – arias, songs and scenas – interspersed with passages of spoken dialogue. In Brechtian fashion, the characters step out of the action to present themselves to the public or perform their songs.* In order to handle such inherently anti-operatic devices, Zemlinsky was obliged to seek new means of musical synthesis. He found them in a system of motivic segregation, rigorously applied, as if in compliance with an unwritten table of motifs. Each of the characters moves within a specific zone of harmony, rhythm, texture and even key. Discontinuous areas of tension and relaxation are generated by interaction between these individual zones. Adorno detected a first vestige of this technique in *Kleider machen Leute*:

One could well believe that Zemlinsky, who certainly knew *The Threepenny Opera*, finally came under its sway and by means of exotic appeal attempted to tone down the brutality of its song form. Truly, the work bears a veneer of the Wiener Werkstatt [i.e. of *Jugendstil*]. But if one considers Zemlinsky's complete line of development, one comes to realize the injustice of such conclusions. The process of reducing everything to its most concise form of musical characterization, which the later Zemlinsky cultivated to the exclusion of expansive music-drama or symphonic techniques, is already clearly detectable in *Kleider machen Leute*. A small adjustment to the stylistic procedure suffices to achieve results similar to those of Brecht

---

* Or vice versa: it would be more accurate to say *Brecht* introduces his characters in *Klabundian* fashion.

and Weill – almost as if Zemlinsky had been the first to evolve the style of *The Threepenny Opera*.[4]

Even if the music of *Der Kreidekreis* includes more *couleur locale* than *Sarema* or *Der Zwerg*, this is very much a picture-book China: a stylized bird call, a melancholy flute tune, the occasional boom of a gong – little more. As Revers has pointed out, to Zemlinsky the 'fears, hopes and fateful decisions' of his protagonists were 'far more important than the superficial stylization of an exotic ambience'.[5] The same goes for the element of jazz in his score. Despite saxophones, banjo, hi-hat and tomtoms, this is no minstrel show, and Zemlinsky makes no conscious effort to 'swing'. When his orchestra does break into dance rhythm, the music is stylized to the point of classicality, far removed from the jazz-inspired musical comedies of Paul Ábrahám, Walter Kollo and Eduard Künnecke popular at the time, or indeed from the shimmies and tangos of Krenek and Weill.

In practice, the principle of 'single characters' tends to cramp Zemlinsky's style. In jettisoning ballast of past styles and techniques, his forms grow rigid, his polyphony acquires a dry, didactic quality. For lack of expansiveness, his natural Viennese *espressivo* is often supplanted by a hard-edged Prussian *staccato*. Song form works only if a song possesses popular appeal. But in this respect Zemlinsky remains true to his proud self and his aversion to writing for the entertainment industry. Few moments in the opera can vie for tunefulness with the slinky saxophone melody and atmospheric 'flower-maiden' song of the opening scene, and none can compete with *Surabaya Johnny* or *Mack the Knife* – nor were they intended to. In the orchestral introduction to act III, which he would gladly have reserved for profounder thoughts, as in *Der Traumgörge* and *Der König Kandaules*, he introduces the corrupt judge Chu-chu with a few pages of riotous parody, affording a glimpse of the latent entertainer. But not until the final apotheosis, where the orchestra abandons its neo-classical reserve, does Zemlinsky come into his true element. Emperor and Empress ascend the Dragon Throne to a rich tableau of post-Romantic orchestral colour, complete with Straussian whooping horns and extravagant harp *glissandos*, against an intricate background of figuration and arabesque. Haitang's miraculous rescue, Pao's untold riches, the joyful wedding bells: Zemlinsky depicts all this as a fairy-tale apotheosis: unreal, improbable, impossible.

End of the Kroll

On Friday 24 October 1929 the US stock market collapsed. Weakened by crippling indemnity payments to the victors of 1918, Stresemann's government had come to depend on American loans. Hence in Germany the Wall Street Crash, which led to a sharp rise in interest rates, caused inflation and unemployment to spiral. Within two months the number of unemployed had doubled to over 3 million, and continued to rise steadily.

Under the circumstances, heavy cuts in public spending became an urgent necessity. In poverty, as Klabund's allegory had confirmed, art can survive and even thrive. But when art is state-subsidized, poverty can cripple or even kill. Several theatres in the Ruhr area were faced with the prospect of amalgamation, and other important provincial houses threatened with closure. Under the circumstances, it no longer seemed feasible or desirable to maintain three opera companies in the capital city. Already in January 1930 members of the Berlin Landtag demanded the closure of the Kroll, but thanks to Klemperer's energetic protests and support from the liberal press, the threat was at first averted. The following months witnessed a valiant struggle for survival, but to no avail. Once arrangements had been made to accommodate the Volksbühne at the Lindenoper, the Landtag voted in favour of closure, a decision that was made public on 6 November. With Klemperer's *Figaro* (brilliantly directed by Gustaf Gründgens), Zemlinsky's *Louise* and *Madama Butterfly* (with beautiful and intelligible designs by Moholy-Nagy), and the German première of Janáček's *From the House of the Dead*, the Kroll's fourth and final season was artistically and financially its most successful. But the die had been cast, and on 3 July 1931, when the curtain fell on the act iv finale of *Figaro*, one of the most stimulating and controversial chapters in the history of opera came to an end.

Due to the annexation of Hesse-Nassau to Prussia – an anomaly of German federalism that had been in effect since 1867 – the city of Wiesbaden came under Prussian jurisdiction. Tietjen had recently been promoted to the rank of Prussian *Staats-Intendant* and was hence also in charge of the Wiesbaden theatre. Obliged to find alternative employment for those members of the Kroll ensemble whose contracts had not yet expired, he offered Zemlinsky Klemperer's former post as Musical Director at Wiesbaden.* On 16 May 1931 Erwin Stein wrote on behalf of Universal Edition to congratulate him on his new appointment, and even sent lists of repertoire suggestions from the UE catalogue, from Berg to Webern and Casella to Weinberger.[6] He was wasting his time.

For thirty years Zemlinsky had dedicated his energies to a conducting career that, as was now clear to him, would never bring the hoped rewards. His engagement book was liberally sprinkled with concerts at home and abroad, work on *Der Kreidekreis* had whetted his appetite for further creative work, he had been offered a class in score-reading at the Berlin Hochschule für Musik (a menial appointment, but one that offered a regular income and a professor's pension), and since marrying Louise he could rely on financial support from the Sachsel family. Now that he had turned sixty, he felt disinclined to squander his

* After the reunification of Germany, lorry-loads of documents were transferred from the East German State Archive in Merseburg to the Prussian State Archive in Berlin-Dahlem. In the course of this operation, the personal files of artists at the Kroll, including Zemlinsky's, appear to have been mislaid. Details of his Kroll contract are hence unavailable.

remaining reserves of energy on conducting in a provincial opera house. Having given Tietjen's offer due consideration, he declined it. For the first time since the death of his father, he was now master of his own will.

Mahagonny

Soon after completing the short score of *Der Kreidekreis* Zemlinsky set off for a Russian tour, with three concerts in Leningrad, on 9, 14 and 17 November. At the end of the month he was in Prague, where on 30 November he conducted a programme of Haydn, Brahms (B♭ major Piano Concerto with Arthur Rubinstein) and Mahler (First Symphony).

As soon as he arrived back in Berlin, rehearsals began for Weill's *Aufstieg und Fall der Stadt Mahagonny*. At the Kroll the luxury of state subsidy had provided for months of rehearsal. This in contrast was a commercial venture, promoted on a shoe-string budget by the impresario Ernst Josef Aufricht. The chosen venue, the Theater am Kurfürstendamm, was strategically placed in the midst of Berlin's night-life and entertainment district. Caspar Neher directed an ensemble that included three Brechtian artists of the first rank: Lotte Lenya, Trude Hesterberg and Harald Paulsen. Since the pit accommodated only fifteen musicians, Weill produced a new, radically reduced version of the score.

Mahagonny in Berlin was a calculated provocation. Performances in Leipzig, Frankfurt and elsewhere had been greeted with storms of right-wing protest, indeed to the extent that Universal Edition had urged the authors to excise or replace the more controversial scenes. Klemperer, though enthusiastic about the original *Songspiel* of 1927, had refused to perform the opera at the Kroll, evidently on moral grounds, and Max Reinhardt, who envisaged a production at the Deutsches Theater with Marlene Dietrich in the role of Jenny, was allegedly paid by the industrialist Fritz Thyssen *not* to go ahead with it.[7] Fearing eclipse by Brecht, and anxious to be accepted as a serious composer in his own right, it was Weill who took the initiative for Berlin. If state-run theatres were reluctant to stage his work, he would side-step officialdom and promote his work on the commercial circuit. His choice of conductor confirmed the seriousness of his intentions, and Aufricht ensured that, for the first time since 1918, the name appeared on billboards and in newspaper announcements complete with the obsolete *Adelsprädikat*, as Alexander von Zemlinsky.

Everything came together in three intensive weeks. 'I am at rehearsal from 9:00 in the morning to 1:00 at night,' wrote Weill to Universal Edition on 14 December, and added, 'Zemlinsky is absolutely great!!!'[8] The composer Rudolf Wagner-Régeny, who attended the dress rehearsal as Weill's guest, recalls a moment of crisis:

After a while there was some nervousness amongst the singers, evidently occasioned by some remark of Zemlinsky's. I saw Brecht, Neher, Weill and Zemlinsky rush on stage, and Weill standing close by with a gloomy look on his face. It was announced that the rehearsal would be interrupted for a whole hour. I had seated myself at a table somewhere outside to wait, when Weill came up to me with some orchestral parts under his arm, [. . .] spread them out on the table, inserted loose sheets of manuscript paper and, with intense care and concentration, started writing music, counting bars, calculating rests, occasionally smiling. In less than an hour, and without resorting to a full score, he had completed a new piece – albeit a short one – and the rehearsal could be resumed.[9]

Despite tensions backstage – during this period the partnership between Brecht and Weill came to an end – the production was a huge success. It opened on 21 December and ran *en suite* for over forty performances. The theatre (which seated 815) played to capacity audiences.[10] It was a milestone in the history of contemporary music-theatre. Weill's most ardent admirers, who had followed the work from one production to the next, knew the score by heart. 'Mahagonny has improved,' wrote Adorno:

Not only clearer in its content and surrealistic form, but also more compact, in a performance that at last reveals the immediacy of the music. It must be admitted that Zemlinsky's conducting makes all the difference. Perhaps because he senses a wellnigh apocryphal relationship to Weill's music via Mahler and the garishness of the banal, he has at last freed it from the misunderstanding of élan, jazz and diabolical amusement, and shows it in its true light, against a weightless, gaudy, yet profoundly sad backdrop, precisely focused to reveal all the cracks and crevices that a musical-comedy public (*Songpublikum*) prefers to ignore; above all in the *sound* that he wrests from this wretched handful of instruments, which possesses an expansive force that exceeds and surpasses the diffuser sound of many a larger orchestra.[11]

In the Recording Studio

Since 1928 Zemlinsky had been in sporadic demand as a recording artist. As none of his radio broadcasts appears to have been preserved (they included a concert of his own music for the RAVAG, Mahler's Second and Eighth Symphonies, *Das Lied von der Erde*, Beethoven's 'Choral' Symphony and the Missa Solemnis for Czech Radio), the only surviving aural evidence of his qualities as an interpreter is provided by a handful of shellac disks. His accompaniments to Puccini and Verdi arias sung by the tenor Rudolf Gerlach-Rusnak rate as little more than workmanlike; a disc with Jarmila Novotná in lollipops by Dvořák and Fibich, though charming, offered him little artistic scope; sour intonation and scrappy ensemble mar his recordings with the orchestra of the Städtische Oper, and in this respect even the playing of the Staatsoper orchestra leaves much to be desired. Two fine recordings with the orchestra of the Staatsoper, the overtures to *Die Fledermaus* and *Der Freischütz*, were never released, because they occupied three sides, and a filler for side 4 was never produced. As testimony to the art of a great conductor, only two productions qualify for serious consideration: the duet for Ford and Falstaff from Nicolai's *Die lustigen Weibe von Windsor*, with Gerhard Hüsch and Eugen Fuchs, recorded in 1932, and Smetana's *Vltava*, coupled with the Polka from Weinberger's *Schwanda the Bagpiper*, recorded with the Berlin Philharmonic approximately two years earlier.

Even so, the Nicolai is more a token than an achievement in its own right. But to hear it is to understand why critics in Vienna, Munich, Prague and Berlin lavished such praise on Zemlinsky's opera conducting, and explains the enthusiasm of such disparate musical personalities as Stravinsky, Schoenberg and Weill. The perfect, unforced ensemble between soloists and orchestra indicates that this is neither the work of a mere accompanist nor of a musical despot. Ensemble of such quality testifies to a deep-seated, unspoken empathy – in this case with two star singers, neither of whom had worked with Zemlinsky before. Naturalness belies technical discipline and artistic sophistication. With a scintillating sense of colour, clarity and flexibility of articulation, often extreme but never wayward *rubato*, above all with a bitter-sweet sense of humour that exactly touches the nerve of the drama, such music-making is pure *joie de vivre*.

In Smetana's *Vltava* the listener is invited to hear the score through the ears of a great orchestrator. Even with the modest means then available, more instrumental detail is audible on this old monaural disk than in many a modern recording. Zemlinsky offers no mere blueprint of the score, however, but a complete picture. He knows how to create a sense of liquid movement, subtly highlighting the all-important flow of semiquavers even in passages where they are usually submerged. With the same unforced precision, he achieves a natural flow of tempo, essential for sustaining Smetana's topographical and dramatic continuity; minute changes of pulse serve to emphasize, articulate and unify. In the celebrated E minor melody the Berlin violins sing out sweetly – perhaps even too vibrantly – but with no trace of sentiment or false pathos. The climax is grand but never bombastic. For depth and luminosity, the sound matches any of the Berlin Philharmonic's best post-war LP recordings.* In Weinberger's Polka the entertainer shines through once more. As in the 'rustic wedding' episode of the Smetana, Zemlinsky and his players perfectly capture the quirky Bohemian lift of the quaver movement; as in the Nicolai, every bar is vibrant with rhythm and colour.

Exodus

At the Reichstag elections on 31 July 1932 over 37 per cent of the electorate voted for the National Socialists. A coalition government led by Franz von

* Richard Warren, custodian of Zemlinsky's personal collection of shellac disks at Harvard University, has pointed out that the transfer to LP and CD (on Schwann mm 4001) is marred by a technical error (the application of RIAA equalization standards to a pre-RIAA recording).

Papen collapsed within a matter of weeks, and new elections were called for 6 November. With the Nazi contingent now slightly reduced, Hindenburg entrusted his military adviser Kurt von Schleicher with the formation of a new government, which took office on 3 December.

Two days later the Berlin Philharmonic Chorus celebrated its fiftieth anniversary with a dinner party at Hotel Esplanade. Eighty-nine guests sat down to a menu of game soup with sherry, stuffed young Styrian turkey and pineapple condé.[12] At the VIP table sat a dazzling array of artists (most of them with their wives): Carl Ebert, Wilhelm Furtwängler, Eugen Jochum, Otto Klemperer, Siegfried Ochs, Günther Ramin, Artur Schnabel, Bruno Walter and Zemlinsky.* Also invited were the conductors Paul Breisach and Karl Rankl, the critics Alfred Einstein and Max Marschalk, the pianist Erich Simon, and the musicologist Georg Schünemann, recently appointed successor to Schreker as Director of the Hochschule für Musik.

On 19 January 1933 Zemlinsky again conducted the 'Choral' Symphony in Prague, sung this time entirely in Czech, and preceded by the overture *Leonore no. 3* – Beethoven's wordless hymn to the triumph of righteousness over political oppression – and *Eine kleine Nachtmusik* – the quintessence of Mozartian equanimity and order.

On 30 January the new coalition government was sworn into office. With Hitler as Chancellor and Göring as minister without portfolio, three of the eleven cabinet ministers were Nazis.

On 8 February the Hochschule für Musik presented a concert with works by pupils from the Schoenberg class. During the performance of a string quartet by Max Jarczyk,[†] Paul Graener, himself a professor of composition at the Hochschule, walked out, denouncing the music as an insult to German culture. Six of his colleagues followed suit.[13]

On 12 February Zemlinsky was again in Prague, this time for a Wagner night. Prominent on the programme, which included the *Faust* overture, *Siegfried Idyll* and the *Tristan* prelude, was Hans Sachs's act III monologue from *Die Meistersinger*: 'Wahn, Wahn, überall Wahn' – 'Madness, madness all around'. Still in Prague, on 23 February he conducted Beethoven's Missa Solemnis, with its prayer in the Agnus Dei 'for personal and universal peace'.

Four days later, on 27 February, the Reichstag went up in flames. At a meeting of the Akademie der Künste on 1 March, Ash Wednesday, Zemlinsky's old friend Max von Schillings announced that the Jewish influence on German art would be broken. Schoenberg stood up and left.

Ousted from his position as Musical Director in Aachen, Paul Pella had

---

* The guests at 'Table A' also included Gertrud Hindemith, Gertrud Schoenberg and the concert agent Luise Wolff.
† Under the name of Michael Jary, Jarczyk later become well known as a composer of popular music.

come to Berlin in the summer of 1932, where he was engaged by the Berlin Reichssender to conduct a studio production of *Kleider machen Leute*. Towards the end of March, after three months of rehearsals, the management suddenly announced that the production had been cancelled.[14] Even the most mindless of optimists will not have failed to grasp the significance of this decision. For Zemlinsky it was the writing on the wall. Once again the grand piano was taken apart and prepared for freighting. Within a few weeks he had left Berlin, never to return.

X

The Humpbacked Mannikin

previous page:
Alexander Zemlinsky
caricature by Fred Dolbin
first published in *Musikblätter des Anbruch*, VII, 1925, 307

Das bucklichte Männlein[1]

(Des Knaben Wunderhorn)

Alexander Zemlinsky

EX. 78

[1] There I stand a-gardening, / watering the onions, / comes this humpbacked
mannikin / coughing and a-sneezing.

2 In I go to get the lunch, / want to stir the hot-pot, / there's this humpbacked mannikin / smashing up the dishes.

3 Off I go to my front room, / want to eat my porridge, / sits that humpbacked mannikin, / he's already scoffed it.

4 There I sit me down to work, / want to turn the spindle, /

there's this humpbacked mannikin / stops the wheel from turning.
5 Up into my room I go, / want to smooth the sheets down, / there's this humpbacked mannikin / chuckling with laughter.

6 There I kneel before my bench, / want to say my prayers, / there's that hump-backed mannikin, / suddenly starts talking: / 'Please my poppet, say a prayer / for the humpbacked mannikin!'

Of all the enigmatic and unearthly verses in *Des Knaben Wunderhorn*, *Das bucklichte Männlein* is arguably the most disquieting, the most calamitous. Hanno, the hyper-sensitive child of Thomas Mann's *Buddenbrooks*, murmurs the first verse in his sleep. Like many a nineteenth-century German schoolboy, he knows the poem from his reading book. 'It's really very awful,' comments his nanny as she stoops over the sleeping child.

This little hunchbacked man is everywhere. He smashes pots, eats the broth, steals the wood, keeps the spinning wheel from turning, makes fun of people – and then, at the end, he asks to be included in people's prayers. Yes, the lad's been fascinated by it. He's been thinking about it all day and all night. [Do you know what he said? Two or three times he said,] 'Don't you see . . . he doesn't do it because he's wicked, not because he's wicked! . . . He does it because he's sad, but that only makes him sadder. And if people pray for him, then he won't have to do it any more.'[2]

The youngest offspring of a once proud dynasty, Hanno dies of typhoid fever while still in his teens. Merely by quoting from the poem, Mann peremptorily seals the boy's fate.

Walter Benjamin considered the poem 'unfathomable'.[3] In his family the mannikin played the role of bogeyman: 'Greetings from the Clumsy One,' his mother would exclaim, if a child were to break a household object or trip and fall.

And now I understand what she meant. She meant the humpbacked mannikin, whose gaze was cast upon me. Whoever this mannikin singles out is heedless. Heedless of himself and of the mannikin. He stands aghast before a heap of rubble.[4]

In adult life Benjamin was relentlessly pursued by the mannikin's gaze. He submitted a brilliant dissertation on German baroque tragedy, only to see it rejected on grounds of incomprehensibility; due to political upheavals and financial difficulties, four of his most ambitious book projects remained unfinished;[5] by turning to the dialectical materialism of Marx he provoked a bitter controversy with his closest friend, the cabbala scholar Gershom Scholem, and another good friend, Adorno, censured him for acclaiming Brecht as the greatest German poet of his age. He lost his savings in the galloping inflation, never to regain them; his publishers went bankrupt, with disastrous consequences for his literary career. Fleeing from Paris in 1939 to avoid the bombing raids, he took refuge in Meaux; but while no bombs fell on Paris at all, Meaux, an assembly point of the French army, was under constant bombardment. In 1940 he acquired an American emergency visa. Lacking the necessary exit permit, he decided to trek across the Pyrenees into Spain. On the day he chose to flee, refugees were being sent back. During the night of 25–6 September he committed suicide in a police cell at Port Bou. One day earlier or a few days later he could have entered Spain with impunity.

Benjamin considered the mannikin a forerunner of the misshapen characters in Kafka:

Odradek [in *The Cares of a Family Man*][6] is the form that things assume when they are overlooked. They grow disfigured. The insect, which we know all too well is Gregor Samsa [in *Metamorphosis* . . .], is disfigured. [. . .] But these Kafkaesque characters are connected via a long line to the archetype of disfigurement, the hunchback. In Kafka's short stories one of the most frequent physical poses is that of the head sagging low over the chest. [In *The Trial*] this is the weariness of the court attendants, the noise of the hotel porters, the low ceiling over the visitors' gallery.[7]

The poem depicts a daily cycle of work, recreation, prayer and sleep. In this context Benjamin perceived sleep as oblivion and, in Kafka, oblivion as neglect. But oblivion, he observed, can also signify loving kindness. To forget is to forgive:

Das bucklichte Männlein symbolizes this very quality. This mannikin is the inmate of a disfigured life. With the advent of the Messiah – of whom a great rabbi once said that He will not change the world by force, but simply rearrange it a little – the mannikin will disappear.[8]

Unlike Benjamin, who saw himself as victim of the hunchback, Zemlinsky presents the mannikin as a drastic caricature of himself: a hapless little man, left standing 'aghast before a heap of rubble', whose lineage can be traced back to Görge, Strapinski and the Dwarf. According to his interpretation, the genderless 'Kindlein' is neither Princess nor Infanta, but the archetypal maiden of German folk poetry: not the sensuous, brown-skinned girl of the Symphonic Songs, however, but the virginal 'Schatz' of Mahler's *Lieder eines fahrenden Gesellen*, buxom, blue-eyed and blond, of whom Adorno once wrote:

The fact that Mahler, a Jew, foresaw fascism decades in advance [. . .] was no doubt the true motivation for the despair of the Wayfarer, who was 'sent out into the big, wide world' by two blue eyes.[9]

Long before the advent of Fascism in Germany, Schoenberg had often felt the sting of anti-Semitism; Zemlinsky, in contrast, had hitherto suffered no personal insult or injury on account of his non-Aryan background. With worldly wisdom, Schoenberg immediately apprehended the threat and acted to safeguard himself and his family; Zemlinsky, lulled like so many others into believing that 'it could never happen here', joined the lemming-like exodus from Germany to Austria.

Himself now a despairing wayfarer, he discovered in the text of *Das bucklichte Männlein* a heartfelt plea for tolerance and loving kindness. Beneath a surface of glassy humour, his song can be read as a dialogue between persecutor and persecuted, Aryan and Jew.

Three drafts of *Das bucklichte Männlein* were written in quick succession on
15 December 1934; presumably the fair copy followed soon after. Each of the
first three verses is 14 bars long; verse 4 is a little longer (17 bars), verse 5 a
little shorter (9 bars); taken together, verse 6 and the non-strophic final stanza
comprise 29 (14 + 15) bars.* Unlike the short score of *Der Kreidekreis*, none of
the *Männlein* manuscripts bears any visible sign of numerical organization. In
Zemlinsky's sense of the word, the underlying 14-bar periodic structure must
have been a coincidence.

While the accompaniment runs an almost operatic gamut of texture, dynamic
and register, the vocal line is of restricted range, and the text underlay (apart
from the single grace note in bar 23) entirely syllabic. Thematic or rhythmic
correspondences between voice and piano are minimal: in bar 17 the piano
twice reiterates the opening phrase of the vocal line, bar 22 in the piano anticipates the vocal line of bars 33–5, and at bar 68, the climax of verse 4, voice
and piano right hand move in rhythmic unison.

As in *Der Kreidekreis*, Zemlinsky characterizes each protagonist with a specific vocabulary of intervals, in this case an octave for the 'liebes Kindlein' and
a semitone for the hunchback: the octave as symbol of purity and consonance,
the semitone as the smallest interval, as source of dissonance and instability.
The confrontation of these two characters, mannikin and child, is articulated by
the play of tension between their two intervals. Initially the semitone corrupts
the purity of the octave; at the close the intervals unite in an optimistic gesture
of atonement.

Each line of text is delineated in the vocal line by an individual cell or
pattern, and each of these is individually varied from one verse to the next (see
EX. 79). Within a system of prosodic equilibrium, interrelationships between
adjacent cells are tenuous,† and the technique of variation applied to one cell
has little bearing on that applied to its neighbours.[10] To seek out one central
idea from which all else follows – whether directly or indirectly – is to discover
two interrelated ideas: the opening cells of verse 1 and of verse 6 (in the nomenclature of EX. 79: 1/i and 6/i). Their relationship recalls the motivic dualities of
Der Traumgörge (EXX. 27A and B) and *Der Zwerg* (EXX. 65A and B), a dialectic
of the straight and the crooked. Initially presented in misshapen form, the
disfigurement is here progressively reduced until the cell finally appears in its
pristine state as a simple triadic figure in B♭ major.

The intervening stages can be followed in EX. 79. Cells 1/i and 2/i follow the
outline of the 'Fate' chord (with an auxiliary C♯), as if the gravitational pull of
the hunchback's semitone had twisted the triad of 6/i out of shape; 3/i softens
the outline to its major-key equivalent, the 'Fortune' chord of *Der Kreidekreis*;

* Zemlinsky omits two verses of the original *Wunderhorn* text.
† Intercellular correspondences are indicated in EX. 79 by dotted lines.

EX. 79

both 4/*i* and 5/*i* further simplify the cell to the outline of a diminished 7th chord.

Cell *ii* inhabits the domain of F♯ minor, from which it scarcely strays. In 5/*ii* the enharmonic ambiguity of F♮ and E♯ serves to cast a bridge between the implied D minor environment of 5/*i* and the sharp-key pentatonicism of 5/*iii*.

The pliant chain of major 2nds in 1/*iii*, spanning a downward F♯ octave, functions as consequent to 1/*ii* and antecedent to 1/*iv*. Underlaid by a text that scarcely changes from verse to verse, cell *iii* is subjected to a wider degree of variation. In 2/*iii* the pitches are rearranged within a D-minor environment; in 3/*iii* the group is presented as image and mirror image; the first five pitches of 4/*iii* follow the line of the 'Fate' chord, now in B♭ minor, and in 5/*iii* the major 2nds of 1/*iii* reappear, but sequentially altered and in a pentatonic context.

In its original shape, cell *iv* imitates cell *i*, but extended by a two-note cadential formula. The harmonic implications of the line range from whole-tone harmony (1/*iv*) and pentatonicism (3/*iv*) to diatonicism (F minor with flattened supertonic in 2/*iv*, B♭ minor in 4/*iv*).

In verse 6 the hierarchy of cells is reduced to a rhythmic skeleton, the divergent harmonic implications of the previous verses give way to a stable, diatonic environment, and the verse-orientated rhythmic structure is replaced by a simple alternation of chorale and quasi-recitative. In each phrase the compass of the vocal line decreases, from octave to minor 6th to perfect 4th to minor 3rd.

Where the vocal line adheres to strophic form, the accompaniment unfolds with minimal regard for regular verse structure. The piano part is entirely the domain of the mannikin. Everything originates directly or indirectly from the hunchback's semitone and an anapaestic rhythm, ♫ ♩ or ♩. ♫ . These two diminutive ideas prove themselves capable of following every turn of events, illustrating every picture. The rhythmic pattern of the mirror canon in bars 1–2 suggests the hunchback's irregular, hobbling gait; a *crescendo*, followed by explosive demisemiquavers and a *ritardando* (bars 13–16) depicts his sneeze and its after-effects; the semitone on its own, reduced to a drone on E–F, becomes the hum of the spinning-wheel, and with a notated *ritardando* in bars 53–7 the anapaest literally 'stops the wheel from turning'. Transformed into an acciaccatura, the semiquaver also serves to portray the mannikin's hysterical laughter (bars 65–75).

In the alteration from implied D minor (bars 1–7, 16–21, 25 and 32) to affirmed D major (bars 8–10, 22–4 and 33–8) and thence to whole-tone harmony (bars 10–13 and 68–9) the accompaniment follows or anticipates the implicit harmony of the vocal line. Until the last verse, however, there is little harmonic rapport between voice and piano, indeed the one occasionally contradicts the other. At bar 40 the 'Fate' chord in the piano clashes defiantly with the B♭ of the voice; at the passage marked *ärgerlich* (bars 55–9), where the voice implies B♭ minor, the piano clings unremittingly to the major-key G♭7/B♭9 pattern of the previous bars.

After bar 12 the anapaestic rhythm submerges, not to return in its original form until the coda. Metamorphoses of the rhythm are found however in the hemiolas of bars 15–16 and 25–6 (further reduced in bars 19–21, middle voice), in the C–D♭ ostinato transition to verse 3 (bars 27–9) and the soft, expletive left-hand chords of bars 39 and 41 (with the second quaver now tied to the minim). Zemlinsky also exploits the suggestion of syncopation in the off-beat right-hand chords of the opening bars. With jerkily syncopated steps the hunchback follows the child from kitchen to living room (bars 33–8); a pathetic, syncopated figure accompanies the turning of the spinning-wheel (bars 44–52, inner parts); syncopated left-hand interjections accompany the hunchback's laughter (bars 65–77).

As his laughter dies away, the anapaest dissolves into a long chain of 3rds, syncopated in the left hand, and coloured in the right hand by plaintive acciaccaturas: musical gestures shared between the mannikin and Mime, the tormented dwarf of Wagner's *Ring*. For all its simplicity, the final page of the piano part is pure music-drama. As the girl kneels to pray, the accompaniment graphically depicts the hunchback prostrating himself before her. With the re-entry of his anapaestic rhythm in bar 82 one can almost visualize him hobbling cautiously towards the child.

As the bass line falls by a semitone to A, voice and piano finally meet in D major. With the anapaest nervously hopping in the background, the mannikin addresses the child. His song of contrition draws on the pitch material of the opening bars, and his vocal line is still disfigured, with the B♭ on 'Kindlein' clashing against the second inversion triad in the accompaniment. The 'Clumsy One' accordingly modifies his phrase by a semitone, but in the wrong direction, to B♮. As if anxious to communicate, the accompaniment shifts to B minor. Bars 93–4 invert the line of 'ach ich bitt', which folds graciously back on itself into the pure, pentatonic curve of the 'World' motif. Beneath a compliant chordal accompaniment, the piano left hand now 'rearranges things a little'. The hunchback's semitone is inverted, transforming the smallest interval into the largest, as if unobtrusively to proclaim the gospel that 'some who are now last will be first, and some who are first will be last'. In the closing bar, with the falling 7th doubled at the octave, conflict between the opposing parties is finally resolved.

To compare Zemlinsky's first drafts with his fair copies or printed editions is to uncover a creative process virtually unconcerned with technical problems, based entirely on intuition. First came the act of spontaneous creation, then followed a process of rationalization and refinement. Most ideas came to him in an advanced state of development, and many took form, no doubt, long before they were committed to paper. His first task was to trace each idea to its origin. Once a lowest common factor had been identified, he would build on it. Even so, the logic of a form often came clear to him only when a work was in its final stages. Werner Loll has shown that Zemlinsky often made last-minute changes that were anything but trivial. In the Second Quartet, for instance, the first scherzo theme (EX. 48G) was a late interpolation, and even the first two bars of the work (EX. 48A) were added as an afterthought.[11]

In *Das bucklichte Männlein* the ingenious glass-bead game of intervals and rhythms emerged intuitively during the course of composition. Even the final gesture of atonement, it transpires, was unpremeditated: the all-important octaves in the last bar were added to the fair copy at a later juncture, and then only in pencil.

From the point where the voice enters, discrepancies between the fair copy and the two main drafts[12] of the song (henceforth identified as *A* and *B*) are slight. In *A* the tritone figure of bars 11–12 (left hand) is doubled in octaves, and the right-hand octave in bar 25 is added only in *B*.* In *B* (but not in *A*)

---

* These changes are of consequence in that the piano part is otherwise devoid of octaves.

much of verse 4 is barred in 3/4 time, and the left-hand interjections in verse 5 are notated as syncopated quavers. In both drafts the interlude before verse 6 was originally only two bars long, and even in the fair copy the extra bars were a subsequent addition, indicated by a repeat sign in blue pencil. The vocal line of *A*, verses 1–3, is substantially identical to the fair copy; apart from a high-pitched *ossia* for bars 82–6, rising to a high B on the word 'reden', *B* differs here only in small details. The discrepancies in the piano introduction are more far-reaching.

In *A* the introduction is 7 bars long (EX. 80A); in *B* the passage is shortened by stages to 4 bars (EX. 80B). The symmetry of bars 1–2 and 3–4 is eliminated, triadic harmony partially replaced by implied polyphony, and a new variant of the opening idea (EX. 80A, bars 5–6) expunged. In *A* the left-hand tritones (bars 1–4), right-hand 3rds and left-hand 5ths (bars 5–6) stake claims to sovereignty almost equal to that of the semitone. In *B* the configuration of tritones and 3rds is discarded, but not until the final version does Zemlinsky find the logical and economical solution of contrary motion in semitones. Raising the salient pitches, Bb and A (bar 2, left hand), to Bb and B♮, served to tauten the motivic logic: now the outer parts mirrored each other exactly, and the asymmetrical voice-leading, with semitones and one whole-tone, matched the irregularity of rhythm.

EX. 80A   first draft, opening

EX. 80B   second draft, opening

EX. 81   second draft, as from bar 71

The same processes of logic and economy apply to the patterns and cells of the vocal line. Astonishing as it may seem, the octave span of the phrase 'Wenn ich an mein Bänklein knie' was added only as an afterthought, in *B*. In other words, Zemlinsky identified the principal motif of the composition *only after he had completed two drafts of it* – and then in the B minor of pain rather than the B♭ major of contentment (EX. 81).

As Schoenberg once wrote, 'The method by which balance is restored seems to me the real *idea* of a composition.'[13] In his essay 'Brahms the Progressive', of which every sentence echoes the artistic credo of his former mentor, he wrote in greater detail of the search for the idea, of the joy and profundity of craftsmanship:

A craftsman likes to be conscious of what he produces; he is proud of the ability of his hands, of the flexibility of his mind, of his subtle sense of balance . . . and last but not least of the profundity of his idea and his capacity of penetrating to the most remote consequences of an idea. One cannot do this with a shallow idea, but one can, and one can *only*, with a profound idea – and there one *must*.[14]

XI

Vienna 1933–1938

Line 38

The Zemlinskys spent the summer of 1933 in a five-room apartment at Casa Camuzzi in Montagnola. Set amid palms and cypresses in a garden overlooking Lake Lugano, the villa had until 1931 had been the home of Hermann Hesse; here, in blessed isolation, he had conceived his great novel *The Glass Bead Game*. At first Zemlinsky was tempted to settle permanently in Tessin – 'Lugano is a pleasure to the eye & an inviting place to live,' he wrote – but soon he missed the pulse of city life. There were practical drawbacks too. For lack of personnel, Hansi had to attend to the household, and Louise struggled valiantly in the kitchen, with Zemlinsky's dog Pepi missing no opportunity to get under her feet. For much of the time it was too cold and damp to sit on the terrace, and dinner – usually a simple meal of ham and eggs – was taken in the salon around an open fire. Even if nothing was quite ideal, they were at least in safety.[1]

For several weeks they enjoyed the company of Louise's brother Otto. Already sickly as a child, at thirty-two he was suffering from the first symptoms of an incurable liver disease. A friend of the family remembered him well:

Tall and incredibly thin, with refined features, reddish-brown hair slightly greying at the temples, a sun-tanned complexion and a small moustache, he had the bearing of an old-world Austrian army officer. [. . .] But the expression in his eyes was sad, and sometimes his cheek muscles would contract with pain.[2]

In mid-September Otto returned to Paris, where he was in charge of the French branch of the family business, while Louise returned to Berlin to supervise the move and attend to the necessary paperwork.[3] Back in Vienna, she and Zemlinsky settled into an apartment at Mariannengasse 28, a few minutes' walk from the Volksoper.

Even if Zemlinsky's departure from Berlin was determined by *force majeure*, his return to Vienna signified the fulfilment of a long-cherished ambition. Vienna was the womb in which his art had gestated, the breast that had nourished him. Politics aside, he was Görge now, bride in hand, returning to his village. 'During the past twenty years,' observes the Viennese musicologist Ernst Hilmar, '[. . .] it had been brought home to him here that neither he nor his artistic experience were really needed.'[4] But Zemlinsky no longer cared whether he was still 'needed'. After an involuntary exile of over twenty years, his fondest wish was to settle on the bank of his beloved millstream – and dream.

Whether needed or not, he soon found work for himself. The recession of 1929 had caused as much hardship in Austria as elsewhere, and drastic cuts in public spending left many artists out of work. In 1931 a group of unemployed musicians pooled their resources to found a privately financed body, the Wiener Konzertorchester, with Hermann Scherchen as Musical Director. In the summer of 1933 Scherchen took up a new appointment as Principal Conductor of the Zurich Radio Orchestra, and Zemlinsky was invited to take over his Viennese commitments.* Even if the orchestra was not of the first rank, and its financial situation precarious, the offer was attractive. He was happy to accept.

His first and most urgent task, however, was to supervise rehearsals for the world première of *Der Kreidekreis* in Zurich. To this end, he returned to Switzerland during the first week of October 1933, accompanied by his old friend Paul Stefan.

Der Kreidekreis *Goes the Rounds*

Universal Edition had drawn up contracts with four German theatres[5] – Berlin, Frankfurt, Cologne and Nuremberg – to stage simultaneous world premières of *Der Kreidekreis*. On the season's roster of operatic novelties the score ranked second in importance only to Strauss's *Arabella* (scheduled for Dresden on 1 July 1933) – but then came the Nazi ban.

With the rise of the Third Reich, the focal point of the avant-garde in Central Europe should by rights have shifted to Austria. But the arts in Vienna had fallen on hard times: money was scarce, tastes were capricious, and even here nobody was entirely safe from Nazi slander. Under the directorship of Clemens Krauss, such funds as were available for new music at the Staatsoper were squandered on sub-Straussian banalities: Julius Bittner's *Das Veilchen*, for instance, premièred in 1934, Marco Frank's *Die fremde Frau*, Bernhard Paumgartner's *Rossini in Neapel* and Jaromír Weinberger's *Wallenstein*, all added to the repertoire in 1937.[6] As an enticement to paying clientele from the private theatres, furthermore, the Staatsoper lifted its statutory ban on operetta for the world première of Lehár's *Giuditta* in January 1934 (*Das Land des Lächelns* followed in January 1938). For progressive composers the outlook was bleak.

In January 1933 Universal Edition sent Krauss a vocal score of *Der Kreidekreis*, but his opinion of the piece was unfavourable, largely on account of the 'extensive passages of spoken dialogue'. Not to be deterred, Zemlinsky drew his attention to the Berlin première and urged him to attend it. Though professing 'great interest in seeing a performance', Krauss ignored the invitation

---

* Initially the first four concerts were offered 'at a very modest fee' to Klemperer (unpublished letter from Klemperer to his wife, 10 May 1933).

and merely sent an emissary, Ministerialrat Wisoko, to the première in Graz. Wisoko's report settled the matter for once and for all:

I do not believe that the work would be a box-office success for the Staatsoper, and from an artistic point of view I see no particular need to perform it.[7]

The rescue of *Der Kreidekreis* by the Zurich Stadttheater was neither the work of Swiss Good Samaritans nor a collective gesture of political protest. Credit went entirely to the First *Kapellmeister*, Robert Kolisko,* seconded by the Director of the Zurich opera, Karl Schmid-Bloss. At his behest Universal Edition had been negotiating since 1931 to mount a production of *Kleider machen Leute*. With the ban in Germany, it now seemed expedient to defer *Kleider machen Leute* and substitute *Der Kreidekreis*. Contrary to expectation, Kolisko was thus delighted to find himself in charge of the world première.

Zemlinsky was not quite so delighted. 'I am just off to rehearsal,' he wrote to Louise on Saturday 7 October:

Today just stage and piano. Act 1 very nice (*sehr nett*). With *our* first act I am *well* satisfied. On stage, with certain exceptions, very atmospheric. But the worst at present is the orchestra. Kolisko is simply not a good conductor, doesn't know how to rehearse. We are contemplating postponement.[8]

The following day Paul Stefan presented a matinée for the Zurich Theaterverein, which included extracts from Zemlinsky's operas, sung at the piano. As Zemlinsky reported to Louise:

The pieces seem to have gone down well, judging at least by individual reactions. Afterwards a splendid lunch party (twelve people), very luxurious & very agreeable. Later I was with Dr Kaufmann, President of the Theaterverein, a fellow with pots of money (*ein reicher Hund*) [. . .], who also took me and P. Stefan for a ride in his car. Now I'm off with Stefan to dinner at Kolisko's.[9]

The première, on 14 October (Zemlinsky's sixty-second birthday), was broadcast live on Radio Zurich. During the final week of rehearsal Kolisko had evidently succeeded in setting his musical house in order, and the production by Schmid-Bloss, which followed Chinese theatre tradition by presenting the singers on a narrow walkway across the orchestra pit, was more than serviceable. Though not the great occasion Zemlinsky and his publishers had hoped for, it was at least an occasion. Willy Schuh wrote in the *Neue Zürcher Zeitung* of a 'trace of refinement that signifies the renunciation of operatic banality',[10] and found that Zemlinsky had 'again assumed the role of lyricist rather than of

---

* Kolisko (1891–1974) studied theory with Zemlinsky, Schoenberg and Schreker. Before his engagement in Zurich he conducted at Klagenfurt, Ulm, Dortmund, Teplitz (Teplice) and, during Zemlinsky's last season, the NDT (Paul Stefan refers to him in his review of the world première as a 'well-known personality in Prague'). After 1945 he was Administrative Director of the Vienna Symphony Orchestra.

gripping dramatist'. '[The opera] seeks no fresh path in the constructive sense,'
reported Herbert Graf from Basle for the *Tageblatt*, 'but stands at the turning
point between impressionism and modernism.'¹¹ While the local press found
little to praise, Paul Stefan filed an enthusiastic review for *Der Auftakt*, in which
he wrote of Zemlinsky as an 'exquisite artist' and cautiously ventured the opinion that this was 'perhaps the finest' of all his operas, 'certainly the most catchy,
and not only valuable but also significant for our time'.¹² His colleague Paul A.
Pisk sent an even more positive report to *Anbruch* in Vienna, of which a shortened version appeared in a Sunday edition of the *New York Times*:

> It appears that [Zemlinsky's] latest work [. . .] may prove his greatest artistic and
> popular success. [. . .] The orchestra sounds beautiful, the melodies are rich and
> tasteful. The Chinese atmosphere is characterized most discreetly by four chords
> and by several kinds of battle drums. The musical impression is, together with the
> action, strong and absorbing. [. . .] The conductor [was] Dr Robert Kolisko, a young
> Viennese artist, who gave careful rehearsals and followed the intentions of the
> composer.* [. . .] Already at the opening performance, after the first act, there was
> a great ovation, while later on the composer was called repeatedly to the stage and
> the success of his work was extraordinary. Zemlinsky's *Kreidekreis* seems to be one
> of the best German operas of the last ten years.¹³

A few days later Zemlinsky was back in Vienna for rehearsals with the Konzertorchester. For his first appearance, a Sunday afternoon concert on 22 October,
he chose a programme of Beethoven and Mahler, in which he was joined by a
friend from Hofoper days, Madame Cahier. Highlights of his November concerts were Hindemith's Concert Music op. 49 for piano, two harps and brass
(12 November, with Eduard Steuermann), *Das Lied von der Erde* (16
November) and Franz Schmidt's Beethoven Variations for piano left-hand and
orchestra (26 November, with Paul Wittgenstein). During the spring of 1934
concerts became more sporadic and the repertoire less enterprising – sure indications of financial straits. In September 1934 Zemlinsky relinquished his post
in favour of a fellow exile from Berlin, Paul Breisach from the Städtische Oper.

Meanwhile in Germany, after the initial reaction of striking out blindly at
anything and everything 'un-German', Hitler and his ideologists were taking
measures to gain control of the unruly SA (culminating in the so-called 'Night
of the Long Knives' of 30 June 1934), to organize every aspect of public life
according to a system of rigid hierarchies, and to draw up jurisdiction on racial
policies (as defined by the Nuremberg *Rassengesetze* of 1935). Efforts were

* During the final week of rehearsals Kolisko evidently received a crash course in orchestral
conducting. Thirty years later he wrote: 'My thoughts are always of Zemlinsky, the master.
What in his eyes counted as the art of interpretation is today scarcely to be found' (letter to
Louise Zemlinsky, c.1963, NLZ Da 30).

meanwhile made to win the confidence of neighbouring states and to present the new regime as a reliable trading partner. Since these latter, pseudo-conciliatory measures also applied to the arts, theatre directors and concert managements were notified that, within certain limits, they could now fulfil their pre-1933 contractual obligations. As abruptly as the ban on *Der Kreidekreis* had been imposed, it was lifted.

The first stage of this unexpected odyssey for Zemlinsky's opera was Stettin, where the *Reichsdeutsche* première was given on 16 January 1934, conducted by Gustav Grossmann and directed by Friedrich Siems. Stuckenschmidt, who had travelled up from Berlin, applauded Zemlinsky's new economy and approachability:

As an artist of experience, he commands a wellnigh inexhaustible range of lyric and dramatic expression. [. . .] With regard to harmony, Zemlinsky strives to compromise between tonality and the unrelenting chromaticism of his earlier works. Compared with the melodic and textural means of expression to which he, as a friend of Mahler and Schoenberg, is normally accustomed, here he has sought and found simpler solutions.[14]

Another Berlin critic, Karl Westermayer, commended the Stettin ensemble, but poured scorn on Klabund and damned Zemlinsky with faint praise:

During this period of transition in our country, performances of this work may be instructive and, for certain sections of the opera audience, even effective. But for the youth of Germany they can be of no interest whatsoever.[15]

The curtain had risen to cat-calls from a group of Brown-shirts, whose protests continued sporadically throughout the performance: reason enough for the Burgomaster to declare the opera 'incompatible with the spirit of the new Germany' and ban all further performances. It was probably Tietjen, fearing cancellation of his première at the Staatsoper, who immediately lodged a protest with the Ministry of Culture. The minister in turn referred the matter to his arbiter on music and drama, the theatre critic Rainer Schlösser, for whom the Nazis had created the post of *Reichsdramaturg*. Having read the libretto,* Schlösser declared it to be 'unobjectionable' (*unbedenklich*), save for a few lines of spoken dialogue in the tea-house scene. These were excised.[†] With this assurance from on high, calculated primarily to censure the wilful act of a small-town politician, further productions opened, as planned, in Coburg

---

* Zemlinsky had entirely overlooked the question of copyright. Fortunately Klabund's widow, Carola Neher, raised no objection (Zemlinsky probably knew her personally through her brother Caspar), and the libretto was published by Phaidon Verlag, Vienna, in 1933.
† As transpires from the Zurich prompter's copy of the vocal score (*LoC* 23/2), Tong's account of his voluntary castration (act I/1), which fell victim to Schlösser's scissors, had already been cut at the world première. Nobody in Nazi Germany appears to have been offended by Wagner's euphemistic treatment of the same theme in *Parsifal*.

(21 January), Berlin (23 January) and Nuremberg (25 January); Graz followed, with a live broadcast, on 9 February.* In Berlin alone *Der Kreidekreis* ran for no fewer than twenty-one performances. For a few weeks Zemlinsky enjoyed a run of success, the like of which he had not experienced in over thirty years.

It had been Klemperer's intention to stage at least one Zemlinsky opera in Berlin, indeed negotiations for *Kleider machen Leute* were all but finalized when the closure of the Kroll caused the project to founder. With an undeniable sense of fair play, the much maligned Tietjen offered to compensate by staging the world première of *Der Kreidekreis* at the Staatsoper. Now that he had been forced to rescind his *ius primae noctis* to Zurich, Zemlinsky in turn compensated for the loss of prestige by composing two additional interludes for the scene changes before and after act III–6. As the dramaturg Julius Kapp argued in his programme note, at least these few pages of orchestral music qualified as a world première.† His explanation for the delay itself was a masterpiece of Orwellian Newspeak:

It would have been unpropitious to deliver such a quiet-spoken, self-willed work into the world on the rising wave of joy and excitement engendered by the final victory of our national uprising. Therefore, with the consent of the author and his publisher, the performance was postponed.[16]

With Robert Heger as conductor, Franz Ludwig Hörth as director, Emil Praetorius as designer, and a fine cast of singers (including Susanne Fischer as Haitang, Fritz Krenn as Ma and Fritz Soot as Tong), the Staatsoper gave of its best. Only the handling of the spoken dialogue, rendered in a bewildering variety of regional dialects, provoked adverse comment.

Several critics who had sent in reports from Stettin were writing about the work for a second time within a matter of days. In his earlier review Stuckenschmidt had cited Mahler and Schoenberg as Zemlinsky's closest musical allies, names that invariably caused Nazi hackles to rise. Anticipating vituperative reactions to the work by his right-wing colleagues, he now wrote, with calculated effrontery, 'One would have to be struck blind and deaf not to acknowledge the high artistic value of this (intentionally restrained) music.'‡[17]

* Further contracts with Frankfurt and Chemnitz remained unfulfilled; Cologne performed *Kleider machen Leute* as a substitute (see p. 173).
† They had in fact already been performed at Stettin and Coburg!
‡ Shortly afterwards Stuckenschmidt was debarred from journalism, and by the autumn he had left the country. Until 1942, when he was called up for active service, he wrote for the *Prager Presse*. With his interest in the 'glass-bead games' of music, it comes as no surprise that he was the first to draw attention to the language of symbols in Zemlinsky's score: '[In the previous review] it was pointed out how ingeniously 4ths harmony is combined with pentatonicism (the five-note scale C–D–E–G–A is after all merely a condensed form of the five-note 4ths chord E–A–D–G–C). No mention was made of the finesse with which the 'Chalk Circle' theme flows into its own mirror image, thus actually turning back on itself to symbolize the circle' (*B.Z. am Mittag*, 24 January 1934).

Westermayer, on the other side of the political fence, pounced on Schlösser's word *unbedenklich*: 'The work is not only unobjectionable in the context of contemporary issues, but tame (*harmlos*) and, viewed in the long term as a work of art, meaningless.'[18] Rudolf Bilke, as if directly responding to Stuckenschmidt's provocation, called attention to the composer's 'degenerate' artistic roots:

Here Zemlinsky is the wolf in sheep's clothing. While masquerading as a serious composer, he is attempting to smuggle that music back into Germany whose leading exponents (Schoenberg, Schreker) have at last left the country. [. . .] To speak approvingly of Zemlinsky would be to support the demand of these other persons to be welcomed back on a red carpet.[19]

Similarly hostile receptions in Berlin for Hindemith's *Mathis der Maler* Symphony (premièred by Furtwängler on 12 March) and Berg's *Lulu* Suite (with Kleiber, on 30 November) showed that the Nazis' new-found tolerance for the avant-garde was mere pretence. The curtain fell for a second time. When it rose again, three-quarters of Germany's opera houses lay in ruins.

In 1940 Herbert Gerick published his *Lexikon der Juden in der Musik*, an exhaustive list of musicians, dead or alive, known or suspected to be of non-Aryan parentage. Zemlinsky was listed with an 'H' (for 'half-Jew', which was inaccurate), with the appended remark that he was 'Jewish by marriage (*jüdisch versippt*); brother-in-law of Arnold Schoenberg, to whose works he lent emphatic support'.

Louise recalled that during the summer of 1933 Schoenberg wrote from France with news of his return to the Jewish faith, urging his former brother-in-law to follow suit. Zemlinsky was uncertain how to react. According to Louise, it was she who dissuaded him, arguing that he had no need to jeopardize his position still further. Whatever the facts – and it must be stressed that they are supported only by tenuous oral evidence – Zemlinsky's unwillingness to follow Schoenberg's call signified the final break. 'I was angry that Schoenberg's love for him was so limited,' said Louise, 'and so I have torn up all the Schoenberg letters. They no longer exist.'[20] A baffling remark, for over 150 holograph letters from Schoenberg exist even today, and she herself watched over their publication with an eagle eye. She may, however, have destroyed letters on the delicate subject of conversion, for apart from a telegram of congratulation on the birth of Ronald Schoenberg,[21] there is a gap of over ten years in the correspondence, from February 1929 until the late autumn of 1939.* How deeply Zemlinsky was troubled by the estrangement can be read, if only between the lines, in his contribution to the Festschrift for Schoenberg's sixtieth birthday, written the following summer. Their friendship had been 'intimate', he recalled; now, from 'bitter struggles' against his adversaries,

* The editor of *Web-Br* offers no explanation for the gap.

Schoenberg had emerged 'as victor'.[22] Alma's remark that Zemlinsky 'became Schoenberg's pupil' may appear malicious, but it did reflect uninformed public opinion: even as perspicacious a writer as Stuckenschmidt detected in Zemlinsky's art the influence of Schoenberg.

Once Zemlinsky had left Berlin, he never again set foot on German soil. Though unwilling to appear before the curtain in Stettin or Nuremberg, he was delighted to acknowledge the enthusiasm of his public in Prague. On 8 December 1934, at a concert broadcast live on Czech Radio, he conducted Novák's Serenade in G op. 36 and Mahler's Second Symphony. The following evening at the NDT, again with a live transmission, he witnessed as fine a performance of his opera as he could have wished for. Directed by Renato Mordo, designed by Emil Pirchan, and with the young Hilde Konetzni in the role of Haitang, the work was in even more capable hands than in Berlin. Star of the evening, as reported in *Bohemia*, was the conductor:

Georg Szell approaches the score with all the élan of his rhythmic decisiveness and with his unique art of sonic differentiation. The delicate outer shell of lyricism remains transparent, the expressive power of the drama undiminished.[23]

Zemlinsky was infuriated to hear that the *Intendant*, Paul Eger,* had scheduled only three further performances. Tacitly admitting that he had underestimated the work's popular appeal, Eger later invited him to conduct an extra performance himself, perhaps to be followed by a more extensive revival. On return from his third and last visit to Russia, in January–February 1935,[†] Zemlinsky replied:

The fact that my opus has been scheduled for a Sunday afternoon will not exactly be beneficial, will it!? But *modest* as I am, I console myself with the prospect of a 'later date'. And *immodest* as I am, I do not think that my work counts as the weakest of modern operas.[24]

'Ich muss wieder einmal in Grinzing sein'[‡]

For the summer of 1934 Louise packed her husband and step-daughter off to Königswart. Left to her own devices, she supervised the clearance of the apart-

---

* Eger (1881–1947) had been associated with the NDT since 1911, when Teweles engaged him as Dramaturg; as staff producer he was also responsible for Zemlinsky's first NDT performances of *Figaro* and *Die Meistersinger*. From 1912 he was *Intendant* at Darmstadt, and from 1918 at Hamburg (Deutsches Schauspielhaus). After the closure of the NDT in 1938 he was appointed Director of the Stadttheater Lucerne, a post he held until shortly before his death.

† It was perhaps symptomatic of the growing hostility towards Western contemporary music that Zemlinsky's Leningrad programmes were more classical on this visit, with Haydn and Mahler (26 January), an all-Beethoven programme (28 January), a concert of Schubert, Brahms and Mozart (31 January) and Handel's *Acis and Galatea*, coupled with a repeat performance of Beethoven's Fifth Symphony (3 February).

‡ 'To Grinzing again I must wend my way': popular song by Ralph Benatzky, composed in 1915.

ment in the Mariannengasse, moved into Pension Columbia (a few blocks away in the Kochgasse) and took charge of the final stages in the building of her new house.

It has always been assumed that Zemlinsky himself purchased a plot of land at Kaasgrabengasse 24 in Grinzing. Yet the property was registered in Louise's name, and it was she who dealt with the building contractors; no doubt it was also her decision to install a 'dream' kitchen, complete with refrigerator, and though she never laboured the point, it would appear that the project was financed largely, if not entirely, by herself and her family. Even if she remained a willing slave, this was one area in which she could assert her independence. Another, incidentally, was transport: following the example of the Bergs, Louise acquired a driving licence and bought herself a small, black Ford.[25]

The stresses and strains of a house-owner *in spe* proved at times almost too much for her. When in early July she sent a few snapshots to Königswart, Zemlinsky found her accompanying letter 'nervous and jittery'.

The pictures are not very clear either, perhaps because of the windows. You haven't mentioned how far they have got with the interior. – The terrace appears not even to have been started. [. . .] Here everything is just fine. The food is very good, but too plentiful. You seem to have given Maria instructions to fatten me up! But I'll have none of it! [. . .] I beg you, try to keep calm, go to a doctor if need be.[26]

By the end of the summer the ordeal was over. The villa stood in its own grounds on a tree-lined side street, pristine and ultra-modern. It was precisely that haven built for two of which Zemlinsky had always dreamed ('a small, subdued living room, cosy – but beautiful, very beautiful', as he once described it to Alma): a synthesis of undogmatic Viennese modernism and cool Bauhaus precision, custom-designed by the young Hoffmann pupil Walter Loos.* To a latter-day observer, jaded by post-war council-estate imitations, the building has all the charm of a concrete box. Its squat, foreshortened façade recalls the artist who once lived in it (the interior is said to have been very beautiful), and whether out of deference or indifference to the outside world, only one window overlooks the street. Placed almost secretively to one side, the entrance admonishes chance callers to keep away: 'I cannot see you now. I am busy.'

Grinzing, with its bosky hills and lively *Heurigen* taverns, had always been a popular destination for ramblers and weekend trippers. Under Lueger the area developed into a modern garden suburb, conveniently accessible from the city centre by tram (line 38). In due course it also became a residential area favoured by the Viennese intelligentsia. Many exiles later found approximations to Grinzing in Hampstead village or Beverly Hills, in the more salubrious suburbs

* See plate 26. The Viennese-born architect and writer Walter Loos (1905–1974, no relation of his celebrated colleague Adolf Loos) specialized in detached and semi-detached private houses. Apart from several projects in Vienna, he also worked in Germany and France. In 1938 he emigrated to Buenos Aires.

of Buenos Aires, Cape Town and Melbourne, or in areas north of downtown Tel Aviv – but for the real thing there was no replacement. Egon Wellesz and his wife Emmy lived three doors away in a spacious *Jugendstil* villa designed by Josef Hoffmann; other close neighbours were Hugo Botstiber, Emil Hertzka's widow Yella,* and Hans Gál; further up the hill, in the Strassergasse, lived Sigmund Freud, and in the village itself Elias and Veza Canetti.

When Louise was busy or preferred to stay at home, Zemlinsky thought nothing of taking line 38 into town, indeed a tram-stop stood conveniently at the end of the street. As the carriage gradually filled with passengers, Canetti would often observe the celebrated maestro, with his 'black, birdlike head and prominent, triangular nose', as he got in and took his seat:

I could never look at him without a sense of awe, I could sense the concentration in that tiny face, marked as it was by purely spiritual processes, stern, almost sparse, with none of the self-importance of the conductor that he actually was. [. . .] When I looked at him, I had no idea that he was also a composer.[27]

Swansong

Yet Zemlinsky had come to Vienna primarily to compose. Educated amateurs such as Canetti should grow aware of him as a creative artist; experts such as Stuckenschmidt, who discovered in his art the influence of Schoenberg, should cease to confuse cause with effect. That was his ambition.

First fruits of his new, more leisurely lifestyle were the Six Songs (originally *Abendlieder*) op. 22, composed in January 1934. Soon afterwards, on 8 March, he started work on a more substantial project, the Sinfonietta op. 23, written as if to order. Several years before, namely, in answer to his complaint that Universal Edition was not doing enough to propagate his music, Hans Heinsheimer had written:

The greatest obstacle is that we have no purely orchestral work of yours. As soon as soloists are involved, marketing becomes far more difficult. It is a crying shame that the wonderful Lyric Symphony is not performed more often. I have already spoken to many conductors about it, and the reason for their disinclination is always the entirely superficial argument of feasibility. Would you not care to write an orchestral work, short and practical in its requirements, hence also easier to market?[28]

Apart from these immutable laws of commerce, it was only logical that Zemlinsky should continue to pursue the clear, economical course of the Symphonic Songs and *Der Kreidekreis*. The essence of his three-movement Sinfonietta is brevity.† For all its textual complexity, with polyphony in as many

* Hertzka had died in 1932.
† Performing times range between *c*.16' (in the Mitropoulos broadcast of 1941) to *c*.24' (in recent CD recordings). Zemlinsky's own estimated timing was 'circa 20 minutes' (unpublished letter to Oswald Kabasta, 24 September 1934, courtesy of Günther Verbeet).

as six or seven rapidly moving strands, textures remain hard-edged and transparent. For all its brilliance and intensity, the orchestra is relatively small: double woodwind, a standard contingent of brass and percussion, one harp. 'Fatten me up! I'll have none of it!' he wrote to Louise soon afterwards. This lean, ascetic outlook of approaching old age applies to much of his later music (one could speak of a 'Grinzing style', were it not that the Sinfonietta was composed before the move to the Kaasgrabengasse): unwillingness to indulge or waste time, coupled – at least in this work – with an almost disturbing readiness to laugh. Like the house itself, Zemlinsky's later style is an absorbing synthesis of Austrian *Gemütlichkeit* and German *Sachlichkeit*: modern music without tears, yet with a nagging awareness of tears forcibly suppressed.

In contrast to the social engagement of the Symphonic Songs, the Sinfonietta is a highly personal creation. For all its outward show of bravura – and this is perhaps Zemlinsky's most virtuosic score – the music often speaks with words. Their meaning, however, is cryptic. Composed only a few weeks after the *Kreidekreis* premières in Stettin and Berlin, the work appears infected by the spirit of that mad carousel which had whirled Zemlinsky's music through the opera houses of the Third Reich. Visions of joy and anxiety, pride and sorrow, humour and grief pass by with bewildering rapidity, intermingle, affirm and negate.

Perhaps as an allusion to the motto of Korngold's Sinfonietta op. 5, the 'motif of a joyous heart' (EX. 38A), the outer movements are encircled by fanfares of 2nds and 4ths, to which Zemlinsky adds a sly, semitonal twist (EX. 82).

The first subject of the opening movement, in Lydian D major, expounds on the 'Self' motif (F♯–G♯–B), but its aggressive upward thrust is immediately answered by the falling-5ths motif of the sixth Maeterlinck Song: 'Wohin gehst du?' In the second movement, a *Ballade* in B♭ minor, the same figure provides the substance for a solemn processional (EX. 83).

Shortly before the climax of the *Ballade*, a line from Haitang's 'Song of the Caged Bird' rings out ominously on muted trumpet and violins –

Verschliess den Käfig! Hüte gut das Haus! / Sonst fliegt der Vogel in den Wald hinaus!

Lock up the cage door, guard the house all day, / or to the woods the bird will fly away!

– while as counter-subject the motif of Görge, the composer's *alter ego*, resounds powerfully in horns and cellos.

The *Rondo* finale is so closely related to the opening *Presto*, both in spirit and letter, as to create the illusion of a Bachian *double*. With their rapid changes of mood and a complex chiaroscuro of timbre and texture, these movements offset a centrepiece of more sombre hue, like matching outer panels of a triptych.

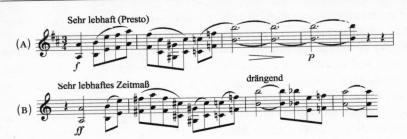

EX. 82   (A) first movement, opening bars; (B) third movement, coda (30⁴)

EX. 83   (A) *Sie kam zum Schloss gegangen* op. 13 no. 6, bars 51–3;
(B) Sinfonietta, first movement 1⁵; (C¹) Symphony in B♭ major, opening bars;
(C) Sinfonietta, second movement, opening bars

Berg, who heard the work in an Austrian Radio broadcast,* immediately recognized the centrifugal force of the *Ballade*:

> Once again a work of colourful sonority and vivid clarity, whose genuine Zemlinsky-tone (palpable in every phrase) in my opinion finds its climax in the second movement. This is the tone that I so love.[29]

* On 4 June 1935, with Zemlinsky conducting the Vienna Symphony Orchestra.

Of the more substantial works composed during these five years as a 'caged bird' in Vienna, the Sinfonietta was the only one to be performed during Zemlinsky's lifetime. He himself conducted it several times, in Vienna, Paris, Barcelona and Lausanne;[30] Jalowetz conducted the world première in Prague, and in 1940–41 Dimitri Mitropoulos gave three performances of scorching intensity with the New York Philharmonic.* 'One sees where Schoenberg learned some of his cute tricks, all right!' chortled Schoenberg's eighteen-year-old pupil Dika Newlin after listening to the broadcast with him in Los Angeles.[31] Writing for the *New York Sun*, Irving Kolodin re-echoed her enthusiasm in dignified East Coast prose:

Paradoxically, out of a list that included the names of Ravel, Hindemith, Casella and Zemlinsky, it was music by the last of these that provided the deepest satisfaction.[†] [. . . The Sinfonietta] has the sure-handedness which one would expect from a musician who was, among other things, Schoenberg's teacher; but it also has a nub of quality, a kernel of expressiveness, which are no common attributes of contemporary writing.[32]

The orchestration of the Sinfonietta was completed on 3 July 1934. Work on the score was interrupted by conducting engagements, including a programme of Mozart and Mahler in Prague on 25 April (*Figaro* overture and the D minor Piano Concerto with the twenty-three-year-old Rudolf Firkušný, followed by the Fifth Symphony) and a concert with Jarmila Novotná and the Vienna Symphony Orchestra at the Musikverein on 11 May, the eve of the fiftieth anniversary of Smetana's death. It was Zemlinsky's habit to reserve the summer months for composition. This year, however, while Louise was occupied with plumbers, gardeners and interior decorators, he simply relaxed, took day trips to Marienbad, rambled with Hansi in the woods, and ate his fill of Maria's *table d'hôte*. A brief article for the Schoenberg Festschrift, 'Jugenderinnerungen' ('Reminiscences of Youth'), was his only creative work.[‡]

On 5 November he conducted the Lyric Symphony and the Maeterlinck Songs with the Prague Radio Symphony Orchestra, followed by an all-Beethoven programme with the Czech Philharmonic. Only three days after the NDT première of *Der Kreidekreis* in December, he composed *Das bucklichte Männlein*, and in early January a setting of Werfel's *Ahnung Beatricens*. In February he was again in Prague, this time to watch over Jalowetz's rehearsals for the Sinfonietta.

The day after the concert, 20 February, the Czech Philharmonic invited him

---

* Wax discs of his live broadcast (29 December 1940) are preserved at the Yale Collection of Historical Sound Recordings.
† The concert on which Kolodin was reporting included music by Brahms, Chausson and Casella (Suite no. 2 from the opera *La donna serpente*); in mentioning Ravel and Hindemith he was comparing the Sinfonietta with other items recently performed by Mitropoulos.
‡ Quoted in part on p. 37.

to step in for Tálich, who was indisposed. On the programme was Wolfgang
Graeser's orchestral transcription of Bach's *Art of Fugue*.* Hitherto, apart from
a solitary performance of the St John Passion,† Zemlinsky had taken little active
interest in the major works of Bach. This chance encounter with the greatest
glass-bead game in the history of music seems to have made a profound impression on him. The affinities were clear: when Bach composed the work, he too
was in his mid-sixties; in a world of disintegrating values, he too felt bound to
uphold time-honoured principles of artistic integrity; in turn, the outside world
saw him as an obscure *Kapellmeister* with outmoded music. Through Graeser's
scholarly but romantic eye, *The Art of Fugue* was not only a demonstration of
craftsmanship at its highest level but also a quixotic gesture of protest and
lament.

One aspect of the event was troubling: for giving preference to a foreigner,
Tálich had come under fire from the Czech press. Since 1911 Zemlinsky had
been accepted, if not venerated, by Czech and German alike. But now, with
headlines such as 'Have we no conductors of our own?', it became clear to him
that, beyond musical circles in Prague, he could expect neither sympathy nor
hospitality.

Concert versions of *The Art of Fugue* often conclude with the chorale
prelude *Vor deinem Thron tret ich hiermit*, dictated by Bach on his deathbed.
Graeser's is no exception, indeed his published score also includes all fifteen
verses of the text by Justinius Gesenius. While standing idly on the rostrum
(Graeser entrusts the piece to solo organ), Zemlinsky may well have read the
opening lines:

*Vor deinem Thron tret ich hiermit, / O Gott und dich demütig bitt: / Wend dein
genädig Angesicht / Von mir betrübtem Sünder nicht.*

Before Thy throne, o Lord, I tread / And humbly unto Thee I plead: / Be merciful,
turn not Thy face / from me, a sinner in distress.‡

Soon after returning to Vienna, his seismographic reaction to the concert and its
aftermath found expression in a setting for chorus, organ and large orchestra of
Psalm 13. In bolder language, the opening verse of the psalm pre-echoes the
humble Pietism of Gesenius:

---

* Graeser also edited *The Art of Fugue* for volume XLVII of the Bach Gesellschaft edition, published in 1924. His 'newly ordered orchestration' of the work, published in 1929, calls for
three flutes, three oboes (doubling cor anglais or oboe da caccia), two bassoons, four trumpets,
six trombones, two harpsichords, organ and strings.
† On 4 May 1919 at the NDT.
‡ As Friedrich Smend has pointed out in his book *Johann Sebastian Bach bei seinem Namen
gerufen* (Kassel, 1950), the sum of the letters BACH is 14, that of JSBACH 41. Smend further
points out that the first melody line of *Vor deinem Thron*, as embellished by Bach, contains 14
notes, and the entire melody 41 notes.

How long wilt thou forget me, o Lord? for ever? how long wilt thou hide thy face from me?

Over an extended pedal D in bassoons, timpani and basses, and a plaintive figure, reiterated fourteen times in the bass clarinet, flutes, clarinets and horns softly intone a theme that opens, like Contrapunctus I of *The Art of Fugue*, with the rising 5th D–A. Where Bach builds his theme from concentric rings of 3rds and 2nds, Zemlinsky returns to the hieratic intervals of his 'Circle' theme from *Der Kreidekreis*, 5ths and 2nds. After a 27-bar introduction, the chorus enters. At first the theme is taken up monodically by the sopranos, over a tortuously chromatic bass line (EX. 86B); but with the entry of the altos and tenors Zemlinsky weaves it into a web of Bach-inspired polyphony:

EX. 84   Psalm 13, bars 43–9 (chorus part)

How long shall I take counsel in my soul, having sorrow in my heart daily? how long shall mine enemy be exalted over me?

The people call with one voice: polyphony gives way to homophony. As their appeal grows more urgent, four-part harmony is supplanted by unison chant, and the pulse increases.

Consider and hear me, o Lord my God: Lighten mine eyes, lest I sleep the sleep of death, lest mine enemy say, I have prevailed against him; and those that trouble me rejoice when I am moved.

Beginning in C minor, the outburst rises and swells, rapidly traversing B minor, E major and C♯ minor to culminate in a D minor battle cry. Underlined by full organ, the plaintive figure of the opening returns as a high-pitched shriek. Gradually, in contemplation of 'the sleep of death', the mood grows pensive, the pulse slackens. The chorus cries out once more, then falls silent. In the orchestra struggle breaks out anew, this time in a prolonged contrapuntal turmoil of voice against voice, idea against idea.

But I have trusted in thy mercy; my heart shall rejoice in thy salvation.

Finally the chorus re-enters, with a full-throated hymn of praise in E♭ major –
the key of transfiguration, the Masonic key, but here above all as a recollection
of the *Hochzeitsgesang* of 1896:

EX. 85   (A) *Hochzeitsgesang*, bars 9–10; (B) Psalm 13, bars 206–8*

I will sing unto the Lord, because he hath dealt bountifully with me.

Once again Zemlinsky recalls the temple music of his youth, the organ that he
played on high days and holidays, the sunlight shining through stained-glass
windows. Psalm 23 invokes these memories as a mystic experience; here, with
almost cinematic realism, they represent a declaration of solidarity with the
Jewish people, less public a gesture than Schoenberg's re-conversion, but no less
sincere. To the accompaniment of four harps and tambourine, the chorus

---

* To appreciate the similarity, the two extracts need to be read at the appropriate tempo:
Hochzeitsgesang with an *andante* crotchet beat (♩ = *c.*66), the passage from Psalm 13 at
approximately the same pulse, but in minims.

breaks into a Semitic dance of joy that rises gradually to a triumphal climax. Like the closing scene of *Der Kreidekreis*, this is an apotheosis from within, a great din of full orchestra, organ, harps and glockenspiel, drowning out the harsh noise of reality.

How long wilt thou forget me, o Lord? for ever?

In November 1935 Zemlinsky confidently announced to a Prague reporter that the world première of Psalm 13 was imminent,[33] but it was not to be. For lack of royalties from Germany, the publishing of serious music had by now truly become an 'all but futile undertaking'. With Kurt von Schuschnigg's Austrian cabinet infiltrated by Nazis, and every influential position in the Viennese musical world occupied by Nazi sympathizers – Karl Böhm, Oswald Kabasta, Leopold Reichwein, to name but a few – the forces required to perform such a score could no longer be mobilized. For thirty-six years, Psalm 13 – one of Zemlinsky's finest works – remained unpublished and unperformed.

2

The Final Synthesis

Now that Zemlinsky was again living within close range of Alma (by car, if not by public transport), contact was relatively frequent.[1] The house on the Hohe Warte was still open to musicians, writers, painters and sculptors, but by now the balance had tilted towards an *haute volée* of diplomats, politicians and high-ranking clergymen. Werfel, in search of seclusion for his work, spent much of his time at Alma's summer house in Breitenstein or at the Villa Mahler in Venice, leaving his wife free to enjoy her latest conquest, a theology professor sixteen years her junior named Johannes Hollnsteiner.

For over a year, her daughter Manon had fought bravely against polio. With her death on Easter Monday 1935, aged eighteen, it seemed to Alma's older, truer friends that hope itself had died. 'Hollnsteiner was a great help,' wrote Alma. 'He beautified the ugliness of her death and gave a wonderful speech at the graveside.'[2] But for the presence of a few genuinely grief-stricken friends, the funeral, at the cemetery in Grinzing, would have degenerated into a society event. Later in the year Alban Berg composed his Violin Concerto as a more fitting memorial to the unfortunate Manon.

'We'll sit together at the piano,' Zemlinsky had once written to Alma. 'Simply, naïvely you'll say: "That I like, that I don't."'[3] Between him and Louise there was never such an exchange. 'Actually I knew none of his music,' she recalled. Even if this was an understatement,* he kept the technicalities of his art to himself, aware that music theory was a topic on which she had squandered little of her schooling. But she helped out where she could, on the practical side:

In Vienna I used to go to the library, where I read plays which I hoped would be of interest to Zemlinsky for his opera. And I was very taken with a work by Gide. At first Zemlinsky was not entirely in agreement, but then he declared himself willing to compose it.[4]

She had discovered a handsome bibliophile edition of André Gide's *Le roi Candaule* in a German adaptation by Franz Blei, published by Insel Verlag in 1905.† During the spring or early summer of 1935 she helped Zemlinsky to copy

---

* Not only did Louise sing in the Prague production of *Der Zwerg*, she also travelled to Zurich for the world première of *Der Kreidekreis*. Doubtless she also attended other performances and heard radio broadcasts of his music.
† Blei's German adaptation was published in a limited edition. The Stadt- und Landesbibliothek is (today) the only public library in Vienna to possess a copy.

out the text and, as with *Der Kreidekreis*, probably also advised him on cuts and alterations. True to form, he made no effort to contact Gide's publishers, let alone set up an agreement with them. For a true artist, he will have argued, such material considerations were irrelevant.*

He began work in July and completed the short score of act I on 15 September. Six days later, a Saturday, he was in Zurich for the Swiss première of *Kleider machen Leute*,⁵ then he doubled across to Brno, where the following Tuesday, assisted by his former pupil Adolf Singer, he was due to start rehearsals for a production of *Figaro* at the Landestheater.

By now the proportion of *Sudetendeutsche* and German-speaking Jews in Brno was considerably higher than in Prague, and with a rising tendency. Like the NDT, the Landestheater was a German-language house, which for many years had been affiliated to the Deutsche Bühnenverein. Leopold Kramer† had just taken over as Director, but so far his presence was scarcely felt. As Zemlinsky reported to Louise, conditions were chaotic:

So far there has been no sign of Herr Singer, and for today, it appears, *no rehearsal has been called*. Instead I read that between my rehearsals an operetta is to be prepared for Saturday. [. . .] One cannot work in such confusion. *If I don't get enough rehearsals, I shan't do it.*

Two days later the news was scarcely more cheering:

Well, I'm still here. What will come of it I cannot tell, but I've already been slaving away. On Wednesday I rehearsed from 10:00 in the morning until 10:00 at night, with only a two-hour lunch break. [. . .] The poor singers are at their last gasp! [. . .] And the theatre is in a bad way! Singer asked for a reimbursement of 60 Kč(!) that had been promised him ages ago, but he couldn't get it on the same day, because the cashier *didn't have the money*!! What is to come of my fee? If I hadn't already run up such expenses, I would return to Vienna straight away.⁶

Somehow he stayed the course until the first night, on 29 September; somehow he made a success of the endeavour.⁷

On 4 October, between performances of *Figaro*, he started work on act II of *Candaules* (for a long time he followed Blei in retaining the French orthography). This section of the score, played by a small stage band of flutes and harps, proved troublesome. On the one hand, the drama called for tedious and repetitive music (after a few bars the King dismisses the musicians with a

---

* Agreements with representatives of the Gide and Blei estates were finalized only in 1998, two years after the world première of the opera.
† Since leaving the NDT Kramer had worked as an actor in German touring ensembles. He remained in office in Brno until the house was closed in 1938. Unable to flee from the Nazis due to ill-health, he died in Vienna in 1942.

gesture of impatience), on the other, after the blood-curdling close of act I, tension had to be sustained, and the musical idea had to be capable of integration into Zemlinsky's network of motifs. At the end of October he made a further attempt at the scene, but this too came to nothing. Before finding a viable solution, a further nine discarded versions followed.

After the confusion of Brno, it must have been a relief to return to the well-ordered world of the Czech Philharmonic, when on 7 November Zemlinsky conducted Mahler's Third Symphony, his first contribution to a Mahler cycle spread over two seasons. In an interview with a Prague newspaper he gave a few vague details of 'the seventh (sic) in the series of his great stage conceptions':

The libretto, by a living, modern French author, will be set to music word for word. It will be an opera without chorus and, following the spirit of the times, simpler in style than all his previous operas.[8]

On his return to Vienna, he continued to struggle with the opening of act II, coming a little further now, with a flat-key ballade in similar vein to the slow movement of the Sinfonietta. Time was short, for he had agreed to spend several weeks in January 1936 at the Teatre Liceu in Barcelona, conducting a festival of Dvořák and Smetana with an ensemble of soloists from the Národní Divadlo.* After a few weeks, work on *Kandaules* ground once again to a halt.

On 11 December the Vienna Symphony Orchestra under Oswald Kabasta gave the long-awaited Viennese première of Berg's *Lulu* Suite. The work had already received eleven performances, but Berg himself had heard only two, and these only in radio transmissions of poor quality. For months he had been suffering from furunculosis. Though in a lamentable state, and inspired with 'nothing but dread'[9] at the prospect of being seen in public, he dragged himself to the concert. Six days later he was admitted to hospital for an emergency blood transfusion. His condition, which was more critical than he or his wife had realized, deteriorated rapidly. In the early hours of Christmas Eve (shortly after the fateful 23rd had passed without incident) he breathed his last.

'I still cannot believe that my dear Alban is gone,' wrote Schoenberg to Helene Berg from Hollywood.[10] Nobody could believe it.† On 28 December, as Elias Canetti recalls, a small crowd of mourners, scarcely more than thirty in all, assembled at the cemetery in Hietzing:

---

* The first production, *The Bartered Bride*, was scheduled for 2 January; Dvořák's *The Jacobin*, with Maria Rajdl (who had sung the Infanta in the Vienna production of *Der Zwerg*) as Julia, followed nine days later (information kindly provided by Albin Hänseroth).
† As is well known, Helene Berg remained in contact with her husband via a medium. Less well known, but supported by independent and reliable sources, is the fact that in later life Louise also held imaginary conversations with Berg.

Ernst Krenek was there, also Egon Wellesz and Willi Reich.* Of the speeches I can only recall that the latter spoke of the deceased as his teacher. [. . .] I paid no attention to the others, who spoke more wisely and with greater composure, for I was in no condition even to understand where we were.[11]

Canetti may not have spotted Zemlinsky and Louise among the mourners, but there can be little doubt that they were there, and that they too were in no condition to understand.

String Quartet no. 4

A few days later Webern set off for Barcelona to attend an ISCM committee meeting. Zemlinsky should have left immediately after Christmas for his season at the Teatre Liceu. Under the circumstances, however, he decided to remain at home and compose a memorial for his dead friend.[†]

Like Berg's Lyric Suite and *Lulu* Suite, the Fourth Quartet is a suite in six movements.[‡] In contrast to the sonata form of the previous quartets or the extended sonata form envisaged for the unfinished Quartet of 1927, the movements are grouped, like those of the Lyric Suite, in thematically related pairs, deploying an untypically large number of themes and motifs in uncharacteristically open-ended structures. As in the Lyric Suite, the proportions of the movements are irregular.[§] Several sections stretch the concept of tonal harmony beyond breaking point, but much of the work adopts that 'genuine Zemlinsky-tone' which Berg so loved. What further distinguishes this work from its predecessors is the absence of internal conflict. Zemlinsky still exploits the dramatic possibilities of the medium, but here the four players ride his waves of tension and relaxation in a spirit of almost unbroken unanimity.

The first movement, *Praeludium*, opens *senza espressione* with a hushed chorale in E minor – a Zemlinskian E minor none the less, that undemonstratively embraces 11 semitones, arrayed in a freely asymmetrical pattern of image

---

* Of Berg's closest friends, the only notable absentees were the Mahler-Werfels, who were in New York for rehearsals of Kurt Weill's *The Eternal Road*. Krenek, who spoke as a representative of the ISCM, was accompanied by his housemaid, 'because for the likes of her there was nothing more exciting than a wedding or a funeral. She returned with tears pouring down her face' (Ernst Krenek, *Im Atem der Zeit. Erinnerungen an die Moderne* (Hamburg, 1998), 916).
† The performances in Barcelona were taken over by a staff conductor from Prague, Karel Nedbal.
‡ In his autograph, Zemlinsky subtitled the work 'Suite'. The epithet is missing from the Universal Edition study score, published in 1971, probably because this edition was prepared from the autograph parts (*MolA*) rather than from the original manuscript (*LoC*).
§ Berg, Lyric Suite (in multiples of 23 or 10): 69, 150, 138, 69, 460 and 46 bars; Zemlinsky, Fourth Quartet: 59, 285, 39, 139, 49 and 195 bars. To a certain degree, the timings (quoted here from the DGG/LaSalle Quartet recordings) relativize these proportions. Berg: 2'55", 5'35", 3'17", 4'59", 4'27" and 5'23"; Zemlinsky: 3'48", 5'01", 2'56", 4'14", 4'44" and 3'11".

and mirror image. Neither the theme nor its timbre are entirely new. The former follows a contour similar to that of the dirge-like fugal counter-subject of
Psalm 13, the latter originates in the second movement of the Quartet op. 19:*

EX. 86   (A) Quartet no. 4, opening; (B) Psalm 13, bar 27;
(C) Quartet no. 3, second movement, variation 7, 11³

During the course of the movement various figures step forward in turn, like
mourners around the open grave. Bar 6 introduces the composer, with his 'Self'
motif, D–E–G. The minor 9th of a new theme, introduced with a *più adagio* in
bars 17–20,† seems to imply the presence of Schoenberg, and bars 26–7 present
a free, impassioned discourse between this idea and the 'Self' motif. Bars 45–54,
with a theme in violin 1 based on A–H–D–E, and a variant of Schoenberg's
'Melisande' theme in the viola, invoke the shade of Mathilde. Between each of
these episodes the principal theme returns, strident at bar 28, but falling with a
glissando in all four instruments to a sudden hush, then at bar 55 distant and
remote, clad in the harmony of the 'Fate' chord. The movement ends softly on
a triad of pure E major.
    The ensuing *Burleske* transforms the opening motif of the *Praeludium* into
an outburst of furious energy. With an accelerated version of the pentatonic

* Though not quoted at pitch until bar 70 of the second movement, the first three melody
notes appear to have been inspired by the first three pitches of Berg's musical monogram,
A–B–A.
† As Loll points out (*ZTuA*, 240–41) the idea can be traced back to bar 5 of the op. 15 Quartet
(see EX. 48A).

'Mathilde' theme a more conciliatory mood is established, and the trio in Lydian D major, whose theme is based on the pitches of the 'Fortune' chord, strikes a distinctly amiable note. Its most pronounced feature, a repeated A♮ (later expanded to A♮–E♭), seems to recall the repeated C♮ ('Do-do') motif of the Lyric Suite; perhaps it can be read as a secret cipher.

In long contrapuntal strands, the *Adagietto* combines a variant of the 'Görge' motif (B♭–C–G) with a rising octave figure derived from the *più adagio* theme of the *Praeludium*. In the ensuing *Intermezzo* the line is transformed into a lithe dance movement in E♭ minor, underpinned by jazz-inspired syncopations in viola and cello. Further episodes follow: a pliantly contrapuntal trio in E major and a more animated second trio with rapid sextuplet movement. In the absence of *da capo* demarcation lines, Zemlinsky reintroduces the original dance measure in the rhythm and texture of its new surroundings, thereby emulating (on a smaller scale) the cumulative A, B, A+B form of Berg's Chamber Concerto. In spirit, the movement comes close to the elegant dance measures of *Der Kreidekreis*.

Where in op. 19 Zemlinsky had composed variations on a theme scarcely worthy of the name, his variation theme for op. 25, a barcarole for solo cello, is carefully structured and generously proportioned (12 long bars), the three variations themselves are an intricate web of counterpoint in radiant D major, establishing a calm, exalted mood reminiscent of late Beethoven. And where in the finale of op. 19 the cello's invitation to fugal discourse was simply ignored, in the finale of op. 25 the players willingly follow the lead of the second violin in an energetic double fugue (the subject originates in the chromatic figure of EX. 85, the counter-subject follows the contour of the *più adagio* theme from the *Praeludium*). Announcing the coda with a fugal stretta *più mosso* (bar 145), Zemlinsky transforms the jagged rhythm of the principal theme into a smooth, mercurial flow of *spiccato* quavers. Here too, as if to stress the spirit of solidarity, the texture is predominantly homophonic.

By now the outlook for new chamber music had grown even bleaker than for large-scale choral works or lieder. In order to hear his new Quartet at all, Zemlinsky was obliged to write out the parts himself (aided by an unidentified amanuensis). According to oral evidence the work was given a private hearing in the US by the Kolisch Quartet.* Whether they also played the work in public is uncertain;† certain is only that no further performance followed until 21 April 1967, when the LaSalle Quartet rediscovered the work for posterity; a further seven years passed before the score appeared in print.

---

* Rudolf Kolisch and his quartet colleagues, Felix Khuner, Jenö Léner and Benar Heifetz, emigrated to the US in 1935.
† Reporting for the *New York Times* on Zemlinsky's arrival in the US, Harald Taubmann wrote: 'A year ago he completed a string quartet which the Kolisch Quartet was playing' (*NYT*, 5 January 1939).

In February 1936 Zemlinsky interrupted work on his Quartet for another visit to Prague, this time to conduct Mahler's Ninth Symphony, preceded by Mozart's *Figaro* overture and A major Piano Concerto (K.488). Since the embarrassment of the previous season, Tálich had evidently put the record straight with those who disapproved of foreign conductors, for he again invited Zemlinsky to deputize for him, this time in a programme of J. C. Bach, Emil Hlobil (Suite no. 2 op. 7, interpreted 'with loving conviction')[12] and Beethoven ('Eroica' Symphony). At the end of February he set out for Barcelona, where on 3 March he conducted the Orquestra Pau Casals in the Catalan première of his Sinfonietta. Back in Prague later in the spring, he made amends for his January cancellation by conducting three performances of *Tannhäuser* at the Národní Divadlo.

Universal Edition was meanwhile confronted with the problem of preparing the full score of *Lulu*, which was due to receive its world première in Zurich the following season. In his letter of condolence to Helene Berg, Schoenberg had spontaneously intimated that, rather than see the orchestration completed (badly, as implied) by 'Krenek or someone else', he would be prepared to offer his own services.[13] Later, however, he withdrew his offer, ostensibly on account of isolated instances of anti-Semitic vocabulary in the libretto, perhaps also because of the painter's suicide scene in act I, which may have reminded him all too vividly of Gerstl.* Erwin Stein, who was handling this delicate matter for UE, had meanwhile approached Webern ('I can't imagine that anything will come of it,' he wrote to Schoenberg) and Zemlinsky. 'As a practical man of the theatre,' reported Stein, the latter seemed at first 'much inclined'.

But after two days' study he decided not to do it and suggested that just what Berg brought to completion should be performed. And that is probably what will happen. We've suggested to the director at Zurich that he present the two finished acts and give a purely symphonic performance of the *Adagio* from the 'Symphonic Pieces' as an epilogue.[14]

Though testifying to his boundless respect, Zemlinsky's suggestion was neither particularly courageous nor, from a theatrical standpoint, particularly convincing.† Nevertheless his word was gospel, particularly for Helene Berg, on whose insistence the act III manuscripts of *Lulu* were then locked away for forty years.

Der König Kandaules

After a further visit to Prague for two performances of Mahler's Eighth Symphony at the end of May, Zemlinsky was at last able to return to *Kandaules*. At first it

---

* The allegedly anti-Semitic aspect of the argument is set out in detail by George Perle in *The Operas of Alban Berg*, vol. 2: *Lulu* (Berkeley–Los Angeles–London, 1989). Perle does not address the question of the Gerstl connection.
† Without the variations on a barrel-organ tune (movement 5 of the *Lulu* Suite), it was almost impossible to establish the milieu of the closing scene.

seemed as if he could compose nothing but funeral marches, but as work progressed his imagination again caught fire for Gide's drama. The final double-bar of act II was signed on 29 August, and act III was completed on 29 December, a year and a day after Berg's funeral.

Now that the short score was complete, Zemlinsky could see that his overall concept was flawed by a break in style. Acts II and III, composed after an interruption of several months, departed to a greater or lesser extent from the 'simpler style' of act I, and drew at times on ideas inspired by his cursory examination of the score of *Lulu*. Berg's scrupulous gradations of song and speech, for example, had inspired him to use a variety of *Sprechstimme* notations, and certain structural features of *Lulu* had influenced his own work. During the course of 1937 he therefore began to rework the first half of the opera, neither altering nor expanding the motivic material, but leaving scarcely a bar of the original unchanged – a remarkable feat both of technique and imagination. By the following spring he had completed 885 bars of the new short score (almost exactly three-quarters of act I), and written out 846 bars of full score in fair copy. After the annexation of Austria by the Nazis in March 1938 he wrote no more.

His remark to a Prague reporter that this was his 'seventh' opera was no slip of the tongue. It was in fact his eighth, but 7 was the number of fulfilment, and with *Kandaules* he clearly intended to set the seal on his creative endeavours. By the time he started work, Zemlinsky must have realized that there was as little chance of such a work being performed in Austria as in Germany. His 'simpler style' might initially have reflected a desire to win acceptance with musicians of more conservative taste, such as Clemens Krauss, but might also have been conceived with a view to performance in the United States. In 1931 Bodanzky had received a medal from the Czech government, and subsequently spent a few days with the Zemlinskys at Königswart: contact, it appears, was as cordial and frequent as ever.* Having resigned his directorship of the Society of the Friends of Music, he was no longer in a position to perform the Symphonic Songs, as promised. But at the Met, where, according to *Time* magazine, 'behind the throne of General Manager Edward Johnson, Bodanzky was a great power [. . . and] had more to say about who should sing what, and how, than anyone else',[15] there was every chance of rallying support for Zemlinsky's new opera.

Before leaving for the US in December 1938, Zemlinsky seems indeed to have evinced a promise that *Kandaules* would be performed at the Met. Seven days after his arrival, during the course of an interview with Harald Taubmann from the *New York Times*, he and Bodanzky discussed the opera, apparently for the first time:

---

* Apart from the summer of 1934, which Bodanzky spent in Italy, he visited Vienna every year. His last visit to Europe was in the summer of 1936.

At the present time he was working on the orchestration of an opera based on a play by André Gide. 'What is the opera like?' Mr Bodanzky asked. 'It is,' Mr Zemlinsky hesitated. 'It is ultra-modern.'[16]

As Hans Heinsheimer recalls:

Zemlinsky showed [Bodanzky] the libretto [. . .], but Bodanzky was of the opinion that a bedroom scene in this opera (though mild) was impossible at the Metropolitan, although there was evidently no objection from that quarter to the first scene of *Rosenkavalier*.[17]

In *Kandaules* there is no 'bedroom scene' as such – the night of love itself is left to the spectator's imagination – but an integral part of the dramatic idea is nudity. For a few moments before the close of act II, Gide requires his heroine to remove every strip of clothing, albeit on a darkened stage. As conductor of German repertoire at the Met, Bodanzky will have witnessed at first hand the battles fought and lost over *Salome*.* For a comparable conflict of morals in connection with a self-avowedly 'ultra-modern' opera by a composer who was scarcely known he could extend no hope. On his advice Zemlinsky set the score aside. Sixty years elapsed before *Kandaules* was seen on stage.

Cast

King Kandaules (dram ten); Nyssia, his queen (dram sop); Gyges, a fisherman (dram bar); Trydo, his wife (silent); Kandaules's guests: Phedros (lyr bar), Syphax (lyr ten), Nicomedes (bar), Pharnaces (bass), Philebos (bass), Simias (ten), Sebas (ten) and Archelaos (bass); cook (bass).

Synopsis

Lydia in ancient times

1 *Banqueting hall in the palace garden*   Gyges enters as prologue, in his net a magnificent fish for the royal banquet. Kandaules, he recalls, was a childhood friend; he is saddened to see him now surrounded by flatterers. With idle talk of fortune and beauty, the guests arrive and take their seats. Greeting them effusively, Kandaules escorts his wife Nyssia to table. He asks her to unveil; reluctantly she complies. Syphax proposes a toast, and Kandaules rejoices that he can share his wife's beauty with others. When the fish is served, Archelaos bites on a ring embedded in its flesh. Examining it more closely, Phedros discovers that it bears an inscription: 'I conceal fortune.' Kandaules, perturbed, sends for Gyges. While he waits, the guests idly observe a hut burning on the seashore. Gyges is ushered in. The hut, he explains, was his, inadvertently set ablaze by his wife, who returned drunk from the

* A chorus of protest, led by Mrs Herbert Satterlee, daughter of the financier J. Pierpont Morgan, led to the withdrawal of *Salome* after just one performance, in January 1907. Mary Garden sang the title role in 1909 at the Manhattan Opera House (and subsequently in other East Coast opera houses), but at the Met itself the ban remained in force until 1933.

palace kitchens. Kandaules orders him to fetch her. Trydo is a wild, dishevelled creature, but Gyges is proud to call her his own. When Sebas casts lewd aspersions on her fidelity, however, he snatches a knife and cuts her throat. Dismissing the guests, Kandaules offers Gyges his friendship.

II *A chamber in the palace, towards nightfall*   Gyges, dressed in finery, drinks wine with the King. Would he like to be rich? asks Kandaules, and did he kill Trydo because Nyssia was more beautiful? Riches mean little to him, the fisherman replies, and he scarcely looked at the Queen; he loved his wife, but could not bear to share her with a rival. Kandaules demonstrates that the ring makes its bearer invisible: with its aid he will share Nyssia's beauty with his friend. Before Gyges can even protest, Kandaules has slipped the ring on to his finger. Nyssia enters, still upset by her unveiling of the previous evening. Observed by the invisible Gyges, Kandaules unbinds her hair and helps her undress, then creeps furtively from the room. Gyges, still invisible, steps hesitantly towards the bed.

III *As in act I, the following morning*   Laughingly Philebos breaks the news to his companions of the ring's magic and the King's feverish search for its invisible bearer. Gyges, torn between love and remorse, overhears Kandaules in conversation with Nyssia: after a night of such passion, she cannot understand his anxiety. While Kandaules resumes his search for the ring, Gyges reveals himself to Nyssia and confesses all. Falling to his knees, he hands her his dagger. She hands it back: it is Kandaules who must die. As the King returns to escort the Queen to her chamber, Gyges strikes him down. Tearing the ring from his finger, he kneels at Kandaules' side, grief-stricken. The guests enter in consternation. Gyges, proclaimed King by Nyssia, harshly orders her to don her veil. With a cry of contempt she tears it to shreds. Syphax raises his glass.

The legend of Kandaules, King of the Lydians, is almost as old as time. The first to recount it was Herodotus (in the opening pages of the *Histories*), followed by Plato (*Politeia*), Justinus and Nicholas of Damascus, Ptolemy and Plutarch. Gide's play is an ingenious compilation of these texts, and also incorporates ideas from associated sources. Kandaules, for instance, is invested with the wealth of Croesus, and the fish with the golden ring (which also swims via *Des Knaben Wunderhorn* into Mahler's *Rheinlegendchen*) originates in Herodotus' account of the fortunes of Polycrates. Gide follows Ptolemy in naming the Queen Nyssia (in Herodotus she is unnamed), while the name Trydo originates in the version by Nicholas of Damascus. For the guests Gide draws primarily on names from Plato, but makes no attempt to match the individuals to their prototypes.* When he wrote *Le roi Candaule*, he evidently knew Théophile Gautier's eponymous short story, but had allegedly not read Hebbel's drama *Gyges und sein Ring*. His play may in turn have inspired Hofmannsthal to a Kandaules project, begun in 1903 but never completed.

* An exhaustive study of source material is found in Hans Schwabl and Hartmut Krones, 'Kandaules: Von Herodot bis Zemlinsky', *Wiener Humanistische Blätter*, vol. 39 (Vienna, 1997).

Written and published in 1899, *Le roi Candaule* was premièred, with the celebrated actor–director Aurelien Lugné-Poe in the title role, at the Nouveau Théâtre in Paris in 1901. If critical acclaim in France was tepid, in Austria and Germany the play was a fiasco: Blei's German adaptation, staged in January 1906 at the Deutsches Volkstheater, ran for only three performances, and a production in Berlin two years later, acted largely in whispers, was shouted down at the first night. A sympathetic review of the Vienna production in *Die Schaubühne* highlighted the strengths and weaknesses: although the writing was often 'sketchy and meagre, too intellectual for a mystic experience, too far elevated above reality to be moving as a true-to-life drama', the play still made a 'deep and powerful impression'.[18] Gide's sparseness, his refusal to motivate the often obscure behaviour of his characters, dehumanized the drama, and by its very nature his Symbolist-eye-view of the legend laid itself open to a multitude of interpretations.

At a personal level, as disclosed by Léon Pierre-Quint, the play chronicles a period during which its author was obliged to share with a friend his love for a younger man. Whether for lack of candour or fear of prosecution, Gide translated this *ménage à trois* into a heterosexual triangle.* Pierre-Quint accordingly interprets the drama as a disastrous attempt to escape from a hopeless situation:

One could venture the opinion that Kandaules wishes not only to rid himself of all that he possesses, but also to retract from his obligations towards his wife. By remaining alone he thus preserves that perfect happiness to which he had won through. [. . .] But Kandaules loves his wife; despite everything he is jealous of her.[19]

In the early years of the century *Le roi Candaule* was viewed as a drama of social inequality, indeed Gide fuelled this particular fire by publishing the play with a Shavian preface that spoke grandly of *communisme* and *les classes dirigeantes*.[†] While *Die Schaubühne* noted that the play was 'essentially a drama of social conflict',[20] later critics tended to seek a less political approach. James C. McClaren interprets the play not as 'the political defeat of capitalism by a communist proletariat' but as 'the defeat of abstraction and illusion by reality'.[21] J. W. Ireland looks at the drama even more candidly –

It is the story of a king who is measurelessly rich, but who can appreciate his riches only as they make it possible for him to enrich others.

– and draws a thought-provoking conclusion:

---

* Gide also changes the gender of his stage band. In 1895 Oscar Wilde encouraged him to a sexual encounter with a fluting boy from an Algerian coffee-house. In the play (and the opera) this episode is translated into the lust of Sebas and Archelaos for *joueuses de flûte* (see Richard Ellmann, 'Corydon and Ménalque', *Golden Codgers: Biographical Speculations* (London, 1973)).
† By the time Zemlinsky became aware of the play, Gide's works had been banned by the Nazis for their allegedly Communist leaning.

Kandaules' problem [. . .] is essentially an artist's problem. [. . .] The more an artist gives the richer he is and the greater and more intense is his experience of his riches. [. . .] The gift that the artist makes is a gift of revelation; and is not the ultimate gift – which is the ultimate revelation – the revelation of what is most hidden, the confiding of some *secret*?[22]

Like Ireland, Klaus Mann understands Kandaules as 'the artist who makes the whole world witness to his most intimate adventure'. If the revelation of Nyssia's nakedness symbolizes the 'ultimate gift', Mann goes further, specifying the nature of that gift and of the crime perpetrated by revealing it:

The high priest who unveils the secret of the temple blasphemes against the Godhead: this is the moral of the Kandaules tragedy.[23]

Though of greater relevance to Zemlinsky than any political interpretation, such a reading still offers no explicit motive for the King's murder at the hand of a friend. And neither a political nor an artistic slant can explain his Queen's gradual transformation from a sweet-natured young woman into a hysterical harridan.

From the standpoint of practicality *Le roi Candaule* was ideal: it required only three principals and a handful of *comprimario* singers, the scenic requirements were modest, and chorus participation was optional. Nevertheless, it is easy to understand that Zemlinsky did not initially share Louise's enthusiasm. *Der Kreidekreis* had not only satisfied his artistic requirements but was also highly successful as a stage work in its own right. Here, in contrast, was a drama of questionable public appeal, with an obscure plot and arid dialogue; and though essentially a tragedy, its consistency was marred by sudden flights of Gallic humour, as if Gide himself had been unwilling to take his characters entirely seriously.*

As a vehicle for Zemlinsky's dramatic vision, however, the play had its merits. Superficially it must have been satisfying for a composer with a predilection for the Lydian mode to discover a drama set in ancient Lydia.† For a work envisaged as a final synthesis, moreover, the idea of returning to his roots by drawing on the first chapter of the first known history of Western civilization may also have appealed. And for an artist searching fervidly for 'the path to success', Gide's opening line – 'He who possesses fortune should hide himself well!' – must have struck a strong note of sympathy. Fortune (*le bonheur*) in all shapes and forms plays the principal role in *Le roi Candaule*: the attainment and safe-

---

* A case in point is the scene of Philebos and the guests (opening of act III), in which Gyges exploits his invisibility for moments of Beaumarchais-inspired slapstick. Needless to say, these episodes are absent from Zemlinsky's libretto.
† Recent archaeological research has shown that Sardis, the capital city of Lydia, was almost certainly the 'Sepharad' mentioned in the prophecies of Obadiah.

guarding of fortune, the irony and joy of fortune, the misery of misfortune, the peril of sharing fortune with others, the capacity of fortune to turn full circle.* As fate would have it, Zemlinsky's full score breaks off at the words 'die Erde mein zu nennen' ('to call the Earth my own'), shortly before the end of Kandaules' vehement monologue on fortune.

Reading the play might also have reminded him of an article on Schoenberg, written by Richard Specht in 1910 for the periodical *Die Musik*. It was an unremarkable but heartfelt piece of propaganda, partly informative, partly adulatory, in which one passage stood out as a flight of literary fancy that ended with a crash-landing:

No doubt about it: he who no longer wishes to serve the old but break through to the new will have to inflict severe wounds on the old. An artist who takes this risk is like King Kandaules who rudely awakens the sleeping world.[24]

Specht had perpetrated a classical howler. Kandaules was the last of the Heraclides, a dynasty descended from Hercules, which ruled over Lydia (according to Herodotus) for 505 years; his overthrow by Gyges marked the ascent of a new dynasty, the Mermnads. In other words, it was Gyges, not Kandaules, who had awoken 'the sleeping world'; Kandaules was left with the 'severe wounds'. Zemlinsky might well have recalled Specht's blunder, and perhaps also the derisive laughter with which it had been greeted by Schoenberg. Whatever the case, there can be little doubt that he began to identify himself with the title role, and to see in Gyges a portrait of his estranged friend. Several aspects of the character corresponded closely: the pride born of poverty, the brusque manner, the purity of thought, the high moral values. In the hedonist, permissive, but magnanimous character of Kandaules Zemlinsky will have discovered the corresponding likeness to himself.

But such similarities alone can scarcely have persuaded him that *Le roi Candaule* was the most appropriate work for his crowning operatic achievement. At face value, Gide's drama presented little more than a standard configuration: a sensuous tenor, a brutish baritone, and between them, in whatever shape or form, *la femme*. *Carmen* and *Werther*, *Tosca* and *Eugene Onegin*, *Die Gezeichneten* and *Die toten Augen* thrived on this simple formula, as did *A Florentine Tragedy*. *Kandaules* had more to offer.

'Each character stands alone and is significant only to itself; but between the characters is a void,' noted *Die Schaubühne*.[25] In this void, Kandaules, Nyssia and Gyges interact on the superhuman plane of allegory. If Haitang in *Der Kreidekreis* could be understood as personifying art in general, Nyssia can be

---

* While Zemlinsky was composing *Kandaules*, across the border in Bavaria Carl Orff was composing a very different discourse on fortune, *Carmina burana*, in a neo-primitive style designed to eliminate from modern German music any remaining traces of 'decadent art'. It was first performed in Frankfurt on 8 June 1937.

seen as specifically representing the art of music. By revealing to the uninitiated the most intimate secrets of that art, Kandaules profanes the Holy of Holies; for this transgression he forfeits his life. Once Gyges has been granted access to the defenceless muse, he violates her – against his better judgement, but no less forcibly – and wins her over for himself. The consequence of Kandaules' rash generosity is irreversible. In one significant detail Zemlinsky therefore departs from Gide: at the close of the play Nyssia obeys Gyges' command to replace her veil; at the close of the opera she refuses.

What bearing do these images have on the art of music? An analogy can be drawn to those of Schoenberg's circle who followed him from the emancipation of the dissonance to the point at which he began to organize pitch material by serial means. Those who hesitated, notably Eisler and Ullmann, found themselves plunged into a severe crisis of allegiance; from his position at the periphery, Zemlinsky looked on with disbelief. Questioned on this very point in New York, he revealed that the controversy still occupied him intensely:

What did he think of Schoenberg's latest music? Mr Zemlinsky did not answer for a moment. Had he failed to understand or was he being tactful? 'The truth is', he replied, 'I was studying Schoenberg's recent work, his quartet [*sic*] for woodwinds, the other day. I studied it measure for measure. To be frank, I do not understand it.'[26]

In an essay on Berg, published in 1930, Ullmann traced the origins of the rift:

At the time Schoenberg found his *ars nova* in the path of polyphony, [. . . but] he soon saw a danger of anarchy lurking amidst this new community of pitches, which could have led to the 'law of the jungle'. He averted this danger by means of a great taboo, the twelve-note system.[27]

Six years later, in an obituary notice on Berg, Ullmann explained what he meant by 'a great taboo':*

Atonality is the musical equivalent to human freedom; it marks the final point in a line of development, at which all that is God-given in music is struck dumb; from here on, mankind produces music only from within. The sounding cosmos falls silent, fades away. Here, at the point of zero, in the gloom, decisions are taken; here only the human ego lights the way. A musician stands before the void.[28]

To impose human order on the art of music was to blaspheme against the divine order.

In their youth, Zemlinsky and Schoenberg had been 'intimate' friends; now

---

* The contact between Ullmann and Zemlinsky after 1927 is scarcely documented. Ullmann's dedication of his *Three Sonnets from the Portuguese* to Zemlinsky in 1940 indicates that their relationship remained cordial, as does the programme of a recital, preserved in *LoC*, given by Ullmann in Prague on 25 November 1936 with the soprano Amelie Duras. Apart from Berg's Piano Sonata, the programme included lieder by Josef Foerster, Mahler, Reger, Schoenberg, Hugo Wolf and Zemlinsky.

Schoenberg had emerged 'as victor'. This was the bitter kernel of *Der König Kandaules*.

A few years after Zemlinsky's death, Louise approached a composer in New York, whom she hoped would complete the full score of *Kandaules*; his reaction was negative. 'Nobody else was prepared to do it,' she recalled.

At this time I was visited by the pianist Eduard Steuermann – I told him of my plan & of my efforts. Herr Steuermann reproached me for being unaware of the importance of *the choice* of the right musician for this task & also of the responsibility that I had taken upon myself. After this conversation I abandoned the plan.[29]

Not until 1981, two years after the world première of the complete *Lulu*, did she take any further action. In view of the unanimous approval that had greeted Friedrich Cerha's reconstruction of Berg's act III, she approached him about *Kandaules*. Having agreed to inspect the manuscript material, Cerha sent her a preliminary report:

There is a considerable amount of material in a state of complete disorder. It includes brief passages and even entire sections from each of the three acts. The state of notation ranges from hasty sketches to passages of short score with indications of the instrumentation.[30]

Contrary to Louise's assertion that the short score was complete, it seemed to him that sizeable portions were missing.* Rather than attempting to bridge the gaps with music of his own, he decided to abandon the project altogether.[31]

   The problem of the short score lay indeed in its confusion. When Zemlinsky's papers were deposited at the Library of Congress in the early 1970s, the library staff went through the entire collection, adding pencilled page numbers in square brackets at the top outer corner of each folio. Many of these obliterated Zemlinsky's own numberings. Fortunately the *Kandaules* manuscripts had been microfilmed in their original state, and copies deposited at public libraries in Munich and Vienna. Although it was scarcely possible on screen to decipher the musical content itself, Zemlinsky's own numbers were clearly visible at the top of each page – and in a state of complete disarray. Pages 1 to 39 were followed by 27 to 34, 33 to 39, 25 to 32, and so on.† Several pages were partially or completely deleted; in some instances, as could be seen by misalignment of staves, new passages had been pasted over old; in others, indicated by darkened edges (which turned out to be rust marks), pins had been used to

* For a long time it was believed that they had been stolen.
† To be more specific, pages 1–39 contain the entire revised portion of act I; 27–34 contain part of the original version of act I (which runs altogether to 52 pages); 33-9 are the final pages of act III; 25–32 are the preceding pages of act III. The situation is further confused by the interpolation of discarded pages, many of which bear the same numbers as their replacements. Each final double-bar is signed and dated.

fasten corrections to the paper. Although the manuscript was in a less than pristine condition, by sorting the pages back into their original order it immediately became clear that the short score was complete.

The lengthy but absorbing task of deciphering was completed by the author in February 1992, almost exactly fifty years after Zemlinsky's death. As Cerha had noted, many passages included notes on the envisaged orchestration. These apply chiefly to special techniques, such as flutter-tonguing or *sul ponticello*, or the use of specific instruments, such as alto saxophone or Eb clarinet. Octave doublings are written out in full, and the density and spacing of chordal passages clearly defined; throughout the score Zemlinsky has taken care to leave a 'window' around the vocal line (a free space of approximately a 5th), which makes it possible – at least in theory – to hear the voices above the orchestra, even in *forte*. Markings of tempo, dynamic and expression are copious and evidently exhaustive. Even in passages devoid of instrumental markings, the scoring is often self-evident, since much depends on register, texture and dynamic. For the rest, Zemlinsky's 800-bar orchestral score served as guide and reference. On 15 May 1992 the prelude to act III and Gyges' act III monologue were performed in a concert of the Wiener Festwochen. The full score of the opera was completed on 14 November 1993, and the world première, at the Hamburg Staatsoper, followed on 6 October 1996.

Given a grain of sensitivity and a grain of technique, Zemlinsky's orchestral style is not difficult to emulate, for like Ravel's it follows a logical system. And wherever the musical argument calls for exceptional effects or unusual colours, Zemlinsky himself notes them down in the short score. Nevertheless, as published and performed, *Kandaules* represents a compromise, less on account of the orchestration (which in performance is anyway subject to variables such as tempo and acoustic) than of the text itself. To make the work performable at all, three-quarters of an older *Kandaules* had to be welded on to the first quarter of a newer one. How far Zemlinsky intended to continue his process of revision is unclear. Presumably he would have made substantial changes to the final scene of act I and reworked the opening of act II, which, as it stands, is the most diffuse passage of the whole work. He might well have sought to differentiate more strongly between the curtain-falls of acts I and II, which, as they stand, are almost interchangeable, and perhaps he would also have worked on the transitions between scenes in act III, which consist merely of silences, fermatas or held chords. On paper these appear perfunctory, but in performance this simple, block structure proves cogent and effective. Indeed, the formal cohesion and cumulative power of act III surpass anything that Zemlinsky had previously written for the theatre.

Shortly before the entry of Gyges in the closing scene of act I, the reconstructed score reverts to the original version of 1935. There is a natural caesura at this point, a *pp* A octave tied over a double-bar, and since in the dia-

EX. 87   (A) vocal score, p. 62; (B) unpublished version (1938)

(*somewhat tired and irritable*) The air is heavy tonight and its desire oppresses me.

sequel the two versions are alike, there is no audible break in musical sense
(EX. 87)*

The main body of act I, which follows the prologue without a break, is divided into four quasi-symphonic units, separated by brief passages of spoken

* For the sake of cohesion, the last 10 bars of Zemlinsky's revised version had to be sacrificed.

logue or melodrama. In act II the forms are more strongly contrasted, the transitions more subtle. The opening scene for Gyges and Kandaules is divided into four sections of slow to moderate tempo,* then follows a fughetta, in which Kandaules recounts his experiences with the magic ring,† and a sequence of free variations on the 'Ring' motif. A prolonged transition now leads to the entrance of Nyssia and thence to the erotic climax of the work, the *scène d'amour*, observed with a mixture of horror and voyeuristic fascination by the invisible Gyges. As Uwe Sommer has shown in his monograph on *Kandaules*,[32] the superimposition in this scene of extended rondo form on a symphonic *adagio* owes much to act II of *Lulu*. Little can be added to his meticulous and exhaustive analysis, except for the unscientific remark that this scene includes some of the most beautiful music that Zemlinsky ever committed to paper.

Berg's influence is also apparent in the revised prologue to act I, which, like that of *Lulu*, presents a concise *défilée* of thematic material.‡ As in *Der Kreidekreis*, Zemlinsky works with 'individual characters' (Adorno's terminology), motifs associated primarily with one specific figure or idea, that can be condensed to a rhythmic signal or pitch class, and are capable of wellnigh endless variation:

EX. 88 (A) Kandaules; (B) Flatterers; (C) Friends; (D) Trydo; (E) Gyges;
(F) Banquet; (G) Ring; (H) Kandaules as young man

Each of these motifs contains a tightly packed nucleus of musical information.

* Only the ballade bears a title, but the ensuing sections could be headed 'funeral march', 'quasi *andante*' (3/4) and 'rhapsody' (6/8), the latter with a prominent part for alto saxophone.
† Here Zemlinsky makes extensive and unconventional use of *Sprechgesang* At the world première (hence also on the CD recording of 1997) the passage was cut.
‡ As the curtain rises, Gyges' entry is preceded by two sharply articulated triads (E♭ minor and A minor). While it is not inconceivable that these were intended to spell out Schoenberg's initials, S–A, they also include the four opening pitches of *Lulu*, B♭–E♭–E♮–A♮. Zemlinsky had already used this musical synonym in the Second Quartet (see EX. 48(P)). For a detailed analysis of the prologue, see Schwabl and Krones, op. cit.

88A, often reduced to its first five pitches, is built around Zemlinsky's cardinal numbers, 5 and 14 (cf. EX. 43).

Like the flatterers and spongers that it represents, 88B mimics, distorts and (literally) diminishes the Kandaules motif.

88C originates in the music for the miller and his neighbours in *Der Traumgörge* (EX. 31A).

88D is a disfigured variant of the motif of 'Joy', first heard in the *Lerchengesang* of 1891 (cf. EXX. 13 and 27A–C).

The major 2nd and triplet semiquaver figure of 88e connect Gyges, the cuckolded husband, with his murderous predecessor Simone (cf. EX. 53A–C).

88F reintroduces the 'Circassian' rhythm of *Sarema* and the 'Self' motif (here F♯–G♯–B).

Rather than the ring itself, 88G, presented *misterioso* on muted trumpet, represents the sinister inscription, 'I conceal fortune.' Reminiscent of a passage in *Elektra*,* the motif appears in no earlier work of Zemlinsky's.

88H, which accompanies Gyges' reminiscences of youth, alludes to the 'Görge' motif. Kandaules makes his first entrance to the motif itself, clad in the rich apparel of *ff* strings and coloured by the imperial Lydian colours of the Emperor's five-note 5ths chord from *Der Kreidekreis* (cf. EX. 25):

EX. 89   *Der König Kandaules*, page 20 (23)

Elsewhere in the score Zemlinsky brings out other talismans from past works. A theme associated with Kandaules' search for a true friend, for instance EX. 90 –

EX. 90

* Cf. *Elektra*, 158⁴, '[dass meine] Augenlider angeschwollen'. The association with Klytemnestra, which was presumably subconscious, might be explained by the fact that she too is bedecked with talismans.

– cites the motif of the Dwarf's love for the Infanta from *Der Zwerg* (EX. 63E), implying that Kandaules' love for Gyges is similarly predestined to destroy him. And where Schoenberg's 'Melisande' theme was quoted in the Fourth Quartet to invoke the shade of Mathilde, in *Kandaules* Zemlinsky underlines the connection by presenting the idea as a token of Gyges' remorse for the death of his wife:

EX. 91   vocal score page 94

[I spoke to her: 'Trydo'], and she said: 'Master'. I believed that she loved me, and I was happy.

Despite these many reminiscences, Zemlinsky goes some way, particularly in acts II and III, to meet his claim that the work was 'ultra-modern'. To illustrate the concept of invisibility, he evolves a harmony of discontinuous chromatic clusters. With demonstratively catholic taste, he also finds appropriate contexts for passages of bitonality and polytonality, polyrhythm and Stravinskian complex metre; at one stage in act I he even indulges in a parody of the song style of Eisler and Weill.* The score knows no taboos – except for serial technique. In the 'invisibility' clusters Zemlinsky avoids any chord groupings that would include all the twelve semitones. And the chord that marks Nyssia's agonized realization of her betrayal, inspired by the 'cry of agony' from the *Adagio* of Mahler's Tenth Symphony, contains only nine of the twelve semitones:

EX. 92   vocal score page 170

But this is a gesture that looks back still further, to act II of *Parsifal*. As befits a work conceived as a final synthesis, the language is selectively retrospective.

For Zemlinsky the *fin-de-siècle* concept of 'decadence' differed only in spirit from the 'degeneracy' of the 1930s. His epithet 'ultra-modern', catchword of the Secessionists, draws the connecting line between the two. But what formerly had been ridiculed and encouraged was now ridiculed and forbidden. *Kandaules* replaces the luxuriant post-*Tristan*esque death wish of the Lyric Symphony and *Der Zwerg* with a new, acute awareness of the horror and inevitability of death. In 1907 Görge could still look to the future, if despondently. Thirty years later, even that slender ray of hope had been extinguished.

---

* Vocal score page 54, at 80², to the words 'doppelsinniger Worte Spiel' (ambiguous play of words).

XII

Lieder III

previous page:
Zemlinsky smiles . . .
caricature by Gedö
first published in *Prager Presse* (undated copy in archive of Universal Edition, Vienna)

When Zemlinsky was asked in October 1932 to comment on the state of new music in Austria and Germany, his views differed only slightly from those he had expressed at the turn of the century. However, where formerly he had complained that 'sickly but delicate nerves' were impeding progress, he now ascribed the stagnation to external pressures:

What we are witnessing at the present time is neither an improvement nor a deterioration in the quality of musical life, for music goes its way unerringly. [. . .] There is, I would say, no sign of decline at all, only of standstill. [. . .] Unfortunately our era has not yet brought forth the one truly great musician who towers above all others. If I am not mistaken, composers of genuine stature almost always lived in periods of calm and stability. [. . .] As soon as the situation shows some sign of normalization, the public, which has grown fickle, will crowd back into the concert halls and opera houses, creative artists will receive fresh impetus, and stagnation will be followed by a new advance – perhaps then we shall also witness the emergence of that one truly great, outstanding personality.[1]

Since the death of Brahms, a new god had ascended in Zemlinsky's musical firmament – Gustav Mahler – and for a time Richard Strauss had stood almost as high in his esteem. But Mahler had been dead for twenty years, Strauss had fallen from grace,* and if Zemlinsky ever seriously considered Schoenberg to be the 'outstanding personality' of his own generation, he was too proud and too humble to acknowledge the fact in print.

As for himself, the divine spark still burned fiercely. Most of his efforts were concentrated on larger-scale compositions for a wider public, but he also maintained a small reserve of energy for works of a more personal nature: lieder and chamber music. His last songs resume the search for Görge's inner 'miracle world' of beauty and imagination. Shuttered off from the real world, protest or self-pity rarely ruffles their Apollonian calm. 'Music', as he stressed, 'goes its way unerringly.'

A few weeks after leaving Germany, during his sojourn at Montagnola, Zemlinsky composed *Und einmal gehst du* to a text by August Eigner. Delicately

---

* On 10 October 1928 Zemlinsky wrote to Louise from Vienna: 'Yesterday I saw *Die ägyptische Helena* [at the Staatsoper] with [Rose] Pauly as guest – very, very dull on the whole, but the orchestra and stage (designs [by Roller]) were wonderful.'

but firmly, with images of autumn – pale sunlight, almond trees heavy with fruit, the crackling of dead leaves – the poet traces the path that 'each of us must one day tread', the approach of old age. With the lightest of brushstrokes Zemlinsky adds pallid colours and soft textures to complete the picture. In Hofmannsthal's *Noch spür' ich ihren Atem* human transience had been something 'too dreadful even to bewail'. Now, seventeen years later, tolling D octaves in conjunction with a tritonal allusion to the 'Fate' chord (D–A♭/G♯) recall the subliminal agitation of the Hofmannsthal song (cf. EX. 59), but in a spirit of equanimity and resignation:

EX. 93   (A) *Noch spür' ich ihren Atem*, opening;
(B) *Und einmal gehst du*, bars 29–32.

Upon my cheeks I still can feel them breathing,
No point delaying, no point in turning back now . . .

On 10–11 January 1934, a few days before the première of *Der Kreidekreis* in Stettin, Zemlinsky wrote two further meditations on the evening of life, provisionally entitled *Abendlieder*, to texts by Christian Morgenstern. Shortly afterwards he set two further Morgenstern texts and two epigrammatic poems by Goethe, making up a cycle of Six Songs op. 22. Four of these were performed in Prague in April 1934; on 13 February 1935 Zemlinsky accompanied Julia

Nessy in the first complete performance at the Kleine Musikvereinsaal in Vienna.* They were published, together with *Das bucklichte Männlein* and *Ahnung Beatricens*,[†] in 1978.

Auf braunen Sammetschuhen depicts the setting sun as a torch that sets the stars ablaze: a metaphor of death as the bridge between life and eternity. As if in answer to the stern austerity of *Und einmal gehst du*, the song ends with words of consolation:

Sei ruhig Herz, sei ruhig. / Das Dunkel kann dir nun kein Leid mehr tun.

Be still, my heart, be still. / The darkness can hurt you now no more.

Thirteen of its 20 bars are harmonized in a predominantly pentatonic G♭ major, with an accompaniment of evenly pulsating crotchets. A flurry of chromatic passing notes in the fourth bar initiates a 9-bar phase of tonal instability, the apex of which is marked by the 'Fate' chord (bar 8). G♭ major is then gradually restored, and the song closes calmly, as it opened, with the 'World' motif, supported by 5th-based pentatonic harmonies.

Abendkelch voll Sonnenlicht again equates day to life and night to death, but now the rays of the setting sun are compared to a glass of wine, the golden 'evening wine of all sorrow' ('alles Herzwehs Abendwein'), of which before nightfall every drop must be drained. The composition, in two sections of 14 bars each, is one of Zemlinsky's most idiosyncratic. The accompaniment moves inexorably through areas of consonant and dissonant harmony, ranging from root-position triads to bitonal composites, in a sequence determined only by the tenuous logic of a semitonal figure defined in the opening bar. D major is implied at the opening and confirmed at the close, but the essence of the piece is tonal asymmetry. The first section passes through F♯ minor to conclude in the vicinity of D♭, and before the tonic again shines through, the harmony is anchored for 6 bars on a pedal E♭. Much of the vocal line is extrapolated from its attendant harmonies; not until the close does the line momentarily free itself, but only to fall 14 semitones from the supertonic to the tonic, as if symbolically to negate the life- and love-affirming conclusion of the Second Quartet.

Feiger Gedanken bängliches Schwanken, to a poem by Goethe, was composed on 18 January, the day on which first critical reactions to *Der Kreidekreis* appeared in the German press:

Feiger Gedanken / bängliches Schwanken, / weibisches Zagen, / ängstliches Klagen / wendet kein Elend, / macht dich nicht frei. / Allen Gewalten / zum Trutz dich erhalten, /

---

* The programme also included arias by Peri, Cavalli, Scarlatti, Paisiello, and songs by Debussy and Schoenberg.
[†] Jacques-Louis Monod was responsible for editing all the later songs except 'Und einmal gehst du', which was first published in 1995.

nimmer sich beugen, / kräftig sich zeigen, / rufet die Arme / der Götter herbei.

Cowardly thinking, / timid reluctance, / weak hesitation, / fearful complaining / ward off no anguish, / make you not free. / Boldly confront every / hostile aggressor, / never surrender, / show yourself fearless, / summon the arms of / the gods to your aid.

A key scheme bounded by the A minor of death and the E♭ major of transfiguration implies that Zemlinsky interpreted the poem as a war cry against finality ('My time will come after my death'). Over the first 7 bars (verse 1) the bass line rises in irregular steps from the subdominant of A minor to a region of 7th-chord harmony between G♭ and D; in the following 7 bars (verse 2) the line descends through A minor 7th chords, passing through areas of D, G♭ and F♭ before reaching the dominant, E major, in the penultimate bar. The final flourish of E♭ major, briefly anticipated in bars 12 and 13, forcibly breaks the death-ridden harmonic circle of the previous 14 bars.

Light-hearted antidotes are offered by *Elfenlied*, composed the following day, and *Volkslied*, composed on 12 January. Their surface of gracefully tripping rhythm and largely diatonic harmony conceals a world of subtlety and refinement. *Elfenlied* is no less a *Nachtstück* than the two *Abendlieder*, but night is now the realm of fantasy, the time when mortals sleep and the 'little people' come out of hiding to sing, dance and dream. In contrast to the monolithic *forte–fortissimo* of *Feiger Gedanken*, the song begins *piano leggiero* and ends in a whispered *pppp*, its substance spun from the tenuous thread of a semitone device articulated by skipping B♭ major–C♭⁷ triads in the opening bars. Oscillating between D major and F major, *Volkslied* is built on a similar semitone figure, articulated in gently swaying 6/8 rhythm. Drawing on a miscellany of erotic images – two lovers and a storm-tossed forest, a necklace of white coral spun with fine red veins, 'a world full of happiness' – Morgenstern preaches a light-hearted sermon of resignation and self-denial:

O Welt, deine süssen Dinge / sind nicht für mich, für mich.

O world, your delightful pleasures / are not for me, for me.

Finally, under the golden light of the summer sun, with the white of sails and swans' wings shining brightly against a bright blue sky, the poet invites the weary and despondent to join him on the ocean of his soul – *Auf dem Meere meiner Seele* – in a joyful regatta. Zemlinsky translates Morgenstern's colours into harmony, mixing white (C major) with the yellowish red 'at maximum intensity' of E major (Ullmann), the greenish blue of E♭ major (bar 16) and the deep purple of A♭ minor (bar 24). The textures themselves remain brittle and lean, with a high-pitched, breathless vocal line and an accompaniment in swiftly moving two-part counterpoint. As a triumphant apotheosis of the first song, the piano erupts at the close in an *accelerando* of Lydian E major: 'The darkness can hurt you now no more.'

Living in Vienna, it was difficult to avoid contact with Alma, and harder still to resist her animal magnetism. Louise recalled that social gatherings *chez* Mahler-Werfel affected Zemlinsky with an indefinable agitation, as if he were fighting to control an upsurge of feelings that long had lain dormant.[2] Beneath a surface of equanimity, his setting of a sonnet by Werfel, *Ahnung Beatricens* ('Intimation of Beatrice'), composed in January 1935 as a companion piece to *Das buck-lichte Männlein*, sensitively reflects the emotional strain of these encounters. Revisiting the 'streets and parks' of his childhood, the poet recalls the tender grip of a beloved hand; 'in lakeside restaurants, in smoky taverns' his erstwhile muse still haunts him. But the vision has grown indistinct, the passion is spent, only the pain lingers on. As in *Das bucklichte Männlein*, semitone and octave contribute substantially to the line, but now in conjunction with a rising minor 3rd figure. Where the role distribution of the *Männlein* required that voice and piano go their separate ways, the texture of *Ahnung Beatricens* is fully integrated: a four-part invention, in which voice and piano frequently cross and entwine. Using the G♯ of the 'Fate' chord as pivotal note, the harmony vacillates between D minor and C♯ minor, the key of lament and longing.* The two keys collide already in the opening bar, with a rising semiquaver figure extracted from the pitches of the 'Fate' chord superimposed on a secondinversion C♯minor triad. Within a freely chromatic context, elements of bitonality serve to confine much of the ensuing musical argument to a tonal no man's land. But at the close it becomes evident that the two keys remain unreconciled:

Und keiner weiss, wie fern wir uns geschehen.

And no one knows how far apart we drift.

The Twelve Songs op. 27 were composed between 31 March and 19 April 1937 in the afterglow of *Der König Kandaules*. Beyond the confines of the 'cage' in Grinzing, the cycle reaches out to points far east and far west, with three texts by German poets, three from the Afro-American of *Afrika singt* and six from the Sanskrit of Amaru and Kalidasa. The latter (taken from Hans Bethge's little-known anthology *Die indische Harfe*) explore new byways of tonal harmony and experiment with ultra-compact forms.

The three European poems are placed at strategic points in the cycle. In George's *Entführung* (from *Das Jahr der Seele*) the singer calls to his beloved to travel with him to far-off places, to bathe in silver lakes and gather flowers in green forests. The journey leads first to India, with three seasonal poems

---

* Cf. *Orientalisches Sonnett* and *Klagen ist der Mond gekommen*, op. 6 no. 2.

(*Sommer, Frühling, Der Wind des Herbstes*) and two romances (*Jetzt ist die Zeit, Die Verschmähte*), then to America, with a contrasting group of Harlem Renaissance poems (*Elend, Harlem Tänzerin* and *Afrikanischer Tanz*). With George's *Gib ein Lied mir wieder* the singer wakes from his dream, troubled that he can no longer find words for his grief. In Kalidasa's melancholy *Regenzeit* the patter of raindrops reminds him of his wanderings, but the illusion of freedom is shattered. In *Wandrers Nachtlied*,* one of Goethe's best-known poems, the singer prays for peace and deliverance.

The seventh song, *Elend* ('Misery'), has become something of a popular favourite. Discovering in it the 'characteristic sensibility of the blues', Cord Garben recorded it (sung in English) with 'crossed legs at the piano [. . . and] a dummy cigarette between the lips',[3] while another duo presented all three Harlem songs on record as 'cabaret classics', side by side with Schoenberg's Brettl-Lieder and authentic cabaret songs by Satie and Weill.[4] Yet Zemlinsky's music knows little of such milieux, indeed the melodic shape of his *Elend* theme has more in common with the first subject of his Clarinet Trio, composed nearly forty years earlier, than with any jazz composition of the 1920s or 1930s.†

The op. 27 songs are the most Janus-faced of Zemlinsky's *œuvre*, rich in musical memories, yet conceived in a spirit of adventure, of a determination to overcome the prevalent artistic stagnation. *Gib ein Lied mir wieder* opens with a juxtaposition of E♭ minor and A major, the keys of Gyges' misery and Kandaules' joy. Here the afterglow of *Kandaules* becomes apparent, and *Regenzeit* even includes a brief quotation from the opera (cf. EX. 87):

Ein schwü - ler Duft er - gießt sich durch den feuch - ten Raum

EX. 94   *Regenzeit*, op. 27 no. 11, bars 7–8

A sultry perfume permeates the humid air.

---

* Zemlinsky set the same poem to music in 1896, but the manuscript is mutilated to the point of illegibility.
† Zemlinsky's new setting of *Afrikanischer Tanz* bears no resemblance to the version in the Symphonic Songs. In order to reproduce the internal rhyme of Hughes's opening lines – 'low' and 'slow' – the German translation sacrifices sense to sound, rhyming 'grollen' (rumble) with 'rollen' (roll), and ignoring the intended effects of tempo and pitch. As Zemlinsky never read the original poems, his settings are therefore neither 'low' nor 'slow' in character.

Like an album of picture postcards, the charm of the exotic poems lies in the diversity of their themes and colours, shapes and sizes. In singing of Afro-America and India, Zemlinsky casts a bridge to two works close to his heart, the Symphonic Songs and the Lyric Symphony. Other pieces delve still further into the past. *Die Verschmähte*, for instance, with its dotted rhythms and carefully organized variative architecture, recalls *Die Beiden* (1916); *Jetzt ist die Zeit* comes close in its Mahlerian spirit to the fifth and sixth Maeterlinck songs (1913); the middle section of *Der Wind des Herbstes* paraphrases a passage from the fourth Dehmel song (1907), and the flat-key colouring at the close of *Wandrers Nachtlied* re-echoes the death wish of *Empfängnis*, composed in 1896.

Gib ein Lied mir wieder, George's 'sad dance',* was the last of the cycle to be completed. Here the real world becomes palpable once more. Realizing that his dream of 'calm and stability' will remain unfulfilled, the poet sings the only song that still remains to him, his own inability to sing:

Du weisst es ja: mir wich der friede / und meine hand ist zag.

You know for sure: I find no peace and / uncertain is my hand.

---

* In *Das Jahr der Seele*, the poem is the third of the section entitled 'Traurige Tänze'.

XIII

The Exile

previous page:
Alexander Zemlinsky
drawing by Emil Orlik

Finis Austriae

The summer of 1937 was long and hot. 'Führer weather' the Germans called it; indeed, since Hitler had taken control, many of them believed the gods to be entirely on their side. Across the border, the Austrians were content simply to swelter. For over twenty years their country had lurched from one crisis to the next; revolutions, assassinations, general strikes and street-fighting were the order of the day. The people, grown impervious, stretched out in the sunshine, opened the daily papers and read of fresh disasters.

In the Mahler-Werfel household tension had meanwhile almost reached breaking point. Seconded by Johannes Hollnsteiner, Alma had become a passionate supporter of Mussolini and Franco, and almost as fervent an admirer of Hitler; Werfel, naturally, held diametrically opposing views. In this atmosphere of disagreement and mistrust, the marriage was in danger of foundering. To Alma's mind, the house on the Hohe Warte had fallen under an evil star, and since Werfel had never found the place conducive to creative work, she decided to sell up and move away. Her farewell party, on 12 June, was the talk of the town. Aristocratic, financial and government circles were well represented, and the guest list was enhanced by distinguished personalities from the world of literature and music: Hermann Broch, Franz Theodor Csokor, Ödon von Horvath and Carl Zuckmayer, Bruno Walter, Egon Wellesz and, naturally, Alexander von Zemlinsky (the *Adelsprädikat* had by now become an almost obligatory part of his name).[1] The official garden party was followed by a *Heurigen* razzle that lasted into the small hours. While Egon Wellesz was drawn into Alma's inner circle, his wife Emmy 'spent most of her time', as she recalled, 'in conversation with Alexander von Zemlinsky, who despite his unattractive appearance so bubbled with wit and charm that one never tired of listening to him'.[2] Shortly afterwards Werfel left the country, never to return. For all her anti-Semitic posturing, Alma joined him on the long trek into exile.

The glorious weather lasted until well into the autumn. Nobody in Austria took much heed of the frenetic activity in state rooms all over Europe, nobody seemed unduly alarmed by Hitler's mobilization of the *Wehrmacht*, and only few rallied to the cause of the Popular Front in Spain. Returning from London in November to pay a final farewell to the city of his birth, Stefan Zweig was amazed to find people going about their daily lives oblivious of the gathering storm clouds:

I knew that the same voices that today called out 'Heil Schuschnigg' would tomorrow be bellowing 'Heil Hitler'. But everyone to whom I spoke in Vienna appeared honestly unconcerned. They invited each other to parties in dinner-jackets and tails (not suspecting that they would soon be wearing concentration-camp uniforms), they overran the shops in search of Christmas gifts for their beautiful homes (not suspecting that only months later these would be confiscated and plundered).[3]

In early December Zemlinsky was back in Prague to conduct the Czech Philharmonic, this time in a programme of Bach's Suite in D, Schumann's Cello Concerto and Mahler's Fourth Symphony. The cello soloist was his old friend Casals, now a fugitive from Falangist Spain. There was a fateful symmetry to this chance encounter: twenty-six years before, Casals had been the star attraction of Zemlinsky's first Prague concert; now they were sharing the stage in what was to be his last.

To celebrate the fiftieth anniversary of the NDT in 1938, Paul Eger planned a series of gala performances conducted by three former musical directors, Blech, Steinberg and Szell. Zemlinsky was not invited; but when Blech cancelled at short notice, he was asked to step in. Thus on 8 January 1938 he took his place in the pit, as he had done so many times in the past, to conduct a performance of *Carmen*. Despite the ignominious circumstances, the public was glad for a last chance to show its respect.

Hitler's humiliation of Schuschnigg at Berchtesgarten on 12 February 1938, Schuschnigg's call for a plebiscite on 13 March to confirm the mandate of his Austrian Fatherland Front, Austria's forcible annexation by the Nazis on 11–12 March: these events are too well documented to need recounting here. At 8 p.m. on the evening of 11 March, the Greissles gathered around the wireless in their Mödling living room to hear Schuschnigg's address to the nation:

On Radio Vienna the disheartened Chancellor capitulated. Having announced his resignation, he ended his speech with words from the Imperial anthem: 'Gott schütze Österreich' ('God protect Austria'). Within a few minutes [. . .] you could hear the rhythmic noise of National Socialist battle songs through coffee-house windows. And on the streets Jews were already being held up, abused and assaulted.[4]

Bruno Walter and his wife followed the broadcast from their hotel in Amsterdam:

After Schuschnigg's parting words, 'Gott schütze Österreich', the land that we had loved faded out to the solemn sound of Haydn's 'Kaiser' Hymn, played by a string quartet. And as speech followed speech [. . .], with the dreadful news of advancing German troops and the occupation of Austrian towns and cities, the gaps were filled with Viennese waltzes. [. . .] All of a sudden this crazy mixture of death-agony and dance music ceased, and a change of tone became apparent. A hard-edged Prussian voice took over, which informed us in short, clipped phrases of the progress of the invaders; in place of waltzes the turn of events was symbolically affirmed by the din of military march music.[5]

Together with millions of others, Zemlinsky and his wife probably also witnessed the fateful events in their own home, over the air. 'When Hitler came to Austria,' Louise remembered,

the next day I decided to go to the American Embassy and apply for a visa. I asked Zemlinsky if he intended to stay in Vienna. He wanted to sleep it over. And the following morning he said to me: I'm coming with you.[6]

Even before the *Anschluss*, members of the Austrian Nazi Party had rung the doorbell, canvassing for support. Hoping that they would leave her in peace, Louise made a donation to party funds.[7] But once the SA had taken over, she knew that other callers would soon follow, and with more sinister intentions. The Zemlinskys' first concern was not for themselves, however, but for Felix Greissle who, as an active member of the Austrian Communist Party, was in immediate danger. Since Schoenberg was unable to underwrite an affidavit for Greissle and his family,* friends in America advised him to apply for a permit to visit his father-in-law and remain in the country, illegally if need be, until he could find employment.† The sole obstacle to this plan was its prohibitive cost. 'Fortunately,' recalls Arnold Greissle-Schönberg,

Uncle Alex and his wife Luise (*sic*) agreed to lend my parents $1,500, which at that time was a fairly substantial sum. In April 1938, as soon as our Papa had received the money, he bought our rail tickets to Antwerp and booked passages to New York. [. . .] Incidentally, since the journey needed to appear like a visit from which he would be coming home, he had to buy return tickets for both train and boat. American travel regulations also required evidence of two-way transit.[8]

Hans Gál recalled seeing Zemlinsky at this time 'on a bench at the roadside in Grinzing. [. . .] He looked very old, very miserable, a broken man.'[9] In the dream world of his op. 27 songs he had longed for distant lands: 'See the world with me, dear child.' But Louise's memories of a husband prepared to follow her to the ends of the earth cannot be substantiated – on the contrary. For several weeks he did nothing at all, then in mid-April he resolved to authenticate his family tree. The documents that he obtained from the Catholic registry office (Leopoldstadt) and the registrar of the Vienna Rathaus are preserved among Louise's own papers:

* According to US Immigration Law, refugees could enter the country either on the 'quota', i.e. within limits specified by Federal Government, or on presentation of an Affidavit of Support, i.e. an undertaking by a US citizen to 'receive, maintain, support the alien(s) after their immigration [. . .], and hereby assume such obligations guaranteeing that none of them will at any time become public charges upon any community in the United States'. Official acceptance of an affidavit was dependent on a means test.
† Before Greissle departed for the US, a letter of recommendation from Schoenberg secured him a job with the New York music publisher G. Schirmer Inc. Later he occupied the post of Director of Serious Music Publications at Schirmer's.

Anton Semlinsky and Cäcilie Pulletz: marriage certificate (23 October 1832),
copy dated 14 April 1938;
ditto: civil marriage certificate (undated);
ditto, baptismal record, copy dated 27 April 1938;
Adolf Semlinsky: birth certificate (23 April 1845), copy dated 27 April 1938.[10]

Each certificate is rubber-stamped: 'Valid only in conjunction with application
for a certificate of Aryan origin (*Ariernachweis*)'. Before the application could
be submitted, two further documents were required: Adolf Zemlinszky's marriage certificate and Zemlinsky's own birth certificate. But these were kept in
black-bound, gold-embossed ledgers at the archive of the Isräelitisches
Kultusgemeinde. And they were in the hands of the Gestapo.

Only now, it seems, did he realize his predicament. Görge's village had been
overrun by thieves and murderers; life and limb were at risk. To struggle against
destiny was futile. He would have to leave.

On 7 May Zemlinsky applied to the authorities in Prague for an entry visa,
writing (in Czech) that as an 'internationally accredited conductor' he had
appeared regularly in Prague and 'familiarized concert audiences the world over
with the music of Smetana, Dvořák and Janáček'; his wife, he wrote, was
Jewish but Prague-born; her relatives were all Czech subjects; he himself was of
Aryan birth; the purpose of his stay was to finalize arrangements for travel to
the USA, where (as he wrote) he was due to take up an engagement with the
New York Philharmonic Orchestra. Towards the end of the month the Czech
immigration authority notified him that with effect from 9 June he had been
granted a four-month residence permit 'for non-commercial purposes'.[11]

On 26 May post arrived from Melanie Guttmann in New York. She had
attempted to obtain an affidavit for Zemlinsky and his family, but her financial
resources had been judged insufficient, and the application rejected. The letter
included a cheque for $110, which was never paid in.[12]

The summer was taken up with paperwork and household administration.
Since Austria was now a province of Germany (the 'Ostmark'), every passport
and identity card in the land had to be renewed. The Nazis also required
prospective emigrants to pay *Reichsfluchtsteuer* (fugitive tax), amounting to
30 per cent of their liquid assets. Together with thousands of others, the
Zemlinskys were therefore obliged to join endless queues, fill in innumerable
application forms and wait patiently for bevies of minor officials to rubber-
stamp and sign them. As they were aware, their property in Grinzing would be
forfeited to the state. Before arranging for shipment of his personal effects,
Zemlinsky sorted through his papers and destroyed everything that might
hinder their passage through customs. Only the letters from Schoenberg were
salvaged, together with a few items of sentimental value, such as his diploma
from the Vienna Conservatoire.

On 20 August he was notified that his *Reichsfluchtsteuer* application had been processed, and that within seven days he was to pay 27,612 Reichsmark to the Deutsche Länderbank. Confirmation of payment was issued on 5 September, and two days later the emigration office issued new passports, valid for twelve months.

Amidst this turmoil, he began to compose. First he sketched out two love songs to texts from Hans Bethge's anthology *Die chinesische Flöte*, then, on 22 August, he began work on a quartet for clarinet and string trio. Before leaving Vienna he had drafted several versions of a first-movement exposition, the most substantial of which extended to 76 bars.

On the morning of Saturday 10 September the Zemlinskys made their way to the Czech Consulate. From there, with new visa stamps in their new passports, they went to the Deutsche Länderbank to withdraw their currency allowance of US $8. By midday they were ready to leave. Shortly after 3 p.m. their passports were again rubber-stamped, this time by German and Czech border guards. Arriving in Prague late in the evening, they made their way to the Sachsel family home at Poděbradova 187 in Karlín.

With the growing threat of Nazi invasion, life in Czechoslovakia was scarcely less precarious than in Austria. Hans Nachod, for instance, who had also just arrived in Prague, was in an even more difficult position than the Zemlinskys, for his residence permit was valid only for fourteen days.* On 16 September he wrote to Schoenberg in California, begging him to obtain an affidavit for him.† 'Here in Prague', he explained,

the utter certainty of a terrible war consumes everyone with dread. One sees weeping women, apprehensive men, but also people prepared in their desperation to do anything. [. . .] We have witnessed the Great War and plenty else. Formerly we had no idea what would happen when war broke out; today we do know, and we await the horrors as if turned to stone.[13]

Having abandoned hope of finding a sponsor for an affidavit, Zemlinsky now resolved to seek a quota permit for the US. This was a slow business, however, for documents had to pass between Prague and the Central Immigration Authority at Staten Island, NY. Since the Czech visas were due to expire on 9 October, he first took steps to secure their extension. The list of visa applications from

---

* Having signed an affidavit for his student friend Moritz Violin, Schoenberg could guarantee support neither for his son Georg nor for his cousin Hans Nachod. After Nachod's release from British internment in October 1945, Schoenberg arranged for him to travel to the US, but Nachod decided to remain in England.
† Schoenberg had written to Nachod, asking him to take care of Georg. Anxious for his own safety, however, Nachod ignored the request, leaving Georg to his own resources. The latter remained in Vienna throughout the Nazi occupation, working at first as a copyist for Universal Edition and later as driver of a delivery van. At one stage he was summoned for transportation to Terezín, but thanks to intervention from his employer, his name was struck off the list.

Austrian Jews had meanwhile passed the 100,000 mark, refugee camps had been set up outside Prague, Brno and Bratislava, and many applications were being turned down outright. Supported by a recommendation from the Ministry of Culture and Education, Zemlinsky wrote another urgent appeal:

We are living with relatives, are unoccupied and have no intention of seeking occupation. [. . .] I, Alexander Zemlinsky, was active in Prague for fifteen years, where I did much for the propagation of Czech music.[14]

Of his other activities during these twelve weeks in Prague – how he celebrated his sixty-seventh birthday, whether he met up with Nachod, Ullmann or other friends – nothing is known. As far as conducting was concerned, Zemlinsky respected the conditions of residence and refrained from seeking employment. For a performance of *Das Lied von der Erde*, planned for the following March with the Czech Philharmonic, he would have needed a special dispensation – but by then he had left the country. There is no evidence of any creative activity during this period either. Certain is only that he attended a performance of Janáček's *Kat'a Kabanová*, with Marta Krásová in the role of Kabanichá, on 4 November at the Národní Divadlo. The following day he wrote in a crabbed, shaky hand to his colleague Václav Tálich:

It was one of the most beautiful operatic performances I ever attended. And it seems to me that this was almost entirely of *your doing*. Thank you for the great pleasure. – The work numbers among the most inspired in the entire operatic literature.[15]

On 11 November the American Vice-Consul issued the long-awaited Immigration Identification Cards. With a US visa stamp in his passport, Zemlinsky now required only transit visas for Belgium and France, together with flight tickets and travel documents. To obtain these took a further fortnight. He and Louise pleaded with Hanna to come with them, but in vain. At sixty-three, she no longer felt capable of such a journey. Unable or unwilling to envisage the consequences, she resolved to let destiny run its course.

On 2 December[16] the Zemlinskys flew to Rotterdam, where they boarded the SS *Statendam*, headed for Boulogne. Thence, on 14 December, they set sail for the New World.

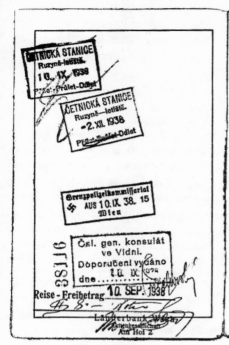

From the passport of Louise Zemlinsky

verso:
Czech arrival stamp, 10 September 1938
Czech departure stamp, 2 December 1938
German departure stamp, Vienna, 10 September 1938, 15:00 hours
Immigration permit, Czech General Consulate, Vienna, 10 September 1938
Dispensation for US $8,– travel allowance in notes, 10 September 1938, Länderbank Wien

recto:
Embarkation stamp, French special commissariat, 14 December 1938
Fifteen-day transit visa, French General Consulate, Prague, 21 November 1938, expiry date
19 December; reason for journey: 'business'
Visa endorsement by French special police commissariat (date illegible)

Succeeding pages include the following entries: Belgian transit visa, Prague 21 September
1938; Date stamp of Riverpolitie Rotterdam, 2 December 1938, with handwritten entry:
'Doerreis naar U.S.A. op 14 Dec 1938 met s.s. Statendam, via Boulogne'; Quota Immigration
Visa No. 23285 dated 11 November 1938, signed Andrew Gilchrist, American Vice-Consul
[Prague].

America

On 23 December the SS *Statendam* docked at Ellis Island. Once the Zemlinskys had been cleared by passport and immigration control, they were met by Melanie Guttmann, who accompanied them to Hotel Hamilton in West 73rd Street. There, with Felix and Trudi Greissle, Arthur Bodanzky and other old friends, they settled in and celebrated their first Christmas in America.

Shortly afterwards, Bodanzky invited Zemlinsky to a lunch date with the critic Harold Taubmann. On 5 January 1939 an account of their meeting appeared in the *New York Times*:

[. . .] A day or two after his arrival here he enrolled in a [language] class for adults. During lunch his interest seemed to be divided equally between the conversation in hand and the immediate absorption of a few fresh nuggets of English enunciation and idiom. [. . .] What did he plan to do here? Mr Bodanzky offered an answer for him: 'Teach composition or conducting or harmony or counterpoint. After all, such a musician can teach anything a musician needs to know.'[1]

Having equipped himself with a supply of Schirmer manuscript paper, Zemlinsky now resumed work on his Clarinet Quartet of the previous summer. He retained only the first 6 bars of the Grinzing fragment, at a more deliberate pace (*Allegro moderato* instead of *Molto allegro*) and with a greater wealth of motivic variation. The surviving 127-bar torso of a first-movement exposition extends the promise – unfulfilled, alas – of a final masterpiece.

On 25 January two crates of furniture, household items, books and manuscripts arrived on board the SS *Hamburg*. Thanks to the efforts of the Zemlinsky's Viennese housekeeper, Frau Zimmermann, everything had survived the journey in good order. At the beginning of February, now that it was possible to set up a home of their own, they moved into an apartment at 46 West 83rd Street.

The change of ambience disrupted work on the Quartet. But there was anyway no time now to be squandered on composing for sheer pleasure. While Louise and Hansi attended to domestic arrangements, Zemlinsky addressed the problem of writing an opera to replace the 'unstageable' *Kandaules*: something with which to establish his reputation in the New World and to earn a few urgently needed dollars. Among the circle of Austro-German refugees in New York, he had met up with the actor and playwright Walter Firner,* brother of

---

* Since the Firners were living close to Hotel Hamilton, at 306 West 73rd Street, it is not inconceivable that they met on the street.

his former assistant at the NDT and the Krolloper, Artur Feinsinger. Before emigrating to the US in 1938, Firner and his wife, the actress Irma Stein, had written a film script based on the Homeric legend of Circe. Later they reworked the text into a three-act opera libretto, which they offered to Richard Strauss. Since his collaboration with Stefan Zweig on *Die schweigsame Frau*, for which he been denounced and discredited by the Nazis, Strauss was scarcely in a position to work with another Jewish librettist. Yet he was enthusiastic about *Circe*, and on his recommendation it was accepted for performance in Zurich – providing, of course, that a composer of repute could be found for the project. Zemlinsky leapt at the idea. Zurich: his friend Schmid-Bloss was still *Intendant* at the Stadttheater; Zurich was the last remaining oasis for progressive composers. Perhaps he could return, perhaps even settle in Switzerland. For in his heart of hearts he knew that America was not for him. He had already abandoned hope of mastering the English language (Walter Firner recalls that he was in the habit of addressing everyone in German, regardless of whether they understood him or not).[2] And one grey winter's day, walking down Broadway, he suddenly turned to Louise and said, 'I wouldn't even want to be buried here.'

No classical theme could have been more appropriate to a fugitive artist than that of the Argonauts stranded on a foreign shore. Praying to Athene, Odysseus gives voice to his misery:

Ich zog durch Länder, fuhr über Meere. [. . .] Auf allen Strassen bin ich gewandert. Und immer irrte mein Fuss. Spottet Ihr meiner, Ihr Götter? Macht mich zum fahrenden Sänger, zum Landstreicher, zum Bettler?

I have travelled by land, sailed the seas. [. . .] Down every pathway I have wandered. And every time I went astray. Do you mock me, you gods? Would you make of me a wandering minstrel, a vagrant, a beggar?

Although the Stein-Firner libretto was written in Europe, the revised version included images of a refugee's America: the statue of Pallas Athene dominating the coastline, for instance, or Circe's palace of white stone, fronted by Grecian columns. As for public decency, the drama presented an ideal corrective to *Kandaules*. This Circe remains immortal, namely, only as long as she abstains from sex. It is not she, the virginal, red-headed enchantress, who transforms men into swine, as in Homer, but the men themselves and their thwarted lust.

The opening of act II, a banquet attended by her devoted retinue of animals, could present a diverting, Muppet-like spectacle. For the rest, the libretto wavers between the inconsequential and the banal. Predictably, Odysseus is consumed by desire for Circe, and saves himself from translation only by getting drunk. The final scene is pure Hollywood: Circe is united in true love with her blond, muscular hero, his comrades are restored, the spell is broken. The captain of a passing ship offers to take the Argonauts on board, but they are happy to remain on the island, exiles in paradise:

Die Liebe kennt kein Mass der Zeit, / kein Ziel die Liebe, sie ist unendlich!

No measure does love know of time, / nor any goal. Love is unending!

Given time to find the collaborator of his choice, Zemlinsky is unlikely to have committed himself to *Circe*. But his capital was almost exhausted, his critical powers were dampened by desperation, and this was the only available straw at which to clutch. On 15 March the Nazis had marched into Prague, making further contact with the Sachsels difficult and uncertain; his health had suffered during the past twelve months, and since he was in no condition to conduct or even to teach, composition was his only feasible source of income. Setting to work with grim determination, he completed the short score of act I in about six weeks; in early April he moved on at the same frantic pace to act II.

He might never have worked faster, but never before had he filled so many pages with so few compelling ideas. Perhaps he planned, as with *Kandaules*, to sketch out the entire work, then return to the opening, filtering and refining until he had uncovered an inner core of beauty and logic. But perhaps he realized, as with *Der Meister von Prag* or *Der Graf von Gleim*, that he was wasting his time. In a second interview for the *New York Times*, published in early September, it was mentioned that 'writing according to his inner feeling, disregarding slogans and currents, [Zemlinsky] is now working on a new opera'.[3] But by that time he had long since laid down his pen.*

Disregarding the niceties of music-drama, Zemlinsky was simply in no state to continue. Having fought the battle for sheer survival, the strain of the past twelve months began to take its toll. 'I fell victim to a severe nervous disorder,' he later explained:

For months I was confined to bed, and in great pain. [. . .] The consequences of what we had experienced & witnessed in Vienna were unavoidable: a complete nervous breakdown.[4]

Louise remembered the spring of 1939 above all as a time of severe material hardship. Cash reserves were running low, the cost of medical treatment was crippling, and neither she nor Hansi had yet found means of supporting themselves. At one stage the situation grew so critical, she recalled, that they saw no alternative to suicide.[5]

On 19 May her brother Otto arrived from Europe. Having closed the Paris

* A remark in the second paragraph of the interview, that Zemlinsky had 'recently arrived in this country' suggests that it was given several months prior to publication. Writing to Schoenberg the following year, Zemlinsky spoke favourably of the libretto, adding that he had already completed 'the first act' (*Web-Br, c.* February 1940, 279).

office in early March, he had hastily returned to Prague to take care of family affairs. Just two days before the Nazis occupied Bohemia, he flew back to Paris and from there to London, in a vain attempt to obtain immigration permits for his mother, his aunt Clara and several of her children. Anxious to save at least his own skin, and perhaps hoping to find treatment for his liver condition, on 8 May he boarded a vessel bound for America.[6] His dream was to buy property in California, build a house and settle there. To this end, he had transferred all his movable assets to a bank in New York.

Otto's arrival was Zemlinsky's salvation. The prospect of moving to California evidently persuaded him that there was a future for him in the US after all. On 2 June, furnished with a testimony by Peter Herman Adler,[7] he applied for American citizenship ('I will renounce for ever all allegiance and fidelity to any foreign prince, potentate, state, or sovereignty; [. . .] I am not an anarchist; I am not a polygamist nor a believer in the practice of polygamy: [. . .] so help me God.').[8] Nevertheless his state of health was precarious, and his doctor held out little hope of him surviving the journey west until he had returned to strength. Otto's condition was graver still, but he struggled on courageously, found employment, and did what he could to help.

Around this time, Bodanzky introduced Zemlinsky to the music publisher Max Dreyfus, managing director of Chappell & Co. As Hans Heinsheimer recalls, the plan was for Zemlinsky to earn his living as a writer of popular songs:

[He] was invited to dine with Bodanzky at Hotel Astor, where Mr Dreyfus, whose business had by that time grown into an empire, held a daily round-table for a select circle of guests. [. . .] Zemlinsky was confused and unbelieving. He could remember the period in his youth, as *Kapellmeister* at the Carltheater, where he was not only obliged to spend four years conducting operettas, but the management also urged him to write some of his own. 'I have no talent for it,' he said at the time, and that memory probably still plagued his conscience. At the insistence of his wife and Bodanzky, [. . .] he signed a contract with Mr Dreyfus, under the American, utterly un-Zemlinskian pseudonym of Al Roberts.[9]

Irma Stein-Firner supplied him with a few charming but unremarkable lyrics – songs of love, parting and farewell – and in June 1939, soon after signing the contract with Chappell, he set to work. Irrespective of whether he was composing for the Tonkünstlerverein or for Tin Pan Alley, his standards of workmanship were as high as ever. Nor had he lost his ability to capture the spirit of a poem, to mould line, harmony and structure into an integrated musical experience. Chappell published the Three Songs in 1940, with a clumsy English translation, at a sheet-music price of 60c. Louise was incensed to discover that, contrary to agreement, the edition bore Zemlinsky's own name; indeed she later disowned the songs altogether. But even if she was acting on her husband's instructions (which cannot be verified), there was no need to be ashamed.

Without compromising Alexander Zemlinsky's artistic integrity, Al Roberts had done his best.

Hans Heinsheimer had also meanwhile made his way to New York. Having found employment with a publisher specializing in music for schools, he suggested to Zemlinsky that he might also investigate the possibilities of this market. To his surprise Zemlinsky agreed; indeed he returned home, as Louise recounted, 'in a mood of complete happiness'.[10] Perhaps it was his fine sense of irony that prompted him, a fugitive in a foreign land, to compose a Hunting Piece for two horns and piano. Ironical too, under the circumstances, was the title of a second, more substantial composition: Humoreske, a rondo in B♭ major for wind quintet. From his years of teaching experience, he knew that youthful enthusiasm thrives on challenge. Accordingly, his two 'school pieces' demand technical skill and ensemble playing of a high level. For his part, he wrote music of wit, charm and technical brilliance (for his personal amusement he even embedded a few of his talismans: the 'Self' motif in the opening theme of the Humoreske, for instance, or a variant of the 'Circle' theme from Der Kreide-kreis in the trio of the Hunting Piece). Only one thing was missing: his courage to explore the outer reaches of tonal harmony. These pieces, the last he was to write, tread the safe ground of Straussian diatonicism. Listening to their catchy tunes and lithe rhythms, it is difficult to imagine that they were written by a man whose nerves were stretched to breaking point.

Since arriving in New York, Zemlinsky had been suffering from chronic hyper-tension, exacerbated by arteriosclerosis.[11] He finished the Humoreske early in July. The next day he suffered a severe cerebral haemorrhage, which left him partially paralysed on the left-hand side of his body.

During the autumn of 1939 one disaster followed another. At the end of September the New York Herald-Tribune broke the news that Otto Klemperer had been admitted to Boston City Hospital for surgery to remove a tumour from a cranial nerve in the right ear.[12] Soon afterwards Zemlinsky heard that his old friend Siegfried Theumann* was dying of cancer of the larynx. And on 28 October his protector and mentor Arthur Bodanzky was taken to hospital suffering from arthritis and heart disease. Unnoticed to all but himself, Bodanzky's health had been failing ever since his son Carl Artur jun. had been killed in a motoring accident on 12 August 1930. 'Few thought of him in terms of failing health, or of health at all,' recalled Irving Kolodin.[13] But during the 1937–8 season at the Met he had been obliged to reduce his workload, engag-ing Erich Leinsdorf, Maurice Abravanel and Karl Riedel to deputize for him. 'When he was feeling impatient he would sometimes drag a performance over

---

* Theumann, who was living in New York, had been a friend since the 1890s, when he played the violin in the world première of Zemlinsky's A major Quartet. From 1913 to 1920 he was engaged as conductor and later as stage director at the NDT.

the jumps as if he were rushing for a train,' wrote *Time* magazine. 'But when Arthur Bodanzky felt just right, he could drive a pack of Valkyries through the Nibelung clouds like Wotan himself.' He died at The New York Hospital on 24 November.

News of Zemlinsky's affliction had meanwhile travelled as far as Los Angeles. On 11 November Schoenberg wrote to his daughter Trudi in New York:

Somebody – Dr Herbert Graf – told me yesterday that Zemlinsky is said to have been ill for some time now. Please write to me about this straight away and give me his address, so that I can write to him.[14]

Trudi did as requested; she also informed Louise of her father's inquiry. Schoenberg wrote soon afterwards, but Louise could not to bring herself to show the letter to her husband. Instead she acknowledged its arrival herself:*

My husband is already able to spend a few hours out of bed every day & can walk around in his room *a little*, but all this has to be taken with great deliberation.[15]

She had still not found the courage to inform him of Bodanzky's death. And after a silence of ten years, she feared that news from Schoenberg, whether good or bad, would only exacerbate his nervous condition. Her fears were not unfounded: on 19 December she read him Schoenberg's letter; the same day he suffered a further collapse.

Ten days earlier, Zemlinsky had enjoyed a half-hour visit from his colleague Fritz Stiedry.[†] In a letter to Schoenberg, Stiedry now recorded his impressions:

I saw Zemlinsky for the first time a fortnight ago. He was sitting in his little bedroom at a table next to the bed, ashamedly hiding his crippled left hand behind the table, his face not actually distorted, but somehow unfamiliar. He spoke slowly, with occasional errors of syntax, but spoke of everything, often with remarkable powers of recall.[16]

Fortunately the effects of this last minor stroke were less severe than had been feared. Gradually his condition improved, and by the end of January he was able to reply to Schoenberg in person,[17] writing of his illness, of Klemperer, Bodanzky (of whose death he was evidently still unaware) and Theumann. On the brighter side, he also mentioned his plans for California. Schoenberg was overjoyed:

I am absolutely sure that you will soon be the same old fellow, namely the youngster that you always were. Do you remember in 1924, when you were conducting my *Erwartung* in Prague, how the two of us jumped over the railing into the orchestra pit, something that younger old fellows would never have dared! I am quite certain that after a week of Californian climate we shall both be jumping again.[18]

* Schoenberg's letter is not preserved; presumably it was among those that Louise later destroyed.
† In 1937, after a three-year period with the Leningrad Philharmonic, Stiedry had taken over Bodanzky's position as Conductor of the Society of the Friends of Music in New York.

Zemlinsky's condition was further strengthened by stirrings of interest in his music. On 4 February the League of Composers* promoted a concert at the Museum of Modern Art with works by refugees. Three of his songs[†] were programmed between longer works by Paul Dessau, Nikolai Lopatnikoff, Karol Rathaus and Stefan Wolpe. Even if his music was ignored by the newspaper critics, considering the number of composers now living in exile in New York, he must have been grateful to be included at all. And even if Elliott Carter, reviewing the concert for *Modern Music*, wrote merely that these were songs 'of the jumpy school'[19] (for one of the profoundest minds in American music, a remark of singular superficiality), Zemlinsky will have consoled himself with the thought that he might soon be 'jumping' on a beach in Santa Monica. Later in the month, after hearing a broadcast of his Maeterlinck Songs and Schoenberg's Second Quartet,[‡] he dictated a letter to his old, new-found friend:

I too am glad to recall the time when we jumped over the railing into the orchestra pit, all the more so after my long illness, at a time when I have to learn to walk all over again. [. . .] Until I am sufficiently restored to health for the strenuous journey to California, my doctor advises me to spend the coming months here, in the country.[20]

It took several months to complete arrangements for moving out of town. Evidently Zemlinsky's doctor had opened Louise's eyes to the gravity of her husband's condition, and though Otto valiantly faced up to his illness, he too was in no state to travel. The subject of California was tacitly dropped. Louise, who had bought herself a Studebaker[21] to explore the surrounding countryside, persuaded her brother that his dream of an American retreat could be fulfilled at Larchmont in Westchester County, a pleasant rural area eighteen miles northeast of New York City. Until the new house was ready, the three of them settled into a ground-floor apartment two miles away, at 68 Kewanee Road, New Rochelle (Hansi decided to stay on in New York City). In the summer of 1940 Otto Sachsel sent a consoling letter to his mother in Prague:

The summer has been very hot here, and about ten days ago we had a record heatwave, but it's much more tolerable here [than in town], especially as it cools off towards six o'clock in the evening. Around that time, we love to sit out in the garden. The surrounding area is entirely green, and the birdsong every morning is

---

* The League of Composers, founded in 1923, was affiliated to the International Composers' Guild, founded by Edgard Varèse. Since 1926, a composer listed as 'Alexander Ziemlinski' had been a member of the Guild's advisory committee (see Louise Varèse, *A Looking-glass Diary* (London, 1973), 164).
† The songs were performed in English: 'Come with me, beloved child' (*Entführung* op. 27 no. L), 'An evening goblet full of sunlight' (*Abendkelch voll Sonnenlicht* op. 22 no. 11) and 'An African Dance' (*Afrikanischer Tanz* op. 27 no. 9). They were sung by Rose Landwehr (soprano), accompanied by Paul Breisach.
‡ Judging by the text of a telegram from Schoenberg to Louis T. Gruenberg, dated 26 February 1940, this might have been a League Broadcast on 24 February.

wonderful. [. . .] Alex grouses from time to time – you know what he's like – but mostly he's in good spirits. Louise is looking very well, and I, so they tell me, am looking better than ever! [. . .] We have a lot of fun with our dog, who runs wild out here, carries large sticks into the house, and barks his head off at all and sundry. But he's a real delight and very good-natured. Alex is particularly fond of him, and spoils him just as much as Pepi. The only thing that bothers me is our canary. It makes such a din that one can scarcely hear one's own voice – and it sings incessantly, from dawn to dusk. [. . .] As you can see, things are not at all bad.[22]

When Schoenberg finally found time to call, on 21 November,* he too found everyone in good spirits: 'ZEMLINSKY BETTER THAN EXPECTED,' he wired to his wife in Los Angeles.[23]

Within a few weeks, however, the political situation had taken a sudden turn for the worse. With the appointment of the notorious Reinhard Heydrich as *Reichsprotektor* of Bohemia and Moravia, Prague was swept by a reign of terror; such reports as still filtered through spoke only of arrests, interrogations and executions. And on 7 December Japanese dive-bombers crippled the American naval and air strength at Pearl Harbor; within two days the US was at war.

Events in the Zemlinsky household, as Fritz Stiedry reported in a letter to Schoenberg dated 17 December, were scarcely less dramatic:

It is my unfortunate duty to inform you that, after terrible agonies, Mrs Zemlinsky's brother [passed away] on Saturday [14 December]. A week ago Zemlinsky himself suffered another severe stroke, and remains semi-comatose. He knows nothing of the death of his brother-in-law, whose body had to be carried through the room only a few feet away from his bed.[24]

Stiedry did at least have some positive news:

On 29 December Mitropoulos will be conducting [Zemlinsky's] Sinfonietta at a Philharmonic Concert here. I am glad that I managed to arrange this performance with Mitropoulos, who was once my assistant.[25]

Whether Zemlinsky was able to hear the broadcast is uncertain; for all eventualities, the technicians at WABC made a wax-disc recording for him to hear at home. As soon as the broadcast was over, Schoenberg cabled from Los Angeles: 'JUST HEARD YOUR WONDERFUL SYMFONIETTA HOPE IT IS THE BEGINNING OF YOUR AMERICAN SUCCESS.'[26] Louise had to read the telegram to Zemlinsky again and again. He was deeply moved. 'I would like to tell you', she wrote in her letter of thanks to Schoenberg,

that my husband – ever since I first met him – has always felt a great and selfless admiration & a profound affection for you.[27]

At Kewanee Road the following months passed almost without event. In July

* Schoenberg was in New York to conduct a performance of *Pierrot lunaire* on 17 November.

Schoenberg sent a brief report to Hans Nachod in Kendal, Westmoreland:

He is very sick. He had several paralytic strokes, from which he recovered recently, but the next might be the end.[28]

By now the decline was palpable, and Louise had come to depend on the services of a full-time nurse. Arnold Greissle-Schönberg, who was seventeen at the time, recalls occasional family visits, the affectionate wave of a feeble hand from a darkened bedroom; doubtless Hansi also called whenever she could. But no Festschrift or special concert, not even a few lines of newsprint marked Zemlinsky's seventieth birthday on 14 October.

Despite Otto's death, work on the dream house in Larchmont continued as planned. It may have taken longer than intended – many a building worker will have been called up for military service – but by the winter of 1942 it was ready. Flanked by tall trees, 81 Willow Avenue was an ideal place of retreat, spacious and comfortable.* Louise took care of everything. She had much experience of house-moving by now, more perhaps than she had bargained for. Once all was ready, a small cortège set out on 11 March to transport the invalid composer to his new home.

It might have been the chill of the Atlantic breeze as they wheeled him across the lawn to the front door; it might have been sheer inner agitation. Whatever the cause, the effect was immediate and fatal: a sudden onset of hypostatic pneumonia. The reflexes began to falter and the vital organs to fail, periods of consciousness grew ever shorter. The fateful 14th day passed without event, but when the doctor drove over from White Plains† the following day, 15 March, there was nothing more that he could do.

An air-raid practice had been called for the whole New York district that evening:

Sirens, factory whistles and even the grim steam whistle of Sing Sing Prison at Ossining helped inform the sprawling area between the Bronx and Putnam County, the Hudson River and Connecticut that the blackout was on.[29]

Even if Zemlinsky could have heard the din, poised as he was on the threshold of his miracle world, he was no longer listening. At 8.15 p.m. he drew a last, shallow breath. Görge had found his Dream-Princess at last.

* See plate 27.
† Dr Gustav Reiter. He had been attending Zemlinsky since November of the previous year.

XIV EPILOGUE

'Zemlinsky can wait'

'Zemlinsky can wait': Schoenberg's ostensibly callous birthday greeting conveys a subtle message of admiration and compassion. '*Can* wait', he had written, not '*must* wait'. 'Can' implies ability; ability is potential; potential is strength. Zemlinsky has the strength to wait. But ability comes from learning, and learning comes from experiencing. Zemlinsky knows to wait. He waits because he has learned that to wait is his destiny: 'My time will come after my death.'

Hoping that her husband's prophecy would soon be fulfilled, during the summer of 1943 Louise wrote to several leading musicians in America, canvassing for support. Two such documents survive from this period, an inquiry addressed to Sergey Koussevitzky in Boston,[1] and a negative reply from Eugene Ormandy in Philadelphia;[2] doubtless there were many more. With one exception, however, a performance in New York of the Third Quartet,[3] her appeals were disregarded. In Europe, old acquaintances or ex-pupils who had risen to positions of authority sporadically attempted to revive interest in his music. Thus on 5 July 1945, just two months after the termination of hostilities, the Maeterlinck Songs were broadcast on Austrian Radio; between 1948 and 1962 the prelude to *A Florentine Tragedy* was heard quite frequently over the air, in 1954 the complete opera was performed in the studios of Radio Bern, and in 1955 *Der Kreidekreis* was not only broadcast by Radio Wien but also staged in Dortmund. But these were events of no lasting significance. Despite the advocacy of Adorno, who included influential essays on Zemlinsky and Schreker in his book *Quasi una fantasia*, published in 1963, the post-war generation knew these composers only as footnotes in the history of the Second Viennese School.

Tastes had changed radically, and many a work hailed in its day as a masterpiece of modernism was now considered mere kitsch. In the era of kidney-shaped tables and white-wall tyres, grandmother's Gallé vases gathered dust in the attic, and grandfather's Bauhaus writing desk was banished to the back room. Already in 1942 Krenek had written that the music of his erstwhile teacher Schreker was 'a thick, over-seasoned stew of heavy, glutinous melodies'.[4] In 1969 Klemperer still remembered Schreker's *Irrelohe* as 'typical inflation music'.[5] Attitudes had scarcely changed. For a generation that found the symphonies of Mahler merely extravagant and eccentric, the music of Zemlinsky was neither desirable nor (emotionally) accessible.

Having waited twenty years for some token of recognition, Louise decided that the time had come to put her husband's manuscripts up for sale. Initially she intended to sell the collection to the son of a well-known Viennese conductor, an aspiring composer who had expressed an interest in completing the score of *Kandaules*. On Steuermann's advice, however, Louise rejected the *Kandaules* offer. Evidently fearing plagiarism, she also requested the return of manuscripts that she had sent to her prospective client in Paris. To confirm her suspicions, when the carton arrived back in New York two items were missing: the autograph vocal score of the Symphonic Songs and the full score of Psalm 13.*

In July 1962, through the mediation of the New York art-dealer Otto Kallir, the collection was sold to a leading American antiquarian, Robert O. Lehman. According to the agreement drawn up between him and Louise, the manuscripts were to be catalogued, efforts were to be made to publish and perform the later works (Psalm 13, Songs opp. 22 and 27, Fourth Quartet), and steps taken to complete the score of *Kandaules*.[6] Naturally Louise also retained the copyright. For the privilege of acquiring the Zemlinsky Collection – three bulky cartons filled to the brim – Senator Lehman paid just $6000. Being himself in no position to undertake the task of sorting and cataloguing such a mountain of paper, he later donated the entire collection to the Library of Congress.

Twenty-five years at Zemlinsky's side had not always been a bed of roses. Yet compared with the twenty-five years that followed, Louise could look back on them as carefree and contented.

Two days before his death, Otto Sachsel had written to friends in Sweden bewailing the fate of his cousins Robert and Paul, separated from their families and forced to shovel snow on the streets of Prague.[7] The following year events went from bad to worse. On 4 June 1942 *Reichsprotektor* Heydrich ('the hangman') died of injuries after a bomb attack by Czech partisans. Nazi vengeance was swift and terrible. Following the massacre at Lidice on 10 June, Jews were rounded up in droves and taken to the ghetto at Terezín, pending liquidation. Louise's mother and Aunt Clara were among those arrested on 14 July. On 14 January 1943 Paul Sachsel managed to wire the following ominous dispatch from Prague to Larchmont:

HA[N]NA KLARA DEPORTED TOGETHER PROBABLY POLAND PARENTS VIA TEREZIN SIMILAR DESTINATION STOP ALL MISSING AFRAID LITTLE HOPE.[8]

And in July 1945, when the first brigade of American soldiers entered Bohemia, Louise received the following radiogram, sent to her by George Lederer, a distant relative who was serving as a Lieutenant-Corporal in the US army:

NEWS FROM PRAGUE VERY SAD APPARENTLY PAUL WITH WIFE AND ROBERT ARE ONLY SURVIVORS OF OUR FAMILY [. . .][9]

On the extermination lists at Auschwitz no record was ever found of Hanna

---

* Thirty-seven years later, at the time of writing, the whereabouts of these manuscripts is still unknown. A microfilm copy of Psalm 13, prepared before the manuscript was sent to Paris, is preserved in the Arturo Toscanini Memorial Collection at the New York Public Library.

Sachsel. Elderly, frail and weakened by six months of detention in Terezín, she probably numbered among the thousands that starved or froze to death in the primitive railway wagons used for transport. In the absence of written evidence, in 1947 Louise was obliged to sign a declaration that her mother had gone missing 'probably at an unknown concentration camp in an Eastern region'.[10]

Later in 1945 Louise sold the house in Larchmont and moved into an apartment at 225 East 54th Street. Her subsequent trail is not easy to follow, nor did she readily talk of this most difficult phase of her life. From her collection of news cuttings it transpires that she found work in 1951 as a concert singer. The following year, furnished with testimonials from Irene Schlemmer-Ambros in Vienna and the Austrian–American musicologist Paul Nettl, she embarked on a career as voice teacher. LP recordings by her pupils Beverly Wesp und Jerome Kopmar reveal that her efforts in this area were by no means unsuccessful.[11] For a time she worked as a saleswoman at an exclusive New York department store and, rediscovering her early talent for the visual arts, she also returned to her easel, producing a substantial output of portraits, nudes and still-lifes. Commissions and exhibitions, including a one-woman show of abstract paintings 'in an Expressionist style'[12] at Gallery Pietrantonio in February 1971, testify to her success.

Hansi's track is harder still to find. Evidently little love was lost between her and her stepmother,* but Louise unfailingly sent her an annual share of the royalties from Zemlinsky's music, even at a time when there was precious little to be divided.[13] Eventually Hansi moved away from New York and settled on a ranch in Virginia. She died there on 30 November 1972.

For many years Louise struggled to obtain indemnity for her stolen property. Shortly before the fall of Vienna, the roof of her house in the Kaasgrabengasse was damaged by a shower of shrapnel. Russian soldiers billeted in the building stole the refrigerator and other movable items, and even tore electric cables from the walls. Once the damage had been repaired, Austrian tenants moved in, and in all seriousness Louise was asked to meet the cost of repairing and renovating the fabric. In 1958, after years of legal wrangling, she agreed to sell the property for the laughable sum of $5000.

In Prague, as heir to the family estate, she was entitled to restitution for the confiscation of her mother's house (valued at 1.5 million Czech crowns), the return of cash deposits, stocks and shares amounting to a further 1.35 million crowns, as well as family silver, carpets and other valuables.[14] Soon after the cessation of hostilities she deposited a claim for compensation at the Czech Consulate in New York. Negotiations dragged on until 1948, when the Communist

* According to Louise, Hansi was 'deaf and slightly backward' (conversation with the author, 20 April 1989); Arnold Greissle-Schönberg mentions only 'a (minor) speech defect or rather peculiarity. [. . .] No, Hansi was no dummy; she was both lively and very friendly, down-to-earth' (letter to the author, 5 August 1998).

regime redirected the claim to the appropriate authority in Germany. After years of waiting, the indemnities that Louise received for the loss of a family and a home scarcely covered the cost of legal advice.

One of Zemlinsky's greatest treasures was a landscape by Egon Schiele, which he acquired from a Viennese art gallery in 1937. With careful attention to its proportions (in its frame the picture was approximately six foot square), he and Louise had redesigned their living room in order to accommodate it. The picture left the country with their other personal effects, but later, due to her precarious financial position, Louise took it to a New York art-dealer for valuation. Three weeks later the proprietor was declared bankrupt, and the picture vanished without trace. For years she attempted to find and reclaim it, but in vain.*

And then, suddenly and unexpectedly, the years of hardship and frustration were over, Zemlinsky's time had come. The miraculous rise of his music during the later 1960s and 1970s was the indirect outcome of innumerable nuances of social and cultural change, enhanced and accelerated by the steadily growing influence of the media. In this process, the first and most decisive phase was the rehabilitation of Mahler, beginning with the centenary celebrations in 1960. Interest in every aspect of *fin-de-siècle* art now began to burgeon, and by the end of the decade the stage was set for Zemlinsky and his contemporaries. Responsibility for the propagation of his music was at first shouldered by a handful of enthusiasts, and concentrated for the most part on specific geographical centres, notably Hamburg, Berlin and Cincinatti. The welcome in Vienna was more hesitant but no less heartfelt.

Zemlinsky, Schreker, Korngold and their contemporaries emerged at first as a single block, hewn roughly from a mine of forgotten scores, some of which, as it soon transpired, were true masterpieces. With growing familiarity it became possible to differentiate more clearly between them. Further excavations revealed the music of Josef Suk, almost forgotten after decades of suppression in Communist Czechoslovakia, and Paul Dukas, long hidden in the shadow of Debussy and Ravel. Deeper understanding of the Viennese post-Romantics and their place in music history also led to a re-evaluation of the Second Viennese School. In the case of Webern, whom post-war composers had approached with the graph-paper-and-slide-rule mentality of their own era, the revival revealed an expressive intensity bordering on hysteria. Illuminated by knowledge of Schreker and Zemlinsky, the music of Berg acquired sharper contours. Schoenberg himself became less difficult to understand.

In July 1985 the Austrian Ministry of Culture organized the final homecoming:

---

* Surviving correspondence on this topic includes a letter from the Guggenheim Museum, dated 29 June 1978 (*NLZ* Ac 38).

Zemlinsky's ashes were to be transferred from Ferncliff Cemetery in Ardsley, where they reposed in a niche next to those of Otto Sachsel, to a grave of honour at the Zentralfriedhof in Vienna. Louise herself accompanied the urn, and she in turn was escorted by Peter Marboe, Director of the Austrian Cultural Institute in New York. On the way to the airport, she asked to stop at a turnout on the freeway. Taking the urn in her arms, she walked away into a nearby field, where she stood in silent dialogue. Perhaps she was enumerating the standing ovations and ecstatic reviews, or telling her husband of the distinguished performers who now enthused over his music. Perhaps she spoke of her life in a colony of anthroposophists, and of her decision to abandon it in favour of a comfortable home for senior citizens. She might also have mentioned her plans for a Vienna-based Alexander Zemlinsky Fund* and a Cincinatti-based Zemlinsky Competition for Composers.† In America she had made a home, she concluded, whereas in Vienna she would always be an outsider. Her place was at Ardsley, next to her brother; she would not be following him on his last journey.

Whatever she told him, it took a long time. As the car finally approached Kennedy airport, the plane to Vienna was already taxiing up the runway.

---

* The Alexander Zemlinsky Fonds bei der Gesellschaft der Musikfreunde in Wien was founded in 1989.
† The Alexander Zemlinsky Composition Prize was established by Louise Zemlinsky in 1990 in conjunction with Cincinatti College–Conservatory of Music. The Prize was first awarded in April 1999.

APPENDIX I

List of Compositions

Items marked * are incomplete or lost; items marked † are held in a portfolio of compositions entitled 'Compositionen von Alex. v. Zemlinsky 1887–1888' (*LoC* 1/1); and items marked ‡ are held in a portfolio of compositions (40 pp.) evidently found among the posthumous papers of Theodor Fuchs (1873–1953). The manuscripts and their contents are described in Mircea Voicana, 'Zemlinsky: un camarade viennois de Georges Enesco', *Revue roumaine d'histoire de l'art*, v, 1968, 155–62. Although the portfolio was housed temporarily in the Romanian State Library, Bucharest, its present location is unknown.

C indicates composition dating and *P* publication dating; *fp* indicates first performance details and *D* any dedication.

*†Piano Sonata (no. 1) in G major (*Allegro*; *Adagio molto*; *Scherzo-Trio*; *Rondo* [incomplete]). Comp. 1887.
*†Piano concerto in B♭ minor. *C* 1888. Sketches.
†Romanze¹ in D♭ major for violin and piano. Violin part dated 28 July 1889.
Seven (Twelve) Songs for voice and piano.² *P* Ricordi, 1995.
Three Songs for voice and piano. *P* Ricordi, 1995.
‡Piano Sonata [no. 2] in C minor. *C* November 1890. MS: Bucharest
Three (Four) Piano Pieces. *C* begun 16 April 1891. *LoC* 1/7.
Four Miniatures for piano.³ *C* ?1891. *LoC* 1/8.
Two (Six) Piano Pieces. *C* ?1891. *LoC* 1/9 and 1/9a.
*‡*Das liebliche Vergissmeinicht* (poet unidentified) for voice and piano. *C* 1891, fragment, not authenticated. MS: Bucharest.
†Symphony (no. 1)⁴ in E minor, movts. 2 and 3 only. Orchestration begun 25 April 1891; completed 26 May 1891. Incomplete. *LoC* 1/10.
Des Mädchens Klage (Vincenz Zusner) for voice and piano. *C* ?May 1891. MS: Gesellschaft der Musikfreunde, Vienna. *P* Ricordi, 1995.
Two (Four) Pieces for piano duet. *C* August ?1891. *LoC* 1/9 and 26/27.
**Die Feier der Tonkunst* (S. Langer), cantata for six-part chorus and large orchestra. *C* 22 August–23 September 1891. Lost. Title page only *LoC* 1/12.
‡Drei leichte Stücke for piano. *C* 1891. MS: Bucharest.

---

1 Original title: '1. Romanze'; possibly intended as the first movement of a suite. The MS includes the complete violin part.
2 Only seven songs have survived. The MS includes a fragment of a further (unidentified) song in E major.
3 No. 4: see Skizze for piano, *P* 1896.
4 It was the wish of Louise Zemlinsky that the symphonies be referred to not by number but by key. The MS catalogued as third movement is an Allegretto in D major and has the character of a finale, i.e. title page and musical content have probably been confused with another, unidentified work.

Ländliche Tänze op. 1, for piano. C ?1891. P Breitkopf und Härtel, 1892.[5]

Der Morgenstern (Vincenz Zusner) for voice and piano. C ?June 1892. LoC 3/1.[6] P Ricordi, 1995.

Frühlingslied (Heinrich Heine) for voice and piano. C 30 July 1892. LoC 1/20. P Ricordi, 1995.

‡Terzet in A major for two violins and viola. C 26 March–27 September 1892. MS: Bucharest.

Wandl' ich im Wald des Abends (Heinrich Heine) for voice and piano. C 18 November ?1892. LoC 1/5. P Ricordi, 1995.

*Piano Quartet in D major. Viola part (complete) and cello part (first movement only): LoC 3/5. fp 20 November 1893, Vienna.

Symphony (no. 2) in D minor.[7] C ?1892–3. LoC 1/13. fp 11 July 1892 (1st movement only); 10 February 1893 (complete), Vienna. P ed. Antony Beaumont, Ricordi, 1995.

Two (Five) Songs to texts by Paul Heyse. C c.November 1892. LoC 1/22. Nos. 2 and 3. P Ricordi, 1995.

Die Folkunger, opera in 4 acts. Text after Solomon H. Mosenthal.[8] C 1893, fragment. LoC 1/22 and 3/4.

*Vor der Stadt[9] (Joseph von Eichendorff) for satb chorus.[10] C 29 March 1893, fragment. LoC 3/8.

Ballades for piano.[11] C 1892–93. D Johann Nepomuk Fuchs. LoC 1/15. P Ricordi, 1996.

String Quartet in E minor. C c. 1893. LoC 3/10–11 (score and parts). P Ricordi, 1996.

*Sonata for cello and piano. fp Vienna, 23 April 1894. Lost.[12]

*String Quintet in D minor.[13] C 6 November 1894.[14] MS incomplete LoC 3/14. First movement. P Ricordi, 1994.

Suite for orchestra: *Legende* (A minor); *Reigen* (A major); *Humoreske* (F major). C ?1895. LoC 4/1–2. fp 18 March 1895, Vienna.

Lustspielouvertüre (to Wartenegg's *Der Ring des Ofterdingen*) for orchestra. C September 1894–15 March 1895. LoC 3/15–16.

---

5 Dances no. 8 and 9 were also published by Breitkopf und Härtel in an undated album: *Salonmusik. N[eue] F[olge]. Ausgewählte Klavierwerke neuerer Komponisten.*

6 Not in Zemlinsky's hand.

7 The score of the finale, written by a copyist, breaks off after 7 pages; the MS continues in Zemlinsky's hand on a separate sheet, but in both scores bar 40 is blank.

8 Only one section of particell survives (85 bars), a monologue for 'Magnus' (King Magnus VII). An approximate dating can be deduced from the title page, which is written on the reverse side of the song *Auf die Nacht*.

9 The song is numbered 'III'.

10 The same text as op. 2/1 no. 6.

11 Designated in the MS as 'op. 2'.

12 LoC 26/19 (*Der Mönch zu Pisa*) contains a concluding fragment in E♭ major for cello and piano, dated '7.1.1894' and marked 'zum Übertragen' ('to be transferred'). This could be a passage from the sonata.

13 Zemlinsky's fair copy of this work is lost. The extant MS includes the entire first movement and sketches for three further movements: *Adagio* (A♭ major, 62 bars), *Scherzando* (C major, 9 bars) and *Finale* (D major, 27 bars).

14 Completion date of the first movement, of which the opening is marked 'am 17.10'. Sketches for three succeeding movements are undated.

Minnelied (Heinrich Heine) for TTBB chorus, 2 flutes, 2 horns and harp. C ?1895. LoC 3/17–18. P Ricordi, 1995.

Sarema, opera in three parts.[15] Libretto [by the composer, Adolf von Zemlinszky and Arnold Schoenberg] after Rudolf von Gottschall. Short score C 7 February–22 June 1893; full score compl. 25 August 1895. D 'to my parents'. MS (full score and vocal score): Bayerische Staatsbibliothek, Munich[16] and LoC 4/9–12, 5/1 and 6/1. P Libretto, Kastner & Lossen, 1897; v.s., Berthé, 1899; rp Ricordi, 1993. fp 10 October 1897, Munich Hofoper.

Albumblatt (Erinnerung aus Wien) for piano. C 26–28 May 1895. D Catharina Maleschewski. LoC 4/3. P Ricordi, 1996.

Orientalisches Sonett (Hans Grasberger) for voice and piano. C 15 October 1895. LoC 4/4. P Ricordi, 1995.

Serenade (Suite) in A major for violin and piano. C 1895. LoC 2/8–9. fp 24 January 1896, Vienna. P Universal Edition, 1984.

Waldgespräch (Joseph von Eichendorff) for soprano, two horns, harp and strings. C 3 January 1896. LoC 4/5–6. fp 2 March 1896, Vienna. P Ricordi, 1995.

Hochzeitsgesang[17] ('Baruch aba'; 'Mi adir'), motet for cantor, SATB chorus and organ. C 29 April [1896]. D Helene Bauer. LoC 3/7. P Ricordi, 1995.

String Quintet in D, finale.[18] C 11 January 1896. LoC 4/7. fp (as new finale of the 1894 Quintet) 5 March 1896, Vienna. P Ricordi, 1994.

Trio op. 3 in D minor for clarinet (or violin), cello and piano. C c.1896. MS sketch: LoC 7/5. P Simrock, 1897. fp 11 December 1896, Vienna.

Herbsten (Paul Wertheimer) for voice and piano. C 29 June 1896. LoC 6/3. P Ricordi, 1995.

Skizze for piano.[19] C c.1896. P as music supplement to *Neue musikalische Presse*, Vienna, no. 40, 4 October 1896; rp Ricordi, 1996.

Frühlingsbegräbnis (Paul Heyse) for soprano and baritone soli, chorus and orchestra. C April–July 1896; orch. c.1897; rev. and re-orch. c.1903. D to the memory of Johannes Brahms. MS: Gesellschaft der Musikfreunde, Vienna[20] and LoC 6/7–10. P (rev. version) Ricordi, 1996. fp original version: 11 February 1900, Vienna; rev. version: 16 March 1997, Cologne.

String Quartet no. 1 in A major op. 4. C begun 9 July 1896. MS sketch: LoC 7/6. P Simrock, 1898. fp 2 December 1896, Vienna.

Wanderers Nachtlied (Johann von Goethe) for voice and piano. C 20 July 1896. MS mutilated. LoC 26/20.[21]

*Untitled operatic fragment.[21] First surviving sketch dated 29 June 1896. LoC 6/3,

---

15 Originally 'Oper in 3 Abtheilungen'.
16 Also original performing materials.
17 The MS is untitled.
18 Composed as new finale for the String Quintet in D minor (1894).
19 A revised and abbreviated version of no. 4 of the Four Miniatures (c.1891).
20 Complete original performing materials.
21 An opera about Desiderius, last king of the Lombards. The most substantial fragment extends to several pages and opens with the words, 'Aufs Haupt geschlagen ist Desider. Es siegt der Langobarden Heer.' The chief character of the opera is 'Almosfrede'. A further fragment, 'Einzug der Jagdgesellschaft', is written on the same folio as the *Hochzeitsgesang*, composed in April 1896; another (LoC 6/3), headed '1. Scene', is preserved on the same folio as the song *Im Lenz* (op. 2/II no. 4) and can hence be approximately dated to July 1896.

26/24 and 26/27.

Frühlingsglaube (Ludwig Uhland) for satb chorus and string orchestra. C October 1896. LoC 7/1–2. P Ricordi, 1995. *fp* 16 June 1988, Cologne.

Geheimnis (poet unidentified) for SATB chorus and string orchestra. C 1896. Short score: LoC 7/1. P orch. Antony Beaumont, Ricordi, 1995. *fp* 2 April 1995, Vienna.

Nun schwillt der See so bang (Paul Wertheimer) for voice and piano. C ?1896. LoC 7/4. P Ricordi, 1995.

Süsse, süsse Sommernacht (Aissa Lynx) for voice and piano. C 6 November 1896. LoC 7/4. P Ricordi, 1995.

Der Tag wird kühl (Paul Heyse) for voice and piano. C June 1897. D Melanie Guttmann. MS: Moldenhauer Archive, Harvard University.[22] P Ricordi, 1995.

Lieder op. 2 for voice and piano. C 1895–6. P Hansen, 1897.[23] MS: Wilhelm Hansen, Copenhagen,[24] LoC 6/5–6 (fragments of nos. I/3; I/7; II/4; II/6) and *MolA* (II/6). D Anton Sistermanns. *fp* (II/5, II/2 and II/3 only) ?17 March 1898, Vienna.

Symphony (no. 3) in B♭ major. C 9 September 1897. LoC 7/8–9. P Universal Edition, 1977. *fp* 5 March 1899, Vienna.

Gesänge op. 5 for voice and piano. C 1896–7. MS: Moldenhauer Collection, Library of Congress[25] and Wilhelm Hansen, Copenhagen. D 'Fr. J.C.' P Hansen, 1898.[26]

Walzer-Gesänge nach toskanischen Liedern von Ferdinand Gregorovius op. 6 for voice and piano: C begun 28 March 1898. LoC 7/12. P (with English trans. by Constance Bache) Simrock, 1899.

*Waldseligkeit (Richard Dehmel) for voice and piano.[27] C ?1898, fragment. LoC 9/12.

Fantasien über Gedichte von Richard Dehmel op. 9 for piano: C 1898. MS: Doblinger, Vienna[28] and LoC 9/10–11. P Doblinger, 1901.

*Erwartung (poet unidentified) for voice and piano. C ?1898, fragment. LoC 26/22.

Irmelin Rose und andere Gesänge for voice and piano op. 7. C 1898–9. MS: LoC 9/6 (fragments of nos. 2 and 3). D Alma Schindler. P Hansen, 1901.[29]

*Ein Grab (Richard Dehmel) for voice and piano. C ?1899, fragment. LoC 9/6.

Turmwächterlied und andere Gesänge for low voice and piano op. 8. C 1898–9.[30] LoC 9/9 (no. 3 only).[31] D Johannes Messchaert. P Hansen, 1901. *fp* (nos. 3 and 4) 1 December 1900, Vienna.

Es war einmal . . ., folk-tale opera in a prologue and three acts. Libretto by

---

22 A further MS of this song, allegedly copied by Arnold Schoenberg, is preserved in *MolA*

23 The contract with W. Hansen was signed on 24 November 1896.

24 Several songs in the Copenhagen MS are not in Zemlinsky's hand. None of the MSS is dated.

25 Fair copy with dedication to Melanie Guttmann ('meiner lieben Mela in Erinnerung an s. St.', dated Vienna, 6 September [?1897]).

26 The contract with W. Hansen was signed on 4 January 1898.

27 Not related to the eponymous Fantasy for piano op. 9 no. 2.

28 The Doblinger autograph is dedicated to Schoenberg, but no dedication is included in the published edition.

29 The contracts for opp. 7 and 8 were signed with W. Hansen in January 1900.

30 According to a letter to Edition Wilhelm Hansen dated 12 January 1898 Zemlinsky had already delivered the MSS of these songs but still wished to revise op. 8 no. 3.

31 Copies of these songs in an unidentified hand (with some autograph markings) are preserved in the *MolA*.

Maximilian Singer after Holger Drachmann. C August 1897–28 March 1899. Further revisions compl. *c.*1912. MSS: ÖNB[32] and *LoC* 9/3–5 and 10/1. P libretto, Künast, 1900; v.s., Eberle, undated [1899]; Ricordi, 1990. *fp* 22 January 1900, Vienna Hofoper.

Nordisches Volkslied (Maximilian Singer) from act II of the opera *Es war einmal* . . . for voice and piano. P as musical supplement to *Neue musikalische Presse*, no. 3, 21 January 1900.

*Mit Toves Stimme flüstert der Wald (Jens Peter Jacobsen, trans. Arnold Franz) for voice and piano. C 1899, fragment. *LoC* 9/18.

*Fridl, singspiel in two scenes for voices and piano. Text ?by the composer. C ?winter 1900. Lost.

Psalm 83, 'Gott! Schweige Dich nicht also', for soli, chorus and orchestra. C July–September 1900. *LoC* 9/13–14. P Universal Edition, 1987. *fp* 5 March 1987, Vienna.

In der Sonnengasse (Arno Holz) for voice and piano.[33] C 22 January 1901. *LoC* 9/15. P Ricordi, 1995.

Herr Bombardil (Rudolf Alexander Schröder) for voice and piano. C 23 January 1901. *LoC* 9/15–16. P Ricordi, 1995.

Two (Three) Songs for male voice and orchestra. C 1900–1901. MS: *LoC* 14/11. P orch. Antony Beaumont, Ricordi, 1999. *fp* 10 October 1999, Cologne.

Ehetanzlied und andere Gesänge for voice and piano op. 10. C 1899–1901.[34] MS: *LoC* 9/17–18. P with English translation by Eleanor Mary Rosé-Bott, Doblinger, [1901].

Ein Lichtstrahl, mime drama with piano. Scenario by Oskar Geller. C 8–17 May 1901; rev. *c.*1902. *LoC* 9/20–21. P Ricordi, 1992; *rp* Ricordi, 1996 (both versions).

*Eine gantz neu Schelmweys (Richard Dehmel) for voice and piano. C May 1901. Lost.[35]

*Die Juli-Hexen (Otto Julius Bierbaum) ?for two female voices and piano. C ?May 1901. Lost.[36]

*Komm, komm ins [?*goldene Korn*] (poet unidentified), for two female voices and piano.[37] C May 1901. Sketch, *LoC* 9/16.

*Der Triumph der Zeit (Hugo von Hofmannsthal), ballet in three acts. C January–July 1901, incomplete.[38] Short score: *LoC* 11/1. See also Menuett, Drei Ballettstücke and *Ein Tanzpoem*.

32 Österreichische Nationalbibliothek; copyist's score with MS revisions by Zemlinsky and further alterations by Mahler; also original performing materials. A vocal score used by Margarethe Michalek, who understudied Selma Kurz in the original Vienna production, is preserved in the British Library. It includes copious handwritten alterations.
33 A sketch for a discarded setting of this poem is found in *LoC* 9/16.
34 As no. 5 was incorporated in the revised version of *Es war einmal* . . ., it must have been composed before 1900.
35 Mentioned in *AZ–AMW c.* 8 June 1901, together with 'eine Pantomime' (i.e. *Ein Lichtstrahl*).
36 Cf. *Web-Br* 20, letter to Schoenberg postmarked 18 December 1901; this was evidently the only Ueberbrettl song of Zemlinsky's to be performed at Wolzogen's Buntes Theater in Berlin.
37 Possibly identical to *Die Juli-Hexen*.
38 Whether Zemlinsky ever completed the short score of act III is unclear; cf. letter from Hofmannsthal to Universal Edition, Vienna, dated 26 January 1926: '. . . Zemlinsky composed either the whole ballet or at least part of it.'

Menuett[39] for piano. C 1901. P in *Musik-Blätter*, Pfingst-Album, III. Jg., Nr. 20, Vienna, 1902; *rp* Ricordi, 1996.

Drei Ballettstücke (Suite from the ballet *Der Triumph der Zeit*). Orch. compl. 1902. *LoC* 11/4–5. P Ricordi, 1992. *fp* 18 February 1903, Vienna.

*Licht in der Nacht (Otto Julius Bierbaum) for voice and piano. C ?1903, fragment. *LoC* 12/4.

Die Seejungfrau, fantasy for orchestra. C February 1902–20 March 1903. MS: private collection, Vienna (first movement); *LoC* 12/2–4. P Universal Edition, 1984. *fp* 25 January 1905, Vienna.

Three (Five) Pieces for piano duet. C 1903. *LoC* 12/6.

*Ein Stück aus dem Leben eines Menschen, Sextet in E♭ minor for two violins, two violas and two cellos, incomplete. C ?1902. *LoC* 26/11.

Maiblumen blühten überall (Richard Dehmel) for soprano and string sextet. C ?1902–3. *LoC* 26/12.[40] P Ricordi, 1996.

Es war ein alter König (Heinrich Heine) for voice and piano. C June 1903, rev. 24 December 1921. *LoC* 12/7. D (1903) Lily Hoffmann; (1921) Louise Sachsel. P Ricordi, 1995.

Ein Tanzpoem, poem for dance[41] in one act by Hugo von Hofmannsthal. Compl. February 1904.[42] *fp* Zurich, 19 January 1992. P Ricordi, 1991.

Mädel, kommst du mit zum Tanz? (Leo Feld) for voice and piano.[43] MS: ÖNB.[44] C c.1904. P Ricordi, 1995.

Über eine Wiege[45] (Detlev von Liliencron) for voice and piano. C April 1904. MS: *LoC* 12/8. P in *Der Merker*, music supplement to Heft 5, II. Jg., 1910. *rp* Ricordi, 1995. *fp* 10 April 1904, Vienna.

Schlummerlied[46] (Richard Beer-Hofmann) for voice and piano. C 6 July 1905. MS: Stadt- und Landesbibliothek, Vienna.[47] P 1911 in *Bohemia*, no. 96, 7 April 1912, 39. *rp* Ricordi, 1995.

*Sieh, wie wunderlich der Abend lacht (poet unidentified) for voice and piano. C ?1905, fragment. *LoC* 110.[48]

Der Traumgörge (op. 11), opera in two acts and a postlude. Libretto by Leo Feld. C c.May 1904–26 October 1906. MSS: ÖNB[49] and *LoC* 12/9, 13 and 14/1–6. P libretto and v.s. (two versions) Karczag und Wallner, 1906; *rp* Ricordi, 1989. *fp* 11 October 1980, Nuremberg Opernhaus.

---

39 An extract from act 1 of *Der Triumph der Zeit*.

40 The first movement of a projected two- or three-movement work, the 167 bars of this composition are a setting of vv. 1 and 2 of Dehmel's 5-verse poem. Zemlinsky's choice of G♯ major suggests a possible link with the E♭ minor of the preceding composition.

41 In Hofmannsthal's revised MS: 'Eine Tanzdichtung'.

42 The final version of the original ballet in three acts *Der Triumph der Zeit*.

43 Text and music of this song are largely identical to Grete's aria in act 1/6 of *Der Traumgörge*.

44 Not in Zemlinsky's hand.

45 The MS title is *Schmetterlinge*, the text being extracted from a longer poem of that name.

46 Title of sketch: *Abendlied*. The text is v2 of the poem *Schlaflied für Mirjam*.

47 The first sketch for this song is contained in a volume of sketches for *Der Traumgörge*, *LoC* 12/9.

48 Included in the sketches for *Der Traumgörge*, *LoC* 12/9.

49 Also original performing materials.

Two Ballads for baritone and piano. *C c.*March–April 1907. *P* Ricordi, 1995.

Five Songs to texts by Richard Dehmel for voice and piano. *C* December 1907.[50] *LoC* 14/10. *P* Ricordi, 1995.

*Quintet in D minor for two violins, viola and two cellos. *C* begun 8 June 1908, fragment. *LoC* 26/7.[51]

Der chinesische Hund (Zemlinsky) for voice and tambourine. *C* June–July 1908. *LoC* 26/23.

Kleider machen Leute (op. 12), opera in a prologue and three acts. Libretto by Leo Feld after Gottfried Keller. *C* April 1907–14 August 1909. MS: *LoC* 15/1–11, Stadt- und Landesbibliothek, Vienna and ÖNB.[52] *P* v.s. Bote und Bock, 1910 (two versions). *fp* 2 December 1910, Vienna Volksoper.

Four Songs to texts by Maurice Maeterlinck [trans. K. L. Ammer and F. von Oppeln-Bronikowski] for voice and piano op. 13.[53] *C* August 1910. *P* Universal Edition, 1914.[54] *fp* 11 December 1910, Vienna.

Psalm 23, 'Der Herr ist mein Hirte', op. 14 for satb chorus and orchestra. Compl. 20 August 1910. MS: ÖNB (also MS v.s.) and *LoC* 16/1. *P* Universal Edition, 1911 (v.s.) and 1922 (score). *fp* 10 December 1910, Vienna.

*Malwa, Opera in two acts. Libretto by 'R.L.' after Maxim Gorky. *C* July–August 1912, fragment. *LoC* 16/11–12.

*Untitled operatic fragment ('*Meister Gottfried*'). Dated 7 May 1913.[55] *LoC* 26/25.

Four Maeterlinck Songs for voice and orchestra op. 13 (nos. 1, 2, 3 and 5). Orchestration compl. *c.* 10 March 1913. MS: ÖNB. *P* Universal Edition, 1923. *fp* 31 March 1913, Vienna.

Two Songs to texts by Maurice Maeterlinck [trans. K. L. Ammer and F. von Oppeln-Bronikowski] for voice and piano op. 13.[56] *C* July 1913. *LoC* 16/6–7. *P* Universal Edition, 1914.

String Quartet no. 2 op. 15. *C* 20 July 1913–12 March 1915. MS: ÖNB and *LoC* 16/7 and 17/1–2. *D* Arnold Schoenberg. *P* Universal Edition, 1916. *fp* 9 April 1918, Vienna.

Incidental music to Shakespeare's *Cymbeline*[57] [trans. unidentified] for tenor solo, speakers and large orchestra. *C c.*December 1913–February 1915. *LoC* 16/14–16.

— Suite from the incidental music to Shakespeare's *Cymbeline*. *P* Ricordi, 1996. *fp* 13 October 1996, Hamburg.

50 This is the sequence as published; Zemlinsky stipulated no specific order for these songs.
51 The MS is headed by a cryptogram: 'D. b. d. a. z. m. n.'
52 Additions to the revised version.
53 Nos. 1, 2, 3 and 5 of the cycle of six. The two further songs were added in 1913.
54 *P* no.1 first as music supplement to *NMZ*, 32 Jg. 1911, Heft 18; no. 3 as music supplement to *Musikblätter des Anbruch*, 2. Jg. 1920, Heft 13; nos. 3 and 5 also in *Das moderne Lied. Eine Sammlung von 50 Gesängen für mittlere Stimme*, edited by J. V. v. Wöss, Universal Edition, 1914.
55 The MS, headed '1. Szene', extends to 17 pages and includes parts for 'Der Ritter,' 'Der Mönch' and 'Der Diener'; it breaks off after a chorus of monks intoning the 'Kyrie eleison'. With the putative title, which is mentioned in an undated letter to Hertzka (UE), Zemlinsky may, according to Clayton, have been referring to Karl von Levetzow's *Der Meister von Prag*, a libretto also considered by Richard Strauss (*ACl*, 248).
56 Nos. 4 and 6 of the cycle begun in 1910.
57 In Zemlinsky's original MS the *Cymbeline* music is numbered 'op. 14': this number was later allocated to Psalm 23.

Eine florentinische Tragödie op. 16, opera in one act. Libretto by Oscar Wilde, trans. Max Meyerfeld. C 14 March 1915–14 March 1916. LoC 18/6–7. P Universal Edition, 1916. fp 30 January 1917, Stuttgart Hofoper.

Four Songs for voice and piano. C July–August 1916. MS: Paul Sacher Stiftung, Basle.[58] P Ricordi, 1995.

Herr Arnes Schatz, opera in three acts. Libretto by Zemlinsky after Selma Lagerlöf. C July–August 1917.[59] MS libretto: LoC 28/15.

Raphael,[60] opera in four scenes. Libretto by Georg Klaren after Honoré de Balzac. C May 1918–July 1919, fragment. LoC 19/1–4.

Aurikelchen (Richard Dehmel) for ssaa chorus. C ?1920. LoC 7/3. P Ricordi, 1995.

Der Zwerg (op. 17), opera in one act. Libretto by Georg Klaren[61] after Oscar Wilde. C July 1919–4 January 1921. LoC 20/1. P Universal Edition, 1921 (v.s. and libretto) and 1922 (score). fp 28 May 1922, Cologne Stadttheater.

— Intrada, March and Intermezzo from *Der Zwerg*. P Universal Edition. fp 22 October 1929, Vienna.

— Spanish Dance from *Der Zwerg* for piano.[62] P in *Berliner Tageblatt* (illustrated weekly supplement), 19 February 1927.

Two Maeterlinck Songs for voice and orchestra op. 13 (nos. 4 and 6). Orchestration compl. ?April 1921. LoC (no. 6 only). P Universal Edition, 1924.[63] fp 4 May 1921, Prague.

Kleider machen Leute, musical comedy in a prelude and two acts, revised ('Prague') version. Libretto by Leo Feld after Gottfried Keller. Compl. 1922. P Universal Edition, 1922. fp 20 April 1922, Prague, Deutsches Landestheater.

— Waltz-Intermezzo from *Kleider machen Leute*. P Universal Edition, 1922. fp 22 October 1929, Vienna.

Lyrische Symphonie op. 18 in seven songs after Rabindranath Tagore [trans. Hans Effenberger] for soprano and baritone soli and large orchestra. C 2 April 1922–29 August 1923. MS: ÖNB and LoC 20/2. P Universal Edition, 1923 (v.s.) and 1926 (orchestral score). fp 4 June 1924, Prague.

String Quartet no. 3 op. 19. C August–September 1924. LoC 20/3. D Friedrich Buxbaum. P Universal Edition, 1925. fp 27 October 1924, Leipzig.

*Untitled operatic fragment ('Der Graf von Gleim').[64] Libretto by Marie Pappen-heim. C ?summer 1925. MS: private collection, Vienna.

58 Further source material, evidently used for performances in Vienna under Webern's supervision on 19 and 20 November 1922, are handwritten copies of nos. 1 and 2 (LoC 16/13 and 12/1) and of nos. 1, 3 and 4 (private collection).
59 Zemlinsky composed the music for a 'scenic prologue', of which the autograph is lost (see *Web-Br* 21 May 1917, 170).
60 Original title: *Das Chagrinleder*.
61 A typescript of Klaren's libretto with alterations (presumably in his hand) is preserved in the Stadt- und Landesbibliothek, Vienna (Handschriftenabteilung).
62 Strictly speaking this is a transcription, for the printed text follows the vocal score by Jalowetz (*Allegro*, p. 116–19) note for note. Presumably the publication was authorized by Zemlinsky.
63 In the orchestral score of the six songs, published in 1923, the sequence of nos. 4 and 5 in the piano version of 1914 is reversed.
64 The MS comprises four sketches and an unfinished particell for '1. Scene', Presto 6/8; the roles are: Karl (bass) and Leonie (soprano). Ernst Hilmar places the work chronologically

Der heilige Vitalis, opera in three acts.[65] Libretto by the composer after Gottfried Keller. Sketches C July 1926–c. 1927. LoC 17/3–8 and 18/1–5.

String Quartet (originally intended as no. 4):[66] two complete movements, four fragments. C 22 July–August 1927. MSS: LoC 20/4 and Stadt- und Landesbibliothek, Vienna. First and second movements. P Ricordi, 1994. fp 19 July 1994, Toblach.

Ernste Stunde (Rainer Maria Rilke) for voice and piano. C 16 April 1928, fragment. LoC 20/5.

Symphonische Gesänge op. 20 for baritone (or alto) voice and orchestra. Texts from *Afrika singt. Eine Auslese neuer afro-amerikanischer Lyrik* [trans. Anna Nussbaum, Hermann Kesser, Josef Luitpold and Anna Siemsen]. C July–August 1929. LoC 20/6 and 21/1. P Universal Edition, 1929. fp 8 April 1935, Brno.

Der Kreidekreis (op. 21), opera in three acts (seven scenes). Libretto by Zemlinsky after Klabund. C 3 July 1930–8 October 1932. LoC 21/1–2, 22/1 and 23/1–2. D Louise Zemlinsky. P libretto, Phaidon Verlag, 1933; v.s. Universal Edition, 1933. fp 14 October 1933, Zurich Stadttheater.

Und einmal gehst du (August Eigner) for voice and piano. C July 1933. LoC 23/3. P Ricordi, 1995.

Six Songs[67] op. 22 for voice and piano. C January 1934. D Eva Freund. MSS: LoC 23/6–7 (fair copies) and *MolA*. P (with English translations by Maurice Wright) Mobart, 1977. fp 1934, Prague.

Sinfonietta op. 23 for orchestra. C 8 March–3 July 1934. MS: ÖNB and LoC 23/5. P Universal Edition, 1935. fp 19 February 1935, Prague.

Das bucklichte Männlein (*Des Knaben Wunderhorn*) for voice and piano.[68] C December 1934. LoC 23/6. P with Six Songs op. 22, Mobart, 1977.

Ahnung Beatricens (Franz Werfel) for voice and piano. C January 1935. LoC 23/8. P with Six Songs op. 22, Mobart, 1977.

Psalm 13, 'Herr, wie lange willst Du mein vergessen?', op. 24 for satb chorus and orchestra. C 2 April 1935. MS: New York Public Library, Toscanini Memorial Collection[69] and LoC 23/10. P Universal Edition, 1971. fp 8 June 1971, Vienna.

String Quartet no. 4 (Suite) op. 25. C January–April 1936. MS (score): LoC 23/11; (parts, some pages autograph) *MolA*. P Universal Edition, 1974. fp 21 April 1967, Vienna.

Der König Kandaules (op. 26), opera in three acts. Libretto by the composer after André Gide, German version by Franz Blei. C begun 14 June 1935, short score compl. 29 December 1936. Orchestration incomplete.[70] LoC 188–92. Score reconstructed and orchestration completed by Antony Beaumont 1992–5. P v.s., Ricordi, 1994. fp 6 October 1996, Staatsoper Hamburg.

---

between *Cymbeline* and *Eine florentinische Tragödie*, i.e. c. 1915 (cf. Hilmar, 'Text und Musik in einem Opernfragment Zemlinskys', *AeSU*, 280–83). Judging by the musical style, however, there can be little doubt that the fragment dates from a later period.

65 Original title: *Der tolle Mönch*, opera in five scenes.

66 In the MS the quartet is not numbered. The published version is listed as 'Two Movements for String Quartet'.

67 The MS title of the collection was *Abendlieder*.

68 Originally intended as op. 22 no. 6.

69 Original MS untraceable; a microfilm is available.

70 The MS material includes 137 pp. of orchestral score and 13 pp. of vocal score.

— Prelude and Monologue from act III of the opera *Der König Kandaules*. Orch. Antony Beaumont. P Ricordi, 1992. *fp* 15 May 1992, Vienna.

Twelve Songs op. 27 for voice and piano. C April 1937. LoC 25/2–3. P (with English translations by Maurice Wright) Mobart, 1978.

*Praeludium and Courante (for piano?). C March 1938, incomplete. LoC 24/3.[71]

*Two songs from the Chinese (trans. Hans Bethge) for voice and piano. C begun August 1938, fragment. LoC 27/27 and 25/4.[72]

*Quartet for clarinet, violin, viola and cello. C begun 22 August 1938,[73] fragments. LoC 25/3–4.

Circe, opera in three acts by Irma Stein-Firner. C begun February 1939. Act I compl. in short score March 1939; act II incomplete. LoC 25/5–8 and 25/10.

Three Songs (Irma Stein-Firner, trans. Alice Mattullath). C c.May 1939. LoC 26/14 (sketches only). P Chappell, 1940. *fp* 5 October 1996, Hamburg.

Hunting Piece ('school piece') for two horns and piano. C c.June–July 1939. LoC 26/1. P Universal Edition, as *Jagdstück*, 1977.

Humoreske (Rondo, 'school piece') for wind quintet. C July 1939. LoC 26/2. P Universal Edition, 1978.

71 Among the sketches for *Der König Kandaules*.
72 The sketch for *Liebestrunken* is on the same folio as the first sketches for the Clarinet Quartet.
73 Some sketches are written on Schirmer Imperial Brand manuscript paper and hence date presumably from after Zemlinsky's arrival in New York (December 1938).

Zemlinsky's Recordings

This discography is published by courtesy of Richard Warren, Yale Collection of Historical Sound Recordings. Items marked * were reissued on Schwann MM 4001 (LP and CD), 1986. Zemlinsky's personal copies of the test pressings listed below, as well as wax discs of the 1940 NBC broadcast of the *Sinfonietta* conducted by Mitropoulos, are housed in the Yale Collection. An invoice sent to Zemlinsky by Universal Edition *c.*1929 lists the Waltz-Intermezzo from *Kleider machen Leute* (on Gramola AM 1661, conductor and orchestra unnamed), evidently the only recording of his music published during his lifetime.

LUDWIG VAN BEETHOVEN
Fidelio overture
Berlin State Opera Orchestra
Polydor 62667
rec. 1929*

ANTONÍN DVOŘÁK
Humoresque, op. 101 no. 7
Jarmila Novotná (soprano)
Vienna Concert Orchestra
Parlophone AR–282, RO–20293
rec. 1935, reissued on
Supraphon 11 1491–2 201 (CD), 1992

ZDENÍK FIBICH
Poem (from *At Twilight* op. 39)
Jarmila Novotná (soprano)
Vienna Concert Orchestra
Parlophone AR-282, RO-20293
rec. 1935, reissued on Supraphon
11 1491–2 201 (CD), 1992

FRIEDRICH VON FLOTOW
Alessandro Stradella overture
Berlin State Opera Orchestra
Polydor 66795 [1]
rec. 1928*

LOUIS AIMÉ MAILLART
Les Dragons de Villars [*Das Glöckchen des Eremiten*] overture
Berlin State Opera Orchestra
Polydor 19796 [2]
rec. 1928*

WOLFGANG AMADEUS MOZART
Così fan tutte overture
Berlin-Charlottenburg Opera Orchestra
Polydor 19796 [3]
rec. 1928*

Don Giovanni overture
Berlin-Charlottenburg Opera Orchestra
Polydor 19796 [4]
rec. 1928*

Die Entführung aus dem Serail overture
Berlin-Charlottenburg Opera Orchestra
Polydor 19796 [5]
rec. 1928*

1 Also test pressings 1374bmI, 1346bmI, T7–1773.
2 Also test pressings 1347bmI, 1348bmI, 1348 1/2bmI, T7–1773.
3 Also test pressings 711bm, 711 1/2bm, T7–1770.
4 Also test pressing T7–1770.
5 Also test pressings 712bm, 712 1/2bm, T7–1770.

OTTO NICOLAI
Die lustigen Weiber von Windsor:
Duet 'In einem Waschkorb'
Gerhard Hüsch (baritone)
Eugen Fuchs (bass)
Berlin-Charlottenburg Opera Orchestra
Columbia DW–3047 (10 inch)
rec. 1932, reissued on
Austro Mechana 890171 (CD), 1993

GIACOMO PUCCINI
Tosca:
'Und es blitzen die Sterne'
('E lucevan le stelle')
'Wie sich die Bilder gleichen'
('Recondita armonia')
Rudolf Gerlach-Rusnak (tenor)
Berlin-Charlottenburg Opera Orchestra
Gramophone EG–2637
rec. ? (after 1931)

GIOACCHINO ROSSINI
La gazza ladra overture
Berlin State Opera Orchestra
Polydor 66856
rec. 1929*

BEDŘICH SMETANA
Prodana nevěsta (*The Bartered Bride*):
Duet: 'Wer in Lieb entbrannt'
('Každy jen tu svou')
Charles Kullmann (tenor)
Eugen Fuchs (baritone)
Berlin-Charlottenburg Opera Orchestra
Columbia DWX 3051
rec. 1931, re-issued on
Austro-Mechana 89057 (CD), 1992

Vltava (*Die Moldau*)
Berlin Philharmonic Orchestra
Ultraphon E–465/6
rec. *c.* 1930 (3 sides)*

JOHANN STRAUSS
Die Fledermaus overture
Berlin State Opera Orchestra
Polydor (tests only)[6]
rec. *c.* 1930

GIUSEPPE VERDI
Il trovatore (*Der Troubador*):
'Dass nur für mich' ('Ah, sì! ben mio')
'Lodern zum Himmel' ('Di quella pira')
Rudolf Gerlach-Rusnak (tenor)
Berlin-Charlottenburg Opera Orchestra
Gramophone EG–2636
rec. ? (after 1931)

CARL MARIA VON WEBER
Der Freischütz overture
Berlin State Opera Orchestra
Polydor (tests only)[7]
rec. *c.* 1929 (3 sides)

JAROMIR WEINBERGER
Schwanda the Bagpiper: Polka
Berlin Philharmonic Orchestra
Ultraphon E–466 Telefunken E-938
rec. *c.* 1930*

---

6 716bm, 717bm, T7–1771.
7 718bm, 719bm, 719 1/2bm, 720bm, 720 1/2bm, T7–1772.

Notes

Introduction

1 Recounted in a letter from Arnold Greissle-Schönberg to Louise Zemlinsky, 6 January 1991 (*NLZ* Da 18). The anecdote is attributed to a friend of Zemlinsky's named Warner Bass.
2 The list of new editions, prepared by G. Ricordi, Munich, includes the following: *Posthumous Songs, Selected Piano Music, Maiblumen blühten überall* (Dehmel) for soprano and string sextet, String Quartet in E minor, Two Movements for String Quintet (1893–6), Two Movements for String Quartet (1927), Clarinet Quartet (fragments), *Aurikelchen* (Dehmel) for female voices, *Minnelied* (Heine) for male voices and small orchestra, *Waldgespräch* (Eichendorff) for soprano and chamber orchestra, Zwei Gesänge for baritone and orchestra (orchestrated from the short score), *Hochzeitslied* for cantor, chorus and organ, *Frühlingsbegräbnis* (Heyse) for solo voices, chorus and orchestra, Symphony in D minor, Prelude to *Es war einmal* . . . (original version), Drei Ballettstücke, Suite from the incidental music to Shakespeare's *Cymbeline*, *Ein Lichtstrahl* (mime drama with piano accompaniment), *Ein Tanzpoem* (ballet in one act). With the exception of the Clarinet Quartet, the chamber works were edited in collaboration with Werner Loll; the Clarinet Quartet fragments remain unpublished, but have been recorded on Thorophon CTH 2376 (1996).
3 A. Beaumont and S. Rode-Breymann (eds.), *Alma Mahler-Werfel Tagebuch-Suiten 1898–1902* (Frankfurt, 1997); abridged English edition: *Alma Mahler-Werfel: Diaries 1898–1902* (London and Ithaca, 1998).
4 Zemlinsky, *Der König Kandaules*, drama in three acts by André Gide, German adaptation by Franz Blei, score reconstructed and orchestration completed by Antony Beaumont (Munich, 1993).
5 Zemlinsky's letters and postcards to Heinrich Jalowetz were acquired in 1990 by the Paul Sacher Stiftung in Basle.
6 See Antony Beaumont, 'Alexander Zemlinsky: *Der Triumph der Zeit* – Drei Ballettstücke – *Ein Tanzpoem*', in S. Harpner and B. Gotzes (eds.) *Über Musiktheater. Eine Festschrift [für Arthur Scherle]* (Munich, 1992), 13–31.

1 Prologue: The Sephardic Diaspora

1 Obadiah, v. 20 (AV). The editors of *The New English Bible* consider the four italicized words spurious and have relegated them to a footnote.
2 Orthographic variants include Šem Tob and Schemtov.
3 *Encyclopaedia Judaica*, v, 970.
4 *Encyclopaedia Judaica*, iv, 1482.
5 Rabbi Dr M. Papo, 'The Sephardi Community of Vienna', in Josef Fraenkel (ed.), *The Jews of Austria. Essays on Their Life, History and Destruction* (London, 1967), 337.
6 *El Correo de Viena*, 15 Tevet 5630 [1870], quoted in Edwin Seroussi, 'Die sephardische Gemeinde in Wien: Geschichte einer orientalisch-jüdischen Enklave in Mitteleuropa', *SPH*, 145–53.
7 Papo, op. cit., 332.
8 Jacob Bauer, foreword to *Shir ha-kavod* (Vienna, 1889).
9 Pierre Genée, *Wiener Synagogen 1825–1938* (Vienna, 1987), 89.
10 Papo, op. cit., 334.
11 In 1898 the journal was renamed *Freiheit*.
12 *Oesterreich-ungarische Cantoren-Zeitung*, 8 February 1882.
13 Ibid., 9 December 1888.
14 Three further relatives, Franz, Hugo and Karl Semlinsky, presumably Adolf's brothers, were resident at the same address, Taborstrasse 59; cf. *Lehmanns allgemeiner Wohnungs-Anzeiger . . .*, ix (Vienna, 1871). Franz Semlinsky (profession cited in *Lehmann*, 1898 and 1901, as 'railway official'), later settled in the Upper Austrian town of Amstetten, where he was employed as stationmaster.
15 There is some evidence that Anton Semlinsky also adopted the new orthography.
16 Alexander Semo lived in the more salubrious *III. Bezirk* (cf. *Lehmann*, op. cit.) Confusingly, *Lehmann* cites the journal as *Wiener Courier*.
17 Alexander Semo died in April 1881. His wife Bianca survived him by thirteen years.
18 Cf. Adolf von Zemlinszky's letter of application to the Vienna Conservatoire on behalf of his son, dated 6 September 1884: 'For twelve years I have been Secretary to the Turkish-Israelite Community in Vienna and rely on an annual income of 600 fl.' (quoted in Otto Biba, 'Alexander Zemlinsky und die Gesellschaft der Musikfreunde in Wien', *AeSU*, 207).
19 In *Lehmann* (Vienna, 1901), Adolf von Zemlinszky is registered as 'Bureau-Chef'.

20 Cf. *Web-ZW*, p. 79. Weber cites *Lehmann* (Vienna, 1873–1900) as his source.
21 'Diverse chronicles of Dr Confusius'.
22 'Simon Crash at the Stock Exchange'.
23 The latter also appeared in *El Correo* as 'La figlia del rabbino'; a further publication in Ladino was 'Il cigno di Toledo' ('The Swan of Toledo').
24 In the programme for the annual Prater parade (*Blumencorso*) of 1887, Zemlinszky published a short story entitled *Der Blumen Bestimmung*.
25 Adolf von Zemlinszky, *Geschichte der türkisch-israelitischen Gemeinde zu Wien von ihrer Gründung bis heute nach historischen Daten* (Vienna, 1888), with Ladino translation by Michael Papo.

II   Vienna 1871–1901

1   Childhood in the Leopoldstadt

1   The birth is recorded in the registry of the Israelitische Kultusgemeinde. Birth certificates for Bianca and Mathilde are preserved in the registry of the Sephardic community.
2   Contemporary euphemism for circumcision. Sigmund Freud's younger brother was named Alexander allegedly 'in recall of Alexander [the Great]'s magnanimity and [. . .] prowess as a military leader' (Peter Gay, *Freud. A Life for Our Time* (London, 1988), 8n).
3   *ACl*, 22.
4   A. J. P. Taylor, 'Empire of Austria', *Encyclopaedia Britannica*, II (London, 1955), 769.
5   Roman Sandgruber, 'Der große Krach', in *Traum und Wirklichkeit. Wien 1870–1930*, exhibition catalogue, 68–75.
6   Quoted by Sandgruber, ibid.; source not specified.
7   April 1874. Recorded cause of death was *Magen-Cholik* (stomach colic).
8   *ASD*, 4 February 1901.
9   Ibid.
10 *Wiener Punsch*, no. 836 (5 April 1892), 6. Heinrich Elias, the composer of the festive motet, was a son of the Sephardic community's benefactor Abraham Elias.
11 According to Heinz Schöny ('Musikgeschichte und Genealogie' no. 56, *Genealogie*, April 1978, vol. 14, 97–101), there was also a twin brother named Matthias.
12 Considering the family's financial hardship, it seems curious that they never made use of the apartment in the new synagogue, which, as von Zemlinszky himself writes – in his *Geschichte der türkisch-israelitischen Gemeinde zu Wien von ihrer Gründung bis heute nach historischen Daten* (Vienna, 1888) – was designated to the Secretary.
13 I.e. from the first surviving letters in 1901 until her death in 1912. In a letter of condolence to Zemlinsky upon the death of his mother, dated 14 June 1912, Webern wrote: 'I always revered your deceased mother. Her great sympathy towards myself, my wife and my children was always such a delight'(*Web-Br*, 281).
14 Only once, in a letter to Schoenberg dated 5 July 1905, does Zemlinsky write more explicitly about his mother: 'The card from M[athilde] seems to imply that mother is living at your place. Isn't that rather a disruption? I hope at least that she doesn't cause you trouble! Is she very bad-tempered? Or does she like it there?' (*Web-Br*, 52).
15 *AZ-AMW*, *c.* 8 July 1901.
16 Letter from Louise Zemlinsky to Helmut Haack, 6 October 1980 (excerpts published in an unidentified concert programme, Heidelberg, 26 January 1988). In 1913, the seven-year-old Elias Canetti attended the school in the Novaragasse, which he describes in his autobiography, *Die gerettete Zunge*: 'Conditions at that school were wretched because the teacher, a poor, wheezing fellow, cut a ridiculous figure, [. . .] he made not the slightest impression upon the pupils, who did whatever they pleased. Of course we learned to read Hebrew and rattled off the prayers in the book at great speed. But we had no idea what the words we were reading actually meant, nobody thought to explain them to us.'
17 Adolf von Zemlinszky, *Geschichte . . .*, op. cit.
18 *BikW*, 13/8: 'In main and extra subjects his mark for the year was a "first".'
19 *ASD*, 4 February 1901. Adolf Zemlinszky's application forms for *Schulgeldbefreiung* (exemption from school fees) are preserved in the archives of the Gesellschaft der Musikfreunde in Wien. They confirm the accuracy of Alma Schindler's report: the first application, in 1884, was rejected; the following year Zemlinszky appended a note signed by the director (*Vorstand*) of the Sephardic community, Leon J. Haim, emphasizing that the applicant was 'comparatively poorly off, as he has to support his family from a low income'. Finally, in 1886, as the result of a glowing annual report on Zemlinsky's progress, the exemption was granted (cf. *BikW*, 11/4, 12/6–8, 13/10–11).
20 *ACl*, 24.
21 *BikW*, 13/6.

2   The Vienna Conservatoire

1   For one unhappy year (1884–5) the seventeen-year-old Ferruccio Busoni studied with the same teacher.
2   Cf. *BikW*, 15/10, Zemlinsky's application for the Rubinstein scholarship, dated 1890, which clearly states that 'during the completed year of study [. . .] he has successfully terminated his first course of *composition*' (author's italics).
3   The diploma certificate is preserved in the Zemlinsky Collection at the Library of Congress.
4   Josef Labor (1842–1924) was Schoenberg's first teacher. From 1895 to 1901 he also taught Alma Schindler.
5   Brahms's comment on Fuchs's opera *Die Teufelsglocke*, performed at the Vienna Hofoper in 1893, from Richard Heuberger, *Erinnerungen an Johannes Brahms. Tagebuchaufzeichnungen aus den Jahren 1875 bis 1897* (Tutzing, 1976), 48. Heuberger also records: 'he [i.e. Brahms] was very pleased that the [Vienna] Philharmonic was to perform Robert Fuchs's First Symphony, for he loves the work and has recommended it to Simrock, who also wishes to publish it' (ibid., 26).
6   Ibid., 142.
7   *ASD*, 26 February 1900.
8   Verwaltungsarchiv, Vienna, June 1912. Translated and quoted by Christopher Hailey in *Franz Schreker, 1878–1934. A cultural biography* (Cambridge 1993), 56.
9   Letter from Sibelius to Martin Wegelius *c.* October 1890, quoted in Erik Tawaststjerna (trans. Robert Layton), *Sibelius*, vol. I (London, 1976), 74.
10   Karl Ekman, *Jean Sibelius. His Life and Personality* (New York, 1946), 97.
11   Letter from Hugo Wolf dated 15 March 1876, quoted in Frank Walker, *Hugo Wolf. A Biography* (London, 1951), 46.
12   Cf. R. Batka and H. Werner (eds.), *Hugo Wolfs musikalische Kritiken* (Leipzig, 1911; rep. Liechtenstein, 1986), 294, 310.
13   Henry-Louis de La Grange, *Mahler*, vol. I (London, 1974), 32.
14   *ASD*, 26 February 1900.
15   Cf. Hailey, op. cit., 22.
16   *BikW*, 16/18.
17   'I am to stop composing songs and for the next lesson I have to compose short movements based on the first thematic groups and whole, single movements of [Beethoven] sonatas.' *ASD*, 26 November 1900.
18   Alma Schindler's opinion of J. N. Fuchs's conducting was anything but flattering: 'I don't know of any conductor more dreadful than he was. Like a cart-horse. All of a sudden he would go wild and brandish his baton with considerable fire and temperament – but not for long. Then he resumed his customary trot. Scarcely a performance came off without a hitch' (*ASD*, 26 February 1900).
19   *Lehrplan und Prüfungs-Vorschrift für das Schuljahr 1891–1892*, 14 (Archive of the Gesellschaft der Musikfreunde in Wien).
20   *BikW*, 15/11.
21   Zemlinsky did however assert that he had begun to compose at the age of eight.
22   Nos. 11–12, bars 67–72.
23   No. 7, bars 28–31; cf. Schoenberg Chamber Symphony no. 1 op. 9, 79⁻⁴ bars before.
24   Nos. 11–12, bars 37–44.
25   'Heart and Brain in Music', *St-Id*, 55.
26   *Wiener Punsch*, no. 836 (5 April 1892), 6.
27   Letter from Louise Zemlinsky to Helmut Haack dated 6 October 1980, published in a cyclostyled concert programme, Heidelberg, 26 January 1988.
28   'One thing, though – if you would like to be my pupil, you should not contemplate publishing your works for some time yet' (*ASD*, 13 November 1900).
29   The score of the first three movements (*LoC*) is the work of a copyist. Of the finale the copyist only wrote out the first six pages, the rest of the score is in Zemlinsky's own hand.
30   *Entretiens*, tape 5; cf. Noel Malcolm, *George Enescu, His Life and Music* (Surbiton, 1990), 41.
31   *Wiener Tageblatt*, 16 February 1893.
32   *Deutsche Kunst- und Musik-Zeitung*, 24 February 1893.
33   *Neue Freie Presse*, 13 February 1893.

3   The Polyhymnia

1   Information kindly supplied by Hofrat Dr Rainer Egger, Director of the Archive at the Austrian War Ministry (letter to the author, 27 June 1994).
2   Conversation with the author, 11 April 1999.
3   Hans Heinsheimer, 'Die scharfe Brille über die Nase [. . .] Meine Erinnerungen an Alexander Zemlinsky', programme book of *Eine florentinische Tragödie* and Schreker's *Der Geburtstag der Infantin*, Hamburg, 1981, 103.
4   Elias Canetti, *Das Augenspiel* (Munich–Vienna, 1985), 301.

5   *AZ–AMW, c.* 9 July 1901.
6   *AZ–AMW, c.* 24 July 1901.
7   *AZ–AMW, c.* June 1901.
8   Arnold Schoenberg, *Berliner Tagebuch*, edited by Josef Rufer (Frankfurt–Berlin–Vienna, 1974); entry for 21 February 1912.
9   From a poem by Pepi Glöckner, dated 24 June 1927 (unpublished typescript, *MolA*).
10 Conversation with the author, 3 December 1990.
11 Bodanzky's papers, which must have included letters from Busoni, Mahler and Schoenberg as well as other invaluable material, were posthumously destroyed by his wife and daughter (information kindly supplied by Bodanzky's granddaughter, Mrs John Arms, New York).
12 Cf. Carl Nemeth, *Franz Schmidt. Ein Meister nach Brahms und Bruckner* (Vienna, 1957), 52–4.
13 Cf. *St-Sch*, 29.
14 Richard Heuberger, *Erinnerungen an Johannes Brahms. Tagebuchaufzeichnungen aus den Jahren 1875 bis 1897* (Tutzing, 1976), 16.
15 According to Ottilie Schoenberg, Webern and others, parts of act III were orchestrated by Schoenberg (cf. *St-Sch*, 30). Ernst Hilmar, who inspected the original manuscript in the early 1970s, maintains that there is no evidence to support this assertion (cf. Hilmar (ed.), *Arnold Schoenberg. Gedenkausstellung 1974* (Vienna, 1974), 170).
16 *Die Fackel*, III/90 (Ende December 1901), 27.
17 Cf. *ASD*, 1 April 1901: 'Orchestra fabulous. Zemlinsky conducted. Had also orchestrated it superbly for Ed.'
18 Gärtner is also known to have participated in an early concert of Schreker (cf. *B–SC*, 14).
19 Concerts on 19 February 1897 and 1 December 1901. *ASD* also refers to private performances, which Alma Schindler did not attend.
20 Egon Wellesz, *Arnold Schoenberg*, edited by Carl Dahlhaus (Wilhelmshaven, 1985), 11–12.
21 Cf. Hilmar, op. cit., 164.
22 Cf. *ASD*, 17 February 1901, for a description of a composition lesson with Hoffmann and another, unidentified, student (probably Karl Weigl): 'The one, Hoffmann, played a sonata of his own composition. – Well [. . .] I have heard more beautiful things.'
23 Cf. Dési Halban and Ursula Ebbers (eds.) *Selma Kurz. Die Sängerin und ihre Zeit* (Stuttgart–Zurich, 1983), 31.
24 *B–SC*, 329.
25 *B–SC*, 14.
26 Paul Stefan, 'Das Leben', *Musikblätter des Anbruch*, II/1–2 (January 1920), 9–11.
27 In lieu of printed programmes the Tonkünstlerverein published an annual report (*Rechenschaftsbericht*), which included the treasurer's report, lists of current active and non-active members and the concert programmes of the preceding season.
28 In his memoirs Flesch makes no mention of the Franck Sonata. Zemlinsky's participation is likewise passed over in silence (see H. Keller (trans. and ed.), *The Memoirs of Carl Flesch* (London, 1957)).
29 *Neue Musikalische Presse*, VIII (1899), no. 17, 1 (quoted in Hilmar, op. cit., 60).
30 Archive of the Ministerium für Kultus und Unterricht in Vienna; quoted in Alfred Clayton, 'Brahms und Zemlinsky', *Bericht des Brahms-Kongresses Wien 1983* (Tutzing, 1984), 86. The score of *Sarema* was submitted to the jury of the Luitpold Prize in Munich on 3 September 1895 (cf. *Web-ZW*, 84). By the time Zemlinsky received the grant, he had long since completed his project.
31 'Sieht überall Talent heraus' (Heuberger, op. cit., 97).
32 Recounted by Louise Zemlinsky, cf. Clayton, op. cit., 86n.
33 Zemlinsky, 'Brahms und die neuere Generation. Persönliche Erinnerungen', *Musikblätter des Anbruch*, IV (March 1922), 69–70. Zemlinsky's account omits to mention that he refused Brahms's offer of financial support.
34 Ibid.
35 *Web-Br*, 144, letter dated September 1915. The concert, which took place on 21 October 1915, also included Schubert's *Rosamunde* Overture and Robert Fuchs's Serenade in E minor.
36 Ibid.
37 Zemlinsky, *Two Movements for String Quintet*, edited by A. Beaumont and W. Loll (Munich, 1993), II/148–52. The opening theme of the first Ballade, *Archibald Douglas*, composed *c.* 1893, also includes the 'World' motif.
38 Cf. *Neue Musikalische Presse*, 1 December 1895, and Ernst Hilmar, 'Zemlinsky und Schönberg', *TiU*, 55–6.
39 *Neue Musikalische Presse*, 15 March 1896.
40 Cf. Hilmar, *Arnold Schoenberg*, op. cit., 166–7. Schoenberg conducted a male-voice choir in Stockerau from 1895 to 1896, and from 1896 to 1898 he was choirmaster of the Mödlinger Arbeitergesangsverein.
41 Quoted in *St-Sch*, 29.
42 Wellesz, op. cit., 18.
43 Zemlinsky, 'Jugenderinnerungen', *Arnold Schönberg zum 60. Geburtstag* (Vienna, 1934), 33

44 Max Graf, 'Das Wiener Café Größenwahn', *Neues Österreich*, II/1951 (quoted in Hilmar, *Arnold Schoenberg*, op. cit., 165).

45 From the *Listener*, 1952; quoted (verbatim?) in *St-Sch*, English version, 31.

46 Max Graf, 'Kammermusik mit Edmund Eysler und Arnold Schönberg', quoted in *Hil-Kat*, 231.

47 Schoenberg, 'Zemlinsky', *St-Id*, 486.

48 The only example preserved is the remark 'sehr gut' on the manuscript of Schoenberg's song 'Das zerbrochene Krüglein' (facsimile in John A. Kimmey Jr., *The Arnold Schoenberg– Hans Nachod Collection*, Detroit Studies in Music Bibliography XLI (Detroit, 1979), 218), but the handwriting cannot positively be identified as Zemlinsky's.

49 Schoenberg, 'My Evolution', *St-Id*, 79.

50 Conversation with the author, 3 December 1990.

51 Schoenberg, 'Notes on the Four String Quartets' in U. von Rauchhaupt (ed.), *The String Quartets. A Documentary Study* (Hamburg, 1971), 32.

52 Webern, 'Schönbergs Musik', *Arnold Schönberg* (Munich, 1912), 22.

53 Robert Fleischmann, 'Alexander von Zemlinsky', *Biographische Skizzen moderner Musiker*, XV (*Monatsblätter für zeitgenössische Musik*), July 1913.

54 The preliminary versions are published in the Schoenberg Complete Edition, 1/2. part 2 (Reihe B). The Lieder op. 1 were published in 1903. Schoenberg presented a copy to Zemlinsky, accompanied by a letter of dedication. The letter, which was inadvertently omitted from *Web-Br*, is reproduced here in full:

Lieber Alex, 'Da stehts, was wir stemmten' [a quotation from *Das Rheingold*]. Wenn's auch nicht das worden ist, was ich hoffte, als ich mir vornahm, dir meine ersten gedruckten Noten zu widmen – vielleicht wird es das später: Lohn das Lehrers durch den Freund! Wien 14. October 1903, zu deinem Geburtstage. Arnold Schönberg.

[Dear Alex, 'Here stands what we strove for.' Even if it's not quite what I was hoping for when I resolved to dedicate my first printed music to you – perhaps later it will be: A teacher's recompense from a friend! Vienna, 14 October 1903, on your birthday. Arnold Schoenberg.]

55 Both songs were raised by a semitone.

56 *Web-Br*, 12.

57 Undated note (in English) at the Schoenberg Archive, Los Angeles; published in Josef Rufer, *Das Werk Arnold Schönbergs* (Kassel, 1959), 154.

58 Cf. *Neue Musikalische Presse*, 1896/XI, 2–3. The jury members were Baron von Perfall, Graf von Hochberg and five conductors: Ernst von Schuch (Dresden), Julius Hofmann (Cologne), Hermann Levi (Munich), Franz Wüllner (Cologne) and Hermann Zumpe (Berlin). On 12 June 1896 Wüllner complained to the organizers that he was having to spend all his free time reading scores for the competition (cf. *ACl*, 52).

59 *Sarema* was revived at Trier (1996) and Kassel (1998).

60 The manuscript arrived in Munich on 3 September 1895 (cf. *Web-ZW*, 84).

61 *Allgemeine Musik-Zeitung*, 22 October 1897.

62 *Neue Musikalische Presse*, 1897/VI, 3.

63 Cf. Clayton, op. cit., 54.

64 *Münchener Freie Presse*, 12 October 1897.

65 *AZ–AMW*, 13 June 1901.

66 *Münchener Neueste Nachrichten*, 12 October 1897.

67 Bars 17–18.

68 Cf. Gösta Neuwirth, 'Musik um 1900' in Jürg Stenzl (ed.), *Art Nouveau, Jugendstil und Musik* (Zurich–Freiburg, 1980), 105, and Peter Andraschke, 'Alexander Zemlinskys Dehmel– Kompositionen' in *AeSU*, 158. As Neuwirth points out, 'The two pieces are so manifestly related that the more deepseated differences between them can easily be overlooked.'

69 *AZ–AMW*, 12 May 1901.

70 *AZ–AMW*, c.26 September 1901.

71 Rabbi Dr M. Papo, 'The Sephardi Community of Vienna', in Josef Fraenkel (ed.), *The Jews of Austria. Essays on Their Life, History and Destruction* (London, 1967), 340.

72 Instead of 'chatan' ('bridegroom') Zemlinsky wrote 'chata'. In the autograph, most of the composition is notated without word underlay.

73 *ZTuA*, 25–40.

74 Zemlinsky, 'Brahms und die neuere Generation. Persönliche Erinnerungen', op. cit., 69–70.

75 *Wiener Tageblatt*, 11 March 1896.

76 *Neue Freie Presse*, 14 March 1896.

77 *Neue Musikalische Presse*, 15 March 1896.

78 *Neues Wiener Tageblatt*, 14 March 1896.

79 *Sonn- und Montagszeitung*, 9 March 1896.

80 In the published score (Simrock, 1897): p. 7, line 4, bar 4 and the ensuing 10 bars.

81 *ZTuA*, 72, 74.

82   Unidentified press cutting (signed 'R.') from Zemlinsky's scrapbook, *MolA*.
83   Walter William Cobbett and Colin Mason (eds.), *Cobbett's Cyclopedic Survey of Chamber Music*, II (London, 1963), 597.
84   *Der Merker*, VIII/1912, 596. In 1924 a young composer named Zabinsky from Breslau tried to pass the work off as his own.
85   *Neue Musikalische Presse*, 1895/XII, 4.
86   *Oesterreichische Rundschau*, 1 April 1895.
87   'S. Th.' in *Neue Musikalische Presse*, 15 March 1896.
88   *Neue Musikalische Presse*, 12 March 1899.
89   *Neues Wiener Journal*, 12 February 1900.

4   Fin de siècle

1   *Web-Br*, letter to Schoenberg, 18 February 1902. Zemlinsky writes in the context of the 'Critics' section from Richard Strauss's *Ein Heldenleben*.
2   Rudolf Stefan Hoffmann, 'Zemlinskys Opern', *AT*, 215.
3   Viktor Ullmann, 'Zur Charakteristik der Tonarten', *Anbruch*, 1935, 211–12.
4   Bernard Grun (ed. and trans.), *Alban Berg. Letters to his Wife* (London–New York, 1971), 19; undated letter (spring 1907).
5   In the published edition of this passage (*Posthumous Songs*, edited by Antony Beaumont) there are two errors: (a) the *crescendo* and *diminuendo* are wrongly placed; (b) the marking *ben ten.* over the penultimate bar is misread. Mea culpa.
6   Theodor Adorno, 'Zemlinsky' (1959) in *Quasi una fantasia. Musikalische Schriften II* (Frankfurt, 1990), 160.
7   *AZ–AMW*, c. 8 July 1901.
8   *ASD*, 2 March 1901.
9   Unidentified press-cutting (*c.* 1897), *MolA*.
10   Letter from the publisher of *Sarema*, Emil Berté, to Ernst von Possart, *Intendant* of the Munich Hoftheater, 6 November 1897, cf. *Web-ZW*, 89.
11   The original version of Drachmann's play, written in 1884, was published in Copenhagen in 1895. Two German translations were subsequently published: translated by Heinrich Zschalig, Dresden, 1894; translated by Marie von Borch, Leipzig, 1897.
12   *Es war einmal, oder Der Prinz von Nordland*, Märchen-Komödie in 5 Aufzügen. Im Auftrag des Verfassers besorgte Uebersetzung von M. v. Borch. Musik von P. G. Lange-Müller. Souffleur- und Regiebuch (Reclam, Leipzig, 1897).
13   Drachmann's play is divided into five acts. The opera libretto, originally in four *Bilder* (tableaux), was eventually divided up into a prologue and three acts.
14   Cf. Henry-Louis de La Grange, *Mahler*, vol. I (London, 1974), 500.
15   The orchestral Prelude is dated 28 March 1899, but the remainder of the full score includes no further dates.
16   Cf. Hanne Marie and Werner Svendsen, *Geschichte der dänischen Literatur* (Neumünster Copenhagen, 1964), 312–20; P. M. Mitchell, *A History of Danish Literature*, 2nd edn (New York, 1971), 179–81.
17   Sometimes translated simply as 'Midsummer Song'.
18   Letter from Drachmann to V. Hegel, 1 July 1884, in Morten Borup (ed.), *Breve fra og til Holger Drachmann* (Copenhagen, 1970), III, 114.
19   Conversation with the author, 10 January 1993.
20   From *Der Zwerg*, scene i.
21   Cf. Prologue: 'Lieb Väterchen, hab' ein wenig Geduld, / nah kam nicht der Rechte, s'ist nicht meine Schuld, / doch nahet ein Mann mit männlichem Sinn, / dem geb' ich mich willig gefangen hin.' ('Dear father, be patient awhile. The right man has not yet come, it's not my fault. But if a really masculine man appears, I'll gladly let him take me prisoner.')
22   Ullmann, op. cit.
23   O. J. Bierbaum (ed.), *Deutsche Chansons (Brettllieder)* (Berlin–Leipzig, 1900), ix.
24   O. J. Bierbaum, *Stilpe. Ein Roman aus der Froschperspektive* (Berlin, 1897); quoted in Walter Rösler, *Das Chanson im deutschen Kabarett 1901–1933* (Berlin, 1980), 57 – cf. footnote 3.
25   Cf. La Grange, op. cit., 550, who cites no source. One of the more radical alterations (in the Prologue), which may have been penned by Lipiner, runs as follows: [Liebe am Markte Töpfe verkaufen, / lieber mit dem Bettelsack laufen, / selbst des ärmsten Mannes Frau]. *Original version*: als solch eines Prinzen, der hohl und schal, / in Prunkgewändern fürstlich Gemahl. *Revised version*: [. . .] als solch eines Schwärmers von Eurem Schlag / Ehgenossin nur einen Tag!
26   *Neue Freie Presse*, 24 January 1900.
27   '*Es war einmal*. Gelegentliches über Zemlinsky und Richard Strauss. 1900', in Eduard Hanslick, *Aus neuer und neuester Zeit. Der modernen Oper ix. Teil* (Berlin, 1900), 44–50; *rp* in Peter Wapnewski (ed.), *Eduard Hanslick, Aus dem Tagebuch eines Rezensenten* (Kassel–Basle, 1989), 203–11.

28   Seven performances were given, three of them conducted by Karl Horwitz, a composition pupil of Schoenberg's.

5   Alma gentil

1   *ASD*, 11 February 1900.
2   *ASD*, 26 February 1900. The dinner party was given by Spitzer at his villa on the Hohe Warte.
3   *ASD*, 10 March 1900.
4   *ASD*, 29 March 1900.
5   *ASD*, 23 April 1900.
6   *ASD*, 22 May 1900.
7   *ASD*, 19 June 1900.
8   *ASD*, 29 June 1900.
9   Rabbi Dr M. Papo, 'The Sephardi Community of Vienna', in Josef Fraenkel (ed.), *The Jews of Austria. Essays on Their Life, History and Destruction* (London, 1967), 341.
10   Vv. 1, 2, 3 (shortened), 13, 14 (sequence reversed) and 18. The rest of the psalm does not lend itself well to musical treatment. The AV cites the name Jehovah, but this is one of the so-called 'Elohim' psalms. Luther's translation avoids problems of nomenclature by using the vocative 'Herr' (Lord).
11   Cf. *Web-Br*, 27–8.
12   'Alexander Zemlinskys Psalmkompositionen in ihrer Zeit', *AeSU*, 67–78.
13   Cf. Verena Keil-Budischowsky, *Die Theater Wiens* (Vienna–Hamburg, 1983), 264–5.
14   *Neue musikalische Presse*, 12 March 1899.
15   Ibid.
16   'Wieder einmal und wohl endgiltig sind die Musiker von ihm [Weinberger] vertrieben worden. Einer von ihnen, der erste Capellmeister des Theaters, soll sich freiwillig vor Herrn Weinberger zurückgezogen, ja sich contractlich gegen die Zumuthung, die Aufführungen der "Diva" zu leiten, gesichert haben' (*Die Fackel*, II/56 (Mitte Oktober 1900), 24–5). *Die Diva* ran for twenty-six performances between 11 October and 18 November. The text, by Bernhard Buchbinder jun., was revised by the dramaturg Johannes Wattke, later also responsible for editing the libretto of *Der Traumgörge*.
17   *AZ–AMW*, 9 August 1900.
18   *ASD*, 6 November 1900.
19   Zemlinsky had to conduct a performance of *Le grand Mogul* the same evening.
20   *ASD*, 8 December 1900.
21   Alma Mahler-Werfel, *Mein Leben* (unabridged edn; Frankfurt am Main, 1963), 29.
22   *ASD*, 7 January 1901. Revising this passage in 1962, Alma Mahler-Werfel added 'horrible' before the word 'smell'.
23   *ASD*, 31 January 1901.
24   *ASD*, 1 February 1901.
25   *ASD*, 24 February 1901.
26   *ASD*, 8 March 1901.
27   *ASD*, 11 March 1901.
28   *ASD*, 12 March 1901.
29   *ASD*, 13 March 1901.
30   *AZ–AMW*, 20 March 1901. In March 1901 Barnum and Bailey's travelling circus (the original 'Greatest Show on Earth') was appearing in Vienna.
31   *AZ–AMW*, 4 April 1901.
32   *ASD*, 10 April 1901. In the original: 'Wir küssten uns, dass die Zähne schmerzten.' The final sentence is entered separately in the margin.
33   A well-researched and detailed history of Wolzogen's 'Buntes Theater' is published in Walter Rösler, *Das Chanson im deutschen Kabarett 1901–1933* (Berlin, 1980), 55–85.
34   Ernst von Wolzogen, *Wie ich mich ums Leben brachte. Erinnerungen und Erfahrungen* (Brunswick, 1923), 200. Wolzogen, who later became a Nazi sympathizer, stressed that all the composers involved in his little 'competition' were Jews.
35   Ibid.
36   Oskar Geller, 'Wie Gustav Mahler nach Wien kam. Eine journalistische "Intrige"', in *Neues Wiener Journal*, 24 May 1931, reprinted in *Die Musik*, May 1932, 633–4.
37   *Ein Lichtstrahl*, bars 373 and 381, cf. Symphony in B♭, bars 5–7.
38   *Ein Lichtstrahl*, bar 368 et seq.
39   The entire closing section of the text is rewritten, replacing the *ménage-à-trois* conclusion of the original version with a more conventional, burlesque variant.

6   Alma crudel

1   *ASD*, 13 April 1901.
2   *ASD*, 18 April 1901.

3   *ASD*, 15 April 1901. The last sentence ('Mich dürstet nach seinem Blut') was deleted by Alma Mahler-Werfel.
4   *ASD*, 19 April 1901.
5   *ASD*, 27 April 1901.
6   *ASD*, 4 May 1901.
7   *AZ–AMW*, undated (spring 1901).
8   *ASD*, 18 May 1901.
9   *ASD*, 30 May 1901.
10 *AZ–AMW*, 22 May 1901.
11 *AZ–AMW*, 27 May 1901.
12 Ibid.
13 *AZ–AMW*, c. 18 June 1901.
14 *AZ–AMW*, 13 June 1901.
15 *AZ–AMW*, 12 August 1901.
16 *ASD*, 15 September 1901.
17 *AZ–AMW*, 22 August 1901.
18 *AZ–AMW*, c. 21 September 1901.
19 *AZ–AMW*, undated (summer 1901).
20 *ASD*, 24 September 1901.
21 Cf. Wolfram Mauser, 'Hofmannsthals "Triumph der Zeit". Zur Bedeutung seiner Ballett- und Pantomiment-Libretti', *Hofmannsthal und das Theater. Symposium Wien 1979* (Vienna, 1981), 143.
22 Letter from Hofmannsthal to Zemlinsky, 18 September 1901, first published in *Autographen*, catalogue no. 580 (Stargardt, Marburg, 1967), 51.
23 Cf. letter from Hofmannsthal to Alfred Roller, in Antony Beaumont, 'Alexander Zemlinsky. "Der Triumph der Zeit – Drei Ballettstücke – Ein Tanzpoem"', in S. G. Harper and Birgit Gotzes (eds.) *Über Musiktheater. Eine Festschrift* (Munich, 1992), 26–7.
24 Letter from Hofmannsthal to Strauss, 14 December 1900; this passage quoted in Beaumont, op. cit., 16.
25 Ibid.
26 Letter to Hofmannsthal, 1 March 1900; ibid. 16–17.
27 *ASD*, 6 March 1901.
28 Letter to Hofmannsthal, 8 March 1901; Beaumont, op. cit., 17.
29 *AZ–AMW*, 29 October 1904.
30 Letter to Hofmannsthal, mid-June 1901; Beaumont, op. cit., 20.
31 *AZ–AMW*, 8 June 1901.
32 *AZ–AMW*, 1 July 1901. Max Reinhardt's ensemble from Berlin was at that time appearing at the Carltheater in a programme of Ibsen, Gerhart Hautpmann, Tolstoy, etc.
33 Letter from Hofmannsthal to Hermann Bahr, 3 July 1901, in *Hugo von Hofmannsthal in der Österreichischen Nationalbibliothek*, exhibition catalogue (Vienna, 1971), 22.
34 Letter to Hofmannsthal, c. 1 August 1901; Beaumont, op. cit., 23.
35 'Wenn das Herz aus Kristall / zerbricht in einem Schrei, / die Ungebornen eilen / wie Sternenglanz herbei' (*Die Frau ohne Schatten*, act III).
36 Mauser, op. cit., 146.
37 Letter from Hofmannsthal to Arthur Schnitzler, 18 July 1901, *Hofmannsthal: Briefe 1900–1909* (Vienna, 1857), 50–51.
38 *AZ–AMW*, 23 June 1901; in Beaumont, op. cit., 19.
39 Letter from Hofmannsthal to Zemlinsky, 18 September 1901 (see note 22).
40 Cf. *Web-Br*, 39.
41 Cf. *Web-Br*, 43.
42 Cf. G. B. Schmid, *'Der Triumph der Zeit' – allegorisches Spiel*, programme book *Ein Tanzpoem – Josephs Legende*, Zürcher Ballett, Opernhaus Zurich, 1992.
43 'Your picture stands before me beneath a bouquet of freshly cut roses' (*AZ–AMW*, 14 October 1901).
44 *AZ–AMW*, 2 June 1901.
45 *AZ–AMW*, 9 July 1901. In the finished score, the horn motif is replaced by a trumpet fanfare. The care Zemlinsky lavished on this particular section of the score is indicated by several further comments in *AZ–AMW*: 'My "youth" will have to be revised. I have already started on it' (c. 24 July 1901); 'The youth has not yet been revised: I had to set it aside for a while – at the moment I can't think of anything better –' (c. 30 July 1901).
46 *AZ–AMW*, [spring–summer] 1910.
47 Zemlinsky, 'Jugenderinnerungen', *Arnold Schönberg zum 60. Geburtstag* (Vienna, 1934).
48 Schoenberg, 'Criteria for the Evaluation of Music', *St-Id*, 131.
49 *ASD*, 19 November 1900.
50 'Seit ich so viele Weiber sah' (Emanuel Schikaneder), written for the Jung-Wien Theater 'zum lieben Augustin'.
51 *ASD*, 5 October 1901. Zemlinsky conducted Zamara's *Die Debütantin*, which had opened the previous night.

52   *ASD*, 7 October 1901.
53   *AZ–AMW*, *c.* 25 October 1901.
54   Alma Mahler-Werfel, *Mein Leben* (unabridged edn; Frankfurt am Main, 1963), 29.
55   *AZ–AMW*, 2 November 1901.
56   *AZ–AMW*, *c.* 4 November 1901.
57   *AZ–AMW*, 6 November 1901.
58   *ASD*, 7 November 1901.
59   *ASD*, 9 November 1901.
60   *ASD*, 19 November 1901.
61   *ASD*, 3 December 1901.
62   *ASD*, 12 December 1901.
63   *ASD*, 16 December 1901.
64   *Web-Br*, 4–5.

III   Lieder (1)

1   *AZ–AMW*, *c.* 5 July 1901.
2   From Scriabin's notebook, 1905, quoted in Faubion Bowers, *Scriabin*, vol. II (Tokyo– Palo Alto, 1969), 61.
3   *AZ–AMW*, 1 June 1901.
4   Cf. Letter from Zemlinsky to W. Hansen, 3 December 1896.
5   Theodor Adorno, 'Zemlinsky' (1959) in *Quasi una fantasia. Musikalische Schriften II* (Frankfurt, 1990), 165.
6   Ibid.
7   *ASD*, 10 March 1900.
8   *AZ–AMW*, *c.* 10 June 1901.
9   *AZ–AMW*, 9 June 1901.
10   *AZ–AMW*, *c.* 4 November 1901.
11   *AZ–AMW*, 12 May 1901.
12   *AZ–AMW*, *c.* 30 July 1901.
13   The list of intended dedications is preserved in *LoC* 9/18.
14   Cf. Rudolf Stephan Hoffmann, 'Zemlinskys Opern', *AT*, 211.

IV   Vienna 1902–1911

1   Symphony of Death

1   Letter from Mahler to Alma Schindler, 19 December 1901, in Henry-Louis de La Grange and Günther Weiss (eds.), *Ein Glück ohne Ruh'. Die Briefe Gustav Mahlers an Alma* (Berlin, 1995), 109.
2   *Die Fackel*, III/95, 28 February 1902, 27.
3   Cf. *Die Fackel*, III/100, 18 April 1902, 24.
4   Letter to Clara Zemlinszky, 5 April 1902, *Web-Br*, 15.
5   Letter to Schoenberg, 18 February 1902, *Web-Br*, 10.
6   Letter to Schoenberg 2 February 1902, *Web-Br*, 7. The concert also included Leone Sinigaglia's Violin Concerto.
7   Letter to Schoenberg, 19 March 1902, *Web-Br*, 12.
8   For a detailed description and analysis of the fragment cf. *ZTuA*, 104–12.
9   Letter to Schoenberg, 13 May 1902, *Web-Br*, 13.
10   Letter to Schoenberg, 18 July 1902, *Web-Br*, 20.
11   Letter to Schoenberg, 14 October 1902, *Web-Br*, 30.
12   Cf. *BikW*, 53 (nos. 100 and 101).
13   Letters to Schoenberg, April 1903 and 21 May 1903, *Web-Br*, 40, 41.
14   Cf. A. Beaumont, preface to the score of *Frühlingsbegräbnis* (Ricordi, Munich, 1997).
15   Ibid.
16   Letter to Schoenberg, 18 February 1902, *Web-Br*, 8.
17   Letter to Schoenberg, 21 February 1903, *Web-Br*, 39.
18   Ibid.
19   Ibid.
20   Letter to Schoenberg, 28 April 1902, *Web-Br*, 14.
21   Cf. Viktor Ullmann, 'Zur Charakteristik der Tonarten', *Anbruch*, 1935, 211–12.
22   Letter to Schoenberg, 30 October 1902, *Web-Br*, 31.
23   In the original: 'famose Zustände'; letter to Schoenberg, 23 June 1903, *Web-Br*, 43.
24   Cf. Paul Stefan, 'Aus Zemlinskys Wiener Zeit', *AT*, 227–8.
25   *BikW*, 55, 31.
26   Paul Stefan, *Das Grab in Wien* (Vienna, 1911), 24 (quoted in *ACl*, 128).

27   Letter to Schoenberg, 29 May 1903, *Web-Br*, 42.
28   Walter Pass, 'Schönberg und die "Vereinigung schaffender Tonkünstler in Wien"', *Österreichische Musikalische Zeitung*, XXIX (1974), 298–303.
29   *AZ–AMW*, 114, dated (by AMW) '1906', addressed 'Liechtensteinstrasse 68'; actual date: spring 1904. From the letter, it transpires that the Vereinigung had been promised a modest donation from the Rothschilds; Alma was asked to approach a friend, Countess Wydenbruck.
30   Gertrud Schoenberg later went to school there (cf. Arnold Greissle-Schönberg, *Arnold Schönberg und sein Wiener Kreis. Erinnerung eines Enkels* (Vienna, 1998), 26).
31   Cf. Egon Wellesz, *Arnold Schoenberg*, edited by Carl Dahlhaus (Wilhelmshaven, 1985), 21.
32   Pass, op. cit. Of the scores submitted, 69 were orchestral pieces, 73 chamber works, 7 choral works and 709 lieder.
33   Pass, op. cit., quotes from announcements published in September and October 1904 in 'almost every Viennese gazette'. The orchestral concerts, scheduled for 23 November 1904, 18 January 1905 and 11 March 1905, were to include works by Hermann Bischoff, Franz Dubitzky, Hausegger, Edgar Istel, Oscar von Posa, Schoenberg, Richard Strauss, Joseph V. von Wöss and Zemlinsky; lieder and chamber music by Hugo Daffner, Robert Gound, Rudolf Stephan Hoffmann, Gerhard von Keussler, Oskar Noe, Hans Pfitzner, Max Reger, Kurt Schindler, Theodor Streicher, Bruno Walter, Karl Weigl and Erich J. Wolff was scheduled for concerts on 20 December 1904, 20 January 1905 and 20 February 1905. The concert of Mahler's orchestral songs, which included the world première of the *Kindertotenlieder*, was given in the smaller hall of the Musikverein on 29 January 1905 and repeated on 3 February 1905. The third orchestral concert was replaced by a lieder recital.
34   Letter from Schoenberg to Mahler, 12 December 1904; here quoted from *St-Sch*, 95–6.
35   *AZ–AMW*, 108, dated '1905', actual date 13 December 1904. As Zemlinsky had to conduct a performance at the Volksoper, he was unable to attend the concert itself. Curiously, Egon Wellesz wrote, 'Even at the final rehearsal, I could see that Schoenberg, Zemlinsky and Webern, who were sitting together, were unmoved by Mahler's music', and gained the impression that their 'conversion' took place only at the Vereinigung concert on 29 January 1905 (Egon und Emmy Wellesz, *Egon Wellesz. Leben und Werk*, edited by Franz Endler (Vienna–Hamburg, 1981), 41–2).
36   Ibid., 43–4.
37   *Neue Musikalische Presse*, 4 February 1905, 41–2.
38   Richard Specht, 'Die Jungwiener Tondichter', *Die Musik*, IX, (July 1910), 10–11.
39   *Mein Leben* (unabridged edn; Frankfurt am Main, 1963), 38.
40   Alma Mahler, *Gustav Mahler. Memories and Letters*, edited by D. Mitchell and K. Martner, translated by B. Creighton (4th edn; London, 1990), 77.

2   **Dreams and Delusions**

1   Rudolf Stephan Hoffmann, 'Die Wiener Volksoper', *Musikblätter des Anbruch*, I, 1919, 106–9.
2   *AZ–AMW*, 42, dated 'Thursday' (?26 September 1901).
3   *AZ–AMW*, 31, dated 'Friday' (19 July 1901).
4   Letter to Ernst Hutschenreiter, date-stamped on arrival 21 April 1903, in *BikW*, 53.
5   *Tagebücher Arthur Schnitzler*, III: 1903–1908 (Vienna, 1991). Entries for 17, 20 and 25 June 1903 and 11 June 1904.
6   Schnitzler refers on several occasions to Zemlinsky in his diaries, notably in 1905, when he consulted him for advice on launching his wife, Olga, as a singer (*Tagebücher*, 13 and 17 June 1905). He also attended the Vereinigung performance of *Die Seejungfrau*: 'Zemlinsky respectable; Posa amateurish, tame; Schoenberg gifted but bemusing – uproar. [?Eugenie] Hirschfeld [said] to me: "a schoolboy prank!"' (ibid., 25 January 1905). In 1908 he briefly considered the possibility of Zemlinsky as composer for his mime drama *Die Verwandlungen des Pierrot* (ibid., 27 May 1908; the music was composed in 1910 by Erno Dohnányi). Their last recorded meeting, in Prague with Werfel, was on 30 October 1922 (*Arthur Schnitzler Briefe 1913–1931*, edited by P. M. Braunwerth et al. (Frankfurt am Main, 1974), 291.)
7   Letter to Schoenberg, 16 September 1902, *Web-Br*, 28.
8   Stefan Zweig, 'Gedächtnis eines Freundes', *Neue Freie Presse*, 16 May 1925, 1–2. In 1923 Feld also wrote librettos for Eugen d'Albert's *Scirocco* (1915, first performed 1921) and Hans Gál's *Die heilige Ente*, both in collaboration with Karl von Lewetzow, his former colleague from the Buntes Theater. The latter work was successfully premièred in 1923 at Düsseldorf under Georg Szell and played in numerous German theatres until, under Nazi rule, it vanished from the repertoire.
9   Letter to Schoenberg, 14 October 1902 (Zemlinsky's thirty-first birthday), *Web-Br*, 30.
10   *AZ–AMW*, 112, dated '1905', (actual date: probably 29 October 1904).
11   Ibid.
12   Letter to Schoenberg, 20 July 1904, *Web-Br*, 45.
13   Letter to Schoenberg, 30 July 1904, *Web-Br*, 51.
14   Letter to Schoenberg, 25 August 1906, *Web-Br*, 54.
15   *AZ–AMW*, 119, dated 'summer 1906, Vienna, Liechtensteinstr. 68, Friday' (actual date 25 August 1905).

16 Rudolf Stephan Hoffmann, 'Zemlinskys Opern', *AT*, 213.
17 Ibid.
18 *ASD*, 26 May 1899.
19 *Frau Sorge* (28 May 1899), *Geschwister* (14 June 1899) and *Es war* (17 June 1899) – dates refer to *ASD*.
20 Written on the lower half of page 92 of the vocal score (*MolA*). Zemlinsky's criticism (in an almost indecipherable hand) appears to be as follows: 'Warum nicht Kaspar selbst??!! Also: fehlt ein Motiv, warum Görge mittun muss!' ('Why not Kaspar himself? Hence: there is no motive for Görge's collaboration.')
21 Vocal score, 117: 'Hündisch, faul, ein Wanst, ein Säufer, [. . .] ein Stückchen Geifer und dazu noch eine Kehle!'
22 Hoffmann, 'Zemlinskys Opern', *AT*, 214.
23 Erich W. Korngold, 'Erinnerungen an Zemlinsky. Aus meiner Lehrzeit', *AT*, 230–31.
24 Cf. *ACl*, 176.
25 Anton Webern, *Der Weg zur neuen Musik*, edited by W. Reich (Vienna, 1960), 52.
26 *AZ–AMW*, 113, *c.*June 1905.
27 *AZ–AMW*, 110, dated '1905' (actual date: December 1904).
28 *AZ–AMW*, 131, May–June 1907.
29 Cf. Carmen Ottner, 'Alexander Zemlinsky und die Wiener Hofoper', *AeSU*, 220–23.
30 Cf. Letter to Schoenberg, 26 August 1907, *Web-Br*, 56.
31 *AZ–AMW*, 128, *c.*May 1907.
32 Published in Alma Mahler, *Gustav Mahler. Memories and Letters*, edited by D. Mitchell and K. Martner, translated by B. Creighton (4th edn; London, 1990), 302.
33 Felix Weingartner, *Lebens Erinnerungen* (Zurich–Leipzig, 1929), II, 159–60.
34 *ACl*, 143.
35 Undated letter to Zemlinsky in Herta Blaukopf (ed.), *Gustav Mahler Briefe* (Vienna, 1982), 337–8. Blaukopf dates the letter, plausibly, to the end of March 1908.
36 Heinrich Teweles, *Theater und Publikum. Erinnerungen und Erfahrungen* (Prague, 1927), 173–4.
37 Undated letter to Emil Hertzka, *c.*1913.
38 Letter to Zemlinsky, 26 August 1919, *Web-Br*, 9, 291.
39 Recounted to the author by Louise Zemlinsky, 3 December 1990.
40 Angelika Wildner-Partsch, 'Traumgörge als passiver Held', programme book for the world première production, Nuremberg, 1980; see also A. Wildner-Partsch, *Das Opernschaffen Alexander Zemlinskys*, unpublished dissertation, Vienna, 1979.

3   Farewell to Vienna

1   Karl Schreder in *Deutsche Volksblatt*, 3 April 1908.
2   *Neues Wiener Journal*, 3 April 1908.
3   Jessica Duchen, *Erich Wolfgang Korngold* (London, 1996), 43.
4   Cf. *AZ–AMW*, 133 (dated '1908').
5   Schoenberg: 'The Programme of String Quartet no. 1 op. 7' in U. v. Rauchhaupt (ed.), *Schoenberg/Berg/Webern. The String Quartets, A Documentary Study* (Hamburg, 1971), 236–7 (English translation by Eugene Hartzell).
6   Cf. Klaus Albrecht Schröder, *Richard Gerstl 1883–1908* (Vienna, 1993). Schröder also tentatively identifies the subject of a *Portrait of a Man in a Field* (92–3) as Alban Berg.
7   *AZ–AMW*, 29, *c.* 8 July 1901.
8   Cf. Arnold Schoenberg, *Berliner Tagebuch*, edited by J. Rufer (Frankfurt, 1974), 10: 'For certain reasons (G), she [i.e. Mathilde] feels the need to pin something on to Webern.'
9   Quoted in Otto Breicha, *Gerstl und Schönberg. Eine Beziehung* (Salzburg, 1993), 24.
10 Schoenberg, 'Testementsentwurf' (unpublished), Arnold Schönberg Center, Vienna.
11 Louise Zemlinsky in conversation with the author, 3 December 1990.
12 H[arold] T[aubmann], 'Zemlinsky comes to live here', *New York Times*, 5 January 1939.
13 *Web-ZW*, 89 (fn). Weber's comment is intended as a correction of information included in two widely used German musical dictionaries, *Riemanns Musiklexikon* (7th and 12th edns) and *Die Musik in Geschichte in Gegenwart*.
14 *Neue Badische Landes-Zeitung*, 25 December 1908.
15 Wilhelm von Wymetal, 'Arthur Bodansky', *Neue Badische Landes-Zeitung*, 31 December 1908.
16 *Kleider machen Leute*, vocal score (1922 version), page 11.
17 Letter from Gottfried Keller to J. V. Widmann, 18 October 1884.
18 Antony Beaumont (ed.), *Ferruccio Busoni Selected Letters* (London, 1987), 224.
19 Rudolf Kelterborn's chamber opera *Julia* is based partly on *Romeo und Julia auf dem Dorfe*, partly on Shakespeare.
20 *LoC*; quoted in *ACl*, 196.
21 Max Brod, *Prager Sternenhimmel. Musik- und Theatererlebnisse der 20er Jahre* (Vienna, 1966), 100.

22   'Trienes', in *Kölnische Zeitung*, 14 December 1934.
23   Bernhard Diebold, in *Neue Züricher Zeitung*, 28 September 1935.
24   Horst Weber, *Alexander Zemlinsky*, Österreichische Komponisten des xx. Jahrhunderts/ix (Vienna, 1977), 51–2.
25   *AMD*, 16 December 1901.
26   *AZ–AMW*, 134, dated '1909'.
27   *AZ–AMW*, 137, dated '1910'.
28   *Web-Br*, 57–8.
29   Richard Batka in *Fremden-Blatt*, 4 December 1910 (quoted in Walter Pass, 'Zemlinskys Wiener Presse bis zum Jahre 1911', *TiU*, 91).
30   *Wiener Allgemeine Zeitung*, 3 December 1910, 4 (Pass, op. cit., 91).
31   Ludwig Karpath in *Neues Wiener Tagblatt*, 3 December 1910 (Pass, op. cit., 90).
32   Rudolf Stephan Hoffmann, 'Alexander von Zemlinsky', *Der Merker*, 2/v, 1910, 193–7.
33   Julius Korngold in *Neue Freie Presse*, 7 December 1910; reprinted in *Deutsches Opernschaffen der Gegenwart* (Vienna, 1922), 240–53.
34   Felix Weingartner, *Lebens Erinnerungen* (Zurich–Leipzig, 1929), 160.
35   Korngold, 'Erinnerungen an Zemlinsky aus meiner Lehrzeit', in *AT*, 230–32.
36   Ibid.
37   Weingartner, op. cit.; quoted in Duchen, op. cit., 38.
38   Cf. *Web-ZW*, 93.
39   Herta Blaukopf (ed.), *Gustav Mahler/Richard Strauss Briefwechsel 1888–1911* (Munich, 1980), 104.
40   Ibid., 105.
41   Knud Martner (ed.), *Selected Letters of Gustav Mahler* (New York, 1979), 353–4.
42   Blaukopf, op. cit., 105.
43   *AZ–AMW*, 134, dated 1909 (*c.* December 1909).
44   *Neue Badische Landes-Zeitung*, 30 November 1909.
45   *AZ–AMW*, 134.
46   *Neue Badische Landes-Zeitung*, 21 December 1909.
47   *Die Musik*, x/22, 1910, 252.
48   *Web-Br*, 60.
49   Cf. *Die Musik*, x/23, 1910, 318–19.
50   *Web-Br*, 60.
51   Ibid.
52   Ibid., 61.
53   Ibid., 62–3; also Alban Berg Archive in *Österreichische Nationalbibliothek*, and Antony Beaumont (ed.), *Busoni: Selected Letters* (London, 1987), 409–13.
54   Peter Heyworth, *Otto Klemperer, His Life and Times*, vol. i: *1885–1933* (Cambridge, 1983), 60.
55   Ibid.
56   Paul Stefan, *Das Grab in Wien* (Vienna, 1911).
57   *Web-Br*, 60.
58   Gottfried Reinhardt, *Der Liebhaber. Erinnerungen eines Sohnes an Max Reinhardt* (Munich, 1973), 146–7.
59   Dante Aleghieri, *Inferno*, i, i.

v   Surface and Symbol

1   *Prager Tagblatt*, 10 June 1917 (quoted in *Tan*, Anh. 1B/5).
2   Hans Heinz Stuckenschmidt, 'Zahlenzauber und Gottsuche in den Neuen Musik', in *Die Musik eines halben Jahrhunderts* (Munich, 1976), 118.
3   Cf. George Perle, 'The Secret Programme of the Lyric Suite', *Musical Times*, 118 (1977), 629–32 and 709–813.
4   Cf. Eric Sams, 'Did Schumann use Cyphers?', *Musical Times* 106 (1965), 584; 'The Schumann Cyphers', *Musical Times* 107 (1966), 392; 'The Schumann Cyphers: a Coda', *Musical Times* 107 (1966), 1,050.
5   The most substantial contributions to research on this subject are those of Eric Sams (see 'Brahms and his Musical Love-letters', *Musical Times* 112 [1971], 329–30; 'Brahms and his Clara-themes', *Musical Times* 112 [1971], 432–3). The school of César Franck exploited a similar device, F.E.A., derived from the motto 'Frères en Art'. All three movements of Franck's Symphony in D minor include themes derived from these initials.
6   *Münchener Neueste Nachrichten*, 12 October 1897.
7   Cf. *Web-ZW* and Arnošt Mahler: 'Alexander Zemlinsky. Das Porträt eines grossen Musikers', *TiU*, 13–26. It was Louise Zemlinsky who drew Mahler's attention to the false date, showing him her husband's passport to prove the point.
8   Cf. Aleister Crowley, 'Gematria', *The Equinox* i, vol. 5, and S. L. McGregor Mathers, *Kabbala desnudata; The Kaballah Unveiled* (London, 1887).

9 Translation by Constance Bache.
10 Letter dated 10 June 1915, *B–SC*, 245.
11 Letter from Berg to Schoenberg, 20 June 1915, ibid., 249.
12 Brenda Dalen, '"Freundschaft, Liebe und Welt": the secret programme of the Chamber Concerto', in D. Jarman (ed.), *The Berg Companion* (Basingstoke–London, 1989), 141–80.
13 Schoenberg, *Berliner Tagebuch*, edited by Josef Rufer (Frankfurt–Berlin–Vienna, 1974), 13.

VI Prague 1911–1918

1 The Musical Director

1 Statistics from Hermann Münch, *Böhmische Tragödie* (Brunswick, 1949), 282; quoted in *Tan* I/1.
2 Otto Teuber, *Geschichte des Prager Theaters* (Prague, 1883–8) (3 vols.), 838; quoted in *Tan* I/1.
3 Franz Werfel, 'Zemlinsky', *AT*, 197. Werfel left Prague the following year, and thereafter resided in the city only for brief periods. During the 1911–12 season, of the works he mentions, he may have heard *Tristan*, which was given three times (between 8 April and 18 July), and *Figaro* (seven times, between 14 January and 16 May). He appears to have attended all other performances to which he refers during a period of sick leave, from November 1915 to May 1916: Zemlinsky conducted a new production of *Carmen* on 19 November 1915 and *Otello*, with Leo Slezak in the title role, on 9 December 1915; a new production of *Così fan tutte* under his direction opened on 12 March 1916.
4 Hermann Grab, *The Town Park and other stories*, translated by Quintin Hoare, with an introduction by Theodor Adorno, (London, 1988)
5 *Web-Br*, September 1921, 228.
6 *Prager Montagsblatt*, 10 October 1932, quoted in Doortje Cramer, *Von Prag nach New York ohne Wiederkehr. Leben und Werk Hermann Grabs* (Frankfurt, 1994), 399.
7 *Prager Tagblatt*, 28 February 1916.
8 *Web-Br*, 27 September 1913, 109.
9 *AZ–AMW*, December [19]19.
10 *Web-Br*, 4 August 1922, 234. Zemlinsky was staying at Villa Hürsch, 112.
11 Cf. *Tan*, app. II/C.
12 Information provided to the author by Státní Ústřední Archiv v Praze, 24 June 1993.
13 *Bohemia*, 26 September 1911.
14 *Prager Tagblatt*, 26 September 1911.
15 Heinrich Teweles, *Theater und Publikum. Erinnerungen und Erfahrungen* (Prague, 1927), 175.
16 Louis Laber, 'Zemlinsky auf dem Theater', *AT*, 223–4.
17 *Bohemia*, 10 March 1912.
18 Ibid., 181–2.
19 Deryck Cooke, *Gustav Mahler. An Introduction to his Music* (London, 1980), 92.
20 Quoted from Arnošt Mahler, 'Alexander Zemlinskys Prager Jahre', *Hudební věda*, 1972, 239.
21 *Bohemia*, 8 December 1912.
22 Korngold, 'Erinnerungen an Zemlinsky. Aus meiner Lehrzeit', *AT*, 232.
23 Unpublished letter from Schoenberg to Alma Mahler, 12 February 1914, *vP/D*.
24 *Bohemia*, 2 January 1914.
25 Unpublished letter from Schoenberg to Alma Mahler, 4 June 1915, *vP/D*.
26 The theme appears prominently at bar 22 *et seq.* in the first movement of the orchestral suite from *Cymbeline* and serves thereafter, also in the fifth movement, as a leitmotiv. In act II of *Der König Kandaules*, Zemlinsky adapts the idea for the section marked 'Andante (balladenhaft)' (vocal score, pages 84–6).
27 *Web-Br*, 6 March 1913, 87.
28 *Web-Br*, 11 March 1913, 89.
29 *Web-Br*, May or June 1913, 94.
30 *Web-Br*, July 1913, 97.
31 *Web-Br*, 23 August 1912, 81–2.
32 *Web-Br*, August 1912, 82.
33 *Web-Br*, 28 July 1913, 99.
34 Fidelio F. Finke, 'Zemlinskys Kammerkunst', *AT*, 219–21.
35 *AZ–AMW*, July 1915 (dated '1914' by AMW).
36 24 to 26.
37 Rudolf Stephan, 'Über Zemlinskys Streichquartette', *TiU*, 122–37.
38 Horst Weber, *Alexander Zemlinsky* (Vienna, 1977).
39 Ibid., 107.
40 *ZTuA*.
41 Ibid., 156.
42 Cf. *ACl*, 245.
43 Oscar Wilde, *A Portrait of Dorian Gray*.
44 *Web-Br*, summer 1911, 328–9.

45   *Web-Br*, 21 November 1913, 107.
46   *Web-Br*, 2 January 1914, 110.
47   *Web-Br*, May/June 1914, 118. Of the numerous unidentified sketches in the Zemlinsky Collection, none can positively be connected with this Hofmannsthal project.
48   *AZ–AMW*, dated 1912 (*c.* May 1914).
49   Richard Ellmann, *Oscar Wilde* (London, 1987), 388. As Wilde indicated in *De Profundis*, his play *La Sainte Courtisane* was written as a counterpart to *A Florentine Tragedy*.
50   Adami and M. Carner (eds.), *Puccini: Letters* (London, 1974), 244.
51   Mosco Carner, *Puccini* (London, 1974), 149–50.
52   Antony Beaumont (ed.), *Busoni: Selected Letters* (London, 1987), 168.
53   *AZ–AMW*, undated (*c.* May 1917).
54   *Bohemia*, 5 March 1917.
55   *Schwäbische Merkur*, 31 January 1917, quoted in the Hamburg programme to *Eine florentinische Tragödie*, 20 September 1981.
56   Unpublished letter from Schoenberg to Alma Mahler, 13 March 1917.
57   Franz Werfel, op. cit. The assertion that music from the opera had 'followed him for years' requires some qualification: Werfel's essay was written only four years after the Vienna première of the opera.

2   Prague in Wartime

1   Hermann Grab, 'Jahrgang 1903 erlebt Musik in Prag', *Prager Montagsblatt*, 30 December 1937, quoted in K. Hobi, *Hermann Grab, Leben und Werk* (dissertation), Freiburg/Argau, 1969, 14–18.
2   *Web-Br*, 31 December 1914, 128.
3   Ibid.
4   *Web-Br*, February 1915, 133.
5   *Web-Br*, April 1915, 135.
6   *Web-Br*, April 1915, 133.
7   Ibid.
8   Shakespeare, *Cymbeline*, v, iv, 101–2.
9   *Web-Br*, 2 January 1914, 111.
10   *AZ–AMW*, 141, dated 1912 (spring 1914).
11   *Web-Br*, 4 May 1914, 119.
12   *Web-Br*, February 1915, 134.
13   *AZ–AMW* (not numbered; February/March 1915).
14   *Web-Br*, 24 May 1915, 136.
15   *Web-Br*, 20 June 1915, 140.
16   Performance on 15 January 1916.
17   *Web-Br*, Webern to Zemlinsky 6, 25 February 1916, 286.
18   Heinrich Teweles, *Theater und Publikum. Erinnerungen und Erfahrungen* (Prague, 1927), 185–6.
19   *Frankfurter Zeitung*, 28 October 1915, quoted in *Web-Br*, 149.
20   *Web-Br*, 23 October 1915, 146. The full text of this letter was published in the *Prager Tagblatt* on 23 January 1916.
21   *Web-Br*, 26 February 1916, 152.
22   Heinrich Jalowetz, 'Alexander Zemlinsky. Skizze zu einer Biographie', *AT*, 201–3.
23   *Bohemia*, 17 November 1916.
24   Performance dates (respectively): 10 January, 29 November and 9 March 1917.
25   Performance date: 25 April 1918.
26   Performance date: 28 November 1918.
27   Hubermann performed the Beethoven Violin Concerto at the NDT on 27 March 1918.
28   Letter from Schreker to Zemlinsky, 10 May 1917. The letter was sold to an unidentified collector by Rudolf Kallir, New York; a summary of its contents is published in *Web-Br*, 331.
29   *Web-Br*, Zemlinsky to Schreker, 12 May 1917, 332.
30   *Web-Br*, Zemlinsky to Schreker, June 1917 (Weber's dating: 'early summer'), 333.
31   *Web-Br*, 2 June 1918, 195.
32   Bernard Grun (ed. and trans.), *Alban Berg. Letters to His Wife* (London–New York, 1971), 529.
33   *Web-Br*, 15 April 1918, 194.
34   Georg Klaren, 'Zemlinsky vom psychologischen Standpunkte', *AT*, 204–7.
35   Ibid.
36   Ibid.
37   Ibid.
38   *Web-Br*, 198.

VII   Lieder (II)

1   *AZ–AMW*, 3 May 1901.
2   *Neuer deutscher Balladenschatz* (*Die Woche*, 8th *Sonderheft*), Berlin, August 1906.
3   Cf. Horst Weber, 'Schönbergs und Zemlinskys Vertonung der Ballade "Jane Grey" von Heinrich Ammann [sic]. Untersuchungen zum Spätstudium der Tonalität', *IMS, Report of the 11th Congress*, Copenhagen, 1972, 705–14.
4   Hugo von Hofmannsthal, 'Der Prophet', published in *Aufzeichnungen* (Frankfurt am Main, 1959), 94.
5   Edward Thomas, *Maurice Maeterlinck* (New York, 1912; *rp*, 1974), 133.
6   *AZ–AMW*, dated 'Kitzbühel, den 2. August' and 1914–15' (actual date 1913).
7   *AZ–AMW*, *c.*26 September 1901, quoted in part II.
8   Leo Tolstoy, *Chto takoye iskusstvo? (What is Art?)* (Moscow, 1898).
9   *Web-Br*, 9 January 1915, 131.
10   *Web-Br*, letter from Webern, 16 May 1919, 288.
11   *Web-Br*, letter from Webern, 24 November 1922, 294–5.
12   Cornelis Witthoefft, *Prag der zwanziger und dreissiger Jahre*, article for the programme to a concert series in Hamburg, 'Musik war Hoffnung auf Leben', 26–27 April 1997.
13   Elizabeth Barrett Browning, Sonnet XXVIII, *Sonnets from the Portuguese* (London, 1850).

VIII   Prague 1918–1927

1   Under Czech Rule

1   *Prager Tagblatt*, 8 September 1918.
2   *Web-Br*, 5 November 1918, 201.
3   Friedrich Prinz: *Geschichte Böhmens 1848–1948* (Munich, 1988), 21; quoted in *Tan*, IV.
4   Christoph Stölzl, *Kafkas böses Böhmen. Zur Sozialgeschichte eines Prager Juden* (Frankfurt, 1989), 106; quoted in *Tan*, IV.
5   M. Lišková and E. Čakrtová: *Nové Německé Divadlo v Praze 1899–1938/39* (Prague, 1990); quoted in *Tan*, I/4.
6   *Web-Br*, *c.*August 1918, 199.
7   Quotation from *Venkov*, a Czech agricultural journal, reprinted in the Zionist newspaper *Selbstwehr*, 15 October 1920 (from *Tan*, I/4).
8   Franz Kafka, *Briefe an Milena*, edited by J. Born and M. Müller (Frankfurt, 1986), 288.
9   *Prager Tagblatt*, 7 December 1920, quoted in *Web-Br*, 218.
10   Cf. Hans Demetz, *Geschichte des Deutschen Theaters in Prag*, VIII/11; unpublished, quoted in *Tan*, I/4.
11   *Web-Br*, November 1918, 201.
12   Cf. *Tan* I/4.
13   Fr. Grasberger and A. Strauss (eds.), *Der Strom der Töne trug mich fort. Die Welt um Richard Strauss in Briefen* (Tutzing, 1967), letter to Pauline Strauss, 29 January 1921, 258.
14   Heinrich Kralik, *Richard Strauss, Weltbürger der Musik* (Vienna, 1963), 255.
15   *Bohemia*, 11 December 1923; quoted in Peter Heyworth, *Otto Klemperer, His Life and Times*, I (Cambridge–London, 1983), 182.
16   *Bohemia*, 8 June 1921; quoted in *Tan*, B5.
17   *Web-Br*, June 1921, 227.
18   *Web-Br*, 22 April 1921, 224.
19   Cf. *Tan*, I/4.
20   Letter to Kramer, 14 September 1920.
21   *Web-Br*, 19 January 1921, 220.
22   Hans Heinsheimer, 'Die scharfe Brille über die Nase . . . Meine Erinnerungen an Alexander Zemlinsky', in the programme book for *Eine florentinische Tragödie* and *Der Geburtstag der Infantin*, Hamburg, 20 September 1981, 18.
23   Cf. Karl Schumann's interview with Rafael Kubelik on DG 2810 004 (originally issued with Kubelik's Mahler cycle).
24   *Web-Br*, letter from Webern, 15 June 1920, 293.
25   Cf. Ivan Vojtěch, 'Der Verein für musikalische Privataufführungen in Prag', in E. Hilmar (ed.), *Arnold Schönberg Gedenkausstellung 1974* (Vienna, 1974), 83–91. Vojtěch describes the membership as consisting of 'civil servants, writers, doctors, lawyers, university and school teachers, businessmen, actors and painters, well-to-do private patrons and the not so well-to-do: students and musicians of all kinds.'
26   *Web-Br*, *c.*24 October 1922, 237.
27   *Web-Br*, 26 October 1922, 238–40.
28   *Web-Br*, November 1916, 155.
29   *AZ–AMW*, December 1919.

30 Richard Specht, 'Die Jungwiener Tondichter', *Die Musik*, IX/7 (1910), 9–12.
31 Richard Specht, 'Neue Musik in Wien', *Musikblätter des Anbruch*, III, 13–14, September 1921, 245–56.
32 *Bik W,* 148, letter to Richard Specht, September 1921, 76. Specht's reply is not preserved.
33 Letter to Schoenberg, 9 July 1920, *B–SC*, 281.
34 Cf. Rosemary Hilmar, *Alban Berg* (Vienna–Cologne–Graz, 1987), 154.
35 Quoted in *Tan* I/4 (no source cited).
36 Letter to Kramer, undated (May 1923).
37 *Web-Br*, 6 June 1923, 249.
38 *B–SC*, letter from Berg to Schoenberg, 6 June 1923, 325–6. Weber asserts (in *Web-Br*) that the Maeterlinck songs were conducted by Pella; this letter indicates clearly enough that Zemlinsky himself was the conductor.

2 Luise

1 Louise Zemlinsky in conversation with the author, 3 December 1990.
2 Burkhard Laugwitz, '"Meine Zeit kommt nach meine Tod". Begegnung mit Louise Zemlinsky', *Das Orchester*, V/1993, 547–50.
3 'Zeugnis von der Akademie der bildenden Künste in Prag' (Akademie Vytvarnych Umění v Praze), 6 July 1920, in *NLZ*.
4 Information from documents in *NLZ*. Laugwitz's account of Luise Sachsel's birth and childhood, op. cit., differs, principally due his falsely locating Novybydzov (sic) in Galicia.
5 Louise Zemlinsky in conversation with the author, 3 December 1990.
6 Rudolf Steiner, *Das Künstlerische in seiner Weltmission* (Dornach, 1961), 117.
7 Richard Ellmann, *Oscar Wilde* (London, 1984), 359.
8 Ibid., 566.
9 Franz Werfel, 'Zemlinsky', *AT*, 199.
10 Georg Klaren, 'Der Zwerg und was er bedeutet', *Kölnische Zeitung*, 17 June 1922.
11 Ibid.
12 Georg Klaren, 'Zemlinsky vom psychologischen Standpunkte', *AT*, 204–7.
13 Otto Weininger, *Geschlecht und Charakter. Eine prinzipielle Untersuchung* (Vienna, 1903; rp, Munich, 1980), xxii (passages quoted here are taken from the table of contents).
14 Stefan Zweig, 'Vorbeigehen an einem unauffälligen Menschen: Otto Weininger' (1926), *Europäisches Erbe* (Frankfurt, 1960).
15 Oswald Spengler, *Der Untergang des Abendlandes* (Munich, 1923).
16 Georg Klaren, *Otto Weininger. Der Mensch, sein Werk und sein Leben* (Vienna, 1924).
17 Georg Klaren, 'Der Zwerg und was er bedeutet', op. cit.
18 Ibid.
19 Ibid.
20 Ibid.
21 Unnamed author (identified as '—n'), 'Zemlinsky über seinen "Zwerg"', *Komödie*, November 1923, 12.
22 *AZ–AMW*, undated (Prague, autumn 1920).
23 Letter to Emil Hertzka (Universal Edition), 23 August 1919.
24 Ibid.
25 Letter to Hertzka, 26 December 1919.
26 *AZ–AMW*, 27 July 1920; *Web-Br*, 23 August 1920, 217.
27 *AZ–AMW*, undated (autumn 1920).
28 Letter to Hertzka, undated (arrival date 3 May 1921).
29 Letter from Klemperer to Zemlinsky (Archiv OK), 17 September 1921.
30 *Web-Br*, 27 May 1922, 233.
31 Letter to Hertzka, 10 May 1921.
32 *Web-Br*, 27 May 1922, 233.
33 Hans Wilhelm Steinberg, 'Early Days with Klemperer', *Saturday Review*, 29 May 1965.
34 *Allgemeine Musikzeitung*, 49. Jg., June 1922, 568.
35 *Kölnische Zeitung* (W. Jacobs), 29 May 1922.
36 *Kölnische Volkszeitung* (Anton Stehle), 30 May 1922.
37 *Allgemeine Musikzeitung*, op cit.
38 Bernard Grun (ed. and trans.), *Alban Berg. Letters to His Wife* (London–New York, 1971), 22 November 1923, 526.
39 Ibid.
40 Ibid.
41 *Alban Berg. Letters to His Wife*, op. cit., 25 November 1923, 528.
42 *Neue Freie Presse*, 25 November 1923.
43 *Neues Wiener Journal*, 25 November 1923.

44 *Illustrierte Kronen Zeitung*, 25 November 1923.
45 Erwin Schaeffer in *Wiener Zeitung*, 27 November 1923.
46 Louise Zemlinsky in conversation with the author, 3 December 1990.
47 Letter to Hertzka, 19 September 1922.
48 Official wording of the Nobel Prize Committee nomination.
49 Tagore, *Letters to a Friend* [C. F. Andrews], 10 August 1894 (London, 1928), 105–6.
50 Krishna Dutta and Andrew Robinson, *Rabindranath Tagore, the Myriad-Minded Man* (London, 1995), 231–2.
51 Tagore, *Letters to a Friend*, 24 June 1894, 102.
52 Zemlinsky, 'Lyrische Symphonie', *Pult und Taktstock*, I/I, 1924, 10–11.
53 Ibid.
54 Weininger, op. cit., 144, 391 and 394.
55 Ferruccio Busoni, 'Junge Klassizität' (Open Letter to Paul Bekker), first published in *Frankfurter Zeitung*, 7 February 1920.
56 Zemlinsky, op. cit.
57 *Web-Br*, 299.
58 Conversation with the author, 3 December 1990.

3   The Spirit of the ISCM

1 Covenant of the League of Nations, Article 10.
2 *Bohemia*, 6 June 1924.
3 Letter from Berg, undated (shortly after 15 June 1924), *Web-Br*, 307.
4 Zemlinsky, 'Einige Worte über das Studium von Schönbergs *Erwartung*', *Pult und Taktstock*, IV, 1927, 44–5.
5 Unpublished letter from Schoenberg to Alma Mahler, 16 November 1910, *vP/D*.
6 Unpublished letter from Schoenberg to Alma Mahler, 27 March 1911, ibid.
7 Salka Viertel, *The Kindness of Strangers* (New York, 1969), 57.
8 *Web-Br*, 6 July 1923, 252.
9 *Web-Br*, c.12 September 1923, 252.
10 Mathilde Schoenberg, death certificate, Arnold Schönberg Center, Vienna.
11 Untitled document (Bio79.TRC), dated 15 November 1923, Arnold Schönberg Center, Vienna.
12 Schoenberg, *Texte* (Vienna, 1926), 32.
13 *Web-Br*, 16 November 1923, 256.
14 Arnold Greissle-Schönberg, *Arnold Schönberg und sein Wiener Kreis. Erinnerung eines Enkels* (Vienna, 1998), 17.
15 Hans Heinz Stuckenschmidt, *Schönberg. Leben, Umwelt, Werk* (Zurich, 1974), 268.
16 *Web-Br*, 16 November 1923, 257.
17 Author's conversations with Nuria Schoenberg-Nono, 20 September 1996, and with Arnold Greissle-Schönberg, 11 April 1999.
18 Quoted in Walter William Cobbett and Colin Mason (eds.), *Cobbett's Cyclopedic Survey of Chamber Music*, II (London, 1963), 597.
19 Horst Weber, *Alexander Zemlinsky*, Österreichische Komponisten des XX. Jahrhunderts/ IX (Vienna, 1977), 109.
20 Rudolf Stephan, 'Über Zemlinskys Streichquartette', *TiU*, 133.
21 Theodor Adorno, 'Zemlinsky' (1959) in *Quasi una fantasia. Musikalische Schriften II* (Frankfurt, 1990), 173.
22 *ZTuA*, 207 *et seq.*
23 Webern to Zemlinsky, 6 October 1924 (*Web-Br*, 301).
24 Webern to Zemlinsky, 22 October 1924 (*Web-Br*, 301).
25 Berg to Schoenberg, 30 March 1928, *B–SC*, 366–7.
26 Cobbett and Mason, op. cit., 596.
27 *Prager Tagblatt*, 22 May 1925.
28 *Der Auftakt*, IV (1924), 196–7, 230–31 and 261.
29 *Bohemia*, 23 June 1925
30 *Prager Tagblatt*, 27 October 1925.
31 *Bohemia*, 4 September 1925.
32 *Bohemia*, 26 February 1926.
33 Concert on 27 January 1927.
34 *AZ–AMW*, dated '1926' (actual date *c.*June 1925).
35 *Der Auftakt*, IV (1924), 322.
36 Ernst Krenek, *Im Atem der Zeit. Erinnerungen an die Moderne* (Hamburg, 1998), 395–6; retranslated from the German (the English original is unpublished).
37 Ibid., 397–8.

38 The letters from Franz Schalk to Alma Mahler are preserved in *vP/D*.
39 Bernard Grun (ed. and trans.), *Alban Berg. Letters to His Wife* (London–New York, 1971), 25 November 1923, 528.
40 *AZ–AMW*, 154 and 153, both undated. Alma Mahler's added typewritten date, '1925', is clearly wrong, as Zemlinsky mentions his plan to perform his 'big Symphony' (i.e. the Lyric Symphony) 'for the first time'.
41 Letter from Schalk to Alma Mahler; cf. note 38.
42 Letter to Universal Edition, with arrival stamp 1 September 1925 and marked '1.000 Kč' (as fee paid to Zemlinsky). In a further letter, dated 6 September 1925, Zemlinsky requests as a further 'perk' (*Draufgabe*), new copies of the scores of Mahler's First, Fifth, Seventh and Eighth Symphonies and *Das Lied von der Erde*.
43 *AZ–AMW*, August 1925 (dated '1926').
44 Deryck Cooke, *Gustav Mahler: A Performing Version of His Tenth Symphony* (London, 1966), xi.
45 See *Tan*, 1/i.
46 Burkhard Laugwitz, '"Meine Zeit kommt nach meine Tod". Begegnung mit Louise Zemlinsky', *Das Orchester*, V/1993, 547–50.
47 *Wiener Zeitung*, 30 December 1926. In the *Neues Wiener Journal* there is no mention of Luise Sachsel.
48 Conversation with the author, 3 December 1990.
49 Letters to Hertzka, arrival dates 10 and 16 April 1926.
50 *Zeitschrift für Musik*, March 1930, 234. The announcement was probably gleaned from an interview with Zemlinsky published in *Prager Presse* on 4 January 1930.
51 Conversation with the author, 3 December 1990.
52 Letter to Berg 17 January 1927, *Web-Br*, 320–23 (with facsimile).
53 *Web-Br*, 7 June 1925.
54 *Web-Br*, June–July 1925.
55 Ibid.
56 See *Alban Berg. Letters to His Wife*, op. cit., 19 May 1925.
57 Erwin Stein (ed.), *Arnold Schönberg Briefe* (Mainz, 1958), 125.
58 Note in Hanns Eisler Archiv, Akademie der Künste, Berlin, first published in Jürgen Schebera, *Hanns Eisler. Ein Bildbiografie* (Berlin, 1981), 30.
59 Hanns Eisler, 'Über moderne Musik', *Die rote Fahne*, X/243, October 1927, 15, reprinted in G. Mayer (ed.), *Hanns Eisler – Musik und Politik*, 1 (Munich, 1973), 31–4.
60 *Rudé Právo*, 7 June 1927.
61 *Bohemia*, 8 June 1927.

IX Berlin 1927–1933

1 At the Krolloper

1   Letter to Berg, 30 August 1927, *Web-Br*, 323.
2   Cf. Letter to Berg, 3 November 1927, *Web-Br*, 324.
3   Cf. Peter Heyworth, *Otto Klemperer, His Life and Times*, vol. 1: *1885–1933* (Cambridge, 1983), 249. As Heyworth points out, the Krolloper was still shut for maintenance, and first rehearsals were actually held at the Lindenoper.
4   Cf. *Tan*, IV/4.
5   *ASD*, 27 May 1900.
6   *AZ–AMW*, original letter, dated 'Berlin, 6.iii.' (?1931).
7   Wilhelm Reinking, *Spiel und Form* (Hamburg, 1979), 113.
8   *Die rote Fahne*, 22 November 1927.
9   *Die rote Fahne*, 29 November 1927.
10 *Berliner Börsen-Courier*, 24 February 1931.
11 *B.Z. am Mittag*, 10 June 1930.
12 Hans Curjel in a radio broadcast, WDR 24 November 1962, quoted in E. Kruttge (ed.), *Experiment Krolloper* (Munich, 1975), 60.
13 Reinking, op. cit., 113–121, as quoted in Heyworth, 350.
14 Cf. *Web-Br*, 14 October 1927, 272.
15 Jan Meyerowitz, *Arnold Schoenberg* (Berlin, 1967), 22–3 and 13.
16 Ernst Bloch, 'Über Hoffmanns Erzählungen (Klemperers Krolloper, Berlin, 1930)', *Zur Philosophie der Musik* (Frankfurt am Main, 1974), 256–60.
17 *B.Z. am Mittag*, 13 February 1929.
18 'Zurück zur Musik', *Prager Presse*, 4 January 1930.
19 Letter to Klara Kwartin, 4 February 1928, *MolA*.
20 Letter to Universal Edition, 21 February 1928; confirmation of dispatch (UE to Zemlinsky), 22 February 1928.
21 Erich H. Müller, *Deutsches Musiker-Lexikon* (Dresden, 1929). NB the entry is preceded by an asterisk,

signifying that its content had not been verified personally by Zemlinsky. The entry also confirms Zemlinsky's engagement from 1909 to 1910 at Mannheim.

22 Cf. *Prager Presse*, 4 January 1930.
23 Quoted in *Prager Presse*, 22 March 1930.
24 'Tschechischer Chauvinismus im Konzertsaal', *Zeitschrift für Musik*, 97/III (1930), 234.
25 Ernst Bloch, op. cit., 258.
26 Cf. *ACl*, 320 (Clayton cites no source for this information).
27 Malcolm S. Cole, '*Afrika singt*: Austro-German Echoes of the Harlem Renaissance', *Journal of the American Musical Society*, XXX/1 (spring 1977), 72–95.
28 Langston Hughes, *Disillusion, The Weary Blues* (New York, 1925).
29 From the foreword to C. Cullen (ed.), *Caroling Dusk. An Anthology of Verse by Black Poets of the Twenties* (New York, 1927; *rp*,1993).
30 Ibid., 145.
31 Langston Hughes, *Uncle Tom, Selected Poems* (New York, 1959), 168.
32 Letter to Universal Edition, arrival stamp 15 August 1930.
33 Letter to Universal Edition, arrival stamp 14 September 1930.
34 Cf. Christopher Hailey, *Franz Schreker, 1878–1934. A Cultural Biography* (Cambridge, 1993) 206–7; thereafter *passim*.
35 Letter to Universal Edition, arrival stamp 15 September 1930.
36 Letter from Universal Edition (Erwin Stein), 13 June 1931.
37 Letter to Universal Edition, 20 June 1931 (arrival stamp 19 June 1931!).
38 Langston Hughes, *Uncle Tom*, op. cit.
39 *Prager Presse*, 4 January 1930.
40 Herbert Fischer, 'Besuch bei Alexander v. Zemlinsky. Aufstieg oder Niedergang des Musiklebens?', *Neues Wiener Journal*, 12 October 1932.
41 Alma Mahler-Werfel, *Mein Leben* (unabridged edn; Frankfurt am Main, 1963), 30.
42 Stefan Zweig, *Die Welt von Gestern* (Stockholm, 1944); quoted from the 1992 Frankfurt edition, 344–5.

2 The Chalk Circle

1   Cf. *AZ–AMW*, original letter dated 'Berlin, 6.iii.'
2   Cf. *ACl*, 325.
3   Peter Revers, 'Zur Ostasienrezeption in Alexander Zemlinskys *Kreidekreis*', *AeSU*, 115.
4   Theodor Adorno, 'Zemlinsky' (1959) in *Quasi una fantasia. Musikalische Schriften II* (Frankfurt, 1990), 180.
5   Ibid., 181.
6   Letter from Universal Edition to Zemlinsky, 13 June 1931.
7   Jürgen Schebera, *Kurt Weill, eine Biographie in Texten, Bildern und Dokumenten* (Leipzig, 1990), 134–5.
8   Ibid.
9   Rudolf Wagner-Régeny, *Begegnungen. Biographische Aufzeichnungen, Tagebücher und sein Briefwechsel mit Caspar Neher* (Berlin, 1968), 62–3.
10 Schebera, op. cit.
11 *Musikblätter des Anbruch*, XIV (1932), 53–4.
12 Buder and D. Gonschorek (eds.), '*Tradition ohne Schlendrian*'. *100 Jahre Philharmonischer Chor Berlin 1882 bis 1982* (Berlin, 1982), 113.
13 Hans Heinz Stuckenschmidt, *Schönberg. Leben, Umwelt, Werk* (Zurich, 1974), 331.
14 Letter from Paul Pella to Alban Berg, 20 March1933 (quoted in Alfred Beaujean, 'Paul Pella, musikalischer Oberleiter des Stadttheaters Aachen 1927 bis 1932', *Die Menorah*, V, September and December 1988, 19–22 and 9–12).

X The Humpbacked Mannikin

1   As reproduced on p. 385–9, the text follows Zemlinsky's fair copy, which diverges slightly from the printed edition of 1977. Apart from a few markings of tempo, dynamics and articulation absent from the Mobart edition, there are three pitch discrepancies:

bar 75, right hand: grace note E♮, not E♭
bar 84, right hand: dyad (B♮–G), not triad
bar 93–4, left hand: added tie (not in Zemlinsky's final manuscript but present in draft *B*)

Whether the song was performed in public during Zemlinsky's lifetime is uncertain. The inclusion of piano fingerings in the composer's hand, entered with blue pencil in the original manuscript, indicate that he at least prepared the song for performance.

2   Thomas Mann, *Buddenbrooks: The Decline of a Family*, translated by John E. Woods (London,

1994), 455. (The passage in square brackets is missing in the translation.)

3   Walter Benjamin, 'Franz Kafka: beim Bau der chinesischen Mauer', *Gesammelte Werke*, II.2, edited by Rolf Tiedemann and Hermann Schweppenhäuser (Frankfurt am Main, 1977), 682.

4   Walter Benjamin, 'Berliner Kindheit um Neunzehnhundert', *Gesammelte Werke*, edited by Tillman Rexroth (Frankfurt am Main, 1972), 303.

5   *Pariser Passagen, Gesammelte Essays zur Literatur, Über das Haschisch* and a volume of letters.

6   Published in the collection of short stories entitled *A Country Doctor*.

7   Walter Benjamin, 'Franz Kafka', op. cit., 431.

8   Ibid. The 'great rabbi' to whom the author refers was his friend Gershom Scholem (cf. 'Peter Haselberg über den Deutschen Walter Benjamin' in G. Scholem, *Walter Benjamin und sein Engel* (Frankfurt am Main, 1967), 183.)

9   Theodor W. Adorno, *Mahler. Eine musikalische Physiognomie* (Frankfurt am Main, 1960), 51. Mahler's text: 'Die zwei blaue Augen von meinem Schatz, / die haben mich in die weite Welt geschickt.'

10 There are two clear exceptions, in cells *iii* and *iv*: in verse 4 (the passage marked *ärgerlich*) melodic segments are carried over from one cell to the next, the first varied, the second transposed; in verse 5 the rising octave leap on F♯ at the end of *iii* is answered by the falling octave (G♯) in *iv*. One further cellular interrelationship is indicated in EX. 79.

11 *ZTuA* 135–55. The interpolated passage in the Second Quartet is located between 46[4] and 48.

12 The manuscripts of the draft versions at *LoC* are both filed under catalogue number 23/7. A further sketch can be found on page 171 of the *Vitalis* folder (*LoC* 17/3).

13 *St-Id*, 'New Music, Outmoded Music, Style and Idea', 123.

14 Ibid., 'Brahms the Progressive', 439.

XI Vienna 1933–1938

1   Line 38

1   Undated letter-poem (recipient unidentified: probably Hanna Sachsel), *NLZ* Aa 11.

2   Letter to Louise Zemlinsky from Mme Regnell (probably the sister-in-law of Louise Zemlinsky's cousin Robert) in Mariehamn (Åland), 23 March 1941, *NLZ* Ac 12.

3   Berlin police record of transfer to Vienna (Alexander, Louise and Johanna Zemlinsky), signed by Louise Zemlinsky, 27 September 1933, *NLZ* Ab 1.

4   Ernst Hilmar, 'Alexander Zemlinsky – die letzten Wiener Jahre', in H. Goertz (ed.), *Österreichische Musiker im Exil* (Kassel, 1990), 111.

5   Paul Stefan, in 'Zemlinskys *Kreidekreis* in Zürich', *AT*, XIII/11–13 (1933), 171–2, cites 'a dozen' theatres. Documents in the archive of Universal Edition cover eight German theatres, plus Zurich, Prague and Bratislava.

6   Cf. Susanne Rode-Breymann, *Die Wiener Staatsoper in den Zwischenkriegsjahren* (Tutzing, 1994).

7   Ibid., 279–80 and 431. Quoted material: receipt of score and vocal score (12 January 1933) in Archive VI–10/1933; letter from Zemlinsky to Krauss (January 1934); letter from Krauss to Zemlinsky (27 January 1934); Wisoko report (February 1934) – all in Archive 1934:120.

8   Letter to Louise Zemlinsky, 7 October 1933, *MolA*.

9   Letter to Louise Zemlinsky, 8 October 1933, *MolA*.

10 *Neue Zürcher Zeitung*, 16 October 1933.

11 *Tageblatt*, date unknown.

12 Paul Stefan, op. cit.

13 *New York Times*, 5 November 1934.

14 *B.Z. am Mittag*, 18 January 1934.

15 Unidentified press cutting *c.*18 January 1934, Theatermuseum Köln.

16 'Alexander Zemlinsky. Schlaglichter auf sein Leben und Werk', in Julius Kapp (ed.), *Blätter der Staatsoper*, XIV/5, January 1934.

17 *B.Z. am Mittag*, 24 January 1934; reprinted in Hans Heinz Stuckenschmidt, *Die Musik eines halben Jahrhunderts 1925–1975* (Munich, 1976).

18 Unidentified press cutting *c.*24 January 1934, Theatermuseum Köln.

19 *Die Musik*, XXVI/6 (March 1934), 445–56.

20 Burkhard Laugwitz, '"Meine Zeit kommt nach meine Tod". Begegnung mit Louise Zemlinsky', *Das Orchester*, V/1993, 547–50. In conversation with the author, Louise Zemlinsky made the same allegation.

21 *Web-Br*, 14 July 1937, 273.

22 Zemlinsky, 'Jugenderinnerungen', *Arnold Schönberg zum 60. Geburtstag* (Vienna, 1934).

23 Review by 'L.S.' in *Bohemia*, 11 December 1934.

24 Letter to Paul Eger, 8 February 1935, published in the programme book to *Der Kreidekreis*, Hamburg, 1985.

25 Cf. letter from Alban Berg, *Web-Br*, *c.* 5 June 1935, 326.

26 Postcard to Luise (*sic*) Zemlinsky, dated 'Thursday', postmarked Bad Königswart, 6 July 1934, *MolA*.
27 Elias Canetti, *Das Augenspiel* (Munich–Vienna, 1985), 300.
28 Letter from Universal Edition to Zemlinsky, 20 June 1931.
29 Letter from Berg, *c.* 5 June 1935, *Web-Br*, 325–6.
30 The performances were on 4 June 1935 (live broadcast of the RAVAG), 12 September 1935 (Salle Pleyel, Paris) and 3 March 1936 (Teatre Liceu, Barcelona); the date of the Lausanne radio broadcast is unknown.
31 Dika Newlin, *Schoenberg Remembered. Diaries and Recollections (1938–76)* (New York, 1980), 294.
32 *New York Sun*, 30 December 1940.
33 'Zemlinsky erzählt', unidentified news cutting, *c.* November 1935 (a Monday), headed 'Theater und Kunst', *MolA*.

2 The Final Synthesis

1   Conversation with Louise Zemlinsky, 3 December 1990.
2   Alma Mahler-Werfel, *Mein Leben* (unabridged edn; Frankfurt am Main, 1963), 250.
3   *AZ–AMW*, undated (summer 1901).
4   Burkhard Laugwitz, '"Meine Zeit kommt nach meine Tod". Begegnung mit Louise Zemlinsky', *Das Orchester*, V/1993, 547–50.
5   Zemlinsky's presence at the première is mentioned in an unidentified review by Bernhard Diebold, date-stamped 28 September 1935, Theatermusem Köln.
6   Postcards to Louise Zemlinsky, postmarked 24 and 26 September 1935.
7   Unidentified review dated 1 October 1935, *MolA*.
8   'Zemlinsky erzählt', unidentified news cutting, *c.* 4 November 1935, headed 'Theater und Kunst', *MolA*.
9   Letter from Berg to Schoenberg, 30 November 1935, *B–SC*, 468.
10 Letter from Schoenberg to Helene Berg, 1 January 1936, *B–SC*, 471.
11 Elias Canetti, *Das Augenspiel* (Munich–Vienna, 1985), 249.
12 *Prager Tageblatt*, 8 February 1936.
13 Ibid.
14 Letter from Erwin Stein to Schoenberg, first published in Walter Szmolyan, 'Zum III. Akt von Alban Bergs *Lulu*', *ÖMZ* XXXII/9 (September), 396; here quoted in George Perle's translation (*The Operas of Alban Berg*, vol. 2: *Lulu* (Berkeley–Los Angeles–London, 1989) 284–5).
15 *Time*, 4 December 1939, 48.
16 'Zemlinsky comes to live here', *New York Times*, 5 January 1939.
17 Hans Heinsheimer, 'Die scharfe Brille über die Nase [. . .] Meine Erinnerungen an Alexander Zemlinsky', programme book of *Eine florentinische Tragödie* and Schreker's *Der Geburtstag der Infantin*, Hamburg, 1981, 15.
18 Willi Handl, 'König Kandaules', *Die Schaubühne*, VII/1906, 195.
19 Léon Pierre-Quint, *André Gide. Der Mensch und sein Leben. Sein Werk* (Darmstadt, 1956), 160.
20 Handl, op. cit., 196.
21 James C. McClaren, *The Theatre of André Gide* (London, 1953), 32.
22 J. W. Ireland, *André Gide. A Study of His Creative Writings* (Oxford, 1970), 164–9.
23 Klaus Mann, *André Gide and the Crisis of Modern Thought* (New York, 1943).
24 *Die Musik*, IX/1909–10, vol. 9, 13.
25 Handl, op. cit., 196.
26 *New York Times*, 5 January 1939.
27 Viktor Ullmann, 'Alban Berg', *Anbruch* XII/2 (subtitled 'Die sogenannte Opernkrise'), February 1930, 50
28 Viktor Ullmann, 'Zum Gedächtnis Alban Bergs', *Das Goetheanum* 15 (1926)/II, 12 January 1936, 14.
29 Letter from Louise Zemlinsky to Friedrich Cerha, 1 December 1982.
30 Letter from Friedrich Cerha to Louise Zemlinsky, 22 November 1984.
31 Letter from Friedrich Cerha to Louise Zemlinsky, 28 September 1986.
32 Uwe Sommer, *Alexander Zemlinsky: Der König Kandaules*, Musik-Konzepte 92/93/94, Munich, 1996, 175–90.

XII Lieder (III)

1   'Besuch bei Alexander Zemlinsky', *Neues Wiener Journal*, 12 October 1932.
2   Louise Zemlinsky in conversation with the author, 3 December 1990.
3   Cord Garben, 'An Advocate's View of Zemlinsky', booklet for *Zemlinsky Lieder*, DG 427 349–2 (Hamburg, 1989).
4   *Jill Gomez in Cabaret Classics*, Unicorn-Kamchana DKP 9055 (London, 1988).

XIII The Exile

1 Finis Austriae

1 *Neues Wiener Journal*, 13 June 1937 (quoted in Peter Stephan Jungk, *Franz Werfel, eine Lebensgeschichte* (Frankfurt am Main, 1987), 409).
2 Egon and Emmy Wellesz, *Egon Wellesz. Leben und Werk*, edited by Franz Endler (Vienna–Hamburg, 1981), 223–34.
3 Stefan Zweig, *Die Welt von Gestern* (Stockholm, 1944); quoted from the 1992 Frankfurt edition, 458.
4 Arnold Greissle-Schönberg, *Arnold Schönberg und sein Wiener Kreis. Erinnerung eines Enkels* (Vienna, 1998), 155.
5 Bruno Walter, *Theme and Variations, an Autobiography* (New York, 1946), 477.
6 Burkhard Laugwitz, '"Meine Zeit kommt nach meine Tod". Begegnung mit Louise Zemlinsky', *Das Orchester*, v/1993, 547–50.
7 A. Beaumont and A. Clayton, 'Alexander Zemlinskys amerikanische Jahre', *AeSU*, 248 (Louise Zemlinsky in conversation with Alfred Clayton).
8 Arnold Greissle-Schonberg, op. cit., 212.
9 From a BBC broadcast, 12 August 1975 (quoted in Beaumont and Clayton, op. cit.).
10 *NLZ* Aa 13–16.
11 Státni Ústřední Archiv v Praze, file z/1015/8/32, box 12376, 1911–1938; details from *Tan* v.
12 *NLZ* Ab 12.
13 Letter from Hans Nachod to Schoenberg, Prague (poste restante), 16 September 1938; from J. A. Kimmey Jr. (ed.), *The Arnold Schoenberg–Hans Nachod Collection*, Detroit Studies in Music Bibliography 41 (Detroit, 1979).
14 *NLZ* Ab 18.
15 Undated letter to Václav Tálich, Tálich Archive, Beroun.
16 The official notification of Zemlinsky's departure was post-dated to 21 April 1939, i.e. several weeks after the occupation of Bohemia and Moravia by the Nazis (Státni Ústřední Archiv, information provided to the author on 24 June 1993).

2 America

1 H[arold] T[aubmann], 'Zemlinsky comes to live here', *New York Times*, 5 January 1939.
2 Walter Firner in conversation with the author, 10 January 1993.
3 Werner Wolff, 'Composer–Conductor of Vienna', *New York Times*, 3 September 1939.
4 Letter to Schoenberg, Web-Br , c. December 1939, 276.
5 Conversation with the author, 3 December 1990.
6 *NLZ* Ac 12.
7 *NLZ* Ab 16.
8 Declaration of Intention No. 2–629673, dated 2 June 1939; *NLZ* (uncatalogued).
9 Hans Heinsheimer, 'Die scharfe Brille über die Nase [. . .] Meine Erinnerungen an Alexander Zemlinsky', programme book of *Eine florentinische Tragödie* and Schreker's *Der Geburtstag der Infantin*, Hamburg, 1981.
10 Ibid.
11 Death certificate, *NLZ* Ab 10.
12 Peter Heyworth, *Otto Klemperer, His Life and Times*, vol. 2: *1933–1973* (Cambridge, 1996), 101.
13 Irving Kolodin, *The Metropolitan Opera 1883–1966* (New York, 1966), 417.
14 Letter from Schoenberg to Trudi Greissle, 11 November 1939, Arnold Schönberg Center, Vienna.
15 Letter from Louise Zemlinsky to Schoenberg, *Web-Br*, c. November–December 1939, 275.
16 Letter from Fritz Stiedry to Schoenberg, 24 December 1939, Arnold Schönberg Center, Vienna.
17 The letter, quoted in part on p. 460, is reproduced in facsimile in *Web-Br*.
18 Letter from Schoenberg, *Web-Br*, 9 February 1940, 278.
19 Else Stone and Kurt Stone (eds.), *The Writings of Elliott Carter* (Bloomington, 1977), 80.
20 Letter to Schoenberg, *Web-Br*, c. 25 February 1940, 278–9.
21 Walter Firner in conversation with the author, 10 January 1993.
22 Letter from Otto Sachsel to Hanna Sachsel, 4 August 1940, *NLZ* Ab 13.
23 Nuria Schoenberg-Nono, *Arnold Schönberg 1874-1951. Lebensgeschichte in Begegnungen* (Klagenfurt 1992), 371.
24 Letter from Fritz Stiedry to Schoenberg, 17 December 1940, Arnold Schönberg Center, Vienna.
25 Ibid.
26 Telegram from Schoenberg, *Web-Br*, 29 December 1940, 279.
27 Letter from Louise Zemlinsky to Schoenberg, *Web-Br*, c. December 1940, 280.
28 Letter from Schoenberg to Hans Nachod, 12 July 1941, John A. Kimmey jun., *The Arnold Schoenberg–Hans Nachod Collection*, Detroit Studies in Music Bibliography no. 41 (Detroit, 1979), 58.
29 *New York Times*, 16 March 1942.

XIV EPILOGUE: 'Zemlinsky can wait'

1   The Library of Congress, Sergey Koussevitzky Collection.
2   *NLZ* Da 48.
3   Mentioned in an unpublished letter from Louise Zemlinsky to Friedrich Cerha, 1 December 1982; no details of the performance are included.
4   Ernst Krenek, *Im Atem der Zeit. Erinnerungen an die Moderne* (Hamburg, 1998), 138.
5   Peter Heyworth (ed.), *Conversations with Klemperer* (London, 1973), 48.
6   *NLZ* Da 36.
7   *NLZ* Ac 12.
8   *NLZ* (uncatalogued).
9   *NLZ* (uncatalogued).
10 *NLZ* Ac 15, dated 1947 (copy dated 12 November 1970).
11 *NLZ* Ae 1, Ae 2.
12 *NLZ* Af 2.
13 *NLZ* Ac 36.
14 *NLZ* Ac 20.

Index